BUS 275 - Business Statistics

Custom Edition For the University of Southern Maine

12e

David R. Anderson | Dennis J. Sweeney
Thomas A. Williams
Jeffrey D. Camm | James J. Cochran

CENGAGE Learning

Australia • Brazil • Japan • Korea • Mexico • Singapore • Spain • United Kingdom • United States

CENGAGE Learning

BUS 275 - Business Statistics: Custom Edition For the University of Southern Maine, 12e

David R. Anderson | Dennis J. Sweeney
Thomas A. Williams
Jeffrey D. Camm | James J. Cochran

Senior Project Development Manager:
Linda deStefano

Market Development Manager:
Heather Kramer

Senior Production/Manufacturing Manager:
Donna M. Brown

Production Editorial Manager:
Kim Fry

Sr. Rights Acquisition Account Manager:
Todd Osborne

Printed in the United States of America

Statistics for Business & Economics, 12th Edition
David R. Anderson | Dennis J. Sweeney | Thomas A. Williams
Jeffrey D. Camm | James J. Cochran

ISBN-13: 978-1-285-91351-3

ISBN-10: 1-285-91351-5

Cengage Learning
5191 Natorp Boulevard
Mason, Ohio 45040
USA

Cengage Learning is a leading provider of customized learning solutions with office locations around the globe, including Singapore, the United Kingdom, Australia, Mexico, Brazil, and Japan. Locate your local office at:
international.cengage.com/region.
Cengage Learning products are represented in Canada by Nelson Education, Ltd.
For your lifelong learning solutions, visit **www.cengage.com/custom.**
Visit our corporate website at **www.cengage.com.**

Brief Contents

Preface

This text is the 12th edition of *STATISTICS FOR BUSINESS AND ECONOMICS.* With this edition we welcome two eminent scholars to our author team: Jeffrey D. Camm of the University of Cincinnati and James J. Cochran of Louisiana Tech University. Both Jeff and Jim are accomplished teachers, researchers, and practitioners in the fields of statistics and business analytics. Jim is a fellow of the American Statistical Association. You can read more about their accomplishments in the About the Authors section which follows this preface. We believe that the addition of Jeff and Jim as our coauthors will both maintain and improve the effectiveness of *Statistics for Business and Economics.*

The purpose of *Statistics for Business and Economics* is to give students, primarily those in the fields of business administration and economics, a conceptual introduction to the field of statistics and its many applications. The text is applications oriented and written with the needs of the nonmathematician in mind; the mathematical prerequisite is knowledge of algebra.

Applications of data analysis and statistical methodology are an integral part of the organization and presentation of the text material. The discussion and development of each technique is presented in an application setting, with the statistical results providing insights to decisions and solutions to problems.

Although the book is applications oriented, we have taken care to provide sound methodological development and to use notation that is generally accepted for the topic being covered. Hence, students will find that this text provides good preparation for the study of more advanced statistical material. A bibliography to guide further study is included as an appendix.

The text introduces the student to the software packages of Minitab 16 and Microsoft® Office Excel 2010 and emphasizes the role of computer software in the application of statistical analysis. Minitab is illustrated as it is one of the leading statistical software packages for both education and statistical practice. Excel is not a statistical software package, but the wide availability and use of Excel make it important for students to understand the statistical capabilities of this package. Minitab and Excel procedures are provided in appendixes so that instructors have the flexibility of using as much computer emphasis as desired for the course. StatTools, a commercial Excel add-in developed by Palisade Corporation, extends the range of statistical options for Excel users. We show how to download and install StatTools in an appendix to Chapter 1, and most chapters include a chapter appendix that shows the steps required to accomplish a statistical procedure using StatTools. We have made the use of StatTools optional so that instructors who want to teach using only the standard tools available in Excel can do so.

Changes in the Twelfth Edition

We appreciate the acceptance and positive response to the previous editions *of Statistics for Business and Economics.* Accordingly, in making modifications for this new edition, we have maintained the presentation style and readability of those editions. There have been many changes made throughout the text to enhance its educational effectiveness. The most significant changes in the new edition are summarized here.

Content Revisions

- **Descriptive Statistics—Chapters 2 and 3.** We have significantly revised these chapters to incorporate new material on data visualization, best practices, and much more. Chapter 2 has been reorganized to include new material on side-by-side and stacked bar charts and a new section has been added on data visualization and best practices in creating effective displays. Chapter 3 now includes coverage of the geometric mean in the section on measures of location. The geometric mean has many applications in the computation of growth rates for financial assets, annual percentage rates, and so on. Chapter 3 also includes a new section on data dashboards and how summary statistics can be incorporated to enhance their effectiveness.

- **Discrete Probability Distributions—Chapter 5.** The introductory material in this chapter has been revised to explain better the role of probability distributions and to show how the material on assigning probabilities in Chapter 4 can be used to develop discrete probability distributions. We point out that the empirical discrete probability distribution is developed by using the relative frequency method to assign probabilities. At the request of many users, we have added a new section (Section 5.4) which covers bivariate discrete distributions and financial applications. We show how financial portfolios can be constructed and analyzed using these distributions.
- **Comparing Multiple Proportions, Tests of Independence, and Goodness of Fit—Chapter 12.** This chapter has undergone a major revision. We have added a new section on testing the equality of three or more population proportions. This section includes a procedure for making multiple comparison tests between all pairs of population proportions. The section on the test of independence has been rewritten to clarify that the test concerns the independence of two categorical variables. Revised appendixes with step-by-step instructions for Minitab, Excel, and StatTools are included.
- **New Case Problems.** We have added 8 new case problems to this edition; the total number of cases is 31. Three new descriptive statistics cases have been added to Chapters 2 and 3. Five new case problems involving regression appear in Chapters 14, 15, and 16. These case problems provide students with the opportunity to analyze larger data sets and prepare managerial reports based on the results of their analysis.
- **New Statistics in Practice Applications.** Each chapter begins with a Statistics in Practice vignette that describes an application of the statistical methodology to be covered in the chapter. New to this edition is a Statistics in Practice for Chapter 2 describing the use of data dashboards and data visualization at the Cincinnati Zoo. We have also added a new Statistics in Practice to Chapter 4 describing how a NASA team used probability to assist the rescue of 33 Chilean miners trapped by a cave-in.
- **New Examples and Exercises based on Real Data.** We continue to make a significant effort to update our text examples and exercises with the most current real data and referenced sources of statistical information. In this edition, we have added approximately 180 new examples and exercises based on real data and referenced sources. Using data from sources also used by *The Wall Street Journal, USA Today, Barron's,* and others, we have drawn from actual studies to develop explanations and to create exercises that demonstrate the many uses of statistics in business and economics. We believe that the use of real data helps generate more student interest in the material and enables the student to learn about both the statistical methodology and its application. The twelfth edition contains over 350 examples and exercises based on real data.

Features and Pedagogy

Authors Anderson, Sweeney, Williams, Camm, and Cochran have continued many of the features that appeared in previous editions. Important ones for students are noted here.

Methods Exercises and Applications Exercises

The end-of-section exercises are split into two parts, Methods and Applications. The Methods exercises require students to use the formulas and make the necessary computations.

The Applications exercises require students to use the chapter material in real-world situations. Thus, students first focus on the computational "nuts and bolts" and then move on to the subtleties of statistical application and interpretation.

Self-Test Exercises

Certain exercises are identified as "Self-Test Exercises." Completely worked-out solutions for these exercises are provided in Appendix D. Students can attempt the Self-Test Exercises and immediately check the solution to evaluate their understanding of the concepts presented in the chapter.

Margin Annotations and Notes and Comments

Margin annotations that highlight key points and provide additional insights for the student are a key feature of this text. These annotations, which appear in the margins, are designed to provide emphasis and enhance understanding of the terms and concepts being presented in the text.

At the end of many sections, we provide Notes and Comments designed to give the student additional insights about the statistical methodology and its application. Notes and Comments include warnings about or limitations of the methodology, recommendations for application, brief descriptions of additional technical considerations, and other matters.

Data Files Accompany the Text

Over 200 data files are available on the website that accompanies the text. The data sets are available in both Minitab and Excel formats. Webfile logos are used in the text to identify the data sets that are available on the website. Data sets for all case problems as well as data sets for larger exercises are included.

Acknowledgments

We would like to acknowledge the work of our reviewers, who provided comments and suggestions of ways to continue to improve our text. Thanks to

AbouEl-Makarim Aboueissa, University of Southern Maine

Kathleen Arano
Fort Hays State University

Musa Ayar
Uw-baraboo/Sauk County

Kathleen Burke
SUNY Cortland

YC Chang
University of Notre Dame

David Chen
Rosemont College and Saint Joseph's University

Margaret E. Cochran
Northwestern State University of Louisiana

Thomas A. Dahlstrom
Eastern University

Anne Drougas
Dominican University

Fesseha Gebremikael
Strayer University/ Calhoun Community College

Malcolm C. Gold
University of Wisconsin—Marshfield/Wood County

Joel Goldstein
Western Connecticut State University

Jim Grant
Lewis & Clark College

Reidar Hagtvedt
University of Alberta School of Business

Clifford B. Hawley
West Virginia University

Vance A. Hughey
Western Nevada College

Tony Hunnicutt
Ouachita Technical College

Stacey M. Jones
Albers School of Business and Economics, Seattle University

Dukpa Kim
University of Virginia

Rajaram Krishnan
Earlham College

Robert J. Lemke
Lake Forest College

Philip J. Mizzi
Arizona State University

Mehdi Mohaghegh
Norwich University

Mihail Motzev
Walla Walla University

Somnath Mukhopadhyay
The University of Texas at El Paso

Kenneth E. Murphy
Chapman University

Ogbonnaya John Nwoha
Grambling State University

Claudiney Pereira
Tulane University

J. G. Pitt
University of Toronto

Scott A. Redenius
Brandeis University

Sandra Robertson
Thomas Nelson Community College

Sunil Sapra
California State University, Los Angeles

Kyle Vann Scott
Snead State Community College

Rodney E. Stanley
Tennessee State University

Jennifer Strehler
Oakton Community College

Ronald Stunda
Valdosta State University

Cindy van Es
Cornell University

Jennifer VanGilder
Ursinus College

Jacqueline Wroughton
Northern Kentucky University

Dmitry Yarushkin
Grand View University

David Zimmer
Western Kentucky University

We continue to owe a debt to our many colleagues and friends for their helpful comments and suggestions in the development of this and earlier editions of our text. Among them are:

Mohammad Ahmadi
University of Tennessee at Chattanooga

Lari Arjomand
Clayton College and State University

Robert Balough
Clarion University

Philip Boudreaux
University of Louisiana

Mike Bourke
Houston Baptist University

James Brannon
University of Wisconsin—Oshkosh

John Bryant
University of Pittsburgh

Peter Bryant
University of Colorado

Terri L. Byczkowski
University of Cincinnati

Robert Carver
Stonehill College

Richard Claycombe
McDaniel College

Robert Cochran
University of Wyoming

Robert Collins
Marquette University

David W. Cravens
Texas Christian University

Tom Dahlstrom
Eastern College

Gopal Dorai
William Patterson University

Nicholas Farnum
California State University—Fullerton

Donald Gren
Salt Lake Community College

Paul Guy
California State University—Chico

Clifford Hawley
West Virginia University

Jim Hightower
California State University, Fullerton

Alan Humphrey
University of Rhode Island

Ann Hussein
Philadelphia College of Textiles and Science

C. Thomas Innis
University of Cincinnati

Ben Isselhardt
Rochester Institute of Technology

Jeffery Jarrett
University of Rhode Island

Ronald Klimberg
St. Joseph's University

David A. Kravitz
George Mason University

David Krueger
St. Cloud State University

John Leschke
University of Virginia

Martin S. Levy
University of Cincinnati

John S. Loucks
St. Edward's University

David Lucking-Reiley
Vanderbilt University

Bala Maniam
Sam Houston State University

Don Marx
University of Alaska, Anchorage

Tom McCullough
University of California—Berkeley

Ronald W. Michener
University of Virginia

Glenn Milligan
Ohio State University

Mitchell Muesham
Sam Houston State University

Roger Myerson
Northwestern University

Richard O'Connell
Miami University of Ohio

Alan Olinsky
Bryant College

Ceyhun Ozgur
Valparaiso University

Tom Pray
Rochester Institute of Technology

Harold Rahmlow
St. Joseph's University

H. V. Ramakrishna
Penn State University at Great Valley

Tom Ryan
Case Western Reserve University

Bill Seaver
University of Tennessee

Alan Smith
Robert Morris College

Willbann Terpening
Gonzaga University

Ted Tsukahara
St. Mary's College of California

Hroki Tsurumi
Rutgers University

David Tufte
University of New Orleans

Victor Ukpolo
Austin Peay State University

Ebenge Usip
Youngstown State University

Cindy Van Es
Cornell University

Jack Vaughn
University of Texas-El Paso

Andrew Welki
John Carroll University

Ari Wijetunga
Morehead State University

J. E. Willis
Louisiana State University

Mustafa Yilmaz
Northeastern University

Gary Yoshimoto
St. Cloud State University

Yan Yu
University of Cincinnati

Charles Zimmerman
Robert Morris College

We thank our associates from business and industry who supplied the Statistics in Practice features. We recognize them individually by a credit line in each of the articles. We are also indebted to our senior acquisitions editor, Charles McCormick Jr.; our developmental editor, Maggie Kubale; our content project manager, Tamborah Moore; our Project Manager at MPS Limited, Lynn Lustberg; our media editor, Chris Valentine; and others at Cengage South-Western for their editorial counsel and support during the preparation of this text.

David R. Anderson
Dennis J. Sweeney
Thomas A. Williams
Jeffrey D. Camm
James J. Cochran

About the Authors

David R. Anderson. David R. Anderson is Professor of Quantitative Analysis in the College of Business Administration at the University of Cincinnati. Born in Grand Forks, North Dakota, he earned his B.S., M.S., and Ph.D. degrees from Purdue University. Professor Anderson has served as Head of the Department of Quantitative Analysis and Operations Management and as Associate Dean of the College of Business Administration at the University of Cincinnati. In addition, he was the coordinator of the College's first Executive Program.

At the University of Cincinnati, Professor Anderson has taught introductory statistics for business students as well as graduate-level courses in regression analysis, multivariate analysis, and management science. He has also taught statistical courses at the Department of Labor in Washington, D.C. He has been honored with nominations and awards for excellence in teaching and excellence in service to student organizations.

Professor Anderson has coauthored 10 textbooks in the areas of statistics, management science, linear programming, and production and operations management. He is an active consultant in the field of sampling and statistical methods.

Dennis J. Sweeney. Dennis J. Sweeney is Professor of Quantitative Analysis and Founder of the Center for Productivity Improvement at the University of Cincinnati. Born in Des Moines, Iowa, he earned a B.S.B.A. degree from Drake University and his M.B.A. and D.B.A. degrees from Indiana University, where he was an NDEA Fellow. Professor Sweeney has worked in the management science group at Procter & Gamble and spent a year as a visiting professor at Duke University. Professor Sweeney served as Head of the Department of Quantitative Analysis and as Associate Dean of the College of Business Administration at the University of Cincinnati.

Professor Sweeney has published more than 30 articles and monographs in the area of management science and statistics. The National Science Foundation, IBM, Procter & Gamble, Federated Department Stores, Kroger, and Cincinnati Gas & Electric have funded his research, which has been published in *Management Science, Operations Research, Mathematical Programming, Decision Sciences,* and other journals.

Professor Sweeney has coauthored 10 textbooks in the areas of statistics, management science, linear programming, and production and operations management.

Thomas A. Williams. Thomas A. Williams is Professor of Management Science in the College of Business at Rochester Institute of Technology. Born in Elmira, New York, he earned his B.S. degree at Clarkson University. He did his graduate work at Rensselaer Polytechnic Institute, where he received his M.S. and Ph.D. degrees.

Before joining the College of Business at RIT, Professor Williams served for seven years as a faculty member in the College of Business Administration at the University of Cincinnati, where he developed the undergraduate program in Information Systems and then served as its coordinator. At RIT he was the first chairman of the Decision Sciences Department. He teaches courses in management science and statistics, as well as graduate courses in regression and decision analysis.

Professor Williams is the coauthor of 11 textbooks in the areas of management science, statistics, production and operations management, and mathematics. He has been a consultant for numerous *Fortune* 500 companies and has worked on projects ranging from the use of data analysis to the development of large-scale regression models.

Jeffrey D. Camm. Jeffrey D. Camm is Professor of Quantitative Analysis, Head of the Department of Operations, Business Analytics, and Information Systems and College of Business Research Fellow in the Carl H. Lindner College of Business at the University of Cincinnati, Born in Cincinnati, Ohio, he holds a B.S. from Xavier University and a Ph.D. from Clemson University. He has been at the University of Cincinnati since 1984 and has been a visiting scholar at Stanford University and a visiting professor of business administration at the Tuck School of Business at Dartmouth College.

Dr. Camm has published over 30 papers in the general area of optimization applied to problems in operations management. He has published his research in *Science, Management Science, Operations Research, Interfaces,* and other professional journals. At the University of Cincinnati, he was named the Dornoff Fellow of Teaching Excellence and he was the 2006 recipient of the INFORMS Prize for the Teaching of Operations Research Practice. A firm believer in practicing what he preaches, he has served as an operations research consultant to numerous companies and government agencies. From 2005 to 2010 he served as editor-in-chief of *Interfaces* and is currently on the editorial board of *INFORMS Transactions on Education.*

James J. Cochran. James J. Cochran is the Bank of Ruston Endowed Research Professor of Quantitative Analysis at Louisiana Tech University. Born in Dayton, Ohio, he earned his B.S., M.S., and M.B.A. degrees from Wright State University and a Ph.D. from the University of Cincinnati. He has been at Louisiana Tech University since 2000 and has been a visiting scholar at Stanford University, Universidad de Talca, and the University of South Africa.

Professor Cochran has published over two dozen papers in the development and application of operations research and statistical methods. He has published his research *in Management Science, The American Statistician, Communications in Statistics—Theory and Methods, European Journal of Operational Research, Journal of Combinatorial Optimization,* and other professional journals. He was the 2008 recipient of the INFORMS Prize for the Teaching of Operations Research Practice and the 2010 recipient of the Mu Sigma Rho Statistical Education Award. Professor Cochran was elected to the International Statistics Institute in 2005 and named a Fellow of the American Statistical Association in 2011. A strong advocate for effective operations research and statistics education as a means of improving the quality of applications to real problems, Professor Cochran has organized and chaired teaching effectiveness workshops in Montevideo, Uruguay; Cape Town, South Africa; Cartagena, Colombia; Jaipur, India; Buenos Aires, Argentina; and Nairobi, Kenya. He has served as an operations research consultant to numerous companies and not-for-profit organizations. He currently serves as editor-in-chief of *INFORMS Transactions on Education* and is on the editorial board of *Interfaces, the Journal of the Chilean Institute of Operations Research,* and *ORiON.*

CHAPTER 7

Sampling and Sampling Distributions

CONTENTS

STATISTICS *in* PRACTICE

MEADWESTVACO CORPORATION*
STAMFORD, CONNECTICUT

MeadWestvaco Corporation, a leading producer of packaging, coated and specialty papers, and specialty chemicals, employs more than 17,000 people. It operates worldwide in 30 countries and serves customers located in approximately 100 countries. MeadWestvaco's internal consulting group uses sampling to provide a variety of information that enables the company to obtain significant productivity benefits and remain competitive.

For example, MeadWestvaco maintains large woodland holdings, which supply the trees, or raw material, for many of the company's products. Managers need reliable and accurate information about the timberlands and forests to evaluate the company's ability to meet its future raw material needs. What is the present volume in the forests? What is the past growth of the forests? What is the projected future growth of the forests? With answers to these important questions MeadWestvaco's managers can develop plans for the future, including long-term planting and harvesting schedules for the trees.

How does MeadWestvaco obtain the information it needs about its vast forest holdings? Data collected from sample plots throughout the forests are the basis for learning about the population of trees owned by the company. To identify the sample plots, the timberland holdings are first divided into three sections based on location and types of trees. Using maps and random numbers, MeadWestvaco analysts identify random samples of 1/5- to 1/7-acre plots in each section of the forest. MeadWestvaco foresters collect data from these sample plots to learn about the forest population.

Random sampling of its forest holdings enables MeadWestvaco Corporation to meet future raw material needs. © Robert Crum/Shutterstock.com.

Foresters throughout the organization participate in the field data collection process. Periodically, two-person teams gather information on each tree in every sample plot. The sample data are entered into the company's continuous forest inventory (CFI) computer system. Reports from the CFI system include a number of frequency distribution summaries containing statistics on types of trees, present forest volume, past forest growth rates, and projected future forest growth and volume. Sampling and the associated statistical summaries of the sample data provide the reports essential for the effective management of MeadWestvaco's forests and timberlands.

In this chapter you will learn about simple random sampling and the sample selection process. In addition, you will learn how statistics such as the sample mean and sample proportion are used to estimate the population mean and population proportion. The important concept of a sampling distribution is also introduced.

*The authors are indebted to Dr. Edward P. Winkofsky for providing this Statistics in Practice.

In Chapter 1 we presented the following definitions of an element, a population, and a sample.

- An *element* is the entity on which data are collected.
- A *population* is the collection of all the elements of interest.
- A *sample* is a subset of the population.

The reason we select a sample is to collect data to make an inference and answer research questions about a population.

Let us begin by citing two examples in which sampling was used to answer a research question about a population.

1. Members of a political party in Texas were considering supporting a particular candidate for election to the U.S. Senate, and party leaders wanted to estimate the proportion of registered voters in the state favoring the candidate. A sample of 400 registered voters in Texas was selected and 160 of the 400 voters indicated a preference for the candidate. Thus, an estimate of the proportion of the population of registered voters favoring the candidate is 160/400 = .40.
2. A tire manufacturer is considering producing a new tire designed to provide an increase in mileage over the firm's current line of tires. To estimate the mean useful life of the new tires, the manufacturer produced a sample of 120 tires for testing. The test results provided a sample mean of 36,500 miles. Hence, an estimate of the mean useful life for the population of new tires was 36,500 miles.

A sample mean provides an estimate of a population mean, and a sample proportion provides an estimate of a population proportion. With estimates such as these, some estimation error can be expected. This chapter provides the basis for determining how large that error might be.

It is important to realize that sample results provide only *estimates* of the values of the corresponding population characteristics. We do not expect exactly .40, or 40%, of the population of registered voters to favor the candidate, nor do we expect the sample mean of 36,500 miles to exactly equal the mean mileage for the population of all new tires produced. The reason is simply that the sample contains only a portion of the population. Some sampling error is to be expected. With proper sampling methods, the sample results will provide "good" estimates of the population parameters. But how good can we expect the sample results to be? Fortunately, statistical procedures are available for answering this question.

Let us define some of the terms used in sampling. The **sampled population** is the population from which the sample is drawn, and a **frame** is a list of the elements that the sample will be selected from. In the first example, the sampled population is all registered voters in Texas, and the frame is a list of all the registered voters. Because the number of registered voters in Texas is a finite number, the first example is an illustration of sampling from a finite population. In Section 7.2, we discuss how a simple random sample can be selected when sampling from a finite population.

The sampled population for the tire mileage example is more difficult to define because the sample of 120 tires was obtained from a production process at a particular point in time. We can think of the sampled population as the conceptual population of all the tires that could have been made by the production process at that particular point in time. In this sense the sampled population is considered infinite, making it impossible to construct a frame to draw the sample from. In Section 7.2, we discuss how to select a random sample in such a situation.

In this chapter, we show how simple random sampling can be used to select a sample from a finite population and describe how a random sample can be taken from an infinite population that is generated by an ongoing process. We then show how data obtained from a sample can be used to compute estimates of a population mean, a population standard deviation, and a population proportion. In addition, we introduce the important concept of a sampling distribution. As we will show, knowledge of the appropriate sampling distribution enables us to make statements about how close the sample estimates are to the corresponding population parameters. The last section discusses some alternatives to simple random sampling that are often employed in practice.

7.1 The Electronics Associates Sampling Problem

The director of personnel for Electronics Associates, Inc. (EAI), has been assigned the task of developing a profile of the company's 2500 managers. The characteristics to be identified include the mean annual salary for the managers and the proportion of managers having completed the company's management training program.

WEB file

EAI

Using the 2500 managers as the population for this study, we can find the annual salary and the training program status for each individual by referring to the firm's personnel records. The data set containing this information for all 2500 managers in the population is in the file named EAI.

Using the EAI data and the formulas presented in Chapter 3, we computed the population mean and the population standard deviation for the annual salary data.

$$\text{Population mean:} \quad \mu = \$51{,}800$$
$$\text{Population standard deviation:} \quad \sigma = \$4000$$

The data for the training program status show that 1500 of the 2500 managers completed the training program.

Numerical characteristics of a population are called **parameters**. Letting p denote the proportion of the population that completed the training program, we see that $p = 1500/2500 = .60$. The population mean annual salary ($\mu = \$51{,}800$), the population standard deviation of annual salary ($\sigma = \$4000$), and the population proportion that completed the training program ($p = .60$) are parameters of the population of EAI managers.

Often the cost of collecting information from a sample is substantially less than from a population, especially when personal interviews must be conducted to collect the information.

Now, suppose that the necessary information on all the EAI managers was not readily available in the company's database. The question we now consider is how the firm's director of personnel can obtain estimates of the population parameters by using a sample of managers rather than all 2500 managers in the population. Suppose that a sample of 30 managers will be used. Clearly, the time and the cost of developing a profile would be substantially less for 30 managers than for the entire population. If the personnel director could be assured that a sample of 30 managers would provide adequate information about the population of 2500 managers, working with a sample would be preferable to working with the entire population. Let us explore the possibility of using a sample for the EAI study by first considering how we can identify a sample of 30 managers.

7.2 Selecting a Sample

In this section we describe how to select a sample. We first describe how to sample from a finite population and then describe how to select a sample from an infinite population.

Sampling from a Finite Population

Other methods of probability sampling are described in Section 7.8

Statisticians recommend selecting a probability sample when sampling from a finite population because a probability sample allows them to make valid statistical inferences about the population. The simplest type of probability sample is one in which each sample of size n has the same probability of being selected. It is called a simple random sample. A simple random sample of size n from a finite population of size N is defined as follows.

SIMPLE RANDOM SAMPLE (FINITE POPULATION)

A **simple random sample** of size n from a finite population of size N is a sample selected such that each possible sample of size n has the same probability of being selected.

We describe how Excel, Minitab, and StatTools can be used to generate a simple random sample in the chapter appendices.

One procedure for selecting a simple random sample from a finite population is to use a table of random numbers to choose the elements for the sample one at a time in such a way that, at each step, each of the elements remaining in the population has the same probability of being selected. Sampling n elements in this way will satisfy the definition of a simple random sample from a finite population.

To select a simple random sample from the finite population of EAI managers, we first construct a frame by assigning each manager a number. For example, we can assign the

TABLE 7.1 RANDOM NUMBERS

63271	59986	71744	51102	15141	80714	58683	93108	13554	79945
88547	09896	95436	79115	08303	01041	20030	63754	08459	28364
55957	57243	83865	09911	19761	66535	40102	26646	60147	15702
46276	87453	44790	67122	45573	84358	21625	16999	13385	22782
55363	07449	34835	15290	76616	67191	12777	21861	68689	03263
69393	92785	49902	58447	42048	30378	87618	26933	40640	16281
13186	29431	88190	04588	38733	81290	89541	70290	40113	08243
17726	28652	56836	78351	47327	18518	92222	55201	27340	10493
36520	64465	05550	30157	82242	29520	69753	72602	23756	54935
81628	36100	39254	56835	37636	02421	98063	89641	64953	99337
84649	48968	75215	75498	49539	74240	03466	49292	36401	45525
63291	11618	12613	75055	43915	26488	41116	64531	56827	30825
70502	53225	03655	05915	37140	57051	48393	91322	25653	06543
06426	24771	59935	49801	11082	66762	94477	02494	88215	27191
20711	55609	29430	70165	45406	78484	31639	52009	18873	96927
41990	70538	77191	25860	55204	73417	83920	69468	74972	38712
72452	36618	76298	26678	89334	33938	95567	29380	75906	91807
37042	40318	57099	10528	09925	89773	41335	96244	29002	46453
53766	52875	15987	46962	67342	77592	57651	95508	80033	69828
90585	58955	53122	16025	84299	53310	67380	84249	25348	04332
32001	96293	37203	64516	51530	37069	40261	61374	05815	06714
62606	64324	46354	72157	67248	20135	49804	09226	64419	29457
10078	28073	85389	50324	14500	15562	64165	06125	71353	77669
91561	46145	24177	15294	10061	98124	75732	00815	83452	97355
13091	98112	53959	79607	52244	63303	10413	63839	74762	50289

managers the numbers 1 to 2500 in the order that their names appear in the EAI personnel file. Next, we refer to the table of random numbers shown in Table 7.1. Using the first row of the table, each digit, 6, 3, 2, . . . , is a random digit having an equal chance of occurring. Because the largest number in the population list of EAI managers, 2500, has four digits, we will select random numbers from the table in sets or groups of four digits. Even though we may start the selection of random numbers anywhere in the table and move systematically in a direction of our choice, we will use the first row of Table 7.1 and move from left to right. The first 7 four-digit random numbers are

The random numbers in the table are shown in groups of five for readability.

6327 1599 8671 7445 1102 1514 1807

Because the numbers in the table are random, these four-digit numbers are equally likely.

We can now use these four-digit random numbers to give each manager in the population an equal chance of being included in the random sample. The first number, 6327, is greater than 2500. It does not correspond to one of the numbered managers in the population, and hence is discarded. The second number, 1599, is between 1 and 2500. Thus the first manager selected for the random sample is number 1599 on the list of EAI managers. Continuing this process, we ignore the numbers 8671 and 7445 before identifying managers number 1102, 1514, and 1807 to be included in the random sample. This process continues until the simple random sample of 30 EAI managers has been obtained.

In implementing this simple random sample selection process, it is possible that a random number used previously may appear again in the table before the complete sample of 30 EAI managers has been selected. Because we do not want to select a manager more than one time, any previously used random numbers are ignored because the corresponding manager is already included in the sample. Selecting a sample in this manner is referred to as **sampling without replacement**. If we selected a sample such that previously used random numbers are acceptable and specific managers could be included in the sample two or more times, we would be **sampling with replacement**. Sampling with replacement is a valid way of identifying a simple random sample. However, sampling without replacement is the sampling procedure used most often in practice. When we refer to simple random sampling, we will assume the sampling is without replacement.

Sampling from an Infinite Population

Sometimes we want to select a sample from a population, but the population is infinitely large or the elements of the population are being generated by an ongoing process for which there is no limit on the number of elements that can be generated. Thus, it is not possible to develop a list of all the elements in the population. This is considered the infinite population case. With an infinite population, we cannot select a simple random sample because we cannot construct a frame consisting of all the elements. In the infinite population case, statisticians recommend selecting what is called a random sample.

RANDOM SAMPLE (INFINITE POPULATION)

A **random sample** of size n from an infinite population is a sample selected such that the following conditions are satisfied.

1. Each element selected comes from the same population.
2. Each element is selected independently.

Care and judgment must be exercised in implementing the selection process for obtaining a random sample from an infinite population. Each case may require a different selection procedure. Let us consider two examples to see what we mean by the conditions (1) each element selected comes from the same population and (2) each element is selected independently.

A common quality control application involves a production process where there is no limit on the number of elements that can be produced. The conceptual population we are sampling from is all the elements that could be produced (not just the ones that are produced) by the ongoing production process. Because we cannot develop a list of all the elements that could be produced, the population is considered infinite. To be more specific, let us consider a production line designed to fill boxes of a breakfast cereal with a mean weight of 24 ounces of breakfast cereal per box. Samples of 12 boxes filled by this process are periodically selected by a quality control inspector to determine if the process is operating properly or if, perhaps, a machine malfunction has caused the process to begin underfilling or overfilling the boxes.

With a production operation such as this, the biggest concern in selecting a random sample is to make sure that condition 1, the sampled elements are selected from the same population, is satisfied. To ensure that this condition is satisfied, the boxes must be selected at approximately the same point in time. This way the inspector avoids the possibility of selecting some boxes when the process is operating properly and other boxes when the process is not operating properly and is underfilling or overfilling the boxes. With a production process such as this, the second condition, each element is selected independently, is satisfied by designing the production process so that each box of cereal is filled independently. With this assumption, the quality control inspector only needs to worry about satisfying the same population condition.

As another example of selecting a random sample from an infinite population, consider the population of customers arriving at a fast-food restaurant. Suppose an employee is asked to select and interview a sample of customers in order to develop a profile of customers who visit the restaurant. The customer arrival process is ongoing and there is no way to obtain a list of all customers in the population. So, for practical purposes, the population for this ongoing process is considered infinite. As long as a sampling procedure is designed so that all the elements in the sample are customers of the restaurant and they are selected independently, a random sample will be obtained. In this case, the employee collecting the sample needs to select the sample from people who come into the restaurant and make a purchase to ensure that the same population condition is satisfied. If, for instance, the employee selected someone for the sample who came into the restaurant just to use the restroom, that person would not be a customer and the same population condition would be violated. So, as long as the interviewer selects the sample from people making a purchase at the restaurant, condition 1 is satisfied. Ensuring that the customers are selected independently can be more difficult.

The purpose of the second condition of the random sample selection procedure (each element is selected independently) is to prevent selection bias. In this case, selection bias would occur if the interviewer were free to select customers for the sample arbitrarily. The interviewer might feel more comfortable selecting customers in a particular age group and might avoid customers in other age groups. Selection bias would also occur if the interviewer selected a group of five customers who entered the restaurant together and asked all of them to participate in the sample. Such a group of customers would be likely to exhibit similar characteristics, which might provide misleading information about the population of customers. Selection bias such as this can be avoided by ensuring that the selection of a particular customer does not influence the selection of any other customer. In other words, the elements (customers) are selected independently.

McDonald's, the fast-food restaurant leader, implemented a random sampling procedure for this situation. The sampling procedure was based on the fact that some customers presented discount coupons. Whenever a customer presented a discount coupon, the next customer served was asked to complete a customer profile questionnaire. Because arriving customers presented discount coupons randomly and independently of other customers, this sampling procedure ensured that customers were selected independently. As a result, the sample satisfied the requirements of a random sample from an infinite population.

Situations involving sampling from an infinite population are usually associated with a process that operates over time. Examples include parts being manufactured on a production line, repeated experimental trials in a laboratory, transactions occurring at a bank, telephone calls arriving at a technical support center, and customers entering a retail store. In each case, the situation may be viewed as a process that generates elements from an infinite population. As long as the sampled elements are selected from the same population and are selected independently, the sample is considered a random sample from an infinite population.

NOTES AND COMMENTS

1. In this section we have been careful to define two types of samples: a simple random sample from a finite population and a random sample from an infinite population. In the remainder of the text, we will generally refer to both of these as either a *random sample* or simply a *sample*. We will not make a distinction of the sample being a "simple" random sample unless it is necessary for the exercise or discussion.
2. Statisticians who specialize in sample surveys from finite populations use sampling methods that provide probability samples. With a probability sample, each possible sample has a known probability of selection and a random process is used to select the elements for the sample. Simple random sampling is one of these methods. In Section 7.8, we describe some other probability sampling methods: stratified random sampling, cluster sampling, and systematic sampling. We use the term "simple" in simple random sampling to clarify that this is the probability sampling method that assures each sample of size n has the same probability of being selected.
3. The number of different simple random samples of size n that can be selected from a finite population of size N is

$$\frac{N!}{n!(N-n)!}$$

In this formula, $N!$ and $n!$ are the factorial formulas discussed in Chapter 4. For the EAI problem with $N = 2500$ and $n = 30$, this expression can be used to show that approximately 2.75×10^{69} different simple random samples of 30 EAI managers can be obtained.

Exercises

Methods

SELF test

1. Consider a finite population with five elements labeled A, B, C, D, and E. Ten possible simple random samples of size 2 can be selected.
   a. List the 10 samples beginning with AB, AC, and so on.
   b. Using simple random sampling, what is the probability that each sample of size 2 is selected?
   c. Assume random number 1 corresponds to A, random number 2 corresponds to B, and so on. List the simple random sample of size 2 that will be selected by using the random digits 8 0 5 7 5 3 2.
2. Assume a finite population has 350 elements. Using the last three digits of each of the following five-digit random numbers (e.g., 601, 022, 448, . . .), determine the first four elements that will be selected for the simple random sample.

   98601 73022 83448 02147 34229 27553 84147 93289 14209

Applications

SELF test

3. *Fortune* publishes data on sales, profits, assets, stockholders' equity, market value, and earnings per share for the 500 largest U.S. industrial corporations (*Fortune* 500, 2012). Assume that you want to select a simple random sample of 10 corporations from the *Fortune* 500 list. Use the last three digits in column 9 of Table 7.1, beginning with 554. Read down the column and identify the numbers of the 10 corporations that would be selected.
4. The 10 most active stocks on the New York Stock Exchange on March 6, 2006, are shown here (*The Wall Street Journal,* March 7, 2006).

AT&T	Lucent	Nortel	Qwest	Bell South
Pfizer	Texas Instruments	Gen. Elect.	iShrMSJpn	LSI Logic

   Exchange authorities decided to investigate trading practices using a sample of three of these stocks.
   a. Beginning with the first random digit in column 6 of Table 7.1, read down the column to select a simple random sample of three stocks for the exchange authorities.
   b. Using the information in the third Note and Comment, determine how many different simple random samples of size 3 can be selected from the list of 10 stocks.
5. A student government organization is interested in estimating the proportion of students who favor a mandatory "pass-fail" grading policy for elective courses. A list of names and addresses of the 645 students enrolled during the current quarter is available from the registrar's office. Using three-digit random numbers in row 10 of Table 7.1 and moving across the row from left to right, identify the first 10 students who would be selected using simple random sampling. The three-digit random numbers begin with 816, 283, and 610.
6. The *County and City Data Book,* published by the Census Bureau, lists information on 3139 counties throughout the United States. Assume that a national study will collect data from 30 randomly selected counties. Use four-digit random numbers from the last column of Table 7.1 to identify the numbers corresponding to the first five counties selected for the sample. Ignore the first digits and begin with the four-digit random numbers 9945, 8364, 5702, and so on.

7. Assume that we want to identify a simple random sample of 12 of the 372 doctors practicing in a particular city. The doctors' names are available from a local medical organization. Use the eighth column of five-digit random numbers in Table 7.1 to identify the 12 doctors for the sample. Ignore the first two random digits in each five-digit grouping of the random numbers. This process begins with random number 108 and proceeds down the column of random numbers.

8. The following stocks make up the Dow Jones Industrial Average (*Barron's,* July 30, 2012).

1. 3M	11. Disney	21. McDonald's
2. AT&T	12. DuPont	22. Merck
3. Alcoa	13. ExxonMobil	23. Microsoft
4. American Express	14. General Electric	24. J.P. Morgan
5. Bank of America	15. Hewlett-Packard	25. Pfizer
6. Boeing	16. Home Depot	26. Procter & Gamble
7. Caterpillar	17. IBM	27. Travelers
8. Chevron	18. Intel	28. United Technologies
9. Cisco Systems	19. Johnson & Johnson	29. Verizon
10. Coca-Cola	20. Kraft Foods	30. Wal-Mart

Suppose you would like to select a sample of six of these companies to conduct an in-depth study of management practices. Use the first two digits in each row of the ninth column of Table 7.1 to select a simple random sample of six companies.

9. *The Wall Street Journal* provides the net asset value, the year-to-date percent return, and the three-year percent return for 555 mutual funds (*The Wall Street Journal,* April 25, 2003). Assume that a simple random sample of 12 of the 555 mutual funds will be selected for a follow-up study on the size and performance of mutual funds. Use the fourth column of the random numbers in Table 7.1, beginning with 51102, to select the simple random sample of 12 mutual funds. Begin with mutual fund 102 and use the *last* three digits in each row of the fourth column for your selection process. What are the numbers of the 12 mutual funds in the simple random sample?

10. Indicate which of the following situations involve sampling from a finite population and which involve sampling from an infinite population. In cases where the sampled population is finite, describe how you would construct a frame.
    a. Obtain a sample of licensed drivers in the state of New York.
    b. Obtain a sample of boxes of cereal produced by the Breakfast Choice company.
    c. Obtain a sample of cars crossing the Golden Gate Bridge on a typical weekday.
    d. Obtain a sample of students in a statistics course at Indiana University.
    e. Obtain a sample of the orders that are processed by a mail-order firm.

7.3 Point Estimation

Now that we have described how to select a simple random sample, let us return to the EAI problem. A simple random sample of 30 managers and the corresponding data on annual salary and management training program participation are as shown in Table 7.2. The notation x_1, x_2, and so on is used to denote the annual salary of the first manager in the sample, the annual salary of the second manager in the sample, and so on. Participation in the management training program is indicated by Yes in the management training program column.

To estimate the value of a population parameter, we compute a corresponding characteristic of the sample, referred to as a **sample statistic**. For example, to estimate the population mean μ and the population standard deviation σ for the annual salary of EAI managers, we use the data in Table 7.2 to calculate the corresponding sample statistics: the

TABLE 7.2 ANNUAL SALARY AND TRAINING PROGRAM STATUS FOR A SIMPLE RANDOM SAMPLE OF 30 EAI MANAGERS

Annual Salary ($)	Management Training Program	Annual Salary ($)	Management Training Program
$x_1 = 49{,}094.30$	Yes	$x_{16} = 51{,}766.00$	Yes
$x_2 = 53{,}263.90$	Yes	$x_{17} = 52{,}541.30$	No
$x_3 = 49{,}643.50$	Yes	$x_{18} = 44{,}980.00$	Yes
$x_4 = 49{,}894.90$	Yes	$x_{19} = 51{,}932.60$	Yes
$x_5 = 47{,}621.60$	No	$x_{20} = 52{,}973.00$	Yes
$x_6 = 55{,}924.00$	Yes	$x_{21} = 45{,}120.90$	Yes
$x_7 = 49{,}092.30$	Yes	$x_{22} = 51{,}753.00$	Yes
$x_8 = 51{,}404.40$	Yes	$x_{23} = 54{,}391.80$	No
$x_9 = 50{,}957.70$	Yes	$x_{24} = 50{,}164.20$	No
$x_{10} = 55{,}109.70$	Yes	$x_{25} = 52{,}973.60$	No
$x_{11} = 45{,}922.60$	Yes	$x_{26} = 50{,}241.30$	No
$x_{12} = 57{,}268.40$	No	$x_{27} = 52{,}793.90$	No
$x_{13} = 55{,}688.80$	Yes	$x_{28} = 50{,}979.40$	Yes
$x_{14} = 51{,}564.70$	No	$x_{29} = 55{,}860.90$	Yes
$x_{15} = 56{,}188.20$	No	$x_{30} = 57{,}309.10$	No

sample mean and the sample standard deviation s. Using the formulas for a sample mean and a sample standard deviation presented in Chapter 3, the sample mean is

$$\bar{x} = \frac{\Sigma x_i}{n} = \frac{1{,}554{,}420}{30} = \$51{,}814$$

and the sample standard deviation is

$$s = \sqrt{\frac{\Sigma(x_i - \bar{x})^2}{n - 1}} = \sqrt{\frac{325{,}009{,}260}{29}} = \$3348$$

To estimate p, the proportion of managers in the population who completed the management training program, we use the corresponding sample proportion $\bar{p}$. Let x denote the number of managers in the sample who completed the management training program. The data in Table 7.2 show that $x = 19$. Thus, with a sample size of $n = 30$, the sample proportion is

$$\bar{p} = \frac{x}{n} = \frac{19}{30} = .63$$

By making the preceding computations, we perform the statistical procedure called *point estimation*. We refer to the sample mean $\bar{x}$ as the **point estimator** of the population mean μ, the sample standard deviation s as the point estimator of the population standard deviation σ, and the sample proportion $\bar{p}$ as the point estimator of the population proportion p. The numerical value obtained for $\bar{x}$, s, or $\bar{p}$ is called the **point estimate**. Thus, for the simple random sample of 30 EAI managers shown in Table 7.2, \$51,814 is the point estimate of μ, \$3348 is the point estimate of σ, and .63 is the point estimate of p. Table 7.3 summarizes the sample results and compares the point estimates to the actual values of the population parameters.

As is evident from Table 7.3, the point estimates differ somewhat from the corresponding population parameters. This difference is to be expected because a sample, and not a census of the entire population, is being used to develop the point estimates. In the next chapter, we will show how to construct an interval estimate in order to provide information about how close the point estimate is to the population parameter.

TABLE 7.3 SUMMARY OF POINT ESTIMATES OBTAINED FROM A SIMPLE RANDOM SAMPLE OF 30 EAI MANAGERS

Population Parameter	Parameter Value	Point Estimator	Point Estimate
μ = Population mean annual salary	\$51,800	$\bar{x}$ = Sample mean annual salary	\$51,814
σ = Population standard deviation for annual salary	\$4000	s = Sample standard deviation for annual salary	\$3348
p = Population proportion having completed the management training program	.60	$\bar{p}$ = Sample proportion having completed the management training program	.63

Practical Advice

The subject matter of most of the rest of the book is concerned with statistical inference. Point estimation is a form of statistical inference. We use a sample statistic to make an inference about a population parameter. When making inferences about a population based on a sample, it is important to have a close correspondence between the sampled population and the target population. The **target population** is the population we want to make inferences about, while the sampled population is the population from which the sample is actually taken. In this section, we have described the process of drawing a simple random sample from the population of EAI managers and making point estimates of characteristics of that same population. So the sampled population and the target population are identical, which is the desired situation. But in other cases, it is not as easy to obtain a close correspondence between the sampled and target populations.

Consider the case of an amusement park selecting a sample of its customers to learn about characteristics such as age and time spent at the park. Suppose all the sample elements were selected on a day when park attendance was restricted to employees of a single company. Then the sampled population would be composed of employees of that company and members of their families. If the target population we wanted to make inferences about were typical park customers over a typical summer, then we might encounter a significant difference between the sampled population and the target population. In such a case, we would question the validity of the point estimates being made. Park management would be in the best position to know whether a sample taken on a particular day was likely to be representative of the target population.

In summary, whenever a sample is used to make inferences about a population, we should make sure that the study is designed so that the sampled population and the target population are in close agreement. Good judgment is a necessary ingredient of sound statistical practice.

Exercises

Methods

SELF test

11. The following data are from a simple random sample.

    5 8 10 7 10 14

    a. What is the point estimate of the population mean?
    b. What is the point estimate of the population standard deviation?

12. A survey question for a sample of 150 individuals yielded 75 Yes responses, 55 No responses, and 20 No Opinions.
    a. What is the point estimate of the proportion in the population who respond Yes?
    b. What is the point estimate of the proportion in the population who respond No?

Applications

SELF test

13. A sample of 5 months of sales data provided the following information:

Month:	1	2	3	4	5
Units Sold:	94	100	85	94	92

   a. Develop a point estimate of the population mean number of units sold per month.
   b. Develop a point estimate of the population standard deviation.

WEB file

MutualFund

14. *BusinessWeek* published information on 283 equity mutual funds (*BusinessWeek,* January 26, 2004). A sample of 40 of those funds is contained in the data set MutualFund. Use the data set to answer the following questions.
   a. Develop a point estimate of the proportion of the *BusinessWeek* equity funds that are load funds.
   b. Develop a point estimate of the proportion of funds that are classified as high risk.
   c. Develop a point estimate of the proportion of funds that have a below-average risk rating.
15. Many drugs used to treat cancer are expensive. *BusinessWeek* reported on the cost per treatment of Herceptin, a drug used to treat breast cancer (*BusinessWeek,* January 30, 2006). Typical treatment costs (in dollars) for Herceptin are provided by a simple random sample of 10 patients.

4376	5578	2717	4920	4495
4798	6446	4119	4237	3814

   a. Develop a point estimate of the mean cost per treatment with Herceptin.
   b. Develop a point estimate of the standard deviation of the cost per treatment with Herceptin.
16. A sample of 426 U.S. adults age 50 and older were asked how important a variety of issues were in choosing whom to vote for in the 2012 presidential election (*AARP Bulletin,* March 2012).
   a. What is the sampled population for this study?
   b. Social Security and Medicare was cited as "very important" by 350 respondents. Estimate the proportion of the population of U.S. adults age 50 and over who believe this issue is very important.
   c. Education was cited as "very important" by 74% of the respondents. Estimate the number of respondents who believe this issue is very important.
   d. Job Growth was cited as "very important" by 354 respondents. Estimate the proportion of U.S. adults age 50 and over who believe job growth is very important.
   e. What is the target population for the inferences being made in parts (b) and (d)? Is it the same as the sampled population you identified in part (a)? Suppose you later learn that the sample was restricted to members of the American Association of Retired People (AARP). Would you still feel the inferences being made in parts (b) and (d) are valid? Why or why not?
17. The American Association of Individual Investors (AAII) polls its subscribers on a weekly basis to determine the number who are bullish, bearish, or neutral on the short-term prospects for the stock market. Their findings for the week ending March 2, 2006, are consistent with the following sample results (AAII website, March 7, 2006).

   Bullish 409 Neutral 299 Bearish 291

   Develop a point estimate of the following population parameters.
   a. The proportion of all AAII subscribers who are bullish on the stock market.
   b. The proportion of all AAII subscribers who are neutral on the stock market.
   c. The proportion of all AAII subscribers who are bearish on the stock market.
   d. What is the sampled population? What is the target population for parts (a), (b), and (c)? Would you be comfortable extending these results to the target population of all investors?

7.4 Introduction to Sampling Distributions

In the preceding section we said that the sample mean $\bar{x}$ is the point estimator of the population mean μ, and the sample proportion $\bar{p}$ is the point estimator of the population proportion p. For the simple random sample of 30 EAI managers shown in Table 7.2, the point estimate of μ is $\bar{x} = \$51,814$ and the point estimate of p is $\bar{p} = .63$. Suppose we select another simple random sample of 30 EAI managers and obtain the following point estimates:

$$\text{Sample mean: } \bar{x} = \$52,670$$
$$\text{Sample proportion: } \bar{p} = .70$$

Note that different values of $\bar{x}$ and $\bar{p}$ were obtained. Indeed, a second simple random sample of 30 EAI managers cannot be expected to provide the same point estimates as the first sample.

The ability to understand the material in subsequent chapters depends heavily on the ability to understand and use the sampling distributions presented in this chapter.

Now, suppose we repeat the process of selecting a simple random sample of 30 EAI managers over and over again, each time computing the values of $\bar{x}$ and $\bar{p}$. Table 7.4 contains a portion of the results obtained for 500 simple random samples, and Table 7.5 shows the frequency and relative frequency distributions for the 500 $\bar{x}$ values. Figure 7.1 shows the relative frequency histogram for the $\bar{x}$ values.

In Chapter 5 we defined a random variable as a numerical description of the outcome of an experiment. If we consider the process of selecting a simple random sample as an

TABLE 7.4 VALUES OF $\bar{x}$ AND $\bar{p}$ FROM 500 SIMPLE RANDOM SAMPLES OF 30 EAI MANAGERS

Sample Number	Sample Mean ($\bar{x}$)	Sample Proportion ($\bar{p}$)
1	51,814	.63
2	52,670	.70
3	51,780	.67
4	51,588	.53
.	.	.
.	.	.
.	.	.
500	51,752	.50

TABLE 7.5 FREQUENCY AND RELATIVE FREQUENCY DISTRIBUTIONS OF $\bar{x}$ FROM 500 SIMPLE RANDOM SAMPLES OF 30 EAI MANAGERS

Mean Annual Salary ($)	Frequency	Relative Frequency
49,500.00–49,999.99	2	.004
50,000.00–50,499.99	16	.032
50,500.00–50,999.99	52	.104
51,000.00–51,499.99	101	.202
51,500.00–51,999.99	133	.266
52,000.00–52,499.99	110	.220
52,500.00–52,999.99	54	.108
53,000.00–53,499.99	26	.052
53,500.00–53,999.99	6	.012
	Totals 500	1.000

FIGURE 7.1 RELATIVE FREQUENCY HISTOGRAM OF $\bar{x}$ VALUES FROM 500 SIMPLE RANDOM SAMPLES OF SIZE 30 EACH

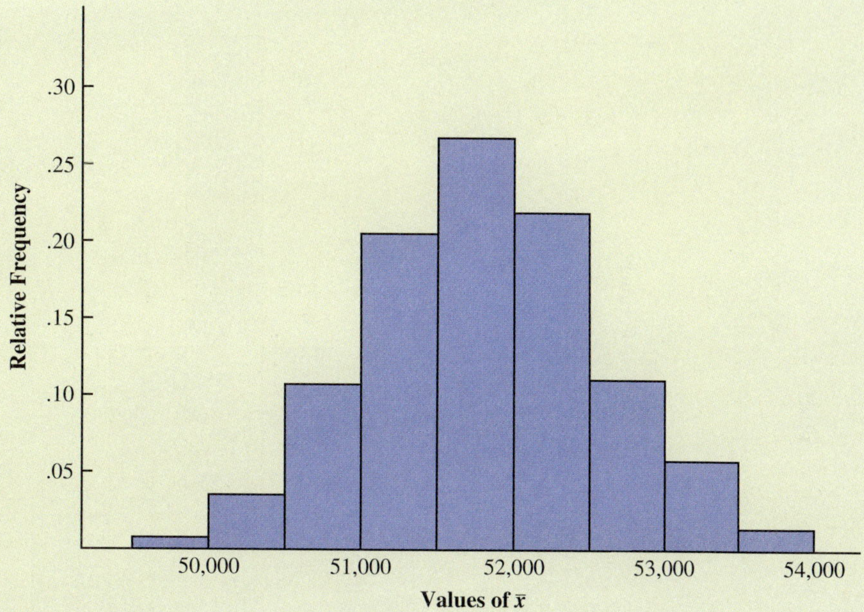

experiment, the sample mean $\bar{x}$ is the numerical description of the outcome of the experiment. Thus, the sample mean $\bar{x}$ is a random variable. As a result, just like other random variables, $\bar{x}$ has a mean or expected value, a standard deviation, and a probability distribution. Because the various possible values of $\bar{x}$ are the result of different simple random samples, the probability distribution of $\bar{x}$ is called the **sampling distribution** of $\bar{x}$. Knowledge of this sampling distribution and its properties will enable us to make probability statements about how close the sample mean $\bar{x}$ is to the population mean μ.

Let us return to Figure 7.1. We would need to enumerate every possible sample of 30 managers and compute each sample mean to completely determine the sampling distribution of $\bar{x}$. However, the histogram of 500 $\bar{x}$ values gives an approximation of this sampling distribution. From the approximation we observe the bell-shaped appearance of the distribution. We note that the largest concentration of the $\bar{x}$ values and the mean of the 500 $\bar{x}$ values is near the population mean $\mu = \$51,800$. We will describe the properties of the sampling distribution of $\bar{x}$ more fully in the next section.

The 500 values of the sample proportion $\bar{p}$ are summarized by the relative frequency histogram in Figure 7.2. As in the case of $\bar{x}$, $\bar{p}$ is a random variable. If every possible sample of size 30 were selected from the population and if a value of $\bar{p}$ were computed for each sample, the resulting probability distribution would be the sampling distribution of $\bar{p}$. The relative frequency histogram of the 500 sample values in Figure 7.2 provides a general idea of the appearance of the sampling distribution of $\bar{p}$.

In practice, we select only one simple random sample from the population. We repeated the sampling process 500 times in this section simply to illustrate that many different samples are possible and that the different samples generate a variety of values for the sample statistics $\bar{x}$ and $\bar{p}$. The probability distribution of any particular sample statistic is called the sampling distribution of the statistic. In Section 7.5 we show the characteristics of the sampling distribution of $\bar{x}$. In Section 7.6 we show the characteristics of the sampling distribution of $\bar{p}$.

FIGURE 7.2 RELATIVE FREQUENCY HISTOGRAM OF $\bar{p}$ VALUES FROM 500 SIMPLE RANDOM SAMPLES OF SIZE 30 EACH

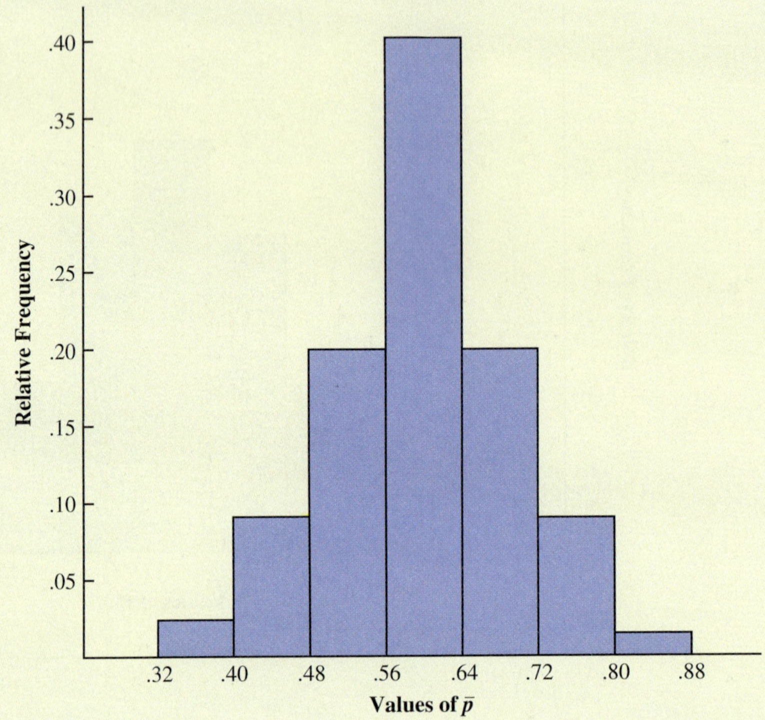

7.5 Sampling Distribution of $\bar{x}$

In the previous section we said that the sample mean $\bar{x}$ is a random variable and its probability distribution is called the sampling distribution of $\bar{x}$.

SAMPLING DISTRIBUTION OF $\bar{x}$

The sampling distribution of $\bar{x}$ is the probability distribution of all possible values of the sample mean $\bar{x}$.

This section describes the properties of the sampling distribution of $\bar{x}$. Just as with other probability distributions we studied, the sampling distribution of $\bar{x}$ has an expected value or mean, a standard deviation, and a characteristic shape or form. Let us begin by considering the mean of all possible $\bar{x}$ values, which is referred to as the expected value of $\bar{x}$.

Expected Value of $\bar{x}$

In the EAI sampling problem we saw that different simple random samples result in a variety of values for the sample mean $\bar{x}$. Because many different values of the random variable $\bar{x}$ are possible, we are often interested in the mean of all possible values of $\bar{x}$ that can be generated by the various simple random samples. The mean of the $\bar{x}$ random variable is the expected value of $\bar{x}$. Let $E(\bar{x})$ represent the expected value of $\bar{x}$ and μ represent the mean of the population from which we are selecting a simple random sample. It can be shown that with simple random sampling, $E(\bar{x})$ and μ are equal.

The expected value of $\bar{x}$ equals the mean of the population from which the sample is selected.

EXPECTED VALUE OF $\bar{x}$

$$E(\bar{x}) = \mu \quad \textbf{(7.1)}$$

where

$$E(\bar{x}) = \text{the expected value of } \bar{x}$$
$$\mu = \text{the population mean}$$

This result shows that with simple random sampling, the expected value or mean of the sampling distribution of $\bar{x}$ is equal to the mean of the population. In Section 7.1 we saw that the mean annual salary for the population of EAI managers is $\mu = \$51{,}800$. Thus, according to equation (7.1), the mean of all possible sample means for the EAI study is also \$51,800.

When the expected value of a point estimator equals the population parameter, we say the point estimator is **unbiased**. Thus, equation (7.1) shows that $\bar{x}$ is an unbiased estimator of the population mean μ.

Standard Deviation of $\bar{x}$

Let us define the standard deviation of the sampling distribution of $\bar{x}$. We will use the following notation.

$$\sigma_{\bar{x}} = \text{the standard deviation of } \bar{x}$$
$$\sigma = \text{the standard deviation of the population}$$
$$n = \text{the sample size}$$
$$N = \text{the population size}$$

It can be shown that the formula for the standard deviation of $\bar{x}$ depends on whether the population is finite or infinite. The two formulas for the standard deviation of $\bar{x}$ follow.

STANDARD DEVIATION OF $\bar{x}$

Finite Population *Infinite Population*

$$\sigma_{\bar{x}} = \sqrt{\frac{N-n}{N-1}}\left(\frac{\sigma}{\sqrt{n}}\right) \qquad \sigma_{\bar{x}} = \frac{\sigma}{\sqrt{n}} \quad \textbf{(7.2)}$$

In comparing the two formulas in (7.2), we see that the factor $\sqrt{(N-n)/(N-1)}$ is required for the finite population case but not for the infinite population case. This factor is commonly referred to as the **finite population correction factor**. In many practical sampling situations, we find that the population involved, although finite, is "large," whereas the sample size is relatively "small." In such cases the finite population correction factor $\sqrt{(N-n)/(N-1)}$ is close to 1. As a result, the difference between the values of the standard deviation of $\bar{x}$ for the finite and infinite population cases becomes negligible. Then, $\sigma_{\bar{x}} = \sigma/\sqrt{n}$ becomes a good approximation to the standard deviation of $\bar{x}$ even though the population is finite. This observation leads to the following general guideline, or rule of thumb, for computing the standard deviation of $\bar{x}$.

USE THE FOLLOWING EXPRESSION TO COMPUTE THE STANDARD DEVIATION OF $\bar{x}$

$$\sigma_{\bar{x}} = \frac{\sigma}{\sqrt{n}} \tag{7.3}$$

whenever

1. The population is infinite; or
2. The population is finite *and* the sample size is less than or equal to 5% of the population size; that is, $n/N \leq .05$.

Problem 21 shows that when $n/N \leq .05$, the finite population correction factor has little effect on the value of $\sigma_{\bar{x}}$.

The term standard error is used throughout statistical inference to refer to the standard deviation of a point estimator.

In cases where $n/N > .05$, the finite population version of formula (7.2) should be used in the computation of $\sigma_{\bar{x}}$. Unless otherwise noted, throughout the text we will assume that the population size is "large," $n/N \leq .05$, and expression (7.3) can be used to compute $\sigma_{\bar{x}}$.

To compute $\sigma_{\bar{x}}$, we need to know σ, the standard deviation of the population. To further emphasize the difference between $\sigma_{\bar{x}}$ and σ, we refer to the standard deviation of $\bar{x}$, $\sigma_{\bar{x}}$, as the **standard error** of the mean. In general, the term *standard error* refers to the standard deviation of a point estimator. Later we will see that the value of the standard error of the mean is helpful in determining how far the sample mean may be from the population mean. Let us now return to the EAI example and compute the standard error of the mean associated with simple random samples of 30 EAI managers.

In Section 7.1 we saw that the standard deviation of annual salary for the population of 2500 EAI managers is $\sigma = 4000$. In this case, the population is finite, with $N = 2500$. However, with a sample size of 30, we have $n/N = 30/2500 = .012$. Because the sample size is less than 5% of the population size, we can ignore the finite population correction factor and use equation (7.3) to compute the standard error.

$$\sigma_{\bar{x}} = \frac{\sigma}{\sqrt{n}} = \frac{4000}{\sqrt{30}} = 730.3$$

Form of the Sampling Distribution of $\bar{x}$

The preceding results concerning the expected value and standard deviation for the sampling distribution of $\bar{x}$ are applicable for any population. The final step in identifying the characteristics of the sampling distribution of $\bar{x}$ is to determine the form or shape of the sampling distribution. We will consider two cases: (1) The population has a normal distribution; and (2) the population does not have a normal distribution.

Population has a normal distribution. In many situations it is reasonable to assume that the population from which we are selecting a random sample has a normal, or nearly normal, distribution. When the population has a normal distribution, the sampling distribution of $\bar{x}$ is normally distributed for any sample size.

Population does not have a normal distribution. When the population from which we are selecting a random sample does not have a normal distribution, the **central limit theorem** is helpful in identifying the shape of the sampling distribution of $\bar{x}$. A statement of the central limit theorem as it applies to the sampling distribution of $\bar{x}$ follows.

CENTRAL LIMIT THEOREM

In selecting random samples of size n from a population, the sampling distribution of the sample mean $\bar{x}$ can be approximated by a *normal distribution* as the sample size becomes large.

Figure 7.3 shows how the central limit theorem works for three different populations; each column refers to one of the populations. The top panel of the figure shows that none of the populations are normally distributed. Population I follows a uniform distribution. Population II is often called the rabbit-eared distribution. It is symmetric, but the more likely

FIGURE 7.3 ILLUSTRATION OF THE CENTRAL LIMIT THEOREM FOR THREE POPULATIONS

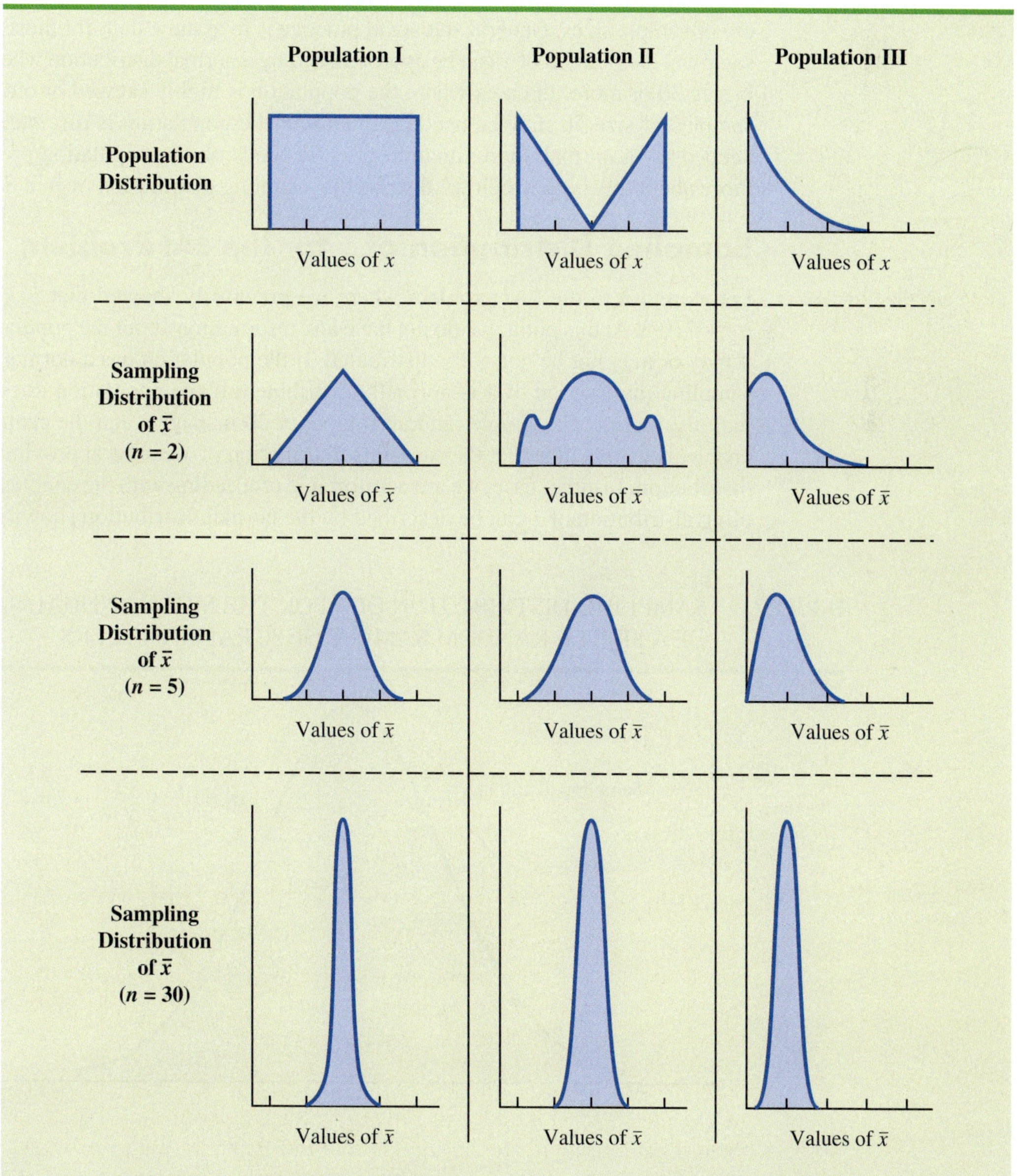

values fall in the tails of the distribution. Population III is shaped like the exponential distribution; it is skewed to the right.

The bottom three panels of Figure 7.3 show the shape of the sampling distribution for samples of size $n = 2$, $n = 5$, and $n = 30$. When the sample size is 2, we see that the shape of each sampling distribution is different from the shape of the corresponding population distribution. For samples of size 5, we see that the shapes of the sampling distributions for populations I and II begin to look similar to the shape of a normal distribution. Even though the shape of the sampling distribution for population III begins to look similar to the shape of a normal distribution, some skewness to the right is still present. Finally, for samples of size 30, the shapes of each of the three sampling distributions are approximately normal.

From a practitioner standpoint, we often want to know how large the sample size needs to be before the central limit theorem applies and we can assume that the shape of the sampling distribution is approximately normal. Statistical researchers have investigated this question by studying the sampling distribution of $\bar{x}$ for a variety of populations and a variety of sample sizes. General statistical practice is to assume that, for most applications, the sampling distribution of $\bar{x}$ can be approximated by a normal distribution whenever the sample is size 30 or more. In cases where the population is highly skewed or outliers are present, samples of size 50 may be needed. Finally, if the population is discrete, the sample size needed for a normal approximation often depends on the population proportion. We say more about this issue when we discuss the sampling distribution of $\bar{p}$ in Section 7.6.

Sampling Distribution of $\bar{x}$ for the EAI Problem

Let us return to the EAI problem where we previously showed that $E(\bar{x}) = \$51,800$ and $\sigma_{\bar{x}} = 730.3$. At this point, we do not have any information about the population distribution; it may or may not be normally distributed. If the population has a normal distribution, the sampling distribution of $\bar{x}$ is normally distributed. If the population does not have a normal distribution, the simple random sample of 30 managers and the central limit theorem enable us to conclude that the sampling distribution of $\bar{x}$ can be approximated by a normal distribution. In either case, we are comfortable proceeding with the conclusion that the sampling distribution of $\bar{x}$ can be described by the normal distribution shown in Figure 7.4.

FIGURE 7.4 SAMPLING DISTRIBUTION OF $\bar{x}$ FOR THE MEAN ANNUAL SALARY OF A SIMPLE RANDOM SAMPLE OF 30 EAI MANAGERS

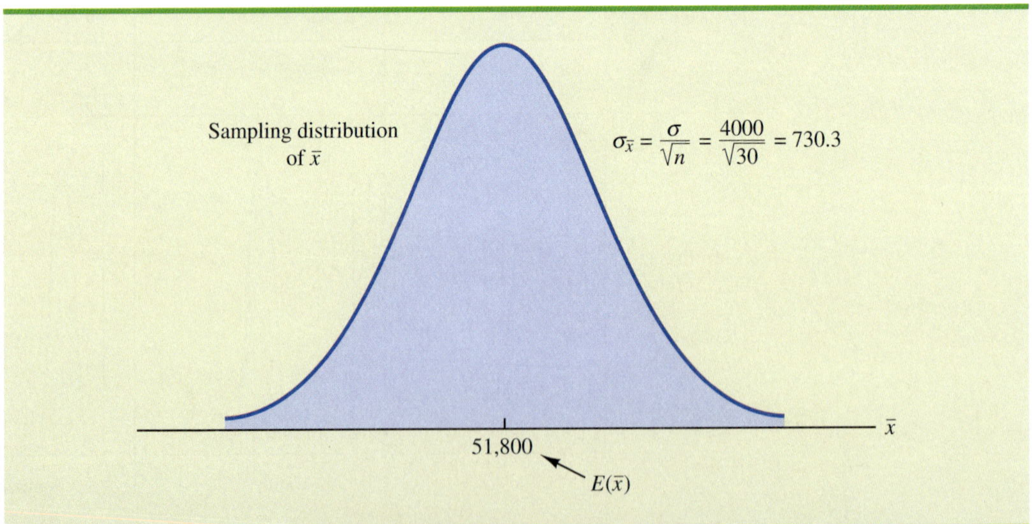

Practical Value of the Sampling Distribution of $\bar{x}$

Whenever a simple random sample is selected and the value of the sample mean is used to estimate the value of the population mean μ, we cannot expect the sample mean to exactly equal the population mean. The practical reason we are interested in the sampling distribution of $\bar{x}$ is that it can be used to provide probability information about the difference between the sample mean and the population mean. To demonstrate this use, let us return to the EAI problem.

Suppose the personnel director believes the sample mean will be an acceptable estimate of the population mean if the sample mean is within \$500 of the population mean. However, it is not possible to guarantee that the sample mean will be within \$500 of the population mean. Indeed, Table 7.5 and Figure 7.1 show that some of the 500 sample means differed by more than \$2000 from the population mean. So we must think of the personnel director's request in probability terms. That is, the personnel director is concerned with the following question: What is the probability that the sample mean computed using a simple random sample of 30 EAI managers will be within \$500 of the population mean?

Because we have identified the properties of the sampling distribution of $\bar{x}$ (see Figure 7.4), we will use this distribution to answer the probability question. Refer to the sampling distribution of $\bar{x}$ shown again in Figure 7.5. With a population mean of \$51,800, the personnel director wants to know the probability that $\bar{x}$ is between \$51,300 and \$52,300. This probability is given by the darkly shaded area of the sampling distribution shown in Figure 7.5. Because the sampling distribution is normally distributed, with mean 51,800 and standard error of the mean 730.3, we can use the standard normal probability table to find the area or probability.

We first calculate the z value at the upper endpoint of the interval (52,300) and use the table to find the area under the curve to the left of that point (left tail area). Then we compute the z value at the lower endpoint of the interval (51,300) and use the table to find the area under the curve to the left of that point (another left tail area). Subtracting the second tail area from the first gives us the desired probability.

At $\bar{x} = 52{,}300$, we have

$$z = \frac{52{,}300 - 51{,}800}{730.30} = .68$$

FIGURE 7.5 PROBABILITY OF A SAMPLE MEAN BEING WITHIN \$500 OF THE POPULATION MEAN FOR A SIMPLE RANDOM SAMPLE OF 30 EAI MANAGERS

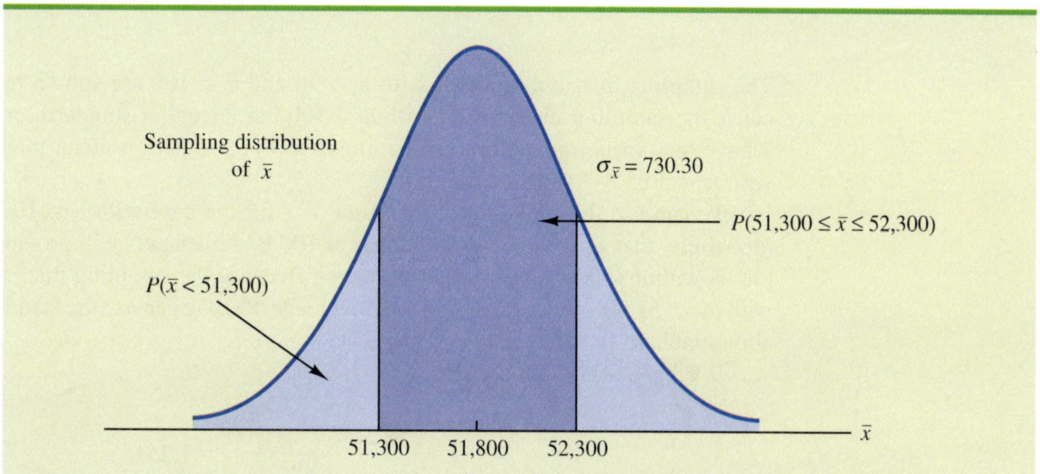

Referring to the standard normal probability table, we find a cumulative probability (area to the left of $z = .68$) of .7517.

At $\bar{x} = 51{,}300$, we have

$$z = \frac{51{,}300 - 51{,}800}{730.30} = -.68$$

The area under the curve to the left of $z = -.68$ is .2483. Therefore, $P(51{,}300 \leq \bar{x} \leq 52{,}300) = P(z \leq .68) - P(z < -.68) = .7517 - .2483 = .5034$.

The sampling distribution of $\bar{x}$ can be used to provide probability information about how close the sample mean $\bar{x}$ is to the population mean μ.

The preceding computations show that a simple random sample of 30 EAI managers has a .5034 probability of providing a sample mean $\bar{x}$ that is within \$500 of the population mean. Thus, there is a $1 - .5034 = .4966$ probability that the difference between $\bar{x}$ and $\mu = \$51{,}800$ will be more than \$500. In other words, a simple random sample of 30 EAI managers has roughly a 50–50 chance of providing a sample mean within the allowable \$500. Perhaps a larger sample size should be considered. Let us explore this possibility by considering the relationship between the sample size and the sampling distribution of $\bar{x}$.

Relationship Between the Sample Size and the Sampling Distribution of $\bar{x}$

Suppose that in the EAI sampling problem we select a simple random sample of 100 EAI managers instead of the 30 originally considered. Intuitively, it would seem that with more data provided by the larger sample size, the sample mean based on $n = 100$ should provide a better estimate of the population mean than the sample mean based on $n = 30$. To see how much better, let us consider the relationship between the sample size and the sampling distribution of $\bar{x}$.

First note that $E(\bar{x}) = \mu$ regardless of the sample size. Thus, the mean of all possible values of $\bar{x}$ is equal to the population mean μ regardless of the sample size n. However, note that the standard error of the mean, $\sigma_{\bar{x}} = \sigma/\sqrt{n}$, is related to the square root of the sample size. Whenever the sample size is increased, the standard error of the mean $\sigma_{\bar{x}}$ decreases. With $n = 30$, the standard error of the mean for the EAI problem is 730.3. However, with the increase in the sample size to $n = 100$, the standard error of the mean is decreased to

$$\sigma_{\bar{x}} = \frac{\sigma}{\sqrt{n}} = \frac{4000}{\sqrt{100}} = 400$$

The sampling distributions of $\bar{x}$ with $n = 30$ and $n = 100$ are shown in Figure 7.6. Because the sampling distribution with $n = 100$ has a smaller standard error, the values of $\bar{x}$ have less variation and tend to be closer to the population mean than the values of $\bar{x}$ with $n = 30$.

We can use the sampling distribution of $\bar{x}$ for the case with $n = 100$ to compute the probability that a simple random sample of 100 EAI managers will provide a sample mean that is within \$500 of the population mean. Because the sampling distribution is normal, with mean 51,800 and standard error of the mean 400, we can use the standard normal probability table to find the area or probability.

At $\bar{x} = 52{,}300$ (see Figure 7.7), we have

$$z = \frac{52{,}300 - 51{,}800}{400} = 1.25$$

FIGURE 7.6 A COMPARISON OF THE SAMPLING DISTRIBUTIONS OF $\bar{x}$ FOR SIMPLE RANDOM SAMPLES OF $n = 30$ AND $n = 100$ EAI MANAGERS

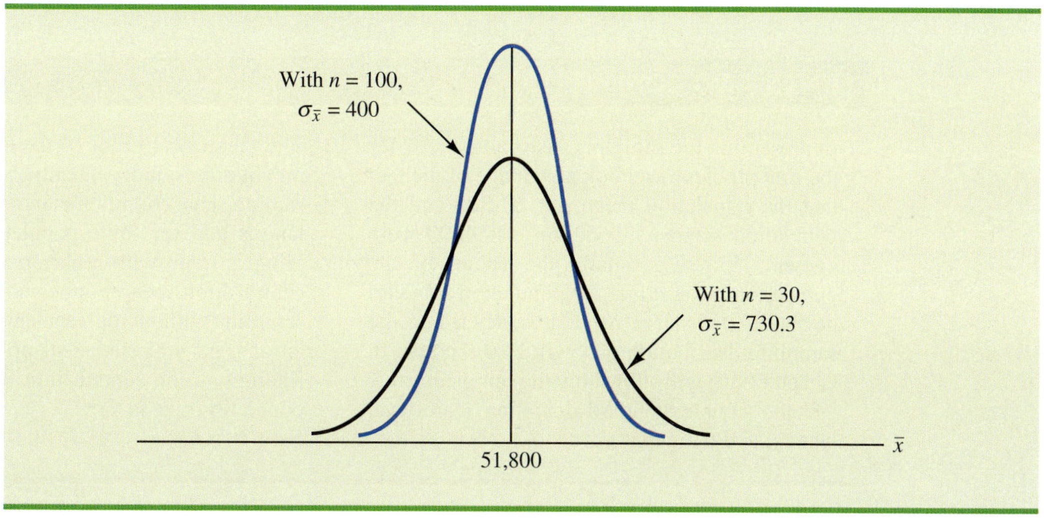

Referring to the standard normal probability table, we find a cumulative probability corresponding to $z = 1.25$ of .8944.

At $\bar{x} = 51{,}300$, we have

$$z = \frac{51{,}300 - 51{,}800}{400} = -1.25$$

The cumulative probability corresponding to $z = -1.25$ is .1056. Therefore, $P(51{,}300 \leq \bar{x} \leq 52{,}300) = P(z \leq 1.25) - P(z \leq -1.25) = .8944 - .1056 = .7888$. Thus, by increasing the sample size from 30 to 100 EAI managers, we increase the probability of obtaining a sample mean within \$500 of the population mean from .5034 to .7888.

FIGURE 7.7 PROBABILITY OF A SAMPLE MEAN BEING WITHIN \$500 OF THE POPULATION MEAN FOR A SIMPLE RANDOM SAMPLE OF 100 EAI MANAGERS

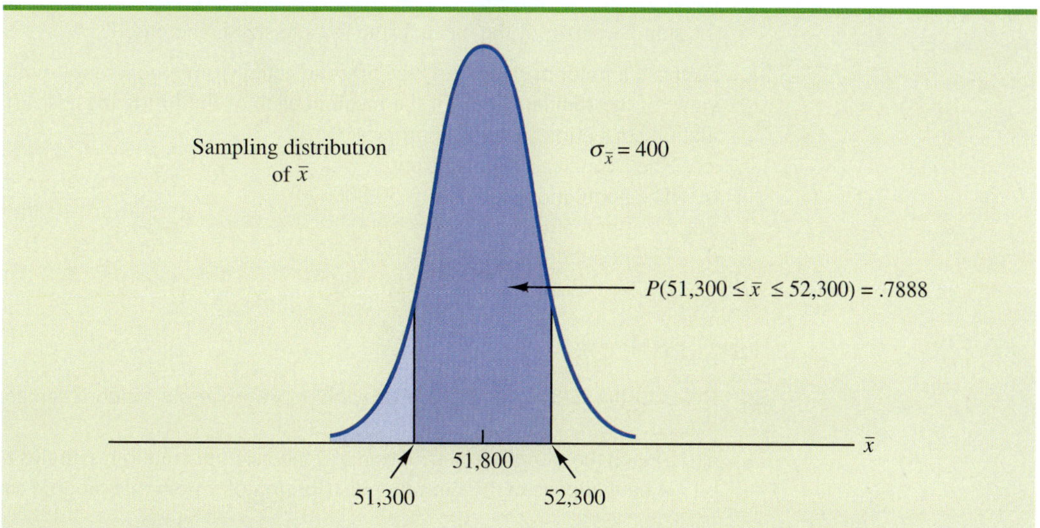

The important point in this discussion is that as the sample size is increased, the standard error of the mean decreases. As a result, the larger sample size provides a higher probability that the sample mean is within a specified distance of the population mean.

NOTES AND COMMENTS

1. In presenting the sampling distribution of $\bar{x}$ for the EAI problem, we took advantage of the fact that the population mean $\mu = 51{,}800$ and the population standard deviation $\sigma = 4000$ were known. However, usually the values of the population mean μ and the population standard deviation σ that are needed to determine the sampling distribution of $\bar{x}$ will be unknown. In Chapter 8 we will show how the sample mean $\bar{x}$ and the sample standard deviation s are used when μ and σ are unknown.

2. The theoretical proof of the central limit theorem requires independent observations in the sample. This condition is met for infinite populations and for finite populations where sampling is done with replacement. Although the central limit theorem does not directly address sampling without replacement from finite populations, general statistical practice applies the findings of the central limit theorem when the population size is large.

Exercises

Methods

18. A population has a mean of 200 and a standard deviation of 50. A sample of size 100 will be taken and the sample mean $\bar{x}$ will be used to estimate the population mean.
    a. What is the expected value of $\bar{x}$?
    b. What is the standard deviation of $\bar{x}$?
    c. Show the sampling distribution of $\bar{x}$.
    d. What does the sampling distribution of $\bar{x}$ show?

SELF test

19. A population has a mean of 200 and a standard deviation of 50. Suppose a sample of size 100 is selected and $\bar{x}$ is used to estimate μ.
    a. What is the probability that the sample mean will be within ± 5 of the population mean?
    b. What is the probability that the sample mean will be within ± 10 of the population mean?

20. Assume the population standard deviation is $\sigma = 25$. Compute the standard error of the mean, $\sigma_{\bar{x}}$, for sample sizes of 50, 100, 150, and 200. What can you say about the size of the standard error of the mean as the sample size is increased?

21. Suppose a random sample of size 50 is selected from a population with $\sigma = 10$. Find the value of the standard error of the mean in each of the following cases (use the finite population correction factor if appropriate).
    a. The population size is infinite.
    b. The population size is $N = 50{,}000$.
    c. The population size is $N = 5000$.
    d. The population size is $N = 500$.

Applications

22. Refer to the EAI sampling problem. Suppose a simple random sample of 60 managers is used.
    a. Sketch the sampling distribution of $\bar{x}$ when simple random samples of size 60 are used.
    b. What happens to the sampling distribution of $\bar{x}$ if simple random samples of size 120 are used?
    c. What general statement can you make about what happens to the sampling distribution of $\bar{x}$ as the sample size is increased? Does this generalization seem logical? Explain.

SELF test

23. In the EAI sampling problem (see Figure 7.5), we showed that for $n = 30$, there was .5034 probability of obtaining a sample mean within $\pm$\$500 of the population mean.
    a. What is the probability that $\bar{x}$ is within \$500 of the population mean if a sample of size 60 is used?
    b. Answer part (a) for a sample of size 120.
24. *Barron's* reported that the average number of weeks an individual is unemployed is 17.5 weeks (*Barron's,* February 18, 2008). Assume that for the population of all unemployed individuals the population mean length of unemployment is 17.5 weeks and that the population standard deviation is 4 weeks. Suppose you would like to select a sample of 50 unemployed individuals for a follow-up study.
    a. Show the sampling distribution of $\bar{x}$, the sample mean average for a sample of 50 unemployed individuals.
    b. What is the probability that a simple random sample of 50 unemployed individuals will provide a sample mean within 1 week of the population mean?
    c. What is the probability that a simple random sample of 50 unemployed individuals will provide a sample mean within 1/2 week of the population mean?
25. The College Board reported the following mean scores for the three parts of the Scholastic Aptitude Test (SAT) (*The World Almanac,* 2009):

Critical Reading	502
Mathematics	515
Writing	494

Assume that the population standard deviation on each part of the test is $\sigma = 100$.
    a. What is the probability a sample of 90 test takers will provide a sample mean test score within 10 points of the population mean of 502 on the Critical Reading part of the test?
    b. What is the probability a sample of 90 test takers will provide a sample mean test score within 10 points of the population mean of 515 on the Mathematics part of the test? Compare this probability to the value computed in part (a).
    c. What is the probability a sample of 100 test takers will provide a sample mean test score within 10 of the population mean of 494 on the writing part of the test? Comment on the differences between this probability and the values computed in parts (a) and (b).
26. The mean annual cost of automobile insurance is \$939 (CNBC, February 23, 2006). Assume that the standard deviation is $\sigma =$ \$245.
    a. What is the probability that a sample of automobile insurance policies will have a sample mean within \$25 of the population mean for each of the following sample sizes: 30, 50, 100, and 400?
    b. What is the advantage of a larger sample size when attempting to estimate the population mean?
27. The Economic Policy Institute periodically issues reports on wages of entry level workers. The institute reported that entry level wages for male college graduates were \$21.68 per hour and for female college graduates were \$18.80 per hour in 2011 (Economic Policy Institute website, March 30, 2012). Assume the standard deviation for male graduates is \$2.30, and for female graduates it is \$2.05.
    a. What is the probability that a sample of 50 male graduates will provide a sample mean within \$.50 of the population mean, \$21.68?
    b. What is the probability that a sample of 50 female graduates will provide a sample mean within \$.50 of the population mean, \$18.80?
    c. In which of the preceding two cases, part (a) or part (b), do we have a higher probability of obtaining a sample estimate within \$.50 of the population mean? Why?
    d. What is the probability that a sample of 120 female graduates will provide a sample mean more than \$.30 below the population mean?

28. The average score for male golfers is 95 and the average score for female golfers is 106 (*Golf Digest,* April 2006). Use these values as the population means for men and women and assume that the population standard deviation is $\sigma = 14$ strokes for both. A sample of 30 male golfers and another sample of 45 female golfers will be taken.
    a. Show the sampling distribution of $\bar{x}$ for male golfers.
    b. What is the probability that the sample mean is within 3 strokes of the population mean for the sample of male golfers?
    c. What is the probability that the sample mean is within 3 strokes of the population mean for the sample of female golfers?
    d. In which case, part (b) or part (c), is the probability of obtaining a sample mean within 3 strokes of the population mean higher? Why?
29. The mean preparation fee H&R Block charged retail customers last year was \$183 (*The Wall Street Journal,* March 7, 2012). Use this price as the population mean and assume the population standard deviation of preparation fees is \$50.
    a. What is the probability that the mean price for a sample of 30 H&R Block retail customers is within \$8 of the population mean?
    b. What is the probability that the mean price for a sample of 50 H&R Block retail customers is within \$8 of the population mean?
    c. What is the probability that the mean price for a sample of 100 H&R Block retail customers is within \$8 of the population mean?
    d. Which, if any, of the sample sizes in parts (a), (b), and (c) would you recommend to have at least a .95 probability that the sample mean is within \$8 of the population mean?
30. To estimate the mean age for a population of 4000 employees, a simple random sample of 40 employees is selected.
    a. Would you use the finite population correction factor in calculating the standard error of the mean? Explain.
    b. If the population standard deviation is $\sigma = 8.2$ years, compute the standard error both with and without the finite population correction factor. What is the rationale for ignoring the finite population correction factor whenever $n/N \le .05$?
    c. What is the probability that the sample mean age of the employees will be within ± 2 years of the population mean age?

7.6 Sampling Distribution of $\bar{p}$

The sample proportion $\bar{p}$ is the point estimator of the population proportion p. The formula for computing the sample proportion is

$$\bar{p} = \frac{x}{n}$$

where

x = the number of elements in the sample that possess the characteristic of interest

n = sample size

As noted in Section 7.4, the sample proportion $\bar{p}$ is a random variable and its probability distribution is called the sampling distribution of $\bar{p}$.

> SAMPLING DISTRIBUTION OF $\bar{p}$
>
> The sampling distribution of $\bar{p}$ is the probability distribution of all possible values of the sample proportion $\bar{p}$.

To determine how close the sample proportion $\bar{p}$ is to the population proportion p, we need to understand the properties of the sampling distribution of $\bar{p}$: the expected value of $\bar{p}$, the standard deviation of $\bar{p}$, and the shape or form of the sampling distribution of $\bar{p}$.

Expected Value of $\bar{p}$

The expected value of $\bar{p}$, the mean of all possible values of $\bar{p}$, is equal to the population proportion p.

EXPECTED VALUE OF $\bar{p}$

$$E(\bar{p}) = p \tag{7.4}$$

where

$E(\bar{p})$ = the expected value of $\bar{p}$
p = the population proportion

Because $E(\bar{p}) = p$, $\bar{p}$ is an unbiased estimator of p. Recall from Section 7.1 we noted that $p = .60$ for the EAI population, where p is the proportion of the population of managers who participated in the company's management training program. Thus, the expected value of $\bar{p}$ for the EAI sampling problem is .60.

Standard Deviation of $\bar{p}$

Just as we found for the standard deviation of $\bar{x}$, the standard deviation of $\bar{p}$ depends on whether the population is finite or infinite. The two formulas for computing the standard deviation of $\bar{p}$ follow.

STANDARD DEVIATION OF $\bar{p}$

Finite Population | *Infinite Population*

$$\sigma_{\bar{p}} = \sqrt{\frac{N-n}{N-1}}\sqrt{\frac{p(1-p)}{n}} \qquad \sigma_{\bar{p}} = \sqrt{\frac{p(1-p)}{n}} \tag{7.5}$$

Comparing the two formulas in (7.5), we see that the only difference is the use of the finite population correction factor $\sqrt{(N-n)/(N-1)}$.

As was the case with the sample mean $\bar{x}$, the difference between the expressions for the finite population and the infinite population becomes negligible if the size of the finite population is large in comparison to the sample size. We follow the same rule of thumb that we recommended for the sample mean. That is, if the population is finite with $n/N \leq .05$, we will use $\sigma_{\bar{p}} = \sqrt{p(1-p)/n}$. However, if the population is finite with $n/N > .05$, the finite population correction factor should be used. Again, unless specifically noted, throughout the text we will assume that the population size is large in relation to the sample size and thus the finite population correction factor is unnecessary.

In Section 7.5 we used the term standard error of the mean to refer to the standard deviation of $\bar{x}$. We stated that in general the term standard error refers to the standard deviation of a point estimator. Thus, for proportions we use *standard error of the proportion* to refer to the standard deviation of $\bar{p}$. Let us now return to the EAI example and compute the standard error of the proportion associated with simple random samples of 30 EAI managers.

For the EAI study we know that the population proportion of managers who participated in the management training program is $p = .60$. With $n/N = 30/2500 = .012$, we can ignore the finite population correction factor when we compute the standard error of the proportion. For the simple random sample of 30 managers, $\sigma_{\bar{p}}$ is

$$\sigma_{\bar{p}} = \sqrt{\frac{p(1-p)}{n}} = \sqrt{\frac{.60(1-.60)}{30}} = .0894$$

Form of the Sampling Distribution of $\bar{p}$

Now that we know the mean and standard deviation of the sampling distribution of $\bar{p}$, the final step is to determine the form or shape of the sampling distribution. The sample proportion is $\bar{p} = x/n$. For a simple random sample from a large population, the value of x is a binomial random variable indicating the number of elements in the sample with the characteristic of interest. Because n is a constant, the probability of x/n is the same as the binomial probability of x, which means that the sampling distribution of $\bar{p}$ is also a discrete probability distribution and that the probability for each value of x/n is the same as the probability of x.

In Chapter 6 we also showed that a binomial distribution can be approximated by a normal distribution whenever the sample size is large enough to satisfy the following two conditions:

$$np \geq 5 \quad \text{and} \quad n(1-p) \geq 5$$

Assuming these two conditions are satisfied, the probability distribution of x in the sample proportion, $\bar{p} = x/n$, can be approximated by a normal distribution. And because n is a constant, the sampling distribution of $\bar{p}$ can also be approximated by a normal distribution. This approximation is stated as follows:

> The sampling distribution of $\bar{p}$ can be approximated by a normal distribution whenever $np \geq 5$ and $n(1-p) \geq 5$.

In practical applications, when an estimate of a population proportion is desired, we find that sample sizes are almost always large enough to permit the use of a normal approximation for the sampling distribution of $\bar{p}$.

Recall that for the EAI sampling problem we know that the population proportion of managers who participated in the training program is $p = .60$. With a simple random sample of size 30, we have $np = 30(.60) = 18$ and $n(1-p) = 30(.40) = 12$. Thus, the sampling distribution of $\bar{p}$ can be approximated by a normal distribution shown in Figure 7.8.

Practical Value of the Sampling Distribution of $\bar{p}$

The practical value of the sampling distribution of $\bar{p}$ is that it can be used to provide probability information about the difference between the sample proportion and the population proportion. For instance, suppose that in the EAI problem the personnel director wants to know the probability of obtaining a value of $\bar{p}$ that is within .05 of the population proportion of EAI managers who participated in the training program. That is, what is the probability of obtaining a sample with a sample proportion $\bar{p}$ between .55 and .65? The darkly shaded

FIGURE 7.8 SAMPLING DISTRIBUTION OF $\bar{p}$ FOR THE PROPORTION OF EAI MANAGERS WHO PARTICIPATED IN THE MANAGEMENT TRAINING PROGRAM

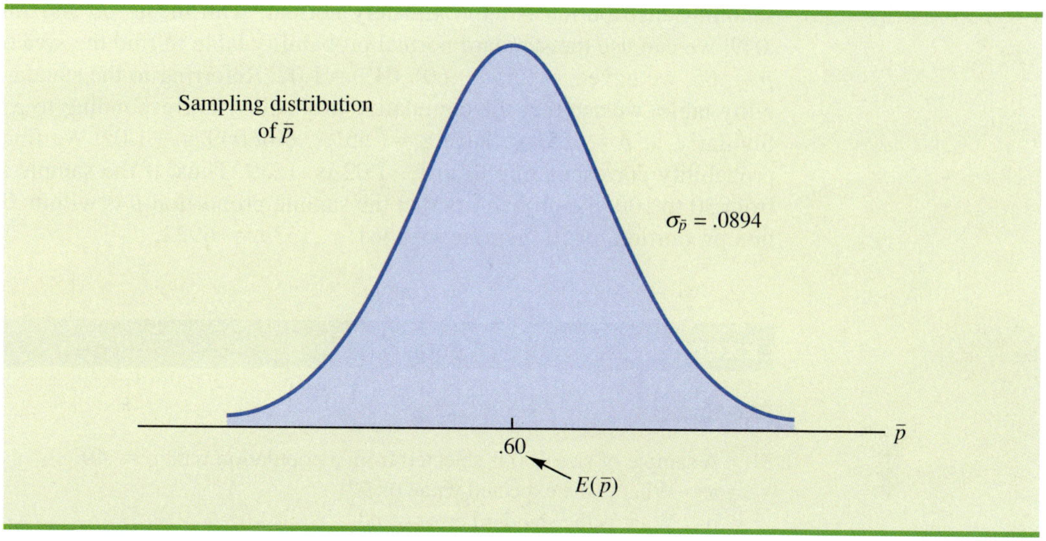

area in Figure 7.9 shows this probability. Using the fact that the sampling distribution of $\bar{p}$ can be approximated by a normal distribution with a mean of .60 and a standard error of the proportion of $\sigma_{\bar{p}} = .0894$, we find that the standard normal random variable corresponding to $\bar{p} = .65$ has a value of $z = (.65 - .60)/.0894 = .56$. Referring to the standard normal probability table, we see that the cumulative probability corresponding to $z = .56$ is .7123. Similarly, at $\bar{p} = .55$, we find $z = (.55 - .60)/.0894 = -.56$. From the standard normal probability table, we find the cumulative probability corresponding to $z = -.56$ is .2877. Thus, the probability of selecting a sample that provides a sample proportion $\bar{p}$ within .05 of the population proportion p is given by $.7123 - .2877 = .4246$.

If we consider increasing the sample size to $n = 100$, the standard error of the proportion becomes

$$\sigma_{\bar{p}} = \sqrt{\frac{.60(1 - .60)}{100}} = .049$$

FIGURE 7.9 PROBABILITY OF OBTAINING $\bar{p}$ BETWEEN .55 AND .65

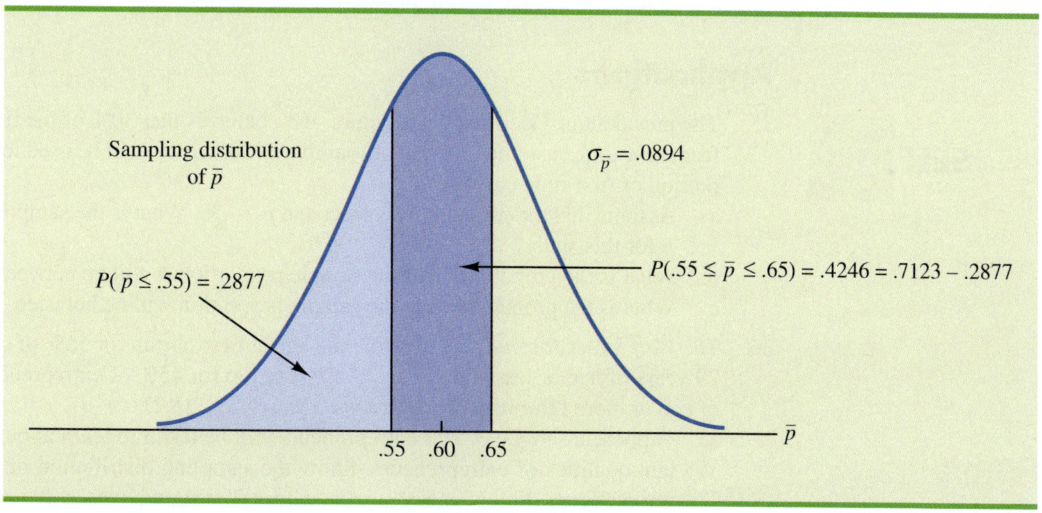

With a sample size of 100 EAI managers, the probability of the sample proportion having a value within .05 of the population proportion can now be computed. Because the sampling distribution is approximately normal, with mean .60 and standard deviation .049, we can use the standard normal probability table to find the area or probability. At $\bar{p} = .65$, we have $z = (.65 - .60)/.049 = 1.02$. Referring to the standard normal probability table, we see that the cumulative probability corresponding to $z = 1.02$ is .8461. Similarly, at $\bar{p} = .55$, we have $z = (.55 - .60)/.049 = -1.02$. We find the cumulative probability corresponding to $z = -1.02$ is .1539. Thus, if the sample size is increased from 30 to 100, the probability that the sample proportion $\bar{p}$ is within .05 of the population proportion p will increase to $.8461 - .1539 = .6922$.

Exercises

Methods

31. A sample of size 100 is selected from a population with $p = .40$.
    a. What is the expected value of $\bar{p}$?
    b. What is the standard error of $\bar{p}$?
    c. Show the sampling distribution of $\bar{p}$.
    d. What does the sampling distribution of $\bar{p}$ show?

SELF test

32. A population proportion is .40. A sample of size 200 will be taken and the sample proportion $\bar{p}$ will be used to estimate the population proportion.
    a. What is the probability that the sample proportion will be within $\pm .03$ of the population proportion?
    b. What is the probability that the sample proportion will be within $\pm .05$ of the population proportion?

33. Assume that the population proportion is .55. Compute the standard error of the proportion, $\sigma_{\bar{p}}$, for sample sizes of 100, 200, 500, and 1000. What can you say about the size of the standard error of the proportion as the sample size is increased?

34. The population proportion is .30. What is the probability that a sample proportion will be within $\pm .04$ of the population proportion for each of the following sample sizes?
    a. $n = 100$
    b. $n = 200$
    c. $n = 500$
    d. $n = 1000$
    e. What is the advantage of a larger sample size?

Applications

SELF test

35. The president of Doerman Distributors, Inc., believes that 30% of the firm's orders come from first-time customers. A random sample of 100 orders will be used to estimate the proportion of first-time customers.
    a. Assume that the president is correct and $p = .30$. What is the sampling distribution of $\bar{p}$ for this study?
    b. What is the probability that the sample proportion $\bar{p}$ will be between .20 and .40?
    c. What is the probability that the sample proportion will be between .25 and .35?

36. *The Wall Street Journal* reported that the age at first startup for 55% of entrepreneurs was 29 years of age or less and the age at first startup for 45% of entrepreneurs was 30 years of age or more (*The Wall Street Journal,* March 19, 2012).
    a. Suppose a sample of 200 entrepreneurs will be taken to learn about the most important qualities of entrepreneurs. Show the sampling distribution of $\bar{p}$ where $\bar{p}$ is the sample proportion of entrepreneurs whose first startup was at 29 years of age or less.

b. What is the probability that the sample proportion in part (a) will be within $\pm.05$ of its population proportion?
c. Suppose a sample of 200 entrepreneurs will be taken to learn about the most important qualities of entrepreneurs. Show the sampling distribution of $\bar{p}$ where $\bar{p}$ is now the sample proportion of entrepreneurs whose first startup was at 30 years of age or more.
d. What is the probability that the sample proportion in part (c) will be within $\pm.05$ of its population proportion?
e Is the probability different in parts (b) and (d)? Why?
f. Answer part (b) for a sample of size 400. Is the probability smaller? Why?

37. People end up tossing 12% of what they buy at the grocery store (*Reader's Digest,* March 2009). Assume this is the true population proportion and that you plan to take a sample survey of 540 grocery shoppers to further investigate their behavior.
    a. Show the sampling distribution of $\bar{p}$, the proportion of groceries thrown out by your sample respondents.
    b. What is the probability that your survey will provide a sample proportion within $\pm.03$ of the population proportion?
    c. What is the probability that your survey will provide a sample proportion within $\pm.015$ of the population proportion?

38. Forty-two percent of primary care doctors think their patients receive unnecessary medical care (*Reader's Digest,* December 2011/January 2012).
    a. Suppose a sample of 300 primary care doctors were taken. Show the sampling distribution of the proportion of the doctors who think their patients receive unnecessary medical care.
    b. What is the probability that the sample proportion will be within $\pm.03$ of the population proportion?
    c. What is the probability that the sample proportion will be within $\pm.05$ of the population proportion?
    d. What would be the effect of taking a larger sample on the probabilities in parts (b) and (c)? Why?

39. In 2008 the Better Business Bureau settled 75% of complaints they received (*USA Today,* March 2, 2009). Suppose you have been hired by the Better Business Bureau to investigate the complaints they received this year involving new car dealers. You plan to select a sample of new car dealer complaints to estimate the proportion of complaints the Better Business Bureau is able to settle. Assume the population proportion of complaints settled for new car dealers is .75, the same as the overall proportion of complaints settled in 2008.
    a. Suppose you select a sample of 450 complaints involving new car dealers. Show the sampling distribution of $\bar{p}$.
    b. Based upon a sample of 450 complaints, what is the probability that the sample proportion will be within .04 of the population proportion?
    c. Suppose you select a sample of 200 complaints involving new car dealers. Show the sampling distribution of $\bar{p}$.
    d. Based upon the smaller sample of only 200 complaints, what is the probability that the sample proportion will be within .04 of the population proportion?
    e. As measured by the increase in probability, how much do you gain in precision by taking the larger sample in part (b)?

40. The Grocery Manufacturers of America reported that 76% of consumers read the ingredients listed on a product's label. Assume the population proportion is $p = .76$ and a sample of 400 consumers is selected from the population.
    a. Show the sampling distribution of the sample proportion $\bar{p}$ where $\bar{p}$ is the proportion of the sampled consumers who read the ingredients listed on a product's label.

b. What is the probability that the sample proportion will be within $\pm .03$ of the population proportion?
c. Answer part (b) for a sample of 750 consumers.

41. The Food Marketing Institute shows that 17% of households spend more than \$100 per week on groceries. Assume the population proportion is $p = .17$ and a sample of 800 households will be selected from the population.
a. Show the sampling distribution of $\bar{p}$, the sample proportion of households spending more than \$100 per week on groceries.
b. What is the probability that the sample proportion will be within $\pm .02$ of the population proportion?
c. Answer part (b) for a sample of 1600 households.

7.7 Properties of Point Estimators

In this chapter we showed how sample statistics such as a sample mean $\bar{x}$, a sample standard deviation s, and a sample proportion $\bar{p}$ can be used as point estimators of their corresponding population parameters μ, σ, and p. It is intuitively appealing that each of these sample statistics is the point estimator of its corresponding population parameter. However, before using a sample statistic as a point estimator, statisticians check to see whether the sample statistic demonstrates certain properties associated with good point estimators. In this section we discuss three properties of good point estimators: unbiased, efficiency, and consistency.

Because several different sample statistics can be used as point estimators of different population parameters, we use the following general notation in this section.

$$\theta = \text{the population parameter of interest}$$
$$\hat{\theta} = \text{the sample statistic or point estimator of } \theta$$

The notation θ is the Greek letter theta, and the notation $\hat{\theta}$ is pronounced "theta-hat." In general, θ represents any population parameter such as a population mean, population standard deviation, population proportion, and so on; $\hat{\theta}$ represents the corresponding sample statistic such as the sample mean, sample standard deviation, and sample proportion.

Unbiased

If the expected value of the sample statistic is equal to the population parameter being estimated, the sample statistic is said to be an *unbiased estimator* of the population parameter.

UNBIASED

The sample statistic $\hat{\theta}$ is an unbiased estimator of the population parameter θ if

$$E(\hat{\theta}) = \theta$$

where

$$E(\hat{\theta}) = \text{the expected value of the sample statistic } \hat{\theta}$$

FIGURE 7.10 EXAMPLES OF UNBIASED AND BIASED POINT ESTIMATORS

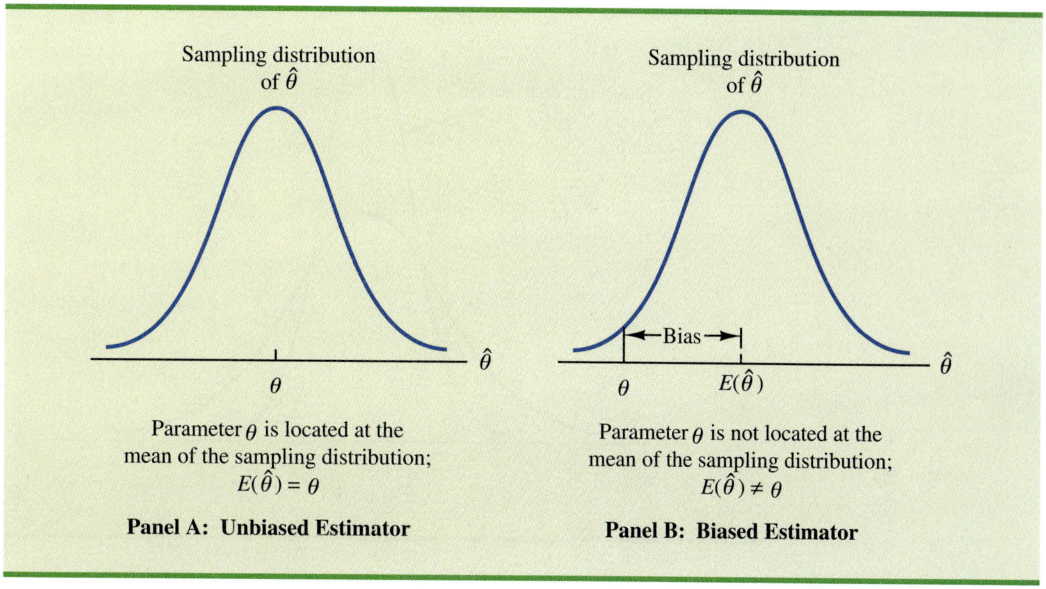

Hence, the expected value, or mean, of all possible values of an unbiased sample statistic is equal to the population parameter being estimated.

Figure 7.10 shows the cases of unbiased and biased point estimators. In the illustration showing the unbiased estimator, the mean of the sampling distribution is equal to the value of the population parameter. The estimation errors balance out in this case, because sometimes the value of the point estimator $\hat{\theta}$ may be less than θ and other times it may be greater than θ. In the case of a biased estimator, the mean of the sampling distribution is less than or greater than the value of the population parameter. In the illustration in Panel B of Figure 7.10, $E(\hat{\theta})$ is greater than θ; thus, the sample statistic has a high probability of overestimating the value of the population parameter. The amount of the bias is shown in the figure.

In discussing the sampling distributions of the sample mean and the sample proportion, we stated that $E(\bar{x}) = \mu$ and $E(\bar{p}) = p$. Thus, both $\bar{x}$ and $\bar{p}$ are unbiased estimators of their corresponding population parameters μ and p.

In the case of the sample standard deviation s and the sample variance s^2, it can be shown that $E(s^2) = \sigma^2$. Thus, we conclude that the sample variance s^2 is an unbiased estimator of the population variance σ^2. In fact, when we first presented the formulas for the sample variance and the sample standard deviation in Chapter 3, $n - 1$ rather than n was used in the denominator. The reason for using $n - 1$ rather than n is to make the sample variance an unbiased estimator of the population variance.

Efficiency

When sampling from a normal population, the standard error of the sample mean is less than the standard error of the sample median. Thus, the sample mean is more efficient than the sample median.

Assume that a simple random sample of n elements can be used to provide two unbiased point estimators of the same population parameter. In this situation, we would prefer to use the point estimator with the smaller standard error, because it tends to provide estimates closer to the population parameter. The point estimator with the smaller standard error is said to have greater **relative efficiency** than the other.

Figure 7.11 shows the sampling distributions of two unbiased point estimators, $\hat{\theta}_1$ and $\hat{\theta}_2$. Note that the standard error of $\hat{\theta}_1$ is less than the standard error of $\hat{\theta}_2$; thus,

FIGURE 7.11 SAMPLING DISTRIBUTIONS OF TWO UNBIASED POINT ESTIMATORS

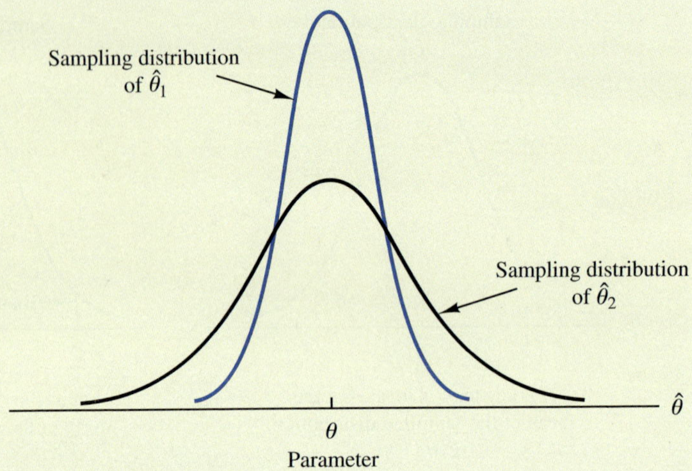

values of $\hat{\theta}_1$ have a greater chance of being close to the parameter θ than do values of $\hat{\theta}_2$. Because the standard error of point estimator $\hat{\theta}_1$ is less than the standard error of point estimator $\hat{\theta}_2$, $\hat{\theta}_1$ is relatively more efficient than $\hat{\theta}_2$ and is the preferred point estimator.

Consistency

A third property associated with good point estimators is **consistency**. Loosely speaking, a point estimator is consistent if the values of the point estimator tend to become closer to the population parameter as the sample size becomes larger. In other words, a large sample size tends to provide a better point estimate than a small sample size. Note that for the sample mean $\bar{x}$, we showed that the standard error of $\bar{x}$ is given by $\sigma_{\bar{x}} = \sigma/\sqrt{n}$. Because $\sigma_{\bar{x}}$ is related to the sample size such that larger sample sizes provide smaller values for $\sigma_{\bar{x}}$, we conclude that a larger sample size tends to provide point estimates closer to the population mean μ. In this sense, we can say that the sample mean $\bar{x}$ is a consistent estimator of the population mean μ. Using a similar rationale, we can also conclude that the sample proportion $\bar{p}$ is a consistent estimator of the population proportion p.

NOTES AND COMMENTS

In Chapter 3 we stated that the mean and the median are two measures of central location. In this chapter we discussed only the mean. The reason is that in sampling from a normal population, where the population mean and population median are identical, the standard error of the median is approximately 25% larger than the standard error of the mean. Recall that in the EAI problem where $n = 30$, the standard error of the mean is $\sigma_{\bar{x}} = 730.3$. The standard error of the median for this problem would be $1.25 \times (730.3) = 913$. As a result, the sample mean is more efficient and will have a higher probability of being within a specified distance of the population mean.

7.8 Other Sampling Methods

This section provides a brief introduction to survey sampling methods other than simple random sampling.

We described simple random sampling as a procedure for sampling from a finite population and discussed the properties of the sampling distributions of $\bar{x}$ and $\bar{p}$ when simple random sampling is used. Other methods such as stratified random sampling, cluster sampling, and systematic sampling provide advantages over simple random sampling in some of these situations. In this section we briefly introduce these alternative sampling methods. A more in-depth treatment is provided in Chapter 22, which is located on the website that accompanies the text.

Stratified Random Sampling

Stratified random sampling works best when the variance among elements in each stratum is relatively small.

In **stratified random sampling**, the elements in the population are first divided into groups called *strata,* such that each element in the population belongs to one and only one stratum. The basis for forming the strata, such as department, location, age, industry type, and so on, is at the discretion of the designer of the sample. However, the best results are obtained when the elements within each stratum are as much alike as possible. Figure 7.12 is a diagram of a population divided into H strata.

After the strata are formed, a simple random sample is taken from each stratum. Formulas are available for combining the results for the individual stratum samples into one estimate of the population parameter of interest. The value of stratified random sampling depends on how homogeneous the elements are within the strata. If elements within strata are alike, the strata will have low variances. Thus relatively small sample sizes can be used to obtain good estimates of the strata characteristics. If strata are homogeneous, the stratified random sampling procedure provides results just as precise as those of simple random sampling by using a smaller total sample size.

Cluster Sampling

Cluster sampling works best when each cluster provides a small-scale representation of the population.

In **cluster sampling**, the elements in the population are first divided into separate groups called *clusters*. Each element of the population belongs to one and only one cluster (see Figure 7.13). A simple random sample of the clusters is then taken. All elements within each sampled cluster form the sample. Cluster sampling tends to provide the best results when the elements within the clusters are not alike. In the ideal case, each cluster is a representative small-scale version of the entire population. The value of cluster sampling depends on how representative each cluster is of the entire population. If all clusters are alike in this regard, sampling a small number of clusters will provide good estimates of the population parameters.

FIGURE 7.12 DIAGRAM FOR STRATIFIED RANDOM SAMPLING

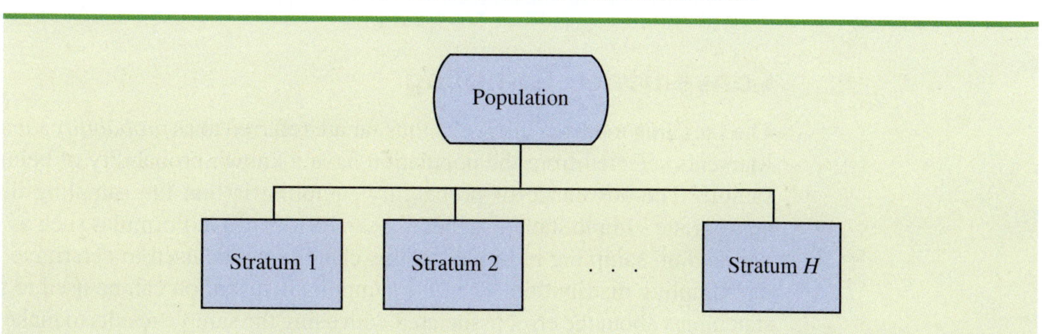

FIGURE 7.13 DIAGRAM FOR CLUSTER SAMPLING

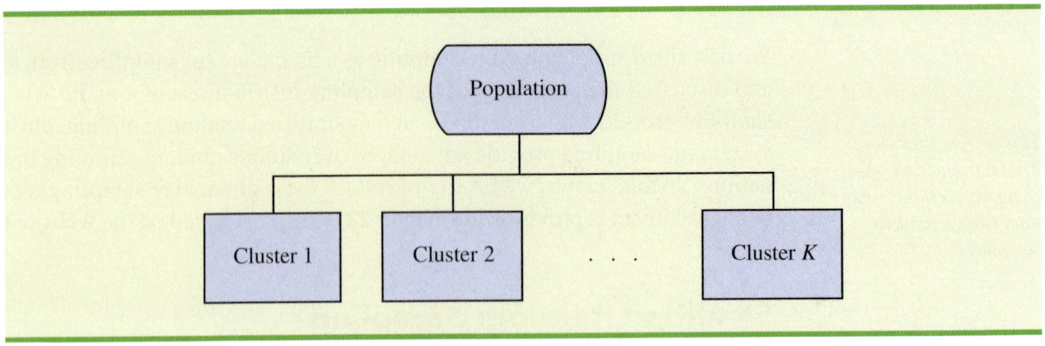

One of the primary applications of cluster sampling is area sampling, where clusters are city blocks or other well-defined areas. Cluster sampling generally requires a larger total sample size than either simple random sampling or stratified random sampling. However, it can result in cost savings because of the fact that when an interviewer is sent to a sampled cluster (e.g., a city-block location), many sample observations can be obtained in a relatively short time. Hence, a larger sample size may be obtainable with a significantly lower total cost.

Systematic Sampling

In some sampling situations, especially those with large populations, it is time-consuming to select a simple random sample by first finding a random number and then counting or searching through the list of the population until the corresponding element is found. An alternative to simple random sampling is **systematic sampling**. For example, if a sample size of 50 is desired from a population containing 5000 elements, we will sample one element for every 5000/50 = 100 elements in the population. A systematic sample for this case involves selecting randomly one of the first 100 elements from the population list. Other sample elements are identified by starting with the first sampled element and then selecting every 100th element that follows in the population list. In effect, the sample of 50 is identified by moving systematically through the population and identifying every 100th element after the first randomly selected element. The sample of 50 usually will be easier to identify in this way than it would be if simple random sampling were used. Because the first element selected is a random choice, a systematic sample is usually assumed to have the properties of a simple random sample. This assumption is especially applicable when the list of elements in the population is a random ordering of the elements.

Convenience Sampling

The sampling methods discussed thus far are referred to as *probability sampling* techniques. Elements selected from the population have a known probability of being included in the sample. The advantage of probability sampling is that the sampling distribution of the appropriate sample statistic generally can be identified. Formulas such as the ones for simple random sampling presented in this chapter can be used to determine the properties of the sampling distribution. Then the sampling distribution can be used to make probability statements about the error associated with using the sample results to make inferences about the population.

Convenience sampling is a *nonprobability sampling* technique. As the name implies, the sample is identified primarily by convenience. Elements are included in the sample without prespecified or known probabilities of being selected. For example, a professor conducting research at a university may use student volunteers to constitute a sample simply because they are readily available and will participate as subjects for little or no cost. Similarly, an inspector may sample a shipment of oranges by selecting oranges haphazardly from among several crates. Labeling each orange and using a probability method of sampling would be impractical. Samples such as wildlife captures and volunteer panels for consumer research are also convenience samples.

Convenience samples have the advantage of relatively easy sample selection and data collection; however, it is impossible to evaluate the "goodness" of the sample in terms of its representativeness of the population. A convenience sample may provide good results or it may not; no statistically justified procedure allows a probability analysis and inference about the quality of the sample results. Sometimes researchers apply statistical methods designed for probability samples to a convenience sample, arguing that the convenience sample can be treated as though it were a probability sample. However, this argument cannot be supported, and we should be cautious in interpreting the results of convenience samples that are used to make inferences about populations.

Judgment Sampling

One additional nonprobability sampling technique is **judgment sampling**. In this approach, the person most knowledgeable on the subject of the study selects elements of the population that he or she feels are most representative of the population. Often this method is a relatively easy way of selecting a sample. For example, a reporter may sample two or three senators, judging that those senators reflect the general opinion of all senators. However, the quality of the sample results depends on the judgment of the person selecting the sample. Again, great caution is warranted in drawing conclusions based on judgment samples used to make inferences about populations.

NOTES AND COMMENTS

We recommend using probability sampling methods when sampling from finite populations: simple random sampling, stratified random sampling, cluster sampling, or systematic sampling. For these methods, formulas are available for evaluating the "goodness" of the sample results in terms of the closeness of the results to the population parameters being estimated. An evaluation of the goodness cannot be made with convenience or judgment sampling. Thus, great care should be used in interpreting the results based on nonprobability sampling methods.

Summary

In this chapter we presented the concepts of sampling and sampling distributions. We demonstrated how a simple random sample can be selected from a finite population and how a random sample can be collected from an infinite population. The data collected from such samples can be used to develop point estimates of population parameters. Because different samples provide different values for the point estimators, point estimators such as $\bar{x}$ and $\bar{p}$ are random variables. The probability distribution of such a random variable is called a sampling distribution. In particular, we described the sampling distributions of the sample mean $\bar{x}$ and the sample proportion $\bar{p}$.

In considering the characteristics of the sampling distributions of $\bar{x}$ and $\bar{p}$, we stated that $E(\bar{x}) = \mu$ and $E(\bar{p}) = p$. Thus $\bar{x}$ and $\bar{p}$ are unbiased estimators. After developing the standard deviation or standard error formulas for these estimators, we described the conditions necessary for the sampling distributions of $\bar{x}$ and $\bar{p}$ to follow a normal distribution. Other sampling methods including stratified random sampling, cluster sampling, systematic sampling, convenience sampling, and judgment sampling were discussed.

Glossary

Sampled population The population from which the sample is taken.

Frame A listing of the elements the sample will be selected from.

Parameter A numerical characteristic of a population, such as a population mean μ, a population standard deviation σ, a population proportion p, and so on.

Simple random sample A simple random sample of size n from a finite population of size N is a sample selected such that each possible sample of size n has the same probability of being selected.

Sampling without replacement Once an element has been included in the sample, it is removed from the population and cannot be selected a second time.

Sampling with replacement Once an element has been included in the sample, it is returned to the population. A previously selected element can be selected again and therefore may appear in the sample more than once.

Random sample A random sample from an infinite population is a sample selected such that the following conditions are satisfied: (1) Each element selected comes from the same population; (2) each element is selected independently.

Sample statistic A sample characteristic, such as a sample mean $\bar{x}$, a sample standard deviation s, a sample proportion $\bar{p}$, and so on. The value of the sample statistic is used to estimate the value of the corresponding population parameter.

Point estimator The sample statistic, such as $\bar{x}$, s, or $\bar{p}$, that provides the point estimate of the population parameter.

Point estimate The value of a point estimator used in a particular instance as an estimate of a population parameter.

Target population The population for which statistical inferences such as point estimates are made. It is important for the target population to correspond as closely as possible to the sampled population.

Sampling distribution A probability distribution consisting of all possible values of a sample statistic.

Unbiased A property of a point estimator that is present when the expected value of the point estimator is equal to the population parameter it estimates.

Finite population correction factor The term $\sqrt{(N - n)/(N - 1)}$ that is used in the formulas for $\sigma_{\bar{x}}$ and $\sigma_{\bar{p}}$ whenever a finite population, rather than an infinite population, is being sampled. The generally accepted rule of thumb is to ignore the finite population correction factor whenever $n/N \leq .05$.

Standard error The standard deviation of a point estimator.

Central limit theorem A theorem that enables one to use the normal probability distribution to approximate the sampling distribution of $\bar{x}$ whenever the sample size is large.

Relative efficiency Given two unbiased point estimators of the same population parameter, the point estimator with the smaller standard error is more efficient.

Consistency A property of a point estimator that is present whenever larger sample sizes tend to provide point estimates closer to the population parameter.

Stratified random sampling A probability sampling method in which the population is first divided into strata and a simple random sample is then taken from each stratum.

Cluster sampling A probability sampling method in which the population is first divided into clusters and then a simple random sample of the clusters is taken.
Systematic sampling A probability sampling method in which we randomly select one of the first k elements and then select every kth element thereafter.
Convenience sampling A nonprobability method of sampling whereby elements are selected for the sample on the basis of convenience.
Judgment sampling A nonprobability method of sampling whereby elements are selected for the sample based on the judgment of the person doing the study.

Key Formulas

Expected Value of $\bar{x}$

$$E(\bar{x}) = \mu \tag{7.1}$$

Standard Deviation of $\bar{x}$ (Standard Error)

Finite Population *Infinite Population*

$$\sigma_{\bar{x}} = \sqrt{\frac{N-n}{N-1}}\left(\frac{\sigma}{\sqrt{n}}\right) \qquad \sigma_{\bar{x}} = \frac{\sigma}{\sqrt{n}} \tag{7.2}$$

Expected Value of $\bar{p}$

$$E(\bar{p}) = p \tag{7.4}$$

Standard Deviation of $\bar{p}$ (Standard Error)

Finite Population *Infinite Population*

$$\sigma_{\bar{p}} = \sqrt{\frac{N-n}{N-1}}\sqrt{\frac{p(1-p)}{n}} \qquad \sigma_{\bar{p}} = \sqrt{\frac{p(1-p)}{n}} \tag{7.5}$$

Supplementary Exercises

42. *U.S. News & World Report* publishes comprehensive information on America's best colleges (*America's Best Colleges,* 2009 ed.). Among other things, they provide a listing of their 133 best national universities. You would like to take a sample of these universities for a follow-up study on their students. Begin at the bottom of the third column of random digits in Table 7.1. Ignoring the first two digits in each five-number group and using the three-digit random numbers beginning with 959 read *up* the column to identify the number (from 1 to 133) of the first seven universities to be included in a simple random sample. Continue by starting at the bottom of the fourth and fifth columns and reading up if necessary.

43. The latest available data showed health expenditures were \$8086 per person in the United States or 17.6% of gross domestic product (Centers for Medicare & Medicaid Services website, April 1, 2012). Use \$8086 as the population mean and suppose a survey research firm will take a sample of 100 people to investigate the nature of their health expenditures. Assume the population standard deviation is \$2500.
    a. Show the sampling distribution of the mean amount of health care expenditures for a sample of 100 people.

b. What is the probability the sample mean will be within ± \$200 of the population mean?
c. What is the probability the sample mean will be greater than \$9000? If the survey research firm reports a sample mean greater than \$9000, would you question whether the firm followed correct sampling procedures? Why or why not?

44. Foot Locker uses sales per square foot as a measure of store productivity. Sales are currently running at an annual rate of \$406 per square foot (*The Wall Street Journal,* March 7, 2012). You have been asked by management to conduct a study of a sample of 64 Foot Locker stores. Assume the standard deviation in annual sales per square foot for the population of all 3400 Foot Locker stores is \$80.
    a. Show the sampling distribution of $\bar{x}$, the sample mean annual sales per square foot for a sample of 64 Foot Locker stores.
    b. What is the probability that the sample mean will be within \$15 of the population mean?
    c. Suppose you find a sample mean of \$380. What is the probability of finding a sample mean of \$380 or less? Would you consider such a sample to be an unusually low performing group of stores?

45. The mean television viewing time for Americans is 15 hours per week (*Money,* November 2003). Suppose a sample of 60 Americans is taken to further investigate viewing habits. Assume the population standard deviation for weekly viewing time is $\sigma = 4$ hours.
    a. What is the probability the sample mean will be within 1 hour of the population mean?
    b. What is the probability the sample mean will be within 45 minutes of the population mean?

46. After deducting grants based on need, the average cost to attend the University of Southern California (USC) is \$27,175 (*U.S. News & World Report, America's Best Colleges,* 2009 ed.). Assume the population standard deviation is \$7400. Suppose that a random sample of 60 USC students will be taken from this population.
    a. What is the value of the standard error of the mean?
    b. What is the probability that the sample mean will be more than \$27,175?
    c. What is the probability that the sample mean will be within \$1000 of the population mean?
    d. How would the probability in part (c) change if the sample size were increased to 100?

47. Three firms carry inventories that differ in size. Firm A's inventory contains 2000 items, firm B's inventory contains 5000 items, and firm C's inventory contains 10,000 items. The population standard deviation for the cost of the items in each firm's inventory is $\sigma = 144$. A statistical consultant recommends that each firm take a sample of 50 items from its inventory to provide statistically valid estimates of the average cost per item. Managers of the small firm state that because it has the smallest population, it should be able to make the estimate from a much smaller sample than that required by the larger firms. However, the consultant states that to obtain the same standard error and thus the same precision in the sample results, all firms should use the same sample size regardless of population size.
    a. Using the finite population correction factor, compute the standard error for each of the three firms given a sample of size 50.
    b. What is the probability that for each firm the sample mean $\bar{x}$ will be within ± 25 of the population mean μ?

48. A researcher reports survey results by stating that the standard error of the mean is 20. The population standard deviation is 500.
    a. How large was the sample used in this survey?
    b. What is the probability that the point estimate was within ± 25 of the population mean?

49. A production process is checked periodically by a quality control inspector. The inspector selects simple random samples of 30 finished products and computes the sample mean product weights $\bar{x}$. If test results over a long period of time show that 5% of the $\bar{x}$ values are over 2.1 pounds and 5% are under 1.9 pounds, what are the mean and the standard deviation for the population of products produced with this process?

50. About 28% of private companies are owned by women (*The Cincinnati Enquirer,* January 26, 2006). Answer the following questions based on a sample of 240 private companies.
    a. Show the sampling distribution of $\bar{p}$, the sample proportion of companies that are owned by women.
    b. What is the probability the sample proportion will be within $\pm.04$ of the population proportion?
    c. What is the probability the sample proportion will be within $\pm.02$ of the population proportion?

51. A market research firm conducts telephone surveys with a 40% historical response rate. What is the probability that in a new sample of 400 telephone numbers, at least 150 individuals will cooperate and respond to the questions? In other words, what is the probability that the sample proportion will be at least 150/400 = .375?

52. Advertisers contract with Internet service providers and search engines to place ads on websites. They pay a fee based on the number of potential customers who click on their ad. Unfortunately, click fraud—the practice of someone clicking on an ad solely for the purpose of driving up advertising revenue—has become a problem. Forty percent of advertisers claim they have been a victim of click fraud (*BusinessWeek,* March 13, 2006). Suppose a simple random sample of 380 advertisers will be taken to learn more about how they are affected by this practice.
    a. What is the probability that the sample proportion will be within $\pm.04$ of the population proportion experiencing click fraud?
    b. What is the probability that the sample proportion will be greater than .45?

53. The proportion of individuals insured by the All-Driver Automobile Insurance Company who received at least one traffic ticket during a five-year period is .15.
    a. Show the sampling distribution of $\bar{p}$ if a random sample of 150 insured individuals is used to estimate the proportion having received at least one ticket.
    b. What is the probability that the sample proportion will be within $\pm.03$ of the population proportion?

54. Lori Jeffrey is a successful sales representative for a major publisher of college textbooks. Historically, Lori obtains a book adoption on 25% of her sales calls. Viewing her sales calls for one month as a sample of all possible sales calls, assume that a statistical analysis of the data yields a standard error of the proportion of .0625.
    a. How large was the sample used in this analysis? That is, how many sales calls did Lori make during the month?
    b. Let $\bar{p}$ indicate the sample proportion of book adoptions obtained during the month. Show the sampling distribution of $\bar{p}$.
    c. Using the sampling distribution of $\bar{p}$, compute the probability that Lori will obtain book adoptions on 30% or more of her sales calls during a one-month period.

Appendix 7.1 The Expected Value and Standard Deviation of $\bar{x}$

In this appendix we present the mathematical basis for the expressions for $E(\bar{x})$, the expected value of $\bar{x}$ as given by equation (7.1), and $\sigma_{\bar{x}}$, the standard deviation of $\bar{x}$ as given by equation (7.2).

Expected Value of $\bar{x}$

Assume a population with mean μ and variance σ^2. A simple random sample of size n is selected with individual observations denoted $x_1, x_2, \ldots, x_n$. A sample mean $\bar{x}$ is computed as follows.

$$\bar{x} = \frac{\Sigma x_i}{n}$$

With repeated simple random samples of size n, $\bar{x}$ is a random variable that assumes different numerical values depending on the specific n items selected. The expected value of the random variable $\bar{x}$ is the mean of all possible $\bar{x}$ values.

$$\begin{aligned}\text{Mean of } \bar{x} = E(\bar{x}) &= E\left(\frac{\Sigma x_i}{n}\right) \\ &= \frac{1}{n}[E(x_1 + x_2 + \cdots + x_n)] \\ &= \frac{1}{n}[E(x_1) + E(x_2) + \cdots + E(x_n)]\end{aligned}$$

For any x_i we have $E(x_i) = \mu$; therefore we can write

$$\begin{aligned}E(\bar{x}) &= \frac{1}{n}(\mu + \mu + \cdots + \mu) \\ &= \frac{1}{n}(n\mu) = \mu\end{aligned}$$

This result shows that the mean of all possible $\bar{x}$ values is the same as the population mean μ. That is, $E(\bar{x}) = \mu$.

Standard Deviation of $\bar{x}$

Again assume a population with mean μ, variance σ^2, and a sample mean given by

$$\bar{x} = \frac{\Sigma x_i}{n}$$

With repeated simple random samples of size n, we know that $\bar{x}$ is a random variable that takes different numerical values depending on the specific n items selected. What follows is the derivation of the expression for the standard deviation of the $\bar{x}$ values, $\sigma_{\bar{x}}$, for the case of an infinite population. The derivation of the expression for $\sigma_{\bar{x}}$ for a finite population when sampling is done without replacement is more difficult and is beyond the scope of this text.

Returning to the infinite population case, recall that a simple random sample from an infinite population consists of observations $x_1, x_2, \ldots, x_n$ that are independent. The following two expressions are general formulas for the variance of random variables.

$$Var(ax) = a^2\, Var(x)$$

where a is a constant and x is a random variable, and

$$Var(x + y) = Var(x) + Var(y)$$

where x and y are *independent* random variables. Using the two preceding equations, we can develop the expression for the variance of the random variable $\bar{x}$ as follows.

$$Var(\bar{x}) = Var\left(\frac{\Sigma x_i}{n}\right) = Var\left(\frac{1}{n}\Sigma x_i\right)$$

Then, with $1/n$ a constant, we have

$$\begin{aligned} Var(\bar{x}) &= \left(\frac{1}{n}\right)^2 Var(\Sigma x_i) \\ &= \left(\frac{1}{n}\right)^2 Var(x_1 + x_2 + \cdots + x_n) \end{aligned}$$

In the infinite population case, the random variables $x_1, x_2, \ldots, x_n$ are independent, which enables us to write

$$Var(\bar{x}) = \left(\frac{1}{n}\right)^2 [Var(x_1) + Var(x_2) + \cdots + Var(x_n)]$$

For any x_i, we have $Var(x_i) = \sigma^2$; therefore we have

$$Var(\bar{x}) = \left(\frac{1}{n}\right)^2 (\sigma^2 + \sigma^2 + \cdots + \sigma^2)$$

With n values of σ^2 in this expression, we have

$$Var(\bar{x}) = \left(\frac{1}{n}\right)^2 (n\sigma^2) = \frac{\sigma^2}{n}$$

Taking the square root provides the formula for the standard deviation of $\bar{x}$.

$$\sigma_{\bar{x}} = \sqrt{Var(\bar{x})} = \frac{\sigma}{\sqrt{n}}$$

Appendix 7.2 Random Sampling with Minitab

If a list of the elements in a population is available in a Minitab file, Minitab can be used to select a simple random sample. For example, a list of the top 100 metropolitan areas in the United States and Canada is provided in column 1 of the data set MetAreas (*Places Rated Almanac—The Millennium Edition 2000*). Column 2 contains the overall rating of each metropolitan area. The first 10 metropolitan areas in the data set and their corresponding ratings are shown in Table 7.6.

Suppose that you would like to select a simple random sample of 30 metropolitan areas in order to do an in-depth study of the cost of living in the United States and Canada. The following steps can be used to select the sample.

Step 1. Select the **Calc** pull-down menu
Step 2. Choose **Random Data**
Step 3. Choose **Sample From Columns**

TABLE 7.6 OVERALL RATING FOR THE FIRST 10 METROPOLITAN AREAS IN THE DATA SET METAREAS

Metropolitan Area	Rating
Albany, NY	64.18
Albuquerque, NM	66.16
Appleton, WI	60.56
Atlanta, GA	69.97
Austin, TX	71.48
Baltimore, MD	69.75
Birmingham, AL	69.59
Boise City, ID	68.36
Boston, MA	68.99
Buffalo, NY	66.10

WEB file
MetAreas

Step 4. When the Sample From Columns dialog box appears:
Enter 30 in the **Number of rows to sample** box
Enter C1 C2 in the **From columns** box below
Enter C3 C4 in the **Store samples in** box
Step 5. Click **OK**

The random sample of 30 metropolitan areas appears in columns C3 and C4.

Appendix 7.3 Random Sampling with Excel

If a list of the elements in a population is available in an Excel file, Excel can be used to select a simple random sample. For example, a list of the top 100 metropolitan areas in the United States and Canada is provided in column A of the data set MetAreas (*Places Rated Almanac—The Millennium Edition 2000*). Column B contains the overall rating of each metropolitan area. The first 10 metropolitan areas in the data set and their corresponding ratings are shown in Table 7.6. Assume that you would like to select a simple random sample of 30 metropolitan areas in order to do an in-depth study of the cost of living in the United States and Canada.

The rows of any Excel data set can be placed in a random order by adding an extra column to the data set and filling the column with random numbers using the =RAND() function. Then, using Excel's sort ascending capability on the random number column, the rows of the data set will be reordered randomly. The random sample of size n appears in the first n rows of the reordered data set.

In the MetAreas data set, labels are in row 1 and the 100 metropolitan areas are in rows 2 to 101. The following steps can be used to select a simple random sample of 30 metropolitan areas.

Step 1. Enter =RAND() in cell C2
Step 2. Copy cell C2 to cells C3:C101
Step 3. Select any cell in Column C
Step 4. Click the **Home** tab on the Ribbon
Step 5. In the **Editing** group, click **Sort & Filter**
Step 6. Click **Sort Smallest to Largest**

The random sample of 30 metropolitan areas appears in rows 2 to 31 of the reordered data set. The random numbers in column C are no longer necessary and can be deleted if desired.

Appendix 7.4 Random Sampling with StatTools

WEB file

MetAreas

If a list of the elements in a population is available in an Excel file, StatTools Random Sample Utility can be used to select a simple random sample. For example, a list of the top 100 metropolitan areas in the United States and Canada is provided in column A of the data set MetAreas (*Places Rated Almanac—The Millennium Edition 2000*). Column B contains the overall rating of each metropolitan area. Assume that you would like to select a simple random sample of 30 metropolitan areas in order to do an in-depth study of the cost of living in the United States and Canada.

Begin by using the Data Set Manager to create a StatTools data set for these data using the procedure described in the appendix to Chapter 1. The following steps will generate a simple random sample of 30 metropolitan areas.

Step 1. Click the **StatTools** tab on the Ribbon
Step 2. In the **Data Group** click **Data Utilities**
Step 3. Choose the **Random Sample** option
Step 4. When the StatTools—Random Sample Utility dialog box appears:
In the **Variables** section:
Select **Metropolitan Area**
Select **Rating**
In the **Options** section:
Enter 1 in the **Number of Samples** box
Enter 30 in the **Sample Size** box
Click **OK**

The random sample of 30 metropolitan areas will appear in columns A and B of the worksheet entitled Random Sample.

CHAPTER 8

Interval Estimation

CONTENTS

STATISTICS *in* PRACTICE

FOOD LION*
SALISBURY, NORTH CAROLINA

Founded in 1957 as Food Town, Food Lion is one of the largest supermarket chains in the United States, with 1300 stores in 11 Southeastern and Mid-Atlantic states. The company sells more than 24,000 different products and offers nationally and regionally advertised brand-name merchandise, as well as a growing number of high-quality private label products manufactured especially for Food Lion. The company maintains its low price leadership and quality assurance through operating efficiencies such as standard store formats, innovative warehouse design, energy-efficient facilities, and data synchronization with suppliers. Food Lion looks to a future of continued innovation, growth, price leadership, and service to its customers.

Being in an inventory-intense business, Food Lion made the decision to adopt the LIFO (last-in, first-out) method of inventory valuation. This method matches current costs against current revenues, which minimizes the effect of radical price changes on profit and loss results. In addition, the LIFO method reduces net income thereby reducing income taxes during periods of inflation.

Food Lion establishes a LIFO index for each of seven inventory pools: Grocery, Paper/Household, Pet Supplies, Health & Beauty Aids, Dairy, Cigarette/Tobacco, and Beer/Wine. For example, a LIFO index of 1.008 for the Grocery pool would indicate that the company's grocery inventory value at current costs reflects a 0.8% increase due to inflation over the most recent one-year period.

A LIFO index for each inventory pool requires that the year-end inventory count for each product be valued at the current year-end cost and at the preceding year-end cost. To avoid excessive time and expense associated with counting the inventory in all 1200 store locations, Food Lion selects a random sample of 50 stores. Year-end physical inventories are taken in each of the sample stores. The current-year and preceding-year costs for each item are then used to construct the required LIFO indexes for each inventory pool.

As an inventory-intense business, Food Lion adopted the LIFO method of inventory valuation. © Bloomberg/Getty Images.

For a recent year, the sample estimate of the LIFO index for the Health & Beauty Aids inventory pool was 1.015. Using a 95% confidence level, Food Lion computed a margin of error of .006 for the sample estimate. Thus, the interval from 1.009 to 1.021 provided a 95% confidence interval estimate of the population LIFO index. This level of precision was judged to be very good.

In this chapter you will learn how to compute the margin of error associated with sample estimates. You will also learn how to use this information to construct and interpret interval estimates of a population mean and a population proportion.

*The authors are indebted to Keith Cunningham, Tax Director, and Bobby Harkey, Staff Tax Accountant, at Food Lion for providing this Statistics in Practice.

In Chapter 7, we stated that a point estimator is a sample statistic used to estimate a population parameter. For instance, the sample mean $\bar{x}$ is a point estimator of the population mean μ and the sample proportion $\bar{p}$ is a point estimator of the population proportion p. Because a point estimator cannot be expected to provide the exact value of the population parameter, an **interval estimate** is often computed by adding and subtracting a value, called the **margin of error**, to the point estimate. The general form of an interval estimate is as follows:

$$\text{Point estimate} \pm \text{Margin of error}$$

The purpose of an interval estimate is to provide information about how close the point estimate, provided by the sample, is to the value of the population parameter.

In this chapter we show how to compute interval estimates of a population mean μ and a population proportion p. The general form of an interval estimate of a population mean is

$$\bar{x} \pm \text{Margin of error}$$

Similarly, the general form of an interval estimate of a population proportion is

$$\bar{p} \pm \text{Margin of error}$$

The sampling distributions of $\bar{x}$ and $\bar{p}$ play key roles in computing these interval estimates.

8.1 Population Mean: σ Known

In order to develop an interval estimate of a population mean, either the population standard deviation σ or the sample standard deviation s must be used to compute the margin of error. In most applications σ is not known, and s is used to compute the margin of error. In some applications, large amounts of relevant historical data are available and can be used to estimate the population standard deviation prior to sampling. Also, in quality control applications where a process is assumed to be operating correctly, or "in control," it is appropriate to treat the population standard deviation as known. We refer to such cases as the **σ known** case. In this section we introduce an example in which it is reasonable to treat σ as known and show how to construct an interval estimate for this case.

Each week Lloyd's Department Store selects a simple random sample of 100 customers in order to learn about the amount spent per shopping trip. With x representing the amount spent per shopping trip, the sample mean $\bar{x}$ provides a point estimate of μ, the mean amount spent per shopping trip for the population of all Lloyd's customers. Lloyd's has been using the weekly survey for several years. Based on the historical data, Lloyd's now assumes a known value of $\sigma = \$20$ for the population standard deviation. The historical data also indicate that the population follows a normal distribution.

WEB file Lloyd's

During the most recent week, Lloyd's surveyed 100 customers ($n = 100$) and obtained a sample mean of $\bar{x} = \$82$. The sample mean amount spent provides a point estimate of the population mean amount spent per shopping trip, μ. In the discussion that follows, we show how to compute the margin of error for this estimate and develop an interval estimate of the population mean.

Margin of Error and the Interval Estimate

In Chapter 7 we showed that the sampling distribution of $\bar{x}$ can be used to compute the probability that $\bar{x}$ will be within a given distance of μ. In the Lloyd's example, the historical data show that the population of amounts spent is normally distributed with a standard deviation of $\sigma = 20$. So, using what we learned in Chapter 7, we can conclude that the sampling distribution of $\bar{x}$ follows a normal distribution with a standard error of $\sigma_{\bar{x}} = \sigma/\sqrt{n} = 20/\sqrt{100} = 2$. This sampling distribution is shown in Figure 8.1.[1] Because

[1]We use the fact that the population of amounts spent has a normal distribution to conclude that the sampling distribution of $\bar{x}$ has a normal distribution. If the population did not have a normal distribution, we could rely on the central limit theorem and the sample size of $n = 100$ to conclude that the sampling distribution of $\bar{x}$ is approximately normal. In either case, the sampling distribution of $\bar{x}$ would appear as shown in Figure 8.1.

FIGURE 8.1 SAMPLING DISTRIBUTION OF THE SAMPLE MEAN AMOUNT SPENT FROM SIMPLE RANDOM SAMPLES OF 100 CUSTOMERS

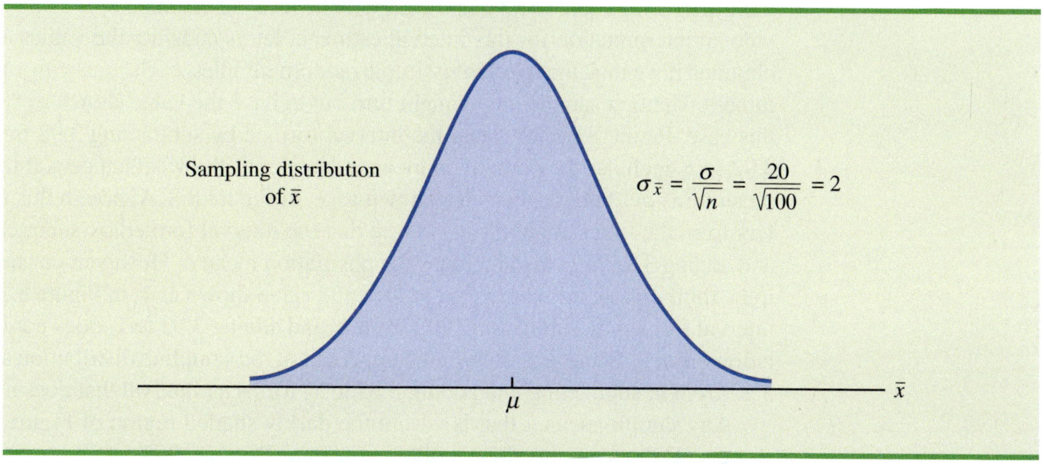

the sampling distribution shows how values of $\bar{x}$ are distributed around the population mean μ, the sampling distribution of $\bar{x}$ provides information about the possible differences between $\bar{x}$ and μ.

Using the standard normal probability table, we find that 95% of the values of any normally distributed random variable are within ± 1.96 standard deviations of the mean. Thus, when the sampling distribution of $\bar{x}$ is normally distributed, 95% of the $\bar{x}$ values must be within $\pm 1.96\sigma_{\bar{x}}$ of the mean μ. In the Lloyd's example we know that the sampling distribution of $\bar{x}$ is normally distributed with a standard error of $\sigma_{\bar{x}} = 2$. Because $\pm 1.96\sigma_{\bar{x}} = 1.96(2) = 3.92$, we can conclude that 95% of all $\bar{x}$ values obtained using a sample size of $n = 100$ will be within ± 3.92 of the population mean μ. See Figure 8.2.

FIGURE 8.2 SAMPLING DISTRIBUTION OF $\bar{x}$ SHOWING THE LOCATION OF SAMPLE MEANS THAT ARE WITHIN 3.92 OF μ

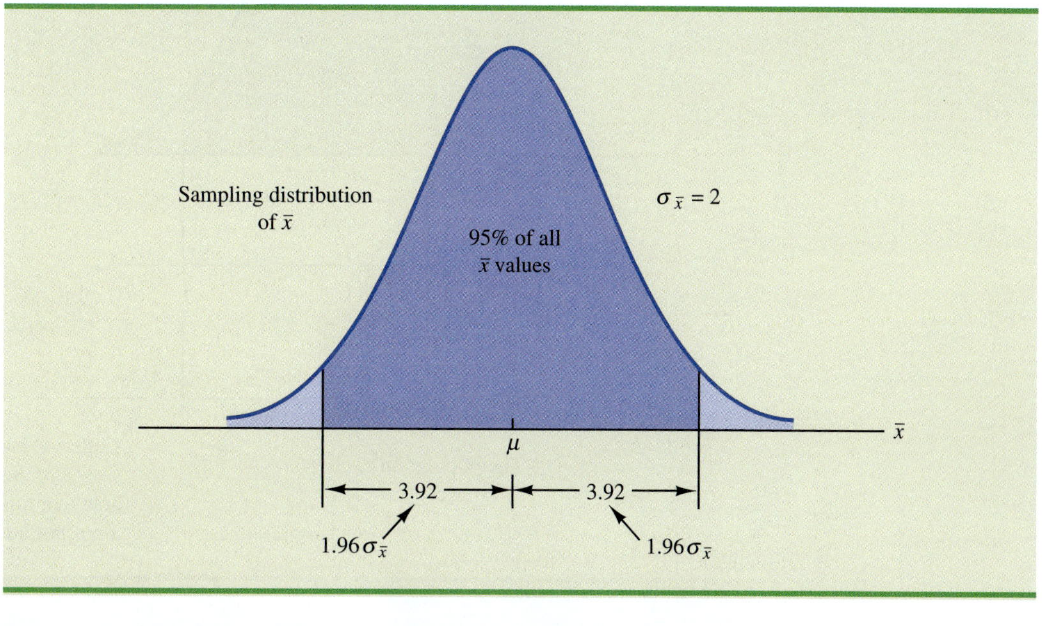

In the introduction to this chapter we said that the general form of an interval estimate of the population mean μ is $\bar{x} \pm$ margin of error. For the Lloyd's example, suppose we set the margin of error equal to 3.92 and compute the interval estimate of μ using $\bar{x} \pm 3.92$. To provide an interpretation for this interval estimate, let us consider the values of $\bar{x}$ that could be obtained if we took three *different* simple random samples, each consisting of 100 Lloyd's customers. The first sample mean might turn out to have the value shown as $\bar{x}_1$ in Figure 8.3. In this case, Figure 8.3 shows that the interval formed by subtracting 3.92 from $\bar{x}_1$ and adding 3.92 to $\bar{x}_1$ includes the population mean μ. Now consider what happens if the second sample mean turns out to have the value shown as $\bar{x}_2$ in Figure 8.3. Although this sample mean differs from the first sample mean, we see that the interval formed by subtracting 3.92 from $\bar{x}_2$ and adding 3.92 to $\bar{x}_2$ also includes the population mean μ. However, consider what happens if the third sample mean turns out to have the value shown as $\bar{x}_3$ in Figure 8.3. In this case, the interval formed by subtracting 3.92 from $\bar{x}_3$ and adding 3.92 to $\bar{x}_3$ does not include the population mean μ. Because $\bar{x}_3$ falls in the upper tail of the sampling distribution and is farther than 3.92 from μ, subtracting and adding 3.92 to $\bar{x}_3$ forms an interval that does not include μ.

Any sample mean $\bar{x}$ that is within the darkly shaded region of Figure 8.3 will provide an interval that contains the population mean μ. Because 95% of all possible sample means are in the darkly shaded region, 95% of all intervals formed by subtracting 3.92 from $\bar{x}$ and adding 3.92 to $\bar{x}$ will include the population mean μ.

Recall that during the most recent week, the quality assurance team at Lloyd's surveyed 100 customers and obtained a sample mean amount spent of $\bar{x} = 82$. Using $\bar{x} \pm 3.92$ to

FIGURE 8.3 INTERVALS FORMED FROM SELECTED SAMPLE MEANS AT LOCATIONS $\bar{x}_1$, $\bar{x}_2$, AND $\bar{x}_3$

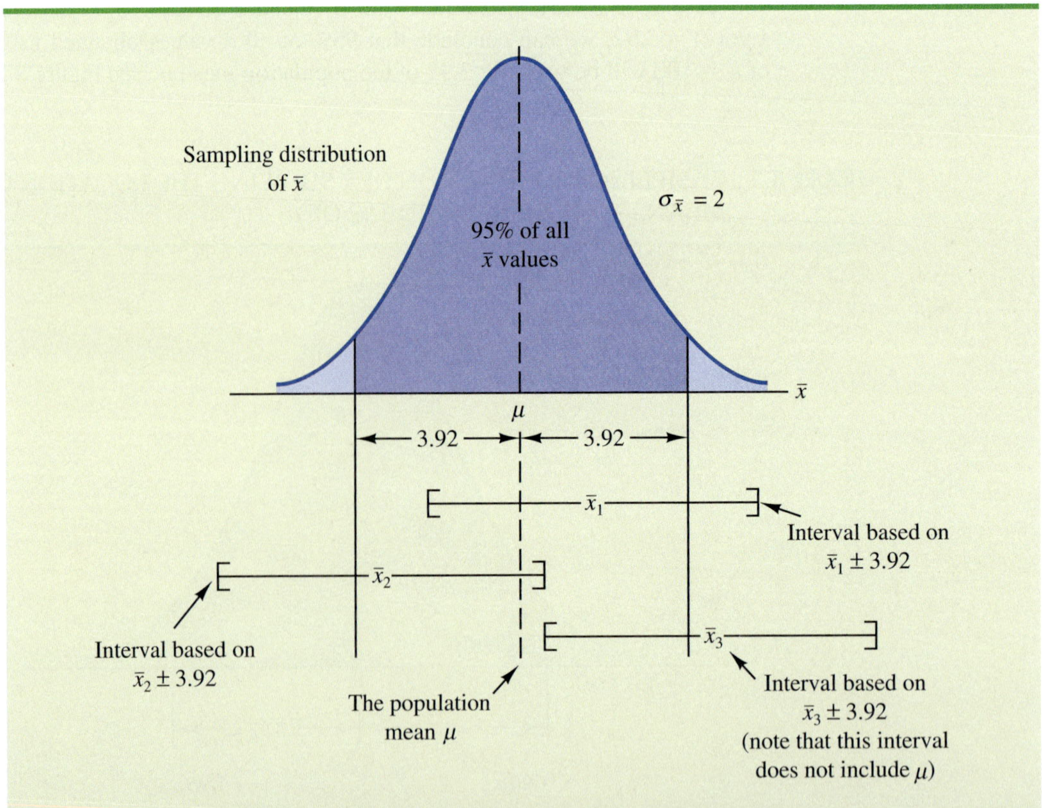

This discussion provides insight as to why the interval is called a 95% confidence interval.

construct the interval estimate, we obtain 82 ± 3.92. Thus, the specific interval estimate of μ based on the data from the most recent week is $82 - 3.92 = 78.08$ to $82 + 3.92 = 85.92$. Because 95% of all the intervals constructed using $\bar{x} \pm 3.92$ will contain the population mean, we say that we are 95% confident that the interval 78.08 to 85.92 includes the population mean μ. We say that this interval has been established at the 95% **confidence level**. The value .95 is referred to as the **confidence coefficient**, and the interval 78.08 to 85.92 is called the 95% **confidence interval**.

With the margin of error given by $z_{\alpha/2}(\sigma/\sqrt{n})$, the general form of an interval estimate of a population mean for the σ known case follows.

INTERVAL ESTIMATE OF A POPULATION MEAN: σ KNOWN

$$\bar{x} \pm z_{\alpha/2}\frac{\sigma}{\sqrt{n}} \tag{8.1}$$

where $(1 - \alpha)$ is the confidence coefficient and $z_{\alpha/2}$ is the z value providing an area of $\alpha/2$ in the upper tail of the standard normal probability distribution.

Let us use expression (8.1) to construct a 95% confidence interval for the Lloyd's example. For a 95% confidence interval, the confidence coefficient is $(1 - \alpha) = .95$ and thus, $\alpha = .05$. Using the standard normal probability table, an area of $\alpha/2 = .05/2 = .025$ in the upper tail provides $z_{.025} = 1.96$. With the Lloyd's sample mean $\bar{x} = 82$, $\sigma = 20$, and a sample size $n = 100$, we obtain

$$82 \pm 1.96\frac{20}{\sqrt{100}}$$

$$82 \pm 3.92$$

Thus, using expression (8.1), the margin of error is 3.92 and the 95% confidence interval is $82 - 3.92 = 78.08$ to $82 + 3.92 = 85.92$.

Although a 95% confidence level is frequently used, other confidence levels such as 90% and 99% may be considered. Values of $z_{\alpha/2}$ for the most commonly used confidence levels are shown in Table 8.1. Using these values and expression (8.1), the 90% confidence interval for the Lloyd's example is

$$82 \pm 1.645\frac{20}{\sqrt{100}}$$

$$82 \pm 3.29$$

TABLE 8.1 VALUES OF $z_{\alpha/2}$ FOR THE MOST COMMONLY USED CONFIDENCE LEVELS

Confidence Level	α	$\alpha/2$	$z_{\alpha/2}$
90%	.10	.05	1.645
95%	.05	.025	1.960
99%	.01	.005	2.576

Thus, at 90% confidence, the margin of error is 3.29 and the confidence interval is $82 - 3.29 = 78.71$ to $82 + 3.29 = 85.29$. Similarly, the 99% confidence interval is

$$82 \pm 2.576 \frac{20}{\sqrt{100}}$$

$$82 \pm 5.15$$

Thus, at 99% confidence, the margin of error is 5.15 and the confidence interval is $82 - 5.15 = 76.85$ to $82 + 5.15 = 87.15$.

Comparing the results for the 90%, 95%, and 99% confidence levels, we see that in order to have a higher degree of confidence, the margin of error and thus the width of the confidence interval must be larger.

Practical Advice

If the population follows a normal distribution, the confidence interval provided by expression (8.1) is exact. In other words, if expression (8.1) were used repeatedly to generate 95% confidence intervals, exactly 95% of the intervals generated would contain the population mean. If the population does not follow a normal distribution, the confidence interval provided by expression (8.1) will be approximate. In this case, the quality of the approximation depends on both the distribution of the population and the sample size.

In most applications, a sample size of $n \geq 30$ is adequate when using expression (8.1) to develop an interval estimate of a population mean. If the population is not normally distributed but is roughly symmetric, sample sizes as small as 15 can be expected to provide good approximate confidence intervals. With smaller sample sizes, expression (8.1) should only be used if the analyst believes, or is willing to assume, that the population distribution is at least approximately normal.

NOTES AND COMMENTS

1. The interval estimation procedure discussed in this section is based on the assumption that the population standard deviation σ is known. By σ known we mean that historical data or other information are available that permit us to obtain a good estimate of the population standard deviation prior to taking the sample that will be used to develop an estimate of the population mean. So technically we don't mean that σ is actually known with certainty. We just mean that we obtained a good estimate of the standard deviation prior to sampling and thus we won't be using the same sample to estimate both the population mean and the population standard deviation.
2. The sample size n appears in the denominator of the interval estimation expression (8.1). Thus, if a particular sample size provides too wide an interval to be of any practical use, we may want to consider increasing the sample size. With n in the denominator, a larger sample size will provide a smaller margin of error, a narrower interval, and greater precision. The procedure for determining the size of a simple random sample necessary to obtain a desired precision is discussed in Section 8.3.

Exercises

Methods

1. A simple random sample of 40 items resulted in a sample mean of 25. The population standard deviation is $\sigma = 5$.
   a. What is the standard error of the mean, $\sigma_{\bar{x}}$?
   b. At 95% confidence, what is the margin of error?

SELF test

2. A simple random sample of 50 items from a population with $\sigma = 6$ resulted in a sample mean of 32.
   a. Provide a 90% confidence interval for the population mean.
   b. Provide a 95% confidence interval for the population mean.
   c. Provide a 99% confidence interval for the population mean.

3. A simple random sample of 60 items resulted in a sample mean of 80. The population standard deviation is $\sigma = 15$.
   a. Compute the 95% confidence interval for the population mean.
   b. Assume that the same sample mean was obtained from a sample of 120 items. Provide a 95% confidence interval for the population mean.
   c. What is the effect of a larger sample size on the interval estimate?

4. A 95% confidence interval for a population mean was reported to be 152 to 160. If $\sigma = 15$, what sample size was used in this study?

Applications

SELF test

WEB file Houston

5. Data were collected on the amount spent by 64 customers for lunch at a major Houston restaurant. These data are contained in the file named Houston. Based upon past studies the population standard deviation is known with $\sigma = \$6$.
   a. At 99% confidence, what is the margin of error?
   b. Develop a 99% confidence interval estimate of the mean amount spent for lunch.

WEB file Nielsen

6. Nielsen Media Research conducted a study of household television viewing times during the 8 P.M. to 11 P.M. time period. The data contained in the file named Nielsen are consistent with the findings reported (*The World Almanac,* 2003). Based upon past studies the population standard deviation is assumed known with $\sigma = 3.5$ hours. Develop a 95% confidence interval estimate of the mean television viewing time per week during the 8 P.M. to 11 P.M. time period.

7. *The Wall Street Journal* reported that automobile crashes cost the United States \$162 billion annually (*The Wall Street Journal,* March 5, 2008). The average cost per person for crashes in the Tampa, Florida, area was reported to be \$1599. Suppose this average cost was based on a sample of 50 persons who had been involved in car crashes and that the population standard deviation is $\sigma = \$600$. What is the margin of error for a 95% confidence interval? What would you recommend if the study required a margin of error of \$150 or less?

8. Studies show that massage therapy has a variety of health benefits and it is not too expensive (*The Wall Street Journal,* March 13, 2012). A sample of 10 typical one-hour massage therapy sessions showed an average charge of \$59. The population standard deviation for a one-hour session is $\sigma = \$5.50$.
   a. What assumptions about the population should we be willing to make if a margin of error is desired?
   b. Using 95% confidence, what is the margin of error?
   c. Using 99% confidence, what is the margin of error?

WEB file TaxReturn

9. AARP reported on a study conducted to learn how long it takes individuals to prepare their federal income tax return (*AARP Bulletin,* April 2008). The data contained in the file named TaxReturn are consistent with the study results. These data provide the time in hours required for 40 individuals to complete their federal income tax returns. Using past years' data, the population standard deviation can be assumed known with $\sigma = 9$ hours. What is the 95% confidence interval estimate of the mean time it takes an individual to complete a federal income tax return?

10. *Playbill* magazine reported that the mean annual household income of its readers is \$119,155 (*Playbill,* January 2006). Assume this estimate of the mean annual household income is based on a sample of 80 households, and based on past studies, the population standard deviation is known to be $\sigma = \$30,000$.

a. Develop a 90% confidence interval estimate of the population mean.
b. Develop a 95% confidence interval estimate of the population mean.
c. Develop a 99% confidence interval estimate of the population mean.
d. Discuss what happens to the width of the confidence interval as the confidence level is increased. Does this result seem reasonable? Explain.

8.2 Population Mean: σ Unknown

When developing an interval estimate of a population mean we usually do not have a good estimate of the population standard deviation either. In these cases, we must use the same sample to estimate both μ and σ. This situation represents the **σ unknown** case. When s is used to estimate σ, the margin of error and the interval estimate for the population mean are based on a probability distribution known as the ***t* distribution**. Although the mathematical development of the t distribution is based on the assumption of a normal distribution for the population we are sampling from, research shows that the t distribution can be successfully applied in many situations where the population deviates significantly from normal. Later in this section we provide guidelines for using the t distribution if the population is not normally distributed.

William Sealy Gosset, writing under the name "Student," is the founder of the t distribution. Gosset, an Oxford graduate in mathematics, worked for the Guinness Brewery in Dublin, Ireland. He developed the t distribution while working on small-scale materials and temperature experiments.

The t distribution is a family of similar probability distributions, with a specific t distribution depending on a parameter known as the **degrees of freedom**. The t distribution with one degree of freedom is unique, as is the t distribution with two degrees of freedom, with three degrees of freedom, and so on. As the number of degrees of freedom increases, the difference between the t distribution and the standard normal distribution becomes smaller and smaller. Figure 8.4 shows t distributions with 10 and 20 degrees of freedom and their relationship to the standard normal probability distribution. Note that a t distribution with more degrees of freedom exhibits less variability and more

FIGURE 8.4 COMPARISON OF THE STANDARD NORMAL DISTRIBUTION WITH t DISTRIBUTIONS HAVING 10 AND 20 DEGREES OF FREEDOM

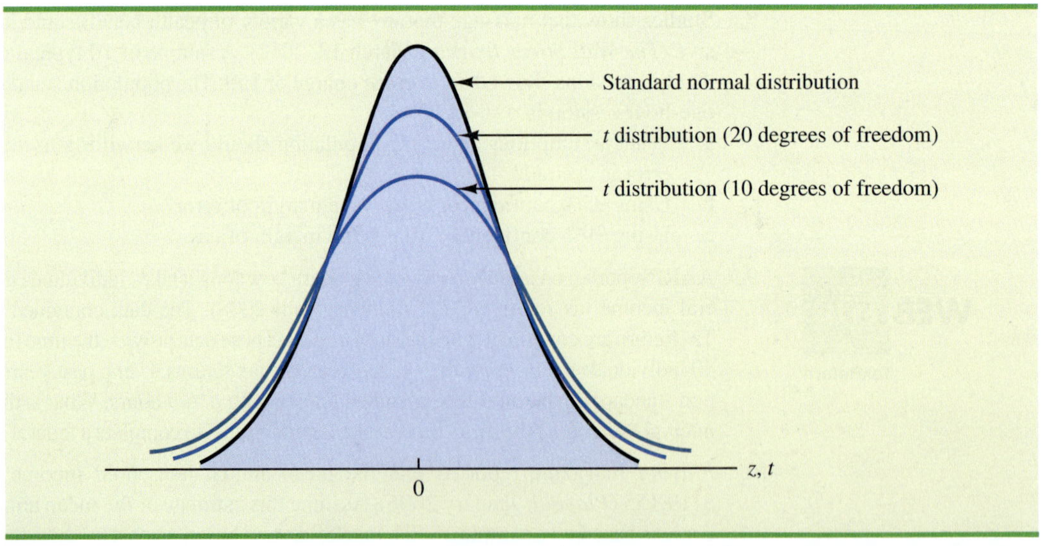

closely resembles the standard normal distribution. Note also that the mean of the t distribution is zero.

We place a subscript on t to indicate the area in the upper tail of the t distribution. For example, just as we used $z_{.025}$ to indicate the z value providing a .025 area in the upper tail of a standard normal distribution, we will use $t_{.025}$ to indicate a .025 area in the upper tail of a t distribution. In general, we will use the notation $t_{\alpha/2}$ to represent a t value with an area of $\alpha/2$ in the upper tail of the t distribution. See Figure 8.5.

As the degrees of freedom increase, the t distribution approaches the standard normal distribution.

Table 2 in Appendix B contains a table for the t distribution. A portion of this table is shown in Table 8.2. Each row in the table corresponds to a separate t distribution with the degrees of freedom shown. For example, for a t distribution with 9 degrees of freedom, $t_{.025} = 2.262$. Similarly, for a t distribution with 60 degrees of freedom, $t_{.025} = 2.000$. As the degrees of freedom continue to increase, $t_{.025}$ approaches $z_{.025} = 1.96$. In fact, the standard normal distribution z values can be found in the infinite degrees of freedom row (labeled ∞) of the t distribution table. If the degrees of freedom exceed 100, the infinite degrees of freedom row can be used to approximate the actual t value; in other words, for more than 100 degrees of freedom, the standard normal z value provides a good approximation to the t value.

Margin of Error and the Interval Estimate

In Section 8.1 we showed that an interval estimate of a population mean for the σ known case is

$$\bar{x} \pm z_{\alpha/2}\frac{\sigma}{\sqrt{n}}$$

To compute an interval estimate of μ for the σ unknown case, the sample standard deviation s is used to estimate σ, and $z_{\alpha/2}$ is replaced by the t distribution value $t_{\alpha/2}$. The margin

FIGURE 8.5 t DISTRIBUTION WITH $\alpha/2$ AREA OR PROBABILITY IN THE UPPER TAIL

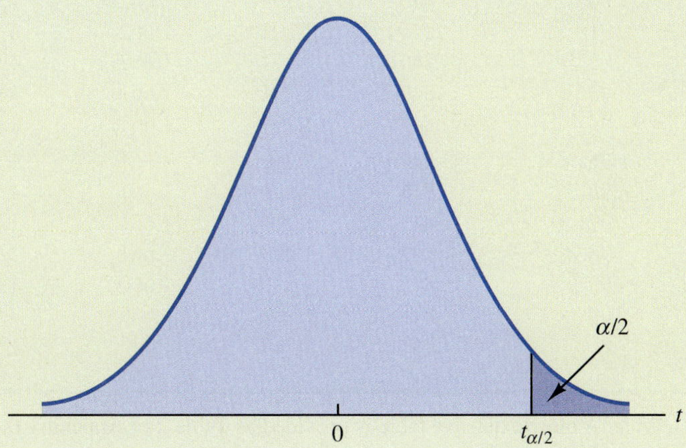

TABLE 8.2 SELECTED VALUES FROM THE *t* DISTRIBUTION TABLE*

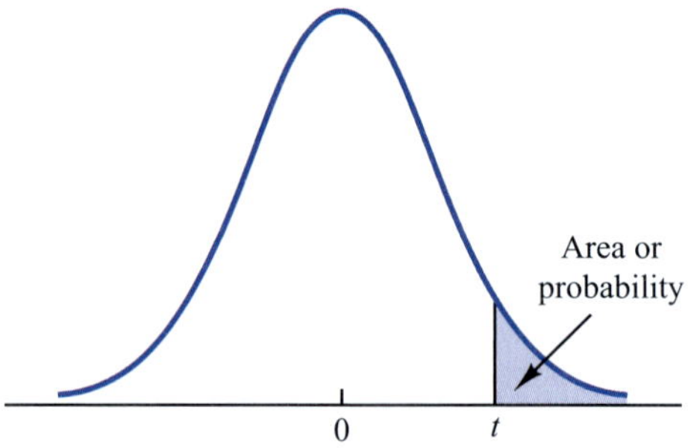

Degrees of Freedom	Area in Upper Tail .20	.10	.05	.025	.01	.005
1	1.376	3.078	6.314	12.706	31.821	63.656
2	1.061	1.886	2.920	4.303	6.965	9.925
3	.978	1.638	2.353	3.182	4.541	5.841
4	.941	1.533	2.132	2.776	3.747	4.604
5	.920	1.476	2.015	2.571	3.365	4.032
6	.906	1.440	1.943	2.447	3.143	3.707
7	.896	1.415	1.895	2.365	2.998	3.499
8	.889	1.397	1.860	2.306	2.896	3.355
9	.883	1.383	1.833	2.262	2.821	3.250
⋮	⋮	⋮	⋮	⋮	⋮	⋮
60	.848	1.296	1.671	2.000	2.390	2.660
61	.848	1.296	1.670	2.000	2.389	2.659
62	.847	1.295	1.670	1.999	2.388	2.657
63	.847	1.295	1.669	1.998	2.387	2.656
64	.847	1.295	1.669	1.998	2.386	2.655
65	.847	1.295	1.669	1.997	2.385	2.654
66	.847	1.295	1.668	1.997	2.384	2.652
67	.847	1.294	1.668	1.996	2.383	2.651
68	.847	1.294	1.668	1.995	2.382	2.650
69	.847	1.294	1.667	1.995	2.382	2.649
⋮	⋮	⋮	⋮	⋮	⋮	⋮
90	.846	1.291	1.662	1.987	2.368	2.632
91	.846	1.291	1.662	1.986	2.368	2.631
92	.846	1.291	1.662	1.986	2.368	2.630
93	.846	1.291	1.661	1.986	2.367	2.630
94	.845	1.291	1.661	1.986	2.367	2.629
95	.845	1.291	1.661	1.985	2.366	2.629
96	.845	1.290	1.661	1.985	2.366	2.628
97	.845	1.290	1.661	1.985	2.365	2.627
98	.845	1.290	1.661	1.984	2.365	2.627
99	.845	1.290	1.660	1.984	2.364	2.626
100	.845	1.290	1.660	1.984	2.364	2.626
∞	.842	1.282	1.645	1.960	2.326	2.576

**Note:* A more extensive table is provided as Table 2 of Appendix B.

of error is then given by $t_{\alpha/2}s/\sqrt{n}$. With this margin of error, the general expression for an interval estimate of a population mean when σ is unknown follows.

INTERVAL ESTIMATE OF A POPULATION MEAN: σ UNKNOWN

$$\bar{x} \pm t_{\alpha/2} \frac{s}{\sqrt{n}} \tag{8.2}$$

where s is the sample standard deviation, $(1 - \alpha)$ is the confidence coefficient, and $t_{\alpha/2}$ is the t value providing an area of $\alpha/2$ in the upper tail of the t distribution with $n - 1$ degrees of freedom.

The reason the number of degrees of freedom associated with the t value in expression (8.2) is $n - 1$ concerns the use of s as an estimate of the population standard deviation σ. The expression for the sample standard deviation is

$$s = \sqrt{\frac{\Sigma(x_i - \bar{x})^2}{n - 1}}$$

Degrees of freedom refer to the number of independent pieces of information that go into the computation of $\Sigma(x_i - \bar{x})^2$. The n pieces of information involved in computing $\Sigma(x_i - \bar{x})^2$ are as follows: $x_1 - \bar{x}, x_2 - \bar{x}, \ldots, x_n - \bar{x}$. In Section 3.2 we indicated that $\Sigma(x_i - \bar{x}) = 0$ for any data set. Thus, only $n - 1$ of the $x_i - \bar{x}$ values are independent; that is, if we know $n - 1$ of the values, the remaining value can be determined exactly by using the condition that the sum of the $x_i - \bar{x}$ values must be 0. Thus, $n - 1$ is the number of degrees of freedom associated with $\Sigma(x_i - \bar{x})^2$ and hence the number of degrees of freedom for the t distribution in expression (8.2).

To illustrate the interval estimation procedure for the σ unknown case, we will consider a study designed to estimate the mean credit card debt for the population of U.S. households. A sample of $n = 70$ households provided the credit card balances shown in Table 8.3. For this situation, no previous estimate of the population standard deviation σ is available. Thus, the sample data must be used to estimate both the population mean and the population standard deviation. Using the data in Table 8.3, we compute the sample mean $\bar{x} = \$9312$ and the sample standard deviation $s = \$4007$. With 95% confidence and $n - 1 = 69$ degrees of

TABLE 8.3 CREDIT CARD BALANCES FOR A SAMPLE OF 70 HOUSEHOLDS

WEB file

NewBalance

9430	14661	7159	9071	9691	11032
7535	12195	8137	3603	11448	6525
4078	10544	9467	16804	8279	5239
5604	13659	12595	13479	5649	6195
5179	7061	7917	14044	11298	12584
4416	6245	11346	6817	4353	15415
10676	13021	12806	6845	3467	15917
1627	9719	4972	10493	6191	12591
10112	2200	11356	615	12851	9743
6567	10746	7117	13627	5337	10324
13627	12744	9465	12557	8372	
18719	5742	19263	6232	7445	

freedom, Table 8.2 can be used to obtain the appropriate value for $t_{.025}$. We want the t value in the row with 69 degrees of freedom, and the column corresponding to .025 in the upper tail. The value shown is $t_{.025} = 1.995$.

We use expression (8.2) to compute an interval estimate of the population mean credit card balance.

$$9312 \pm 1.995 \frac{4007}{\sqrt{70}}$$

$$9312 \pm 955$$

The point estimate of the population mean is \$9312, the margin of error is \$955, and the 95% confidence interval is 9312 − 955 = \$8357 to 9312 + 955 = \$10,267. Thus, we are 95% confident that the mean credit card balance for the population of all households is between \$8357 and \$10,267.

The procedures used by Minitab, Excel and StatTools to develop confidence intervals for a population mean are described in Appendixes 8.1, 8.2 and 8.3. For the household credit card balances study, the results of the Minitab interval estimation procedure are shown in Figure 8.6. The sample of 70 households provides a sample mean credit card balance of \$9312, a sample standard deviation of \$4007, a standard error of the mean of \$479, and a 95% confidence interval of \$8357 to \$10,267.

Practical Advice

If the population follows a normal distribution, the confidence interval provided by expression (8.2) is exact and can be used for any sample size. If the population does not follow a normal distribution, the confidence interval provided by expression (8.2) will be approximate. In this case, the quality of the approximation depends on both the distribution of the population and the sample size.

Larger sample sizes are needed if the distribution of the population is highly skewed or includes outliers.

In most applications, a sample size of $n \geq 30$ is adequate when using expression (8.2) to develop an interval estimate of a population mean. However, if the population distribution is highly skewed or contains outliers, most statisticians would recommend increasing the sample size to 50 or more. If the population is not normally distributed but is roughly symmetric, sample sizes as small as 15 can be expected to provide good approximate confidence intervals. With smaller sample sizes, expression (8.2) should only be used if the analyst believes, or is willing to assume, that the population distribution is at least approximately normal.

Using a Small Sample

In the following example we develop an interval estimate for a population mean when the sample size is small. As we already noted, an understanding of the distribution of the population becomes a factor in deciding whether the interval estimation procedure provides acceptable results.

Scheer Industries is considering a new computer-assisted program to train maintenance employees to do machine repairs. In order to fully evaluate the program, the director of

FIGURE 8.6 MINITAB CONFIDENCE INTERVAL FOR THE CREDIT CARD BALANCE SURVEY

Variable	N	Mean	StDev	SE Mean	95% CI
NewBalance	70	9312	4007	479	(8357, 10267)

TABLE 8.4 TRAINING TIME IN DAYS FOR A SAMPLE OF 20 SCHEER INDUSTRIES EMPLOYEES

WEB file
Scheer

52	59	54	42
44	50	42	48
55	54	60	55
44	62	62	57
45	46	43	56

manufacturing requested an estimate of the population mean time required for maintenance employees to complete the computer-assisted training.

A sample of 20 employees is selected, with each employee in the sample completing the training program. Data on the training time in days for the 20 employees are shown in Table 8.4. A histogram of the sample data appears in Figure 8.7. What can we say about the distribution of the population based on this histogram? First, the sample data do not support the conclusion that the distribution of the population is normal, yet we do not see any evidence of skewness or outliers. Therefore, using the guidelines in the previous subsection, we conclude that an interval estimate based on the t distribution appears acceptable for the sample of 20 employees.

We continue by computing the sample mean and sample standard deviation as follows.

$$\bar{x} = \frac{\Sigma x_i}{n} = \frac{1030}{20} = 51.5 \text{ days}$$

$$s = \sqrt{\frac{\Sigma(x_i - \bar{x})^2}{n - 1}} = \sqrt{\frac{889}{20 - 1}} = 6.84 \text{ days}$$

FIGURE 8.7 HISTOGRAM OF TRAINING TIMES FOR THE SCHEER INDUSTRIES SAMPLE

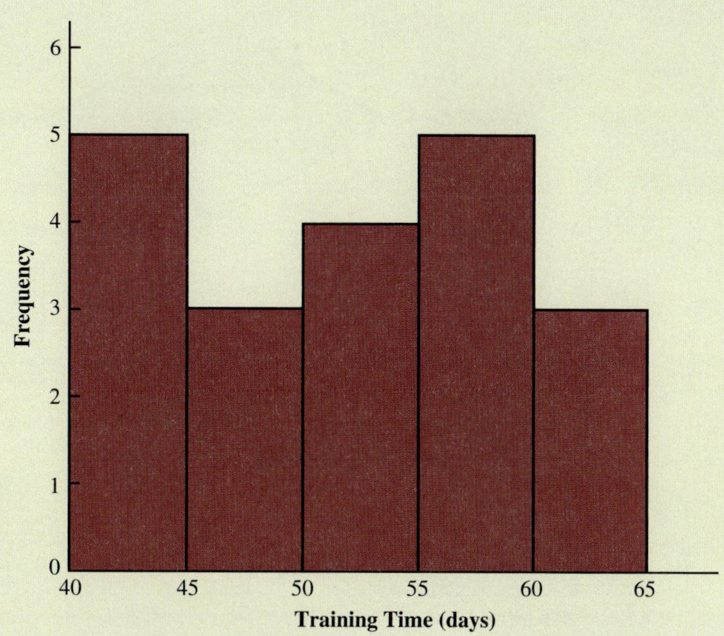

For a 95% confidence interval, we use Table 2 of Appendix B and $n - 1 = 19$ degrees of freedom to obtain $t_{.025} = 2.093$. Expression (8.2) provides the interval estimate of the population mean.

$$51.5 \pm 2.093\left(\frac{6.84}{\sqrt{20}}\right)$$

$$51.5 \pm 3.2$$

The point estimate of the population mean is 51.5 days. The margin of error is 3.2 days and the 95% confidence interval is $51.5 - 3.2 = 48.3$ days to $51.5 + 3.2 = 54.7$ days.

Using a histogram of the sample data to learn about the distribution of a population is not always conclusive, but in many cases it provides the only information available. The histogram, along with judgment on the part of the analyst, can often be used to decide whether expression (8.2) can be used to develop the interval estimate.

Summary of Interval Estimation Procedures

We provided two approaches to developing an interval estimate of a population mean. For the σ known case, σ and the standard normal distribution are used in expression (8.1) to compute the margin of error and to develop the interval estimate. For the σ unknown case, the sample standard deviation s and the t distribution are used in expression (8.2) to compute the margin of error and to develop the interval estimate.

A summary of the interval estimation procedures for the two cases is shown in Figure 8.8. In most applications, a sample size of $n \geq 30$ is adequate. If the population has a normal or approximately normal distribution, however, smaller sample sizes may be used.

FIGURE 8.8 SUMMARY OF INTERVAL ESTIMATION PROCEDURES FOR A POPULATION MEAN

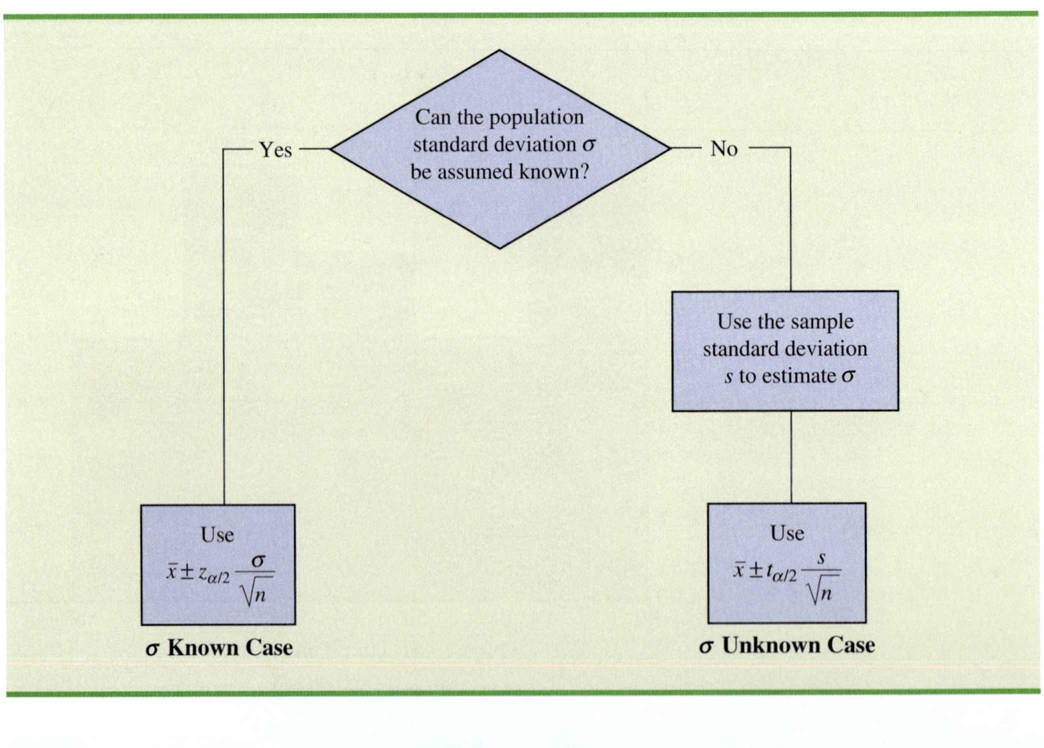

For the σ unknown case a sample size of $n \geq 50$ is recommended if the population distribution is believed to be highly skewed or has outliers.

NOTES AND COMMENTS

1. When σ is known, the margin of error, $z_{\alpha/2}(\sigma/\sqrt{n})$, is fixed and is the same for all samples of size n. When σ is unknown, the margin of error, $t_{\alpha/2}(s/\sqrt{n})$, varies from sample to sample. This variation occurs because the sample standard deviation s varies depending upon the sample selected. A large value for s provides a larger margin of error, while a small value for s provides a smaller margin of error.
2. What happens to confidence interval estimates when the population is skewed? Consider a population that is skewed to the right with large data values stretching the distribution to the right. When such skewness exists, the sample mean $\bar{x}$ and the sample standard deviation s are positively correlated. Larger values of s tend to be associated with larger values of $\bar{x}$. Thus, when $\bar{x}$ is larger than the population mean, s tends to be larger than σ. This skewness causes the margin of error, $t_{\alpha/2}(s/\sqrt{n})$, to be larger than it would be with σ known. The confidence interval with the larger margin of error tends to include the population mean μ more often than it would if the true value of σ were used. But when $\bar{x}$ is smaller than the population mean, the correlation between $\bar{x}$ and s causes the margin of error to be small. In this case, the confidence interval with the smaller margin of error tends to miss the population mean more than it would if we knew σ and used it. For this reason, we recommend using larger sample sizes with highly skewed population distributions.

Exercises

Methods

11. For a t distribution with 16 degrees of freedom, find the area, or probability, in each region.
    a. To the right of 2.120
    b. To the left of 1.337
    c. To the left of -1.746
    d. To the right of 2.583
    e. Between -2.120 and 2.120
    f. Between -1.746 and 1.746
12. Find the t value(s) for each of the following cases.
    a. Upper tail area of .025 with 12 degrees of freedom
    b. Lower tail area of .05 with 50 degrees of freedom
    c. Upper tail area of .01 with 30 degrees of freedom
    d. Where 90% of the area falls between these two t values with 25 degrees of freedom
    e. Where 95% of the area falls between these two t values with 45 degrees of freedom

SELF test

13. The following sample data are from a normal population: 10, 8, 12, 15, 13, 11, 6, 5.
    a. What is the point estimate of the population mean?
    b. What is the point estimate of the population standard deviation?
    c. With 95% confidence, what is the margin of error for the estimation of the population mean?
    d. What is the 95% confidence interval for the population mean?
14. A simple random sample with $n = 54$ provided a sample mean of 22.5 and a sample standard deviation of 4.4.
    a. Develop a 90% confidence interval for the population mean.
    b. Develop a 95% confidence interval for the population mean.

c. Develop a 99% confidence interval for the population mean.
d. What happens to the margin of error and the confidence interval as the confidence level is increased?

Applications

SELF test

15. Sales personnel for Skillings Distributors submit weekly reports listing the customer contacts made during the week. A sample of 65 weekly reports showed a sample mean of 19.5 customer contacts per week. The sample standard deviation was 5.2. Provide 90% and 95% confidence intervals for the population mean number of weekly customer contacts for the sales personnel.

WEB file CorporateBonds

16. A sample containing years to maturity and yield for 40 corporate bonds are contained in the data file named CorporateBonds (*Barron's,* April 2, 2012).
    a. What is the sample mean years to maturity for corporate bonds and what is the sample standard deviation?
    b. Develop a 95% confidence interval for the population mean years to maturity.
    c. What is the sample mean yield on corporate bonds and what is the sample standard deviation?
    d. Develop a 95% confidence interval for the population mean yield on corporate bonds.

17. The International Air Transport Association surveys business travelers to develop quality ratings for transatlantic gateway airports. The maximum possible rating is 10. Suppose a simple random sample of 50 business travelers is selected and each traveler is asked to provide a rating for the Miami International Airport. The ratings obtained from the sample of 50 business travelers follow.

WEB file Miami

6	4	6	8	7	7	6	3	3	8	10	4	8
7	8	7	5	9	5	8	4	3	8	5	5	4
4	4	8	4	5	6	2	5	9	9	8	4	8
9	9	5	9	7	8	3	10	8	9	6		

Develop a 95% confidence interval estimate of the population mean rating for Miami.

WEB file JobSearch

18. Older people often have a hard time finding work. AARP reported on the number of weeks it takes a worker aged 55 plus to find a job. The data on number of weeks spent searching for a job contained in the file JobSearch are consistent with the AARP findings (*AARP Bulletin,* April 2008).
    a. Provide a point estimate of the population mean number of weeks it takes a worker aged 55 plus to find a job.
    b. At 95% confidence, what is the margin of error?
    c. What is the 95% confidence interval estimate of the mean?
    d. Discuss the degree of skewness found in the sample data. What suggestion would you make for a repeat of this study?

19. The average cost per night of a hotel room in New York City is $273 (*SmartMoney,* March 2009). Assume this estimate is based on a sample of 45 hotels and that the sample standard deviation is $65.
    a. With 95% confidence, what is the margin of error?
    b. What is the 95% confidence interval estimate of the population mean?
    c. Two years ago the average cost of a hotel room in New York City was $229. Discuss the change in cost over the two-year period.

WEB file Program

20. Is your favorite TV program often interrupted by advertising? CNBC presented statistics on the average number of programming minutes in a half-hour sitcom (CNBC, February 23, 2006). The following data (in minutes) are representative of their findings.

21.06	22.24	20.62
21.66	21.23	23.86
23.82	20.30	21.52
21.52	21.91	23.14
20.02	22.20	21.20
22.37	22.19	22.34
23.36	23.44	

Assume the population is approximately normal. Provide a point estimate and a 95% confidence interval for the mean number of programming minutes during a half-hour television sitcom.

WEB file Alcohol

21. Consumption of alcoholic beverages by young women of drinking age in the United Kingdom, the United States, and Europe was reported (*The Wall Street Journal,* February 15, 2006). Data (annual consumption in liters) consistent with the findings reported in *The Wall Street Journal* article are shown for a sample of 20 European young women.

266	82	199	174	97
170	222	115	130	169
164	102	113	171	0
93	0	93	110	130

Assuming the population is roughly symmetric, construct a 95% confidence interval for the mean annual consumption of alcoholic beverages by European young women.

22. Disney's *Hannah Montana: The Movie* opened on Easter weekend in April 2009. Over the three-day weekend, the movie became the number-one box office attraction (*The Wall Street Journal,* April 13, 2009). The ticket sales revenue in dollars for a sample of 25 theaters is as follows.

WEB file TicketSales

20,200	10,150	13,000	11,320	9700
8350	7300	14,000	9940	11,200
10,750	6240	12,700	7430	13,500
13,900	4200	6750	6700	9330
13,185	9200	21,400	11,380	10,800

a. What is the 95% confidence interval estimate for the mean ticket sales revenue per theater? Interpret this result.
b. Using the movie ticket price of \$7.16 per ticket, what is the estimate of the mean number of customers per theater?
c. The movie was shown in 3118 theaters. Estimate the total number of customers who saw *Hannah Montana: The Movie* and the total box office ticket sales for the three-day weekend.

8.3 Determining the Sample Size

If a desired margin of error is selected prior to sampling, the procedures in this section can be used to determine the sample size necessary to satisfy the margin of error requirement.

In providing practical advice in the two preceding sections, we commented on the role of the sample size in providing good approximate confidence intervals when the population is not normally distributed. In this section, we focus on another aspect of the sample size issue. We describe how to choose a sample size large enough to provide a desired margin of error. To understand how this process works, we return to the σ known case presented in Section 8.1. Using expression (8.1), the interval estimate is

$$\bar{x} \pm z_{\alpha/2}\frac{\sigma}{\sqrt{n}}$$

The quantity $z_{\alpha/2}(\sigma/\sqrt{n})$ is the margin of error. Thus, we see that $z_{\alpha/2}$, the population standard deviation σ, and the sample size n combine to determine the margin of error. Once we select a confidence coefficient $1 - \alpha$, $z_{\alpha/2}$ can be determined. Then, if we have a value for σ, we can determine the sample size n needed to provide any desired margin of error. Development of the formula used to compute the required sample size n follows.

Let E = the desired margin of error:

$$E = z_{\alpha/2} \frac{\sigma}{\sqrt{n}}$$

Solving for $\sqrt{n}$, we have

$$\sqrt{n} = \frac{z_{\alpha/2}\sigma}{E}$$

Squaring both sides of this equation, we obtain the following expression for the sample size.

Equation (8.3) can be used to provide a good sample size recommendation. However, judgment on the part of the analyst should be used to determine whether the final sample size should be adjusted upward.

SAMPLE SIZE FOR AN INTERVAL ESTIMATE OF A POPULATION MEAN

$$n = \frac{(z_{\alpha/2})^2\sigma^2}{E^2} \tag{8.3}$$

This sample size provides the desired margin of error at the chosen confidence level.

In equation (8.3), E is the margin of error that the user is willing to accept, and the value of $z_{\alpha/2}$ follows directly from the confidence level to be used in developing the interval estimate. Although user preference must be considered, 95% confidence is the most frequently chosen value ($z_{.025} = 1.96$).

Finally, use of equation (8.3) requires a value for the population standard deviation σ. However, even if σ is unknown, we can use equation (8.3) provided we have a preliminary or *planning value* for σ. In practice, one of the following procedures can be chosen.

A planning value for the population standard deviation σ must be specified before the sample size can be determined. Three methods of obtaining a planning value for σ are discussed here.

1. Use the estimate of the population standard deviation computed from data of previous studies as the planning value for σ.
2. Use a pilot study to select a preliminary sample. The sample standard deviation from the preliminary sample can be used as the planning value for σ.
3. Use judgment or a "best guess" for the value of σ. For example, we might begin by estimating the largest and smallest data values in the population. The difference between the largest and smallest values provides an estimate of the range for the data. Finally, the range divided by 4 is often suggested as a rough approximation of the standard deviation and thus an acceptable planning value for σ.

Let us demonstrate the use of equation (8.3) to determine the sample size by considering the following example. A previous study that investigated the cost of renting automobiles in the United States found a mean cost of approximately \$55 per day for renting a midsize automobile. Suppose that the organization that conducted this study would like to conduct a new study in order to estimate the population mean daily rental cost for a midsize automobile in the United States. In designing the new study, the project director specifies that the population mean daily rental cost be estimated with a margin of error of \$2 and a 95% level of confidence.

The project director specified a desired margin of error of $E = 2$, and the 95% level of confidence indicates $z_{.025} = 1.96$. Thus, we only need a planning value for the population standard deviation σ in order to compute the required sample size. At this point, an analyst reviewed the sample data from the previous study and found that the sample standard deviation for the daily rental cost was \$9.65. Using 9.65 as the planning value for σ, we obtain

Equation (8.3) provides the minimum sample size needed to satisfy the desired margin of error requirement. If the computed sample size is not an integer, rounding up to the next integer value will provide a margin of error slightly smaller than required.

$$n = \frac{(z_{\alpha/2})^2\sigma^2}{E^2} = \frac{(1.96)^2(9.65)^2}{2^2} = 89.43$$

Thus, the sample size for the new study needs to be at least 89.43 midsize automobile rentals in order to satisfy the project director's $2 margin-of-error requirement. In cases where the computed n is not an integer, we round up to the next integer value; hence, the recommended sample size is 90 midsize automobile rentals.

Exercises

Methods

23. How large a sample should be selected to provide a 95% confidence interval with a margin of error of 10? Assume that the population standard deviation is 40.

SELF test

24. The range for a set of data is estimated to be 36.
    a. What is the planning value for the population standard deviation?
    b. At 95% confidence, how large a sample would provide a margin of error of 3?
    c. At 95% confidence, how large a sample would provide a margin of error of 2?

Applications

SELF test

25. Refer to the Scheer Industries example in Section 8.2. Use 6.84 days as a planning value for the population standard deviation.
    a. Assuming 95% confidence, what sample size would be required to obtain a margin of error of 1.5 days?
    b. If the precision statement was made with 90% confidence, what sample size would be required to obtain a margin of error of 2 days?
26. The U.S. Energy Information Administration (US EIA) reported that the average price for a gallon of regular gasoline is $3.94 (US EIA website, April 6, 2012). The US EIA updates its estimates of average gas prices on a weekly basis. Assume the standard deviation is $.25 for the price of a gallon of regular gasoline and recommend the appropriate sample size for the US EIA to use if they wish to report each of the following margins of error at 95% confidence.
    a. The desired margin of error is $.10.
    b. The desired margin of error is $.07.
    c. The desired margin of error is $.05.
27. Annual starting salaries for college graduates with degrees in business administration are generally expected to be between $30,000 and $45,000. Assume that a 95% confidence interval estimate of the population mean annual starting salary is desired. What is the planning value for the population standard deviation? How large a sample should be taken if the desired margin of error is
    a. $500?
    b. $200?
    c. $100?
    d. Would you recommend trying to obtain the $100 margin of error? Explain.
28. An online survey by ShareBuilder, a retirement plan provider, and Harris Interactive reported that 60% of female business owners are not confident they are saving enough for retirement (*SmallBiz*, Winter 2006). Suppose we would like to do a follow-up study to determine how much female business owners are saving each year toward retirement and want to use $100 as the desired margin of error for an interval estimate of the population mean. Use $1100 as a planning value for the standard deviation and recommend a sample size for each of the following situations.
    a. A 90% confidence interval is desired for the mean amount saved.
    b. A 95% confidence interval is desired for the mean amount saved.

c. A 99% confidence interval is desired for the mean amount saved.
d. When the desired margin of error is set, what happens to the sample size as the confidence level is increased? Would you recommend using a 99% confidence interval in this case? Discuss.

29. The travel-to-work time for residents of the 15 largest cities in the United States is reported in the *2003 Information Please Almanac.* Suppose that a preliminary simple random sample of residents of San Francisco is used to develop a planning value of 6.25 minutes for the population standard deviation.
    a. If we want to estimate the population mean travel-to-work time for San Francisco residents with a margin of error of 2 minutes, what sample size should be used? Assume 95% confidence.
    b. If we want to estimate the population mean travel-to-work time for San Francisco residents with a margin of error of 1 minute, what sample size should be used? Assume 95% confidence.

30. There has been a trend toward less driving in the last few years, especially by young people. From 2001 to 2009 the annual vehicle miles traveled by people from 16 to 34 years of age decreased from 10,300 to 7900 miles per person (U.S. PIRG and Education Fund website, April 6, 2012). Assume the standard deviation was 2000 miles in 2009. Suppose you would like to conduct a survey to develop a 95% confidence interval estimate of the annual vehicle-miles per person for people 16 to 34 years of age at the current time. A margin of error of 100 miles is desired. How large a sample should be used for the current survey?

8.4 Population Proportion

In the introduction to this chapter we said that the general form of an interval estimate of a population proportion p is

$$\bar{p} \pm \text{Margin of error}$$

The sampling distribution of $\bar{p}$ plays a key role in computing the margin of error for this interval estimate.

In Chapter 7 we said that the sampling distribution of $\bar{p}$ can be approximated by a normal distribution whenever $np \geq 5$ and $n(1 - p) \geq 5$. Figure 8.9 shows the normal approximation

FIGURE 8.9 NORMAL APPROXIMATION OF THE SAMPLING DISTRIBUTION OF $\bar{p}$

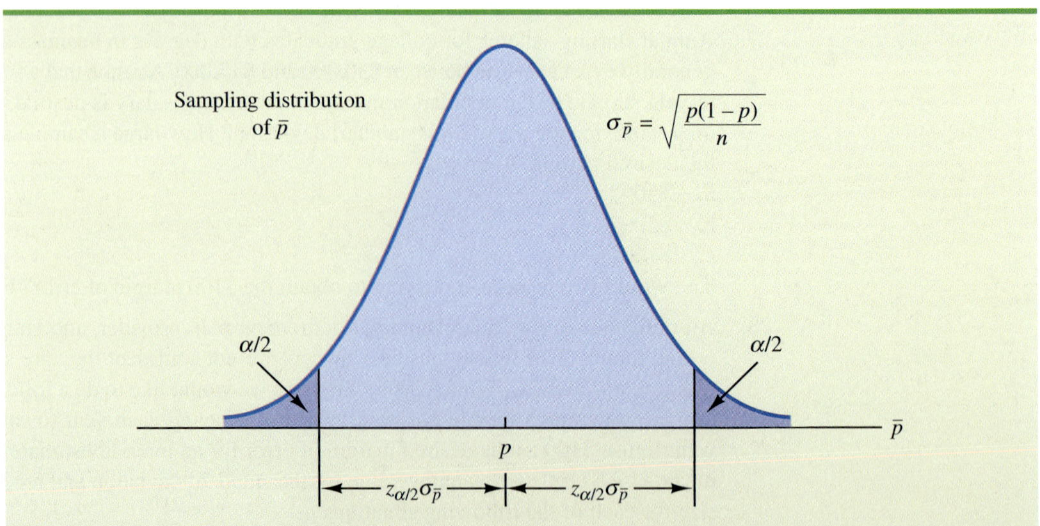

of the sampling distribution of $\bar{p}$. The mean of the sampling distribution of $\bar{p}$ is the population proportion p, and the standard error of $\bar{p}$ is

$$\sigma_{\bar{p}} = \sqrt{\frac{p(1-p)}{n}} \tag{8.4}$$

Because the sampling distribution of $\bar{p}$ is normally distributed, if we choose $z_{\alpha/2}\sigma_{\bar{p}}$ as the margin of error in an interval estimate of a population proportion, we know that $100(1-\alpha)\%$ of the intervals generated will contain the true population proportion. But $\sigma_{\bar{p}}$ cannot be used directly in the computation of the margin of error because p will not be known; p is what we are trying to estimate. So $\bar{p}$ is substituted for p and the margin of error for an interval estimate of a population proportion is given by

$$\text{Margin of error} = z_{\alpha/2}\sqrt{\frac{\bar{p}(1-\bar{p})}{n}} \tag{8.5}$$

With this margin of error, the general expression for an interval estimate of a population proportion is as follows.

When developing confidence intervals for proportions, the quantity $z_{\alpha/2}\sqrt{\bar{p}(1-\bar{p})/n}$ provides the margin of error.

INTERVAL ESTIMATE OF A POPULATION PROPORTION

$$\bar{p} \pm z_{\alpha/2}\sqrt{\frac{\bar{p}(1-\bar{p})}{n}} \tag{8.6}$$

where $1-\alpha$ is the confidence coefficient and $z_{\alpha/2}$ is the z value providing an area of $\alpha/2$ in the upper tail of the standard normal distribution.

WEB file

TeeTimes

The following example illustrates the computation of the margin of error and interval estimate for a population proportion. A national survey of 900 women golfers was conducted to learn how women golfers view their treatment at golf courses in the United States. The survey found that 396 of the women golfers were satisfied with the availability of tee times. Thus, the point estimate of the proportion of the population of women golfers who are satisfied with the availability of tee times is $396/900 = .44$. Using expression (8.6) and a 95% confidence level,

$$\bar{p} \pm z_{\alpha/2}\sqrt{\frac{\bar{p}(1-\bar{p})}{n}}$$

$$.44 \pm 1.96\sqrt{\frac{.44(1-.44)}{900}}$$

$$.44 \pm .0324$$

Thus, the margin of error is .0324 and the 95% confidence interval estimate of the population proportion is .4076 to .4724. Using percentages, the survey results enable us to state with 95% confidence that between 40.76% and 47.24% of all women golfers are satisfied with the availability of tee times.

Determining the Sample Size

Let us consider the question of how large the sample size should be to obtain an estimate of a population proportion at a specified level of precision. The rationale for the sample size determination in developing interval estimates of p is similar to the rationale used in Section 8.3 to determine the sample size for estimating a population mean.

Previously in this section we said that the margin of error associated with an interval estimate of a population proportion is $z_{\alpha/2}\sqrt{\bar{p}(1 - \bar{p})/n}$. The margin of error is based on the value of $z_{\alpha/2}$, the sample proportion $\bar{p}$, and the sample size n. Larger sample sizes provide a smaller margin of error and better precision.

Let E denote the desired margin of error.

$$E = z_{\alpha/2}\sqrt{\frac{\bar{p}(1 - \bar{p})}{n}}$$

Solving this equation for n provides a formula for the sample size that will provide a margin of error of size E.

$$n = \frac{(z_{\alpha/2})^2\bar{p}(1 - \bar{p})}{E^2}$$

Note, however, that we cannot use this formula to compute the sample size that will provide the desired margin of error because $\bar{p}$ will not be known until after we select the sample. What we need, then, is a planning value for $\bar{p}$ that can be used to make the computation. Using p^* to denote the planning value for $\bar{p}$, the following formula can be used to compute the sample size that will provide a margin of error of size E.

SAMPLE SIZE FOR AN INTERVAL ESTIMATE OF A POPULATION PROPORTION

$$n = \frac{(z_{\alpha/2})^2p^*(1 - p^*)}{E^2} \tag{8.7}$$

In practice, the planning value p^* can be chosen by one of the following procedures.

1. Use the sample proportion from a previous sample of the same or similar units.
2. Use a pilot study to select a preliminary sample. The sample proportion from this sample can be used as the planning value, p^*.
3. Use judgment or a "best guess" for the value of p^*.
4. If none of the preceding alternatives apply, use a planning value of $p^* = .50$.

Let us return to the survey of women golfers and assume that the company is interested in conducting a new survey to estimate the current proportion of the population of women golfers who are satisfied with the availability of tee times. How large should the sample be if the survey director wants to estimate the population proportion with a margin of error of .025 at 95% confidence? With $E = .025$ and $z_{\alpha/2} = 1.96$, we need a planning value p^* to answer the sample size question. Using the previous survey result of $\bar{p} = .44$ as the planning value p^*, equation (8.7) shows that

$$n = \frac{(z_{\alpha/2})^2p^*(1 - p^*)}{E^2} = \frac{(1.96)^2(.44)(1 - .44)}{(.025)^2} = 1514.5$$

TABLE 8.5 SOME POSSIBLE VALUES FOR $p^*(1 - p^*)$

p^*	$p^*(1 - p^*)$	
.10	(.10)(.90) = .09	
.30	(.30)(.70) = .21	
.40	(.40)(.60) = .24	
.50	(.50)(.50) = .25	← Largest value for $p^*(1 - p^*)$
.60	(.60)(.40) = .24	
.70	(.70)(.30) = .21	
.90	(.90)(.10) = .09	

Thus, the sample size must be at least 1514.5 women golfers to satisfy the margin of error requirement. Rounding up to the next integer value indicates that a sample of 1515 women golfers is recommended to satisfy the margin of error requirement.

The fourth alternative suggested for selecting a planning value p^* is to use $p^* = .50$. This value of p^* is frequently used when no other information is available. To understand why, note that the numerator of equation (8.7) shows that the sample size is proportional to the quantity $p^*(1 - p^*)$. A larger value for the quantity $p^*(1 - p^*)$ will result in a larger sample size. Table 8.5 gives some possible values of $p^*(1 - p^*)$. Note that the largest value of $p^*(1 - p^*)$ occurs when $p^* = .50$. Thus, in case of any uncertainty about an appropriate planning value, we know that $p^* = .50$ will provide the largest sample size recommendation. In effect, we play it safe by recommending the largest necessary sample size. If the sample proportion turns out to be different from the .50 planning value, the margin of error will be smaller than anticipated. Thus, in using $p^* = .50$, we guarantee that the sample size will be sufficient to obtain the desired margin of error.

In the survey of women golfers example, a planning value of $p^* = .50$ would have provided the sample size

$$n = \frac{(z_{\alpha/2})^2 p^*(1 - p^*)}{E^2} = \frac{(1.96)^2(.50)(1 - .50)}{(.025)^2} = 1536.6$$

Thus, a slightly larger sample size of 1537 women golfers would be recommended.

NOTES AND COMMENTS

The desired margin of error for estimating a population proportion is almost always .10 or less. In national public opinion polls conducted by organizations such as Gallup and Harris, a .03 or .04 margin of error is common. With such margins of error, equation (8.7) will almost always provide a sample size that is large enough to satisfy the requirements of $np \geq 5$ and $n(1 - p) \geq 5$ for using a normal distribution as an approximation for the sampling distribution of $\bar{x}$.

Exercises

Methods

SELF test

31. A simple random sample of 400 individuals provides 100 Yes responses.
    a. What is the point estimate of the proportion of the population that would provide Yes responses?
    b. What is your estimate of the standard error of the proportion, $\sigma_{\bar{p}}$?
    c. Compute the 95% confidence interval for the population proportion.

32. A simple random sample of 800 elements generates a sample proportion $\bar{p} = .70$.
    a. Provide a 90% confidence interval for the population proportion.
    b. Provide a 95% confidence interval for the population proportion.
33. In a survey, the planning value for the population proportion is $p^* = .35$. How large a sample should be taken to provide a 95% confidence interval with a margin of error of .05?
34. At 95% confidence, how large a sample should be taken to obtain a margin of error of .03 for the estimation of a population proportion? Assume that past data are not available for developing a planning value for p^*.

Applications

SELF test

35. The Consumer Reports National Research Center conducted a telephone survey of 2000 adults to learn about the major economic concerns for the future (*Consumer Reports,* January 2009). The survey results showed that 1760 of the respondents think the future health of Social Security is a major economic concern.
    a. What is the point estimate of the population proportion of adults who think the future health of Social Security is a major economic concern.
    b. At 90% confidence, what is the margin of error?
    c. Develop a 90% confidence interval for the population proportion of adults who think the future health of Social Security is a major economic concern.
    d. Develop a 95% confidence interval for this population proportion.
36. According to statistics reported on CNBC, a surprising number of motor vehicles are not covered by insurance (CNBC, February 23, 2006). Sample results, consistent with the CNBC report, showed 46 of 200 vehicles were not covered by insurance.
    a. What is the point estimate of the proportion of vehicles not covered by insurance?
    b. Develop a 95% confidence interval for the population proportion.
37. Towers Perrin, a New York human resources consulting firm, conducted a survey of 1100 employees at medium-sized and large companies to determine how dissatisfied employees were with their jobs (*The Wall Street Journal,* January 29, 2003). Representative data are shown in the file JobSatisfaction. A response of Yes indicates the employee strongly disliked the current work experience.

WEB file

JobSatisfaction

    a. What is the point estimate of the proportion of the population of employees who strongly dislike their current work experience?
    b. At 95% confidence, what is the margin of error?
    c. What is the 95% confidence interval for the proportion of the population of employees who strongly dislike their current work experience?
    d. Towers Perrin estimates that it costs employers one-third of an hourly employee's annual salary to find a successor and as much as 1.5 times the annual salary to find a successor for a highly compensated employee. What message did this survey send to employers?
38. According to Thomson Financial, through January 25, 2006, the majority of companies reported profits had beaten estimates (*BusinessWeek,* February 6, 2006). A sample of 162 companies showed 104 beat estimates, 29 matched estimates, and 29 fell short.
    a. What is the point estimate of the proportion that fell short of estimates?
    b. Determine the margin of error and provide a 95% confidence interval for the proportion that beat estimates.
    c. How large a sample is needed if the desired margin of error is .05?

SELF test

39. The percentage of people not covered by health care insurance in 2003 was 15.6% (*Statistical Abstract of the United States*, 2006). A congressional committee has been charged with conducting a sample survey to obtain more current information.
    a. What sample size would you recommend if the committee's goal is to estimate the current proportion of individuals without health care insurance with a margin of error of .03? Use a 95% confidence level.
    b. Repeat part (a) using a 99% confidence level.

40. For many years businesses have struggled with the rising cost of health care. But recently, the increases have slowed due to less inflation in health care prices and employees paying for a larger portion of health care benefits. A recent Mercer survey showed that 52% of U.S. employers were likely to require higher employee contributions for health care coverage in 2009 (*BusinessWeek,* February 16, 2009). Suppose the survey was based on a sample of 800 companies. Compute the margin of error and a 95% confidence interval for the proportion of companies likely to require higher employee contributions for health care coverage in 2009.
41. Fewer young people are driving. In 1983, 87% of 19-year-olds had a driver's license. Twenty-five years later that percentage had dropped to 75% (University of Michigan Transportation Research Institute website, April 7, 2012). Suppose these results are based on a random sample of 1200 19-year-olds in 1983 and again in 2008.
    a. At 95% confidence, what is the margin of error and the interval estimate of the number of 19-year-old drivers in 1983?
    b. At 95% confidence, what is the margin of error and the interval estimate of the number of 19-year-old drivers in 2008?
    c. Is the margin of error the same in parts (a) and (b)? Why or why not?
42. A poll for the presidential campaign sampled 491 potential voters in June. A primary purpose of the poll was to obtain an estimate of the proportion of potential voters who favored each candidate. Assume a planning value of $p^* = .50$ and a 95% confidence level.
    a. For $p^* = .50$, what was the planned margin of error for the June poll?
    b. Closer to the November election, better precision and smaller margins of error are desired. Assume the following margins of error are requested for surveys to be conducted during the presidential campaign. Compute the recommended sample size for each survey.

Survey	Margin of Error
September	.04
October	.03
Early November	.02
Pre-Election Day	.01

43. A Phoenix Wealth Management/Harris Interactive survey of 1500 individuals with net worth of $1 million or more provided a variety of statistics on wealthy people (*BusinessWeek,* September 22, 2003). The previous three-year period had been bad for the stock market, which motivated some of the questions asked.
    a. The survey reported that 53% of the respondents lost 25% or more of their portfolio value over the past three years. Develop a 95% confidence interval for the proportion of wealthy people who lost 25% or more of their portfolio value over the past three years.
    b. The survey reported that 31% of the respondents feel they have to save more for retirement to make up for what they lost. Develop a 95% confidence interval for the population proportion.
    c. Five percent of the respondents gave $25,000 or more to charity over the previous year. Develop a 95% confidence interval for the proportion who gave $25,000 or more to charity.
    d. Compare the margin of error for the interval estimates in parts (a), (b), and (c). How is the margin of error related to $\bar{p}$? When the same sample is being used to estimate a variety of proportions, which of the proportions should be used to choose the planning value p^*? Why do you think $p^* = .50$ is often used in these cases?

Summary

In this chapter we presented methods for developing interval estimates of a population mean and a population proportion. A point estimator may or may not provide a good estimate of a population parameter. The use of an interval estimate provides a measure of the precision of an estimate. Both the interval estimate of the population mean and the population proportion are of the form: point estimate $\pm$ margin of error.

We presented interval estimates for a population mean for two cases. In the σ known case, historical data or other information is used to develop an estimate of σ prior to taking a sample. Analysis of new sample data then proceeds based on the assumption that σ is known. In the σ unknown case, the sample data are used to estimate both the population mean and the population standard deviation. The final choice of which interval estimation procedure to use depends upon the analyst's understanding of which method provides the best estimate of σ.

In the σ known case, the interval estimation procedure is based on the assumed value of σ and the use of the standard normal distribution. In the σ unknown case, the interval estimation procedure uses the sample standard deviation s and the t distribution. In both cases the quality of the interval estimates obtained depends on the distribution of the population and the sample size. If the population is normally distributed the interval estimates will be exact in both cases, even for small sample sizes. If the population is not normally distributed, the interval estimates obtained will be approximate. Larger sample sizes will provide better approximations, but the more highly skewed the population is, the larger the sample size needs to be to obtain a good approximation. Practical advice about the sample size necessary to obtain good approximations was included in Sections 8.1 and 8.2. In most cases a sample of size 30 or more will provide good approximate confidence intervals.

The general form of the interval estimate for a population proportion is $\bar{p} \pm$ margin of error. In practice the sample sizes used for interval estimates of a population proportion are generally large. Thus, the interval estimation procedure is based on the standard normal distribution.

Often a desired margin of error is specified prior to developing a sampling plan. We showed how to choose a sample size large enough to provide the desired precision.

Glossary

Interval estimate An estimate of a population parameter that provides an interval believed to contain the value of the parameter. For the interval estimates in this chapter, it has the form: point estimate $\pm$ margin of error.

Margin of error The $\pm$ value added to and subtracted from a point estimate in order to develop an interval estimate of a population parameter.

σ known The case when historical data or other information provides a good value for the population standard deviation prior to taking a sample. The interval estimation procedure uses this known value of σ in computing the margin of error.

Confidence level The confidence associated with an interval estimate. For example, if an interval estimation procedure provides intervals such that 95% of the intervals formed using the procedure will include the population parameter, the interval estimate is said to be constructed at the 95% confidence level.

Confidence coefficient The confidence level expressed as a decimal value. For example, .95 is the confidence coefficient for a 95% confidence level.

Confidence interval Another name for an interval estimate.

σ unknown The more common case when no good basis exists for estimating the population standard deviation prior to taking the sample. The interval estimation procedure uses the sample standard deviation s in computing the margin of error.

t distribution A family of probability distributions that can be used to develop an interval estimate of a population mean whenever the population standard deviation σ is unknown and is estimated by the sample standard deviation s.

Degrees of freedom A parameter of the t distribution. When the t distribution is used in the computation of an interval estimate of a population mean, the appropriate t distribution has $n - 1$ degrees of freedom, where n is the size of the sample.

Key Formulas

Interval Estimate of a Population Mean: σ Known

$$\bar{x} \pm z_{\alpha/2} \frac{\sigma}{\sqrt{n}} \tag{8.1}$$

Interval Estimate of a Population Mean: σ Unknown

$$\bar{x} \pm t_{\alpha/2} \frac{s}{\sqrt{n}} \tag{8.2}$$

Sample Size for an Interval Estimate of a Population Mean

$$n = \frac{(z_{\alpha/2})^2 \sigma^2}{E^2} \tag{8.3}$$

Interval Estimate of a Population Proportion

$$\bar{p} \pm z_{\alpha/2} \sqrt{\frac{\bar{p}(1 - \bar{p})}{n}} \tag{8.6}$$

Sample Size for an Interval Estimate of a Population Proportion

$$n = \frac{(z_{\alpha/2})^2 p^*(1 - p^*)}{E^2} \tag{8.7}$$

Supplementary Exercises

44. A sample survey of 54 discount brokers showed that the mean price charged for a trade of 100 shares at \$50 per share was \$33.77 (*AAII Journal,* February 2006). The survey is conducted annually. With the historical data available, assume a known population standard deviation of \$15.
    a. Using the sample data, what is the margin of error associated with a 95% confidence interval?
    b. Develop a 95% confidence interval for the mean price charged by discount brokers for a trade of 100 shares at \$50 per share.
45. A survey conducted by the American Automobile Association showed that a family of four spends an average of \$215.60 per day while on vacation. Suppose a sample of 64 families of four vacationing at Niagara Falls resulted in a sample mean of \$252.45 per day and a sample standard deviation of \$74.50.
    a. Develop a 95% confidence interval estimate of the mean amount spent per day by a family of four visiting Niagara Falls.
    b. Based on the confidence interval from part (a), does it appear that the population mean amount spent per day by families visiting Niagara Falls differs from the mean reported by the American Automobile Association? Explain.
46. The 92 million Americans of age 50 and over control 50 percent of all discretionary income (*AARP Bulletin,* March 2008). AARP estimated that the average annual expenditure on restaurants and carryout food was \$1873 for individuals in this age group. Suppose this estimate is based on a sample of 80 persons and that the sample standard deviation is \$550.
    a. At 95% confidence, what is the margin of error?
    b. What is the 95% confidence interval for the population mean amount spent on restaurants and carryout food?
    c. What is your estimate of the total amount spent by Americans of age 50 and over on restaurants and carryout food?
    d. If the amount spent on restaurants and carryout food is skewed to the right, would you expect the median amount spent to be greater or less than \$1873?

47. Many stock market observers say that when the P/E ratio for stocks gets over 20 the market is overvalued. The P/E ratio is the stock price divided by the most recent 12 months of earnings. Suppose you are interested in seeing whether the current market is overvalued and would also like to know what proportion of companies pay dividends. A random sample of 30 companies listed on the New York Stock Exchange (NYSE) is provided (*Barron's,* January 19, 2004).

WEB file NYSEStocks

Company	Dividend	P/E Ratio	Company	Dividend	P/E Ratio
Albertsons	Yes	14	NY Times A	Yes	25
BRE Prop	Yes	18	Omnicare	Yes	25
CityNtl	Yes	16	PallCp	Yes	23
DelMonte	No	21	PubSvcEnt	Yes	11
EnrgzHldg	No	20	SensientTch	Yes	11
Ford Motor	Yes	22	SmtProp	Yes	12
Gildan A	No	12	TJX Cos	Yes	21
HudsnUtdBcp	Yes	13	Thomson	Yes	30
IBM	Yes	22	USB Hldg	Yes	12
JeffPilot	Yes	16	US Restr	Yes	26
KingswayFin	No	6	Varian Med	No	41
Libbey	Yes	13	Visx	No	72
MasoniteIntl	No	15	Waste Mgt	No	23
Motorola	Yes	68	Wiley A	Yes	21
Ntl City	Yes	10	Yum Brands	No	18

a. What is a point estimate of the P/E ratio for the population of stocks listed on the New York Stock Exchange? Develop a 95% confidence interval.
b. Based on your answer to part (a), do you believe that the market is overvalued?
c. What is a point estimate of the proportion of companies on the NYSE that pay dividends? Is the sample size large enough to justify using the normal distribution to construct a confidence interval for this proportion? Why or why not?

WEB file Flights

48. US Airways conducted a number of studies that indicated a substantial savings could be obtained by encouraging Dividend Miles frequent flyer customers to redeem miles and schedule award flights online (*US Airways Attaché,* February 2003). One study collected data on the amount of time required to redeem miles and schedule an award flight over the telephone. A sample showing the time in minutes required for each of 150 award flights scheduled by telephone is contained in the data set Flights. Use Minitab or Excel to help answer the following questions.
a. What is the sample mean number of minutes required to schedule an award flight by telephone?
b. What is the 95% confidence interval for the population mean time to schedule an award flight by telephone?
c. Assume a telephone ticket agent works 7.5 hours per day. How many award flights can one ticket agent be expected to handle a day?
d. Discuss why this information supported US Airways' plans to use an online system to reduce costs.

WEB file Standing

49. A recent article reported that there are approximately 11 minutes of actual playing time in a typical National Football League (NFL) game (*The Wall Street Journal,* January 15, 2010). The article included information about the amount of time devoted to replays, the amount of time devoted to commercials, and the amount of time the players spend standing around between plays. Data consistent with the findings published in *The Wall Street Journal* are in the file named Standing. These data provide the amount of time players spend standing around between plays for a sample of 60 NFL games.
a. Use the Standing data set to develop a point estimate of the number of minutes during an NFL game that players are standing around between plays. Compare this to the actual playing time reported in the article. Are you surprised?
b. What is the sample standard deviation?

c. Develop a 95% confidence interval for the number of minutes players spend standing around between plays.

50. Mileage tests are conducted for a particular model of automobile. If a 98% confidence interval with a margin of error of 1 mile per gallon is desired, how many automobiles should be used in the test? Assume that preliminary mileage tests indicate the standard deviation is 2.6 miles per gallon.

51. In developing patient appointment schedules, a medical center wants to estimate the mean time that a staff member spends with each patient. How large a sample should be taken if the desired margin of error is two minutes at a 95% level of confidence? How large a sample should be taken for a 99% level of confidence? Use a planning value for the population standard deviation of eight minutes.

52. Annual salary plus bonus data for chief executive officers are presented in the *BusinessWeek* Annual Pay Survey. A preliminary sample showed that the standard deviation is \$675 with data provided in thousands of dollars. How many chief executive officers should be in a sample if we want to estimate the population mean annual salary plus bonus with a margin of error of \$100,000? (*Note:* The desired margin of error would be $E = 100$ if the data are in thousands of dollars.) Use 95% confidence.

53. The National Center for Education Statistics reported that 47% of college students work to pay for tuition and living expenses. Assume that a sample of 450 college students was used in the study.
    a. Provide a 95% confidence interval for the population proportion of college students who work to pay for tuition and living expenses.
    b. Provide a 99% confidence interval for the population proportion of college students who work to pay for tuition and living expenses.
    c. What happens to the margin of error as the confidence is increased from 95% to 99%?

54. A *USA Today*/CNN/Gallup survey of 369 working parents found 200 who said they spend too little time with their children because of work commitments.
    a. What is the point estimate of the proportion of the population of working parents who feel they spend too little time with their children because of work commitments?
    b. At 95% confidence, what is the margin of error?
    c. What is the 95% confidence interval estimate of the population proportion of working parents who feel they spend too little time with their children because of work commitments?

55. Which would be hardest for you to give up: Your computer or your television? In a recent survey of 1677 U.S. Internet users, 74% of the young tech elite (average age of 22) say their computer would be very hard to give up (*PC Magazine,* February 3, 2004). Only 48% say their television would be very hard to give up.
    a. Develop a 95% confidence interval for the proportion of the young tech elite that would find it very hard to give up their computer.
    b. Develop a 99% confidence interval for the proportion of the young tech elite that would find it very hard to give up their television.
    c. In which case, part (a) or part (b), is the margin of error larger? Explain why.

56. Cincinnati/Northern Kentucky International Airport had the second highest on-time arrival rate for 2005 among the nation's busiest airports (*The Cincinnati Enquirer,* February 3, 2006). Assume the findings were based on 455 on-time arrivals out of a sample of 550 flights.
    a. Develop a point estimate of the on-time arrival rate (proportion of flights arriving on time) for the airport.
    b. Construct a 95% confidence interval for the on-time arrival rate of the population of all flights at the airport during 2005.

57. The *2003 Statistical Abstract of the United States* reported the percentage of people 18 years of age and older who smoke. Suppose that a study designed to collect new data on smokers and nonsmokers uses a preliminary estimate of the proportion who smoke of .30.
    a. How large a sample should be taken to estimate the proportion of smokers in the population with a margin of error of .02? Use 95% confidence.

b. Assume that the study uses your sample size recommendation in part (a) and finds 520 smokers. What is the point estimate of the proportion of smokers in the population?
c. What is the 95% confidence interval for the proportion of smokers in the population?

58. A well-known bank credit card firm wishes to estimate the proportion of credit card holders who carry a nonzero balance at the end of the month and incur an interest charge. Assume that the desired margin of error is .03 at 98% confidence.
   a. How large a sample should be selected if it is anticipated that roughly 70% of the firm's card holders carry a nonzero balance at the end of the month?
   b. How large a sample should be selected if no planning value for the proportion could be specified?
59. Workers in several industries were surveyed to determine the proportion of workers who feel their industry is understaffed. In the government sector, 37% of the respondents said they were understaffed, in the health care sector 33% said they were understaffed, and in the education sector 28% said they were understaffed (*USA Today,* January 11, 2010). Suppose that 200 workers were surveyed in each industry.
   a. Construct a 95% confidence interval for the proportion of workers in each of these industries who feel their industry is understaffed.
   b. Assuming the same sample size will be used in each industry, how large would the sample need to be to ensure that the margin of error is .05 or less for each of the three confidence intervals?
60. Although airline schedules and cost are important factors for business travelers when choosing an airline carrier, a *USA Today* survey found that business travelers list an airline's frequent flyer program as the most important factor. From a sample of $n = 1993$ business travelers who responded to the survey, 618 listed a frequent flyer program as the most important factor.
   a. What is the point estimate of the proportion of the population of business travelers who believe a frequent flyer program is the most important factor when choosing an airline carrier?
   b. Develop a 95% confidence interval estimate of the population proportion.
   c. How large a sample would be required to report the margin of error of .01 at 95% confidence? Would you recommend that *USA Today* attempt to provide this degree of precision? Why or why not?

Case Problem 1 Young Professional Magazine

Young Professional magazine was developed for a target audience of recent college graduates who are in their first 10 years in a business/professional career. In its two years of publication, the magazine has been fairly successful. Now the publisher is interested in expanding the magazine's advertising base. Potential advertisers continually ask about the demographics and interests of subscribers to *Young Professional*. To collect this information, the magazine commissioned a survey to develop a profile of its subscribers. The survey results will be used to help the magazine choose articles of interest and provide advertisers with a profile of subscribers. As a new employee of the magazine, you have been asked to help analyze the survey results.

Some of the survey questions follow:

WEB file
Professional

1. What is your age?
2. Are you: Male________ Female___________
3. Do you plan to make any real estate purchases in the next two years? Yes______ No______
4. What is the approximate total value of financial investments, exclusive of your home, owned by you or members of your household?
5. How many stock/bond/mutual fund transactions have you made in the past year?

TABLE 8.6 PARTIAL SURVEY RESULTS FOR *YOUNG PROFESSIONAL* MAGAZINE

Age	Gender	Real Estate Purchases	Value of Investments($)	Number of Transactions	Broadband Access	Household Income($)	Children
38	Female	No	12200	4	Yes	75200	Yes
30	Male	No	12400	4	Yes	70300	Yes
41	Female	No	26800	5	Yes	48200	No
28	Female	Yes	19600	6	No	95300	No
31	Female	Yes	15100	5	No	73300	Yes
⋮	⋮	⋮	⋮	⋮	⋮	⋮	⋮

6. Do you have broadband access to the Internet at home? Yes______ No______
7. Please indicate your total household income last year. ___________
8. Do you have children? Yes______ No______

The file entitled Professional contains the responses to these questions. Table 8.6 shows the portion of the file pertaining to the first five survey respondents.

Managerial Report

Prepare a managerial report summarizing the results of the survey. In addition to statistical summaries, discuss how the magazine might use these results to attract advertisers. You might also comment on how the survey results could be used by the magazine's editors to identify topics that would be of interest to readers. Your report should address the following issues, but do not limit your analysis to just these areas.

1. Develop appropriate descriptive statistics to summarize the data.
2. Develop 95% confidence intervals for the mean age and household income of subscribers.
3. Develop 95% confidence intervals for the proportion of subscribers who have broadband access at home and the proportion of subscribers who have children.
4. Would *Young Professional* be a good advertising outlet for online brokers? Justify your conclusion with statistical data.
5. Would this magazine be a good place to advertise for companies selling educational software and computer games for young children?
6. Comment on the types of articles you believe would be of interest to readers of *Young Professional*.

Case Problem 2 Gulf Real Estate Properties

Gulf Real Estate Properties, Inc., is a real estate firm located in southwest Florida. The company, which advertises itself as "expert in the real estate market," monitors condominium sales by collecting data on location, list price, sale price, and number of days it takes to sell each unit. Each condominium is classified as *Gulf View* if it is located directly on the Gulf of Mexico or *No Gulf View* if it is located on the bay or a golf course, near but not on the Gulf. Sample data from the Multiple Listing Service in Naples, Florida, provided recent sales data for 40 Gulf View condominiums and 18 No Gulf View condominiums. Prices are in thousands of dollars. The data are shown in Table 8.7.

Managerial Report

1. Use appropriate descriptive statistics to summarize each of the three variables for the 40 Gulf View condominiums.

TABLE 8.7 SALES DATA FOR GULF REAL ESTATE PROPERTIES

WEB file GulfProp

Gulf View Condominiums			No Gulf View Condominiums		
List Price	Sale Price	Days to Sell	List Price	Sale Price	Days to Sell
495.0	475.0	130	217.0	217.0	182
379.0	350.0	71	148.0	135.5	338
529.0	519.0	85	186.5	179.0	122
552.5	534.5	95	239.0	230.0	150
334.9	334.9	119	279.0	267.5	169
550.0	505.0	92	215.0	214.0	58
169.9	165.0	197	279.0	259.0	110
210.0	210.0	56	179.9	176.5	130
975.0	945.0	73	149.9	144.9	149
314.0	314.0	126	235.0	230.0	114
315.0	305.0	88	199.8	192.0	120
885.0	800.0	282	210.0	195.0	61
975.0	975.0	100	226.0	212.0	146
469.0	445.0	56	149.9	146.5	137
329.0	305.0	49	160.0	160.0	281
365.0	330.0	48	322.0	292.5	63
332.0	312.0	88	187.5	179.0	48
520.0	495.0	161	247.0	227.0	52
425.0	405.0	149			
675.0	669.0	142			
409.0	400.0	28			
649.0	649.0	29			
319.0	305.0	140			
425.0	410.0	85			
359.0	340.0	107			
469.0	449.0	72			
895.0	875.0	129			
439.0	430.0	160			
435.0	400.0	206			
235.0	227.0	91			
638.0	618.0	100			
629.0	600.0	97			
329.0	309.0	114			
595.0	555.0	45			
339.0	315.0	150			
215.0	200.0	48			
395.0	375.0	135			
449.0	425.0	53			
499.0	465.0	86			
439.0	428.5	158			

2. Use appropriate descriptive statistics to summarize each of the three variables for the 18 No Gulf View condominiums.
3. Compare your summary results. Discuss any specific statistical results that would help a real estate agent understand the condominium market.
4. Develop a 95% confidence interval estimate of the population mean sales price and population mean number of days to sell for Gulf View condominiums. Interpret your results.

5. Develop a 95% confidence interval estimate of the population mean sales price and population mean number of days to sell for No Gulf View condominiums. Interpret your results.
6. Assume the branch manager requested estimates of the mean selling price of Gulf View condominiums with a margin of error of \$40,000 and the mean selling price of No Gulf View condominiums with a margin of error of \$15,000. Using 95% confidence, how large should the sample sizes be?
7. Gulf Real Estate Properties just signed contracts for two new listings: a Gulf View condominium with a list price of \$589,000 and a No Gulf View condominium with a list price of \$285,000. What is your estimate of the final selling price and number of days required to sell each of these units?

Case Problem 3 Metropolitan Research, Inc.

Metropolitan Research, Inc., a consumer research organization, conducts surveys designed to evaluate a wide variety of products and services available to consumers. In one particular study, Metropolitan looked at consumer satisfaction with the performance of automobiles produced by a major Detroit manufacturer. A questionnaire sent to owners of one of the manufacturer's full-sized cars revealed several complaints about early transmission problems. To learn more about the transmission failures, Metropolitan used a sample of actual transmission repairs provided by a transmission repair firm in the Detroit area. The following data show the actual number of miles driven for 50 vehicles at the time of transmission failure.

WEB file Auto

85,092	32,609	59,465	77,437	32,534	64,090	32,464	59,902
39,323	89,641	94,219	116,803	92,857	63,436	65,605	85,861
64,342	61,978	67,998	59,817	101,769	95,774	121,352	69,568
74,276	66,998	40,001	72,069	25,066	77,098	69,922	35,662
74,425	67,202	118,444	53,500	79,294	64,544	86,813	116,269
37,831	89,341	73,341	85,288	138,114	53,402	85,586	82,256
77,539	88,798						

Managerial Report

1. Use appropriate descriptive statistics to summarize the transmission failure data.
2. Develop a 95% confidence interval for the mean number of miles driven until transmission failure for the population of automobiles with transmission failure. Provide a managerial interpretation of the interval estimate.
3. Discuss the implication of your statistical findings in terms of the belief that some owners of the automobiles experienced early transmission failures.
4. How many repair records should be sampled if the research firm wants the population mean number of miles driven until transmission failure to be estimated with a margin of error of 5000 miles? Use 95% confidence.
5. What other information would you like to gather to evaluate the transmission failure problem more fully?

Appendix 8.1 Interval Estimation with Minitab

We describe the use of Minitab in constructing confidence intervals for a population mean and a population proportion.

Population Mean: σ Known

WEB file
Lloyd's

We illustrate interval estimation using the Lloyd's example in Section 8.1. The amounts spent per shopping trip for the sample of 100 customers are in column C1 of a Minitab worksheet. The population standard deviation $\sigma = 20$ is assumed known. The following steps can be used to compute a 95% confidence interval estimate of the population mean.

Step 1. Select the **Stat** menu
Step 2. Choose **Basic Statistics**
Step 3. Choose **1-Sample Z**
Step 4. When the 1-Sample Z dialog box appears:
Enter C1 in the **Samples in columns** box
Enter 20 in the **Standard deviation** box
Step 5. Click **OK**

The Minitab default is a 95% confidence level. In order to specify a different confidence level such as 90%, add the following to step 4.

Select **Options**
When the 1-Sample Z-Options dialog box appears:
Enter 90 in the **Confidence level** box
Click **OK**

Population Mean: σ Unknown

WEB file
NewBalance

We illustrate interval estimation using the data in Table 8.3 showing the credit card balances for a sample of 70 households. The data are in column C1 of a Minitab worksheet. In this case the population standard deviation σ will be estimated by the sample standard deviation s. The following steps can be used to compute a 95% confidence interval estimate of the population mean.

Step 1. Select the **Stat** menu
Step 2. Choose **Basic Statistics**
Step 3. Choose **1-Sample t**
Step 4. When the 1-Sample t dialog box appears:
Enter C1 in the **Samples in columns** box
Step 5. Click **OK**

The Minitab default is a 95% confidence level. In order to specify a different confidence level such as 90%, add the following to step 4.

Select **Options**
When the 1-Sample t-Options dialog box appears:
Enter 90 in the **Confidence level** box
Click **OK**

Population Proportion

WEB file
TeeTimes

We illustrate interval estimation using the survey data for women golfers presented in Section 8.4. The data are in column C1 of a Minitab worksheet. Individual responses are recorded as Yes if the golfer is satisfied with the availability of tee times and No otherwise. The following steps can be used to compute a 95% confidence interval estimate of the proportion of women golfers who are satisfied with the availability of tee times.

Step 1. Select the **Stat** menu
Step 2. Choose **Basic Statistics**
Step 3. Choose **1 Proportion**

Step 4. When the 1 Proportion dialog box appears:
Enter C1 in the **Samples in columns** box
Step 5. Select **Options**
Step 6. When the 1 Proportion-Options dialog box appears:
Select **Use test and interval based on normal distribution**
Click **OK**
Step 7. Click **OK**

The Minitab default is a 95% confidence level. In order to specify a different confidence level such as 90%, enter 90 in the **Confidence Level** box when the 1 Proportion-Options dialog box appears in step 6.

Note: Minitab's 1 Proportion routine uses an alphabetical ordering of the responses and selects the *second response* for the population proportion of interest. In the women golfers example, Minitab used the alphabetical ordering No-Yes and then provided the confidence interval for the proportion of Yes responses. Because Yes was the response of interest, the Minitab output was fine. However, if Minitab's alphabetical ordering does not provide the response of interest, select any cell in the column and use the sequence: Editor > Column > Value Order. It will provide you with the option of entering a user-specified order, but you must list the response of interest second in the define-an-order box.

Appendix 8.2 Interval Estimation Using Excel

We describe the use of Excel in constructing confidence intervals for a population mean and a population proportion.

Population Mean: σ Known

WEB file
Lloyd's

We illustrate interval estimation using the Lloyd's example in Section 8.1. The population standard deviation $\sigma = 20$ is assumed known. The amounts spent for the sample of 100 customers are in column A of an Excel worksheet. Excel's AVERAGE and CONFIDENCE.NORM functions can be used to compute the point estimate and the margin of error for an estimate of the population mean.

Step 1. Select cell C1 and enter the Excel formula =AVERAGE(A2:A101)
Step 2. Select cell C2 and enter the Excel formula =CONFIDENCE.NORM(.05,20,100)

The three inputs of the CONFIDENCE.NORM function are

Alpha = 1 − confidence coefficient = 1 − .95 = .05
The population standard deviation = 20
The sample size = 100

The point estimate of the population mean (82) in cell C1 and the margin of error (3.92) in cell C2 allow the confidence interval for the population mean to be easily computed.

Population Mean: σ Unknown

WEB file
NewBalance

We illustrate interval estimation using the data in Table 8.3, which show the credit card balances for a sample of 70 households. The data are in column A of an Excel worksheet. The following steps can be used to compute the point estimate and the margin of error for an interval estimate of a population mean. We will use Excel's Descriptive Statistics Tool described in Chapter 3.

FIGURE 8.10 INTERVAL ESTIMATION OF THE POPULATION MEAN CREDIT CARD BALANCE USING EXCEL

	A	B	C	D	E	F
1	**NewBalance**		*NewBalance*			
2	9430				Point Estimate	
3	7535		Mean	9312		
4	4078		Standard Error	478.9281		
5	5604		Median	9466		
6	5179		Mode	13627		
7	4416		Standard Deviation	4007		
8	10676		Sample Variance	16056048		
9	1627		Kurtosis	-0.2960		
10	10112		Skewness	0.1879		
11	6567		Range	18648		
12	13627		Minimum	615		
13	18719		Maximum	19263		
14	14661		Sum	651840		
15	12195		Count	70	Margin of Error	
16	10544		Confidence Level(95.0%)	955		
17	13659					
70	9743					
71	10324					
72						

Note: Rows 18 to 69 are hidden.

Step 1. Click the **Data** tab on the Ribbon
Step 2. In the **Analysis** group, click **Data Analysis**
Step 3. Choose **Descriptive Statistics** from the list of Analysis Tools
Step 4. When the Descriptive Statistics dialog box appears:
Enter A1:A71 in the **Input Range** box
Select **Grouped by Columns**
Select **Labels in First Row**
Select **Output Range**
Enter C1 in the Output Range box
Select **Summary Statistics**
Select **Confidence Level for Mean**
Enter 95 in the Confidence Level for Mean box
Click **OK**

The summary statistics will appear in columns C and D. The point estimate of the population mean appears in cell D3. The margin of error, labeled "Confidence Level(95.0%)," appears in cell D16. The point estimate ($9312) and the margin of error ($955) allow the confidence interval for the population mean to be easily computed. The output from this Excel procedure is shown in Figure 8.10.

FIGURE 8.11 EXCEL TEMPLATE FOR INTERVAL ESTIMATION OF A POPULATION PROPORTION

	A	B	C	D	E
1	Response		Interval Estimate of a Population Proportion		
2	Yes				
3	No		Sample Size	=COUNTA(A2:A901)	
4	Yes		Response of Interest	Yes	
5	Yes		Count for Response	=COUNTIF(A2:A901,D4)	
6	No		Sample Proportion	=D5/D3	
7	No				
8	No		Confidence Coefficient	0.95	
9	Yes		z Value	=NORM.S.INV(0.5+D8/2)	
10	Yes				
11	Yes		Standard Error	=SQRT(D6*(1-D6)/D3)	
12	No		Margin of Error	=D9*D11	
13	No				
14	Yes		Point Estimate	=D6	
15	No		Lower Limit	=D14-D12	
16	No		Upper Limit	=D14+D12	
17	Yes				
18	No				
901	Yes				
902					

	A	B	C	D	E	F	G
1	Response		Interval Estimate of a Population Proportion				
2	Yes						
3	No		Sample Size	900	Enter the response of interest		
4	Yes		Response of Interest	Yes			
5	Yes		Count for Response	396			
6	No		Sample Proportion	0.4400			
7	No				Enter the confidence coefficient		
8	No		Confidence Coefficient	0.95			
9	Yes		z Value	1.960			
10	Yes						
11	Yes		Standard Error	0.0165			
12	No		Margin of Error	0.0324			
13	No						
14	Yes		Point Estimate	0.4400			
15	No		Lower Limit	0.4076			
16	No		Upper Limit	0.4724			
17	Yes						
18	No						
901	Yes						
902							

WEB file
TeeTimes

Note: Rows 19 to 900 are hidden.

Population Proportion

WEB file
Interval p

We illustrate interval estimation using the survey data for women golfers presented in Section 8.4. The data are in column A of an Excel worksheet. Individual responses are recorded as Yes if the golfer is satisfied with the availability of tee times and No otherwise. Excel does not offer a built-in routine to handle the estimation of a population proportion; however, it is relatively easy to develop an Excel template that can be used for this purpose. The template shown in Figure 8.11 provides the 95% confidence interval estimate of the proportion of women golfers who are satisfied with the availability of tee times. Note that the background worksheet in Figure 8.11 shows the cell formulas that provide the interval estimation results shown in the foreground worksheet. The following steps are necessary to use the template for this data set.

Step 1. Enter the data range A2:A901 into the =COUNTA cell formula in cell D3
Step 2. Enter Yes as the response of interest in cell D4
Step 3. Enter the data range A2:A901 into the =COUNTIF cell formula in cell D5
Step 4. Enter .95 as the confidence coefficient in cell D8

The template automatically provides the confidence interval in cells D15 and D16.

This template can be used to compute the confidence interval for a population proportion for other applications. For instance, to compute the interval estimate for a new data set, enter the new sample data into column A of the worksheet and then make the changes to the four cells as shown. If the new sample data have already been summarized, the sample data do not have to be entered into the worksheet. In this case, enter the sample size into cell D3 and the sample proportion into cell D6; the worksheet template will then provide the confidence interval for the population proportion. The worksheet in Figure 8.11 is available in the file Interval p on the website that accompanies this book.

Appendix 8.3 Interval Estimation with StatTools

In this appendix we show how StatTools can be used to develop an interval estimate of a population mean for the σ unknown case and determine the sample size needed to provide a desired margin of error.

Population Mean: σ Unknown Case

In this case the population standard deviation σ will be estimated by the sample standard deviation s. We use the credit card balance data in Table 8.3 to illustrate. Begin by using the Data Set Manager to create a StatTools data set for these data using the procedure described in the appendix to Chapter 1. The following steps can be used to compute a 95% confidence interval estimate of the population mean.

WEB file
NewBalance

Step 1. Click the **StatTools** tab on the Ribbon
Step 2. In the **Analyses** group, click **Statistical Inference**
Step 3. Choose the **Confidence Interval** option
Step 4. Choose Mean/Std. Deviation
Step 5. When the StatTools-Confidence Interval for Mean/Std. Deviation dialog box appears:
For **Analysis Type** choose **One-Sample Analysis**
In the **Variables** section, select **NewBalance**
In the **Confidence Intervals to Calculate** section:
Select the **For the Mean** option
Select 95% for the **Confidence Level**
Click **OK**

Some descriptive statistics and the confidence interval will appear.

Determining the Sample Size

In Section 8.3 we showed how to determine the sample size needed to provide a desired margin of error. The example used involved a study designed to estimate the population mean daily rental cost for a midsize automobile in the United States. The project director specified that the population mean daily rental cost be estimated with a margin of error of

$2 and a 95% level of confidence. Sample data from a previous study provided a sample standard deviation of $9.65; this value was used as the planning value for the population standard deviation. The following steps can be used to compute the recommended sample size required to provide a 95% confidence interval estimate of the population mean with a margin of error of $2.

The half-length of interval is the margin of error.

Step 1. Click the **StatTools** tab on the Ribbon
Step 2. In the **Analyses** group, click **Statistical Inference**
Step 3. Choose the **Sample Size Selection** option
Step 4. When the StatTools-Sample Size Selection dialog box appears:
In the **Parameter to Estimate** section, select **Mean**
In the **Confidence Interval Specification** section:
Select **95%** for the **Confidence Level**
Enter **2** in the **Half-Length of Interval** box
Enter **9.65** in the **Estimated Std Dev** box
Click **OK**

The output showing a recommended sample size of 90 will appear.

Population Proportion

We illustrate using the survey data for women golfers presented in Section 8.4. Begin by using the Data Set Manager to create a StatTools data set for these data using the procedure described in the appendix to Chapter 1. The following steps can be used to compute a 95% confidence interval estimate of the population mean.

WEB file
Tee Times

Step 1. Click the **StatTools** tab on the Ribbon
Step 2. In the **Analyses** group, click **Statistical Inference**
Step 3. Choose **Confidence Interval**
Step 4. Choose **Proportion**
Step 5. When the StatTools-Confidence Interval for Proportion dialog box appears:
For **Analysis Type** choose **One-Sample Analysis**
In the **Variables** section, select **Response**
In the **Categories to Analyze** section, select **Yes**
In the **Options** section, enter 95% in the **Confidence Level** box
Click **OK**

Some descriptive statistics and the confidence interval will appear.

StatTools also provides a capability for determining the appropriate sample size to provide a desired margin of error. The steps are similar to those for determining the sample size in the previous subsection.

CHAPTER 9

Hypothesis Tests

CONTENTS

STATISTICS *in* PRACTICE

JOHN MORRELL & COMPANY*
CINCINNATI, OHIO

John Morrell & Company, which began in England in 1827, is considered the oldest continuously operating meat manufacturer in the United States. It is a wholly owned and independently managed subsidiary of Smithfield Foods, Smithfield, Virginia. John Morrell & Company offers an extensive product line of processed meats and fresh pork to consumers under 13 regional brands including John Morrell, E-Z-Cut, Tobin's First Prize, Dinner Bell, Hunter, Kretschmar, Rath, Rodeo, Shenson, Farmers Hickory Brand, Iowa Quality, and Peyton's. Each regional brand enjoys high brand recognition and loyalty among consumers.

Market research at Morrell provides up-to-date information on their various products and how they compare with competing brands. © Jeff Greenberg/Alamy Limited.

Market research at Morrell provides management with up-to-date information on the company's various products and how the products compare with competing brands of similar products. A recent study compared a Beef Pot Roast made by Morrell to similar beef products from two major competitors. In the three-product comparison test, a sample of consumers was used to indicate how the products rated in terms of taste, appearance, aroma, and overall preference.

One research question concerned whether the Beef Pot Roast made by Morrell was the preferred choice of more than 50% of the consumer population. Letting p indicate the population proportion preferring Morrell's product, the hypothesis test for the research question is as follows:

$$H_0: p \leq .50$$
$$H_a: p > .50$$

The null hypothesis H_0 indicates the preference for Morrell's product is less than or equal to 50%. If the sample data support rejecting H_0 in favor of the alternative hypothesis H_a, Morrell will draw the research conclusion that in a three-product comparison, their Beef Pot Roast is preferred by more than 50% of the consumer population.

In an independent taste test study using a sample of 224 consumers in Cincinnati, Milwaukee, and Los Angeles, 150 consumers selected the Beef Pot Roast made by Morrell as the preferred product. Using statistical hypothesis testing procedures, the null hypothesis H_0 was rejected. The study provided statistical evidence supporting H_a and the conclusion that the Morrell product is preferred by more than 50% of the consumer population.

The point estimate of the population proportion was $\bar{p} = 150/224 = .67$. Thus, the sample data provided support for a food magazine advertisement showing that in a three-product taste comparison, Beef Pot Roast made by Morrell was "preferred 2 to 1 over the competition."

In this chapter we will discuss how to formulate hypotheses and how to conduct tests like the one used by Morrell. Through the analysis of sample data, we will be able to determine whether a hypothesis should or should not be rejected.

*The authors are indebted to Marty Butler, Vice President of Marketing, John Morrell, for providing this Statistics in Practice.

In Chapters 7 and 8 we showed how a sample could be used to develop point and interval estimates of population parameters. In this chapter we continue the discussion of statistical inference by showing how hypothesis testing can be used to determine whether a statement about the value of a population parameter should or should not be rejected.

In hypothesis testing we begin by making a tentative assumption about a population parameter. This tentative assumption is called the **null hypothesis** and is denoted by H_0. We then define another hypothesis, called the **alternative hypothesis**, which is the opposite of what is stated in the null hypothesis. The alternative hypothesis is denoted by H_a.

The hypothesis testing procedure uses data from a sample to test the two competing statements indicated by H_0 and H_a.

This chapter shows how hypothesis tests can be conducted about a population mean and a population proportion. We begin by providing examples that illustrate approaches to developing null and alternative hypotheses.

9.1 Developing Null and Alternative Hypotheses

It is not always obvious how the null and alternative hypotheses should be formulated. Care must be taken to structure the hypotheses appropriately so that the hypothesis testing conclusion provides the information the researcher or decision maker wants. The context of the situation is very important in determining how the hypotheses should be stated. All hypothesis testing applications involve collecting a sample and using the sample results to provide evidence for drawing a conclusion. Good questions to consider when formulating the null and alternative hypotheses are, What is the purpose of collecting the sample? What conclusions are we hoping to make?

Learning to correctly formulate hypotheses will take some practice. Expect some initial confusion over the proper choice of the null and alternative hypotheses. The examples in this section are intended to provide guidelines.

In the chapter introduction, we stated that the null hypothesis H_0 is a tentative assumption about a population parameter such as a population mean or a population proportion. The alternative hypothesis H_a is a statement that is the opposite of what is stated in the null hypothesis. In some situations it is easier to identify the alternative hypothesis first and then develop the null hypothesis. In other situations it is easier to identify the null hypothesis first and then develop the alternative hypothesis. We will illustrate these situations in the following examples.

The Alternative Hypothesis as a Research Hypothesis

Many applications of hypothesis testing involve an attempt to gather evidence in support of a research hypothesis. In these situations, it is often best to begin with the alternative hypothesis and make it the conclusion that the researcher hopes to support. Consider a particular automobile that currently attains a fuel efficiency of 24 miles per gallon in city driving. A product research group has developed a new fuel injection system designed to increase the miles-per-gallon rating. The group will run controlled tests with the new fuel injection system looking for statistical support for the conclusion that the new fuel injection system provides more miles per gallon than the current system.

Several new fuel injection units will be manufactured, installed in test automobiles, and subjected to research-controlled driving conditions. The sample mean miles per gallon for these automobiles will be computed and used in a hypothesis test to determine if it can be concluded that the new system provides more than 24 miles per gallon. In terms of the population mean miles per gallon μ, the research hypothesis $\mu > 24$ becomes the alternative hypothesis. Since the current system provides an average or mean of 24 miles per gallon, we will make the tentative assumption that the new system is not any better than the current system and choose $\mu \leq 24$ as the null hypothesis. The null and alternative hypotheses are:

$$H_0: \mu \leq 24$$
$$H_a: \mu > 24$$

If the sample results lead to the conclusion to reject H_0, the inference can be made that $H_a: \mu > 24$ is true. The researchers have the statistical support to state that the new fuel injection system increases the mean number of miles per gallon. The production of automobiles with the new fuel injection system should be considered. However, if the sample results lead to the conclusion that H_0 cannot be rejected, the researchers cannot conclude

The conclusion that the research hypothesis is true is made if the sample data provide sufficient evidence to show that the null hypothesis can be rejected.

that the new fuel injection system is better than the current system. Production of automobiles with the new fuel injection system on the basis of better gas mileage cannot be justified. Perhaps more research and further testing can be conducted.

Successful companies stay competitive by developing new products, new methods, new systems, and the like, that are better than what is currently available. Before adopting something new, it is desirable to conduct research to determine if there is statistical support for the conclusion that the new approach is indeed better. In such cases, the research hypothesis is stated as the alternative hypothesis. For example, a new teaching method is developed that is believed to be better than the current method. The alternative hypothesis is that the new method is better. The null hypothesis is that the new method is no better than the old method. A new sales force bonus plan is developed in an attempt to increase sales. The alternative hypothesis is that the new bonus plan increases sales. The null hypothesis is that the new bonus plan does not increase sales. A new drug is developed with the goal of lowering blood pressure more than an existing drug. The alternative hypothesis is that the new drug lowers blood pressure more than the existing drug. The null hypothesis is that the new drug does not provide lower blood pressure than the existing drug. In each case, rejection of the null hypothesis H_0 provides statistical support for the research hypothesis. We will see many examples of hypothesis tests in research situations such as these throughout this chapter and in the remainder of the text.

The Null Hypothesis as an Assumption to Be Challenged

Of course, not all hypothesis tests involve research hypotheses. In the following discussion we consider applications of hypothesis testing where we begin with a belief or an assumption that a statement about the value of a population parameter is true. We will then use a hypothesis test to challenge the assumption and determine if there is statistical evidence to conclude that the assumption is incorrect. In these situations, it is helpful to develop the null hypothesis first. The null hypothesis H_0 expresses the belief or assumption about the value of the population parameter. The alternative hypothesis H_a is that the belief or assumption is incorrect.

As an example, consider the situation of a manufacturer of soft drink products. The label on a soft drink bottle states that it contains 67.6 fluid ounces. We consider the label correct provided the population mean filling weight for the bottles is *at least* 67.6 fluid ounces. Without any reason to believe otherwise, we would give the manufacturer the benefit of the doubt and assume that the statement provided on the label is correct. Thus, in a hypothesis test about the population mean fluid weight per bottle, we would begin with the assumption that the label is correct and state the null hypothesis as $\mu \geq 67.6$. The challenge to this assumption would imply that the label is incorrect and the bottles are being underfilled. This challenge would be stated as the alternative hypothesis $\mu < 67.6$. Thus, the null and alternative hypotheses are:

$$H_0\colon \mu \geq 67.6$$
$$H_a\colon \mu < 67.6$$

A manufacturer's product information is usually assumed to be true and stated as the null hypothesis. The conclusion that the information is incorrect can be made if the null hypothesis is rejected.

A government agency with the responsibility for validating manufacturing labels could select a sample of soft drinks bottles, compute the sample mean filling weight, and use the sample results to test the preceding hypotheses. If the sample results lead to the conclusion to reject H_0, the inference that $H_a\colon \mu < 67.6$ is true can be made. With this statistical support, the agency is justified in concluding that the label is incorrect and underfilling of the bottles is occurring. Appropriate action to force the manufacturer to comply with labeling standards would be considered. However, if the sample results indicate H_0 cannot be rejected, the assumption that the manufacturer's labeling is correct cannot be rejected. With this conclusion, no action would be taken.

Let us now consider a variation of the soft drink bottle filling example by viewing the same situation from the manufacturer's point of view. The bottle-filling operation has been designed to fill soft drink bottles with 67.6 fluid ounces as stated on the label. The company does not want to underfill the containers because that could result in an underfilling complaint from customers or, perhaps, a government agency. However, the company does not want to overfill containers either because putting more soft drink than necessary into the containers would be an unnecessary cost. The company's goal would be to adjust the bottle-filling operation so that the population mean filling weight per bottle is 67.6 fluid ounces as specified on the label.

Although this is the company's goal, from time to time any production process can get out of adjustment. If this occurs in our example, underfilling or overfilling of the soft drink bottles will occur. In either case, the company would like to know about it in order to correct the situation by readjusting the bottle-filling operation to the designed 67.6 fluid ounces. In a hypothesis testing application, we would again begin with the assumption that the production process is operating correctly and state the null hypothesis as $\mu = 67.6$ fluid ounces. The alternative hypothesis that challenges this assumption is that $\mu \neq 67.6$, which indicates either overfilling or underfilling is occurring. The null and alternative hypotheses for the manufacturer's hypothesis test are:

$$H_0\colon \mu = 67.6$$
$$H_a\colon \mu \neq 67.6$$

Suppose that the soft drink manufacturer uses a quality control procedure to periodically select a sample of bottles from the filling operation and computes the sample mean filling weight per bottle. If the sample results lead to the conclusion to reject H_0, the inference is made that $H_a\colon \mu \neq 67.6$ is true. We conclude that the bottles are not being filled properly and the production process should be adjusted to restore the population mean to 67.6 fluid ounces per bottle. However, if the sample results indicate H_0 cannot be rejected, the assumption that the manufacturer's bottle filling operation is functioning properly cannot be rejected. In this case, no further action would be taken and the production operation would continue to run.

The two preceding forms of the soft drink manufacturing hypothesis test show that the null and alternative hypotheses may vary depending upon the point of view of the researcher or decision maker. To correctly formulate hypotheses it is important to understand the context of the situation and structure the hypotheses to provide the information the researcher or decision maker wants.

Summary of Forms for Null and Alternative Hypotheses

The hypothesis tests in this chapter involve two population parameters: the population mean and the population proportion. Depending on the situation, hypothesis tests about a population parameter may take one of three forms: two use inequalities in the null hypothesis; the third uses an equality in the null hypothesis. For hypothesis tests involving a population mean, we let μ_0 denote the hypothesized value and we must choose one of the following three forms for the hypothesis test.

The three possible forms of hypotheses H_0 and H_a are shown here. Note that the equality always *appears in the null hypothesis H_0.*

$$H_0\colon \mu \geq \mu_0 \qquad H_0\colon \mu \leq \mu_0 \qquad H_0\colon \mu = \mu_0$$
$$H_a\colon \mu < \mu_0 \qquad H_a\colon \mu > \mu_0 \qquad H_a\colon \mu \neq \mu_0$$

For reasons that will be clear later, the first two forms are called one-tailed tests. The third form is called a two-tailed test.

In many situations, the choice of H_0 and H_a is not obvious and judgment is necessary to select the proper form. However, as the preceding forms show, the equality part of the expression (either $\geq$, $\leq$, or $=$) *always* appears in the null hypothesis. In selecting the proper form of H_0 and H_a, keep in mind that the alternative hypothesis is often what the test is attempting to establish. Hence, asking whether the user is looking for evidence to support $\mu < \mu_0$, $\mu > \mu_0$, or $\mu \neq \mu_0$ will help determine H_a. The following exercises are designed to provide practice in choosing the proper form for a hypothesis test involving a population mean.

Exercises

1. The manager of the Danvers-Hilton Resort Hotel stated that the mean guest bill for a weekend is \$600 or less. A member of the hotel's accounting staff noticed that the total charges for guest bills have been increasing in recent months. The accountant will use a sample of future weekend guest bills to test the manager's claim.
   a. Which form of the hypotheses should be used to test the manager's claim? Explain.

$$H_0: \mu \geq 600 \qquad H_0: \mu \leq 600 \qquad H_0: \mu = 600$$
$$H_a: \mu < 600 \qquad H_a: \mu > 600 \qquad H_a: \mu \neq 600$$

   b. What conclusion is appropriate when H_0 cannot be rejected?
   c. What conclusion is appropriate when H_0 can be rejected?

SELF test

2. The manager of an automobile dealership is considering a new bonus plan designed to increase sales volume. Currently, the mean sales volume is 14 automobiles per month. The manager wants to conduct a research study to see whether the new bonus plan increases sales volume. To collect data on the plan, a sample of sales personnel will be allowed to sell under the new bonus plan for a one-month period.
   a. Develop the null and alternative hypotheses most appropriate for this situation.
   b. Comment on the conclusion when H_0 cannot be rejected.
   c. Comment on the conclusion when H_0 can be rejected.
3. A production line operation is designed to fill cartons with laundry detergent to a mean weight of 32 ounces. A sample of cartons is periodically selected and weighed to determine whether underfilling or overfilling is occurring. If the sample data lead to a conclusion of underfilling or overfilling, the production line will be shut down and adjusted to obtain proper filling.
   a. Formulate the null and alternative hypotheses that will help in deciding whether to shut down and adjust the production line.
   b. Comment on the conclusion and the decision when H_0 cannot be rejected.
   c. Comment on the conclusion and the decision when H_0 can be rejected.
4. Because of high production-changeover time and costs, a director of manufacturing must convince management that a proposed manufacturing method reduces costs before the new method can be implemented. The current production method operates with a mean cost of \$220 per hour. A research study will measure the cost of the new method over a sample production period.
   a. Develop the null and alternative hypotheses most appropriate for this study.
   b. Comment on the conclusion when H_0 cannot be rejected.
   c. Comment on the conclusion when H_0 can be rejected.

9.2 Type I and Type II Errors

The null and alternative hypotheses are competing statements about the population. Either the null hypothesis H_0 is true or the alternative hypothesis H_a is true, but not both. Ideally the hypothesis testing procedure should lead to the acceptance of H_0 when H_0 is true and the

TABLE 9.1 ERRORS AND CORRECT CONCLUSIONS IN HYPOTHESIS TESTING

		Population Condition	
		H_0 True	H_a True
Conclusion	Accept H_0	Correct Conclusion	Type II Error
	Reject H_0	Type I Error	Correct Conclusion

rejection of H_0 when H_a is true. Unfortunately, the correct conclusions are not always possible. Because hypothesis tests are based on sample information, we must allow for the possibility of errors. Table 9.1 illustrates the two kinds of errors that can be made in hypothesis testing.

The first row of Table 9.1 shows what can happen if the conclusion is to accept H_0. If H_0 is true, this conclusion is correct. However, if H_a is true, we make a **Type II error**; that is, we accept H_0 when it is false. The second row of Table 9.1 shows what can happen if the conclusion is to reject H_0. If H_0 is true, we make a **Type I error**; that is, we reject H_0 when it is true. However, if H_a is true, rejecting H_0 is correct.

Recall the hypothesis testing illustration discussed in Section 9.1 in which an automobile product research group developed a new fuel injection system designed to increase the miles-per-gallon rating of a particular automobile. With the current model obtaining an average of 24 miles per gallon, the hypothesis test was formulated as follows.

$$H_0: \mu \leq 24$$
$$H_a: \mu > 24$$

The alternative hypothesis, $H_a: \mu > 24$, indicates that the researchers are looking for sample evidence to support the conclusion that the population mean miles per gallon with the new fuel injection system is greater than 24.

In this application, the Type I error of rejecting H_0 when it is true corresponds to the researchers claiming that the new system improves the miles-per-gallon rating ($\mu > 24$) when in fact the new system is not any better than the current system. In contrast, the Type II error of accepting H_0 when it is false corresponds to the researchers concluding that the new system is not any better than the current system ($\mu \leq 24$) when in fact the new system improves miles-per-gallon performance.

For the miles-per-gallon rating hypothesis test, the null hypothesis is $H_0: \mu \leq 24$. Suppose the null hypothesis is true as an equality; that is, $\mu = 24$. The probability of making a Type I error when the null hypothesis is true as an equality is called the **level of significance**. Thus, for the miles-per-gallon rating hypothesis test, the level of significance is the probability of rejecting H_0: $\mu \leq 24$ when $\mu = 24$. Because of the importance of this concept, we now restate the definition of level of significance.

LEVEL OF SIGNIFICANCE

The level of significance is the probability of making a Type I error when the null hypothesis is true as an equality.

The Greek symbol α (alpha) is used to denote the level of significance, and common choices for α are .05 and .01.

In practice, the person responsible for the hypothesis test specifies the level of significance. By selecting α, that person is controlling the probability of making a Type I error. If the cost of making a Type I error is high, small values of α are preferred. If the cost of making a Type I error is not too high, larger values of α are typically used. Applications of hypothesis testing that only control for the Type I error are called *significance tests.* Many applications of hypothesis testing are of this type.

If the sample data are consistent with the null hypothesis H_0, we will follow the practice of concluding "do not reject H_0." This conclusion is preferred over "accept H_0," because the conclusion to accept H_0 puts us at risk of making a Type II error.

Although most applications of hypothesis testing control for the probability of making a Type I error, they do not always control for the probability of making a Type II error. Hence, if we decide to accept H_0, we cannot determine how confident we can be with that decision. Because of the uncertainty associated with making a Type II error when conducting significance tests, statisticians usually recommend that we use the statement "do not reject H_0" instead of "accept H_0." Using the statement "do not reject H_0" carries the recommendation to withhold both judgment and action. In effect, by not directly accepting H_0, the statistician avoids the risk of making a Type II error. Whenever the probability of making a Type II error has not been determined and controlled, we will not make the statement "accept H_0." In such cases, only two conclusions are possible: *do not reject* H_0 or *reject* H_0.

Although controlling for a Type II error in hypothesis testing is not common, it can be done. In Sections 9.7 and 9.8 we will illustrate procedures for determining and controlling the probability of making a Type II error. If proper controls have been established for this error, action based on the "accept H_0" conclusion can be appropriate.

NOTES AND COMMENTS

Walter Williams, syndicated columnist and professor of economics at George Mason University, points out that the possibility of making a Type I or a Type II error is always present in decision making (*The Cincinnati Enquirer,* August 14, 2005). He notes that the Food and Drug Administration (FDA) runs the risk of making these errors in its drug approval process. The FDA must either approve a new drug or not approve it. Thus the FDA runs the risk of making a Type I error by approving a new drug that is not safe and effective, or making a Type II error by failing to approve a new drug that is safe and effective. Regardless of the decision made, the possibility of making a costly error cannot be eliminated.

Exercises

SELF test

5. Duke Energy reported that the cost of electricity for an efficient home in a particular neighborhood of Cincinnati, Ohio, was \$104 per month (*Home Energy Report,* Duke Energy, March 2012). A researcher believes that the cost of electricity for a comparable neighborhood in Chicago, Illinois, is higher. A sample of homes in this Chicago neighborhood will be taken and the sample mean monthly cost of electricity will be used to test the following null and alternative hypotheses.

$$H_0: \mu \leq 104$$
$$H_a: \mu > 104$$

   a. Assume the sample data led to rejection of the null hypothesis. What would be your conclusion about the cost of electricity in the Chicago neighborhood?
   b. What is the Type I error in this situation? What are the consequences of making this error?
   c. What is the Type II error in this situation? What are the consequences of making this error?

6. The label on a 3-quart container of orange juice states that the orange juice contains an average of 1 gram of fat or less. Answer the following questions for a hypothesis test that could be used to test the claim on the label.
   a. Develop the appropriate null and alternative hypotheses.
   b. What is the Type I error in this situation? What are the consequences of making this error?
   c. What is the Type II error in this situation? What are the consequences of making this error?
7. Carpetland salespersons average \$8000 per week in sales. Steve Contois, the firm's vice president, proposes a compensation plan with new selling incentives. Steve hopes that the results of a trial selling period will enable him to conclude that the compensation plan increases the average sales per salesperson.
   a. Develop the appropriate null and alternative hypotheses.
   b. What is the Type I error in this situation? What are the consequences of making this error?
   c. What is the Type II error in this situation? What are the consequences of making this error?
8. Suppose a new production method will be implemented if a hypothesis test supports the conclusion that the new method reduces the mean operating cost per hour.
   a. State the appropriate null and alternative hypotheses if the mean cost for the current production method is \$220 per hour.
   b. What is the Type I error in this situation? What are the consequences of making this error?
   c. What is the Type II error in this situation? What are the consequences of making this error?

9.3 Population Mean: σ Known

In Chapter 8 we said that the σ known case corresponds to applications in which historical data and/or other information are available that enable us to obtain a good estimate of the population standard deviation prior to sampling. In such cases the population standard deviation can, for all practical purposes, be considered known. In this section we show how to conduct a hypothesis test about a population mean for the σ known case.

The methods presented in this section are exact if the sample is selected from a population that is normally distributed. In cases where it is not reasonable to assume the population is normally distributed, these methods are still applicable if the sample size is large enough. We provide some practical advice concerning the population distribution and the sample size at the end of this section.

One-Tailed Test

One-tailed tests about a population mean take one of the following two forms.

Lower Tail Test	Upper Tail Test
$H_0: \mu \geq \mu_0$	$H_0: \mu \leq \mu_0$
$H_a: \mu < \mu_0$	$H_a: \mu > \mu_0$

Let us consider an example involving a lower tail test.

The Federal Trade Commission (FTC) periodically conducts statistical studies designed to test the claims that manufacturers make about their products. For example, the label on a large can of Hilltop Coffee states that the can contains 3 pounds of coffee. The FTC knows that Hilltop's production process cannot place exactly 3 pounds of coffee in each can, even if the mean filling weight for the population of all cans filled is 3 pounds per can. However, as long as the population mean filling weight is at least 3 pounds per can, the rights of consumers will be protected. Thus, the FTC interprets the label information on a large can of coffee as a claim by Hilltop that the population mean filling weight is at least 3 pounds per can. We will show how the FTC can check Hilltop's claim by conducting a lower tail hypothesis test.

The first step is to develop the null and alternative hypotheses for the test. If the population mean filling weight is at least 3 pounds per can, Hilltop's claim is correct. This establishes the null hypothesis for the test. However, if the population mean weight is less than 3 pounds per can, Hilltop's claim is incorrect. This establishes the alternative hypothesis. With μ denoting the population mean filling weight, the null and alternative hypotheses are as follows:

$$H_0: \mu \geq 3$$
$$H_a: \mu < 3$$

Note that the hypothesized value of the population mean is $\mu_0 = 3$.

If the sample data indicate that H_0 cannot be rejected, the statistical evidence does not support the conclusion that a label violation has occurred. Hence, no action should be taken against Hilltop. However, if the sample data indicate H_0 can be rejected, we will conclude that the alternative hypothesis, H_a: $\mu < 3$, is true. In this case a conclusion of underfilling and a charge of a label violation against Hilltop would be justified.

Suppose a sample of 36 cans of coffee is selected and the sample mean $\bar{x}$ is computed as an estimate of the population mean μ. If the value of the sample mean $\bar{x}$ is less than 3 pounds, the sample results will cast doubt on the null hypothesis. What we want to know is how much less than 3 pounds must $\bar{x}$ be before we would be willing to declare the difference significant and risk making a Type I error by falsely accusing Hilltop of a label violation. A key factor in addressing this issue is the value the decision maker selects for the level of significance.

As noted in the preceding section, the level of significance, denoted by α, is the probability of making a Type I error by rejecting H_0 when the null hypothesis is true as an equality. The decision maker must specify the level of significance. If the cost of making a Type I error is high, a small value should be chosen for the level of significance. If the cost is not high, a larger value is more appropriate. In the Hilltop Coffee study, the director of the FTC's testing program made the following statement: "If the company is meeting its weight specifications at $\mu = 3$, I do not want to take action against them. But, I am willing to risk a 1% chance of making such an error." From the director's statement, we set the level of significance for the hypothesis test at $\alpha = .01$. Thus, we must design the hypothesis test so that the probability of making a Type I error when $\mu = 3$ is .01.

For the Hilltop Coffee study, by developing the null and alternative hypotheses and specifying the level of significance for the test, we carry out the first two steps required in conducting every hypothesis test. We are now ready to perform the third step of hypothesis testing: collect the sample data and compute the value of what is called a test statistic.

Test statistic For the Hilltop Coffee study, previous FTC tests show that the population standard deviation can be assumed known with a value of $\sigma = .18$. In addition, these tests also show that the population of filling weights can be assumed to have a normal distribution. From the study of sampling distributions in Chapter 7 we know that if the population from which we are sampling is normally distributed, the sampling distribution of $\bar{x}$ will also be normally distributed. Thus, for the Hilltop Coffee study, the sampling distribution of $\bar{x}$ is normally distributed. With a known value of $\sigma = .18$ and a sample size of $n = 36$, Figure 9.1 shows the sampling distribution of $\bar{x}$ when the null hypothesis is true as an equality; that is, when $\mu = \mu_0 = 3$.[1] Note that the standard error of $\bar{x}$ is given by $\sigma_{\bar{x}} = \sigma/\sqrt{n} = .18/\sqrt{36} = .03$.

The standard error of $\bar{x}$ is the standard deviation of the sampling distribution of $\bar{x}$.

Because the sampling distribution of $\bar{x}$ is normally distributed, the sampling distribution of

$$z = \frac{\bar{x} - \mu_0}{\sigma_{\bar{x}}} = \frac{\bar{x} - 3}{.03}$$

[1] In constructing sampling distributions for hypothesis tests, it is assumed that H_0 is satisfied as an equality.

FIGURE 9.1 SAMPLING DISTRIBUTION OF $\bar{x}$ FOR THE HILLTOP COFFEE STUDY WHEN THE NULL HYPOTHESIS IS TRUE AS AN EQUALITY ($\mu = 3$)

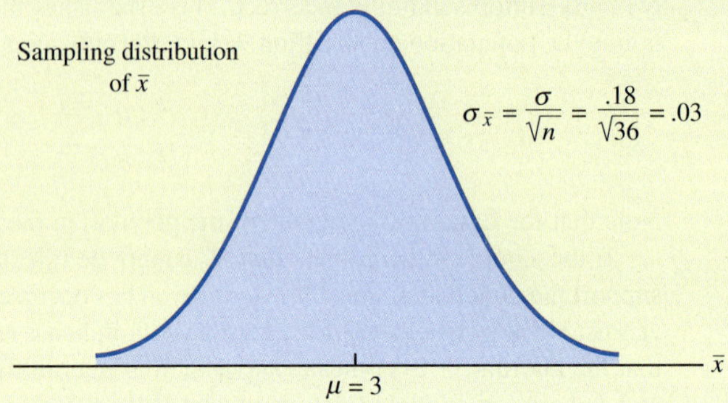

is a standard normal distribution. A value of $z = -1$ means that the value of $\bar{x}$ is one standard error below the hypothesized value of the mean, a value of $z = -2$ means that the value of $\bar{x}$ is two standard errors below the hypothesized value of the mean, and so on. We can use the standard normal probability table to find the lower tail probability corresponding to any z value. For instance, the lower tail area at $z = -3.00$ is .0013. Hence, the probability of obtaining a value of z that is three or more standard errors below the mean is .0013. As a result, the probability of obtaining a value of $\bar{x}$ that is 3 or more standard errors below the hypothesized population mean $\mu_0 = 3$ is also .0013. Such a result is unlikely if the null hypothesis is true.

For hypothesis tests about a population mean in the σ known case, we use the standard normal random variable z as a **test statistic** to determine whether $\bar{x}$ deviates from the hypothesized value of μ enough to justify rejecting the null hypothesis. With $\sigma_{\bar{x}} = \sigma/\sqrt{n}$, the test statistic is as follows.

TEST STATISTIC FOR HYPOTHESIS TESTS ABOUT A POPULATION MEAN: σ KNOWN

$$z = \frac{\bar{x} - \mu_0}{\sigma/\sqrt{n}} \quad (9.1)$$

The key question for a lower tail test is, How small must the test statistic z be before we choose to reject the null hypothesis? Two approaches can be used to answer this question: the p-value approach and the critical value approach.

***p*-value approach** The p-value approach uses the value of the test statistic z to compute a probability called a ***p*-value**.

A small p-value indicates the value of the test statistic is unusual given the assumption that H_0 is true.

p-VALUE

A p-value is a probability that provides a measure of the evidence against the null hypothesis provided by the sample. Smaller p-values indicate more evidence against H_0.

The p-value is used to determine whether the null hypothesis should be rejected.

Let us see how the p-value is computed and used. The value of the test statistic is used to compute the p-value. The method used depends on whether the test is a lower tail, an upper tail, or a two-tailed test. For a lower tail test, the p-value is the probability of obtaining a value for the test statistic as small as or smaller than that provided by the sample. Thus, to compute the p-value for the lower tail test in the σ known case, we use the standard normal distribution to find the probability that z is less than or equal to the value of the test statistic. After computing the p-value, we must then decide whether it is small enough to reject the null hypothesis; as we will show, this decision involves comparing the p-value to the level of significance.

WEB file Coffee

Let us now compute the p-value for the Hilltop Coffee lower tail test. Suppose the sample of 36 Hilltop coffee cans provides a sample mean of $\bar{x} = 2.92$ pounds. Is $\bar{x} = 2.92$ small enough to cause us to reject H_0? Because this is a lower tail test, the p-value is the area under the standard normal curve for values of $z \leq$ the value of the test statistic. Using $\bar{x} = 2.92$, $\sigma = .18$, and $n = 36$, we compute the value of the test statistic z.

$$z = \frac{\bar{x} - \mu_0}{\sigma/\sqrt{n}} = \frac{2.92 - 3}{.18/\sqrt{36}} = -2.67$$

Thus, the p-value is the probability that z is less than or equal to -2.67 (the lower tail area corresponding to the value of the test statistic).

Using the standard normal probability table, we find that the lower tail area at $z = -2.67$ is .0038. Figure 9.2 shows that $\bar{x} = 2.92$ corresponds to $z = -2.67$ and a p-value $= .0038$. This p-value indicates a small probability of obtaining a sample mean of $\bar{x} = 2.92$ (and a test statistic of -2.67) or smaller when sampling from a population with $\mu = 3$. This

FIGURE 9.2 p-VALUE FOR THE HILLTOP COFFEE STUDY WHEN $\bar{x} = 2.92$ AND $z = -2.67$

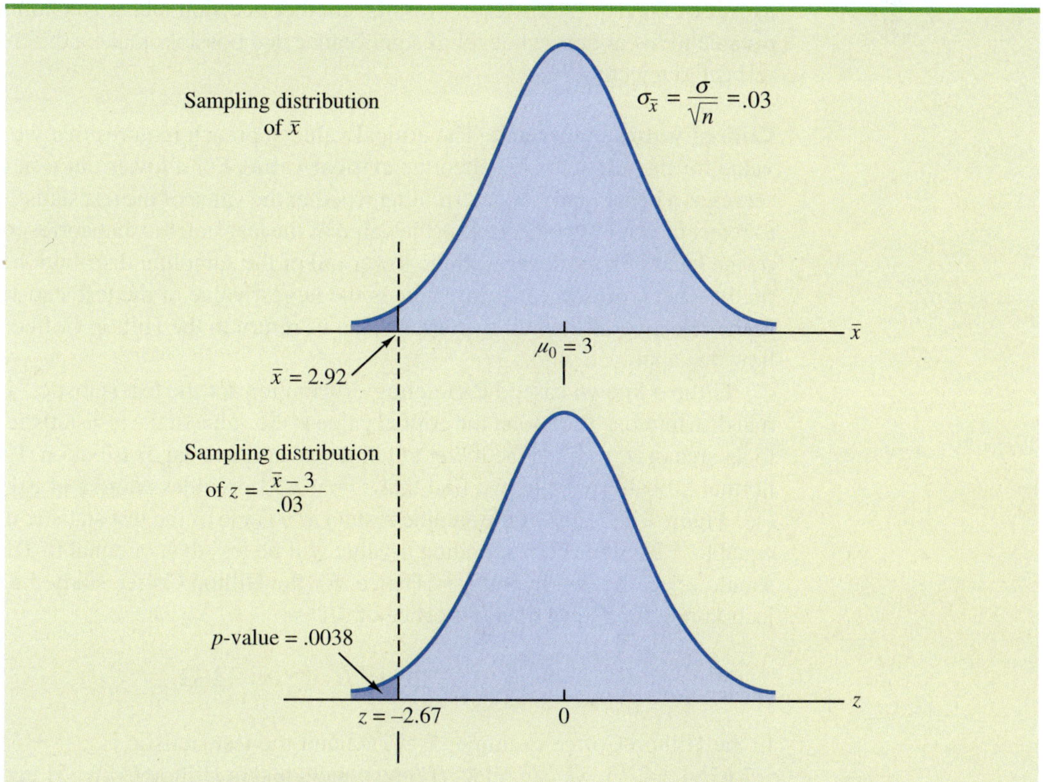

p-value does not provide much support for the null hypothesis, but is it small enough to cause us to reject H_0? The answer depends upon the level of significance for the test.

As noted previously, the director of the FTC's testing program selected a value of .01 for the level of significance. The selection of $\alpha = .01$ means that the director is willing to tolerate a probability of .01 of rejecting the null hypothesis when it is true as an equality ($\mu_0 = 3$). The sample of 36 coffee cans in the Hilltop Coffee study resulted in a p-value $=$ .0038, which means that the probability of obtaining a value of $\bar{x} = 2.92$ or less when the null hypothesis is true as an equality is .0038. Because .0038 is less than or equal to $\alpha = .01$, we reject H_0. Therefore, we find sufficient statistical evidence to reject the null hypothesis at the .01 level of significance.

We can now state the general rule for determining whether the null hypothesis can be rejected when using the p-value approach. For a level of significance α, the rejection rule using the p-value approach is as follows:

REJECTION RULE USING p-VALUE

$$\text{Reject } H_0 \text{ if } p\text{-value} \leq \alpha$$

In the Hilltop Coffee test, the p-value of .0038 resulted in the rejection of the null hypothesis. Although the basis for making the rejection decision involves a comparison of the p-value to the level of significance specified by the FTC director, the observed p-value of .0038 means that we would reject H_0 for any value of $\alpha \geq .0038$. For this reason, the p-value is also called the *observed level of significance.*

Different decision makers may express different opinions concerning the cost of making a Type I error and may choose a different level of significance. By providing the p-value as part of the hypothesis testing results, another decision maker can compare the reported p-value to his or her own level of significance and possibly make a different decision with respect to rejecting H_0.

Critical value approach The critical value approach requires that we first determine a value for the test statistic called the **critical value**. For a lower tail test, the critical value serves as a benchmark for determining whether the value of the test statistic is small enough to reject the null hypothesis. It is the value of the test statistic that corresponds to an area of α (the level of significance) in the lower tail of the sampling distribution of the test statistic. In other words, the critical value is the largest value of the test statistic that will result in the rejection of the null hypothesis. Let us return to the Hilltop Coffee example and see how this approach works.

In the σ known case, the sampling distribution for the test statistic z is a standard normal distribution. Therefore, the critical value is the value of the test statistic that corresponds to an area of $\alpha = .01$ in the lower tail of a standard normal distribution. Using the standard normal probability table, we find that $z = -2.33$ provides an area of .01 in the lower tail (see Figure 9.3). Thus, if the sample results in a value of the test statistic that is less than or equal to -2.33, the corresponding p-value will be less than or equal to .01; in this case, we should reject the null hypothesis. Hence, for the Hilltop Coffee study the critical value rejection rule for a level of significance of .01 is

$$\text{Reject } H_0 \text{ if } z \leq -2.33$$

In the Hilltop Coffee example, $\bar{x} = 2.92$ and the test statistic is $z = -2.67$. Because $z = -2.67 < -2.33$, we can reject H_0 and conclude that Hilltop Coffee is underfilling cans.

FIGURE 9.3 CRITICAL VALUE = −2.33 FOR THE HILLTOP COFFEE HYPOTHESIS TEST

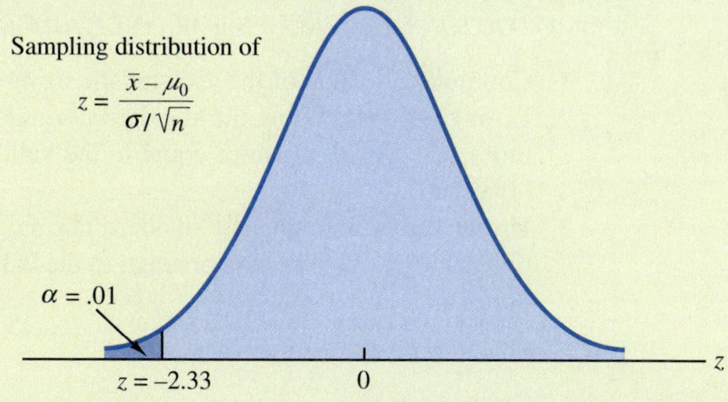

We can generalize the rejection rule for the critical value approach to handle any level of significance. The rejection rule for a lower tail test follows.

REJECTION RULE FOR A LOWER TAIL TEST: CRITICAL VALUE APPROACH

$$\text{Reject } H_0 \text{ if } z \leq -z_\alpha$$

where $-z_\alpha$ is the critical value; that is, the z value that provides an area of α in the lower tail of the standard normal distribution.

Summary The p-value approach to hypothesis testing and the critical value approach will always lead to the same rejection decision; that is, whenever the p-value is less than or equal to α, the value of the test statistic will be less than or equal to the critical value. The advantage of the p-value approach is that the p-value tells us *how* significant the results are (the observed level of significance). If we use the critical value approach, we only know that the results are significant at the stated level of significance.

At the beginning of this section, we said that one-tailed tests about a population mean take one of the following two forms:

Lower Tail Test	Upper Tail Test
$H_0\colon \mu \geq \mu_0$	$H_0\colon \mu \leq \mu_0$
$H_a\colon \mu < \mu_0$	$H_a\colon \mu > \mu_0$

We used the Hilltop Coffee study to illustrate how to conduct a lower tail test. We can use the same general approach to conduct an upper tail test. The test statistic z is still computed using equation (9.1). But, for an upper tail test, the p-value is the probability of obtaining a value for the test statistic as large as or larger than that provided by the sample. Thus, to compute the p-value for the upper tail test in the σ known case, we must use the standard normal distribution to find the probability that z is greater than or equal to the value of the test statistic. Using the critical value approach causes us to reject the null hypothesis if the value of the test statistic is greater than or equal to the critical value z_α; in other words, we reject H_0 if $z \geq z_\alpha$.

Let us summarize the steps involved in computing p-values for one-tailed hypothesis tests.

COMPUTATION OF p-VALUES FOR ONE-TAILED TESTS

1. Compute the value of the test statistic using equation (9.1).
2. **Lower tail test:** Using the standard normal distribution, compute the probability that z is less than or equal to the value of the test statistic (area in the lower tail).
3. **Upper tail test:** Using the standard normal distribution, compute the probability that z is greater than or equal to the value of the test statistic (area in the upper tail).

Two-Tailed Test

In hypothesis testing, the general form for a **two-tailed test** about a population mean is as follows:

$$H_0: \mu = \mu_0$$
$$H_a: \mu \neq \mu_0$$

In this subsection we show how to conduct a two-tailed test about a population mean for the σ known case. As an illustration, we consider the hypothesis testing situation facing MaxFlight, Inc.

The U.S. Golf Association (USGA) establishes rules that manufacturers of golf equipment must meet if their products are to be acceptable for use in USGA events. MaxFlight uses a high-technology manufacturing process to produce golf balls with a mean driving distance of 295 yards. Sometimes, however, the process gets out of adjustment and produces golf balls with a mean driving distance different from 295 yards. When the mean distance falls below 295 yards, the company worries about losing sales because the golf balls do not provide as much distance as advertised. When the mean distance passes 295 yards, MaxFlight's golf balls may be rejected by the USGA for exceeding the overall distance standard concerning carry and roll.

MaxFlight's quality control program involves taking periodic samples of 50 golf balls to monitor the manufacturing process. For each sample, a hypothesis test is conducted to determine whether the process has fallen out of adjustment. Let us develop the null and alternative hypotheses. We begin by assuming that the process is functioning correctly; that is, the golf balls being produced have a mean distance of 295 yards. This assumption establishes the null hypothesis. The alternative hypothesis is that the mean distance is not equal to 295 yards. With a hypothesized value of $\mu_0 = 295$, the null and alternative hypotheses for the MaxFlight hypothesis test are as follows:

$$H_0: \mu = 295$$
$$H_a: \mu \neq 295$$

If the sample mean $\bar{x}$ is significantly less than 295 yards or significantly greater than 295 yards, we will reject H_0. In this case, corrective action will be taken to adjust the manufacturing process. On the other hand, if $\bar{x}$ does not deviate from the hypothesized mean $\mu_0 = 295$ by a significant amount, H_0 will not be rejected and no action will be taken to adjust the manufacturing process.

The quality control team selected $\alpha = .05$ as the level of significance for the test. Data from previous tests conducted when the process was known to be in adjustment show that

FIGURE 9.4 SAMPLING DISTRIBUTION OF $\bar{x}$ FOR THE MAXFLIGHT HYPOTHESIS TEST

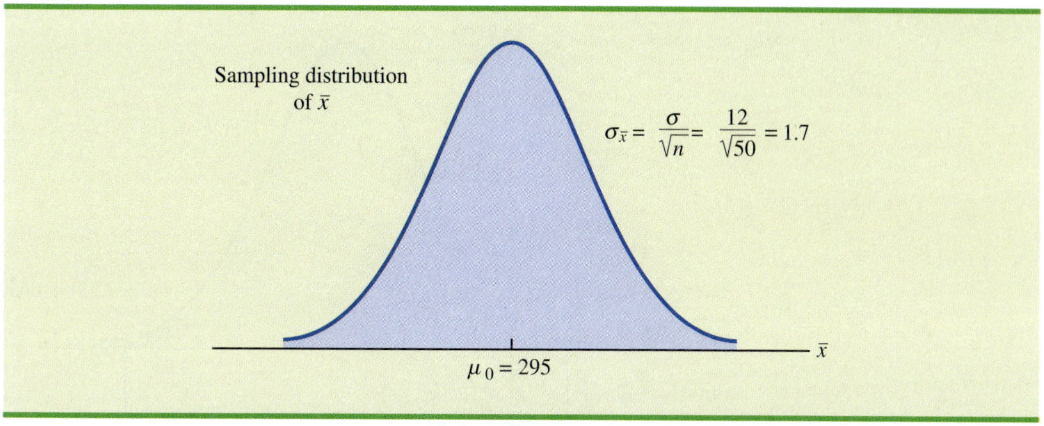

the population standard deviation can be assumed known with a value of $\sigma = 12$. Thus, with a sample size of $n = 50$, the standard error of $\bar{x}$ is

$$\sigma_{\bar{x}} = \frac{\sigma}{\sqrt{n}} = \frac{12}{\sqrt{50}} = 1.7$$

Because the sample size is large, the central limit theorem (see Chapter 7) allows us to conclude that the sampling distribution of $\bar{x}$ can be approximated by a normal distribution. Figure 9.4 shows the sampling distribution of $\bar{x}$ for the MaxFlight hypothesis test with a hypothesized population mean of $\mu_0 = 295$.

WEB file

GolfTest

Suppose that a sample of 50 golf balls is selected and that the sample mean is $\bar{x} = 297.6$ yards. This sample mean provides support for the conclusion that the population mean is larger than 295 yards. Is this value of $\bar{x}$ enough larger than 295 to cause us to reject H_0 at the .05 level of significance? In the previous section we described two approaches that can be used to answer this question: the p-value approach and the critical value approach.

p-value approach Recall that the p-value is a probability used to determine whether the null hypothesis should be rejected. For a two-tailed test, values of the test statistic in *either* tail provide evidence against the null hypothesis. For a two-tailed test, the p-value is the probability of obtaining a value for the test statistic *as unlikely as or more unlikely than* that provided by the sample. Let us see how the p-value is computed for the MaxFlight hypothesis test.

First we compute the value of the test statistic. For the σ known case, the test statistic z is a standard normal random variable. Using equation (9.1) with $\bar{x} = 297.6$, the value of the test statistic is

$$z = \frac{\bar{x} - \mu_0}{\sigma/\sqrt{n}} = \frac{297.6 - 295}{12/\sqrt{50}} = 1.53$$

Now to compute the p-value we must find the probability of obtaining a value for the test statistic *at least as unlikely as* $z = 1.53$. Clearly values of $z \geq 1.53$ are *at least as unlikely.* But, because this is a two-tailed test, values of $z \leq -1.53$ are also *at least as unlikely as* the value of the test statistic provided by the sample. In Figure 9.5, we see that the two-tailed p-value in this case is given by $P(z \leq -1.53) + P(z \geq 1.53)$. Because the normal curve is symmetric, we can compute this probability by finding the upper tail area at $z = 1.53$ and doubling it. The table for the standard normal distribution shows that $P(z < 1.53) = .9370$. Thus, the upper tail area is $P(z \geq 1.53) = 1.0000 - .9370 = .0630$. Doubling this, we find the p-value for the MaxFlight two-tailed hypothesis test is p-value $= 2(.0630) = .1260$.

FIGURE 9.5 p-VALUE FOR THE MAXFLIGHT HYPOTHESIS TEST

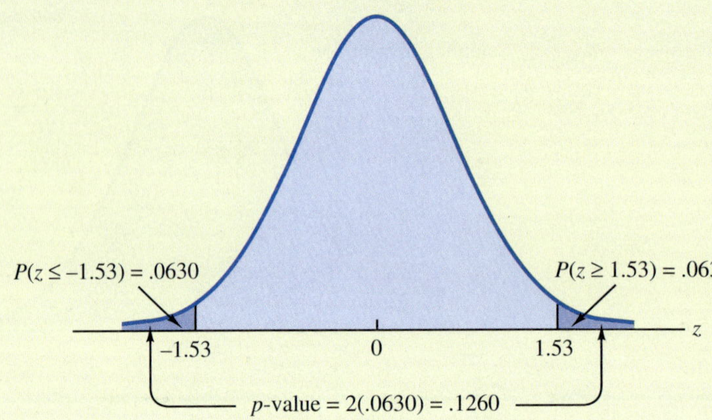

Next we compare the p-value to the level of significance to see whether the null hypothesis should be rejected. With a level of significance of $\alpha = .05$, we do not reject H_0 because the p-value $= .1260 > .05$. Because the null hypothesis is not rejected, no action will be taken to adjust the MaxFlight manufacturing process.

The computation of the p-value for a two-tailed test may seem a bit confusing as compared to the computation of the p-value for a one-tailed test. But it can be simplified by following three steps.

COMPUTATION OF p-VALUES FOR TWO-TAILED TESTS

1. Compute the value of the test statistic using equation (9.1).
2. If the value of the test statistic is in the upper tail, compute the probability that z is greater than or equal to the value of the test statistic (the upper tail area). If the value of the test statistic is in the lower tail, compute the probability that z is less than or equal to the value of the test statistic (the lower tail area).
3. Double the probability (or tail area) from step 2 to obtain the p-value.

Critical value approach Before leaving this section, let us see how the test statistic z can be compared to a critical value to make the hypothesis testing decision for a two-tailed test. Figure 9.6 shows that the critical values for the test will occur in both the lower and upper tails of the standard normal distribution. With a level of significance of $\alpha = .05$, the area in each tail corresponding to the critical values is $\alpha/2 = .05/2 = .025$. Using the standard normal probability table, we find the critical values for the test statistic are $-z_{.025} = -1.96$ and $z_{.025} = 1.96$. Thus, using the critical value approach, the two-tailed rejection rule is

$$\text{Reject } H_0 \text{ if } z \le -1.96 \text{ or if } z \ge 1.96$$

Because the value of the test statistic for the MaxFlight study is $z = 1.53$, the statistical evidence will not permit us to reject the null hypothesis at the .05 level of significance.

Summary and Practical Advice

We presented examples of a lower tail test and a two-tailed test about a population mean. Based upon these examples, we can now summarize the hypothesis testing procedures about a population mean for the σ known case as shown in Table 9.2. Note that μ_0 is the hypothesized value of the population mean.

FIGURE 9.6 CRITICAL VALUES FOR THE MAXFLIGHT HYPOTHESIS TEST

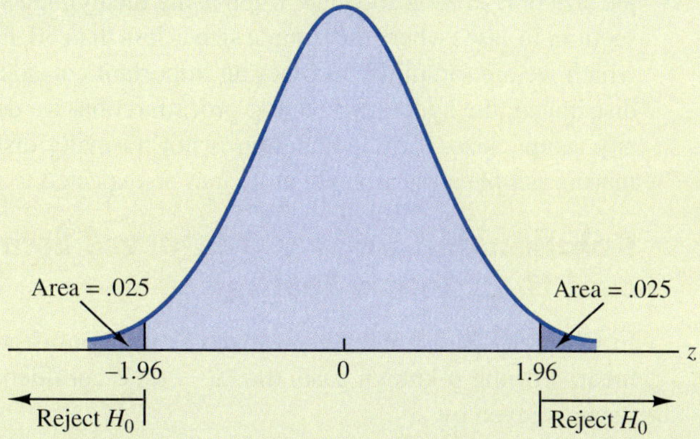

TABLE 9.2 SUMMARY OF HYPOTHESIS TESTS ABOUT A POPULATION MEAN: σ KNOWN CASE

	Lower Tail Test	**Upper Tail Test**	**Two-Tailed Test**
Hypotheses	$H_0: \mu \geq \mu_0$ $H_a: \mu < \mu_0$	$H_0: \mu \leq \mu_0$ $H_a: \mu > \mu_0$	$H_0: \mu = \mu_0$ $H_a: \mu \neq \mu_0$
Test Statistic	$z = \frac{\bar{x} - \mu_0}{\sigma/\sqrt{n}}$	$z = \frac{\bar{x} - \mu_0}{\sigma/\sqrt{n}}$	$z = \frac{\bar{x} - \mu_0}{\sigma/\sqrt{n}}$
Rejection Rule: *p*-Value Approach	Reject H_0 if p-value $\leq \alpha$	Reject H_0 if p-value $\leq \alpha$	Reject H_0 if p-value $\leq \alpha$
Rejection Rule: Critical Value Approach	Reject H_0 if $z \leq -z_\alpha$	Reject H_0 if $z \geq z_\alpha$	Reject H_0 if $z \leq -z_{\alpha/2}$ or if $z \geq z_{\alpha/2}$

The hypothesis testing steps followed in the two examples presented in this section are common to every hypothesis test.

STEPS OF HYPOTHESIS TESTING

Step 1. Develop the null and alternative hypotheses.
Step 2. Specify the level of significance.
Step 3. Collect the sample data and compute the value of the test statistic.

p-Value Approach

Step 4. Use the value of the test statistic to compute the p-value.
Step 5. Reject H_0 if the p-value $\leq \alpha$.
Step 6. Interpret the statistical conclusion in the context of the application.

Critical Value Approach

Step 4. Use the level of significance to determine the critical value and the rejection rule.
Step 5. Use the value of the test statistic and the rejection rule to determine whether to reject H_0.
Step 6. Interpret the statistical conclusion in the context of the application.

Practical advice about the sample size for hypothesis tests is similar to the advice we provided about the sample size for interval estimation in Chapter 8. In most applications, a sample size of $n \geq 30$ is adequate when using the hypothesis testing procedure described in this section. In cases where the sample size is less than 30, the distribution of the population from which we are sampling becomes an important consideration. If the population is normally distributed, the hypothesis testing procedure that we described is exact and can be used for any sample size. If the population is not normally distributed but is at least roughly symmetric, sample sizes as small as 15 can be expected to provide acceptable results.

Relationship Between Interval Estimation and Hypothesis Testing

In Chapter 8 we showed how to develop a confidence interval estimate of a population mean. For the σ known case, the $(1 - \alpha)\%$ confidence interval estimate of a population mean is given by

$$\bar{x} \pm z_{\alpha/2} \frac{\sigma}{\sqrt{n}}$$

In this chapter, we showed that a two-tailed hypothesis test about a population mean takes the following form:

$$H_0: \mu = \mu_0$$
$$H_a: \mu \neq \mu_0$$

where μ_0 is the hypothesized value for the population mean.

Suppose that we follow the procedure described in Chapter 8 for constructing a $100(1 - \alpha)\%$ confidence interval for the population mean. We know that $100(1 - \alpha)\%$ of the confidence intervals generated will contain the population mean and $100\alpha\%$ of the confidence intervals generated will not contain the population mean. Thus, if we reject H_0 whenever the confidence interval does not contain μ_0, we will be rejecting the null hypothesis when it is true ($\mu = \mu_0$) with probability α. Recall that the level of significance is the probability of rejecting the null hypothesis when it is true. So constructing a $100(1 - \alpha)\%$ confidence interval and rejecting H_0 whenever the interval does not contain μ_0 is equivalent to conducting a two-tailed hypothesis test with α as the level of significance. The procedure for using a confidence interval to conduct a two-tailed hypothesis test can now be summarized.

For a two-tailed hypothesis test, the null hypothesis can be rejected if the confidence interval does not include μ_0.

A CONFIDENCE INTERVAL APPROACH TO TESTING A HYPOTHESIS OF THE FORM

$$H_0: \mu = \mu_0$$
$$H_a: \mu \neq \mu_0$$

1. Select a simple random sample from the population and use the value of the sample mean $\bar{x}$ to develop the confidence interval for the population mean μ.

$$\bar{x} \pm z_{\alpha/2} \frac{\sigma}{\sqrt{n}}$$

2. If the confidence interval contains the hypothesized value μ_0, do not reject H_0. Otherwise, reject[2] H_0.

[2]To be consistent with the rule for rejecting H_0 when the p-value $\leq \alpha$, we would also reject H_0 using the confidence interval approach if μ_0 happens to be equal to one of the end points of the $100(1 - \alpha)\%$ confidence interval.

Let us illustrate by conducting the MaxFlight hypothesis test using the confidence interval approach. The MaxFlight hypothesis test takes the following form:

$$H_0: \mu = 295$$
$$H_a: \mu \neq 295$$

To test these hypotheses with a level of significance of $\alpha = .05$, we sampled 50 golf balls and found a sample mean distance of $\bar{x} = 297.6$ yards. Recall that the population standard deviation is $\sigma = 12$. Using these results with $z_{.025} = 1.96$, we find that the 95% confidence interval estimate of the population mean is

$$\bar{x} \pm z_{.025} \frac{\sigma}{\sqrt{n}}$$
$$297.6 \pm 1.96 \frac{12}{\sqrt{50}}$$
$$297.6 \pm 3.3$$

or

$$294.3 \text{ to } 300.9$$

This finding enables the quality control manager to conclude with 95% confidence that the mean distance for the population of golf balls is between 294.3 and 300.9 yards. Because the hypothesized value for the population mean, $\mu_0 = 295$, is in this interval, the hypothesis testing conclusion is that the null hypothesis, H_0: $\mu = 295$, cannot be rejected.

Note that this discussion and example pertain to two-tailed hypothesis tests about a population mean. However, the same confidence interval and two-tailed hypothesis testing relationship exists for other population parameters. The relationship can also be extended to one-tailed tests about population parameters. Doing so, however, requires the development of one-sided confidence intervals, which are rarely used in practice.

NOTES AND COMMENTS

We have shown how to use p-values. The smaller the p-value the greater the evidence against H_0 and the more the evidence in favor of H_a. Here are some guidelines statisticians suggest for interpreting small p-values.

- Less than .01—Overwhelming evidence to conclude H_a is true.
- Between .01 and .05—Strong evidence to conclude H_a is true.
- Between .05 and .10—Weak evidence to conclude H_a is true.
- Greater than .10—Insufficient evidence to conclude H_a is true.

Exercises

Note to Student: Some of the exercises that follow ask you to use the p-value approach and others ask you to use the critical value approach. Both methods will provide the same hypothesis testing conclusion. We provide exercises with both methods to give you practice using both. In later sections and in following chapters, we will generally emphasize the p-value approach as the preferred method, but you may select either based on personal preference.

Methods

9. Consider the following hypothesis test:

$$H_0: \mu \geq 20$$
$$H_a: \mu < 20$$

A sample of 50 provided a sample mean of 19.4. The population standard deviation is 2.

a. Compute the value of the test statistic.
b. What is the p-value?
c. Using $\alpha = .05$, what is your conclusion?
d. What is the rejection rule using the critical value? What is your conclusion?

SELF test

10. Consider the following hypothesis test:

$$H_0: \mu \leq 25$$
$$H_a: \mu > 25$$

A sample of 40 provided a sample mean of 26.4. The population standard deviation is 6.

a. Compute the value of the test statistic.
b. What is the p-value?
c. At $\alpha = .01$, what is your conclusion?
d. What is the rejection rule using the critical value? What is your conclusion?

SELF test

11. Consider the following hypothesis test:

$$H_0: \mu = 15$$
$$H_a: \mu \neq 15$$

A sample of 50 provided a sample mean of 14.15. The population standard deviation is 3.

a. Compute the value of the test statistic.
b. What is the p-value?
c. At $\alpha = .05$, what is your conclusion?
d. What is the rejection rule using the critical value? What is your conclusion?

12. Consider the following hypothesis test:

$$H_0: \mu \geq 80$$
$$H_a: \mu < 80$$

A sample of 100 is used and the population standard deviation is 12. Compute the p-value and state your conclusion for each of the following sample results. Use $\alpha = .01$.

a. $\bar{x} = 78.5$
b. $\bar{x} = 77$
c. $\bar{x} = 75.5$
d. $\bar{x} = 81$

13. Consider the following hypothesis test:

$$H_0: \mu \leq 50$$
$$H_a: \mu > 50$$

A sample of 60 is used and the population standard deviation is 8. Use the critical value approach to state your conclusion for each of the following sample results. Use $\alpha = .05$.

a. $\bar{x} = 52.5$
b. $\bar{x} = 51$
c. $\bar{x} = 51.8$

14. Consider the following hypothesis test:

$$H_0: \mu = 22$$
$$H_a: \mu \neq 22$$

A sample of 75 is used and the population standard deviation is 10. Compute the p-value and state your conclusion for each of the following sample results. Use $\alpha = .01$.

a. $\bar{x} = 23$
b. $\bar{x} = 25.1$
c. $\bar{x} = 20$

Applications

SELF test

15. Individuals filing federal income tax returns prior to March 31 received an average refund of $1056. Consider the population of "last-minute" filers who mail their tax return during the last five days of the income tax period (typically April 10 to April 15).
   a. A researcher suggests that a reason individuals wait until the last five days is that on average these individuals receive lower refunds than do early filers. Develop appropriate hypotheses such that rejection of H_0 will support the researcher's contention.
   b. For a sample of 400 individuals who filed a tax return between April 10 and 15, the sample mean refund was $910. Based on prior experience a population standard deviation of $\sigma = \$1600$ may be assumed. What is the p-value?
   c. At $\alpha = .05$, what is your conclusion?
   d. Repeat the preceding hypothesis test using the critical value approach.

16. In a study entitled How Undergraduate Students Use Credit Cards, it was reported that undergraduate students have a mean credit card balance of $3173 (*Sallie Mae*, April 2009). This figure was an all-time high and had increased 44% over the previous five years. Assume that a current study is being conducted to determine if it can be concluded that the mean credit card balance for undergraduate students has continued to increase compared to the April 2009 report. Based on previous studies, use a population standard deviation $\sigma = \$1000$.
   a. State the null and alternative hypotheses.
   b. What is the p-value for a sample of 180 undergraduate students with a sample mean credit card balance of $3325?
   c. Using a .05 level of significance, what is your conclusion?

17. The mean hourly wage for employees in goods-producing industries is currently $24.57 (Bureau of Labor Statistics website, April, 12, 2012). Suppose we take a sample of employees from the manufacturing industry to see if the mean hourly wage differs from the reported mean of $24.57 for the goods-producing industries.
   a. State the null and alternative hypotheses we should use to test whether the population mean hourly wage in the manufacturing industry differs from the population mean hourly wage in the goods-producing industries.
   b. Suppose a sample of 30 employees from the manufacturing industry showed a sample mean of $23.89 per hour. Assume a population standard deviation of $2.40 per hour and compute the p-value.
   c. With $\alpha = .05$ as the level of significance, what is your conclusion?
   d. Repeat the preceding hypothesis test using the critical value approach.

18. The average annual total return for U.S. Diversified Equity mutual funds from 1999 to 2003 was 4.1% (*BusinessWeek*, January 26, 2004). A researcher would like to conduct a

hypothesis test to see whether the returns for mid-cap growth funds over the same period are significantly different from the average for U.S. Diversified Equity funds.

a. Formulate the hypotheses that can be used to determine whether the mean annual return for mid-cap growth funds differ from the mean for U.S. Diversified Equity funds.
b. A sample of 40 mid-cap growth funds provides a mean return of $\bar{x} = 3.4\%$. Assume the population standard deviation for mid-cap growth funds is known from previous studies to be $\sigma = 2\%$. Use the sample results to compute the test statistic and p-value for the hypothesis test.
c. At $\alpha = .05$, what is your conclusion?

19. The Internal Revenue Service (IRS) provides a toll-free help line for taxpayers to call in and get answers to questions as they prepare their tax returns. In recent years, the IRS has been inundated with taxpayer calls and has redesigned its phone service as well as posted answers to frequently asked questions on its website (*The Cincinnati Enquirer*, January 7, 2010). According to a report by a taxpayer advocate, callers using the new system can expect to wait on hold for an unreasonably long time of 12 minutes before being able to talk to an IRS employee. Suppose you select a sample of 50 callers after the new phone service has been implemented; the sample results show a mean waiting time of 10 minutes before an IRS employee comes on the line. Based upon data from past years, you decide it is reasonable to assume that the standard deviation of waiting time is 8 minutes. Using your sample results, can you conclude that the actual mean waiting time turned out to be significantly less than the 12-minute claim made by the taxpayer advocate? Use $\alpha = .05$.

20. For the United States, the mean monthly Internet bill is \$32.79 per household (CNBC, January 18, 2006). A sample of 50 households in a southern state showed a sample mean of \$30.63. Use a population standard deviation of $\sigma = \$5.60$.
    a. Formulate hypotheses for a test to determine whether the sample data support the conclusion that the mean monthly Internet bill in the southern state is less than the national mean of \$32.79.
    b. What is the value of the test statistic?
    c. What is the p-value?
    d. At $\alpha = .01$, what is your conclusion?

WEB file
Fowle

21. Fowle Marketing Research, Inc., bases charges to a client on the assumption that telephone surveys can be completed in a mean time of 15 minutes or less. If a longer mean survey time is necessary, a premium rate is charged. A sample of 35 surveys provided the survey times shown in the file named Fowle. Based upon past studies, the population standard deviation is assumed known with $\sigma = 4$ minutes. Is the premium rate justified?
    a. Formulate the null and alternative hypotheses for this application.
    b. Compute the value of the test statistic.
    c. What is the p-value?
    d. At $\alpha = .01$, what is your conclusion?

22. CCN and ActMedia provided a television channel targeted to individuals waiting in supermarket checkout lines. The channel showed news, short features, and advertisements. The length of the program was based on the assumption that the population mean time a shopper stands in a supermarket checkout line is 8 minutes. A sample of actual waiting times will be used to test this assumption and determine whether actual mean waiting time differs from this standard.
    a. Formulate the hypotheses for this application.
    b. A sample of 120 shoppers showed a sample mean waiting time of 8.4 minutes. Assume a population standard deviation of $\sigma = 3.2$ minutes. What is the p-value?
    c. At $\alpha = .05$, what is your conclusion?
    d. Compute a 95% confidence interval for the population mean. Does it support your conclusion?

9.4 Population Mean: σ Unknown

In this section we describe how to conduct hypothesis tests about a population mean for the σ unknown case. Because the σ unknown case corresponds to situations in which an estimate of the population standard deviation cannot be developed prior to sampling, the sample must be used to develop an estimate of both μ and σ. Thus, to conduct a hypothesis test about a population mean for the σ unknown case, the sample mean $\bar{x}$ is used as an estimate of μ and the sample standard deviation s is used as an estimate of σ.

The steps of the hypothesis testing procedure for the σ unknown case are the same as those for the σ known case described in Section 9.3. But, with σ unknown, the computation of the test statistic and p-value is a bit different. Recall that for the σ known case, the sampling distribution of the test statistic has a standard normal distribution. For the σ unknown case, however, the sampling distribution of the test statistic follows the t distribution; it has slightly more variability because the sample is used to develop estimates of both μ and σ.

In Section 8.2 we showed that an interval estimate of a population mean for the σ unknown case is based on a probability distribution known as the t distribution. Hypothesis tests about a population mean for the σ unknown case are also based on the t distribution. For the σ unknown case, the test statistic has a t distribution with $n - 1$ degrees of freedom.

TEST STATISTIC FOR HYPOTHESIS TESTS ABOUT A POPULATION MEAN: σ UNKNOWN

$$t = \frac{\bar{x} - \mu_0}{s/\sqrt{n}} \tag{9.2}$$

In Chapter 8 we said that the t distribution is based on an assumption that the population from which we are sampling has a normal distribution. However, research shows that this assumption can be relaxed considerably when the sample size is large enough. We provide some practical advice concerning the population distribution and sample size at the end of the section.

One-Tailed Test

WEB file AirRating

Let us consider an example of a one-tailed test about a population mean for the σ unknown case. A business travel magazine wants to classify transatlantic gateway airports according to the mean rating for the population of business travelers. A rating scale with a low score of 0 and a high score of 10 will be used, and airports with a population mean rating greater than 7 will be designated as superior service airports. The magazine staff surveyed a sample of 60 business travelers at each airport to obtain the ratings data. The sample for London's Heathrow Airport provided a sample mean rating of $\bar{x} = 7.25$ and a sample standard deviation of $s = 1.052$. Do the data indicate that Heathrow should be designated as a superior service airport?

We want to develop a hypothesis test for which the decision to reject H_0 will lead to the conclusion that the population mean rating for the Heathrow Airport is *greater* than 7. Thus, an upper tail test with H_a: $\mu > 7$ is required. The null and alternative hypotheses for this upper tail test are as follows:

$$H_0: \mu \leq 7$$
$$H_a: \mu > 7$$

We will use $\alpha = .05$ as the level of significance for the test.

Using equation (9.2) with $\bar{x} = 7.25$, $\mu_0 = 7$, $s = 1.052$, and $n = 60$, the value of the test statistic is

$$t = \frac{\bar{x} - \mu_0}{s/\sqrt{n}} = \frac{7.25 - 7}{1.052/\sqrt{60}} = 1.84$$

The sampling distribution of t has $n - 1 = 60 - 1 = 59$ degrees of freedom. Because the test is an upper tail test, the p-value is $P\,(t \geq 1.84)$, that is, the upper tail area corresponding to the value of the test statistic.

The t distribution table provided in most textbooks will not contain sufficient detail to determine the exact p-value, such as the p-value corresponding to $t = 1.84$. For instance, using Table 2 in Appendix B, the t distribution with 59 degrees of freedom provides the following information.

Area in Upper Tail	**.20**	**.10**	**.05**	**.025**	**.01**	**.005**
***t* Value (59 *df*)**	.848	1.296	1.671	2.001	2.391	2.662

$t = 1.84$

We see that $t = 1.84$ is between 1.671 and 2.001. Although the table does not provide the exact p-value, the values in the "Area in Upper Tail" row show that the p-value must be less than .05 and greater than .025. With a level of significance of $\alpha = .05$, this placement is all we need to know to make the decision to reject the null hypothesis and conclude that Heathrow should be classified as a superior service airport.

Appendix F shows how to compute p-values using Excel or Minitab.

Because it is cumbersome to use a t table to compute p-values, and only approximate values are obtained, we show how to compute the exact p-value using Excel or Minitab. The directions can be found in Appendix F at the end of this text. Using Excel or Minitab with $t = 1.84$ provides the upper tail p-value of .0354 for the Heathrow Airport hypothesis test. With $.0354 < .05$, we reject the null hypothesis and conclude that Heathrow should be classified as a superior service airport.

The decision whether to reject the null hypothesis in the σ unknown case can also be made using the critical value approach. The critical value corresponding to an area of $\alpha = .05$ in the upper tail of a t distribution with 59 degrees of freedom is $t_{.05} = 1.671$. Thus the rejection rule using the critical value approach is to reject H_0 if $t \geq 1.671$. Because $t = 1.84 > 1.671$, H_0 is rejected. Heathrow should be classified as a superior service airport.

Two-Tailed Test

To illustrate how to conduct a two-tailed test about a population mean for the σ unknown case, let us consider the hypothesis testing situation facing Holiday Toys. The company manufactures and distributes its products through more than 1000 retail outlets. In planning production levels for the coming winter season, Holiday must decide how many units of each product to produce prior to knowing the actual demand at the retail level. For this year's most important new toy, Holiday's marketing director is expecting demand to average 40 units per retail outlet. Prior to making the final production decision based upon this estimate, Holiday decided to survey a sample of 25 retailers in order to develop more information about the demand for the new product. Each retailer was provided with information about the features of the new toy along with the cost and the suggested selling price. Then each retailer was asked to specify an anticipated order quantity.

With μ denoting the population mean order quantity per retail outlet, the sample data will be used to conduct the following two-tailed hypothesis test:

$$H_0: \mu = 40$$
$$H_a: \mu \neq 40$$

If H_0 cannot be rejected, Holiday will continue its production planning based on the marketing director's estimate that the population mean order quantity per retail outlet will be $\mu = 40$ units. However, if H_0 is rejected, Holiday will immediately reevaluate its production plan for the product. A two-tailed hypothesis test is used because Holiday wants to reevaluate the production plan if the population mean quantity per retail outlet is less than anticipated or greater than anticipated. Because no historical data are available (it's a new product), the population mean μ and the population standard deviation must both be estimated using $\bar{x}$ and s from the sample data.

WEB file Orders

The sample of 25 retailers provided a mean of $\bar{x} = 37.4$ and a standard deviation of $s = 11.79$ units. Before going ahead with the use of the t distribution, the analyst constructed a histogram of the sample data in order to check on the form of the population distribution. The histogram of the sample data showed no evidence of skewness or any extreme outliers, so the analyst concluded that the use of the t distribution with $n - 1 = 24$ degrees of freedom was appropriate. Using equation (9.2) with $\bar{x} = 37.4$, $\mu_0 = 40$, $s = 11.79$, and $n = 25$, the value of the test statistic is

$$t = \frac{\bar{x} - \mu_0}{s/\sqrt{n}} = \frac{37.4 - 40}{11.79/\sqrt{25}} = -1.10$$

Because we have a two-tailed test, the p-value is two times the area under the curve of the t distribution for $t \leq -1.10$. Using Table 2 in Appendix B, the t distribution table for 24 degrees of freedom provides the following information.

Area in Upper Tail	**.20**	**.10**	**.05**	**.025**	**.01**	**.005**
***t*-Value (24 *df*)**	.857	1.318	1.711	2.064	2.492	2.797

$t = 1.10$

The t distribution table only contains positive t values. Because the t distribution is symmetric, however, the upper tail area at $t = 1.10$ is the same as the lower tail area at $t = -1.10$. We see that $t = 1.10$ is between 0.857 and 1.318. From the "Area in Upper Tail" row, we see that the area in the upper tail at $t = 1.10$ is between .20 and .10. When we double these amounts, we see that the p-value must be between .40 and .20. With a level of significance of $\alpha = .05$, we now know that the p-value is greater than α. Therefore, H_0 cannot be rejected. Sufficient evidence is not available to conclude that Holiday should change its production plan for the coming season.

Appendix F shows how the p-value for this test can be computed using Excel or Minitab. The p-value obtained is .2822. With a level of significance of $\alpha = .05$, we cannot reject H_0 because $.2822 > .05$.

The test statistic can also be compared to the critical value to make the two-tailed hypothesis testing decision. With $\alpha = .05$ and the t distribution with 24 degrees of freedom, $-t_{.025} = -2.064$ and $t_{.025} = 2.064$ are the critical values for the two-tailed test. The rejection rule using the test statistic is

$$\text{Reject } H_0 \text{ if } t \leq -2.064 \text{ or if } t \geq 2.064$$

TABLE 9.3 SUMMARY OF HYPOTHESIS TESTS ABOUT A POPULATION MEAN: σ UNKNOWN CASE

	Lower Tail Test	Upper Tail Test	Two-Tailed Test
Hypotheses	$H_0: \mu \geq \mu_0$ $H_a: \mu < \mu_0$	$H_0: \mu \leq \mu_0$ $H_a: \mu > \mu_0$	$H_0: \mu = \mu_0$ $H_a: \mu \neq \mu_0$
Test Statistic	$t = \dfrac{\bar{x} - \mu_0}{s/\sqrt{n}}$	$t = \dfrac{\bar{x} - \mu_0}{s/\sqrt{n}}$	$t = \dfrac{\bar{x} - \mu_0}{s/\sqrt{n}}$
Rejection Rule: *p*-Value Approach	Reject H_0 if p-value $\leq \alpha$	Reject H_0 if p-value $\leq \alpha$	Reject H_0 if p-value $\leq \alpha$
Rejection Rule: Critical Value Approach	Reject H_0 if $t \leq -t_\alpha$	Reject H_0 if $t \geq t_\alpha$	Reject H_0 if $t \leq -t_{\alpha/2}$ or if $t \geq t_{\alpha/2}$

Based on the test statistic $t = -1.10$, H_0 cannot be rejected. This result indicates that Holiday should continue its production planning for the coming season based on the expectation that $\mu = 40$.

Summary and Practical Advice

Table 9.3 provides a summary of the hypothesis testing procedures about a population mean for the σ unknown case. The key difference between these procedures and the ones for the σ known case is that s is used, instead of σ, in the computation of the test statistic. For this reason, the test statistic follows the t distribution.

The applicability of the hypothesis testing procedures of this section is dependent on the distribution of the population being sampled from and the sample size. When the population is normally distributed, the hypothesis tests described in this section provide exact results for any sample size. When the population is not normally distributed, the procedures are approximations. Nonetheless, we find that sample sizes of 30 or greater will provide good results in most cases. If the population is approximately normal, small sample sizes (e.g., $n < 15$) can provide acceptable results. If the population is highly skewed or contains outliers, sample sizes approaching 50 are recommended.

Exercises

Methods

23. Consider the following hypothesis test:

$$H_0: \mu \leq 12$$
$$H_a: \mu > 12$$

A sample of 25 provided a sample mean $\bar{x} = 14$ and a sample standard deviation $s = 4.32$.

a. Compute the value of the test statistic.
b. Use the t distribution table (Table 2 in Appendix B) to compute a range for the p-value.
c. At $\alpha = .05$, what is your conclusion?
d. What is the rejection rule using the critical value? What is your conclusion?

SELF test

24. Consider the following hypothesis test:

$$H_0: \mu = 18$$
$$H_a: \mu \neq 18$$

A sample of 48 provided a sample mean $\bar{x} = 17$ and a sample standard deviation $s = 4.5$.
   a. Compute the value of the test statistic.
   b. Use the t distribution table (Table 2 in Appendix B) to compute a range for the p-value.
   c. At $\alpha = .05$, what is your conclusion?
   d. What is the rejection rule using the critical value? What is your conclusion?

25. Consider the following hypothesis test:

$$H_0: \mu \geq 45$$
$$H_a: \mu < 45$$

A sample of 36 is used. Identify the p-value and state your conclusion for each of the following sample results. Use $\alpha = .01$.
   a. $\bar{x} = 44$ and $s = 5.2$
   b. $\bar{x} = 43$ and $s = 4.6$
   c. $\bar{x} = 46$ and $s = 5.0$

26. Consider the following hypothesis test:

$$H_0: \mu = 100$$
$$H_a: \mu \neq 100$$

A sample of 65 is used. Identify the p-value and state your conclusion for each of the following sample results. Use $\alpha = .05$.
   a. $\bar{x} = 103$ and $s = 11.5$
   b. $\bar{x} = 96.5$ and $s = 11.0$
   c. $\bar{x} = 102$ and $s = 10.5$

Applications

SELF test

27. The Employment and Training Administration reported that the U.S. mean unemployment insurance benefit was \$238 per week (*The World Almanac,* 2003). A researcher in the state of Virginia anticipated that sample data would show evidence that the mean weekly unemployment insurance benefit in Virginia was below the national average.
   a. Develop appropriate hypotheses such that rejection of H_0 will support the researcher's contention.
   b. For a sample of 100 individuals, the sample mean weekly unemployment insurance benefit was \$231 with a sample standard deviation of \$80. What is the p-value?
   c. At $\alpha = .05$, what is your conclusion?
   d. Repeat the preceding hypothesis test using the critical value approach.

28. A shareholders' group, in lodging a protest, claimed that the mean tenure for a chief executive office (CEO) was at least nine years. A survey of companies reported in *The Wall Street Journal* found a sample mean tenure of $\bar{x} = 7.27$ years for CEOs with a standard deviation of $s = 6.38$ years (*The Wall Street Journal*, January 2, 2007).
   a. Formulate hypotheses that can be used to challenge the validity of the claim made by the shareholders' group.
   b. Assume 85 companies were included in the sample. What is the p-value for your hypothesis test?
   c. At $\alpha = .01$, what is your conclusion?

WEB file
Administrator

29. The national mean annual salary for a school administrator is \$90,000 a year (*The Cincinnati Enquirer*, April 7, 2012). A school official took a sample of 25 school administrators in the state of Ohio to learn about salaries in that state to see if they differed from the national average.
    a. Formulate hypotheses that can be used to determine whether the population mean annual administrator salary in Ohio differs from the national mean of \$90,000.
    b. The sample data for 25 Ohio administrators is contained in the file named Administrator. What is the p-value for your hypothesis test in part (a)?
    c. At $\alpha = .05$, can your null hypothesis be rejected? What is your conclusion?
    d. Repeat the preceding hypothesis test using the critical value approach.

WEB file
ChildCare

30. The time married men with children spend on child care averages 6.4 hours per week (*Time*, March 12, 2012). You belong to a professional group on family practices that would like to do its own study to determine if the time married men in your area spend on child care per week differs from the reported mean of 6.4 hours per week. A sample of 40 married couples will be used with the data collected showing the hours per week the husband spends on child care. The sample data are contained in the file ChildCare.
    a. What are the hypotheses if your group would like to determine if the population mean number of hours married men are spending in child care differs from the mean reported by *Time* in your area?
    b. What is the sample mean and the p-value?
    c. Select your own level of significance. What is your conclusion?

31. The Coca-Cola Company reported that the mean per capita annual sales of its beverages in the United States was 423 eight-ounce servings (Coca-Cola Company website, February 3, 2009). Suppose you are curious whether the consumption of Coca-Cola beverages is higher in Atlanta, Georgia, the location of Coca-Cola's corporate headquarters. A sample of 36 individuals from the Atlanta area showed a sample mean annual consumption of 460.4 eight-ounce servings with a standard deviation of $s = 101.9$ ounces. Using $\alpha = .05$, do the sample results support the conclusion that mean annual consumption of Coca-Cola beverage products is higher in Atlanta?

WEB file
UsedCars

32. According to the National Automobile Dealers Association, the mean price for used cars is \$10,192. A manager of a Kansas City used car dealership reviewed a sample of 50 recent used car sales at the dealership in an attempt to determine whether the population mean price for used cars at this particular dealership differed from the national mean. The prices for the sample of 50 cars are shown in the file named UsedCars.
    a. Formulate the hypotheses that can be used to determine whether a difference exists in the mean price for used cars at the dealership.
    b. What is the p-value?
    c. At $\alpha = .05$, what is your conclusion?

33. Annual per capita consumption of milk is 21.6 gallons (*Statistical Abstract of the United States: 2006*). Being from the Midwest, you believe milk consumption is higher there and wish to support your opinion. A sample of 16 individuals from the midwestern town of Webster City showed a sample mean annual consumption of 24.1 gallons with a standard deviation of $s = 4.8$.
    a. Develop a hypothesis test that can be used to determine whether the mean annual consumption in Webster City is higher than the national mean.
    b. What is a point estimate of the difference between mean annual consumption in Webster City and the national mean?
    c. At $\alpha = .05$, test for a significant difference. What is your conclusion?

34. Joan's Nursery specializes in custom-designed landscaping for residential areas. The estimated labor cost associated with a particular landscaping proposal is based on the number of plantings of trees, shrubs, and so on to be used for the project. For cost-estimating purposes, managers use two hours of labor time for the planting of a

medium-sized tree. Actual times from a sample of 10 plantings during the past month follow (times in hours).

1.7	1.5	2.6	2.2	2.4	2.3	2.6	3.0	1.4	2.3

With a .05 level of significance, test to see whether the mean tree-planting time differs from two hours.

a. State the null and alternative hypotheses.
b. Compute the sample mean.
c. Compute the sample standard deviation.
d. What is the p-value?
e. What is your conclusion?

9.5 Population Proportion

In this section we show how to conduct a hypothesis test about a population proportion p. Using p_0 to denote the hypothesized value for the population proportion, the three forms for a hypothesis test about a population proportion are as follows.

$$\begin{array}{lll} H_0\colon p \geq p_0 & H_0\colon p \leq p_0 & H_0\colon p = p_0 \\ H_a\colon p < p_0 & H_a\colon p > p_0 & H_a\colon p \neq p_0 \end{array}$$

The first form is called a lower tail test, the second form is called an upper tail test, and the third form is called a two-tailed test.

Hypothesis tests about a population proportion are based on the difference between the sample proportion $\bar{p}$ and the hypothesized population proportion p_0. The methods used to conduct the hypothesis test are similar to those used for hypothesis tests about a population mean. The only difference is that we use the sample proportion and its standard error to compute the test statistic. The p-value approach or the critical value approach is then used to determine whether the null hypothesis should be rejected.

Let us consider an example involving a situation faced by Pine Creek golf course. Over the past year, 20% of the players at Pine Creek were women. In an effort to increase the proportion of women players, Pine Creek implemented a special promotion designed to attract women golfers. One month after the promotion was implemented, the course manager requested a statistical study to determine whether the proportion of women players at Pine Creek had increased. Because the objective of the study is to determine whether the proportion of women golfers increased, an upper tail test with $H_a\colon p > .20$ is appropriate. The null and alternative hypotheses for the Pine Creek hypothesis test are as follows:

$$\begin{array}{l} H_0\colon p \leq .20 \\ H_a\colon p > .20 \end{array}$$

If H_0 can be rejected, the test results will give statistical support for the conclusion that the proportion of women golfers increased and the promotion was beneficial. The course manager specified that a level of significance of $\alpha = .05$ be used in carrying out this hypothesis test.

The next step of the hypothesis testing procedure is to select a sample and compute the value of an appropriate test statistic. To show how this step is done for the Pine Creek upper tail test, we begin with a general discussion of how to compute the value of the test statistic for any form of a hypothesis test about a population proportion. The sampling distribution of $\bar{p}$, the point estimator of the population parameter p, is the basis for developing the test statistic.

When the null hypothesis is true as an equality, the expected value of $\bar{p}$ equals the hypothesized value p_0; that is, $E(\bar{p}) = p_0$. The standard error of $\bar{p}$ is given by

$$\sigma_{\bar{p}} = \sqrt{\frac{p_0(1 - p_0)}{n}}$$

In Chapter 7 we said that if $np \geq 5$ and $n(1 - p) \geq 5$, the sampling distribution of $\bar{p}$ can be approximated by a normal distribution.[3] Under these conditions, which usually apply in practice, the quantity

$$z = \frac{\bar{p} - p_0}{\sigma_{\bar{p}}} \tag{9.3}$$

has a standard normal probability distribution. With $\sigma_{\bar{p}} = \sqrt{p_0(1 - p_0)/n}$, the standard normal random variable z is the test statistic used to conduct hypothesis tests about a population proportion.

TEST STATISTIC FOR HYPOTHESIS TESTS ABOUT A POPULATION PROPORTION

$$z = \frac{\bar{p} - p_0}{\sqrt{\dfrac{p_0(1 - p_0)}{n}}} \tag{9.4}$$

WEB file WomenGolf

We can now compute the test statistic for the Pine Creek hypothesis test. Suppose a random sample of 400 players was selected, and that 100 of the players were women. The proportion of women golfers in the sample is

$$\bar{p} = \frac{100}{400} = .25$$

Using equation (9.4), the value of the test statistic is

$$z = \frac{\bar{p} - p_0}{\sqrt{\dfrac{p_0(1 - p_0)}{n}}} = \frac{.25 - .20}{\sqrt{\dfrac{.20(1 - .20)}{400}}} = \frac{.05}{.02} = 2.50$$

Because the Pine Creek hypothesis test is an upper tail test, the p-value is the probability that z is greater than or equal to $z = 2.50$; that is, it is the upper tail area corresponding to $z \geq 2.50$. Using the standard normal probability table, we find that the area to the left of $z = 2.50$ is .9938. Thus, the p-value for the Pine Creek test is $1.0000 - .9938 = .0062$. Figure 9.7 shows this p-value calculation.

Recall that the course manager specified a level of significance of $\alpha = .05$. A p-value $= .0062 < .05$ gives sufficient statistical evidence to reject H_0 at the .05 level of significance. Thus, the test provides statistical support for the conclusion that the special promotion increased the proportion of women players at the Pine Creek golf course.

[3]In most applications involving hypothesis tests of a population proportion, sample sizes are large enough to use the normal approximation. The exact sampling distribution of $\bar{p}$ is discrete with the probability for each value of $\bar{p}$ given by the binomial distribution. So hypothesis testing is a bit more complicated for small samples when the normal approximation cannot be used.

FIGURE 9.7 CALCULATION OF THE p-VALUE FOR THE PINE CREEK HYPOTHESIS TEST

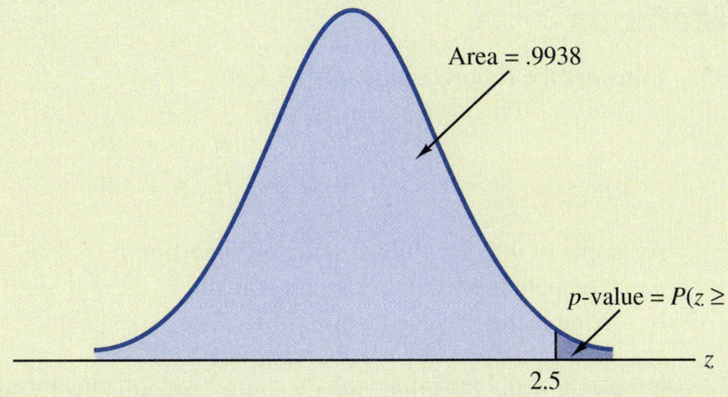

The decision whether to reject the null hypothesis can also be made using the critical value approach. The critical value corresponding to an area of .05 in the upper tail of a normal probability distribution is $z_{.05} = 1.645$. Thus, the rejection rule using the critical value approach is to reject H_0 if $z \geq 1.645$. Because $z = 2.50 > 1.645$, H_0 is rejected.

Again, we see that the p-value approach and the critical value approach lead to the same hypothesis testing conclusion, but the p-value approach provides more information. With a p-value $= .0062$, the null hypothesis would be rejected for any level of significance greater than or equal to .0062.

Summary

The procedure used to conduct a hypothesis test about a population proportion is similar to the procedure used to conduct a hypothesis test about a population mean. Although we only illustrated how to conduct a hypothesis test about a population proportion for an upper tail test, similar procedures can be used for lower tail and two-tailed tests. Table 9.4 provides a summary of the hypothesis tests about a population proportion. We assume that $np \geq 5$ and $n(1 - p) \geq 5$; thus the normal probability distribution can be used to approximate the sampling distribution of $\bar{p}$.

TABLE 9.4 SUMMARY OF HYPOTHESIS TESTS ABOUT A POPULATION PROPORTION

	Lower Tail Test	**Upper Tail Test**	**Two-Tailed Test**
Hypotheses	$H_0: p \geq p_0$ $H_a: p < p_0$	$H_0: p \leq p_0$ $H_a: p > p_0$	$H_0: p = p_0$ $H_a: p \neq p_0$
Test Statistic	$z = \dfrac{\bar{p} - p_0}{\sqrt{\dfrac{p_0(1 - p_0)}{n}}}$	$z = \dfrac{\bar{p} - p_0}{\sqrt{\dfrac{p_0(1 - p_0)}{n}}}$	$z = \dfrac{\bar{p} - p_0}{\sqrt{\dfrac{p_0(1 - p_0)}{n}}}$
Rejection Rule: *p*-Value Approach	Reject H_0 if p-value $\leq \alpha$	Reject H_0 if p-value $\leq \alpha$	Reject H_0 if p-value $\leq \alpha$
Rejection Rule: Critical Value Approach	Reject H_0 if $z \leq -z_\alpha$	Reject H_0 if $z \geq z_\alpha$	Reject H_0 if $z \leq -z_{\alpha/2}$ or if $z \geq z_{\alpha/2}$

Exercises

Methods

35. Consider the following hypothesis test:

$$H_0: p = .20$$
$$H_a: p \neq .20$$

A sample of 400 provided a sample proportion $\bar{p} = .175$.

a. Compute the value of the test statistic.
b. What is the p-value?
c. At $\alpha = .05$, what is your conclusion?
d. What is the rejection rule using the critical value? What is your conclusion?

SELF test

36. Consider the following hypothesis test:

$$H_0: p \geq .75$$
$$H_a: p < .75$$

A sample of 300 items was selected. Compute the p-value and state your conclusion for each of the following sample results. Use $\alpha = .05$.

a. $\bar{p} = .68$
b. $\bar{p} = .72$
c. $\bar{p} = .70$
d. $\bar{p} = .77$

Applications

37. A study found that, in 2005, 12.5% of U.S. workers belonged to unions (*The Wall Street Journal,* January 21, 2006). Suppose a sample of 400 U.S. workers is collected in 2006 to determine whether union efforts to organize have increased union membership.
   a. Formulate the hypotheses that can be used to determine whether union membership increased in 2006.
   b. If the sample results show that 52 of the workers belonged to unions, what is the p-value for your hypothesis test?
   c. At $\alpha = .05$, what is your conclusion?

SELF test

38. A study by *Consumer Reports* showed that 64% of supermarket shoppers believe supermarket brands to be as good as national name brands. To investigate whether this result applies to its own product, the manufacturer of a national name-brand ketchup asked a sample of shoppers whether they believed that supermarket ketchup was as good as the national brand ketchup.
   a. Formulate the hypotheses that could be used to determine whether the percentage of supermarket shoppers who believe that the supermarket ketchup was as good as the national brand ketchup differed from 64%.
   b. If a sample of 100 shoppers showed 52 stating that the supermarket brand was as good as the national brand, what is the p-value?
   c. At $\alpha = .05$, what is your conclusion?
   d. Should the national brand ketchup manufacturer be pleased with this conclusion? Explain.

WEB file
AgeGroup

39. According to the Pew Internet & American Life Project, 75% of American adults use the Internet (Pew Internet website, April 19, 2008). The Pew project authors also reported on the percentage of Americans who use the Internet by age group. The data in the file AgeGroup are consistent with their findings. These data were obtained from a sample of 100 Internet users in the 30–49 age group and 200 Internet users in the 50–64 age group. A Yes indicates the survey repondent had used the Internet; a No indicates the survey repondent had not.

a. Formulate hypotheses that could be used to determine whether the percentage of Internet users in the two age groups differs from the overall average of 75%
b. Estimate the proportion of Internet users in the 30–49 age group. Does this proportion differ significantly from the overall proportion of .75? Use $\alpha = .05$
c. Estimate the proportion of Internet users in the 50–64 age group. Does this proportion differ significantly from the overall proportion of .75? Use $\alpha = .05$
d. Would you expect the proportion of users in the 18–29 age group to be larger or smaller than the proportion for the 30–49 age group? Support you conclusion with the results obtained in parts (b) and (c).

40. In 2008, 46% of business owners gave a holiday gift to their employees. A 2009 survey of business owners indicated that 35% planned to provide a holiday gift to their employees (Radio WEZV, Myrtle Beach, SC, November 11, 2009). Suppose the survey results are based on a sample of 60 business owners.
    a. How many business owners in the survey planned to provide a holiday gift to their employees in 2009?
    b. Suppose the business owners in the sample did as they planned. Compute the p-value for a hypothesis test that can be used to determine if the proportion of business owners providing holiday gifts had decreased from the 2008 level.
    c. Using a .05 level of significance, would you conclude that the proportion of business owners providing gifts decreased? What is the smallest level of significance for which you could draw such a conclusion?

41. Speaking to a group of analysts in January 2006, a brokerage firm executive claimed that at least 70% of investors are currently confident of meeting their investment objectives. A UBS Investor Optimism Survey, conducted over the period January 2 to January 15, found that 67% of investors were confident of meeting their investment objectives (CNBC, January 20, 2006).
    a. Formulate the hypotheses that can be used to test the validity of the brokerage firm executive's claim.
    b. Assume the UBS Investor Optimism Survey collected information from 300 investors. What is the p-value for the hypothesis test?
    c. At $\alpha = .05$, should the executive's claim be rejected?

42. According to the University of Nevada Center for Logistics Management, 6% of all merchandise sold in the United States gets returned (*BusinessWeek,* January 15, 2007). A Houston department store sampled 80 items sold in January and found that 12 of the items were returned.
    a. Construct a point estimate of the proportion of items returned for the population of sales transactions at the Houston store.
    b. Construct a 95% confidence interval for the porportion of returns at the Houston store.
    c. Is the proportion of returns at the Houston store significantly different from the returns for the nation as a whole? Provide statistical support for your answer.

WEB file
Eagle

43. Eagle Outfitters is a chain of stores specializing in outdoor apparel and camping gear. They are considering a promotion that involves mailing discount coupons to all their credit card customers. This promotion will be considered a success if more than 10% of those receiving the coupons use them. Before going national with the promotion, coupons were sent to a sample of 100 credit card customers.
    a. Develop hypotheses that can be used to test whether the population proportion of those who will use the coupons is sufficient to go national.
    b. The file Eagle contains the sample data. Develop a point estimate of the population proportion.
    c. Use $\alpha = .05$ to conduct your hypothesis test. Should Eagle go national with the promotion?

WEB file
Drowsy

44. In a cover story, *BusinessWeek* published information about sleep habits of Americans (*BusinessWeek,* January 26, 2004). The article noted that sleep deprivation causes a number of problems, including highway deaths. Fifty-one percent of adult drivers admit to

driving while drowsy. A researcher hypothesized that this issue was an even bigger problem for night shift workers.

a. Formulate the hypotheses that can be used to help determine whether more than 51% of the population of night shift workers admit to driving while drowsy.
b. A sample of 400 night shift workers identified those who admitted to driving while drowsy. See the Drowsy file. What is the sample proportion? What is the p-value?
c. At $\alpha = .01$, what is your conclusion?

45. Many investors and financial analysts believe the Dow Jones Industrial Average (DJIA) provides a good barometer of the overall stock market. On January 31, 2006, 9 of the 30 stocks making up the DJIA increased in price (*The Wall Street Journal,* February 1, 2006). On the basis of this fact, a financial analyst claims we can assume that 30% of the stocks traded on the New York Stock Exchange (NYSE) went up the same day.
    a. Formulate null and alternative hypotheses to test the analyst's claim.
    b. A sample of 50 stocks traded on the NYSE that day showed that 24 went up. What is your point estimate of the population proportion of stocks that went up?
    c. Conduct your hypothesis test using $\alpha = .01$ as the level of significance. What is your conclusion?

9.6 Hypothesis Testing and Decision Making

In the previous sections of this chapter we have illustrated hypothesis testing applications that are considered significance tests. After formulating the null and alternative hypotheses, we selected a sample and computed the value of a test statistic and the associated p-value. We then compared the p-value to a controlled probability of a Type I error, α, which is called the level of significance for the test. If p-value $\leq \alpha$, we made the conclusion "reject H_0" and declared the results significant; otherwise, we made the conclusion "do not reject H_0." With a significance test, we control the probability of making the Type I error, but not the Type II error. Thus, we recommended the conclusion "do not reject H_0" rather than "accept H_0" because the latter puts us at risk of making the Type II error of accepting H_0 when it is false. With the conclusion "do not reject H_0," the statistical evidence is considered inconclusive and is usually an indication to postpone a decision or action until further research and testing can be undertaken.

However, if the purpose of a hypothesis test is to make a decision when H_0 is true and a different decision when H_a is true, the decision maker may want to, and in some cases be forced to, take action with both the conclusion *do not reject* H_0 and the conclusion *reject* H_0. If this situation occurs, statisticians generally recommend controlling the probability of making a Type II error. With the probabilities of both the Type I and Type II error controlled, the conclusion from the hypothesis test is either to *accept* H_0 or *reject* H_0. In the first case, H_0 is concluded to be true, while in the second case, H_a is concluded true. Thus, a decision and appropriate action can be taken when either conclusion is reached.

A good illustration of hypothesis testing for decision making is lot-acceptance sampling, a topic we will discuss in more depth in Chapter 20. For example, a quality control manager must decide to accept a shipment of batteries from a supplier or to return the shipment because of poor quality. Assume that design specifications require batteries from the supplier to have a mean useful life of at least 120 hours. To evaluate the quality of an incoming shipment, a sample of 36 batteries will be selected and tested. On the basis of the sample, a decision must be made to accept the shipment of batteries or to return it to the supplier because of poor quality. Let μ denote the mean number of hours of useful life for batteries in the shipment. The null and alternative hypotheses about the population mean follow.

$$H_0: \mu \geq 120$$
$$H_a: \mu < 120$$

If H_0 is rejected, the alternative hypothesis is concluded to be true. This conclusion indicates that the appropriate action is to return the shipment to the supplier. However, if H_0 is not rejected, the decision maker must still determine what action should be taken. Thus, without directly concluding that H_0 is true, but merely by not rejecting it, the decision maker will have made the decision to accept the shipment as being of satisfactory quality.

In such decision-making situations, it is recommended that the hypothesis testing procedure be extended to control the probability of making a Type II error. Because a decision will be made and action taken when we do not reject H_0, knowledge of the probability of making a Type II error will be helpful. In Sections 9.7 and 9.8 we explain how to compute the probability of making a Type II error and how the sample size can be adjusted to help control the probability of making a Type II error.

9.7 Calculating the Probability of Type II Errors

In this section we show how to calculate the probability of making a Type II error for a hypothesis test about a population mean. We illustrate the procedure by using the lot-acceptance example described in Section 9.6. The null and alternative hypotheses about the mean number of hours of useful life for a shipment of batteries are H_0: $\mu \geq 120$ and H_a: $\mu < 120$. If H_0 is rejected, the decision will be to return the shipment to the supplier because the mean hours of useful life are less than the specified 120 hours. If H_0 is not rejected, the decision will be to accept the shipment.

Suppose a level of significance of $\alpha = .05$ is used to conduct the hypothesis test. The test statistic in the σ known case is

$$z = \frac{\bar{x} - \mu_0}{\sigma/\sqrt{n}} = \frac{\bar{x} - 120}{\sigma/\sqrt{n}}$$

Based on the critical value approach and $z_{.05} = 1.645$, the rejection rule for the lower tail test is

$$\text{Reject } H_0 \text{ if } z \leq -1.645$$

Suppose a sample of 36 batteries will be selected and based upon previous testing the population standard deviation can be assumed known with a value of $\sigma = 12$ hours. The rejection rule indicates that we will reject H_0 if

$$z = \frac{\bar{x} - 120}{12/\sqrt{36}} \leq -1.645$$

Solving for $\bar{x}$ in the preceding expression indicates that we will reject H_0 if

$$\bar{x} \leq 120 - 1.645\left(\frac{12}{\sqrt{36}}\right) = 116.71$$

Rejecting H_0 when $\bar{x} \leq 116.71$ means that we will make the decision to accept the shipment whenever

$$\bar{x} > 116.71$$

With this information, we are ready to compute probabilities associated with making a Type II error. First, recall that we make a Type II error whenever the true shipment mean is less than 120 hours and we make the decision to accept H_0: $\mu \geq 120$. Hence, to compute the probability of making a Type II error, we must select a value of μ less than 120 hours.

FIGURE 9.8 PROBABILITY OF A TYPE II ERROR WHEN $\mu = 112$

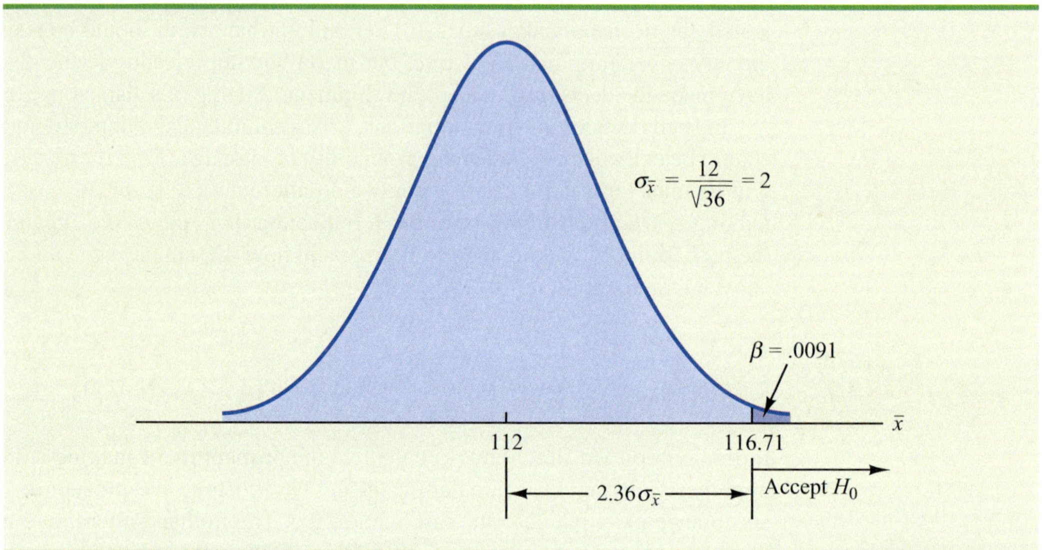

For example, suppose the shipment is considered to be of poor quality if the batteries have a mean life of $\mu = 112$ hours. If $\mu = 112$ is really true, what is the probability of accepting H_0: $\mu \geq 120$ and hence committing a Type II error? Note that this probability is the probability that the sample mean $\bar{x}$ is greater than 116.71 when $\mu = 112$.

Figure 9.8 shows the sampling distribution of $\bar{x}$ when the mean is $\mu = 112$. The shaded area in the upper tail gives the probability of obtaining $\bar{x} > 116.71$. Using the standard normal distribution, we see that at $\bar{x} = 116.71$

$$z = \frac{\bar{x} - \mu}{\sigma/\sqrt{n}} = \frac{116.71 - 112}{12/\sqrt{36}} = 2.36$$

The standard normal probability table shows that with $z = 2.36$, the area in the upper tail is $1.0000 - .9909 = .0091$. Thus, .0091 is the probability of making a Type II error when $\mu = 112$. Denoting the probability of making a Type II error as β, we see that when $\mu = 112$, $\beta = .0091$. Therefore, we can conclude that if the mean of the population is 112 hours, the probability of making a Type II error is only .0091.

We can repeat these calculations for other values of μ less than 120. Doing so will show a different probability of making a Type II error for each value of μ. For example, suppose the shipment of batteries has a mean useful life of $\mu = 115$ hours. Because we will accept H_0 whenever $\bar{x} > 116.71$, the z value for $\mu = 115$ is given by

$$z = \frac{\bar{x} - \mu}{\sigma/\sqrt{n}} = \frac{116.71 - 115}{12/\sqrt{36}} = .86$$

From the standard normal probability table, we find that the area in the upper tail of the standard normal distribution for $z = .86$ is $1.0000 - .8051 = .1949$. Thus, the probability of making a Type II error is $\beta = .1949$ when the true mean is $\mu = 115$.

In Table 9.5 we show the probability of making a Type II error for a variety of values of μ less than 120. Note that as μ increases toward 120, the probability of making a Type II error increases toward an upper bound of .95. However, as μ decreases to values farther below 120, the probability of making a Type II error diminishes. This pattern is what we

TABLE 9.5 PROBABILITY OF MAKING A TYPE II ERROR FOR THE LOT-ACCEPTANCE HYPOTHESIS TEST

Value of μ	$z = \dfrac{116.71 - \mu}{12/\sqrt{36}}$	Probability of a Type II Error (β)	Power $(1 - \beta)$
112	2.36	.0091	.9909
114	1.36	.0869	.9131
115	.86	.1949	.8051
116.71	.00	.5000	.5000
117	−.15	.5596	.4404
118	−.65	.7422	.2578
119.999	−1.645	.9500	.0500

As Table 9.5 shows, the probability of a Type II error depends on the value of the population mean μ. For values of μ near μ_0, the probability of making the Type II error can be high.

should expect. When the true population mean μ is close to the null hypothesis value of $\mu = 120$, the probability is high that we will make a Type II error. However, when the true population mean μ is far below the null hypothesis value of $\mu = 120$, the probability is low that we will make a Type II error.

The probability of correctly rejecting H_0 when it is false is called the **power** of the test. For any particular value of μ, the power is $1 - \beta$; that is, the probability of correctly rejecting the null hypothesis is 1 minus the probability of making a Type II error. Values of power are also listed in Table 9.5. On the basis of these values, the power associated with each value of μ is shown graphically in Figure 9.9. Such a graph is called a **power curve**. Note that the power curve extends over the values of μ for which the null hypothesis is false. The height of the power curve at any value of μ indicates the probability of correctly rejecting H_0 when H_0 is false.[4]

FIGURE 9.9 POWER CURVE FOR THE LOT-ACCEPTANCE HYPOTHESIS TEST

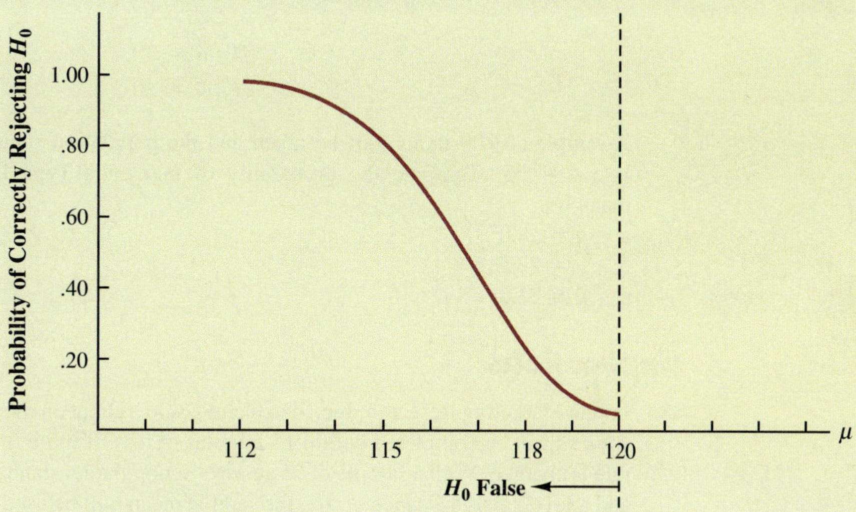

[4]Another graph, called the operating characteristic curve, is sometimes used to provide information about the probability of making a Type II error. The operating characteristic curve shows the probability of accepting H_0 and thus provides β for the values of μ where the null hypothesis is false. The probability of making a Type II error can be read directly from this graph.

In summary, the following step-by-step procedure can be used to compute the probability of making a Type II error in hypothesis tests about a population mean.

1. Formulate the null and alternative hypotheses.
2. Use the level of significance α and the critical value approach to determine the critical value and the rejection rule for the test.
3. Use the rejection rule to solve for the value of the sample mean corresponding to the critical value of the test statistic.
4. Use the results from step 3 to state the values of the sample mean that lead to the acceptance of H_0. These values define the acceptance region for the test.
5. Use the sampling distribution of $\bar{x}$ for a value of μ satisfying the alternative hypothesis, and the acceptance region from step 4, to compute the probability that the sample mean will be in the acceptance region. This probability is the probability of making a Type II error at the chosen value of μ.

Exercises

Methods

SELF test

46. Consider the following hypothesis test.

$$H_0: \mu \geq 10$$
$$H_a: \mu < 10$$

The sample size is 120 and the population standard deviation is assumed known with $\sigma = 5$. Use $\alpha = .05$.

a. If the population mean is 9, what is the probability that the sample mean leads to the conclusion *do not reject* H_0?
b. What type of error would be made if the actual population mean is 9 and we conclude that H_0: $\mu \geq 10$ is true?
c. What is the probability of making a Type II error if the actual population mean is 8?

47. Consider the following hypothesis test.

$$H_0: \mu = 20$$
$$H_a: \mu \neq 20$$

A sample of 200 items will be taken and the population standard deviation is $\sigma = 10$. Use $\alpha = .05$. Compute the probability of making a Type II error if the population mean is:

a. $\mu = 18.0$
b. $\mu = 22.5$
c. $\mu = 21.0$

Applications

48. Fowle Marketing Research, Inc., bases charges to a client on the assumption that telephone surveys can be completed within 15 minutes or less. If more time is required, a premium rate is charged. With a sample of 35 surveys, a population standard deviation of 4 minutes, and a level of significance of .01, the sample mean will be used to test the null hypothesis H_0: $\mu \leq 15$.

a. What is your interpretation of the Type II error for this problem? What is its impact on the firm?
b. What is the probability of making a Type II error when the actual mean time is $\mu = 17$ minutes?

c. What is the probability of making a Type II error when the actual mean time is $\mu = 18$ minutes?
d. Sketch the general shape of the power curve for this test.

SELF test

49. A consumer research group is interested in testing an automobile manufacturer's claim that a new economy model will travel at least 25 miles per gallon of gasoline (H_0: $\mu \geq 25$).
a. With a .02 level of significance and a sample of 30 cars, what is the rejection rule based on the value of $\bar{x}$ for the test to determine whether the manufacturer's claim should be rejected? Assume that σ is 3 miles per gallon.
b. What is the probability of committing a Type II error if the actual mileage is 23 miles per gallon?
c. What is the probability of committing a Type II error if the actual mileage is 24 miles per gallon?
d. What is the probability of committing a Type II error if the actual mileage is 25.5 miles per gallon?

50. *Young Adult* magazine states the following hypotheses about the mean age of its subscribers.

$$H_0\colon \mu = 28$$
$$H_a\colon \mu \neq 28$$

a. What would it mean to make a Type II error in this situation?
b. The population standard deviation is assumed known at $\sigma = 6$ years and the sample size is 100. With $\alpha = .05$, what is the probability of accepting H_0 for μ equal to 26, 27, 29, and 30?
c. What is the power at $\mu = 26$? What does this result tell you?

51. A production line operation is tested for filling weight accuracy using the following hypotheses.

Hypothesis	Conclusion and Action
H_0: $\mu = 16$	Filling okay; keep running
H_a: $\mu \neq 16$	Filling off standard; stop and adjust machine

The sample size is 30 and the population standard deviation is $\sigma = .8$. Use $\alpha = .05$.
a. What would a Type II error mean in this situation?
b. What is the probability of making a Type II error when the machine is overfilling by .5 ounces?
c. What is the power of the statistical test when the machine is overfilling by .5 ounces?
d. Show the power curve for this hypothesis test. What information does it contain for the production manager?

52. Refer to exercise 48. Assume the firm selects a sample of 50 surveys and repeat parts (b) and (c). What observation can you make about how increasing the sample size affects the probability of making a Type II error?

53. Sparr Investments, Inc., specializes in tax-deferred investment opportunities for its clients. Recently Sparr offered a payroll deduction investment program for the employees of a particular company. Sparr estimates that the employees are currently averaging \$100 or less per month in tax-deferred investments. A sample of 40 employees will be used to test Sparr's hypothesis about the current level of investment activity among the population of employees. Assume the employee monthly tax-deferred investment amounts have a standard deviation of \$75 and that a .05 level of significance will be used in the hypothesis test.
a. What is the Type II error in this situation?
b. What is the probability of the Type II error if the actual mean employee monthly investment is \$120?
c. What is the probability of the Type II error if the actual mean employee monthly investment is \$130?
d. Assume a sample size of 80 employees is used and repeat parts (b) and (c).

9.8 Determining the Sample Size for a Hypothesis Test About a Population Mean

Assume that a hypothesis test is to be conducted about the value of a population mean. The level of significance specified by the user determines the probability of making a Type I error for the test. By controlling the sample size, the user can also control the probability of making a Type II error. Let us show how a sample size can be determined for the following lower tail test about a population mean.

$$H_0: \mu \geq \mu_0$$
$$H_a: \mu < \mu_0$$

The upper panel of Figure 9.10 is the sampling distribution of $\bar{x}$ when H_0 is true with $\mu = \mu_0$. For a lower tail test, the critical value of the test statistic is denoted $-z_\alpha$. In the upper panel of the figure the vertical line, labeled c, is the corresponding value of $\bar{x}$. Note that, if we reject H_0 when $\bar{x} \leq c$, the probability of a Type I error will be α. With z_α representing the z value corresponding to an area of α in the upper tail of the standard normal distribution, we compute c using the following formula:

$$c = \mu_0 - z_\alpha \frac{\sigma}{\sqrt{n}} \tag{9.5}$$

FIGURE 9.10 DETERMINING THE SAMPLE SIZE FOR SPECIFIED LEVELS OF THE TYPE I (α) AND TYPE II (β) ERRORS

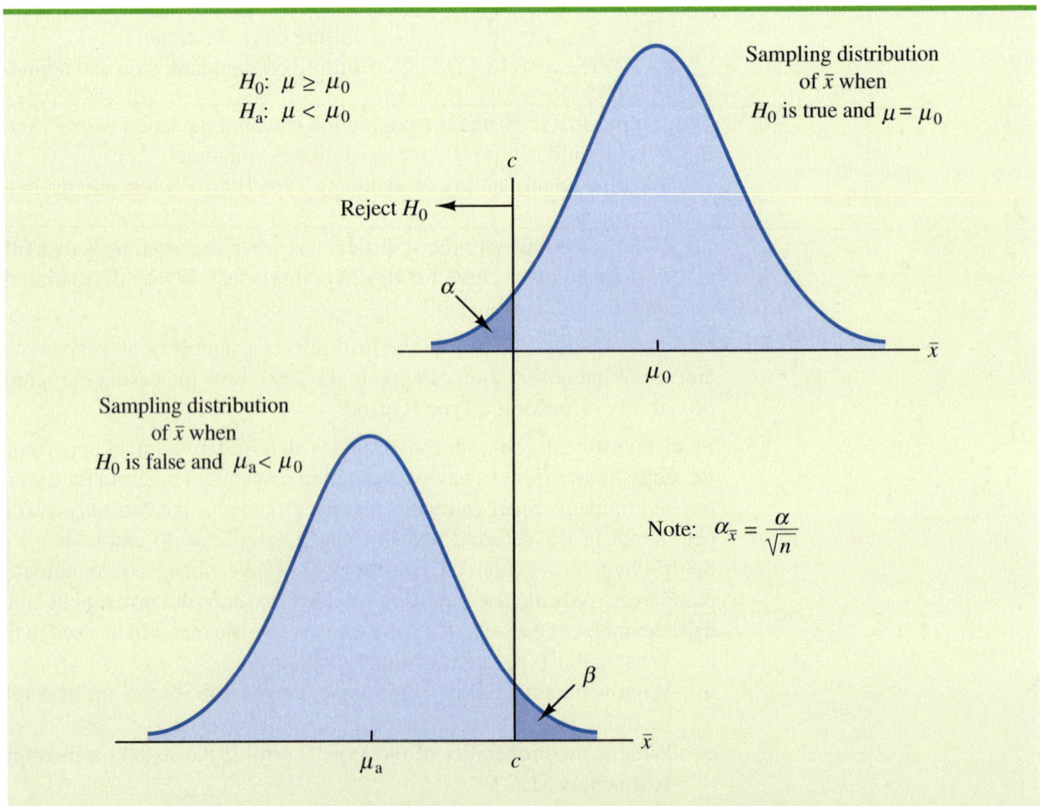

The lower panel of Figure 9.10 is the sampling distribution of $\bar{x}$ when the alternative hypothesis is true with $\mu = \mu_a < \mu_0$. The shaded region shows β, the probability of a Type II error that the decision maker will be exposed to if the null hypothesis is accepted when $\bar{x} > c$. With z_β representing the z value corresponding to an area of β in the upper tail of the standard normal distribution, we compute c using the following formula:

$$c = \mu_a + z_\beta \frac{\sigma}{\sqrt{n}} \tag{9.6}$$

Now what we want to do is to select a value for c so that when we reject H_0 and accept H_a, the probability of a Type I error is equal to the chosen value of α and the probability of a Type II error is equal to the chosen value of β. Therefore, both equations (9.5) and (9.6) must provide the same value for c, and the following equation must be true.

$$\mu_0 - z_\alpha \frac{\sigma}{\sqrt{n}} = \mu_a + z_\beta \frac{\sigma}{\sqrt{n}}$$

To determine the required sample size, we first solve for the $\sqrt{n}$ as follows.

$$\mu_0 - \mu_a = z_\alpha \frac{\sigma}{\sqrt{n}} + z_\beta \frac{\sigma}{\sqrt{n}}$$

$$\mu_0 - \mu_a = \frac{(z_\alpha + z_\beta)\sigma}{\sqrt{n}}$$

and

$$\sqrt{n} = \frac{(z_\alpha + z_\beta)\sigma}{(\mu_0 - \mu_a)}$$

Squaring both sides of the expression provides the following sample size formula for a one-tailed hypothesis test about a population mean.

SAMPLE SIZE FOR A ONE-TAILED HYPOTHESIS TEST ABOUT A POPULATION MEAN

$$n = \frac{(z_\alpha + z_\beta)^2\sigma^2}{(\mu_0 - \mu_a)^2} \tag{9.7}$$

where

z_α = z value providing an area of α in the upper tail of a standard normal distribution
z_β = z value providing an area of β in the upper tail of a standard normal distribution
σ = the population standard deviation
μ_0 = the value of the population mean in the null hypothesis
μ_a = the value of the population mean used for the Type II error

Note: In a two-tailed hypothesis test, use (9.7) with $z_{\alpha/2}$ replacing z_α.

Although the logic of equation (9.7) was developed for the hypothesis test shown in Figure 9.10, it holds for any one-tailed test about a population mean. In a two-tailed hypothesis test about a population mean, $z_{\alpha/2}$ is used instead of z_α in equation (9.7).

Let us return to the lot-acceptance example from Sections 9.6 and 9.7. The design specification for the shipment of batteries indicated a mean useful life of at least 120 hours for the batteries. Shipments were rejected if H_0: $\mu \geq 120$ was rejected. Let us assume that the quality control manager makes the following statements about the allowable probabilities for the Type I and Type II errors.

Type I error statement: If the mean life of the batteries in the shipment is $\mu = 120$, I am willing to risk an $\alpha = .05$ probability of rejecting the shipment.

Type II error statement: If the mean life of the batteries in the shipment is 5 hours under the specification (i.e., $\mu = 115$), I am willing to risk a $\beta = .10$ probability of accepting the shipment.

These statements are based on the judgment of the manager. Someone else might specify different restrictions on the probabilities. However, statements about the allowable probabilities of both errors must be made before the sample size can be determined.

In the example, $\alpha = .05$ and $\beta = .10$. Using the standard normal probability distribution, we have $z_{.05} = 1.645$ and $z_{.10} = 1.28$. From the statements about the error probabilities, we note that $\mu_0 = 120$ and $\mu_a = 115$. Finally, the population standard deviation was assumed known at $\sigma = 12$. By using equation (9.7), we find that the recommended sample size for the lot-acceptance example is

$$n = \frac{(1.645 + 1.28)^2(12)^2}{(120 - 115)^2} = 49.3$$

Rounding up, we recommend a sample size of 50.

Because both the Type I and Type II error probabilities have been controlled at allowable levels with $n = 50$, the quality control manager is now justified in using the *accept* H_0 and *reject* H_0 statements for the hypothesis test. The accompanying inferences are made with allowable probabilities of making Type I and Type II errors.

We can make three observations about the relationship among α, β, and the sample size n.

1. Once two of the three values are known, the other can be computed.
2. For a given level of significance α, increasing the sample size will reduce β.
3. For a given sample size, decreasing α will increase β, whereas increasing α will decrease β.

The third observation should be kept in mind when the probability of a Type II error is not being controlled. It suggests that one should not choose unnecessarily small values for the level of significance α. For a given sample size, choosing a smaller level of significance means more exposure to a Type II error. Inexperienced users of hypothesis testing often think that smaller values of α are always better. They are better if we are concerned only about making a Type I error. However, smaller values of α have the disadvantage of increasing the probability of making a Type II error.

Exercises

Methods

SELF test

54. Consider the following hypothesis test.

$$H_0: \mu \geq 10$$
$$H_a: \mu < 10$$

The sample size is 120 and the population standard deviation is 5. Use $\alpha = .05$. If the actual population mean is 9, the probability of a Type II error is .2912. Suppose the researcher wants to reduce the probability of a Type II error to .10 when the actual population mean is 9. What sample size is recommended?

55. Consider the following hypothesis test.

$$H_0: \mu = 20$$
$$H_a: \mu \neq 20$$

The population standard deviation is 10. Use $\alpha = .05$. How large a sample should be taken if the researcher is willing to accept a .05 probability of making a Type II error when the actual population mean is 22?

Applications

56. Suppose the project director for the Hilltop Coffee study (see Section 9.3) asked for a .10 probability of claiming that Hilltop was not in violation when it really was underfilling by 1 ounce ($\mu_a = 2.9375$ pounds). What sample size would have been recommended?

SELF test

57. A special industrial battery must have a life of at least 400 hours. A hypothesis test is to be conducted with a .02 level of significance. If the batteries from a particular production run have an actual mean use life of 385 hours, the production manager wants a sampling procedure that only 10% of the time would show erroneously that the batch is acceptable. What sample size is recommended for the hypothesis test? Use 30 hours as an estimate of the population standard deviation.

58. *Young Adult* magazine states the following hypotheses about the mean age of its subscribers.

$$H_0: \mu = 28$$
$$H_a: \mu \neq 28$$

If the manager conducting the test will permit a .15 probability of making a Type II error when the true mean age is 29, what sample size should be selected? Assume $\sigma = 6$ and a .05 level of significance.

59. An automobile mileage study tested the following hypotheses.

Hypothesis	Conclusion
$H_0: \mu \geq 25$ mpg	Manufacturer's claim supported
$H_a: \mu < 25$ mpg	Manufacturer's claim rejected; average mileage per gallon less than stated

For $\sigma = 3$ and a .02 level of significance, what sample size would be recommended if the researcher wants an 80% chance of detecting that μ is less than 25 miles per gallon when it is actually 24?

Summary

Hypothesis testing is a statistical procedure that uses sample data to determine whether a statement about the value of a population parameter should or should not be rejected. The hypotheses are two competing statements about a population parameter. One statement is called the null hypothesis (H_0), and the other statement is called the alternative hypothesis (H_a). In Section 9.1 we provided guidelines for developing hypotheses for situations frequently encountered in practice.

Whenever historical data or other information provides a basis for assuming that the population standard deviation is known, the hypothesis testing procedure for the population mean is based on the standard normal distribution. Whenever σ is unknown, the sample standard deviation s is used to estimate σ and the hypothesis testing procedure is based on the t distribution. In both cases, the quality of results depends on both the form of the population distribution and the sample size. If the population has a normal distribution, both hypothesis testing procedures are applicable, even with small sample sizes. If the population is not normally distributed, larger sample sizes are needed. General guidelines about the sample size were provided in Sections 9.3 and 9.4. In the case of hypothesis tests about a population proportion, the hypothesis testing procedure uses a test statistic based on the standard normal distribution.

In all cases, the value of the test statistic can be used to compute a p-value for the test. A p-value is a probability used to determine whether the null hypothesis should be rejected. If the p-value is less than or equal to the level of significance α, the null hypothesis can be rejected.

Hypothesis testing conclusions can also be made by comparing the value of the test statistic to a critical value. For lower tail tests, the null hypothesis is rejected if the value of the test statistic is less than or equal to the critical value. For upper tail tests, the null hypothesis is rejected if the value of the test statistic is greater than or equal to the critical value. Two-tailed tests consist of two critical values: one in the lower tail of the sampling distribution and one in the upper tail. In this case, the null hypothesis is rejected if the value of the test statistic is less than or equal to the critical value in the lower tail or greater than or equal to the critical value in the upper tail.

Extensions of hypothesis testing procedures to include an analysis of the Type II error were also presented. In Section 9.7 we showed how to compute the probability of making a Type II error. In Section 9.8 we showed how to determine a sample size that will control for the probability of making both a Type I error and a Type II error.

Glossary

Null hypothesis The hypothesis tentatively assumed true in the hypothesis testing procedure.

Alternative hypothesis The hypothesis concluded to be true if the null hypothesis is rejected.

Type II error The error of accepting H_0 when it is false.

Type I error The error of rejecting H_0 when it is true.

Level of significance The probability of making a Type I error when the null hypothesis is true as an equality.

One-tailed test A hypothesis test in which rejection of the null hypothesis occurs for values of the test statistic in one tail of its sampling distribution.

Test statistic A statistic whose value helps determine whether a null hypothesis should be rejected.

***p*-value** A probability that provides a measure of the evidence against the null hypothesis given by the sample. Smaller p-values indicate more evidence against H_0. For a lower tail test, the p-value is the probability of obtaining a value for the test statistic as small as or smaller than that provided by the sample. For an upper tail test, the p-value is the probability of obtaining a value for the test statistic as large as or larger than that provided by the sample. For a two-tailed test, the p-value is the probability of obtaining a value for the test statistic at least as unlikely as or more unlikely than that provided by the sample.

Critical value A value that is compared with the test statistic to determine whether H_0 should be rejected.

Two-tailed test A hypothesis test in which rejection of the null hypothesis occurs for values of the test statistic in either tail of its sampling distribution.

Power The probability of correctly rejecting H_0 when it is false.

Power curve A graph of the probability of rejecting H_0 for all possible values of the population parameter not satisfying the null hypothesis. The power curve provides the probability of correctly rejecting the null hypothesis.

Key Formulas

Test Statistic for Hypothesis Tests About a Population Mean: σ Known

$$z = \frac{\bar{x} - \mu_0}{\sigma/\sqrt{n}} \tag{9.1}$$

Test Statistic for Hypothesis Tests About a Population Mean: σ Unknown

$$t = \frac{\bar{x} - \mu_0}{s/\sqrt{n}} \tag{9.2}$$

Test Statistic for Hypothesis Tests About a Population Proportion

$$z = \frac{\bar{p} - p_0}{\sqrt{\dfrac{p_0(1 - p_0)}{n}}} \tag{9.4}$$

Sample Size for a One-Tailed Hypothesis Test About a Population Mean

$$n = \frac{(z_\alpha + z_\beta)^2\sigma^2}{(\mu_0 - \mu_a)^2} \tag{9.7}$$

In a two-tailed test, replace z_α with $z_{\alpha/2}$.

Supplementary Exercises

60. A production line operates with a mean filling weight of 16 ounces per container. Overfilling or underfilling presents a serious problem and when detected requires the operator to shut down the production line to readjust the filling mechanism. From past data, a population standard deviation $\sigma = .8$ ounces is assumed. A quality control inspector selects a sample of 30 items every hour and at that time makes the decision of whether to shut down the line for readjustment. The level of significance is $\alpha = .05$.
    a. State the hypothesis test for this quality control application.
    b. If a sample mean of $\bar{x} = 16.32$ ounces were found, what is the p-value? What action would you recommend?
    c. If a sample mean of $\bar{x} = 15.82$ ounces were found, what is the p-value? What action would you recommend?
    d. Use the critical value approach. What is the rejection rule for the preceding hypothesis testing procedure? Repeat parts (b) and (c). Do you reach the same conclusion?

61. At Western University the historical mean of scholarship examination scores for freshman applications is 900. A historical population standard deviation $\sigma = 180$ is assumed known. Each year, the assistant dean uses a sample of applications to determine whether the mean examination score for the new freshman applications has changed.
    a. State the hypotheses.
    b. What is the 95% confidence interval estimate of the population mean examination score if a sample of 200 applications provided a sample mean $\bar{x} = 935$?
    c. Use the confidence interval to conduct a hypothesis test. Using $\alpha = .05$, what is your conclusion?
    d. What is the p-value?

62. *Playbill* is a magazine distributed around the country to people attending musicals and other theatrical productions. The mean annual household income for the population of *Playbill* readers is $119,155 (*Playbill,* January 2006). Assume the standard deviation is

σ = \$20,700. A San Francisco civic group has asserted that the mean for theatergoers in the Bay Area is higher. A sample of 60 theater attendees in the Bay Area showed a sample mean household income of \$126,100.

a. Develop hypotheses that can be used to determine whether the sample data support the conclusion that theater attendees in the Bay Area have a higher mean household income than that for all *Playbill* readers.
b. What is the p-value based on the sample of 60 theater attendees in the Bay Area?
c. Use $\alpha = .01$ as the level of significance. What is your conclusion?

63. On Friday, Wall Street traders were anxiously awaiting the federal government's release of numbers on the January increase in nonfarm payrolls. The early consensus estimate among economists was for a growth of 250,000 new jobs (CNBC, February 3, 2006). However, a sample of 20 economists taken Thursday afternoon provided a sample mean of 266,000 with a sample standard deviation of 24,000. Financial analysts often call such a sample mean, based on late-breaking news, the *whisper number*. Treat the "consensus estimate" as the population mean. Conduct a hypothesis test to determine whether the whisper number justifies a conclusion of a statistically significant increase in the consensus estimate of economists. Use $\alpha = .01$ as the level of significance.

WEB file
FirstBirth

64. Data released by the National Center for Health Statistics showed that the mean age at which women had their first child was 25.0 in 2006 (*The Wall Street Journal,* February 4, 2009). The reporter, Sue Shellenbarger, noted that this was the first decrease in the average age at which women had their first child in several years. A recent sample of 42 women provided the data in the website file named FirstBirth concerning the age at which these women had their first child. Do the data indicate a change from 2006 in the mean age at which women had their first child? Use $\alpha = .05$.

WEB file
WeeklyPay

65. A recent issue of the *AARP Bulletin* reported that the average weekly pay for a woman with a high school school degree is \$520 (*AARP Bulletin*, January–February, 2010). Suppose you would like to determine if the average weekly pay for all working women is significantly greater than that for women with a high school degree. Data providing the weekly pay for a sample of 50 working women are available in the file named WeeklyPay. These data are consistent with the findings reported in the AARP article.
   a. State the hypotheses that should be used to test whether the mean weekly pay for all women is significantly greater than the mean weekly pay for women with a high school degree.
   b. Use the data in the file named WeeklyPay to compute the sample mean, the test statistic, and the p-value.
   c. Use $\alpha = .05$. What is your conclusion?
   d. Repeat the hypothesis test using the critical value approach.

66. The chamber of commerce of a Florida Gulf Coast community advertises that area residential property is available at a mean cost of \$125,000 or less per lot. Suppose a sample of 32 properties provided a sample mean of \$130,000 per lot and a sample standard deviation of \$12,500. Use a .05 level of significance to test the validity of the advertising claim.

67. In Hamilton County, Ohio, the mean number of days needed to sell a house is 86 days (Cincinnati Multiple Listing Service, April, 2012). Data for the sale of 40 houses in a nearby county showed a sample mean of 80 days with a sample standard deviation of 20 days. Conduct a hypothesis test to determine whether the mean number of days until a house is sold is different than the Hamilton County mean of 86 days in the nearby county. Use $\alpha = .05$ for the level of significance, and state your conclusion.

68. On December 25, 2009, an airline passenger was subdued while attempting to blow up a Northwest Airlines flight headed for Detroit, Michigan. The passenger had smuggled explosives hidden in his underwear past a metal detector at an airport screening facility. As a result, the Transportation Security Administration (TSA) proposed installing full-body scanners to replace the metal detectors at the nation's largest airports. This proposal resulted in strong objections from privacy advocates who considered the scanners an invasion of privacy.

On January 5–6, 2010, *USA Today* conducted a poll of 542 adults to learn what proportion of airline travelers approved of using full-body scanners (*USA Today,* January 11, 2010). The poll results showed that 455 of the respondents felt that full-body scanners would improve airline security and 423 indicated that they approved of using the devices.

a. Conduct a hypothesis test to determine if the results of the poll justify concluding that over 80% of airline travelers feel that the use of full-body scanners will improve airline security. Use $\alpha = .05$.
b. Suppose the TSA will go forward with the installation and mandatory use of full-body scanners if over 75% of airline travelers approve of using the devices. You have been told to conduct a statistical analysis using the poll results to determine if the TSA should require mandatory use of the full-body scanners. Because this is viewed as a very sensitive decision, use $\alpha = .01$. What is your recommendation?

69. An airline promotion to business travelers is based on the assumption that two-thirds of business travelers use a laptop computer on overnight business trips.
    a. State the hypotheses that can be used to test the assumption.
    b. What is the sample proportion from an American Express sponsored survey that found 355 of 546 business travelers use a laptop computer on overnight business trips?
    c. What is the p-value?
    d. Use $\alpha = .05$. What is your conclusion?

70. Virtual call centers are staffed by individuals working out of their homes. Most home agents earn \$10 to \$15 per hour without benefits versus \$7 to \$9 per hour with benefits at a traditional call center (*BusinessWeek,* January 23, 2006). Regional Airways is considering employing home agents, but only if a level of customer satisfaction greater than 80% can be maintained. A test was conducted with home service agents. In a sample of 300 customers, 252 reported that they were satisfied with service.
    a. Develop hypotheses for a test to determine whether the sample data support the conclusion that customer service with home agents meets the Regional Airways criterion.
    b. What is your point estimate of the percentage of satisfied customers?
    c. What is the p-value provided by the sample data?
    d. What is your hypothesis testing conclusion? Use $\alpha = .05$ as the level of significance.

71. During the 2004 election year, new polling results were reported daily. In an IBD/TIPP poll of 910 adults, 503 respondents reported that they were optimistic about the national outlook, and President Bush's leadership index jumped 4.7 points to 55.3 (*Investor's Business Daily,* January 14, 2004).
    a. What is the sample proportion of respondents who are optimistic about the national outlook?
    b. A campaign manager wants to claim that this poll indicates that the majority of adults are optimistic about the national outlook. Construct a hypothesis test so that rejection of the null hypothesis will permit the conclusion that the proportion optimistic is greater than 50%.
    c. Use the polling data to compute the p-value for the hypothesis test in part (b). Explain to the manager what this p-value means about the level of significance of the results.

72. A radio station in Myrtle Beach announced that at least 90% of the hotels and motels would be full for the Memorial Day weekend. The station advised listeners to make reservations in advance if they planned to be in the resort over the weekend. On Saturday night a sample of 58 hotels and motels showed 49 with a no-vacancy sign and 9 with vacancies. What is your reaction to the radio station's claim after seeing the sample evidence? Use $\alpha = .05$ in making the statistical test. What is the p-value?

73. According to the federal government, 24% of workers covered by their company's health care plan were not required to contribute to the premium (*Statistical Abstract of the United*

States: 2006). A recent study found that 81 out of 400 workers sampled were not required to contribute to their company's health care plan.

a. Develop hypotheses that can be used to test whether the percent of workers not required to contribute to their company's health care plan has declined.
b. What is a point estimate of the proportion receiving free company-sponsored health care insurance?
c. Has a statistically significant decline occurred in the proportion of workers receiving free company-sponsored health care insurance? Use $\alpha = .05$.

74. Shorney Construction Company bids on projects assuming that the mean idle time per worker is 72 or fewer minutes per day. A sample of 30 construction workers will be used to test this assumption. Assume that the population standard deviation is 20 minutes.
    a. State the hypotheses to be tested.
    b. What is the probability of making a Type II error when the population mean idle time is 80 minutes?
    c. What is the probability of making a Type II error when the population mean idle time is 75 minutes?
    d. What is the probability of making a Type II error when the population mean idle time is 70 minutes?
    e. Sketch the power curve for this problem.
75. A federal funding program is available to low-income neighborhoods. To qualify for the funding, a neighborhood must have a mean household income of less than \$15,000 per year. Neighborhoods with mean annual household income of \$15,000 or more do not qualify. Funding decisions are based on a sample of residents in the neighborhood. A hypothesis test with a .02 level of significance is conducted. If the funding guidelines call for a maximum probability of .05 of not funding a neighborhood with a mean annual household income of \$14,000, what sample size should be used in the funding decision study? Use $\sigma = \$4000$ as a planning value.
76. H_0: $\mu = 120$ and H_a: $\mu \neq 120$ are used to test whether a bath soap production process is meeting the standard output of 120 bars per batch. Use a .05 level of significance for the test and a planning value of 5 for the standard deviation.
    a. If the mean output drops to 117 bars per batch, the firm wants to have a 98% chance of concluding that the standard production output is not being met. How large a sample should be selected?
    b. With your sample size from part (a), what is the probability of concluding that the process is operating satisfactorily for each of the following actual mean outputs: 117, 118, 119, 121, 122, and 123 bars per batch? That is, what is the probability of a Type II error in each case?

Case Problem 1 Quality Associates, Inc.

Quality Associates, Inc., a consulting firm, advises its clients about sampling and statistical procedures that can be used to control their manufacturing processes. In one particular application, a client gave Quality Associates a sample of 800 observations taken during a time in which that client's process was operating satisfactorily. The sample standard deviation for these data was .21; hence, with so much data, the population standard deviation was assumed to be .21. Quality Associates then suggested that random samples of size 30 be taken periodically to monitor the process on an ongoing basis. By analyzing the new samples, the client could quickly learn whether the process was operating satisfactorily. When the process was not operating satisfactorily, corrective action could be taken to eliminate the problem. The design specification indicated the mean for the process should be 12. The hypothesis test suggested by Quality Associates follows.

$$H_0: \mu = 12$$
$$H_a: \mu \neq 12$$

Corrective action will be taken any time H_0 is rejected.

The following samples were collected at hourly intervals during the first day of operation of the new statistical process control procedure. These data are available in the data set Quality.

WEB file

Quality

Sample 1	Sample 2	Sample 3	Sample 4
11.55	11.62	11.91	12.02
11.62	11.69	11.36	12.02
11.52	11.59	11.75	12.05
11.75	11.82	11.95	12.18
11.90	11.97	12.14	12.11
11.64	11.71	11.72	12.07
11.80	11.87	11.61	12.05
12.03	12.10	11.85	11.64
11.94	12.01	12.16	12.39
11.92	11.99	11.91	11.65
12.13	12.20	12.12	12.11
12.09	12.16	11.61	11.90
11.93	12.00	12.21	12.22
12.21	12.28	11.56	11.88
12.32	12.39	11.95	12.03
11.93	12.00	12.01	12.35
11.85	11.92	12.06	12.09
11.76	11.83	11.76	11.77
12.16	12.23	11.82	12.20
11.77	11.84	12.12	11.79
12.00	12.07	11.60	12.30
12.04	12.11	11.95	12.27
11.98	12.05	11.96	12.29
12.30	12.37	12.22	12.47
12.18	12.25	11.75	12.03
11.97	12.04	11.96	12.17
12.17	12.24	11.95	11.94
11.85	11.92	11.89	11.97
12.30	12.37	11.88	12.23
12.15	12.22	11.93	12.25

Managerial Report

1. Conduct a hypothesis test for each sample at the .01 level of significance and determine what action, if any, should be taken. Provide the test statistic and p-value for each test.
2. Compute the standard deviation for each of the four samples. Does the assumption of .21 for the population standard deviation appear reasonable?
3. Compute limits for the sample mean $\bar{x}$ around $\mu = 12$ such that, as long as a new sample mean is within those limits, the process will be considered to be operating satisfactorily. If $\bar{x}$ exceeds the upper limit or if $\bar{x}$ is below the lower limit, corrective action will be taken. These limits are referred to as upper and lower control limits for quality control purposes.
4. Discuss the implications of changing the level of significance to a larger value. What mistake or error could increase if the level of significance is increased?

Case Problem 2 Ethical Behavior of Business Students at Bayview University

During the global recession of 2008 and 2009, there were many accusations of unethical behavior by Wall Street executives, financial managers, and other corporate officers. At that time, an article appeared that suggested that part of the reason for such unethical business behavior may stem from the fact that cheating has become more prevalent among business students (*Chronicle of Higher Education*, February 10, 2009). The article reported that 56 percent of business students admitted to cheating at some time during their academic career as compared to 47 percent of nonbusiness students.

Cheating has been a concern of the dean of the College of Business at Bayview University for several years. Some faculty members in the college believe that cheating is more widespread at Bayview than at other universities, while other faculty members think that cheating is not a major problem in the college. To resolve some of these issues, the dean commissioned a study to assess the current ethical behavior of business students at Bayview. As part of this study, an anonymous exit survey was administered to a sample of 90 business students from this year's graduating class. Responses to the following questions were used to obtain data regarding three types of cheating.

During your time at Bayview, did you ever present work copied off the Internet as your own?

Yes ________ No ________

During your time at Bayview, did you ever copy answers off another student's exam?

Yes ________ No ________

During your time at Bayview, did you ever collaborate with other students on projects that were supposed to be completed individually?

Yes ________ No ________

Any student who answered Yes to one or more of these questions was considered to have been involved in some type of cheating. A portion of the data collected follows. The complete data set is in the file named Bayview.

WEB file Bayview

Student	Copied from Internet	Copied on Exam	Collaborated on Individual Project	Gender
1	No	No	No	Female
2	No	No	No	Male
3	Yes	No	Yes	Male
4	Yes	Yes	No	Male
5	No	No	Yes	Male
6	Yes	No	No	Female
.	.	.	.	.
.	.	.	.	.
.	.	.	.	.
88	No	No	No	Male
89	No	Yes	Yes	Male
90	No	No	No	Female

Managerial Report

Prepare a report for the dean of the college that summarizes your assessment of the nature of cheating by business students at Bayview University. Be sure to include the following items in your report.

1. Use descriptive statistics to summarize the data and comment on your findings.
2. Develop 95% confidence intervals for the proportion of all students, the proportion of male students, and the proportion of female students who were involved in some type of cheating.
3. Conduct a hypothesis test to determine if the proportion of business students at Bayview University who were involved in some type of cheating is less than that of business students at other institutions as reported by the *Chronicle of Higher Education*.
4. Conduct a hypothesis test to determine if the proportion of business students at Bayview University who were involved in some form of cheating is less than that of nonbusiness students at other institutions as reported by the *Chronicle of Higher Education*.
5. What advice would you give to the dean based upon your analysis of the data?

Appendix 9.1 Hypothesis Testing with Minitab

We describe the use of Minitab to conduct hypothesis tests about a population mean and a population proportion.

Population Mean: σ Known

We illustrate using the MaxFlight golf ball distance example in Section 9.3. The data are in column C1 of a Minitab worksheet. The population standard deviation $\sigma = 12$ is assumed known and the level of significance is $\alpha = .05$. The following steps can be used to test the hypothesis H_0: $\mu = 295$ versus H_a: $\mu \neq 295$.

WEB file
GolfTest

Step 1. Select the **Stat** menu
Step 2. Choose **Basic Statistics**
Step 3. Choose **1-Sample Z**
Step 4. When the 1-Sample Z dialog box appears:
Enter C1 in the **Samples in columns** box
Enter 12 in the **Standard deviation** box
Select **Perform Hypothesis Test**
Enter 295 in the **Hypothesized mean** box
Select **Options**
Step 5. When the 1-Sample Z-Options dialog box appears:
Enter 95 in the **Confidence level** box*
Select **not equal** in the **Alternative** box
Click **OK**
Step 6. Click **OK**

In addition to the hypothesis testing results, Minitab provides a 95% confidence interval for the population mean.

*Minitab provides both hypothesis testing and interval estimation results simultaneously. The user may select any confidence level for the interval estimate of the population mean: 95% confidence is suggested here.

The procedure can be easily modified for a one-tailed hypothesis test by selecting the less than or greater than option in the **Alternative** box in step 5.

Population Mean: σ Unknown

WEB file **AirRating**

The ratings that 60 business travelers gave for Heathrow Airport are entered in column C1 of a Minitab worksheet. The level of significance for the test is $\alpha = .05$, and the population standard deviation σ will be estimated by the sample standard deviation s. The following steps can be used to test the hypothesis H_0: $\mu \leq 7$ against H_a: $\mu > 7$.

Step 1. Select the **Stat** menu
Step 2. Choose **Basic Statistics**
Step 3. Choose **1-Sample t**
Step 4. When the 1-Sample t dialog box appears:
  Enter C1 in the **Samples in columns** box
  Select **Perform Hypothesis Test**
  Enter 7 in the **Hypothesized mean** box
  Select **Options**
Step 5. When the 1-Sample t-Options dialog box appears:
  Enter 95 in the **Confidence level** box
  Select **greater than** in the **Alternative** box
  Click **OK**
Step 6. Click **OK**

The Heathrow Airport rating study involved a greater than alternative hypothesis. The preceding steps can be easily modified for other hypothesis tests by selecting the less than or not equal options in the **Alternative** box in step 5.

Population Proportion

WEB file **WomenGolf**

We illustrate using the Pine Creek golf course example in Section 9.5. The data with responses Female and Male are in column C1 of a Minitab worksheet. Minitab uses an alphabetical ordering of the responses and selects the *second response* for the population proportion of interest. In this example, Minitab uses the alphabetical ordering Female-Male to provide results for the population proportion of Male responses. Because Female is the response of interest, we change Minitab's ordering as follows: Select any cell in the column and use the sequence: Editor > Column > Value Order. Then choose the option of entering a user-specified order. Enter Male-Female in the **Define-an-order** box and click OK. Minitab's 1 Proportion routine will then provide the hypothesis test results for the population proportion of female golfers. We proceed as follows:

Step 1. Select the **Stat** menu
Step 2. Choose **Basic Statistics**
Step 3. Choose **1 Proportion**
Step 4. When the 1 Proportion dialog box appears:
  Enter C1 in the **Samples in Columns** box
  Select **Perform Hypothesis Test**
  Enter .20 in the **Hypothesized proportion** box
  Select **Options**
Step 5. When the 1 Proportion-Options dialog box appears:
  Enter 95 in the **Confidence level** box
  Select greater than in the **Alternative** box
  Select **Use test and interval based on normal distribution**
  Click **OK**
Step 6. Click **OK**

Appendix 9.2 Hypothesis Testing with Excel

Excel does not provide built-in routines for the hypothesis tests presented in this chapter. To handle these situations, we present Excel worksheets that we designed to use as templates for testing hypotheses about a population mean and a population proportion. The worksheets are easy to use and can be modified to handle any sample data. The worksheets are available on the website that accompanies this book.

Population Mean: σ Known

We illustrate using the MaxFlight golf ball distance example in Section 9.3. The data are in column A of an Excel worksheet. The population standard deviation $\sigma = 12$ is assumed known and the level of significance is $\alpha = .05$. The following steps can be used to test the hypothesis H_0: $\mu = 295$ versus H_a: $\mu \neq 295$.

WEB file
Hyp Sigma Known

Refer to Figure 9.11 as we describe the procedure. The worksheet in the background shows the cell formulas used to compute the results shown in the foreground worksheet. The data are entered into cells A2:A51. The following steps are necessary to use the template for this data set.

Step 1. Enter the data range A2:A51 into the =COUNT cell formula in cell D4
Step 2. Enter the data range A2:A51 into the =AVERAGE cell formula in cell D5
Step 3. Enter the population standard deviation $\sigma = 12$ into cell D7
Step 4. Enter the hypothesized value for the population mean 295 into cell D8

The remaining cell formulas automatically provide the standard error, the value of the test statistic z, and three p-values. Because the alternative hypothesis ($\mu_0 \neq 295$) indicates a two-tailed test, the p-value (Two Tail) in cell D15 is used to make the rejection decision. With p-value $= .1255 > \alpha = .05$, the null hypothesis cannot be rejected. The p-values in cells D13 or D14 would be used if the hypotheses involved a one-tailed test.

This template can be used to make hypothesis testing computations for other applications. For instance, to conduct a hypothesis test for a new data set, enter the new sample data into column A of the worksheet. Modify the formulas in cells D4 and D5 to correspond to the new data range. Enter the population standard deviation into cell D7 and the hypothesized value for the population mean into cell D8 to obtain the results. If the new sample data have already been summarized, the new sample data do not have to be entered into the worksheet. In this case, enter the sample size into cell D4, the sample mean into cell D5, the population standard deviation into cell D7, and the hypothesized value for the population mean into cell D8 to obtain the results. The worksheet in Figure 9.11 is available in the file Hyp Sigma Known on the website that accompanies this book.

Population Mean: σ Unknown

We illustrate using the Heathrow Airport rating example in Section 9.4. The data are in column A of an Excel worksheet. The population standard deviation σ is unknown and will be estimated by the sample standard deviation s. The level of significance is $\alpha = .05$. The following steps can be used to test the hypothesis H_0: $\mu \leq 7$ versus H_a: $\mu > 7$.

WEB file
Hyp Sigma Unknown

Refer to Figure 9.12 as we describe the procedure. The background worksheet shows the cell formulas used to compute the results shown in the foreground version of the worksheet. The data are entered into cells A2:A61. The following steps are necessary to use the template for this data set.

Step 1. Enter the data range A2:A61 into the =COUNT cell formula in cell D4
Step 2. Enter the data range A2:A61 into the =AVERAGE cell formula in cell D5
Step 3. Enter the data range A2:A61 into the =STDEV cell formula in cell D6
Step 4. Enter the hypothesized value for the population mean 7 into cell D8

FIGURE 9.11 EXCEL WORKSHEET FOR HYPOTHESIS TESTS ABOUT A POPULATION MEAN WITH σ KNOWN

	A	B	C	D	E
1	**Yards**		**Hypothesis Test about a Population Mean:**		
2	303		**σ Known Case**		
3	282				
4	289		**Sample Size**	=COUNT(A2:A51)	
5	298		**Sample Mean**	=AVERAGE(A2:A51)	
6	283				
7	317		**Population Standard Deviation**	12	
8	297		**Hypothesized Value**	295	
9	308				
10	317		**Standard Error**	=D7/SQRT(D4)	
11	293		**Test Statistic z**	=(D5-D8)/D10	
12	284				
13	290		***p*-value (Lower Tail)**	=NORM.S.DIST(D11,TRUE)	
14	304		***p*-value (Upper Tail)**	=1-D13	
15	290		***p*-value (Two Tail)**	=2*(MIN(D13,D14))	
16	311				
50	301				
51	292				
52					

	A	B	C	D	E
1	**Yards**		**Hypothesis Test about a Population Mean:**		
2	303		**σ Known Case**		
3	282				
4	289		**Sample Size**	50	
5	298		**Sample Mean**	297.6	
6	283				
7	317		**Population Standard Deviation**	12	
8	297		**Hypothesized Value**	295	
9	308				
10	317		**Standard Error**	1.70	
11	293		**Test Statistic z**	1.53	
12	284				
13	290		***p*-value (Lower Tail)**	0.9372	
14	304		***p*-value (Upper Tail)**	0.0628	
15	290		***p*-value (Two Tail)**	0.1255	
16	311				
50	301				
51	292				
52					

Note: Rows 17 to 49 are hidden.

The remaining cell formulas automatically provide the standard error, the value of the test statistic t, the number of degrees of freedom, and three p-values. Because the alternative hypothesis ($\mu > 7$) indicates an upper tail test, the p-value (Upper Tail) in cell D15 is used to make the decision. With p-value $= .0353 < \alpha = .05$, the null hypothesis is rejected. The p-values in cells D14 or D16 would be used if the hypotheses involved a lower tail test or a two-tailed test.

This template can be used to make hypothesis testing computations for other applications. For instance, to conduct a hypothesis test for a new data set, enter the new sample data into column A of the worksheet and modify the formulas in cells D4, D5, and D6 to

FIGURE 9.12 EXCEL WORKSHEET FOR HYPOTHESIS TESTS ABOUT A POPULATION MEAN WITH σ UNKNOWN

	A	B	C	D	E
1	**Rating**		**Hypothesis Test About a Population Mean**		
2	5		**With σ Unknown**		
3	7				
4	8		**Sample Size**	=COUNT(A2:A61)	
5	7		**Sample Mean**	=AVERAGE(A2:A61)	
6	8		**Sample Std. Deviation**	=STDEV(A2:A61)	
7	8				
8	8		**Hypothesized Value**	7	
9	7				
10	8		**Standard Error**	=D6/SQRT(D4)	
11	10		**Test Statistic *t***	=(D5-D8)/D10	
12	6		**Degrees of Freedom**	=D4-1	
13	7				
14	8		***p*-value (Lower Tail)**	=T.DIST(D11,D12,TRUE)	
15	8		***p*-value (Upper Tail)**	=1-D14	
16	9		***p*-value (Two Tail)**	=2*(MIN(D14,D15))	
17	7				
59	7				
60	7				
61	8				
62					

	A	B	C	D	E	F
1	**Rating**		**Hypothesis Test About a Population Mean**			
2	5		**With σ Unknown**			
3	7					
4	8		**Sample Size**	60		
5	7		**Sample Mean**	7.25		
6	8		**Sample Std. Deviation**	1.05		
7	8					
8	8		**Hypothesized Value**	7		
9	7					
10	8		**Standard Error**	0.136		
11	10		**Test Statistic *t***	1.841		
12	6		**Degrees of Freedom**	59		
13	7					
14	8		***p*-value (Lower Tail)**	0.9647		
15	8		***p*-value (Upper Tail)**	0.0353		
16	9		***p*-value (Two Tail)**	0.0706		
17	7					
59	7					
60	7					
61	8					
62						

Note: Rows 18 to 58 are hidden.

correspond to the new data range. Enter the hypothesized value for the population mean into cell D8 to obtain the results. If the new sample data have already been summarized, the new sample data do not have to be entered into the worksheet. In this case, enter the sample size into cell D4, the sample mean into cell D5, the sample standard deviation into cell D6, and the hypothesized value for the population mean into cell D8 to obtain the results. The worksheet in Figure 9.12 is available in the file Hyp Sigma Unknown on the website that accompanies this book.

FIGURE 9.13 EXCEL WORKSHEET FOR HYPOTHESIS TESTS ABOUT A POPULATION PROPORTION

	A	B	C	D	E
1	Golfer		**Hypothesis Test about a Population Proportion**		
2	Female				
3	Male		**Sample Size**	=COUNTA(A2:A401)	
4	Female		**Response of Interest**	Female	
5	Male		**Count for Response**	=COUNTIF(A2:A903,D4)	
6	Male		**Sample Proportion**	=D5/D3	
7	Female				
8	Male		**Hypothesized Value**	0.2	
9	Male				
10	Female		**Standard Error**	=SQRT(D8*(1-D8)/D3)	
11	Male		**Test Statistic *z***	=(D6-D8)/D10	
12	Male				
13	Male		***p*-value (Lower Tail)**	=NORM.S.DIST(D11,TRUE)	
14	Male		***p*-value (Upper Tail)**	=1-D13	
15	Male		***p*-value (TwoTail)**	=2*MIN(D13,D14)	
16	Female				
400	Male				
401	Male				
402					

	A	B	C	D	E	F
1	Golfer		**Hypothesis Test about a Population Proportion**			
2	Female					
3	Male		**Sample Size**	400		
4	Female		**Response of Interest**	Female		
5	Male		**Count for Response**	100		
6	Male		**Sample Proportion**	0.25		
7	Female					
8	Male		**Hypothesized Value**	0.20		
9	Male					
10	Female		**Standard Error**	0.02		
11	Male		**Test Statistic *z***	2.5000		
12	Male					
13	Male		***p*-value (Lower Tail)**	0.9938		
14	Male		***p*-value (Upper Tail)**	0.0062		
15	Male		***p*-value (TwoTail)**	0.0124		
16	Female					
400	Male					
401	Male					
402						

Note: Rows 17 to 399 are hidden.

Population Proportion

WEB file
Hypothesis p

We illustrate using the Pine Creek golf course survey data presented in Section 9.5. The data of Male or Female golfer are in column A of an Excel worksheet. Refer to Figure 9.13 as we describe the procedure. The background worksheet shows the cell formulas used to compute the results shown in the foreground worksheet. The data are entered into cells A2:A401. The following steps can be used to test the hypothesis H_0: $p \leq .20$ versus H_a: $p > .20$.

Step 1. Enter the data range A2:A401 into the =COUNTA cell formula in cell D3
Step 2. Enter Female as the response of interest in cell D4
Step 3. Enter the data range A2:A401 into the =COUNTIF cell formula in cell D5
Step 4. Enter the hypothesized value for the population proportion .20 into cell D8

The remaining cell formulas automatically provide the standard error, the value of the test statistic z, and three p-values. Because the alternative hypothesis ($p > .20$) indicates an upper tail test, the p-value (Upper Tail) in cell D14 is used to make the decision. With p-value $= .0062 < \alpha = .05$, the null hypothesis is rejected. The p-values in cells D13 or D15 would be used if the hypothesis involved a lower tail test or a two-tailed test.

This template can be used to make hypothesis testing computations for other applications. For instance, to conduct a hypothesis test for a new data set, enter the new sample data into column A of the worksheet. Modify the formulas in cells D3 and D5 to correspond to the new data range. Enter the response of interest into cell D4 and the hypothesized value for the population proportion into cell D8 to obtain the results. If the new sample data have already been summarized, the new sample data do not have to be entered into the worksheet. In this case, enter the sample size into cell D3, the sample proportion into cell D6, and the hypothesized value for the population proportion into cell D8 to obtain the results. The worksheet in Figure 9.13 is available in the file Hypothesis p on the website that accompanies this book.

Appendix 9.3 Hypothesis Testing with StatTools

In this appendix we show how StatTools can be used to conduct hypothesis tests about a population mean for the σ unknown case

Population Mean: σ Unknown Case

WEB file
AirRating

In this case the population standard deviation σ will be estimated by the sample standard deviation s. We use the example discussed in Section 9.4 involving ratings that 60 business travelers gave for Heathrow Airport.

Begin by using the Data Set Manager to create a StatTools data set for these data using the procedure described in the appendix in Chapter 1. The following steps can be used to test the hypothesis H_0: $\mu \leq 7$ against H_a: $\mu > 7$.

Step 1. Click the **StatTools** tab on the Ribbon
Step 2. In the **Analyses** group, click **Statistical Inference**
Step 3. Choose the **Hypothesis Test** option
Step 4. Choose Mean/Std. Deviation
Step 5. When the StatTools-Hypothesis Test for Mean/Std. Deviation dialog box appears:
For **Analysis Type,** choose **One-Sample Analysis**
In the **Variables** section, select **Rating**
In the **Hypothesis Tests to Perform** section:
Select the **Mean** option
Enter 7 in the **Null Hypothesis Value** box
Select **Greater Than Null Value (One-Tailed Test)** in the **Alternative Hypothesis Type** box
If selected, remove the check in the **Standard Deviation** box
Click **OK**

The results from the hypothesis test will appear. They include the p-value and the value of the test statistic.

Population Proportion

We illustrate using the Pine Creek golf course example in Section 9.5. Begin by using the Data Set Manager to create a StatTools data set for these data using the procedure described in the appendix to Chapter 1. The following steps can be used to conduct a hypothesis test of the population proportion.

WEB file

WomenGolf

Step 1. Click the **StatTools** tab on the Ribbon
Step 2. In the **Analyses** group, click **Statistical Inference**
Step 3. Choose **Hypothesis Test**
Step 4. Choose **Proportion**
Step 5. When the StatTools-Hypothesis Test for Proportion dialog box appears:
  For **Analysis Type** choose **One-Sample Analysis**
  In the **Variables** section, select **Golfer**
  In the **Categories to Analyze** section, select **Female**
  In the **Hypotheses About Proportion** section:
    Enter .20 in the **Null Hypothesis Value** box
    In the **Alternaive Hypothesis Type** box, choose **Greater Than Null Value (One-Tailed Test)**
 Click **OK**

The results from the hypothesis test will appear. They include the *p*-value and the value of the test statistic.

CHAPTER 10

Inference About Means and Proportions with Two Populations

CONTENTS

STATISTICS *in* PRACTICE

U.S. FOOD AND DRUG ADMINISTRATION
WASHINGTON, D.C.

It is the responsibility of the U.S. Food and Drug Administration (FDA), through its Center for Drug Evaluation and Research (CDER), to ensure that drugs are safe and effective. But CDER does not do the actual testing of new drugs itself. It is the responsibility of the company seeking to market a new drug to test it and submit evidence that it is safe and effective. CDER statisticians and scientists then review the evidence submitted.

Companies seeking approval of a new drug conduct extensive statistical studies to support their application. The testing process in the pharmaceutical industry usually consists of three stages: (1) preclinical testing, (2) testing for long-term usage and safety, and (3) clinical efficacy testing. At each successive stage, the chance that a drug will pass the rigorous tests decreases; however, the cost of further testing increases dramatically. Industry surveys indicate that on average the research and development for one new drug costs $250 million and takes 12 years. Hence, it is important to eliminate unsuccessful new drugs in the early stages of the testing process, as well as to identify promising ones for further testing.

Statistics plays a major role in pharmaceutical research, where government regulations are stringent and rigorously enforced. In preclinical testing, a two- or three-population statistical study typically is used to determine whether a new drug should continue to be studied in the long-term usage and safety program. The populations may consist of the new drug, a control, and a standard drug. The preclinical testing process begins when a new drug is sent to the pharmacology group for evaluation of efficacy—the capacity of the drug to produce the desired effects. As part of the process, a statistician is asked to design an experiment that can be used to test the new drug. The design must specify the sample size and the statistical methods of analysis. In a two-population study, one sample is used to obtain data on the efficacy of the new drug (population 1) and a second sample is used to obtain data on the efficacy of a standard drug (population 2). Depending on the intended use, the new and standard drugs are tested in such disciplines as neurology, cardiology, and immunology. In most studies, the statistical method involves hypothesis testing for the difference between the means of the new drug population and the standard drug population. If a new drug lacks efficacy or produces undesirable effects in comparison with the standard drug, the new drug is rejected and withdrawn from further testing. Only new drugs that show promising comparisons with the standard drugs are forwarded to the long-term usage and safety testing program.

Statistical methods are used to test and develop new drugs. © Lisa S./Shutterstock.com.

Further data collection and multipopulation studies are conducted in the long-term usage and safety testing program and in the clinical testing programs. The FDA requires that statistical methods be defined prior to such testing to avoid data-related biases. In addition, to avoid human biases, some of the clinical trials are double or triple blind. That is, neither the subject nor the investigator knows what drug is administered to whom. If the new drug meets all requirements in relation to the standard drug, a new drug application (NDA) is filed with the FDA. The application is rigorously scrutinized by statisticians and scientists at the agency.

In this chapter you will learn how to construct interval estimates and make hypothesis tests about means and proportions with two populations. Techniques will be presented for analyzing independent random samples as well as matched samples.

In Chapters 8 and 9 we showed how to develop interval estimates and conduct hypothesis tests for situations involving a single population mean and a single population proportion. In this chapter we continue our discussion of statistical inference by showing how interval estimates and hypothesis tests can be developed for situations involving two populations when the difference between the two population means or the two population proportions is of prime importance. For example, we may want to develop an interval estimate of the difference between the mean starting salary for a population of men and the mean starting salary for a population of women or conduct a hypothesis test to determine whether any difference is present between the proportion of defective parts in a population of parts produced by supplier A and the proportion of defective parts in a population of parts produced by supplier B. We begin our discussion of statistical inference about two populations by showing how to develop interval estimates and conduct hypothesis tests about the difference between the means of two populations when the standard deviations of the two populations are assumed known.

10.1 Inferences About the Difference Between Two Population Means: σ_1 and σ_2 Known

Letting μ_1 denote the mean of population 1 and μ_2 denote the mean of population 2, we will focus on inferences about the difference between the means: $\mu_1 - \mu_2$. To make an inference about this difference, we select a simple random sample of n_1 units from population 1 and a second simple random sample of n_2 units from population 2. The two samples, taken separately and independently, are referred to as **independent simple random samples**. In this section, we assume that information is available such that the two population standard deviations, σ_1 and σ_2, can be assumed known prior to collecting the samples. We refer to this situation as the σ_1 and σ_2 known case. In the following example we show how to compute a margin of error and develop an interval estimate of the difference between the two population means when σ_1 and σ_2 are known.

Interval Estimation of $\mu_1 - \mu_2$

Greystone Department Stores, Inc., operates two stores in Buffalo, New York: One is in the inner city and the other is in a suburban shopping center. The regional manager noticed that products that sell well in one store do not always sell well in the other. The manager believes this situation may be attributable to differences in customer demographics at the two locations. Customers may differ in age, education, income, and so on. Suppose the manager asks us to investigate the difference between the mean ages of the customers who shop at the two stores.

Let us define population 1 as all customers who shop at the inner-city store and population 2 as all customers who shop at the suburban store.

μ_1 = mean of population 1 (i.e., the mean age of all customers who shop at the inner-city store)

μ_2 = mean of population 2 (i.e., the mean age of all customers who shop at the suburban store)

The difference between the two population means is $\mu_1 - \mu_2$.

To estimate $\mu_1 - \mu_2$, we will select a simple random sample of n_1 customers from population 1 and a simple random sample of n_2 customers from population 2. We then compute the two sample means.

$\bar{x}_1$ = sample mean age for the simple random sample of n_1 inner-city customers

$\bar{x}_2$ = sample mean age for the simple random sample of n_2 suburban customers

The point estimator of the difference between the two population means is the difference between the two sample means.

POINT ESTIMATOR OF THE DIFFERENCE BETWEEN TWO POPULATION MEANS

$$\bar{x}_1 - \bar{x}_2 \tag{10.1}$$

Figure 10.1 provides an overview of the process used to estimate the difference between two population means based on two independent simple random samples.

The standard error of $\bar{x}_1 - \bar{x}_2$ is the standard deviation of the sampling distribution of $\bar{x}_1 - \bar{x}_2$.

As with other point estimators, the point estimator $\bar{x}_1 - \bar{x}_2$ has a standard error that describes the variation in the sampling distribution of the estimator. With two independent simple random samples, the standard error of $\bar{x}_1 - \bar{x}_2$ is as follows:

STANDARD ERROR OF $\bar{x}_1 - \bar{x}_2$

$$\sigma_{\bar{x}_1 - \bar{x}_2} = \sqrt{\frac{\sigma_1^2}{n_1} + \frac{\sigma_2^2}{n_2}} \tag{10.2}$$

If both populations have a normal distribution, or if the sample sizes are large enough that the central limit theorem enables us to conclude that the sampling distributions of $\bar{x}_1$ and $\bar{x}_2$ can be approximated by a normal distribution, the sampling distribution of $\bar{x}_1 - \bar{x}_2$ will have a normal distribution with mean given by $\mu_1 - \mu_2$.

As we showed in Chapter 8, an interval estimate is given by a point estimate ± a margin of error. In the case of estimation of the difference between two population means, an interval estimate will take the following form:

$$\bar{x}_1 - \bar{x}_2 \pm \text{Margin of error}$$

FIGURE 10.1 ESTIMATING THE DIFFERENCE BETWEEN TWO POPULATION MEANS

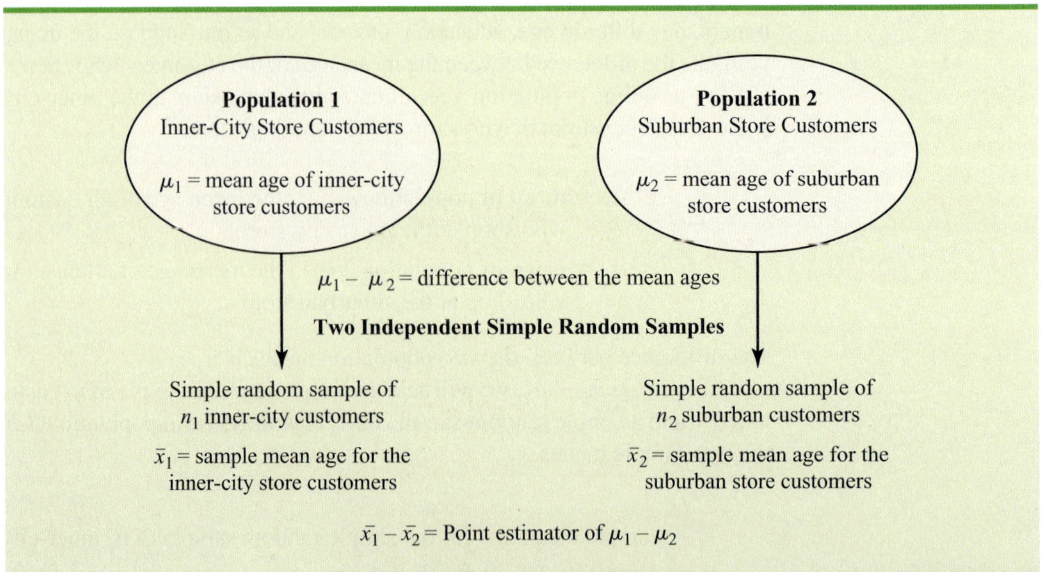

With the sampling distribution of $\bar{x}_1 - \bar{x}_2$ having a normal distribution, we can write the margin of error as follows:

The margin of error is given by multiplying the standard error by $z_{\alpha/2}$.

$$\text{Margin of error} = z_{\alpha/2}\sigma_{\bar{x}_1-\bar{x}_2} = z_{\alpha/2}\sqrt{\frac{\sigma_1^2}{n_1} + \frac{\sigma_2^2}{n_2}} \tag{10.3}$$

Thus the interval estimate of the difference between two population means is as follows:

INTERVAL ESTIMATE OF THE DIFFERENCE BETWEEN TWO POPULATION MEANS: σ_1 AND σ_2 KNOWN

$$\bar{x}_1 - \bar{x}_2 \pm z_{\alpha/2}\sqrt{\frac{\sigma_1^2}{n_1} + \frac{\sigma_2^2}{n_2}} \tag{10.4}$$

where $1 - \alpha$ is the confidence coefficient.

Let us return to the Greystone example. Based on data from previous customer demographic studies, the two population standard deviations are known with $\sigma_1 = 9$ years and $\sigma_2 = 10$ years. The data collected from the two independent simple random samples of Greystone customers provided the following results.

	Inner City Store	Suburban Store
Sample Size	$n_1 = 36$	$n_2 = 49$
Sample Mean	$\bar{x}_1 = 40$ years	$\bar{x}_2 = 35$ years

Using expression (10.1), we find that the point estimate of the difference between the mean ages of the two populations is $\bar{x}_1 - \bar{x}_2 = 40 - 35 = 5$ years. Thus, we estimate that the customers at the inner-city store have a mean age five years greater than the mean age of the suburban store customers. We can now use expression (10.4) to compute the margin of error and provide the interval estimate of $\mu_1 - \mu_2$. Using 95% confidence and $z_{\alpha/2} = z_{.025} = 1.96$, we have

$$\bar{x}_1 - \bar{x}_2 \pm z_{\alpha/2}\sqrt{\frac{\sigma_1^2}{n_1} + \frac{\sigma_2^2}{n_2}}$$

$$40 - 35 \pm 1.96\sqrt{\frac{9^2}{36} + \frac{10^2}{49}}$$

$$5 \pm 4.06$$

Thus, the margin of error is 4.06 years and the 95% confidence interval estimate of the difference between the two population means is $5 - 4.06 = .94$ years to $5 + 4.06 = 9.06$ years.

Hypothesis Tests About $\mu_1 - \mu_2$

Let us consider hypothesis tests about the difference between two population means. Using D_0 to denote the hypothesized difference between μ_1 and μ_2, the three forms for a hypothesis test are as follows:

$$H_0: \mu_1 - \mu_2 \geq D_0 \qquad H_0: \mu_1 - \mu_2 \leq D_0 \qquad H_0: \mu_1 - \mu_2 = D_0$$
$$H_a: \mu_1 - \mu_2 < D_0 \qquad H_a: \mu_1 - \mu_2 > D_0 \qquad H_a: \mu_1 - \mu_2 \neq D_0$$

In many applications, $D_0 = 0$. Using the two-tailed test as an example, when $D_0 = 0$ the null hypothesis is H_0: $\mu_1 - \mu_2 = 0$. In this case, the null hypothesis is that μ_1 and μ_2 are equal. Rejection of H_0 leads to the conclusion that H_a: $\mu_1 - \mu_2 \neq 0$ is true; that is, μ_1 and μ_2 are not equal.

The steps for conducting hypothesis tests presented in Chapter 9 are applicable here. We must choose a level of significance, compute the value of the test statistic and find the p-value to determine whether the null hypothesis should be rejected. With two independent simple random samples, we showed that the point estimator $\bar{x}_1 - \bar{x}_2$ has a standard error $\sigma_{\bar{x}_1 - \bar{x}_2}$ given by expression (10.2) and, when the sample sizes are large enough, the distribution of $\bar{x}_1 - \bar{x}_2$ can be described by a normal distribution. In this case, the test statistic for the difference between two population means when σ_1 and σ_2 are known is as follows.

TEST STATISTIC FOR HYPOTHESIS TESTS ABOUT $\mu_1 - \mu_2$: σ_1 AND σ_2 KNOWN

$$z = \frac{(\bar{x}_1 - \bar{x}_2) - D_0}{\sqrt{\dfrac{\sigma_1^2}{n_1} + \dfrac{\sigma_2^2}{n_2}}} \tag{10.5}$$

Let us demonstrate the use of this test statistic in the following hypothesis testing example.

As part of a study to evaluate differences in education quality between two training centers, a standardized examination is given to individuals who are trained at the centers. The difference between the mean examination scores is used to assess quality differences between the centers. The population means for the two centers are as follows.

μ_1 = the mean examination score for the population of individuals trained at center A

μ_2 = the mean examination score for the population of individuals trained at center B

We begin with the tentative assumption that no difference exists between the training quality provided at the two centers. Hence, in terms of the mean examination scores, the null hypothesis is that $\mu_1 - \mu_2 = 0$. If sample evidence leads to the rejection of this hypothesis, we will conclude that the mean examination scores differ for the two populations. This conclusion indicates a quality differential between the two centers and suggests that a follow-up study investigating the reason for the differential may be warranted. The null and alternative hypotheses for this two-tailed test are written as follows.

$$H_0: \mu_1 - \mu_2 = 0$$
$$H_a: \mu_1 - \mu_2 \neq 0$$

The standardized examination given previously in a variety of settings always resulted in an examination score standard deviation near 10 points. Thus, we will use this information to assume that the population standard deviations are known with $\sigma_1 = 10$ and $\sigma_2 = 10$. An $\alpha = .05$ level of significance is specified for the study.

WEB file ExamScores

Independent simple random samples of $n_1 = 30$ individuals from training center A and $n_2 = 40$ individuals from training center B are taken. The respective sample means are $\bar{x}_1 = 82$ and $\bar{x}_2 = 78$. Do these data suggest a significant difference between the population means at the two training centers? To help answer this question, we compute the test statistic using equation (10.5).

$$z = \frac{(\bar{x}_1 - \bar{x}_2) - D_0}{\sqrt{\frac{\sigma_1^2}{n_1} + \frac{\sigma_2^2}{n_2}}} = \frac{(82 - 78) - 0}{\sqrt{\frac{10^2}{30} + \frac{10^2}{40}}} = 1.66$$

Next let us compute the p-value for this two-tailed test. Because the test statistic z is in the upper tail, we first compute the area under the curve to the right of $z = 1.66$. Using the standard normal distribution table, the area to the left of $z = 1.66$ is .9515. Thus, the area in the upper tail of the distribution is $1.0000 - .9515 = .0485$. Because this test is a two-tailed test, we must double the tail area: p-value $= 2(.0485) = .0970$. Following the usual rule to reject H_0 if p-value $\leq \alpha$, we see that the p-value of .0970 does not allow us to reject H_0 at the .05 level of significance. The sample results do not provide sufficient evidence to conclude the training centers differ in quality.

In this chapter we will use the p-value approach to hypothesis testing as described in Chapter 9. However, if you prefer, the test statistic and the critical value rejection rule may be used. With $\alpha = .05$ and $z_{\alpha/2} = z_{.025} = 1.96$, the rejection rule employing the critical value approach would be reject H_0 if $z \leq -1.96$ or if $z \geq 1.96$. With $z = 1.66$, we reach the same do not reject H_0 conclusion.

In the preceding example, we demonstrated a two-tailed hypothesis test about the difference between two population means. Lower tail and upper tail tests can also be considered. These tests use the same test statistic as given in equation (10.5). The procedure for computing the p-value and the rejection rules for these one-tailed tests are the same as those presented in Chapter 9.

Practical Advice

In most applications of the interval estimation and hypothesis testing procedures presented in this section, random samples with $n_1 \geq 30$ and $n_2 \geq 30$ are adequate. In cases where either or both sample sizes are less than 30, the distributions of the populations become important considerations. In general, with smaller sample sizes, it is more important for the analyst to be satisfied that it is reasonable to assume that the distributions of the two populations are at least approximately normal.

Exercises

Methods

SELF test

1. The following results come from two independent random samples taken of two populations.

Sample 1	Sample 2
$n_1 = 50$	$n_2 = 35$
$\bar{x}_1 = 13.6$	$\bar{x}_2 = 11.6$
$\sigma_1 = 2.2$	$\sigma_2 = 3.0$

a. What is the point estimate of the difference between the two population means?
b. Provide a 90% confidence interval for the difference between the two population means.
c. Provide a 95% confidence interval for the difference between the two population means.

SELF test

2. Consider the following hypothesis test.

$$H_0: \mu_1 - \mu_2 \leq 0$$
$$H_a: \mu_1 - \mu_2 > 0$$

The following results are for two independent samples taken from the two populations.

Sample 1	Sample 2
$n_1 = 40$	$n_2 = 50$
$\bar{x}_1 = 25.2$	$\bar{x}_2 = 22.8$
$\sigma_1 = 5.2$	$\sigma_2 = 6.0$

a. What is the value of the test statistic?
b. What is the p-value?
c. With $\alpha = .05$, what is your hypothesis testing conclusion?

3. Consider the following hypothesis test.

$$H_0: \mu_1 - \mu_2 = 0$$
$$H_a: \mu_1 - \mu_2 \neq 0$$

The following results are for two independent samples taken from the two populations.

Sample 1	Sample 2
$n_1 = 80$	$n_2 = 70$
$\bar{x}_1 = 104$	$\bar{x}_2 = 106$
$\sigma_1 = 8.4$	$\sigma_2 = 7.6$

a. What is the value of the test statistic?
b. What is the p-value?
c. With $\alpha = .05$, what is your hypothesis testing conclusion?

Applications

SELF test

4. *Condé Nast Traveler* conducts an annual survey in which readers rate their favorite cruise ship. All ships are rated on a 100-point scale, with higher values indicating better service. A sample of 37 ships that carry fewer than 500 passengers resulted in an average rating of 85.36, and a sample of 44 ships that carry 500 or more passengers provided an average rating of 81.40 (*Condé Nast Traveler,* February 2008). Assume that the population standard deviation is 4.55 for ships that carry fewer than 500 passengers and 3.97 for ships that carry 500 or more passengers.
   a. What is the point estimate of the difference between the population mean rating for ships that carry fewer than 500 passengers and the population mean rating for ships that carry 500 or more passengers?
   b. At 95% confidence, what is the margin of error?
   c. What is a 95% confidence interval estimate of the difference between the population mean ratings for the two sizes of ships?
5. The average expenditure on Valentine's Day was expected to be \$100.89 (*USA Today,* February 13, 2006). Do male and female consumers differ in the amounts they spend? The average expenditure in a sample survey of 40 male consumers was \$135.67, and the average expenditure in a sample survey of 30 female consumers was \$68.64. Based on past surveys, the standard deviation for male consumers is assumed to be \$35, and the standard deviation for female consumers is assumed to be \$20.

a. What is the point estimate of the difference between the population mean expenditure for males and the population mean expenditure for females?
b. At 99% confidence, what is the margin of error?
c. Develop a 99% confidence interval for the difference between the two population means.

6. Suppose that you are responsible for making arrangements for a business convention. Because of budget cuts due to the recent recession, you have been charged with choosing a city for the convention that has the least expensive hotel rooms. You have narrowed your choices to Atlanta and Houston. The file named Hotel contains samples of prices for rooms in Atlanta and Houston that are consistent with the results reported by Smith Travel Research (*SmartMoney,* March 2009). Because considerable historical data on the prices of rooms in both cities are available, the population standard deviations for the prices can be assumed to be \$20 in Atlanta and \$25 in Houston. Based on the sample data, can you conclude that the mean price of a hotel room in Atlanta is lower than one in Houston?

WEB file
Hotel

7. *Consumer Reports* uses a survey of readers to obtain customer satisfaction ratings for the nation's largest retailers (*Consumer Reports,* March 2012). Each survey respondent is asked to rate a specified retailer in terms of six factors: quality of products, selection, value, checkout efficiency, service, and store layout. An overall satisfaction score summarizes the rating for each respondent with 100 meaning the respondent is completely satisfied in terms of all six factors. Sample data representative of independent samples of Target and Walmart customers are shown below.

Target	Walmart
$n_1 = 25$	$n_2 = 30$
$\bar{x}_1 = 79$	$\bar{x}_2 = 71$

a. Formulate the null and alternative hypotheses to test whether there is a difference between the population mean customer satisfaction scores for the two retailers.
b. Assume that experience with the *Consumer Reports* satisfaction rating scale indicates that a population standard deviation of 12 is a reasonable assumption for both retailers. Conduct the hypothesis test and report the p-value. At a .05 level of significance what is your conclusion?
c. Which retailer, if either, appears to have the greater customer satisfaction? Provide a 95% confidence interval for the difference between the population mean customer satisfaction scores for the two retailers.

8. Will improving customer service result in higher stock prices for the companies providing the better service? "When a company's satisfaction score has improved over the prior year's results and is above the national average (currently 75.7), studies show its shares have a good chance of outperforming the broad stock market in the long run" (*Businessweek,* March 2, 2009). The following satisfaction scores of three companies for the 4th quarters of 2007 and 2008 were obtained from the American Customer Satisfaction Index. Assume that the scores are based on a poll of 60 customers from each company. Because the polling has been done for several years, the standard deviation can be assumed to equal 6 points in each case.

Company	2007 Score	2008 Score
Rite Aid	73	76
Expedia	75	77
J.C. Penney	77	78

a. For Rite Aid, is the increase in the satisfaction score from 2007 to 2008 statistically significant? Use $\alpha = .05$. What can you conclude?
b. Can you conclude that the 2008 score for Rite Aid is above the national average of 75.7? Use $\alpha = .05$.
c. For Expedia, is the increase from 2007 to 2008 statistically significant? Use $\alpha = .05$.
d. When conducting a hypothesis test with the values given for the standard deviation, sample size, and α, how large must the increase from 2007 to 2008 be for it to be statistically significant?
e. Use the result of part (d) to state whether the increase for J.C. Penney from 2007 to 2008 is statistically significant.

10.2 Inferences About the Difference Between Two Population Means: σ_1 and σ_2 Unknown

In this section we extend the discussion of inferences about the difference between two population means to the case when the two population standard deviations, σ_1 and σ_2, are unknown. In this case, we will use the sample standard deviations, s_1 and s_2, to estimate the unknown population standard deviations. When we use the sample standard deviations, the interval estimation and hypothesis testing procedures will be based on the t distribution rather than the standard normal distribution.

Interval Estimation of $\mu_1 - \mu_2$

In the following example we show how to compute a margin of error and develop an interval estimate of the difference between two population means when σ_1 and σ_2 are unknown. Clearwater National Bank is conducting a study designed to identify differences between checking account practices by customers at two of its branch banks. A simple random sample of 28 checking accounts is selected from the Cherry Grove Branch and an independent simple random sample of 22 checking accounts is selected from the Beechmont Branch. The current checking account balance is recorded for each of the checking accounts. A summary of the account balances follows:

WEB file CheckAcct

	Cherry Grove	Beechmont
Sample Size	$n_1 = 28$	$n_2 = 22$
Sample Mean	$\bar{x}_1 = \$1025$	$\bar{x}_2 = \$910$
Sample Standard Deviation	$s_1 = \$150$	$s_2 = \$125$

Clearwater National Bank would like to estimate the difference between the mean checking account balance maintained by the population of Cherry Grove customers and the population of Beechmont customers. Let us develop the margin of error and an interval estimate of the difference between these two population means.

In Section 10.1, we provided the following interval estimate for the case when the population standard deviations, σ_1 and σ_2, are known.

$$\bar{x}_1 - \bar{x}_2 \pm z_{\alpha/2}\sqrt{\frac{\sigma_1^2}{n_1} + \frac{\sigma_2^2}{n_2}}$$

When σ_1 and σ_2 are estimated by s_1 and s_2, the t distribution is used to make inferences about the difference between two population means.

With σ_1 and σ_2 unknown, we will use the sample standard deviations s_1 and s_2 to estimate σ_1 and σ_2 and replace $z_{\alpha/2}$ with $t_{\alpha/2}$. As a result, the interval estimate of the difference between two population means is given by the following expression:

INTERVAL ESTIMATE OF THE DIFFERENCE BETWEEN TWO POPULATION MEANS: σ_1 AND σ_2 UNKNOWN

$$\bar{x}_1 - \bar{x}_2 \pm t_{\alpha/2}\sqrt{\frac{s_1^2}{n_1} + \frac{s_2^2}{n_2}} \tag{10.6}$$

where $1 - \alpha$ is the confidence coefficient.

In this expression, the use of the t distribution is an approximation, but it provides excellent results and is relatively easy to use. The only difficulty that we encounter in using expression (10.6) is determining the appropriate degrees of freedom for $t_{\alpha/2}$. Statistical software packages compute the appropriate degrees of freedom automatically. The formula used is as follows:

DEGREES OF FREEDOM: t DISTRIBUTION WITH TWO INDEPENDENT RANDOM SAMPLES

$$df = \frac{\left(\dfrac{s_1^2}{n_1} + \dfrac{s_2^2}{n_2}\right)^2}{\dfrac{1}{n_1 - 1}\left(\dfrac{s_1^2}{n_1}\right)^2 + \dfrac{1}{n_2 - 1}\left(\dfrac{s_2^2}{n_2}\right)^2} \tag{10.7}$$

Let us return to the Clearwater National Bank example and show how to use expression (10.6) to provide a 95% confidence interval estimate of the difference between the population mean checking account balances at the two branch banks. The sample data show $n_1 = 28$, $\bar{x}_1 = \$1025$, and $s_1 = \$150$ for the Cherry Grove branch, and $n_2 = 22$, $\bar{x}_2 = \$910$, and $s_2 = \$125$ for the Beechmont branch. The calculation for degrees of freedom for $t_{\alpha/2}$ is as follows:

$$df = \frac{\left(\dfrac{s_1^2}{n_1} + \dfrac{s_2^2}{n_2}\right)^2}{\dfrac{1}{n_1 - 1}\left(\dfrac{s_1^2}{n_1}\right)^2 + \dfrac{1}{n_2 - 1}\left(\dfrac{s_2^2}{n_2}\right)^2} = \frac{\left(\dfrac{150^2}{28} + \dfrac{125^2}{22}\right)^2}{\dfrac{1}{28 - 1}\left(\dfrac{150^2}{28}\right)^2 + \dfrac{1}{22 - 1}\left(\dfrac{125^2}{22}\right)^2} = 47.8$$

We round the noninteger degrees of freedom *down* to 47 to provide a larger t-value and a more conservative interval estimate. Using the t distribution table with 47 degrees of freedom, we find $t_{.025} = 2.012$. Using expression (10.6), we develop the 95% confidence interval estimate of the difference between the two population means as follows.

$$\bar{x}_1 - \bar{x}_2 \pm t_{.025}\sqrt{\frac{s_1^2}{n_1} + \frac{s_2^2}{n_2}}$$

$$1025 - 910 \pm 2.012\sqrt{\frac{150^2}{28} + \frac{125^2}{22}}$$

$$115 \pm 78$$

The point estimate of the difference between the population mean checking account balances at the two branches is \$115. The margin of error is \$78, and the 95% confidence interval estimate of the difference between the two population means is 115 − 78 = \$37 to 115 + 78 = \$193.

This suggestion should help if you are using equation (10.7) to calculate the degrees of freedom by hand.

The computation of the degrees of freedom (equation (10.7)) is cumbersome if you are doing the calculation by hand, but it is easily implemented with a computer software package. However, note that the expressions s_1^2/n_1 and s_2^2/n_2 appear in both expression (10.6) and equation (10.7). These values only need to be computed once in order to evaluate both (10.6) and (10.7).

Hypothesis Tests About $\mu_1 - \mu_2$

Let us now consider hypothesis tests about the difference between the means of two populations when the population standard deviations σ_1 and σ_2 are unknown. Letting D_0 denote the hypothesized difference between μ_1 and μ_2, Section 10.1 showed that the test statistic used for the case where σ_1 and σ_2 are known is as follows.

$$z = \frac{(\bar{x}_1 - \bar{x}_2) - D_0}{\sqrt{\dfrac{\sigma_1^2}{n_1} + \dfrac{\sigma_2^2}{n_2}}}$$

The test statistic, z, follows the standard normal distribution.

When σ_1 and σ_2 are unknown, we use s_1 as an estimator of σ_1 and s_2 as an estimator of σ_2. Substituting these sample standard deviations for σ_1 and σ_2 provides the following test statistic when σ_1 and σ_2 are unknown.

TEST STATISTIC FOR HYPOTHESIS TESTS ABOUT $\mu_1 - \mu_2$: σ_1 AND σ_2 UNKNOWN

$$t = \frac{(\bar{x}_1 - \bar{x}_2) - D_0}{\sqrt{\dfrac{s_1^2}{n_1} + \dfrac{s_2^2}{n_2}}} \qquad \textbf{(10.8)}$$

The degrees of freedom for t are given by equation (10.7).

Let us demonstrate the use of this test statistic in the following hypothesis testing example.

Consider a new computer software package developed to help systems analysts reduce the time required to design, develop, and implement an information system. To evaluate the benefits of the new software package, a random sample of 24 systems analysts is selected. Each analyst is given specifications for a hypothetical information system. Then 12 of the analysts are instructed to produce the information system by using current technology. The other 12 analysts are trained in the use of the new software package and then instructed to use it to produce the information system.

This study involves two populations: a population of systems analysts using the current technology and a population of systems analysts using the new software package. In terms of the time required to complete the information system design project, the population means are as follow.

μ_1 = the mean project completion time for systems analysts using the current technology

μ_2 = the mean project completion time for systems analysts using the new software package

The researcher in charge of the new software evaluation project hopes to show that the new software package will provide a shorter mean project completion time. Thus, the researcher is looking for evidence to conclude that μ_2 is less than μ_1; in this case, the

TABLE 10.1 COMPLETION TIME DATA AND SUMMARY STATISTICS FOR THE SOFTWARE TESTING STUDY

WEB file
SoftwareTest

	Current Technology	**New Software**
	300	274
	280	220
	344	308
	385	336
	372	198
	360	300
	288	315
	321	258
	376	318
	290	310
	301	332
	283	263
Summary Statistics		
Sample size	$n_1 = 12$	$n_2 = 12$
Sample mean	$\bar{x}_1 = 325$ hours	$\bar{x}_2 = 286$ hours
Sample standard deviation	$s_1 = 40$	$s_2 = 44$

difference between the two population means, $\mu_1 - \mu_2$, will be greater than zero. The research hypothesis $\mu_1 - \mu_2 > 0$ is stated as the alternative hypothesis. Thus, the hypothesis test becomes

$$H_0: \mu_1 - \mu_2 \leq 0$$
$$H_a: \mu_1 - \mu_2 > 0$$

We will use $\alpha = .05$ as the level of significance.

Suppose that the 24 analysts complete the study with the results shown in Table 10.1. Using the test statistic in equation (10.8), we have

$$t = \frac{(\bar{x}_1 - \bar{x}_2) - D_0}{\sqrt{\dfrac{s_1^2}{n_1} + \dfrac{s_2^2}{n_2}}} = \frac{(325 - 286) - 0}{\sqrt{\dfrac{40^2}{12} + \dfrac{44^2}{12}}} = 2.27$$

Computing the degrees of freedom using equation (10.7), we have

$$df = \frac{\left(\dfrac{s_1^2}{n_1} + \dfrac{s_2^2}{n_2}\right)^2}{\dfrac{1}{n_1 - 1}\left(\dfrac{s_1^2}{n_1}\right)^2 + \dfrac{1}{n_2 - 1}\left(\dfrac{s_2^2}{n_2}\right)^2} = \frac{\left(\dfrac{40^2}{12} + \dfrac{44^2}{12}\right)^2}{\dfrac{1}{12 - 1}\left(\dfrac{40^2}{12}\right)^2 + \dfrac{1}{12 - 1}\left(\dfrac{44^2}{12}\right)^2} = 21.8$$

Rounding down, we will use a t distribution with 21 degrees of freedom. This row of the t distribution table is as follows:

Area in Upper Tail	**.20**	**.10**	**.05**	**.025**	**.01**	**.005**
***t*-Value (21 *df*)**	0.859	1.323	1.721	2.080	2.518	2.831

$t = 2.27$

FIGURE 10.2 MINITAB OUTPUT FOR THE HYPOTHESIS TEST OF THE CURRENT AND NEW SOFTWARE TECHNOLOGY

```
Two-sample T for Current vs New

          N     Mean    StDev   SE Mean
Current   12    325.0    40.0        12
New       12    286.0    44.0        13

Difference = mu Current - mu New
Estimate for difference:  39.0000
95% lower bound for difference = 9.5
T-Test of difference = 0 (vs >):  T-Value = 2.27  P-Value = 0.017  DF = 21
```

Using the t distribution table, we can only determine a range for the p-value. Use of Excel or Minitab shows the exact p-value = .017.

With an upper tail test, the *p*-value is the area in the upper tail to the right of $t = 2.27$. From the above results, we see that the *p*-value is between .025 and .01. Thus, the *p*-value is less than $\alpha = .05$ and H_0 is rejected. The sample results enable the researcher to conclude that $\mu_1 - \mu_2 > 0$, or $\mu_1 > \mu_2$. Thus, the research study supports the conclusion that the new software package provides a smaller population mean completion time.

Minitab or Excel can be used to analyze data for testing hypotheses about the difference between two population means. The Minitab output comparing the current and new software technology is shown in Figure 10.2. The last line of the output shows $t = 2.27$ and *p*-value $= .017$. Note that Minitab used equation (10.7) to compute 21 degrees of freedom for this analysis.

Practical Advice

Whenever possible, equal sample sizes, $n_1 = n_2$, are recommended.

The interval estimation and hypothesis testing procedures presented in this section are robust and can be used with relatively small sample sizes. In most applications, equal or nearly equal sample sizes such that the total sample size $n_1 + n_2$ is at least 20 can be expected to provide very good results even if the populations are not normal. Larger sample sizes are recommended if the distributions of the populations are highly skewed or contain outliers. Smaller sample sizes should only be used if the analyst is satisfied that the distributions of the populations are at least approximately normal.

NOTES AND COMMENTS

Another approach used to make inferences about the difference between two population means when σ_1 and σ_2 are unknown is based on the assumption that the two population standard deviations are *equal* ($\sigma_1 = \sigma_2 = \sigma$). Under this assumption, the two sample standard deviations are combined to provide the following *pooled sample variance:*

$$s_p^2 = \frac{(n_1 - 1)s_1^2 + (n_2 - 1)s_2^2}{n_1 + n_2 - 2}$$

The *t* test statistic becomes

$$t = \frac{(\bar{x}_1 - \bar{x}_2) - D_0}{s_p\sqrt{\dfrac{1}{n_1} + \dfrac{1}{n_2}}}$$

and has $n_1 + n_2 - 2$ degrees of freedom. At this point, the computation of the *p*-value and the interpretation of the sample results are identical to the procedures discussed earlier in this section.

A difficulty with this procedure is that the assumption that the two population standard deviations are equal is usually difficult to verify. Unequal population standard deviations are frequently encountered. Using the pooled procedure may not provide satisfactory results, especially if the sample sizes n_1 and n_2 are quite different.

The *t* procedure that we presented in this section does not require the assumption of equal population standard deviations and can be applied whether the population standard deviations are equal or not. It is a more general procedure and is recommended for most applications.

Exercises

Methods

SELF test

9. The following results are for independent random samples taken from two populations.

Sample 1	Sample 2
$n_1 = 20$	$n_2 = 30$
$\bar{x}_1 = 22.5$	$\bar{x}_2 = 20.1$
$s_1 = 2.5$	$s_2 = 4.8$

a. What is the point estimate of the difference between the two population means?
b. What is the degrees of freedom for the t distribution?
c. At 95% confidence, what is the margin of error?
d. What is the 95% confidence interval for the difference between the two population means?

SELF test

10. Consider the following hypothesis test.

$$H_0: \mu_1 - \mu_2 = 0$$
$$H_a: \mu_1 - \mu_2 \neq 0$$

The following results are from independent samples taken from two populations.

Sample 1	Sample 2
$n_1 = 35$	$n_2 = 40$
$\bar{x}_1 = 13.6$	$\bar{x}_2 = 10.1$
$s_1 = 5.2$	$s_2 = 8.5$

a. What is the value of the test statistic?
b. What is the degrees of freedom for the t distribution?
c. What is the p-value?
d. At $\alpha = .05$, what is your conclusion?

11. Consider the following data for two independent random samples taken from two normal populations.

Sample 1	10	7	13	7	9	8
Sample 2	8	7	8	4	6	9

a. Compute the two sample means.
b. Compute the two sample standard deviations.
c. What is the point estimate of the difference between the two population means?
d. What is the 90% confidence interval estimate of the difference between the two population means?

Applications

SELF test

12. The U.S. Department of Transportation provides the number of miles that residents of the 75 largest metropolitan areas travel per day in a car. Suppose that for a simple random sample of 50 Buffalo residents the mean is 22.5 miles a day and the standard deviation is

8.4 miles a day, and for an independent simple random sample of 40 Boston residents the mean is 18.6 miles a day and the standard deviation is 7.4 miles a day.

a. What is the point estimate of the difference between the mean number of miles that Buffalo residents travel per day and the mean number of miles that Boston residents travel per day?
b. What is the 95% confidence interval for the difference between the two population means?

WEB file

CollegeCosts

13. The average annual cost (including tuition, room, board, books, and fees) to attend a public college takes nearly a third of the annual income of a typical family with college-age children (*Money,* April 2012). At private colleges, the average annual cost is equal to about 60% of the typical family's income. The following random samples show the annual cost of attending private and public colleges. Data are in thousands of dollars.

Private Colleges

52.8	43.2	45.0	33.3	44.0	
30.6	45.8	37.8	50.5	42.0	

Public Colleges

20.3	22.0	28.2	15.6	24.1	28.5
22.8	25.8	18.5	25.6	14.4	21.8

a. Compute the sample mean and sample standard deviation for private and public colleges.
b. What is the point estimate of the difference between the two population means? Interpret this value in terms of the annual cost of attending private and public colleges.
c. Develop a 95% confidence interval of the difference between the mean annual cost of attending private and pubic colleges.

14. Are nursing salaries in Tampa, Florida, lower than those in Dallas, Texas? Salary data show staff nurses in Tampa earn less than staff nurses in Dallas (*The Tampa Tribune,* January 15, 2007). Suppose that in a follow-up study of 40 staff nurses in Tampa and 50 staff nurses in Dallas you obtain the following results.

Tampa	Dallas
$n_1 = 40$	$n_2 = 50$
$\bar{x}_1 = \$56,100$	$\bar{x}_2 = \$59,400$
$s_1 = \$6000$	$s_2 = \$7000$

a. Formulate hypothesis so that, if the null hypothesis is rejected, we can conclude that salaries for staff nurses in Tampa are significantly lower than for those in Dallas. Use $\alpha = .05$.
b. What is the value of the test statistic?
c. What is the p-value?
d. What is your conclusion?

15. Commercial real estate prices and rental rates suffered substantial declines in 2008 and 2009 (*Newsweek,* July 27, 2009). These declines were particularly severe in Asia; annual lease rates in Tokyo, Hong Kong, and Singapore declined by 40% or more. Even with such large declines, annual lease rates in Asia were still higher than those in many cities in Europe. Annual lease rates for a sample of 30 commercial properties in Hong Kong showed a mean of $1,114 per square meter with a standard deviation of $230.

Annual lease rates for a sample of 40 commercial properties in Paris showed a mean lease rate of \$989 per square meter with a standard deviation of \$195.

a. On the basis of the sample results, can we conclude that the mean annual lease rate is higher in Hong Kong than in Paris? Develop appropriate null and alternative hypotheses.
b. Use $\alpha = .01$. What is your conclusion?

WEB file SATMath

16. The College Board provided comparisons of Scholastic Aptitude Test (SAT) scores based on the highest level of education attained by the test taker's parents. A research hypothesis was that students whose parents had attained a higher level of education would on average score higher on the SAT. The overall mean SAT math score was 514 (College Board website, January 8, 2012). SAT math scores for independent samples of students follow. The first sample shows the SAT math test scores for students whose parents are college graduates with a bachelor's degree. The second sample shows the SAT math test scores for students whose parents are high school graduates but do not have a college degree.

Student's Parents			
College Grads		High School Grads	
485	487	442	492
534	533	580	478
650	526	479	425
554	410	486	485
550	515	528	390
572	578	524	535
497	448		
592	469		

a. Formulate the hypotheses that can be used to determine whether the sample data support the hypothesis that students show a higher population mean math score on the SAT if their parents attained a higher level of education.
b. What is the point estimate of the difference between the means for the two populations?
c. Compute the p-value for the hypothesis test.
d. At $\alpha = .05$, what is your conclusion?

17. Periodically, Merrill Lynch customers are asked to evaluate Merrill Lynch financial consultants and services. Higher ratings on the client satisfaction survey indicate better service, with 7 the maximum service rating. Independent samples of service ratings for two financial consultants are summarized here. Consultant A has 10 years of experience, whereas consultant B has 1 year of experience. Use $\alpha = .05$ and test to see whether the consultant with more experience has the higher population mean service rating.

Consultant A	Consultant B
$n_1 = 16$	$n_2 = 10$
$\bar{x}_1 = 6.82$	$\bar{x}_2 = 6.25$
$s_1 = .64$	$s_2 = .75$

a. State the null and alternative hypotheses.
b. Compute the value of the test statistic.
c. What is the p-value?
d. What is your conclusion?

WEB file

AirDelay

18. Researchers at Purdue University and Wichita State University found that airlines are doing a better job of getting passengers to their destinations on time (Associated Press, April 2, 2012). AirTran Airways and Southwest Airlines were among the leaders in on-time arrivals with both having 88% of their flights arriving on time. But for the 12% of flights that were delayed, how many minutes were these flights late? Sample data showing the number of minutes that delayed flights were late are provided in the file named AirDelay. Data are shown for both airlines.
    a. Formulate the hypotheses that can be used to test for a difference between the population mean minutes late for delayed flights by these two airlines.
    b. What is the sample mean number of minutes late for delayed flights for each of these two airlines?
    c. Using a .05 level of significance, what is the *p*-value and what is your conclusion?

10.3 Inferences About the Difference Between Two Population Means: Matched Samples

Suppose employees at a manufacturing company can use two different methods to perform a production task. To maximize production output, the company wants to identify the method with the smaller population mean completion time. Let μ_1 denote the population mean completion time for production method 1 and μ_2 denote the population mean completion time for production method 2. With no preliminary indication of the preferred production method, we begin by tentatively assuming that the two production methods have the same population mean completion time. Thus, the null hypothesis is H_0: $\mu_1 - \mu_2 = 0$. If this hypothesis is rejected, we can conclude that the population mean completion times differ. In this case, the method providing the smaller mean completion time would be recommended. The null and alternative hypotheses are written as follows.

$$H_0: \mu_1 - \mu_2 = 0$$
$$H_a: \mu_1 - \mu_2 \neq 0$$

In choosing the sampling procedure that will be used to collect production time data and test the hypotheses, we consider two alternative designs. One is based on independent samples and the other is based on **matched samples**.

1. *Independent sample design:* A simple random sample of workers is selected and each worker in the sample uses method 1. A second independent simple random sample of workers is selected and each worker in this sample uses method 2. The test of the difference between population means is based on the procedures in Section 10.2.
2. *Matched sample design:* One simple random sample of workers is selected. Each worker first uses one method and then uses the other method. The order of the two methods is assigned randomly to the workers, with some workers performing method 1 first and others performing method 2 first. Each worker provides a pair of data values, one value for method 1 and another value for method 2.

In the matched sample design the two production methods are tested under similar conditions (i.e., with the same workers); hence this design often leads to a smaller sampling error than the independent sample design. The primary reason is that in a matched sample design, variation between workers is eliminated because the same workers are used for both production methods.

Let us demonstrate the analysis of a matched sample design by assuming it is the method used to test the difference between population means for the two production methods.

TABLE 10.2 TASK COMPLETION TIMES FOR A MATCHED SAMPLE DESIGN

Worker	Completion Time for Method 1 (minutes)	Completion Time for Method 2 (minutes)	Difference in Completion Times (d_i)
1	6.0	5.4	.6
2	5.0	5.2	−.2
3	7.0	6.5	.5
4	6.2	5.9	.3
5	6.0	6.0	.0
6	6.4	5.8	.6

WEB file

Matched

A random sample of six workers is used. The data on completion times for the six workers are given in Table 10.2. Note that each worker provides a pair of data values, one for each production method. Also note that the last column contains the difference in completion times d_i for each worker in the sample.

The key to the analysis of the matched sample design is to realize that we consider only the column of differences. Therefore, we have six data values (.6, −.2, .5, .3, .0, and .6) that will be used to analyze the difference between population means of the two production methods.

Let μ_d = the mean of the *difference* in values for the population of workers. With this notation, the null and alternative hypotheses are rewritten as follows.

$$H_0: \mu_d = 0$$
$$H_a: \mu_d \neq 0$$

If H_0 is rejected, we can conclude that the population mean completion times differ.

Other than the use of the d notation, the formulas for the sample mean and sample standard deviation are the same ones used previously in the text.

The d notation is a reminder that the matched sample provides *difference* data. The sample mean and sample standard deviation for the six difference values in Table 10.2 follow.

$$\bar{d} = \frac{\Sigma d_i}{n} = \frac{1.8}{6} = .30$$

$$s_d = \sqrt{\frac{\Sigma(d_i - \bar{d})^2}{n - 1}} = \sqrt{\frac{.56}{5}} = .335$$

It is not necessary to make the assumption that the population has a normal distribution if the sample size is large. Sample size guidelines for using the t distribution were presented in Chapters 8 and 9.

With the small sample of $n = 6$ workers, we need to make the assumption that the population of differences has a normal distribution. This assumption is necessary so that we may use the t distribution for hypothesis testing and interval estimation procedures. Based on this assumption, the following test statistic has a t distribution with $n - 1$ degrees of freedom.

TEST STATISTIC FOR HYPOTHESIS TESTS INVOLVING MATCHED SAMPLES

$$t = \frac{\bar{d} - \mu_d}{s_d/\sqrt{n}} \qquad \textbf{(10.9)}$$

Once the difference data are computed, the t distribution procedure for matched samples is the same as the one-population estimation and hypothesis testing procedures described in Chapters 8 and 9.

Let us use equation (10.9) to test the hypotheses $H_0: \mu_d = 0$ and $H_a: \mu_d \neq 0$, using $\alpha = .05$. Substituting the sample results $\bar{d} = .30$, $s_d = .335$, and $n = 6$ into equation (10.9), we compute the value of the test statistic.

$$t = \frac{\bar{d} - \mu_d}{s_d/\sqrt{n}} = \frac{.30 - 0}{.335/\sqrt{6}} = 2.20$$

Now let us compute the p-value for this two-tailed test. Because $t = 2.20 > 0$, the test statistic is in the upper tail of the t distribution. With $t = 2.20$, the area in the upper tail to the right of the test statistic can be found by using the t distribution table with degrees of freedom $= n - 1 = 6 - 1 = 5$. Information from the 5 degrees of freedom row of the t distribution table is as follows:

Area in Upper Tail	.20	.10	.05	.025	.01	.005
t-Value (5 *df*)	0.920	1.476	2.015	2.571	3.365	4.032

$t = 2.20$

Thus, we see that the area in the upper tail is between .05 and .025. Because this test is a two-tailed test, we double these values to conclude that the p-value is between .10 and .05. This p-value is greater than $\alpha = .05$. Thus, the null hypothesis $H_0: \mu_d = 0$ is not rejected. Using Excel or Minitab and the data in Table 10.2, we find the exact p-value $= .080$.

In addition we can obtain an interval estimate of the difference between the two population means by using the single population methodology of Chapter 8. At 95% confidence, the calculation follows.

$$\bar{d} \pm t_{.025}\frac{s_d}{\sqrt{n}}$$

$$.3 \pm 2.571\left(\frac{.335}{\sqrt{6}}\right)$$

$$.3 \pm .35$$

Thus, the margin of error is .35 and the 95% confidence interval for the difference between the population means of the two production methods is $-.05$ minutes to .65 minutes.

NOTES AND COMMENTS

1. In the example presented in this section, workers performed the production task with first one method and then the other method. This example illustrates a matched sample design in which each sampled element (worker) provides a pair of data values. It is also possible to use different but "similar" elements to provide the pair of data values. For example, a worker at one location could be matched with a similar worker at another location (similarity based on age, education, gender, experience, etc.). The pairs of workers would provide the difference data that could be used in the matched sample analysis.
2. A matched sample procedure for inferences about two population means generally provides better precision than the independent sample approach; therefore it is the recommended design. However, in some applications the matching cannot be achieved, or perhaps the time and cost associated with matching are excessive. In such cases, the independent sample design should be used.

Exercises

Methods

SELF test

19. Consider the following hypothesis test.

$$H_0: \mu_d \leq 0$$
$$H_a: \mu_d > 0$$

The following data are from matched samples taken from two populations.

	Population	
Element	**1**	**2**
1	21	20
2	28	26
3	18	18
4	20	20
5	26	24

a. Compute the difference value for each element.
b. Compute $\bar{d}$.
c. Compute the standard deviation s_d.
d. Conduct a hypothesis test using $\alpha = .05$. What is your conclusion?

20. The following data are from matched samples taken from two populations.

	Population	
Element	**1**	**2**
1	11	8
2	7	8
3	9	6
4	12	7
5	13	10
6	15	15
7	15	14

a. Compute the difference value for each element.
b. Compute $\bar{d}$.
c. Compute the standard deviation s_d.
d. What is the point estimate of the difference between the two population means?
e. Provide a 95% confidence interval for the difference between the two population means.

Applications

SELF test

21. A market research firm used a sample of individuals to rate the purchase potential of a particular product before and after the individuals saw a new television commercial about the product. The purchase potential ratings were based on a 0 to 10 scale, with higher values indicating a higher purchase potential. The null hypothesis stated that the mean rating "after" would be less than or equal to the mean rating "before." Rejection of this hypothesis would show that the commercial improved the mean purchase potential rating. Use $\alpha = .05$ and the following data to test the hypothesis and comment on the value of the commercial.

Individual	Purchase Rating After	Purchase Rating Before	Individual	Purchase Rating After	Purchase Rating Before
1	6	5	5	3	5
2	6	4	6	9	8
3	7	7	7	7	5
4	4	3	8	6	6

WEB file StockPrices

22. The price per share of stock for a sample of 25 companies was recorded at the beginning of 2012 and then again at the end of the 1st quarter of 2012 (*The Wall Street Journal,* April 2, 2012). How stocks perform during the 1st quarter is an indicator of what is ahead for the stock market and the economy. Use the sample data in the file entitled StockPrices to answer the following.
    a. Let d_i denote the change in price per share for company i where d_i = 1st quarter of 2012 price per share minus the beginning of 2012 price per share. Use the sample mean of these values to estimate the dollar amount a share of stock has changed during the 1st quarter.
    b. What is the 95% confidence interval estimate of the population mean change in the price per share of stock during the first quarter? Interpret this result.
23. Bank of America's Consumer Spending Survey collected data on annual credit card charges in seven different categories of expenditures: transportation, groceries, dining out, household expenses, home furnishings, apparel, and entertainment. Using data from a sample of 42 credit card accounts, assume that each account was used to identify the annual credit card charges for groceries (population 1) and the annual credit card charges for dining out (population 2). Using the difference data, the sample mean difference was $\bar{d}$ = \$850, and the sample standard deviation was s_d = \$1123.
    a. Formulate the null and alternative hypotheses to test for no difference between the population mean credit card charges for groceries and the population mean credit card charges for dining out.
    b. Use a .05 level of significance. Can you conclude that the population means differ? What is the p-value?
    c. Which category, groceries or dining out, has a higher population mean annual credit card charge? What is the point estimate of the difference between the population means? What is the 95% confidence interval estimate of the difference between the population means?

WEB file BusinessTravel

24. The Global Business Travel Association reported the domestic airfare for business travel for the current year and the previous year (*INC. Magazine,* February 2012). Below is a sample of 12 flights with their domestic airfares shown for both years.

Current Year	Previous Year	Current Year	Previous Year
345	315	635	585
526	463	710	650
420	462	605	545
216	206	517	547
285	275	570	508
405	432	610	580

    a. Formulate the hypotheses and test for a significant increase in the mean domestic airfare for business travel for the one-year period. What is the p-value? Using a .05 level of significance, what is your conclusion?
    b. What is the sample mean domestic airfare for business travel for each year?
    c. What is the percentage change in the airfare for the one-year period?
25. The College Board SAT college entrance exam consists of three parts: math, writing, and critical reading (*The World Almanac,* 2012). Sample data showing the math and writing scores for a sample of 12 students who took the SAT follow.

WEB file

TestScores

Student	Math	Writing	Student	Math	Writing
1	540	474	7	480	430
2	432	380	8	499	459
3	528	463	9	610	615
4	574	612	10	572	541
5	448	420	11	390	335
6	502	526	12	593	613

a. Use a .05 level of significance and test for a difference between the population mean for the math scores and the population mean for the writing scores. What is the p-value and what is your conclusion?

b. What is the point estimate of the difference between the mean scores for the two tests? What are the estimates of the population mean scores for the two tests? Which test reports the higher mean score?

26. Scores in the first and fourth (final) rounds for a sample of 20 golfers who competed in PGA tournaments are shown in the following table (*Golfweek,* February 14, 2009, and February 28, 2009). Suppose you would like to determine if the mean score for the first round of a PGA Tour event is significantly different than the mean score for the fourth and final round. Does the pressure of playing in the final round cause scores to go up? Or does the increased player concentration cause scores to come down?

WEB file

GolfScores

Player	First Round	Final Round	Player	First Round	Final Round
Michael Letzig	70	72	Aron Price	72	72
Scott Verplank	71	72	Charles Howell	72	70
D. A. Points	70	75	Jason Dufner	70	73
Jerry Kelly	72	71	Mike Weir	70	77
Soren Hansen	70	69	Carl Pettersson	68	70
D. J. Trahan	67	67	Bo Van Pelt	68	65
Bubba Watson	71	67	Ernie Els	71	70
Reteif Goosen	68	75	Cameron Beckman	70	68
Jeff Klauk	67	73	Nick Watney	69	68
Kenny Perry	70	69	Tommy Armour III	67	71

a. Use $\alpha = .10$ to test for a statistically significantly difference between the population means for first- and fourth-round scores. What is the p-value? What is your conclusion?

b. What is the point estimate of the difference between the two population means? For which round is the population mean score lower?

c. What is the margin of error for a 90% confidence interval estimate for the difference between the population means? Could this confidence interval have been used to test the hypothesis in part (a)? Explain.

27. A manufacturer produces both a deluxe and a standard model of an automatic sander designed for home use. Selling prices obtained from a sample of retail outlets follow.

Retail Outlet	Model Price ($) Deluxe	Model Price ($) Standard	Retail Outlet	Model Price ($) Deluxe	Model Price ($) Standard
1	39	27	5	40	30
2	39	28	6	39	34
3	45	35	7	35	29
4	38	30			

a. The manufacturer's suggested retail prices for the two models show a \$10 price differential. Use a .05 level of significance and test that the mean difference between the prices of the two models is \$10.
b. What is the 95% confidence interval for the difference between the mean prices of the two models?

10.4 Inferences About the Difference Between Two Population Proportions

Letting p_1 denote the proportion for population 1 and p_2 denote the proportion for population 2, we next consider inferences about the difference between the two population proportions: $p_1 - p_2$. To make an inference about this difference, we will select two independent random samples consisting of n_1 units from population 1 and n_2 units from population 2.

Interval Estimation of $p_1 - p_2$

In the following example, we show how to compute a margin of error and develop an interval estimate of the difference between two population proportions.

A tax preparation firm is interested in comparing the quality of work at two of its regional offices. By randomly selecting samples of tax returns prepared at each office and verifying the sample returns' accuracy, the firm will be able to estimate the proportion of erroneous returns prepared at each office. Of particular interest is the difference between these proportions.

p_1 = proportion of erroneous returns for population 1 (office 1)
p_2 = proportion of erroneous returns for population 2 (office 2)
$\bar{p}_1$ = sample proportion for a simple random sample from population 1
$\bar{p}_2$ = sample proportion for a simple random sample from population 2

The difference between the two population proportions is given by $p_1 - p_2$. The point estimator of $p_1 - p_2$ is as follows.

POINT ESTIMATOR OF THE DIFFERENCE BETWEEN TWO POPULATION PROPORTIONS

$$\bar{p}_1 - \bar{p}_2 \tag{10.10}$$

Thus, the point estimator of the difference between two population proportions is the difference between the sample proportions of two independent simple random samples.

As with other point estimators, the point estimator $\bar{p}_1 - \bar{p}_2$ has a sampling distribution that reflects the possible values of $\bar{p}_1 - \bar{p}_2$ if we repeatedly took two independent random samples. The mean of this sampling distribution is $p_1 - p_2$ and the standard error of $\bar{p}_1 - \bar{p}_2$ is as follows:

STANDARD ERROR OF $\bar{p}_1 - \bar{p}_2$

$$\sigma_{\bar{p}_1 - \bar{p}_2} = \sqrt{\frac{p_1(1 - p_1)}{n_1} + \frac{p_2(1 - p_2)}{n_2}} \tag{10.11}$$

If the sample sizes are large enough that n_1p_1, $n_1(1 - p_1)$, n_2p_2, and $n_2(1 - p_2)$ are all greater than or equal to 5, the sampling distribution of $\bar{p}_1 - \bar{p}_2$ can be approximated by a normal distribution.

As we showed previously, an interval estimate is given by a point estimate $\pm$ a margin of error. In the estimation of the difference between two population proportions, an interval estimate will take the following form:

$$\bar{p}_1 - \bar{p}_2 \pm \text{Margin of error}$$

With the sampling distribution of $\bar{p}_1 - \bar{p}_2$ approximated by a normal distribution, we would like to use $z_{\alpha/2}\sigma_{\bar{p}_1 - \bar{p}_2}$ as the margin of error. However, $\sigma_{\bar{p}_1 - \bar{p}_2}$ given by equation (10.11) cannot be used directly because the two population proportions, p_1 and p_2, are unknown. Using the sample proportion $\bar{p}_1$ to estimate p_1 and the sample proportion $\bar{p}_2$ to estimate p_2, the margin of error is as follows.

$$\text{Margin of error} = z_{\alpha/2}\sqrt{\frac{\bar{p}_1(1 - \bar{p}_1)}{n_1} + \frac{\bar{p}_2(1 - \bar{p}_2)}{n_2}} \tag{10.12}$$

The general form of an interval estimate of the difference between two population proportions is as follows.

INTERVAL ESTIMATE OF THE DIFFERENCE BETWEEN TWO POPULATION PROPORTIONS

$$\bar{p}_1 - \bar{p}_2 \pm z_{\alpha/2}\sqrt{\frac{\bar{p}_1(1 - \bar{p}_1)}{n_1} + \frac{\bar{p}_2(1 - \bar{p}_2)}{n_2}} \tag{10.13}$$

where $1 - \alpha$ is the confidence coefficient.

Returning to the tax preparation example, we find that independent simple random samples from the two offices provide the following information.

Office 1	**Office 2**
$n_1 = 250$	$n_2 = 300$
Number of returns with errors = 35	Number of returns with errors = 27

WEB file
TaxPrep

The sample proportions for the two offices follow.

$$\bar{p}_1 = \frac{35}{250} = .14$$

$$\bar{p}_2 = \frac{27}{300} = .09$$

The point estimate of the difference between the proportions of erroneous tax returns for the two populations is $\bar{p}_1 - \bar{p}_2 = .14 - .09 = .05$. Thus, we estimate that office 1 has a .05, or 5%, greater error rate than office 2.

Expression (10.13) can now be used to provide a margin of error and interval estimate of the difference between the two population proportions. Using a 90% confidence interval with $z_{\alpha/2} = z_{.05} = 1.645$, we have

$$\bar{p}_1 - \bar{p}_2 \pm z_{\alpha/2}\sqrt{\frac{\bar{p}_1(1-\bar{p}_1)}{n_1} + \frac{\bar{p}_2(1-\bar{p}_2)}{n_2}}$$

$$.14 - .09 \pm 1.645\sqrt{\frac{.14(1-.14)}{250} + \frac{.09(1-.09)}{300}}$$

$$.05 \pm .045$$

Thus, the margin of error is .045, and the 90% confidence interval is .005 to .095.

Hypothesis Tests About $p_1 - p_2$

Let us now consider hypothesis tests about the difference between the proportions of two populations. We focus on tests involving no difference between the two population proportions. In this case, the three forms for a hypothesis test are as follows:

All hypotheses considered use 0 as the difference of interest.

$$H_0: p_1 - p_2 \geq 0 \qquad H_0: p_1 - p_2 \leq 0 \qquad H_0: p_1 - p_2 = 0$$
$$H_a: p_1 - p_2 < 0 \qquad H_a: p_1 - p_2 > 0 \qquad H_a: p_1 - p_2 \neq 0$$

When we assume H_0 is true as an equality, we have $p_1 - p_2 = 0$, which is the same as saying that the population proportions are equal, $p_1 = p_2$.

We will base the test statistic on the sampling distribution of the point estimator $\bar{p}_1 - \bar{p}_2$. In equation (10.11), we showed that the standard error of $\bar{p}_1 - \bar{p}_2$ is given by

$$\sigma_{\bar{p}_1-\bar{p}_2} = \sqrt{\frac{p_1(1-p_1)}{n_1} + \frac{p_2(1-p_2)}{n_2}}$$

Under the assumption H_0 is true as an equality, the population proportions are equal and $p_1 = p_2 = p$. In this case, $\sigma_{\bar{p}_1-\bar{p}_2}$ becomes

STANDARD ERROR OF $\bar{p}_1 - \bar{p}_2$ WHEN $p_1 = p_2 = p$

$$\sigma_{\bar{p}_1-\bar{p}_2} = \sqrt{\frac{p(1-p)}{n_1} + \frac{p(1-p)}{n_2}} = \sqrt{p(1-p)\left(\frac{1}{n_1} + \frac{1}{n_2}\right)} \qquad \textbf{(10.14)}$$

With p unknown, we pool, or combine, the point estimators from the two samples ($\bar{p}_1$ and $\bar{p}_2$) to obtain a single point estimator of p as follows:

POOLED ESTIMATOR OF p WHEN $p_1 = p_2 = p$

$$\bar{p} = \frac{n_1\bar{p}_1 + n_2\bar{p}_2}{n_1 + n_2} \qquad \textbf{(10.15)}$$

This **pooled estimator of *p*** is a weighted average of $\bar{p}_1$ and $\bar{p}_2$.

Substituting $\bar{p}$ for p in equation (10.14), we obtain an estimate of the standard error of $\bar{p}_1 - \bar{p}_2$. This estimate of the standard error is used in the test statistic. The general form of the test statistic for hypothesis tests about the difference between two population proportions is the point estimator divided by the estimate of $\sigma_{\bar{p}_1-\bar{p}_2}$.

TEST STATISTIC FOR HYPOTHESIS TESTS ABOUT $p_1 - p_2$

$$z = \frac{(\bar{p}_1 - \bar{p}_2)}{\sqrt{\bar{p}(1 - \bar{p})\left(\frac{1}{n_1} + \frac{1}{n_2}\right)}} \tag{10.16}$$

This test statistic applies to large sample situations where n_1p_1, $n_1(1 - p_1)$, n_2p_2, and $n_2(1 - p_2)$ are all greater than or equal to 5.

Let us return to the tax preparation firm example and assume that the firm wants to use a hypothesis test to determine whether the error proportions differ between the two offices. A two-tailed test is required. The null and alternative hypotheses are as follows:

$$H_0: p_1 - p_2 = 0$$
$$H_a: p_1 - p_2 \neq 0$$

If H_0 is rejected, the firm can conclude that the error rates at the two offices differ. We will use $\alpha = .10$ as the level of significance.

The sample data previously collected showed $\bar{p}_1 = .14$ for the $n_1 = 250$ returns sampled at office 1 and $\bar{p}_2 = .09$ for the $n_2 = 300$ returns sampled at office 2. We continue by computing the pooled estimate of p.

$$\bar{p} = \frac{n_1\bar{p}_1 + n_2\bar{p}_2}{n_1 + n_2} = \frac{250(.14) + 300(.09)}{250 + 300} = .1127$$

Using this pooled estimate and the difference between the sample proportions, the value of the test statistic is as follows.

$$z = \frac{(\bar{p}_1 - \bar{p}_2)}{\sqrt{\bar{p}(1 - \bar{p})\left(\frac{1}{n_1} + \frac{1}{n_2}\right)}} = \frac{(.14 - .09)}{\sqrt{.1127(1 - .1127)\left(\frac{1}{250} + \frac{1}{300}\right)}} = 1.85$$

In computing the p-value for this two-tailed test, we first note that $z = 1.85$ is in the upper tail of the standard normal distribution. Using $z = 1.85$ and the standard normal distribution table, we find the area in the upper tail is $1.0000 - .9678 = .0322$. Doubling this area for a two-tailed test, we find the p-value $= 2(.0322) = .0644$. With the p-value less than $\alpha = .10$, H_0 is rejected at the .10 level of significance. The firm can conclude that the error rates differ between the two offices. This hypothesis testing conclusion is consistent with the earlier interval estimation results that showed the interval estimate of the difference between the population error rates at the two offices to be .005 to .095, with Office 1 having the higher error rate.

Exercises

Methods

SELF test

28. Consider the following results for independent samples taken from two populations.

Sample 1	Sample 2
$n_1 = 400$	$n_2 = 300$
$\bar{p}_1 = .48$	$\bar{p}_2 = .36$

a. What is the point estimate of the difference between the two population proportions?
b. Develop a 90% confidence interval for the difference between the two population proportions.
c. Develop a 95% confidence interval for the difference between the two population proportions.

SELF test

29. Consider the hypothesis test

$$H_0: p_1 - p_2 \le 0$$
$$H_a: p_1 - p_2 > 0$$

The following results are for independent samples taken from the two populations.

Sample 1	Sample 2
$n_1 = 200$	$n_2 = 300$
$\bar{p}_1 = .22$	$\bar{p}_2 = .16$

a. What is the p-value?
b. With $\alpha = .05$, what is your hypothesis testing conclusion?

Applications

SELF test

30. A *Businessweek*/Harris survey asked senior executives at large corporations their opinions about the economic outlook for the future. One question was, "Do you think that there will be an increase in the number of full-time employees at your company over the next 12 months?" In the current survey, 220 of 400 executives answered Yes, while in a previous year survey, 192 of 400 executives had answered Yes. Provide a 95% confidence interval estimate for the difference between the proportions at the two points in time. What is your interpretation of the interval estimate?

31. The Professional Golf Association (PGA) measured the putting accuracy of professional golfers playing on the PGA Tour and the best amateur golfers playing in the World Amateur Championship (*Golf Magazine,* January 2007). A sample of 1075 6-foot putts by professional golfers found 688 made puts. A sample of 1200 6-foot putts by amateur golfers found 696 made putts.
    a. Estimate the proportion of made 6-foot putts by professional golfers. Estimate the proportion of made 6-foot putts by amateur golfers. Which group had a better putting accuracy?
    b. What is the point estimate of the difference between the proportions of the two populations? What does this estimate tell you about the percentage of putts made by the two groups of golfers?
    c. What is the 95% confidence interval for the difference between the two population proportions? Interpret his confidence interval in terms of the percentage of putts made by the two groups of golfers.

32. An American Automobile Association (AAA) study investigated the question of whether a man or a woman was more likely to stop and ask for directions (AAA, January 2006). The situation referred to in the study stated the following: "If you and your spouse are driving together and become lost, would you stop and ask for directions?" A sample representative of the data used by AAA showed 300 of 811 women said that they would stop and ask for directions, while 255 of 750 men said that they would stop and ask for directions.
    a. The AAA research hypothesis was that women would be more likely to say that they would stop and ask for directions. Formulate the null and alternative hypotheses for this study.
    b. What is the percentage of women who indicated that they would stop and ask for directions?

c. What is the percentage of men who indicated that they would stop and ask for directions?
d. At $\alpha = .05$, test the hypothesis. What is the p-value, and what conclusion would you expect AAA to draw from this study?

33. Chicago O'Hare and Atlanta Hartsfield-Jackson are the two busiest airports in the United States. The congestion often leads to delayed flight arrivals as well as delayed flight departures. The Bureau of Transportation tracks the on-time and delayed performance at major airports (*Travel & Leisure,* November 2006). A flight is considered delayed if it is more than 15 minutes behind schedule. The following sample data show the delayed departures at Chicago O'Hare and Atlanta Hartsfield-Jackson airports.

	Chicago O'Hare	**Atlanta Hartsfield-Jackson**
Flights	900	1200
Delayed Departures	252	312

a. State the hypotheses that can be used to determine whether the population proportions of delayed departures differ at these two airports.
b. What is the point estimate of the proportion of flights that have delayed departures at Chicago O'Hare?
c. What is the point estimate of the proportion of flights that have delayed departures at Atlanta Hartsfield-Jackson?
d. What is the p-value for the hypothesis test? What is your conclusion?

34. *Businessweek* reported that there seems to be a difference by age group in how well people like life in Russia (*Businessweek,* March 10, 2008). The following sample data are consistent with the *Businessweek* findings and show the responses by age group to the question: "Do you like life in Russia?"

	Russian Age Group	
	17–26	40 and over
Sample	300	260
Responded Yes	192	117

a. What is the point estimate of the proportion of Russians aged 17 to 26 who like life in Russia?
b. What is the point estimate of the proportion of Russians aged 40 and over who like life in Russia?
c. Provide a 95% confidence interval estimate of the difference between the proportion of young Russians aged 17 to 26 and older Russians aged 40 and over who like life in Russia.

35. In a test of the quality of two television commercials, each commercial was shown in a separate test area six times over a one-week period. The following week a telephone survey was conducted to identify individuals who had seen the commercials. Those individuals were asked to state the primary message in the commercials. The following results were recorded.

	Commercial A	**Commercial B**
Number Who Saw Commercial	150	200
Number Who Recalled Message	63	60

a. Use $\alpha = .05$ and test the hypothesis that there is no difference in the recall proportions for the two commercials.
b. Compute a 95% confidence interval for the difference between the recall proportions for the two populations.

36. Winter visitors are extremely important to the economy of Southwest Florida. Hotel occupancy is an often-reported measure of visitor volume and visitor activity (*Naples Daily News,* March 22, 2012). Hotel occupancy data for February in two consecutive years are as follows.

	Current Year	Previous Year
Occupied Rooms	1470	1458
Total Rooms	1750	1800

a. Formulate the hypothesis test that can be used to determine if there has been an increase in the proportion of rooms occupied over the one-year period.
b. What is the estimated proportion of hotel rooms occupied each year?
c. Using a .05 level of significance, what is your hypothesis test conclusion? What is the *p*-value?
d. What is the 95% confidence interval estimate of the change in occupancy for the one-year period? Do you think area officials would be pleased with the results?

37. The Adecco Workplace Insights Survey sampled men and women workers and asked if they expected to get a raise or promotion this year (*USA Today,* February 16, 2012). Suppose the survey sampled 200 men and 200 women. If 104 of the men replied Yes and 74 of the women replied Yes, are the results statistically significant in that you can conclude a greater proportion of men are expecting to get a raise or a promotion this year?
a. State the hypothesis test in terms of the population proportion of men and the population proportion of women?
b. What is the sample proportion for men? For women?
c. Use a .01 level of significance. What is the *p*-value and what is your conclusion?

Summary

In this chapter we discussed procedures for developing interval estimates and conducting hypothesis tests involving two populations. First, we showed how to make inferences about the difference between two population means when independent simple random samples are selected. We first considered the case where the population standard deviations, σ_1 and σ_2, could be assumed known. The standard normal distribution z was used to develop the interval estimate and served as the test statistic for hypothesis tests. We then considered the case where the population standard deviations were unknown and estimated by the sample standard deviations s_1 and s_2. In this case, the t distribution was used to develop the interval estimate and served as the test statistic for hypothesis tests.

Inferences about the difference between two population means were then discussed for the matched sample design. In the matched sample design each element provides a pair of data values, one from each population. The difference between the paired data values is then used in the statistical analysis. The matched sample design is generally preferred to the independent sample design because the matched-sample procedure often improves the precision of the estimate.

Finally, interval estimation and hypothesis testing about the difference between two population proportions were discussed. Statistical procedures for analyzing the difference between two population proportions are similar to the procedures for analyzing the difference between two population means.

Glossary

Independent simple random samples Samples selected from two populations in such a way that the elements making up one sample are chosen independently of the elements making up the other sample.
Matched samples Samples in which each data value of one sample is matched with a corresponding data value of the other sample.
Pooled estimator of p An estimator of a population proportion obtained by computing a weighted average of the point estimators obtained from two independent samples.

Key Formulas

Point Estimator of the Difference Between Two Population Means

$$\bar{x}_1 - \bar{x}_2 \tag{10.1}$$

Standard Error of $\bar{x}_1 - \bar{x}_2$

$$\sigma_{\bar{x}_1 - \bar{x}_2} = \sqrt{\frac{\sigma_1^2}{n_1} + \frac{\sigma_2^2}{n_2}} \tag{10.2}$$

Interval Estimate of the Difference Between Two Population Means: σ_1 and σ_2 Known

$$\bar{x}_1 - \bar{x}_2 \pm z_{\alpha/2}\sqrt{\frac{\sigma_1^2}{n_1} + \frac{\sigma_2^2}{n_2}} \tag{10.4}$$

Test Statistic for Hypothesis Tests About $\mu_1 - \mu_2$: σ_1 and σ_2 Known

$$z = \frac{(\bar{x}_1 - \bar{x}_2) - D_0}{\sqrt{\frac{\sigma_1^2}{n_1} + \frac{\sigma_2^2}{n_2}}} \tag{10.5}$$

Interval Estimate of the Difference Between Two Population Means: σ_1 and σ_2 Unknown

$$\bar{x}_1 - \bar{x}_2 \pm t_{\alpha/2}\sqrt{\frac{s_1^2}{n_1} + \frac{s_2^2}{n_2}} \tag{10.6}$$

Degrees of Freedom: t Distribution with Two Independent Random Samples

$$df = \frac{\left(\frac{s_1^2}{n_1} + \frac{s_2^2}{n_2}\right)^2}{\frac{1}{n_1 - 1}\left(\frac{s_1^2}{n_1}\right)^2 + \frac{1}{n_2 - 1}\left(\frac{s_2^2}{n_2}\right)^2} \tag{10.7}$$

Test Statistic for Hypothesis Tests About $\mu_1 - \mu_2$: σ_1 and σ_2 Unknown

$$t = \frac{(\bar{x}_1 - \bar{x}_2) - D_0}{\sqrt{\frac{s_1^2}{n_1} + \frac{s_2^2}{n_2}}} \tag{10.8}$$

Test Statistic for Hypothesis Tests Involving Matched Samples

$$t = \frac{\bar{d} - \mu_d}{s_d/\sqrt{n}} \tag{10.9}$$

Point Estimator of the Difference Between Two Population Proportions

$$\bar{p}_1 - \bar{p}_2 \tag{10.10}$$

Standard Error of $\bar{p}_1 - \bar{p}_2$

$$\sigma_{\bar{p}_1-\bar{p}_2} = \sqrt{\frac{p_1(1-p_1)}{n_1} + \frac{p_2(1-p_2)}{n_2}} \tag{10.11}$$

Interval Estimate of the Difference Between Two Population Proportions

$$\bar{p}_1 - \bar{p}_2 \pm z_{\alpha/2}\sqrt{\frac{\bar{p}_1(1-\bar{p}_1)}{n_1} + \frac{\bar{p}_2(1-\bar{p}_2)}{n_2}} \tag{10.13}$$

Standard Error of $\bar{p}_1 - \bar{p}_2$ when $p_1 = p_2 = p$

$$\sigma_{\bar{p}_1-\bar{p}_2} = \sqrt{p(1-p)\left(\frac{1}{n_1} + \frac{1}{n_2}\right)} \tag{10.14}$$

Pooled Estimator of p when $p_1 = p_2 = p$

$$\bar{p} = \frac{n_1\bar{p}_1 + n_2\bar{p}_2}{n_1 + n_2} \tag{10.15}$$

Test Statistic for Hypothesis Tests About $p_1 - p_2$

$$z = \frac{(\bar{p}_1 - \bar{p}_2)}{\sqrt{\bar{p}(1-\bar{p})\left(\frac{1}{n_1} + \frac{1}{n_2}\right)}} \tag{10.16}$$

Supplementary Exercises

38. Safegate Foods, Inc., is redesigning the checkout lanes in its supermarkets throughout the country and is considering two designs. Tests on customer checkout times conducted at two stores where the two new systems have been installed result in the following summary of the data.

System A	System B
$n_1 = 120$	$n_2 = 100$
$\bar{x}_1 = 4.1$ minutes	$\bar{x}_2 = 3.4$ minutes
$\sigma_1 = 2.2$ minutes	$\sigma_2 = 1.5$ minutes

Test at the .05 level of significance to determine whether the population mean checkout times of the two systems differ. Which system is preferred?

WEB file
HomePrices

39. Home values tend to increase over time under normal conditions, but the recession of 2008 and 2009 has reportedly caused the sales price of existing homes to fall nationwide (*Businessweek,* March 9, 2009). You would like to see if the data support this conclusion. The file HomePrices contains data on 30 existing home sales in 2006 and 40 existing home sales in 2009.
    a. Provide a point estimate of the difference between the population mean prices for the two years.
    b. Develop a 99% confidence interval estimate of the difference between the resale prices of houses in 2006 and 2009.
    c. Would you feel justified in concluding that resale prices of existing homes have declined from 2006 to 2009? Why or why not?

40. Mutual funds are classified as *load* or *no-load* funds. Load funds require an investor to pay an initial fee based on a percentage of the amount invested in the fund. The no-load funds do not require this initial fee. Some financial advisors argue that the load mutual funds may be worth the extra fee because these funds provide a higher mean rate of return than the no-load mutual funds. A sample of 30 load mutual funds and a sample of 30 no-load mutual funds were selected. Data were collected on the annual return for the funds over a five-year period. The data are contained in the data set Mutual. The data for the first five load and first five no-load mutual funds are as follows.

WEB file
Mutual

Mutual Funds—Load	Return	Mutual Funds—No Load	Return
American National Growth	15.51	Amana Income Fund	13.24
Arch Small Cap Equity	14.57	Berger One Hundred	12.13
Bartlett Cap Basic	17.73	Columbia International Stock	12.17
Calvert World International	10.31	Dodge & Cox Balanced	16.06
Colonial Fund A	16.23	Evergreen Fund	17.61

    a. Formulate H_0 and H_a such that rejection of H_0 leads to the conclusion that the load mutual funds have a higher mean annual return over the five-year period.
    b. Use the 60 mutual funds in the data set Mutual to conduct the hypothesis test. What is the p-value? At $\alpha = .05$, what is your conclusion?

41. The National Association of Home Builders provided data on the cost of the most popular home remodeling projects. Sample data on cost in thousands of dollars for two types of remodeling projects are as follows.

Kitchen	Master Bedroom	Kitchen	Master Bedroom
25.2	18.0	23.0	17.8
17.4	22.9	19.7	24.6
22.8	26.4	16.9	21.0
21.9	24.8	21.8	
19.7	26.9	23.6	

    a. Develop a point estimate of the difference between the population mean remodeling costs for the two types of projects.
    b. Develop a 90% confidence interval for the difference between the two population means.

42. In early 2009, the economy was experiencing a recession. But how was the recession affecting the stock market? Shown are data from a sample of 15 companies. Shown for each company is the price per share of stock on January 1 and April 30 (*The Wall Street Journal,* May 1, 2009).

WEB file
PriceChange

Company	January 1 ($)	April 30 ($)
Applied Materials	10.13	12.21
Bank of New York	28.33	25.48
Chevron	73.97	66.10
Cisco Systems	16.30	19.32
Coca-Cola	45.27	43.05
Comcast	16.88	15.46
Ford Motors	2.29	5.98
General Electric	16.20	12.65
Johnson & Johnson	59.83	52.36
JP Morgan Chase	31.53	33.00
Microsoft	19.44	20.26
Oracle	17.73	19.34
Pfizer	17.71	13.36
Philip Morris	43.51	36.18
Procter & Gamble	61.82	49.44

a. What is the change in the mean price per share of stock over the four-month period?
b. Provide a 90% confident interval estimate of the change in the mean price per share of stock. Interpret the results.
c. What was the percentage change in the mean price per share of stock over the four-month period?
d. If this same percentage change were to occur for the next four months and again for the four months after that, what would be the mean price per share of stock at the end of the year 2009?

43. Country Financial, a financial services company, uses surveys of adults age 18 and older to determine if personal financial fitness is changing over time (*USA Today,* April 4, 2012). In February 2012, a sample of 1000 adults showed 410 indicating that their financial security was more than fair. In February 2010, a sample of 900 adults showed 315 indicating that their financial security was more than fair.
a. State the hypotheses that can be used to test for a significant difference between the population proportions for the two years.
b. What is the sample proportion indicating that their financial security was more than fair in 2012? In 2010?
c. Conduct the hypothesis test and compute the p-value. At a .05 level of significance, what is your conclusion?
d. What is the 95% confidence interval estimate of the difference between the two population proportions?

44. A large automobile insurance company selected samples of single and married male policyholders and recorded the number who made an insurance claim over the preceding three-year period.

Single Policyholders	Married Policyholders
$n_1 = 400$	$n_2 = 900$
Number making claims = 76	Number making claims = 90

a. Use $\alpha = .05$. Test to determine whether the claim rates differ between single and married male policyholders.
b. Provide a 95% confidence interval for the difference between the proportions for the two populations.

45. Medical tests were conducted to learn about drug-resistant tuberculosis. Of 142 cases tested in New Jersey, 9 were found to be drug-resistant. Of 268 cases tested in Texas, 5 were found

to be drug-resistant. Do these data suggest a statistically significant difference between the proportions of drug-resistant cases in the two states? Use a .02 level of significance. What is the p-value, and what is your conclusion?

WEB file Occupancy

46. Vacation occupancy rates were expected to be up during March 2008 in Myrtle Beach, South Carolina (*The Sun News,* February 29, 2008). Data in the file Occupancy will allow you to replicate the findings presented in the newspaper. The data show units rented and not rented for a random sample of vacation properties during the first week of March 2007 and March 2008.
    a. Estimate the proportion of units rented during the first week of March 2007 and the first week of March 2008.
    b. Provide a 95% confidence interval for the difference in proportions.
    c. On the basis of your findings, does it appear March rental rates for 2008 will be up from those a year earlier?
47. For the week ended January 15, 2009, the bullish sentiment of individual investors was 27.6% (*AAII Journal,* February 2009). The bullish sentiment was reported to be 48.7% one week earlier and 39.7% one month earlier. The sentiment measures are based on a poll conducted by the American Assocation of Individual Investors. Assume that each of the bullish sentiment measures was based on a sample size of 240.
    a. Develop a 95% confidence interval for the difference between the bullish sentiment measures for the most recent two weeks.
    b. Develop hypotheses so that rejection of the null hypothesis will allow us to conclude that the most recent bullish sentiment is weaker than that of one month ago.
    c. Conduct a hypotheses test of part (b) using $\alpha = .01$. What is your conclusion?

Case Problem Par, Inc.

Par, Inc., is a major manufacturer of golf equipment. Management believes that Par's market share could be increased with the introduction of a cut-resistant, longer-lasting golf ball. Therefore, the research group at Par has been investigating a new golf ball coating designed to resist cuts and provide a more durable ball. The tests with the coating have been promising.

One of the researchers voiced concern about the effect of the new coating on driving distances. Par would like the new cut-resistant ball to offer driving distances comparable to those of the current-model golf ball. To compare the driving distances for the two balls, 40 balls of both the new and current models were subjected to distance tests. The testing was performed with a mechanical hitting machine so that any difference between the mean distances for the two models could be attributed to a difference in the two models. The results of the tests, with distances measured to the nearest yard, follow. These data are available on the website that accompanies the text.

WEB file Golf

Model		Model		Model		Model	
Current	New	Current	New	Current	New	Current	New
264	277	270	272	263	274	281	283
261	269	287	259	264	266	274	250
267	263	289	264	284	262	273	253
272	266	280	280	263	271	263	260
258	262	272	274	260	260	275	270
283	251	275	281	283	281	267	263
258	262	265	276	255	250	279	261
266	289	260	269	272	263	274	255
259	286	278	268	266	278	276	263
270	264	275	262	268	264	262	279

Managerial Report

1. Formulate and present the rationale for a hypothesis test that Par could use to compare the driving distances of the current and new golf balls.
2. Analyze the data to provide the hypothesis testing conclusion. What is the *p*-value for your test? What is your recommendation for Par, Inc.?
3. Provide descriptive statistical summaries of the data for each model.
4. What is the 95% confidence interval for the population mean driving distance of each model, and what is the 95% confidence interval for the difference between the means of the two populations?
5. Do you see a need for larger sample sizes and more testing with the golf balls? Discuss.

Appendix 10.1 Inferences About Two Populations Using Minitab

We describe the use of Minitab to develop interval estimates and conduct hypothesis tests about the difference between two population means and the difference between two population proportions. Minitab provides both interval estimation and hypothesis testing results within the same module. Thus, the Minitab procedure is the same for both types of inferences. In the examples that follow, we will demonstrate interval estimation and hypothesis testing for the same two samples. We note that Minitab does not provide a routine for inferences about the difference between two population means when the population standard deviations σ_1 and σ_2 are known.

Difference Between Two Population Means: σ_1 and σ_2 Unknown

WEB file
CheckAcct

We will use the data for the checking account balances example presented in Section 10.2. The checking account balances at the Cherry Grove branch are in column C1, and the checking account balances at the Beechmont branch are in column C2. In this example, we will use the Minitab 2-Sample *t* procedure to provide a 95% confidence interval estimate of the difference between population means for the checking account balances at the two branch banks. The output of the procedure also provides the *p*-value for the hypothesis test: H_0: $\mu_1 - \mu_2 = 0$ versus H_a: $\mu_1 - \mu_2 \neq 0$. The following steps are necessary to execute the procedure:

Step 1. Select the **Stat** menu
Step 2. Choose **Basic Statistics**
Step 3. Choose **2-Sample t**
Step 4. When the 2-Sample t (Test and Confidence Interval) dialog box appears:
Select **Samples in different columns**
Enter C1 in the **First** box
Enter C2 in the **Second** box
Select **Options**
Step 5. When the 2-Sample t - Options dialog box appears:
Enter 95 in the **Confidence level** box
Enter 0 in the **Test difference** box
Enter not equal in the **Alternative** box
Click **OK**
Step 6. Click **OK**

The 95% confidence interval estimate is \$37 to \$193, as described in Section 10.2. The *p*-value = .005 shows the null hypothesis of equal population means can be rejected at the α = .01 level of significance. In other applications, step 5 may be modified to provide different confidence levels, different hypothesized values, and different forms of the hypotheses.

Difference Between Two Population Means with Matched Samples

WEB file
Matched

We use the data on production times in Table 10.2 to illustrate the matched-sample procedure. The completion times for method 1 are entered into column C1 and the completion times for method 2 are entered into column C2. The Minitab steps for a matched sample are as follows:

Step 1. Select the **Stat** menu
Step 2. Choose **Basic Statistics**
Step 3. Choose **Paired t**
Step 4. When the Paired t (Test and Confidence Interval) dialog box appears:
Select **Samples in columns**
Enter C1 in the **First sample** box
Enter C2 in the **Second sample** box
Select **Options**
Step 5. When the Paired t - Options dialog box appears:
Enter 95 in the **Confidence level**
Enter 0 in the **Test mean** box
Enter not equal in the **Alternative** box
Click **OK**
Step 6. Click **OK**

The 95% confidence interval estimate is $-.05$ to .65, as described in Section 10.3. The p-value $= .08$ shows that the null hypothesis of no difference in completion times cannot be rejected at $\alpha = .05$. Step 5 may be modified to provide different confidence levels, different hypothesized values, and different forms of the hypothesis.

Difference Between Two Population Proportions

WEB file
TaxPrep

We will use the data on tax preparation errors presented in Section 10.4. The sample results for 250 tax returns prepared at Office 1 are in column C_1 and the sample results for 300 tax returns prepared at Office 2 are in column C_2. Yes denotes an error was found in the tax return and No indicates no error was found. The procedure we describe provides both a 95% confidence interval estimate of the difference between the two population proportions and hypothesis testing results for H_0: $p_1 - p_2 = 0$ and H_a: $p_1 - p_2 \neq 0$.

Step 1. Select the **Stat** menu
Step 2. Choose **Basic Statistics**
Step 3. Choose **2 Proportions**
Step 4. When the 2 Proportions (Test and Confidence Interval) dialog box appears:
Select **Samples in different columns**
Enter C1 in the **First** box
Enter C2 in the **Second** box
Select **Options**
Step 5. When the 2 Proportions-Options dialog box appears:
Enter 90 in the **Confidence level** box
Enter 0 in the **Test difference** box
Enter not equal in the **Alternative** box
Select **Use pooled estimate of p for test**
Click **OK**
Step 6. Click **OK**

The 90% confidence interval estimate is .005 to .095, as described in Section 10.4. The p-value $= .065$ shows the null hypothesis of no difference in error rates can be rejected at

$\alpha = .10$. Step 5 may be modified to provide different confidence levels, different hypothesized values, and different forms of the hypotheses.

In the tax preparation example, the data are categorical. Yes and No are used to indicate whether an error is present. In modules involving proportions, Minitab calculates proportions for the response coming second in alphabetic order. Thus, in the tax preparation example, Minitab computes the proportion of Yes responses, which is the proportion we wanted.

If Minitab's alphabetical ordering does not compute the proportion for the response of interest, we can fix it. Select any cell in the data column, go to the Minitab menu bar, and select Editor > Column > Value Order. This sequence will provide the option of entering a user-specified order. Simply make sure that the response of interest is listed second in the define-an-order box. Minitab's 2 Proportion routine will then provide the confidence interval and hypothesis testing results for the population proportion of interest.

Finally, we note that Minitab's 2 Proportion routine uses a computational procedure different from the procedure described in the text. Thus, the Minitab output can be expected to provide slightly different interval estimates and slightly different p-values. However, results from the two methods should be close and are expected to provide the same interpretation and conclusion.

Appendix 10.2 Inferences About Two Populations Using Excel

We describe the use of Excel to conduct hypothesis tests about the difference between two population means.* We begin with inferences about the difference between the means of two populations when the population standard deviations σ_1 and σ_2 are known.

Difference Between Two Population Means: σ_1 and σ_2 Known

WEB file

ExamScores

We will use the examination scores for the two training centers discussed in Section 10.1. The label Center A is in cell A1 and the label Center B is in cell B1. The examination scores for Center A are in cells A2:A31 and examination scores for Center B are in cells B2:B41. The population standard deviations are assumed known with $\sigma_1 = 10$ and $\sigma_2 = 10$. The Excel routine will request the input of variances which are $\sigma_1^2 = 100$ and $\sigma_2^2 = 100$. The following steps can be used to conduct a hypothesis test about the difference between the two population means.

Step 1. Click the **Data** tab on the Ribbon
Step 2. In the **Analysis** group, click **Data Analysis**
Step 3. When the Data Analysis dialog box appears:
Choose **z-Test: Two Sample for Means**
Step 4. When the z-Test: Two Sample for Means dialog box appears:
Enter A1:A31 in the **Variable 1 Range** box
Enter B1:B41 in the **Variable 2 Range** box
Enter 0 in the **Hypothesized Mean Difference** box
Enter 100 in the **Variable 1 Variance (known)** box
Enter 100 in the **Variable 2 Variance (known)** box
Select **Labels**
Enter .05 in the **Alpha** box
Select **Output Range** and enter C1 in the box
Click **OK**

*Excel's data analysis tools provide hypothesis testing procedures for the difference between two population means. No routines are available for interval estimation of the difference between two population means nor for inferences about the difference between two population proportions.

The two-tailed p-value is denoted P(Z<=z) two-tail. Its value of .0977 does not allow us to reject the null hypothesis at $\alpha = .05$.

Difference Between Two Population Means: σ_1 and σ_2 Unknown

WEB file SoftwareTest

We use the data for the software testing study in Table 10.1. The data are already entered into an Excel worksheet with the label Current in cell A1 and the label New in cell B1. The completion times for the current technology are in cells A2:A13, and the completion times for the new software are in cells B2:B13. The following steps can be used to conduct a hypothesis test about the difference between two population means with σ_1 and σ_2 unknown.

Step 1. Click the **Data** tab on the Ribbon
Step 2. In the **Analysis** group, click **Data Analysis**
Step 3. When the Data Analysis dialog box appears:
Choose **t-Test: Two Sample Assuming Unequal Variances**
Step 4. When the t-Test: Two Sample Assuming Unequal Variances dialog box appears:
Enter A1:A13 in the **Variable 1 Range** box
Enter B1:B13 in the **Variable 2 Range** box
Enter 0 in the **Hypothesized Mean Difference** box
Select **Labels**
Enter .05 in the **Alpha** box
Select **Output Range** and enter C1 in the box
Click **OK**

The appropriate p-value is denoted P(T<=t) one-tail. Its value of .017 allows us to reject the null hypothesis at $\alpha = .05$.

Difference Between Two Population Means with Matched Samples

WEB file Matched

We use the matched-sample completion times in Table 10.2 to illustrate. The data are entered into a worksheet with the label Method 1 in cell A1 and the label Method 2 in cell B2. The completion times for method 1 are in cells A2:A7 and the completion times for method 2 are in cells B2:B7. The Excel procedure uses the steps previously described for the t-Test except the user chooses the **t-Test: Paired Two Sample for Means** data analysis tool in step 3. The variable 1 range is A1:A7 and the variable 2 range is B1:B7.

The appropriate p-value is denoted P(T<=t) two-tail. Its value of .08 does not allow us to reject the null hypothesis at $\alpha = .05$.

Appendix 10.3 Inferences About Two Populations Using StatTools

In this appendix we show how StatTools can be used to develop interval estimates and conduct hypothesis tests about the difference between two population means for the σ_1 and σ_2 unknown case.

Interval Estimation of μ_1 and μ_2

WEB file CheckAcct

We will use the data for the checking account balances example presented in Section 10.2. Begin by using the Data Set Manager to create a StatTools data set for these data using the procedure described in the appendix in Chapter 1. The following steps can be used to compute a 95% confidence interval estimate of the difference between the two population means.

Step 1. Click the **StatTools** tab on the Ribbon
Step 2. In the **Analyses** group, click **Statistical Inference**
Step 3. Select the **Confidence Interval** option
Step 4. Choose Mean/Std. Deviation
Step 5. When the StatTools-Confidence Interval for Mean/Std. Deviation dialog box appears:
For **Analysis Type**, choose **Two-Sample Analysis**
In the **Variables** section,
Select **Cherry Grove**
Select **Beechmont**
In the **Confidence Intervals to Calculate** section,
Select the **For the Difference of Means** option
Select 95% for the **Confidence Level**
Click **OK**

Because the sample size for Cherry Grove ($n_1 = 28$) differs from the sample size for Beechmont ($n_2 = 22$), StatTools will inform you of this difference after you click OK. A dialog box will appear saying "The variable Beechmont contains missing data. This analysis will ignore the missing data." Click OK. A Choose Variable Ordering dialog box then appears, indicating that the analysis will compare the difference between the Cherry Grove data set and the Beechmont data set. Click OK and the StatTools interval estimation output will appear.

Hypothesis Tests About μ_1 and μ_2

WEB file
SoftwareTest

We will use the software evaluation example and the completion time data presented in Table 10.1. Begin by using the Data Set Manager to create a StatTools data set for these data using the procedure described in the appendix in Chapter 1. The following steps can be used to test the hypothesis: H_0: $\mu_1 - \mu_2 \leq 0$ against H_a: $\mu_1 - \mu_2 > 0$.

Step 1. Click the **StatTools** tab on the Ribbon
Step 2. In the **Analyses** group, click **Statistical Inference**
Step 3. Select the **Hypothesis Test** option
Step 4. Choose Mean/Std. Deviation
Step 5. When the StatTools-Hypothesis Test for Mean/Std. Deviation dialog box appears:
For **Analysis Type**, choose **Two-Sample Analysis**
In the **Variables** section,
Select **Current**
Select **New**
In the **Hypothesis Test to Perform** section,
Select **Difference of Means**
Enter 0 in the **Null Hypothesis Value** box
Select **Greater Than Null Value (One-Tailed Test)** in the **Alternative Hypothesis Type** box
Click **OK**
When the Choose Variable Ordering dialog box appears, click **OK**

The results of the hypothesis test will then appear.

Inferences About the Difference Between Two Population Means: Matched Samples

WEB file
Matched

StatTools can be used to develop interval estimates and conduct hypothesis tests for the difference between population means for the matched samples case. We will use the matched-sample completion times in Table 10.2 to illustrate.

Begin by using the Data Set Manager to create a StatTools data set for these data using the procedure described in the appendix in Chapter 1. The following steps can be used to compute a 95% confidence interval estimate of the difference between the population mean completion times.

Step 1. Click the **StatTools** tab on the Ribbon
Step 2. In the **Analyses** group, click **Statistical Inference**
Step 3. Select the **Confidence Interval** option
Step 4. Choose Mean/Std. Deviation
Step 5. When the StatTools-Confidence Interval for Mean/Std. Deviation dialog box appears:
For **Analysis Type**, choose **Paired-Sample Analysis**
In the **Variables** section,
Select **Method 1**
Select **Method 2**
In the **Confidence Intervals to Calculate** section,
Select the **For the Difference of Means** option
Select 95% for the **Confidence Level**
If selected, remove the check in the **For the Standard Deviation box**
Click **OK**
When the Choose Variable Ordering dialog box appears, click **OK**

The confidence interval will appear.

Conducting hypothesis tests for the matched samples case is very similar to conducting hypothesis tests for the difference in two means shown previously. Choose the Hypothesis Test option in step 3. Then when the Hypothesis Test for Mean/Std. Deviation dialog box appears in step 5, describe the type of hypothesis test desired.

CHAPTER 11

Inferences About Population Variances

CONTENTS

STATISTICS *in* PRACTICE

U.S. GOVERNMENT ACCOUNTABILITY OFFICE*
WASHINGTON, D.C.

The U.S. Government Accountability Office (GAO) is an independent, nonpolitical audit organization in the legislative branch of the federal government. GAO evaluators determine the effectiveness of current and proposed federal programs. To carry out their duties, evaluators must be proficient in records review, legislative research, and statistical analysis techniques.

In one case, GAO evaluators studied a Department of Interior program established to help clean up the nation's rivers and lakes. As part of this program, federal grants were made to small cities throughout the United States. Congress asked the GAO to determine how effectively the program was operating. To do so, the GAO examined records and visited the sites of several waste treatment plants.

One objective of the GAO audit was to ensure that the effluent (treated sewage) at the plants met certain standards. Among other things, the audits reviewed sample data on the oxygen content, the pH level, and the amount of suspended solids in the effluent. A requirement of the program was that a variety of tests be taken daily at each plant and that the collected data be sent periodically to the state engineering department. The GAO's investigation of the data showed whether various characteristics of the effluent were within acceptable limits.

For example, the mean or average pH level of the effluent was examined carefully. In addition, the variance in the reported pH levels was reviewed. The following hypothesis test was conducted about the variance in pH level for the population of effluent.

$$H_0: \sigma^2 = \sigma_0^2$$
$$H_a: \sigma^2 \neq \sigma_0^2$$

In this test, σ_0^2 is the population variance in pH level expected at a properly functioning plant. In one particular plant, the null hypothesis was rejected. Further analysis showed that this plant had a variance in pH level that was significantly less than normal.

Effluent at this facility must fall within a statistically determined pH range. © ZUMA Wire Service/Alamy Limited.

The auditors visited the plant to examine the measuring equipment and to discuss their statistical findings with the plant manager. The auditors found that the measuring equipment was not being used because the operator did not know how to work it. Instead, the operator had been told by an engineer what level of pH was acceptable and had simply recorded similar values without actually conducting the test. The unusually low variance in this plant's data resulted in rejection of H_0. The GAO suspected that other plants might have similar problems and recommended an operator training program to improve the data collection aspect of the pollution control program.

In this chapter you will learn how to conduct statistical inferences about the variances of one and two populations. Two new distributions, the chi-square distribution and the F distribution, will be introduced and used to make interval estimates and hypothesis tests about population variances.

*The authors thank Mr. Art Foreman and Mr. Dale Ledman of the U.S. Government Accountability Office for providing this Statistics in Practice.

In the preceding four chapters we examined methods of statistical inference involving population means and population proportions. In this chapter we expand the discussion to situations involving inferences about population variances. As an example of a case in which a variance can provide important decision-making information, consider the production process of filling containers with a liquid detergent product. The filling mechanism for the process is adjusted so that the mean filling weight is 16 ounces per container. Although a mean of 16 ounces is desired, the variance of the filling weights is also critical.

That is, even with the filling mechanism properly adjusted for the mean of 16 ounces, we cannot expect every container to have exactly 16 ounces. By selecting a sample of containers, we can compute a sample variance for the number of ounces placed in a container. This value will serve as an estimate of the variance for the population of containers being filled by the production process. If the sample variance is modest, the production process will be continued. However, if the sample variance is excessive, overfilling and underfilling may be occurring even though the mean is correct at 16 ounces. In this case, the filling mechanism will be readjusted in an attempt to reduce the filling variance for the containers.

In many manufacturing applications, controlling the process variance is extremely important in maintaining quality.

In the first section we consider inferences about the variance of a single population. Subsequently, we will discuss procedures that can be used to make inferences about the variances of two populations.

11.1 Inferences About a Population Variance

The sample variance

$$s^2 = \frac{\Sigma(x_i - \bar{x})^2}{n - 1} \tag{11.1}$$

is the point estimator of the population variance σ^2. In using the sample variance as a basis for making inferences about a population variance, the sampling distribution of the quantity $(n - 1)s^2/\sigma^2$ is helpful. This sampling distribution is described as follows.

SAMPLING DISTRIBUTION OF $(n - 1)s^2/\sigma^2$

Whenever a simple random sample of size n is selected from a normal population, the sampling distribution of

$$\frac{(n - 1)s^2}{\sigma^2} \tag{11.2}$$

has a chi-square distribution with $n - 1$ degrees of freedom.

The chi-square distribution is based on sampling from a normal population.

Figure 11.1 shows some possible forms of the sampling distribution of $(n - 1)s^2/\sigma^2$.

Since the sampling distribution of $(n - 1)s^2/\sigma^2$ is known to have a chi-square distribution whenever a simple random sample of size n is selected from a normal population, we can use the chi-square distribution to develop interval estimates and conduct hypothesis tests about a population variance.

Interval Estimation

To show how the chi-square distribution can be used to develop a confidence interval estimate of a population variance σ^2, suppose that we are interested in estimating the population variance for the production filling process mentioned at the beginning of this chapter. A sample of 20 containers is taken, and the sample variance for the filling quantities is found to be $s^2 = .0025$. However, we know we cannot expect the variance of a sample of 20 containers to provide the exact value of the variance for the population of containers filled by the production process. Hence, our interest will be in developing an interval estimate for the population variance.

FIGURE 11.1 EXAMPLES OF THE SAMPLING DISTRIBUTION OF $(n - 1)s^2/\sigma^2$ (A CHI-SQUARE DISTRIBUTION)

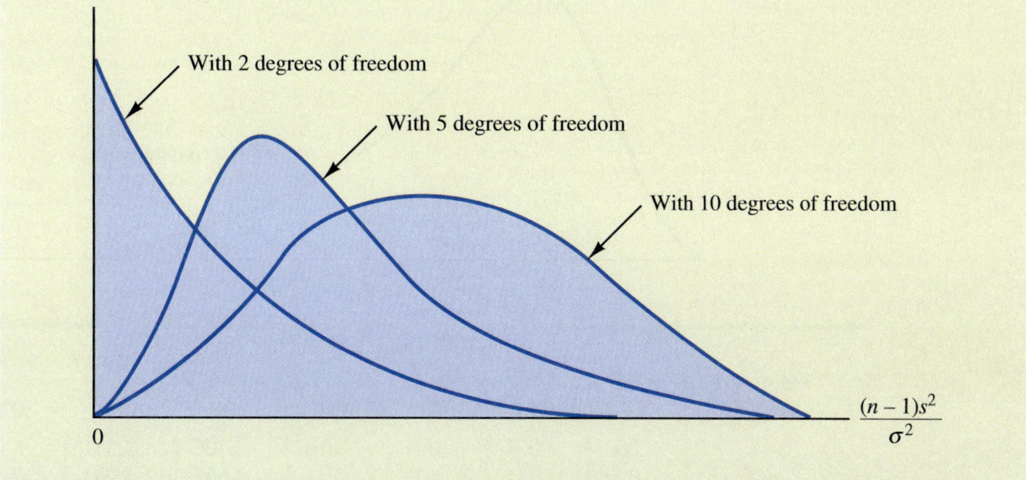

We will use the notation χ^2_α to denote the value for the chi-square distribution that provides an area or probability of α to the *right* of the χ^2_α value. For example, in Figure 11.2 the chi-square distribution with 19 degrees of freedom is shown with $\chi^2_{.025} = 32.852$ indicating that 2.5% of the chi-square values are to the right of 32.852, and $\chi^2_{.975} = 8.907$ indicating that 97.5% of the chi-square values are to the right of 8.907. Tables of areas or probabilities are readily available for the chi-square distribution. Refer to Table 11.1 and verify that these chi-square values with 19 degrees of freedom (19th row of the table) are correct. Table 3 of Appendix B provides a more extensive table of chi-square values.

From the graph in Figure 11.2 we see that .95, or 95%, of the chi-square values are between $\chi^2_{.975}$ and $\chi^2_{.025}$. That is, there is a .95 probability of obtaining a χ^2 value such that

$$\chi^2_{.975} \leq \chi^2 \leq \chi^2_{.025}$$

FIGURE 11.2 A CHI-SQUARE DISTRIBUTION WITH 19 DEGREES OF FREEDOM

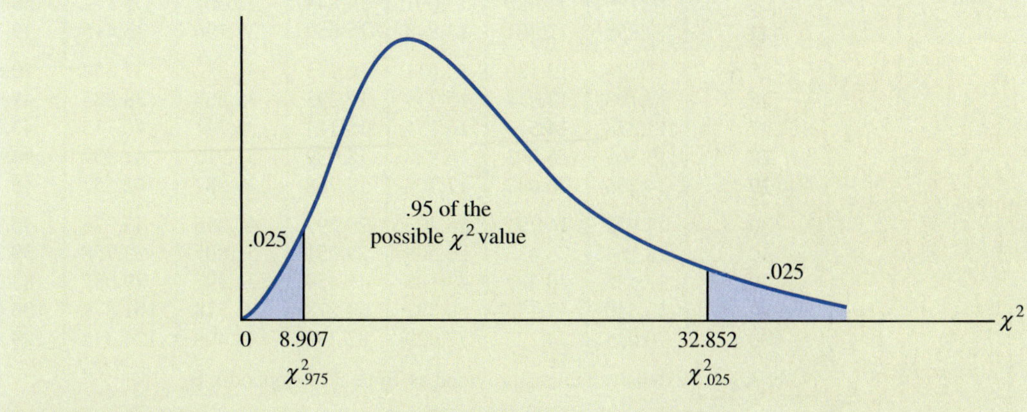

TABLE 11.1 SELECTED VALUES FROM THE CHI-SQUARE DISTRIBUTION TABLE*

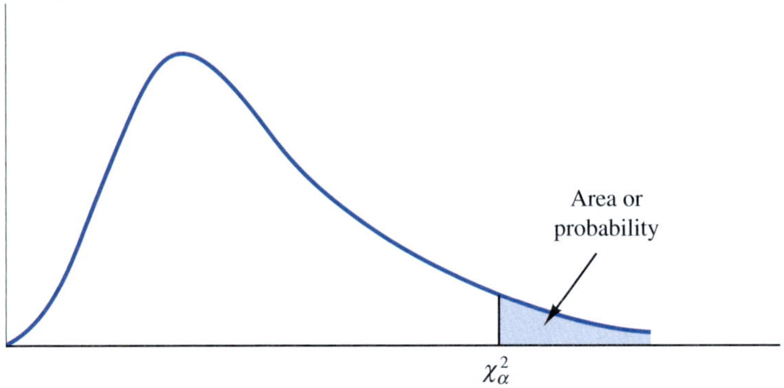

Degrees of Freedom	Area in Upper Tail .99	.975	.95	.90	.10	.05	.025	.01
1	.000	.001	.004	.016	2.706	3.841	5.024	6.635
2	.020	.051	.103	.211	4.605	5.991	7.378	9.210
3	.115	.216	.352	.584	6.251	7.815	9.348	11.345
4	.297	.484	.711	1.064	7.779	9.488	11.143	13.277
5	.554	.831	1.145	1.610	9.236	11.070	12.832	15.086
6	.872	1.237	1.635	2.204	10.645	12.592	14.449	16.812
7	1.239	1.690	2.167	2.833	12.017	14.067	16.013	18.475
8	1.647	2.180	2.733	3.490	13.362	15.507	17.535	20.090
9	2.088	2.700	3.325	4.168	14.684	16.919	19.023	21.666
10	2.558	3.247	3.940	4.865	15.987	18.307	20.483	23.209
11	3.053	3.816	4.575	5.578	17.275	19.675	21.920	24.725
12	3.571	4.404	5.226	6.304	18.549	21.026	23.337	26.217
13	4.107	5.009	5.892	7.041	19.812	22.362	24.736	27.688
14	4.660	5.629	6.571	7.790	21.064	23.685	26.119	29.141
15	5.229	6.262	7.261	8.547	22.307	24.996	27.488	30.578
16	5.812	6.908	7.962	9.312	23.542	26.296	28.845	32.000
17	6.408	7.564	8.672	10.085	24.769	27.587	30.191	33.409
18	7.015	8.231	9.390	10.865	25.989	28.869	31.526	34.805
19	7.633	8.907	10.117	11.651	27.204	30.144	32.852	36.191
20	8.260	9.591	10.851	12.443	28.412	31.410	34.170	37.566
21	8.897	10.283	11.591	13.240	29.615	32.671	35.479	38.932
22	9.542	10.982	12.338	14.041	30.813	33.924	36.781	40.289
23	10.196	11.689	13.091	14.848	32.007	35.172	38.076	41.638
24	10.856	12.401	13.848	15.659	33.196	36.415	39.364	42.980
25	11.524	13.120	14.611	16.473	34.382	37.652	40.646	44.314
26	12.198	13.844	15.379	17.292	35.563	38.885	41.923	45.642
27	12.878	14.573	16.151	18.114	36.741	40.113	43.195	46.963
28	13.565	15.308	16.928	18.939	37.916	41.337	44.461	48.278
29	14.256	16.047	17.708	19.768	39.087	42.557	45.722	49.588
30	14.953	16.791	18.493	20.599	40.256	43.773	46.979	50.892
40	22.164	24.433	26.509	29.051	51.805	55.758	59.342	63.691
60	37.485	40.482	43.188	46.459	74.397	79.082	83.298	88.379
80	53.540	57.153	60.391	64.278	96.578	101.879	106.629	112.329
100	70.065	74.222	77.929	82.358	118.498	124.342	129.561	135.807

**Note:* A more extensive table is provided as Table 3 of Appendix B.

We stated in expression (11.2) that $(n - 1)s^2/\sigma^2$ follows a chi-square distribution; therefore we can substitute $(n - 1)s^2/\sigma^2$ for χ^2 and write

$$\chi^2_{.975} \leq \frac{(n-1)s^2}{\sigma^2} \leq \chi^2_{.025} \tag{11.3}$$

In effect, expression (11.3) provides an interval estimate in that .95, or 95%, of all possible values for $(n - 1)s^2/\sigma^2$ will be in the interval $\chi^2_{.975}$ to $\chi^2_{.025}$. We now need to do some algebraic manipulations with expression (11.3) to develop an interval estimate for the population variance σ^2. Working with the leftmost inequality in expression (11.3), we have

$$\chi^2_{.975} \leq \frac{(n-1)s^2}{\sigma^2}$$

Thus

$$\sigma^2\chi^2_{.975} \leq (n-1)s^2$$

or

$$\sigma^2 \leq \frac{(n-1)s^2}{\chi^2_{.975}} \tag{11.4}$$

Performing similar algebraic manipulations with the rightmost inequality in expression (11.3) gives

$$\frac{(n-1)s^2}{\chi^2_{.025}} \leq \sigma^2 \tag{11.5}$$

The results of expressions (11.4) and (11.5) can be combined to provide

$$\frac{(n-1)s^2}{\chi^2_{.025}} \leq \sigma^2 \leq \frac{(n-1)s^2}{\chi^2_{.975}} \tag{11.6}$$

Because expression (11.3) is true for 95% of the $(n - 1)s^2/\sigma^2$ values, expression (11.6) provides a 95% confidence interval estimate for the population variance σ^2.

Let us return to the problem of providing an interval estimate for the population variance of filling quantities. Recall that the sample of 20 containers provided a sample variance of $s^2 = .0025$. With a sample size of 20, we have 19 degrees of freedom. As shown in Figure 11.2, we have already determined that $\chi^2_{.975} = 8.907$ and $\chi^2_{.025} = 32.852$. Using these values in expression (11.6) provides the following interval estimate for the population variance.

$$\frac{(19)(.0025)}{32.852} \leq \sigma^2 \leq \frac{(19)(.0025)}{8.907}$$

or

$$.0014 \leq \sigma^2 \leq .0053$$

A confidence interval for a population standard deviation can be found by computing the square roots of the lower limit and upper limit of the confidence interval for the population variance.

Taking the square root of these values provides the following 95% confidence interval for the population standard deviation.

$$.0380 \leq \sigma \leq .0730$$

Thus, we illustrated the process of using the chi-square distribution to establish interval estimates of a population variance and a population standard deviation. Note specifically that because $\chi^2_{.975}$ and $\chi^2_{.025}$ were used, the interval estimate has a .95 confidence coefficient. Extending expression (11.6) to the general case of any confidence coefficient, we have the following interval estimate of a population variance.

INTERVAL ESTIMATE OF A POPULATION VARIANCE

$$\frac{(n-1)s^2}{\chi^2_{\alpha/2}} \leq \sigma^2 \leq \frac{(n-1)s^2}{\chi^2_{(1-\alpha/2)}} \tag{11.7}$$

where the χ^2 values are based on a chi-square distribution with $n - 1$ degrees of freedom and where $1 - \alpha$ is the confidence coefficient.

Hypothesis Testing

Using σ_0^2 to denote the hypothesized value for the population variance, the three forms for a hypothesis test about a population variance are as follows:

$$\begin{array}{lll} H_0\colon \sigma^2 \geq \sigma_0^2 & H_0\colon \sigma^2 \leq \sigma_0^2 & H_0\colon \sigma^2 = \sigma_0^2 \\ H_a\colon \sigma^2 < \sigma_0^2 & H_a\colon \sigma^2 > \sigma_0^2 & H_a\colon \sigma^2 \neq \sigma_0^2 \end{array}$$

These three forms are similar to the three forms that we used to conduct one-tailed and two-tailed hypothesis tests about population means and proportions in Chapters 9 and 10.

The procedure for conducting a hypothesis test about a population variance uses the hypothesized value for the population variance σ_0^2 and the sample variance s^2 to compute the value of a χ^2 test statistic. Assuming that the population has a normal distribution, the test statistic is as follows:

TEST STATISTIC FOR HYPOTHESIS TESTS ABOUT A POPULATION VARIANCE

$$\chi^2 = \frac{(n-1)s^2}{\sigma_0^2} \tag{11.8}$$

where χ^2 has a chi-square distribution with $n - 1$ degrees of freedom.

After computing the value of the χ^2 test statistic, either the p-value approach or the critical value approach may be used to determine whether the null hypothesis can be rejected.

Let us consider the following example. The St. Louis Metro Bus Company wants to promote an image of reliability by encouraging its drivers to maintain consistent schedules. As a standard policy the company would like arrival times at bus stops to have low variability. In terms of the variance of arrival times, the company standard specifies an arrival time variance of 4 or less when arrival times are measured in minutes. The following hypothesis test is formulated to help the company determine whether the arrival time population variance is excessive.

$$\begin{aligned} H_0&\colon \sigma^2 \leq 4 \\ H_a&\colon \sigma^2 > 4 \end{aligned}$$

In tentatively assuming H_0 is true, we are assuming that the population variance of arrival times is within the company guideline. We reject H_0 if the sample evidence indicates that the population variance exceeds the guideline. In this case, follow-up steps should be taken to reduce the population variance. We conduct the hypothesis test using a level of significance of $\alpha = .05$.

WEB file BusTimes

Suppose that a random sample of 24 bus arrivals taken at a downtown intersection provides a sample variance of $s^2 = 4.9$. Assuming that the population distribution of arrival times is approximately normal, the value of the test statistic is as follows.

$$\chi^2 = \frac{(n-1)s^2}{\sigma_0^2} = \frac{(24-1)(4.9)}{4} = 28.18$$

The chi-square distribution with $n - 1 = 24 - 1 = 23$ degrees of freedom is shown in Figure 11.3. Because this is an upper tail test, the area under the curve to the right of the test statistic $\chi^2 = 28.18$ is the p-value for the test.

Like the t distribution table, the chi-square distribution table does not contain sufficient detail to enable us to determine the p-value exactly. However, we can use the chi-square distribution table to obtain a range for the p-value. For example, using Table 11.1, we find the following information for a chi-square distribution with 23 degrees of freedom.

Area in Upper Tail	.10	.05	.025	.01
χ^2 Value (23 df)	32.007	35.172	38.076	41.638

$\chi^2 = 28.18$ (arrow pointing to the left of 32.007)

Because $\chi^2 = 28.18$ is less than 32.007, the area in upper tail (the p-value) is greater than .10. With the p-value $> \alpha = .05$, we cannot reject the null hypothesis. The sample does not support the conclusion that the population variance of the arrival times is excessive.

Because of the difficulty of determining the exact p-value directly from the chi-square distribution table, a computer software package such as Minitab or Excel is helpful. Appendix F, at the back of the book, describes how to compute p-values. In the appendix, we show that the exact p-value corresponding to $\chi^2 = 28.18$ is .2091.

As with other hypothesis testing procedures, the critical value approach can also be used to draw the hypothesis testing conclusion. With $\alpha = .05$, $\chi^2_{.05}$ provides the critical value for

FIGURE 11.3 CHI-SQUARE DISTRIBUTION FOR THE ST. LOUIS METRO BUS EXAMPLE

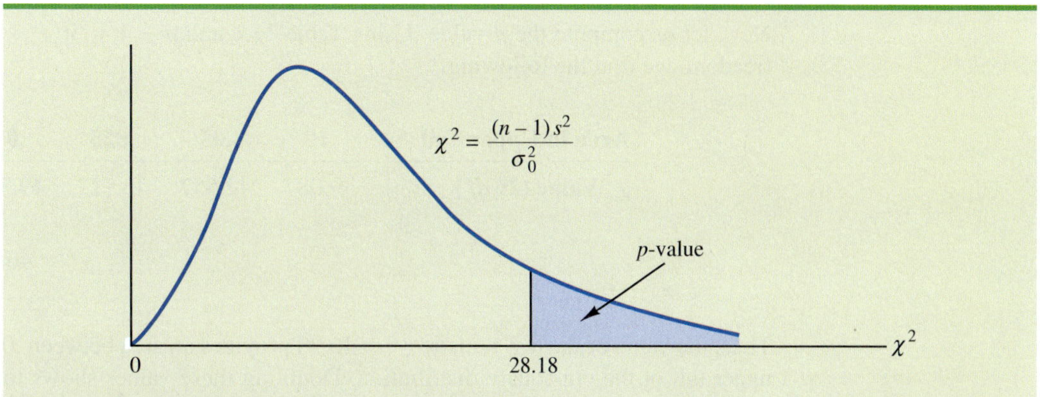

the upper tail hypothesis test. Using Table 11.1 and 23 degrees of freedom, $\chi^2_{.05} = 35.172$. Thus, the rejection rule for the bus arrival time example is as follows:

$$\text{Reject } H_0 \text{ if } \chi^2 \geq 35.172$$

Because the value of the test statistic is $\chi^2 = 28.18$, we cannot reject the null hypothesis.

In practice, upper tail tests as presented here are the most frequently encountered tests about a population variance. In situations involving arrival times, production times, filling weights, part dimensions, and so on, low variances are desirable, whereas large variances are unacceptable. With a statement about the maximum allowable population variance, we can test the null hypothesis that the population variance is less than or equal to the maximum allowable value against the alternative hypothesis that the population variance is greater than the maximum allowable value. With this test structure, corrective action will be taken whenever rejection of the null hypothesis indicates the presence of an excessive population variance.

As we saw with population means and proportions, other forms of hypothesis tests can be developed. Let us demonstrate a two-tailed test about a population variance by considering a situation faced by a bureau of motor vehicles. Historically, the variance in test scores for individuals applying for driver's licenses has been $\sigma^2 = 100$. A new examination with new test questions has been developed. Administrators of the bureau of motor vehicles would like the variance in the test scores for the new examination to remain at the historical level. To evaluate the variance in the new examination test scores, the following two-tailed hypothesis test has been proposed.

$$H_0\colon \sigma^2 = 100$$
$$H_a\colon \sigma^2 \neq 100$$

Rejection of H_0 will indicate that a change in the variance has occurred and suggest that some questions in the new examination may need revision to make the variance of the new test scores similar to the variance of the old test scores. A sample of 30 applicants for driver's licenses will be given the new version of the examination. We will use a level of significance $\alpha = .05$ to conduct the hypothesis test.

The sample of 30 examination scores provided a sample variance $s^2 = 162$. The value of the chi-square test statistic is as follows:

$$\chi^2 = \frac{(n-1)s^2}{\sigma_0^2} = \frac{(30-1)(162)}{100} = 46.98$$

Now, let us compute the p-value. Using Table 11.1 and $n - 1 = 30 - 1 = 29$ degrees of freedom, we find the following.

Area in Upper Tail	**.10**	**.05**	**.025**	**.01**
χ^2 Value (29 *df*)	39.087	42.557	45.722	49.588

$\chi^2 = 46.98$ (between 45.722 and 49.588)

Thus, the value of the test statistic $\chi^2 = 46.98$ provides an area between .025 and .01 in the upper tail of the chi-square distribution. Doubling these values shows that the two-tailed

TABLE 11.2 SUMMARY OF HYPOTHESIS TESTS ABOUT A POPULATION VARIANCE

	Lower Tail Test	Upper Tail Test	Two-Tailed Test
Hypotheses	$H_0: \sigma^2 \geq \sigma_0^2$ $H_a: \sigma^2 < \sigma_0^2$	$H_0: \sigma^2 \leq \sigma_0^2$ $H_a: \sigma^2 > \sigma_0^2$	$H_0: \sigma^2 = \sigma_0^2$ $H_a: \sigma^2 \neq \sigma_0^2$
Test Statistic	$\chi^2 = \dfrac{(n-1)s^2}{\sigma_0^2}$	$\chi^2 = \dfrac{(n-1)s^2}{\sigma_0^2}$	$\chi^2 = \dfrac{(n-1)s^2}{\sigma_0^2}$
Rejection Rule: *p*-value Approach	Reject H_0 if p-value $\leq \alpha$	Reject H_0 if p-value $\leq \alpha$	Reject H_0 if p-value $\leq \alpha$
Rejection Rule: Critical Value Approach	Reject H_0 if $\chi^2 \leq \chi^2_{(1-\alpha)}$	Reject H_0 if $\chi^2 \geq \chi^2_{\alpha}$	Reject H_0 if $\chi^2 \leq \chi^2_{(1-\alpha/2)}$ or if $\chi^2 \geq \chi^2_{\alpha/2}$

p-value is between .05 and .02. Excel or Minitab can be used to show the exact p-value = .0374. With p-value $\leq \alpha = .05$, we reject H_0 and conclude that the new examination test scores have a population variance different from the historical variance of $\sigma^2 = 100$. A summary of the hypothesis testing procedures for a population variance is shown in Table 11.2.

Exercises

Methods

1. Find the following chi-square distribution values from Table 11.1 or Table 3 of Appendix B.
   a. $\chi^2_{.05}$ with $df = 5$
   b. $\chi^2_{.025}$ with $df = 15$
   c. $\chi^2_{.975}$ with $df = 20$
   d. $\chi^2_{.01}$ with $df = 10$
   e. $\chi^2_{.95}$ with $df = 18$

SELF test

2. A sample of 20 items provides a sample standard deviation of 5.
   a. Compute the 90% confidence interval estimate of the population variance.
   b. Compute the 95% confidence interval estimate of the population variance.
   c. Compute the 95% confidence interval estimate of the population standard deviation.

3. A sample of 16 items provides a sample standard deviation of 9.5. Test the following hypotheses using $\alpha = .05$. What is your conclusion? Use both the p-value approach and the critical value approach.

$$H_0: \sigma^2 \leq 50$$
$$H_a: \sigma^2 > 50$$

Applications

4. The variance in drug weights is critical in the pharmaceutical industry. For a specific drug, with weights measured in grams, a sample of 18 units provided a sample variance of $s^2 = .36$.
   a. Construct a 90% confidence interval estimate of the population variance for the weight of this drug.
   b. Construct a 90% confidence interval estimate of the population standard deviation.

5. John Calipari, head basketball coach for the 2012 national champion University of Kentucky Wildcats, is the highest paid coach in college basketball with an annual salary of $5.4 million (*USA Today,* March 29, 2012). The sample below shows the head basketball coach's salary for a sample of 10 schools playing NCAA Division I basketball. Salary data are in millions of dollars.

University	Coach's Salary	University	Coach's Salary
Indiana	2.2	Syracuse	1.5
Xavier	.5	Murray State	.2
Texas	2.4	Florida State	1.5
Connecticut	2.7	South Dakota State	.1
West Virginia	2.0	Vermont	.2

a. Use the sample mean for the 10 schools to estimate the population mean annual salary for head basketball coaches at colleges and universities playing NCAA Division I basketball.
b. Use the data to estimate the population standard deviation for the annual salary for head basketball coaches.
c. What is the 95% confidence interval for the population variance?
d. What is the 95% confidence interval for the population standard deviation?

WEB file
Halloween

6. Americans spend nearly $7 billion on Halloween costumes and decorations (*The Wall Street Journal,* October 27, 2011). Sample data showing the amount, in dollars, 16 adults spent on a Halloween costume are as follows.

12	69	22	64
33	36	31	44
52	16	13	98
45	32	63	26

a. What is the estimate of the population mean amount adults spend on a Halloween costume?
b. What is the sample standard deviation?
c. Provide a 95% confidence interval estimate of the population standard deviation for the amount adults spend on a Halloween costume?

7. To analyze the risk, or volatility, associated with investing in General Electric common stock, a sample of the eight quarterly percent total returns was identified as shown below (Charles Schwab website, January 2012). The percent total return includes the stock price change plus the dividend payment for the quarter.

20.0	−20.5	12.2	12.6	10.5	−5.8	−18.7	15.3

a. What is the value of the sample mean? What is its interpretation?
b. Compute the sample variance and sample standard deviation as measures of volatility for the quarterly return for General Electric?
c. Construct a 95% confidence interval for the population variance?
d. Construct a 95% confidence interval for the population standard deviation?

8. March 4, 2009, was one of the few good days for the stock market in early 2009. The Dow Jones Industrial Average went up 149.82 points (*The Wall Street Journal,* March 5, 2009). The following table shows the stock price changes for a sample of 12 companies on that day.
a. Compute the sample variance for the daily price change.

WEB file
PriceChange

Company	Price Change ($)	Company	Price Change ($)
Aflac	0.81	John.&John.	1.46
Bank of Am.	−0.05	Loews Cp	0.92
Cablevision	0.41	Nokia	0.21
Diageo	1.32	SmpraEngy	0.97
Flour Cp	2.37	Sunoco	0.52
Goodrich	0.3	Tyson Food	0.12

b. Compute the sample standard deviation for the price change.
c. Provide 95% confidence interval estimates of the population variance and the population standard deviation.

SELF test

9. An automotive part must be machined to close tolerances to be acceptable to customers. Production specifications call for a maximum variance in the lengths of the parts of .0004. Suppose the sample variance for 30 parts turns out to be $s^2 = .0005$. Use $\alpha = .05$ to test whether the population variance specification is being violated.

WEB file
Costco

10. *Consumer Reports* uses a 100-point customer satisfaction score to rate the nation's major chain stores. Assume that from past experience with the satisfaction rating score, a population standard deviation of $\sigma = 12$ is expected. In 2012, Costco with its 432 warehouses in 40 states was the only chain store to earn an outstanding rating for overall quality (*Consumer Reports,* March 2012). A sample of 15 Costco customer satisfaction scores follows.

95	90	83	75	95
98	80	83	82	93
86	80	94	64	62

a. What is the sample mean customer satisfaction score for Costco?
b. What is the sample variance?
c. What is the sample standard deviation?
d. Construct a hypothesis test to determine whether the population standard deviation of $\sigma = 12$ should be rejected for Costco. With a .05 level of significance, what is your conclusion?

11. At the end of 2008, the variance in the semiannual yields of overseas government bond was $\sigma^2 = .70$. A group of bond investors met at that time to discuss future trends in overseas bond yields. Some expected the variability in overseas bond yields to increase and others took the opposite view. The following table shows the semiannual yields for 12 overseas countries as of March 6, 2009 (*Barron's,* March 9, 2009).

WEB file
Yields

Country	Yield (%)	Country	Yield (%)
Australia	3.98	Italy	4.51
Belgium	3.78	Japan	1.32
Canada	2.95	Netherlands	3.53
Denmark	3.55	Spain	3.90
France	3.44	Sweden	2.48
Germany	3.08	U.K.	3.76

a. Compute the mean, variance, and standard deviation of the overseas bond yields as of March 6, 2009.
b. Develop hypotheses to test whether the sample data indicate that the variance in bond yields has changed from that at the end of 2008.
c. Use $\alpha = .05$ to conduct the hypothesis test formulated in part (b). What is your conclusion?

12. A *Fortune* study found that the variance in the number of vehicles owned or leased by subscribers to *Fortune* magazine is .94. Assume a sample of 12 subscribers to another

magazine provided the following data on the number of vehicles owned or leased: 2, 1, 2, 0, 3, 2, 2, 1, 2, 1, 0, and 1.

a. Compute the sample variance in the number of vehicles owned or leased by the 12 subscribers.
b. Test the hypothesis H_0: $\sigma^2 = .94$ to determine whether the variance in the number of vehicles owned or leased by subscribers of the other magazine differs from $\sigma^2 = .94$ for *Fortune*. At a .05 level of significance, what is your conclusion?

11.2 Inferences About Two Population Variances

In some statistical applications we may want to compare the variances in product quality resulting from two different production processes, the variances in assembly times for two assembly methods, or the variances in temperatures for two heating devices. In making comparisons about the two population variances, we will be using data collected from two independent random samples, one from population 1 and another from population 2. The two sample variances s_1^2 and s_2^2 will be the basis for making inferences about the two population variances σ_1^2 and σ_2^2. Whenever the variances of two normal populations are equal ($\sigma_1^2 = \sigma_2^2$), the sampling distribution of the ratio of the two sample variances s_1^2/s_2^2 is as follows.

SAMPLING DISTRIBUTION OF s_1^2/s_2^2 WHEN $\sigma_1^2 = \sigma_2^2$

Whenever independent simple random samples of sizes n_1 and n_2 are selected from two normal populations with equal variances, the sampling distribution of

$$\frac{s_1^2}{s_2^2} \tag{11.9}$$

The F distribution is based on sampling from two normal populations.

has an F distribution with $n_1 - 1$ degrees of freedom for the numerator and $n_2 - 1$ degrees of freedom for the denominator; s_1^2 is the sample variance for the random sample of n_1 items from population 1, and s_2^2 is the sample variance for the random sample of n_2 items from population 2.

Figure 11.4 is a graph of the F distribution with 20 degrees of freedom for both the numerator and denominator. As indicated by this graph, the F distribution is not symmetric,

FIGURE 11.4 *F* DISTRIBUTION WITH 20 DEGREES OF FREEDOM FOR THE NUMERATOR AND 20 DEGREES OF FREEDOM FOR THE DENOMINATOR

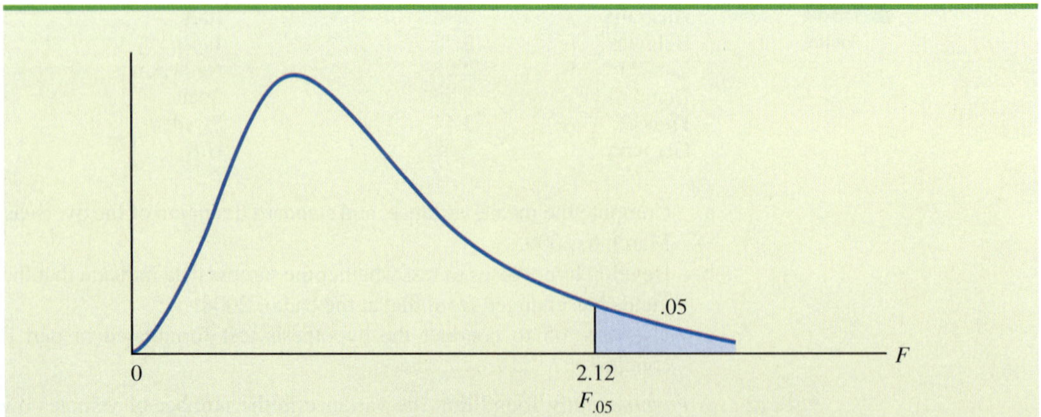

and the F values can never be negative. The shape of any particular F distribution depends on its numerator and denominator degrees of freedom.

We will use F_α to denote the value of F that provides an area or probability of α in the upper tail of the distribution. For example, as noted in Figure 11.4, $F_{.05}$ denotes the upper tail area of .05 for an F distribution with 20 degrees of freedom for the numerator and 20 degrees of freedom for the denominator. The specific value of $F_{.05}$ can be found by referring to the F distribution table, a portion of which is shown in Table 11.3. Using 20 degrees of freedom for the numerator, 20 degrees of freedom for the denominator, and the row corresponding to an area of .05 in the upper tail, we find $F_{.05} = 2.12$. Note that the

TABLE 11.3 SELECTED VALUES FROM THE *F* DISTRIBUTION TABLE*

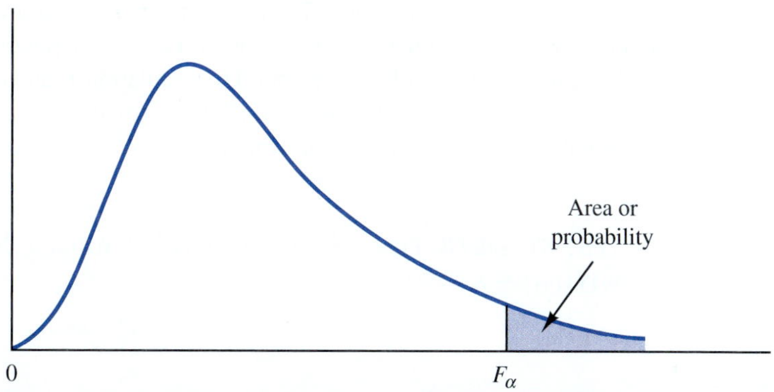

Denominator Degrees of Freedom	Area in Upper Tail	Numerator Degrees of Freedom 10	15	20	25	30
10	.10	2.32	2.24	2.20	2.17	2.16
	.05	2.98	2.85	2.77	2.73	2.70
	.025	3.72	3.52	3.42	3.35	3.31
	.01	4.85	4.56	4.41	4.31	4.25
15	.10	2.06	1.97	1.92	1.89	1.87
	.05	2.54	2.40	2.33	2.28	2.25
	.025	3.06	2.86	2.76	2.69	2.64
	.01	3.80	3.52	3.37	3.28	3.21
20	.10	1.94	1.84	1.79	1.76	1.74
	.05	2.35	2.20	2.12	2.07	2.04
	.025	2.77	2.57	2.46	2.40	2.35
	.01	3.37	3.09	2.94	2.84	2.78
25	.10	1.87	1.77	1.72	1.68	1.66
	.05	2.24	2.09	2.01	1.96	1.92
	.025	2.61	2.41	2.30	2.23	2.18
	.01	3.13	2.85	2.70	2.60	2.54
30	.10	1.82	1.72	1.67	1.63	1.61
	.05	2.16	2.01	1.93	1.88	1.84
	.025	2.51	2.31	2.20	2.12	2.07
	.01	2.98	2.70	2.55	2.45	2.39

**Note:* A more extensive table is provided as Table 4 of Appendix B.

table can be used to find F values for upper tail areas of .10, .05, .025, and .01. See Table 4 of Appendix B for a more extensive table for the F distribution.

Let us show how the F distribution can be used to conduct a hypothesis test about the variances of two populations. We begin with a test of the equality of two population variances. The hypotheses are stated as follows.

$$H_0\colon \sigma_1^2 = \sigma_2^2$$
$$H_a\colon \sigma_1^2 \neq \sigma_2^2$$

We make the tentative assumption that the population variances are equal. If H_0 is rejected, we will draw the conclusion that the population variances are not equal.

The procedure used to conduct the hypothesis test requires two independent random samples, one from each population. The two sample variances are then computed. We refer to the population providing the *larger* sample variance as population 1. Thus, a sample size of n_1 and a sample variance of s_1^2 correspond to population 1, and a sample size of n_2 and a sample variance of s_2^2 correspond to population 2. Based on the assumption that both populations have a normal distribution, the ratio of sample variances provides the following F test statistic.

TEST STATISTIC FOR HYPOTHESIS TESTS ABOUT POPULATION VARIANCES WITH $\sigma_1^2 = \sigma_2^2$

$$F = \frac{s_1^2}{s_2^2} \tag{11.10}$$

Denoting the population with the larger sample variance as population 1, the test statistic has an F distribution with $n_1 - 1$ degrees of freedom for the numerator and $n_2 - 1$ degrees of freedom for the denominator.

Because the F test statistic is constructed with the larger sample variance s_1^2 in the numerator, the value of the test statistic will be in the upper tail of the F distribution. Therefore, the F distribution table as shown in Table 11.3 and in Table 4 of Appendix B need only provide upper tail areas or probabilities. If we did not construct the test statistic in this manner, lower tail areas or probabilities would be needed. In this case, additional calculations or more extensive F distribution tables would be required. Let us now consider an example of a hypothesis test about the equality of two population variances.

Dullus County Schools is renewing its school bus service contract for the coming year and must select one of two bus companies, the Milbank Company or the Gulf Park Company. We will use the variance of the arrival or pickup/delivery times as a primary measure of the quality of the bus service. Low variance values indicate the more consistent and higher-quality service. If the variances of arrival times associated with the two services are equal, Dullus School administrators will select the company offering the better financial terms. However, if the sample data on bus arrival times for the two companies indicate a significant difference between the variances, the administrators may want to give special consideration to the company with the better or lower variance service. The appropriate hypotheses follow.

$$H_0\colon \sigma_1^2 = \sigma_2^2$$
$$H_a\colon \sigma_1^2 \neq \sigma_2^2$$

If H_0 can be rejected, the conclusion of unequal service quality is appropriate. We will use a level of significance of $\alpha = .10$ to conduct the hypothesis test.

WEB file
SchoolBus

A sample of 26 arrival times for the Milbank service provides a sample variance of 48 and a sample of 16 arrival times for the Gulf Park service provides a sample variance of 20. Because the Milbank sample provided the larger sample variance, we will denote Milbank as population 1. Using equation (11.10), we find the value of the test statistic:

$$F = \frac{s_1^2}{s_2^2} = \frac{48}{20} = 2.40$$

The corresponding F distribution has $n_1 - 1 = 26 - 1 = 25$ numerator degrees of freedom and $n_2 - 1 = 16 - 1 = 15$ denominator degrees of freedom.

As with other hypothesis testing procedures, we can use the p-value approach or the critical value approach to obtain the hypothesis testing conclusion. Table 11.3 shows the following areas in the upper tail and corresponding F values for an F distribution with 25 numerator degrees of freedom and 15 denominator degrees of freedom.

Area in Upper Tail	**.10**	**.05**	**.025**	**.01**
***F* Value (df_1 = 25, df_2 = 15)**	1.89	2.28	2.69	3.28

$F = 2.40$

Because $F = 2.40$ is between 2.28 and 2.69, the area in the upper tail of the distribution is between .05 and .025. For this two-tailed test, we double the upper tail area, which results in a p-value between .10 and .05. Because we selected $\alpha = .10$ as the level of significance, the p-value $< \alpha = .10$. Thus, the null hypothesis is rejected. This finding leads to the conclusion that the two bus services differ in terms of pickup/delivery time variances. The recommendation is that the Dullus County School administrators give special consideration to the better or lower variance service offered by the Gulf Park Company.

We can use Excel or Minitab to show that the test statistic $F = 2.40$ provides a two-tailed p-value $= .0811$. With $.0811 < \alpha = .10$, the null hypothesis of equal population variances is rejected.

To use the critical value approach to conduct the two-tailed hypothesis test at the $\alpha = .10$ level of significance, we would select critical values with an area of $\alpha/2 = .10/2 = .05$ in each tail of the distribution. Because the value of the test statistic computed using equation (11.10) will always be in the upper tail, we only need to determine the upper tail critical value. From Table 11.3, we see that $F_{.05} = 2.28$. Thus, even though we use a two-tailed test, the rejection rule is stated as follows.

$$\text{Reject } H_0 \text{ if } F \geq 2.28$$

Because the test statistic $F = 2.40$ is greater than 2.28, we reject H_0 and conclude that the two bus services differ in terms of pickup/delivery time variances.

One-tailed tests involving two population variances are also possible. In this case, we use the F distribution to determine whether one population variance is significantly greater than the other. A one-tailed hypothesis test about two population variances will always be formulated as an *upper tail* test:

A one-tailed hypothesis test about two population variances can always be formulated as an upper tail test. This approach eliminates the need for lower tail F values.

$$H_0: \sigma_1^2 \leq \sigma_2^2$$
$$H_a: \sigma_1^2 > \sigma_2^2$$

This form of the hypothesis test always places the p-value and the critical value in the upper tail of the F distribution. As a result, only upper tail F values will be needed, simplifying both the computations and the table for the F distribution.

Let us demonstrate the use of the F distribution to conduct a one-tailed test about the variances of two populations by considering a public opinion survey. Samples of 31 men and 41 women will be used to study attitudes about current political issues. The researcher conducting the study wants to test to see whether the sample data indicate that women show a greater variation in attitude on political issues than men. In the form of the one-tailed hypothesis test given previously, women will be denoted as population 1 and men will be denoted as population 2. The hypothesis test will be stated as follows.

$$H_0: \sigma^2_{\text{women}} \leq \sigma^2_{\text{men}}$$
$$H_a: \sigma^2_{\text{women}} > \sigma^2_{\text{men}}$$

A rejection of H_0 gives the researcher the statistical support necessary to conclude that women show a greater variation in attitude on political issues.

With the sample variance for women in the numerator and the sample variance for men in the denominator, the F distribution will have $n_1 - 1 = 41 - 1 = 40$ numerator degrees of freedom and $n_2 - 1 = 31 - 1 = 30$ denominator degrees of freedom. We will use a level of significance $\alpha = .05$ to conduct the hypothesis test. The survey results provide a sample variance of $s_1^2 = 120$ for women and a sample variance of $s_2^2 = 80$ for men. The test statistic is as follows.

$$F = \frac{s_1^2}{s_2^2} = \frac{120}{80} = 1.50$$

Referring to Table 4 in Appendix B, we find that an F distribution with 40 numerator degrees of freedom and 30 denominator degrees of freedom has $F_{.10} = 1.57$. Because the test statistic $F = 1.50$ is less than 1.57, the area in the upper tail must be greater than .10. Thus, we can conclude that the p-value is greater than .10. Using Excel or Minitab provides a p-value $= .1256$. Because the p-value $> \alpha = .05$, H_0 cannot be rejected. Hence, the sample results do not support the conclusion that women show greater variation in attitude on political issues than men. Table 11.4 provides a summary of hypothesis tests about two population variances.

TABLE 11.4 SUMMARY OF HYPOTHESIS TESTS ABOUT TWO POPULATION VARIANCES

	Upper Tail Test	Two-Tailed Test
Hypotheses	$H_0: \sigma_1^2 \leq \sigma_2^2$ $H_a: \sigma_1^2 > \sigma_2^2$	$H_0: \sigma_1^2 = \sigma_2^2$ $H_a: \sigma_1^2 \neq \sigma_2^2$ Note: Population 1 has the larger sample variance
Test Statistic	$F = \frac{s_1^2}{s_2^2}$	$F = \frac{s_1^2}{s_2^2}$
Rejection Rule: p-value	Reject H_0 if p-value $\leq \alpha$	Reject H_0 if p-value $\leq \alpha$
Rejection Rule: Critical Value Approach	Reject H_0 if $F \geq F_\alpha$	Reject H_0 if $F \geq F_{\alpha/2}$

NOTES AND COMMENTS

Research confirms the fact that the F distribution is sensitive to the assumption of normal populations. The F distribution should not be used unless it is reasonable to assume that both populations are at least approximately normally distributed.

Exercises

Methods

13. Find the following F distribution values from Table 4 of Appendix B.
    a. $F_{.05}$ with degrees of freedom 5 and 10
    b. $F_{.025}$ with degrees of freedom 20 and 15
    c. $F_{.01}$ with degrees of freedom 8 and 12
    d. $F_{.10}$ with degrees of freedom 10 and 20

14. A sample of 16 items from population 1 has a sample variance $s_1^2 = 5.8$ and a sample of 21 items from population 2 has a sample variance $s_2^2 = 2.4$. Test the following hypotheses at the .05 level of significance.

$$H_0: \sigma_1^2 \leq \sigma_2^2$$
$$H_a: \sigma_1^2 > \sigma_2^2$$

    a. What is your conclusion using the p-value approach?
    b. Repeat the test using the critical value approach.

SELF test

15. Consider the following hypothesis test.

$$H_0: \sigma_1^2 = \sigma_2^2$$
$$H_a: \sigma_1^2 \neq \sigma_2^2$$

    a. What is your conclusion if $n_1 = 21$, $s_1^2 = 8.2$, $n_2 = 26$, and $s_2^2 = 4.0$? Use $\alpha = .05$ and the p-value approach.
    b. Repeat the test using the critical value approach.

Applications

16. Investors commonly use the standard deviation of the monthly percentage return for a mutual fund as a measure of the risk for the fund; in such cases, a fund that has a larger standard deviation is considered more risky than a fund with a lower standard deviation. The standard deviation for the American Century Equity Growth fund and the standard deviation for the Fidelity Growth Discovery fund were recently reported to be 15.0% and 18.9%, respectively (*The Top Mutual Funds*, AAII, 2009). Assume that each of these standard deviations is based on a sample of 60 months of returns. Do the sample results support the conclusion that the Fidelity fund has a larger population variance than the American Century fund? Which fund is more risky?

SELF test

17. Most individuals are aware of the fact that the average annual repair cost for an automobile depends on the age of the automobile. A researcher is interested in finding out whether the variance of the annual repair costs also increases with the age of the automobile. A sample of 26 automobiles 4 years old showed a sample standard deviation for annual repair costs of \$170 and a sample of 25 automobiles 2 years old showed a sample standard deviation for annual repair costs of \$100.
    a. State the null and alternative versions of the research hypothesis that the variance in annual repair costs is larger for the older automobiles.
    b. At a .01 level of significance, what is your conclusion? What is the p-value? Discuss the reasonableness of your findings.

18. Data were collected on the top 1000 financial advisers by *Barron's* (*Barron's*, February 9, 2009). Merrill Lynch had 239 people on the list and Morgan Stanley had 121 people on the list. A sample of 16 of the Merrill Lynch advisers and 10 of the Morgan Stanley advisers showed that the advisers managed many very large accounts with a large variance in the total amount of funds managed. The standard deviation of the amount managed by the Merrill Lynch advisers was $s_1 = \$587$ million. The standard deviation of the amount managed by the Morgan Stanley advisers was $s_2 = \$489$ million. Conduct a hypothesis test at $\alpha = .10$ to determine if there is a significant difference in the population variances for the amounts managed by the two companies. What is your conclusion about the variability in the amount of funds managed by advisers from the two firms?

19. The variance in a production process is an important measure of the quality of the process. A large variance often signals an opportunity for improvement in the process by finding ways to reduce the process variance. Conduct a statistical test to determine whether there is a significant difference between the variances in the bag weights for two machines. Use a .05 level of significance. What is your conclusion? Which machine, if either, provides the greater opportunity for quality improvements?

WEB file
Bags

Machine 1	2.95	3.45	3.50	3.75	3.48	3.26	3.33	3.20
	3.16	3.20	3.22	3.38	3.90	3.36	3.25	3.28
	3.20	3.22	2.98	3.45	3.70	3.34	3.18	3.35
	3.12							
Machine 2	3.22	3.30	3.34	3.28	3.29	3.25	3.30	3.27
	3.38	3.34	3.35	3.19	3.35	3.05	3.36	3.28
	3.30	3.28	3.30	3.20	3.16	3.33		

20. On the basis of data provided by a Romac salary survey, the variance in annual salaries for seniors in public accounting firms is approximately 2.1 and the variance in annual salaries for managers in public accounting firms is approximately 11.1. The salary data were provided in thousands of dollars. Assuming that the salary data were based on samples of 25 seniors and 26 managers, test the hypothesis that the population variances in the salaries are equal. At a .05 level of significance, what is your conclusion?

WEB file
BatteryTime

21. Many smartphones, especially those of the LTE-enabled persuasion, have earned a bad rap for exceptionally poor battery life. Battery life between charges for the Motorola Droid Razr Max averages 20 hours when the primary use is talk time and 7 hours when the primary use is Internet applications (*The Wall Street Journal*, March 7, 2012). Since the mean hours for talk time usage is greater than the mean hours for Internet usage, the question was raised as to whether the variance in hours of usage is also greater when the primary use is talk time. Sample data showing battery hours of use for the two applications follows.

Primary Use: Talking

35.8	22.2	4.0	32.6	8.5	42.5
8.0	3.8	30.0	12.8	10.3	35.5

Primary Use: Internet

14.0	12.5	16.4	1.9	9.9
5.4	1.0	15.2	4.0	4.7

a. Formulate hypotheses about the two population variances that can be used to determine if the population variance in battery hours of use is greater for the talk time application.
b. What are the standard deviations of battery hours of use for the two samples?
c. Conduct the hypothesis test and compute the p-value. Using a .05 level of significance, what is your conclusion?

22. A research hypothesis is that the variance of stopping distances of automobiles on wet pavement is substantially greater than the variance of stopping distances of automobiles on dry pavement. In the research study, 16 automobiles traveling at the same speeds are tested for stopping distances on wet pavement and then tested for stopping distances on dry pavement. On wet pavement, the standard deviation of stopping distances is 32 feet. On dry pavement, the standard deviation is 16 feet.
    a. At a .05 level of significance, do the sample data justify the conclusion that the variance in stopping distances on wet pavement is greater than the variance in stopping distances on dry pavement? What is the p-value?
    b. What are the implications of your statistical conclusions in terms of driving safety recommendations?

Summary

In this chapter we presented statistical procedures that can be used to make inferences about population variances. In the process we introduced two new probability distributions: the chi-square distribution and the F distribution. The chi-square distribution can be used as the basis for interval estimation and hypothesis tests about the variance of a normal population.

We illustrated the use of the F distribution in hypothesis tests about the variances of two normal populations. In particular, we showed that with independent simple random samples of sizes n_1 and n_2 selected from two normal populations with equal variances $\sigma_1^2 = \sigma_2^2$, the sampling distribution of the ratio of the two sample variances s_1^2/s_2^2 has an F distribution with $n_1 - 1$ degrees of freedom for the numerator and $n_2 - 1$ degrees of freedom for the denominator.

Key Formulas

Interval Estimate of a Population Variance

$$\frac{(n-1)s^2}{\chi^2_{\alpha/2}} \leq \sigma^2 \leq \frac{(n-1)s^2}{\chi^2_{(1-\alpha/2)}} \tag{11.7}$$

Test Statistic for Hypothesis Tests About a Population Variance

$$\chi^2 = \frac{(n-1)s^2}{\sigma_0^2} \tag{11.8}$$

Test Statistic for Hypothesis Tests About Population Variances with $\sigma_1^2 = \sigma_2^2$

$$F = \frac{s_1^2}{s_2^2} \tag{11.10}$$

Supplementary Exercises

23. Because of staffing decisions, managers of the Gibson-Marimont Hotel are interested in the variability in the number of rooms occupied per day during a particular season of the year. A sample of 20 days of operation shows a sample mean of 290 rooms occupied per day and a sample standard deviation of 30 rooms.
    a. What is the point estimate of the population variance?
    b. Provide a 90% confidence interval estimate of the population variance.
    c. Provide a 90% confidence interval estimate of the population standard deviation.

24. Initial public offerings (IPOs) of stocks are on average underpriced. The standard deviation measures the dispersion, or variation, in the underpricing-overpricing indicator. A sample of 13 Canadian IPOs that were subsequently traded on the Toronto Stock Exchange had a standard deviation of 14.95. Develop a 95% confidence interval estimate of the population standard deviation for the underpricing-overpricing indicator.

25. The estimated daily living costs for an executive traveling to various major cities follow. The estimates include a single room at a four-star hotel, beverages, breakfast, taxi fares, and incidental costs.

WEB file Travel

City	Daily Living Cost ($)	City	Daily Living Cost ($)
Bangkok	242.87	Mexico City	212.00
Bogotá	260.93	Milan	284.08
Cairo	194.19	Mumbai	139.16
Dublin	260.76	Paris	436.72
Frankfurt	355.36	Rio de Janeiro	240.87
Hong Kong	346.32	Seoul	310.41
Johannesburg	165.37	Tel Aviv	223.73
Lima	250.08	Toronto	181.25
London	326.76	Warsaw	238.20
Madrid	283.56	Washington, D.C.	250.61

a. Compute the sample mean.
b. Compute the sample standard deviation.
c. Compute a 95% confidence interval for the population standard deviation.

26. Part variability is critical in the manufacturing of ball bearings. Large variances in the size of the ball bearings cause bearing failure and rapid wearout. Production standards call for a maximum variance of .0001 when the bearing sizes are measured in inches. A sample of 15 bearings shows a sample standard deviation of .014 inches.
   a. Use $\alpha = .10$ to determine whether the sample indicates that the maximum acceptable variance is being exceeded.
   b. Compute the 90% confidence interval estimate of the variance of the ball bearings in the population.

27. The filling variance for boxes of cereal is designed to be .02 or less. A sample of 41 boxes of cereal shows a sample standard deviation of .16 ounces. Use $\alpha = .05$ to determine whether the variance in the cereal box fillings is exceeding the design specification.

28. City Trucking, Inc., claims consistent delivery times for its routine customer deliveries. A sample of 22 truck deliveries shows a sample variance of 1.5. Test to determine whether H_0: $\sigma^2 \leq 1$ can be rejected. Use $\alpha = .10$.

29. A sample of 9 days over the past six months showed that a dentist treated the following numbers of patients: 22, 25, 20, 18, 15, 22, 24, 19, and 26. If the number of patients seen per day is normally distributed, would an analysis of these sample data reject the hypothesis that the variance in the number of patients seen per day is equal to 10? Use a .10 level of significance. What is your conclusion?

30. A sample standard deviation for the number of passengers taking a particular airline flight is 8. A 95% confidence interval estimate of the population standard deviation is 5.86 passengers to 12.62 passengers.
   a. Was a sample size of 10 or 15 used in the statistical analysis?
   b. Suppose the sample standard deviation of $s = 8$ was based on a sample of 25 flights. What change would you expect in the confidence interval for the population standard deviation? Compute a 95% confidence interval estimate of σ with a sample size of 25.

31. Is there any difference in the variability in golf scores for players on the LPGA Tour (the women's professional golf tour) and players on the PGA Tour (the men's professional golf tour)? A sample of 20 tournament scores from LPGA events showed a standard deviation of 2.4623 strokes, and a sample of 30 tournament scores from PGA events showed a standard deviation of 2.2118 (*Golfweek*, February 7, 2009, and March 7, 2009). Conduct a hypothesis test for equal population variances to determine if there is any statistically significant difference in the variability of golf scores for male and female professional golfers. Use $\alpha = .10$. What is your conclusion?

32. The grade point averages of 352 students who completed a college course in financial accounting have a standard deviation of .940. The grade point averages of 73 students who dropped out of the same course have a standard deviation of .797. Do the data indicate a difference between the variances of grade point averages for students who completed a financial accounting course and students who dropped out? Use a .05 level of significance. *Note:* $F_{.025}$ with 351 and 72 degrees of freedom is 1.466.

33. The accounting department analyzes the variance of the weekly unit costs reported by two production departments. A sample of 16 cost reports for each of the two departments shows cost variances of 2.3 and 5.4, respectively. Is this sample sufficient to conclude that the two production departments differ in terms of unit cost variance? Use $\alpha = .10$.

34. Two new assembly methods are tested and the variances in assembly times are reported. Use $\alpha = .10$ and test for equality of the two population variances.

	Method A	**Method B**
Sample Size	$n_1 = 31$	$n_2 = 25$
Sample Variation	$s_1^2 = 25$	$s_2^2 = 12$

Case Problem Air Force Training Program

An Air Force introductory course in electronics uses a personalized system of instruction whereby each student views a videotaped lecture and then is given a programmed instruction text. The students work independently with the text until they have completed the training and passed a test. Of concern is the varying pace at which the students complete this portion of their training program. Some students are able to cover the programmed instruction text relatively quickly, whereas other students work much longer with the text and require additional time to complete the course. The fast students wait until the slow students complete the introductory course before the entire group proceeds together with other aspects of their training.

A proposed alternative system involves use of computer-assisted instruction. In this method, all students view the same videotaped lecture and then each is assigned to a computer terminal for further instruction. The computer guides the student, working independently, through the self-training portion of the course.

To compare the proposed and current methods of instruction, an entering class of 122 students was assigned randomly to one of the two methods. One group of 61 students used the current programmed-text method and the other group of 61 students used the proposed computer-assisted method. The time in hours was recorded for each student in the study. The following data are provided in the data set Training.

Course Completion Times (hours) for Current Training Method

76	76	77	74	76	74	74	77	72	78	73
78	75	80	79	72	69	79	72	70	70	81
76	78	72	82	72	73	71	70	77	78	73
79	82	65	77	79	73	76	81	69	75	75
77	79	76	78	76	76	73	77	84	74	74
69	79	66	70	74	72					

WEB file

Training

Course Completion Times (hours) for Proposed Computer-Assisted Method

74	75	77	78	74	80	73	73	78	76	76
74	77	69	76	75	72	75	72	76	72	77
73	77	69	77	75	76	74	77	75	78	72
77	78	78	76	75	76	76	75	76	80	77
76	75	73	77	77	77	79	75	75	72	82
76	76	74	72	78	71					

Managerial Report

1. Use appropriate descriptive statistics to summarize the training time data for each method. What similarities or differences do you observe from the sample data?
2. Use the methods of Chapter 10 to comment on any difference between the population means for the two methods. Discuss your findings.
3. Compute the standard deviation and variance for each training method. Conduct a hypothesis test about the equality of population variances for the two training methods. Discuss your findings.
4. What conclusion can you reach about any differences between the two methods? What is your recommendation? Explain.
5. Can you suggest other data or testing that might be desirable before making a final decision on the training program to be used in the future?

Appendix 11.1 Population Variances with Minitab

Here we describe how to use Minitab to conduct a hypothesis test involving two population variances.

WEB file

SchoolBus

We will use the data for the Dullus County School bus study in Section 11.2. The arrival times for Milbank appear in column C1, and the arrival times for Gulf Park appear in column C2. The following Minitab procedure can be used to conduct the hypothesis test H_0: $\sigma_1^2 = \sigma_2^2$ and H_a: $\sigma_1^2 \neq \sigma_2^2$.

Step 1. Select the **Stat** menu
Step 2. Choose **Basic Statistics**
Step 3. Choose **2-Variances**
Step 4. When the 2-Variances (Test and Confidence Interval) dialog box appears:
Select **Samples in different columns** in the **Data** box
Enter C1 in the **First** box
Enter C2 in the **Second** box
Select **Options**

Step 5. When the 2-Variances-Options dialog box appears:
Enter 95 in the **Confidence level** box
Select **Variance 1/Variance 2** in the **Hypothesized ratio** box
Enter 1 in the **Value** box
Select **not equal** in the **Alternative** box
Click **OK**
Click **OK**

The F test results show the test statistic $F = 2.40$ and the p-value $= .081$. The procedure may be used for either one-tailed or two-tailed tests and the output provides confidence intervals for the ratio of the variances as well as the ratio of the standard deviations.

Appendix 11.2 Population Variances with Excel

Here we describe how to use Excel to conduct a hypothesis test involving two population variances.

WEB file SchoolBus

We will use the data for the Dullus County School bus study in Section 11.2. The Excel worksheet has the label Milbank in cell A1 and the label Gulf Park in cell B1. The times for the Milbank sample are in cells A2:A27 and the times for the Gulf Park sample are in cells B2:B17. The steps to conduct the hypothesis test H_0: $\sigma_1^2 = \sigma_2^2$ and H_a: $\sigma_1^2 \neq \sigma_2^2$ are as follows:

Step 1. Click the **Data** tab on the Ribbon
Step 2. In the **Analysis** group, click **Data Analysis**
Step 3. When the Data Analysis dialog box appears:
Choose **F-Test Two-Sample for Variances**
Step 4. When the F-Test Two Sample for Variances dialog box appears:
Enter A1:A27 in the **Variable 1 Range** box
Enter B1:B17 in the **Variable 2 Range** box
Select **Labels**
Enter .05 in the **Alpha** box
(*Note:* This Excel procedure uses alpha as the area in the upper tail.)
Select **Output Range** and enter C1 in the box
Click **OK**

The output P(F<=f) one-tail = .0405 is the one-tailed area associated with the test statistic $F = 2.40$. Thus, the two-tailed p-value is 2(.0405) = .081. If the hypothesis test had been a one-tailed test, the one-tailed area in the cell labeled P(F<=f) one-tail provides the information necessary to determine the p-value for the test.

Appendix 11.3 Single Population Standard Deviation with StatTools

WEB file BusTimes

In this appendix we show how StatTools can be used to conduct hypothesis tests about a population standard deviation. StatTools conducts hypothesis tests on the population standard deviation, not on the population variance directly. We use the example discussed in Section 11.1 involving bus arrival times at a downtown intersection to illustrate.

Begin by using the Data Set Manager to create a StatTools data set for the BusTimes data using the procedure described in the appendix in Chapter 1. The following steps can be used to test the hypothesis $H_0 : \sigma \leq 2$ against $H_a : \sigma > 2$.

Step 1. Click the **StatTools** tab on the Ribbon
Step 2. In the **Analyses** group, click **Statistical Inference**

Step 3. Choose the **Hypothesis Test** option

Step 4. Choose **Mean/Std. Deviation**

Step 5. When the StatTools-Hypothesis Test for Mean/Std. Deviation dialog box appears:

For **Analysis Type,** choose **One-Sample Analysis**
In the variables section, select **Times**
In the **Hypothesis Tests to Perform** section:
Remove the check mark from the **Mean** box
Select the **Standard Deviation** option
Enter 2 in the **Null Hypothesis Value** box
Select **Greater Than Null Value (One-Tailed Test)** in the **Alternative Hypothesis Type** box
Click **OK**

The results from the hypothesis test will appear. They include the p-value and the value of the χ^2 test statistic.

CHAPTER 12

Comparing Multiple Proportions, Test of Independence and Goodness of Fit

CONTENTS

STATISTICS *in* PRACTICE

UNITED WAY*
ROCHESTER, NEW YORK

United Way of Greater Rochester is a nonprofit organization dedicated to improving the quality of life for all people in the seven counties it serves by meeting the community's most important human care needs.

The annual United Way/Red Cross fund-raising campaign funds hundreds of programs offered by more than 200 service providers. These providers meet a wide variety of human needs—physical, mental, and social—and serve people of all ages, backgrounds, and economic means.

The United Way of Greater Rochester decided to conduct a survey to learn more about community perceptions of charities. Focus-group interviews were held with professional, service, and general worker groups to obtain preliminary information on perceptions. The information obtained was then used to help develop the questionnaire for the survey. The questionnaire was pretested, modified, and distributed to 440 individuals.

A variety of descriptive statistics, including frequency distributions and crosstabulations, were provided from the data collected. An important part of the analysis involved the use of chi-square tests of independence. One use of such statistical tests was to determine whether perceptions of administrative expenses were independent of the occupation of the respondent.

The hypotheses for the test of independence were:

H_0: Perception of United Way administrative expenses is independent of the occupation of the respondent.

H_a: Perception of United Way administrative expenses is not independent of the occupation of the respondent.

Two questions in the survey provided categorical data for the statistical test. One question obtained data on perceptions of the percentage of funds going to administrative expenses (up to 10%, 11–20%, and 21% or more). The other question asked for the occupation of the respondent.

United Way programs meet the needs of children as well as adults. © Jim West/Alamy.

The test of independence led to rejection of the null hypothesis and to the conclusion that perception of United Way administrative expenses is not independent of the occupation of the respondent. Actual administrative expenses were less than 9%, but 35% of the respondents perceived that administrative expenses were 21% or more. Hence, many respondents had inaccurate perceptions of administrative expenses. In this group, production-line, clerical, sales, and professional-technical employees had the more inaccurate perceptions.

The community perceptions study helped United Way of Rochester develop adjustments to its programs and fund-raising activities. In this chapter, you will learn how tests, such as described here, are conducted.

*The authors are indebted to Dr. Philip R. Tyler, marketing consultant to the United Way, for providing this Statistics in Practice.

In Chapters 9, 10, and 11 we introduced methods of statistical inference for hypothesis tests about the means, proportions, and variances of one and two populations. In this chapter, we introduce three additional hypothesis-testing procedures that expand our capacity for making statistical inferences about populations.

The test statistic used in conducting the hypothesis tests in this chapter is based on the chi-square (χ^2) distribution. In all cases, the data are categorical. These chi-square tests are versatile and expand hypothesis testing with the following applications.

1. Testing the equality of population proportions for three or more populations
2. Testing the independence of two categorical variables
3. Testing whether a probability distribution for a population follows a specific historical or theoretical probability distribution

We begin by considering hypothesis tests for the equality of population proportions for three or more populations.

12.1 Testing the Equality of Population Proportions for Three or More Populations

In Section 10.2 we introduced methods of statistical inference for population proportions with two populations where the hypothesis test conclusion was based on the standard normal (z) test statistic. We now show how the chi-square (χ^2) test statistic can be used to make statistical inferences about the equality of population proportions for three or more populations. Using the notation

$$p_1 = \text{population proportion for population 1}$$
$$p_2 = \text{population proportion for population 2}$$

and

$$p_k = \text{population proportion for population } k$$

the hypotheses for the equality of population proportions for $k \geq 3$ populations are as follows:

$$H_0: p_1 = p_2 = \cdots = p_k$$
$$H_a: \text{Not all population proportions are equal}$$

If the sample data and the chi-square test computations indicate H_0 cannot be rejected, we cannot detect a difference among the k population proportions. However, if the sample data and the chi-square test computations indicate H_0 can be rejected, we have the statistical evidence to conclude that not all k population proportions are equal; that is, one or more population proportions differ from the other population proportions. Further analyses can be done to conclude which population proportion or proportions are significantly different from others. Let us demonstrate this chi-square test by considering an application.

Organizations such as J.D. Power and Associates use the proportion of owners likely to repurchase a particular automobile as an indication of customer loyalty for the automobile. An automobile with a greater proportion of owners likely to repurchase is concluded to have greater customer loyalty. Suppose that in a particular study we want to compare the customer loyalty for three automobiles: Chevrolet Impala, Ford Fusion, and Honda Accord. The current owners of each of the three automobiles form the three populations for the study. The three population proportions of interest are as follows:

p_1 = proportion likely to repurchase an Impala for the population of Chevrolet Impala owners

p_2 = proportion likely to repurchase a Fusion for the population of Ford Fusion owners

p_3 = proportion likely to repurchase an Accord for the population of Honda Accord owners

TABLE 12.1 SAMPLE RESULTS OF LIKELY TO REPURCHASE FOR THREE POPULATIONS OF AUTOMOBILE OWNERS (OBSERVED FREQUENCIES)

WEB file

AutoLoyalty

		Automobile Owners			
		Chevrolet Impala	**Ford Fusion**	**Honda Accord**	**Total**
Likely to Repurchase	**Yes**	69	120	123	312
	No	56	80	52	188
	Total	125	200	175	500

The hypotheses are stated as follows:

$$H_0: p_1 = p_2 = p_3$$
$$H_a: \text{Not all population proportions are equal}$$

To conduct this hypothesis test we begin by taking a sample of owners from each of the three populations. Thus we will have a sample of Chevrolet Impala owners, a sample of Ford Fusion owners, and a sample of Honda Accord owners. Each sample provides categorical data indicating whether the respondents are likely or not likely to repurchase the automobile. The data for samples of 125 Chevrolet Impala owners, 200 Ford Fusion owners, and 175 Honda Accord owners are summarized in the tabular format shown in Table 12.1. This table has two rows for the responses Yes and No and three columns, one corresponding to each of the populations. The observed frequencies are summarized in the six cells of the table corresponding to each combination of the likely to repurchase responses and the three populations.

In studies such as these, we often use the same sample size for each population. We have chosen different sample sizes in this example to show that the chi-square test is not restricted to equal sample sizes for each of the k populations.

Using Table 12.1, we see that 69 of the 125 Chevrolet Impala owners indicated that they were likely to repurchase a Chevrolet Impala. One hundred and twenty of the 200 Ford Fusion owners and 123 of the 175 Honda Accord owners indicated that they were likely to repurchase their current automobile. Also, across all three samples, 312 of the 500 owners in the study indicated that they were likely to repurchase their current automobile. The question now is how do we analyze the data in Table 12.1 to determine if the hypothesis H_0: $p_1 = p_2 = p_3$ should be rejected?

The data in Table 12.1 are the *observed frequencies* for each of the six cells that represent the six combinations of the likely to repurchase response and the owner population. If we can determine the *expected frequencies under the assumption H_0 is true*, we can use the chi-square test statistic to determine whether there is a significant difference between the observed and expected frequencies. If a significant difference exists between the observed and expected frequencies, the hypothesis H_0 can be rejected and there is evidence that not all the population proportions are equal.

Expected frequencies for the six cells of the table are based on the following rationale. First, we assume that the null hypothesis of equal population proportions is true. Then we note that in the entire sample of 500 owners, a total of 312 owners indicated that they were likely to repurchase their current automobile. Thus, 312/500 = .624 is the overall sample proportion of owners indicating they are likely to repurchase their current automobile. If H_0: $p_1 = p_2 = p_3$ is true, .624 would be the best estimate of the proportion responding likely to repurchase for each of the automobile owner populations. So if the assumption of H_0 is true, we would expect .624 of the 125 Chevrolet Impala owners, or .624(125) = 78 owners to indicate they are likely to repurchase the Impala. Using the .624 overall sample proportion, we would expect .624(200) = 124.8 of the 200 Ford Fusion owners and .624(175) = 109.2

of the Honda Accord owners to respond that they are likely to repurchase their respective model of automobile.

Let us generalize the approach to computing expected frequencies by letting e_{ij} denote the expected frequency for the cell in row i and column j of the table. With this notation, now reconsider the expected frequency calculation for the response of likely to repurchase Yes (row 1) for Chevrolet Impala owners (column 1), that is, the expected frequency e_{11}.

Note that 312 is the total number of Yes responses (row 1 total), 175 is the total sample size for Chevrolet Impala owners (column 1 total), and 500 is the total sample size. Following the logic in the preceding paragraph, we can show

$$e_{11} = \left(\frac{\text{Row 1 Total}}{\text{Total Sample Size}}\right)(\text{Column 1 Total}) = \left(\frac{312}{500}\right)125 = (.624)125 = 78$$

Starting with the first part of the above expression, we can write

$$e_{11} = \frac{(\text{Row 1 Total})(\text{Column 1 Total})}{\text{Total Sample Size}}$$

Generalizing this expression shows that the following formula can be used to provide the expected frequencies under the assumption H_0 is true.

EXPECTED FREQUENCIES UNDER THE ASSUMPTION H_0 IS TRUE

$$e_{ij} = \frac{(\text{Row } i \text{ Total})(\text{Column } j \text{ Total})}{\text{Total Sample Size}} \tag{12.1}$$

Using equation (12.1), we see that the expected frequency of Yes responses (row 1) for Honda Accord owners (column 3) would be e_{13} = (Row 1 Total)(Column 3 Total)/(Total Sample Size) = (312)(175)/500 = 109.2. Use equation (12.1) to verify the other expected frequencies are as shown in Table 12.2.

The test procedure for comparing the observed frequencies of Table 12.1 with the expected frequencies of Table 12.2 involves the computation of the following chi-square statistic:

CHI-SQUARE TEST STATISTIC

$$\chi^2 = \sum_i \sum_j \frac{(f_{ij} - e_{ij})^2}{e_{ij}} \tag{12.2}$$

where

f_{ij} = observed frequency for the cell in row i and column j

e_{ij} = expected frequency for the cell in row i and column j under the assumption H_0 is true

Note: In a chi-square test involving the equality of k population proportions, the above test statistic has a chi-square distribution with $k - 1$ degrees of freedom provided the expected frequency is 5 *or more* for each cell.

TABLE 12.2 EXPECTED FREQUENCIES FOR LIKELY TO REPURCHASE FOR THREE POPULATIONS OF AUTOMOBILE OWNERS IF H_0 IS TRUE

		Automobile Owners			
		Chevrolet Impala	**Ford Fusion**	**Honda Accord**	**Total**
Likely to Repurchase	**Yes**	78	124.8	109.2	312
	No	47	75.2	65.8	188
	Total	125	200	175	500

Reviewing the expected frequencies in Table 12.2, we see that the expected frequency is at least five for each cell in the table. We therefore proceed with the computation of the chi-square test statistic. The calculations necessary to compute the value of the test statistic are shown in Table 12.3. In this case, we see that the value of the test statistic is $\chi^2 = 7.89$.

In order to understand whether or not $\chi^2 = 7.89$ leads us to reject H_0: $p_1 = p_2 = p_3$, you will need to understand and refer to values of the chi-square distribution. Table 12.4 shows the general shape of the chi-square distribution, but note that the shape of a specific chi-square distribution depends upon the number of degrees of freedom. The table shows the upper tail areas of .10, .05, .025, .01, and .005 for chi-square distributions with up to 15 degrees of freedom. This version of the chi-square table will enable you to conduct the hypothesis tests presented in this chapter.

Since the expected frequencies shown in Table 12.2 are based on the assumption that H_0: $p_1 = p_2 = p_3$ is true, observed frequencies, f_{ij}, that are in agreement with expected frequencies, e_{ij}, provide small values of $(f_{ij} - e_{ij})^2$ in equation (12.2). If this is the case, the value of the chi-square test statistic will be relatively small and H_0 cannot be rejected. On the other hand, if the differences between the observed and expected frequencies are *large*, values of $(f_{ij} - e_{ij})^2$ and the computed value of the test statistic will be large. In this case, the null hypothesis of equal population proportions can be rejected. Thus a chi-square test for equal population proportions will always be an upper tail test with rejection of H_0 occurring when the test statistic is in the upper tail of the chi-square distribution.

The chi-square test presented in this section is always a one-tailed test with the rejection of H_0 occurring in the upper tail of the chi-square distribution.

We can use the upper tail area of the appropriate chi-square distribution and the p-value approach to determine whether the null hypothesis can be rejected. In the automobile brand loyalty study, the three owner populations indicate that the appropriate chi-square

TABLE 12.3 COMPUTATION OF THE CHI-SQUARE TEST STATISTIC FOR THE TEST OF EQUAL POPULATION PROPORTIONS

Likely to Repurchase?	**Automobile Owner**	**Observed Frequency (f_{ij})**	**Expected Frequency (e_{ij})**	**Difference ($f_{ij} - e_{ij}$)**	**Squared Difference ($f_{ij} - e_{ij}$)^2**	**Squared Difference Divided by Expected Frequency $(f_{ij} - e_{ij})^2/e_{ij}$**
Yes	Impala	69	78.0	−9.0	81.00	1.04
Yes	Fusion	120	124.8	−4.8	23.04	0.18
Yes	Accord	123	109.2	13.8	190.44	1.74
No	Impala	56	47.0	9.0	81.00	1.72
No	Fusion	80	75.2	4.8	23.04	0.31
No	Accord	52	65.8	−13.8	190.44	2.89
	Total	500	500			$\chi^2 = 7.89$

TABLE 12.4 SELECTED VALUES OF THE CHI-SQUARE DISTRIBUTION

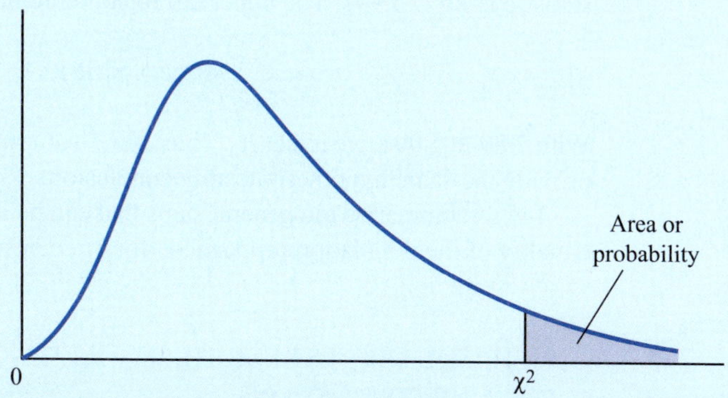

Degrees of Freedom	Area in Upper Tail .10	.05	.025	.01	.005
1	2.706	3.841	5.024	6.635	7.879
2	4.605	5.991	7.378	9.210	10.597
3	6.251	7.815	9.348	11.345	12.838
4	7.779	9.488	11.143	13.277	14.860
5	9.236	11.070	12.832	15.086	16.750
6	10.645	12.592	14.449	16.812	18.548
7	12.017	14.067	16.013	18.475	20.278
8	13.362	15.507	17.535	20.090	21.955
9	14.684	16.919	19.023	21.666	23.589
10	15.987	18.307	20.483	23.209	25.188
11	17.275	19.675	21.920	24.725	26.757
12	18.549	21.026	23.337	26.217	28.300
13	19.812	22.362	24.736	27.688	29.819
14	21.064	23.685	26.119	29.141	31.319
15	22.307	24.996	27.488	30.578	32.801

distribution has $k - 1 = 3 - 1 = 2$ degrees of freedom. Using row two of the chi-square distribution table, we have the following:

Area in Upper Tail	**.10**	**.05**	**.025**	**.01**	**.005**
χ^2 Value (2 *df*)	4.605	5.991	7.378	9.210	10.597

$\chi^2 = 7.89$ (between 7.378 and 9.210)

We see the upper tail area at $\chi^2 = 7.89$ is between .025 and .01. Thus, the corresponding upper tail area or p-value must be between .025 and .01. With p-value $\leq .05$, we reject H_0 and conclude that the three population proportions are not all equal and thus there is a difference in brand loyalties among the Chevrolet Impala, Ford Fusion, and Honda Accord owners. Minitab or Excel procedures provided in Appendix F can be used to show $\chi^2 = 7.89$ with 2 degrees of freedom yields a p-value $= .0193$.

Instead of using the p-value, we could use the critical value approach to draw the same conclusion. With $\alpha = .05$ and 2 degrees of freedom, the critical value for the chi-square test statistic is $\chi^2 = 5.991$. The upper tail rejection region becomes

$$\text{Reject } H_0 \text{ if } \chi^2 \geq 5.991$$

With $7.89 \geq 5.991$, we reject H_0. Thus, the p-value approach and the critical value approach provide the same hypothesis-testing conclusion.

Let us summarize the general steps that can be used to conduct a chi-square test for the equality of the population proportions for three or more populations.

A CHI-SQUARE TEST FOR THE EQUALITY OF POPULATION PROPORTIONS FOR $k \geq 3$ POPULATIONS

1. State the null and alternative hypotheses

   H_0: $p_1 = p_2 = \cdots = p_k$
   H_a: Not all population proportions are equal

2. Select a random sample from each of the populations and record the observed frequencies, f_{ij}, in a table with 2 rows and k columns
3. Assume the null hypothesis is true and compute the expected frequencies, e_{ij}
4. If the expected frequency, e_{ij}, is 5 or more for each cell, compute the test statistic:

$$\chi^2 = \sum_i \sum_j \frac{(f_{ij} - e_{ij})^2}{e_{ij}}$$

5. Rejection rule:

p-value approach:	Reject H_0 if p-value $\leq \alpha$
Critical value approach:	Reject H_0 if $\chi^2 \geq \chi^2_\alpha$

   where the chi-square distribution has $k - 1$ degrees of freedom and α is the level of significance for the test.

A Multiple Comparison Procedure

We have used a chi-square test to conclude that the population proportions for the three populations of automobile owners are not all equal. Thus, some differences among the population proportions exist and the study indicates that customer loyalties are not all the same for the Chevrolet Impala, Ford Fusion, and Honda Accord owners. To identify where the differences between population proportions exist, we can begin by computing the three sample proportions as follows:

Brand Loyalty Sample Proportions

Chevrolet Impala	$\bar{p}_1 = 69/125 = .5520$
Ford Fusion	$\bar{p}_2 = 120/200 = .6000$
Honda Accord	$\bar{p}_3 = 123/175 = .7029$

Since the chi-square test indicated that not all population proportions are equal, it is reasonable for us to proceed by attempting to determine where differences among the population proportions exist. For this we will rely on a multiple comparison procedure that can be used to conduct statistical tests between all pairs of population proportions. In the following, we discuss a multiple comparison procedure known as the **Marascuilo procedure**. This is a relatively straightforward procedure for making pairwise comparisons of all pairs of population proportions. We will demonstrate the computations required by this multiple comparison test procedure for the automobile customer loyalty study.

We begin by computing the absolute value of the pairwise difference between sample proportions for each pair of populations in the study. In the three-population automobile brand loyalty study we compare populations 1 and 2, populations 1 and 3, and then populations 2 and 3 using the sample proportions as follows:

Chevrolet Impala and Ford Fusion

$$|\bar{p}_1 - \bar{p}_2| = |.5520 - .6000| = .0480$$

Chevrolet Impala and Honda Accord

$$|\bar{p}_1 - \bar{p}_3| = |.5520 - .7029| = .1509$$

Ford Fusion and Honda Accord

$$|\bar{p}_2 - \bar{p}_3| = |.6000 - .7029| = .1029$$

In a second step, we select a level of significance and compute the corresponding critical value for each pairwise comparison using the following expression.

CRITICAL VALUES FOR THE MARASCUILO PAIRWISE COMPARISON PROCEDURE FOR k POPULATION PROPORTIONS

For each pairwise comparison compute a critical value as follows:

$$CV_{ij} = \sqrt{\chi^2_\alpha}\sqrt{\frac{\bar{p}_i(1 - \bar{p}_i)}{n_i} + \frac{\bar{p}_j(1 - \bar{p}_j)}{n_j}} \qquad \textbf{(12.3)}$$

where

χ^2_α = chi-square with a level of significance α and $k - 1$ degrees of freedom

$\bar{p}_i$ and $\bar{p}_j$ = sample proportions for populations i and j

n_i and n_j = sample sizes for populations i and j

Using the chi-square distribution in Table 12.4, $k - 1 = 3 - 1 = 2$ degrees of freedom, and a .05 level of significance, we have $\chi^2_{.05} = 5.991$. Now using the sample proportions $\bar{p}_1 = .5520$, $\bar{p}_2 = .6000$, and $\bar{p}_3 = .7029$, the critical values for the three pairwise comparison tests are as follows:

Chevrolet Impala and Ford Fusion

$$CV_{12} = \sqrt{5.991}\sqrt{\frac{.5520(1 - .5520)}{125} + \frac{.6000(1 - .6000)}{200}} = .1380$$

Chevrolet Impala and Honda Accord

$$CV_{13} = \sqrt{5.991}\sqrt{\frac{.5520(1 - .5520)}{125} + \frac{.7029(1 - .7029)}{175}} = .1379$$

TABLE 12.5 PAIRWISE COMPARISON TESTS FOR THE AUTOMOBILE BRAND LOYALTY STUDY

Pairwise Comparison	$\lvert\bar{p}_i - \bar{p}_j\rvert$	CV_{ij}	Significant if $\lvert\bar{p}_i - \bar{p}_j\rvert > CV_{ij}$
Chevrolet Impala vs. Ford Fusion	.0480	.1380	Not significant
Chevrolet Impala vs. Honda Accord	.1509	.1379	Significant
Ford Fusion vs. Honda Accord	.1029	.1198	Not significant

Ford Fusion and Honda Accord

$$CV_{23} = \sqrt{5.991}\sqrt{\frac{.6000(1 - .6000)}{200} + \frac{.7029(1 - .7029)}{175}} = .1198$$

If the absolute value of any pairwise sample proportion difference $\lvert\bar{p}_i - \bar{p}_j\rvert$ exceeds its corresponding critical value, CV_{ij}, the pairwise difference is significant at the .05 level of significance and we can conclude that the two corresponding population proportions are different. The final step of the pairwise comparison procedure is summarized in Table 12.5.

The conclusion from the pairwise comparison procedure is that the only significant difference in customer loyalty occurs between the Chevrolet Impala and the Honda Accord. Our sample results indicate that the Honda Accord had a greater population proportion of owners who say they are likely to repurchase the Honda Accord. Thus, we can conclude that the Honda Accord ($\bar{p}_3 = .7029$) has a greater customer loyalty than the Chevrolet Impala ($\bar{p}_1 = .5520$).

The results of the study are inconclusive as to the comparative loyalty of the Ford Fusion. While the Ford Fusion did not show significantly different results when compared to the Chevrolet Impala or Honda Accord, a larger sample may have revealed a significant difference between Ford Fusion and the other two automobiles in terms of customer loyalty. It is not uncommon for a multiple comparison procedure to show significance for some pairwise comparisons and yet not show significance for other pairwise comparisons in the study.

NOTES AND COMMENTS

1. In Chapter 10, we used the standard normal distribution and the z test statistic to conduct hypothesis tests about the proportions of two populations. However, the chi-square test introduced in this section can also be used to conduct the hypothesis test that the proportions of two populations are equal. The results will be the same under both test procedures and the value of the test statistic χ^2 will be equal to the square of the value of the test statistic z. An advantage of the methodology in Chapter 10 is that it can be used for either a one-tailed or a two-tailed hypothesis about the proportions of two populations whereas the chi-square test in this section can be used only for two-tailed tests. Exercise 12.6 will give you a chance to use the chi-square test for the hypothesis that the proportions of two populations are equal.
2. Each of the k populations in this section had two response outcomes, Yes or No. In effect, each population had a binomial distribution with parameter p the population proportion of Yes responses. An extension of the chi-square procedure in this section applies when each of the k populations has three or more possible responses. In this case, each population is said to have a multinomial distribution. The chi-square calculations for the expected frequencies, e_{ij}, and the test statistic, χ^2, are the same as shown in expressions (12.1) and (12.2). The only difference is that the null hypothesis assumes that the multinomial distribution for the response variable is the same for all populations. With r responses for each of the k populations, the chi-square test statistic has $(r - 1)(k - 1)$ degrees of freedom. Exercise 12.8 will give you a chance to use the chi-square test to compare three populations with multinomial distributions.

Exercises

Methods

SELF test

1. Use the sample data below to test the hypotheses

$$H_0: p_1 = p_2 = p_3$$
$$H_a\text{: Not all population proportions are equal}$$

where p_i is the population proportion of Yes responses for population i. Using a .05 level of significance, what is the p-value and what is your conclusion?

	Populations		
Response	**1**	**2**	**3**
Yes	150	150	96
No	100	150	104

SELF test

2. Reconsider the observed frequencies in exercise 1
   a. Compute the sample proportion for each population.
   b. Use the multiple comparison procedure to determine which population proportions differ significantly. Use a .05 level of significance.

Applications

3. The sample data below represent the number of late and on time flights for Delta, United, and US Airways (*Bureau of Transportation Statistics,* March 2012).

	Airline		
Flight	**Delta**	**United**	**US Airways**
Late	39	51	56
On Time	261	249	344

   a. Formulate the hypotheses for a test that will determine if the population proportion of late flights is the same for all three airlines.
   b. Conduct the hypothesis test with a .05 level of significance. What is the p-value and what is your conclusion?
   c. Compute the sample proportion of late flights for each airline. What is the overall proportion of late flights for the three airlines?

SELF test

4. Benson Manufacturing is considering ordering electronic components from three different suppliers. The suppliers may differ in terms of quality in that the proportion or percentage of defective components may differ among the suppliers. To evaluate the proportion of defective components for the suppliers, Benson has requested a sample shipment of 500 components from each supplier. The number of defective components and the number of good components found in each shipment are as follows.

	Supplier		
Component	**A**	**B**	**C**
Defective	15	20	40
Good	485	480	460

a. Formulate the hypotheses that can be used to test for equal proportions of defective components provided by the three suppliers.
b. Using a .05 level of significance, conduct the hypothesis test. What is the p-value and what is your conclusion?
c. Conduct a multiple comparison test to determine if there is an overall best supplier or if one supplier can be eliminated because of poor quality.

5. Kate Sanders, a researcher in the department of biology at IPFW University, studied the effect of agriculture contaminants on the stream fish population in Northeastern Indiana (April 2012). Specially designed traps collected samples of fish at each of four stream locations. A research question was, Did the differences in agricultural contaminants found at the four locations alter the proportion of the fish population by gender? Observed frequencies were as follows.

	Stream Locations			
Gender	**A**	**B**	**C**	**D**
Male	49	44	49	39
Female	41	46	36	44

a. Focusing on the proportion of male fish at each location, test the hypothesis that the population proportions are equal for all four locations. Use a .05 level of significance. What is the p-value and what is your conclusion?
b. Does it appear that differences in agricultural contaminants found at the four locations altered the fish population by gender?

Exercise 6 shows a chi-square test can be used when the hypothesis is about the equality of two population proportions.

6. A tax preparation firm is interested in comparing the quality of work at two of its regional offices. The observed frequencies showing the number of sampled returns with errors and the number of sampled returns that were correct are as follows.

	Regional Office	
Return	**Office 1**	**Office 2**
Error	35	27
Correct	215	273

a. What are the sample proportions of returns with errors at the two offices?
b. Use the chi-square test procedure to see if there is a significant difference between the population proportion of error rates for the two offices. Test the null hypothesis H_0: $p_1 = p_2$ with a .10 level of significance. What is the p-value and what is your conclusion? *Note*: We generally use the chi-square test of equal proportions when there are three or more populations, but this example shows that the same chi-square test can be used for testing equal proportions with two populations.
c. In the Section 10.2, a z test was used to conduct the above test. Either a χ^2 test statistic or a z test statistic may be used to test the hypothesis. However, when we want to make inferences about the proportions for two populations, we generally prefer the z test statistic procedure. Refer to the Notes and Comments at the end of this section and comment on why the z test statistic provides the user with more options for inferences about the proportions of two populations.

7. Social networking is becoming more and more popular around the world. Pew Research Center used a survey of adults in several countries to determine the percentage of adults who use social networking sites (*USA Today,* February 8, 2012). Assume that the results for surveys in Great Britain, Israel, Russia, and United States are as follows.

Use Social Networking Sites	Country			
	Great Britain	Israel	Russia	United States
Yes	344	265	301	500
No	456	235	399	500

a. Conduct a hypothesis test to determine whether the proportion of adults using social networking sites is equal for all four countries. What is the *p*-value? Using a .05 level of significance, what is your conclusion?

b. What are the sample proportions for each of the four countries? Which country has the largest proportion of adults using social networking sites?

c. Using a .05 level of significance, conduct multiple pairwise comparison tests among the four countries. What is your conclusion?

Exercise 8 shows a chi-square test can also be used for multiple population tests when the categorical response variable has three or more outcomes.

8. A manufacturer is considering purchasing parts from three different suppliers. The parts received from the suppliers are classified as having a minor defect, having a major defect, or being good. Test results from samples of parts received from each of the three suppliers are shown below. Note that any test with these data is no longer a test of proportions for the three supplier populations because the categorical response variable has three outcomes: minor defect, major defect, and good.

Part Tested	Supplier		
	A	B	C
Minor Defect	15	13	21
Major Defect	5	11	5
Good	130	126	124

Using the data above, conduct a hypothesis test to determine if the distribution of defects is the same for the three suppliers. Use the chi-square test calculations as presented in this section with the exception that a table with r rows and c columns results in a chi-square test statistic with $(r - 1)(c - 1)$ degrees of freedom. Using a .05 level of significance, what is the *p*-value and what is your conclusion?

12.2 Test of Independence

An important application of a chi-square test involves using sample data to test for the independence of two categorical variables. For this test we take one sample from a population and record the observations for two categorical variables. We will summarize the data by counting the number of responses for each combination of a category for variable 1 and a category for variable 2. The null hypothesis for this test is that the two categorical variables are independent. Thus, the test is referred to as a **test of independence**. We will illustrate this test with the following example.

A beer industry association conducts a survey to determine the preferences of beer drinkers for light, regular, and dark beers. A sample of 200 beer drinkers is taken with each person in the sample asked to indicate a preference for one of the three types of beers: light, regular, or dark. At the end of the survey questionnaire, the respondent is asked to provide information on a variety of demographics including gender: male or female. A research question of interest to the association is whether preference for the three types of beer is independent of the gender of the beer drinker. If the two categorical variables, beer preference and gender, are independent, beer preference does not depend on gender and the preference for light, regular, and dark beer can be expected to be the same for male and female beer drinkers. However, if the test conclusion is that the two categorical variables are not independent, we have evidence that beer preference is associated or dependent upon the gender of the beer drinker. As a result, we can expect beer preferences to differ for male and female beer drinkers. In this case, a beer manufacturer could use this information to customize its promotions and advertising for the different target markets of male and female beer drinkers.

The hypotheses for this test of independence are as follows:

H_0: Beer preference is independent of gender

H_a: Beer preference is not independent of gender

The sample data will be summarized in a two-way table with beer preferences of light, regular, and dark as one of the variables and gender of male and female as the other variable. Since an objective of the study is to determine if there is difference between the beer preferences for male and female beer drinkers, we consider gender an explanatory variable and follow the usual practice of making the explanatory variable the column variable in the data tabulation table. The beer preference is the categorical response variable and is shown as the row variable. The sample results of the 200 beer drinkers in the study are summarized in Table 12.6.

The sample data are summarized based on the combination of beer preference and gender for the individual respondents. For example, 51 individuals in the study were males who preferred light beer, 56 individuals in the study were males who preferred regular beer, and so on. Let us now analyze the data in the table and test for independence of beer preference and gender.

First of all, since we selected a sample of beer drinkers, summarizing the data for each variable separately will provide some insights into the characteristics of the beer drinker population. For the categorical variable gender, we see 132 of the 200 in the sample were male. This gives us the estimate that 132/200 = .66, or 66%, of the beer drinker population is male. Similarly we estimate that 68/200 = .34, or 34%, of the beer drinker population is female. Thus male beer drinkers appear to outnumber female beer drinkers approximately 2 to 1. Sample proportions or percentages for the three types of beer are

Prefer Light Beer	90/200 = .450, or 45.0%
Prefer Regular Beer	77/200 = .385, or 38.5%
Prefer Dark Beer	33/200 = .165, or 16.5%

Across all beer drinkers in the sample, light beer is preferred most often and dark beer is preferred least often.

Let us now conduct the chi-square test to determine if beer preference and gender are independent. The computations and formulas used are the same as those used for the

TABLE 12.6 SAMPLE RESULTS FOR BEER PREFERENCES OF MALE AND FEMALE BEER DRINKERS (OBSERVED FREQUENCIES)

WEB file

BeerPreference

		Gender		
		Male	**Female**	**Total**
Beer Preference	**Light**	51	39	90
	Regular	56	21	77
	Dark	25	8	33
	Total	132	68	200

TABLE 12.7 EXPECTED FREQUENCIES IF BEER PREFERENCE IS INDEPENDENT OF THE GENDER OF THE BEER DRINKER

		Gender		
		Male	**Female**	**Total**
Beer Preference	**Light**	59.40	30.60	90
	Regular	50.82	26.18	77
	Dark	21.78	11.22	33
	Total	132	68	200

chi-square test in Section 12.1. Utilizing the observed frequencies in Table 12.6 for row i and column j, f_{ij}, we compute the expected frequencies, e_{ij}, under the assumption that the beer preferences and gender are independent. The computation of the expected frequencies follows the same logic and formula used in Section 12.1. Thus the expected frequency for row i and column j is given by

$$e_{ij} = \frac{(\text{Row } i \text{ Total})(\text{Column } j \text{ Total})}{\text{Sample Size}} \tag{12.4}$$

For example, $e_{11} = (90)(132)/200 = 59.40$ is the expected frequency for male beer drinkers who would prefer light beer if beer preference is independent of gender. Show that equation (12.4) can be used to find the other expected frequencies shown in Table 12.7.

Following the chi-square test procedure discussed in Section 12.1, we use the following expression to compute the value of the chi-square test statistic.

$$\chi^2 = \sum_i \sum_j \frac{(f_{ij} - e_{ij})^2}{e_{ij}} \tag{12.5}$$

With r rows and c columns in the table, the chi-square distribution will have $(r-1)(c-1)$ degrees of freedom provided the expected frequency is at least 5 for each cell. Thus, in this application we will use a chi-square distribution with $(3-1)(2-1) = 2$ degrees of freedom. The complete steps to compute the chi-square test statistic are summarized in Table 12.8.

We can use the upper tail area of the chi-square distribution with 2 degrees of freedom and the p-value approach to determine whether the null hypothesis that beer preference

TABLE 12.8 COMPUTATION OF THE CHI-SQUARE TEST STATISTIC FOR THE TEST OF INDEPENDENCE BETWEEN BEER PREFERENCE AND GENDER

Beer Preference	Gender	Observed Frequency f_{ij}	Expected Frequency e_{ij}	Difference $(f_{ij} - e_{ij})$	Squared Difference $(f_{ij} - e_{ij})^2$	Squared Difference Divided by Expected Frequency $(f_{ij} - e_{ij})^2/e_{ij}$
Light	Male	51	59.40	−8.40	70.56	1.19
Light	Female	39	30.60	8.40	70.56	2.31
Regular	Male	56	50.82	5.18	26.83	.53
Regular	Female	21	26.18	−5.18	26.83	1.02
Dark	Male	25	21.78	3.22	10.37	.48
Dark	Female	8	11.22	−3.22	10.37	.92
	Total	200	200			$\chi^2 = 6.45$

is independent of gender can be rejected. Using row two of the chi-square distribution table shown in Table 12.4, we have the following:

Area in Upper Tail	**.10**	**.05**	**.025**	**.01**	**.005**
χ^2 Value (2 *df*)	4.605	5.991	7.378	9.210	10.597

$\chi^2 = 6.45$

Thus, we see the upper tail area at $\chi^2 = 6.45$ is between .05 and .025, and so the corresponding upper tail area or p-value must be between .05 and .025. With p-value $\leq .05$, we reject H_0 and conclude that beer preference is not independent of the gender of the beer drinker. Stated another way, the study shows that beer preference can be expected to differ for male and female beer drinkers. Minitab or Excel procedures provided in Appendix F can be used to show $\chi^2 = 6.45$ with two degrees of freedom yields a p-value $= .0398$.

Instead of using the p-value, we could use the critical value approach to draw the same conclusion. With $\alpha = .05$ and 2 degrees of freedom, the critical value for the chi-square test statistic is $\chi^2_{.05} = 5.991$. The upper tail rejection region becomes

$$\text{Reject } H_0 \text{ if } \geq 5.991$$

With $6.45 \geq 5.991$, we reject H_0. Again we see that the p-value approach and the critical value approach provide the same conclusion.

While we now have evidence that beer preference and gender are not independent, we will need to gain additional insight from the data to assess the nature of the association between these two variables. One way to do this is to compute the probability of the beer preference responses for males and females separately. These calculations are as follows:

Beer Preference	**Male**	**Female**
Light	51/132 = .3864, or 38.64%	39/68 = .5735, or 57.35%
Regular	56/132 = .4242, or 42.42%	21/68 = .3088, or 30.88%
Dark	25/132 = .1894, or 18.94%	8/68 = .1176, or 11.76%

The bar chart for male and female beer drinkers of the three kinds of beer is shown in Figure 12.1.

FIGURE 12.1 BAR CHART COMPARISON OF BEER PREFERENCE BY GENDER

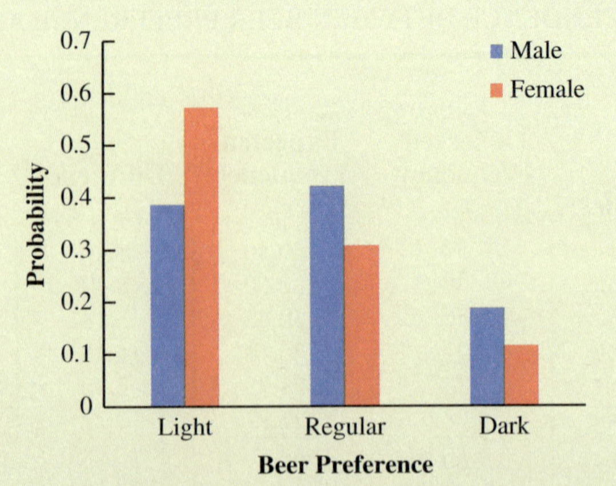

What observations can you make about the association between beer preference and gender? For female beer drinkers in the sample, the highest preference is for light beer at 57.35%. For male beer drinkers in the sample, regular beer is most frequently preferred at 42.42%. While female beer drinkers have a higher preference for light beer than males, male beer drinkers have a higher preference for both regular beer and dark beer. Data visualization through bar charts such as shown in Figure 12.1 is helpful in gaining insight as to how two categorical variables are associated.

Before we leave this discussion, we summarize the steps for a test of independence.

The expected frequencies must all be 5 or more for the chi-square test to be valid.

This chi-square test is also a one-tailed test with rejection of H_0 occurring in the upper tail of a chi-square distribution with $(r - 1)(c - 1)$ degrees of freedom.

CHI-SQUARE TEST FOR INDEPENDENCE OF TWO CATEGORICAL VARIABLES

1. State the null and alternative hypotheses.

   H_0: The two categorical variables are independent

   H_a: The two categorical variables are not independent

2. Select a random sample from the population and collect data for both variables for every element in the sample. Record the observed frequencies, f_{ij}, in a table with r rows and c columns.
3. Assume the null hypothesis is true and compute the expected frequencies, e_{ij}
4. If the expected frequency, e_{ij}, is 5 or more for each cell, compute the test statistic:

$$\chi^2 = \sum_i \sum_j \frac{(f_{ij} - e_{ij})^2}{e_{ij}}$$

5. Rejection rule:

   p-value approach: Reject H_0 if p-value $\leq \alpha$

   Critical value approach: Reject H_0 if $\chi^2 \geq \chi^2_\alpha$

   where the chi-square distribution has $(r - 1)(c - 1)$ degrees of freedom and α is the level of significance for the test.

Finally, if the null hypothesis of independence is rejected, summarizing the probabilities as shown in the above example will help the analyst determine where the association or dependence exists for the two categorical variables.

Exercises

Methods

SELF test

9. The following table contains observed frequencies for a sample of 200. Test for independence of the row and column variables using $\alpha = .05$.

	Column Variable		
Row Variable	**A**	**B**	**C**
P	20	44	50
Q	30	26	30

10. The following table contains observed frequencies for a sample of 240. Test for independence of the row and column variables using $\alpha = .05$.

	Column Variable		
Row Variable	**A**	**B**	**C**
P	20	30	20
Q	30	60	25
R	10	15	30

Applications

SELF test

11. A *Bloomberg Businessweek* subscriber study asked, "In the past 12 months, when traveling for business, what type of airline ticket did you purchase most often?" A second question asked if the type of airline ticket purchased most often was for domestic or international travel. Sample data obtained are shown in the following table.

	Type of Flight	
Type of Ticket	**Domestic**	**International**
First class	29	22
Business class	95	121
Economy class	518	135

a. Using a .05 level of significance, is the type of ticket purchased independent of the type of flight? What is your conclusion?
b. Discuss any dependence that exists between the type of ticket and type of flight.

WEB file

WorkforcePlan

12. A Deloitte employment survey asked a sample of human resource executives how their company planned to change its workforce over the next 12 months (*INC. Magazine*, February 2012). A categorical response variable showed three options: The company plans to hire and add to the number of employees, the company plans no change in the number of employees, or the company plans to lay off and reduce the number of employees. Another categorical variable indicated if the company was private or public. Sample data for 180 companies are summarized as follows.

	Company	
Employment Plan	**Private**	**Public**
Add Employees	37	32
No Change	19	34
Lay Off Employees	16	42

a. Conduct a test of independence to determine if the employment plan for the next 12 months is independent of the type of company. At a .05 level of significance, what is your conclusion?
b. Discuss any differences in the employment plans for private and public companies over the next 12 months.

13. Health insurance benefits vary by the size of the company (*Atlanta Business Chronicle*, December 31, 2010). The sample data below show the number of companies providing health insurance for small, medium, and large companies. For purposes of this study, small companies are companies that have fewer than 100 employees. Medium-sized companies have 100 to 999 employees, and large companies have 1000 or more employees. The

questionnaire sent to 225 employees asked whether or not the employee had health insurance and then asked the employee to indicate the size of the company.

	Size of the Company		
Health Insurance	**Small**	**Medium**	**Large**
Yes	36	65	88
No	14	10	12

a. Conduct a test of independence to determine whether health insurance coverage is independent of the size of the company. What is the p-value? Using a .05 level of significance, what is your conclusion?

b. A newspaper article indicated employees of small companies are more likely to lack health insurance coverage. Use percentages based on the above data to support this conclusion.

WEB file
AutoQuality

14. A vehicle quality survey asked new owners a variety of questions about their recently purchased automobile (J.D. Power and Associates, March 2012). One question asked for the owner's rating of the vehicle using categorical responses of average, outstanding, and exceptional. Another question asked for the owner's education level with the categorical responses some high school, high school graduate, some college, and college graduate. Assume the sample data below are for 500 owners who had recently purchased an automobile.

	Education			
Quality Rating	**Some HS**	**HS Grad**	**Some College**	**College Grad**
Average	35	30	20	60
Outstanding	45	45	50	90
Exceptional	20	25	30	50

a. Use a .05 level of significance and a test of independence to determine if a new owner's vehicle quality rating is independent of the owner's education. What is the p-value and what is your conclusion?

b. Use the overall percentage of average, outstanding, and exceptional ratings to comment upon how new owners rate the quality of their recently purchased automobiles.

15. *The Wall Street Journal* Corporate Perceptions Study 2011 surveyed readers and asked how each rated the quality of management and the reputation of the company for over 250 worldwide corporations. Both the quality of management and the reputation of the company were rated on an excellent, good, and fair categorical scale. Assume the sample data for 200 respondents below applies to this study.

	Reputation of Company		
Quality of Management	**Excellent**	**Good**	**Fair**
Excellent	40	25	5
Good	35	35	10
Fair	25	10	15

a. Use a .05 level of significance and test for independence of the quality of management and the reputation of the company. What is the p-value and what is your conclusion?

b. If there is a dependence or association between the two ratings, discuss and use probabilities to justify your answer.

16. As the price of oil rises, there is increased worldwide interest in alternate sources of energy. A *Financial Times*/Harris Poll surveyed people in six countries to assess attitudes toward a variety of alternate forms of energy (Harris Interactive website, February 27, 2008). The data in the following table are a portion of the poll's findings concerning whether people favor or oppose the building of new nuclear power plants.

	Country					
Response	**Great Britain**	**France**	**Italy**	**Spain**	**Germany**	**United States**
Strongly favor	141	161	298	133	128	204
Favor more than oppose	348	366	309	222	272	326
Oppose more than favor	381	334	219	311	322	316
Strongly oppose	217	215	219	443	389	174

a. How large was the sample in this poll?
b. Conduct a hypothesis test to determine whether people's attitude toward building new nuclear power plants is independent of country. What is your conclusion?
c. Using the percentage of respondents who "strongly favor" and "favor more than oppose," which country has the most favorable attitude toward building new nuclear power plants? Which country has the least favorable attitude?

17. The National Sleep Foundation used a survey to determine whether hours of sleep per night are independent of age (*Newsweek*, January 19, 2004). A sample of individuals was asked to indicate the number of hours of sleep per night with categorical options: fewer than 6 hours, 6 to 6.9 hours, 7 to 7.9 hours, and 8 hours or more. Later in the survey, the individuals were asked to indicate their age with categorical options: age 39 or younger and age 40 or older. Sample data follow.

	Age Group	
Hours of Sleep	**39 or younger**	**40 or older**
Fewer than 6	38	36
6 to 6.9	60	57
7 to 7.9	77	75
8 or more	65	92

a. Conduct a test of independence to determine whether hours of sleep are independent of age. Using a .05 level of significance, what is the p-value and what is your conclusion?
b. What is your estimate of the percentages of individuals who sleep fewer than 6 hours, 6 to 6.9 hours, 7 to 7.9 hours, and 8 hours or more per night?

18. On a syndicated television show the two hosts often create the impression that they strongly disagree about which movies are best. Each movie review is categorized as Pro ("thumbs up"), Con ("thumbs down"), or Mixed. The results of 160 movie ratings by the two hosts are shown here.

	Host B		
Host A	**Con**	**Mixed**	**Pro**
Con	24	8	13
Mixed	8	13	11
Pro	10	9	64

Use a test of independence with a .01 level of significance to analyze the data. What is your conclusion?

12.3 Goodness of Fit Test

In this section we use a chi-square test to determine whether a population being sampled has a specific probability distribution. We first consider a population with a historical multinomial probability distribution and use a goodness of fit test to determine if new sample data indicate there has been a change in the population distribution compared to the historical distribution. We then consider a situation where an assumption is made that a population has a normal probability distribution. In this case, we use a goodness of fit test to determine if sample data indicate that the assumption of a normal probability distribution is or is not appropriate. Both tests are referred to as **goodness of fit tests**.

Multinomial Probability Distribution

The multinomial probability distribution is an extension of the binomial probability distribution to the case where there are three or more outcomes per trial.

With a **multinomial probability distribution**, each element of a population is assigned to one and only one of three or more categories. As an example, consider the market share study being conducted by Scott Marketing Research. Over the past year, market shares for a certain product have stabilized at 30% for company A, 50% for company B, and 20% for company C. Since each customer is classified as buying from one of these companies, we have a multinomial probability distribution with three possible outcomes. The probability for each of the three outcomes is as follows.

$$p_A = \text{probability a customer purchases the company A product}$$
$$p_B = \text{probability a customer purchases the company B product}$$
$$p_C = \text{probability a customer purchases the company C product}$$

The sum of the probabilities for a multinomial probability distribution equal 1.

Using the historical market shares, we have multinomial probability distribution with $p_A = .30$, $p_B = .50$, and $p_C = .20$.

Company C plans to introduce a "new and improved" product to replace its current entry in the market. Company C has retained Scott Marketing Research to determine whether the new product will alter or change the market shares for the three companies. Specifically, the Scott Marketing Research study will introduce a sample of customers to the new company C product and then ask the customers to indicate a preference for the company A product, the company B product, or the new company C product. Based on the sample data, the following hypothesis test can be used to determine if the new company C product is likely to change the historical market shares for the three companies.

$$H_0\text{: } p_A = .30,\ p_B = .50,\text{ and } p_C = .20$$
$$H_a\text{: The population proportions are not } p_A = .30,\ p_B = .50,\text{ and } p_C = .20$$

The null hypothesis is based on the historical multinomial probability distribution for the market shares. If sample results lead to the rejection of H_0, Scott Marketing Research will have evidence to conclude that the introduction of the new company C product will change the market shares.

Let us assume that the market research firm has used a consumer panel of 200 customers. Each customer was asked to specify a purchase preference among the three alternatives: company A's product, company B's product, and company C's new product. The 200 responses are summarized here.

Observed Frequency		
Company A's Product	**Company B's Product**	**Company C's New Product**
48	98	54

We now can perform a goodness of fit test that will determine whether the sample of 200 customer purchase preferences is consistent with the null hypothesis. Like other chi-square tests, the goodness of fit test is based on a comparison of observed frequencies with the expected frequencies under the assumption that the null hypothesis is true. Hence, the next step is to compute expected purchase preferences for the 200 customers under the assumption that H_0: $p_A = .30$, $p_B = .50$, and $p_C = .20$ is true. Doing so provides the expected frequencies as follows.

	Expected Frequency	
Company A's Product	**Company B's Product**	**Company C's New Product**
200(.30) = 60	200(.50) = 100	200(.20) = 40

Note that the expected frequency for each category is found by multiplying the sample size of 200 by the hypothesized proportion for the category.

The goodness of fit test now focuses on the differences between the observed frequencies and the expected frequencies. Whether the differences between the observed and expected frequencies are "large" or "small" is a question answered with the aid of the following chi-square test statistic.

TEST STATISTIC FOR GOODNESS OF FIT

$$\chi^2 = \sum_{i=1}^{k} \frac{(f_i - e_i)^2}{e_i} \tag{12.6}$$

where

f_i = observed frequency for category i

e_i = expected frequency for category i

k = the number of categories

Note: The test statistic has a chi-square distribution with $k - 1$ degrees of freedom provided that the expected frequencies are 5 *or more* for all categories.

Let us continue with the Scott Marketing Research example and use the sample data to test the hypothesis that the multinomial population has the market share proportions $p_A = .30$, $p_B = .50$, and $p_C = .20$. We will use an $\alpha = .05$ level of significance. We proceed by using the observed and expected frequencies to compute the value of the test statistic. With the expected frequencies all 5 or more, the computation of the chi-square test statistic is shown in Table 12.9. Thus, we have $\chi^2 = 7.34$.

The test for goodness of fit is always a one-tailed test with the rejection occurring in the upper tail of the chi-square distribution.

We will reject the null hypothesis if the differences between the observed and expected frequencies are large. Thus the test of goodness of fit will always be an upper tail test. We can use the upper tail area for the test statistic and the p-value approach to determine whether the null hypothesis can be rejected. With $k - 1 = 3 - 1 = 2$ degrees of freedom,

TABLE 12.9 COMPUTATION OF THE CHI-SQUARE TEST STATISTIC FOR THE SCOTT MARKETING RESEARCH MARKET SHARE STUDY

Category	Hypothesized Proportion	Observed Frequency (f_i)	Expected Frequency (e_i)	Difference $(f_i - e_i)$	Squared Difference $(f_i - e_i)^2$	Squared Difference Divided by Expected Frequency $(f_i - e_i)^2/e_i$
Company A	.30	48	60	−12	144	2.40
Company B	.50	98	100	−2	4	0.04
Company C	.20	54	40	14	196	4.90
Total		200				$\chi^2 = 7.34$

row two of the chi-square distribution table in Table 12.4 provides the following:

Area in Upper Tail	**.10**	**.05**	**.025**	**.01**	**.005**
χ^2 Value (2 *df*)	4.605	5.991	7.378	9.210	10.597

$\chi^2 = 7.34$ (between 5.991 and 7.378)

The test statistic $\chi^2 = 7.34$ is between 5.991 and 7.378. Thus, the corresponding upper tail area or p-value must be between .05 and .025. With p-value $\leq .05$, we reject H_0 and conclude that the introduction of the new product by company C will alter the historical market shares. Minitab or Excel procedures provided in Appendix F can be used to show $\chi^2 = 7.34$ provides a p-value $= .0255$.

Instead of using the p-value, we could use the critical value approach to draw the same conclusion. With $\alpha = .05$ and 2 degrees of freedom, the critical value for the test statistic is $\chi^2_{.05} = 5.991$. The upper tail rejection rule becomes

$$\text{Reject } H_0 \text{ if } \chi^2 \geq 5.991$$

With $7.34 > 5.991$, we reject H_0. The p-value approach and critical value approach provide the same hypothesis testing conclusion.

Now that we have concluded the introduction of a new company C product will alter the market shares for the three companies, we are interested in knowing more about how the market shares are likely to change. Using the historical market shares and the sample data, we summarize the data as follows:

Company	Historical Market Share (%)	Sample Data Market Share (%)
A	30	48/200 = .24, or 24
B	50	98/200 = .49, or 49
C	20	54/200 = .27, or 27

The historical market shares and the sample market shares are compared in the bar chart shown in Figure 12.2. This data visualization process shows that the new product will likely increase the market share for company C. Comparisons for the other two companies indicate that company C's gain in market share will hurt company A more than company B.

FIGURE 12.2 BAR CHART OF MARKET SHARES BY COMPANY BEFORE AND AFTER THE NEW PRODUCT FOR COMPANY C

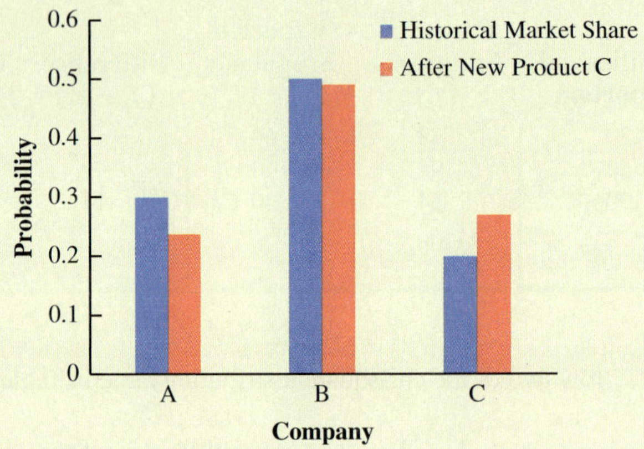

Let us summarize the steps that can be used to conduct a goodness of fit test for a hypothesized multinomial population distribution.

MULTINOMIAL PROBABILITY DISTRIBUTION GOODNESS OF FIT TEST

1. State the null and alternative hypotheses.

   H_0: The population follows a multinomial probability distribution with specified probabilities for each of the k categories

   H_a: The population does not follow a multinomial distribution with the specified probabilities for each of the k categories

2. Select a random sample and record the observed frequencies f_i for each category.
3. Assume the null hypothesis is true and determine the expected frequency e_i in each category by multiplying the category probability by the sample size.
4. If the expected frequency e_i is at least 5 for each category, compute the value of the test statistic.

$$\chi^2 = \sum_{i=1}^{k} \frac{(f_i - e_i)^2}{e_i}$$

5. Rejection rule:

   p-value approach: Reject H_0 if p-value $\leq \alpha$

   Critical value approach: Reject H_0 if $\chi^2 \geq \chi^2_\alpha$

   where α is the level of significance for the test and there are $k - 1$ degrees of freedom.

Normal Probability Distribution

The goodness of fit test for a normal probability distribution is also based on the use of the chi-square distribution. In particular, observed frequencies for several categories of sample data are compared to expected frequencies under the assumption that the population has a

TABLE 12.10 CHEMLINE EMPLOYEE APTITUDE TEST SCORES FOR 50 RANDOMLY CHOSEN JOB APPLICANTS

71	66	61	65	54	93
60	86	70	70	73	73
55	63	56	62	76	54
82	79	76	68	53	58
85	80	56	61	61	64
65	62	90	69	76	79
77	54	64	74	65	65
61	56	63	80	56	71
79	84				

normal probability distribution. Because the normal probability distribution is continuous, we must modify the way the categories are defined and how the expected frequencies are computed. Let us demonstrate the goodness of fit test for a normal distribution by considering the job applicant test data for Chemline, Inc., shown in Table 12.10.

Chemline hires approximately 400 new employees annually for its four plants located throughout the United States. The personnel director asks whether a normal distribution applies for the population of test scores. If such a distribution can be used, the distribution would be helpful in evaluating specific test scores; that is, scores in the upper 20%, lower 40%, and so on, could be identified quickly. Hence, we want to test the null hypothesis that the population of test scores has a normal distribution.

Let us first use the data in Table 12.10 to develop estimates of the mean and standard deviation of the normal distribution that will be considered in the null hypothesis. We use the sample mean $\bar{x}$ and the sample standard deviation s as point estimators of the mean and standard deviation of the normal distribution. The calculations follow.

$$\bar{x} = \frac{\Sigma x_i}{n} = \frac{3421}{50} = 68.42$$

$$s = \sqrt{\frac{\Sigma(x_i - \bar{x})^2}{n - 1}} = \sqrt{\frac{5310.0369}{49}} = 10.41$$

WEB file Chemline

Using these values, we state the following hypotheses about the distribution of the job applicant test scores.

H_0: The population of test scores has a normal distribution with mean 68.42 and standard deviation 10.41

H_a: The population of test scores does not have a normal distribution with mean 68.42 and standard deviation 10.41

The hypothesized normal distribution is shown in Figure 12.3.

With the continuous normal probability distribution, we must use a different procedure for defining the categories. We need to define the categories in terms of *intervals* of test scores.

With a continuous probability distribution, establish intervals such that each interval has an expected frequency of five or more.

Recall the rule of thumb for an expected frequency of at least five in each interval or category. We define the categories of test scores such that the expected frequencies will be at least five for each category. With a sample size of 50, one way of establishing categories

FIGURE 12.3 HYPOTHESIZED NORMAL DISTRIBUTION OF TEST SCORES FOR THE CHEMLINE JOB APPLICANTS

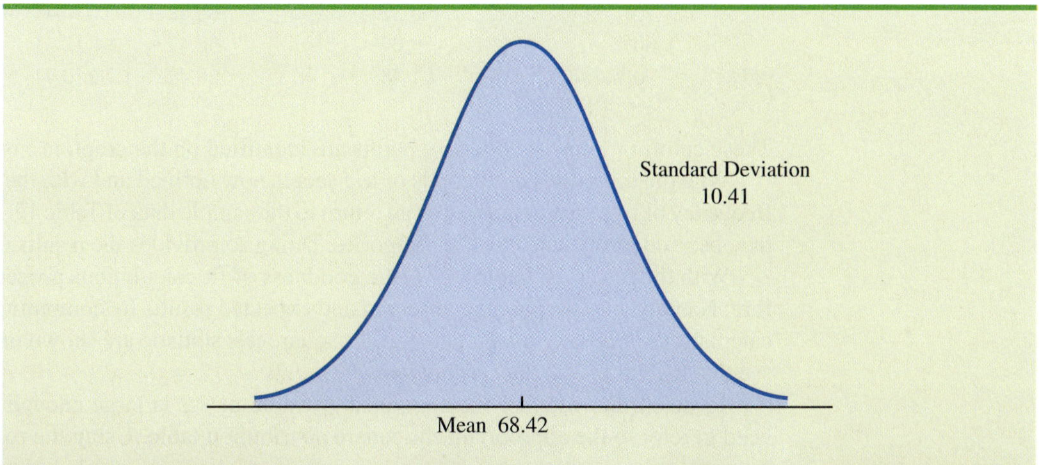

FIGURE 12.4 NORMAL DISTRIBUTION FOR THE CHEMLINE EXAMPLE WITH 10 EQUAL-PROBABILITY INTERVALS

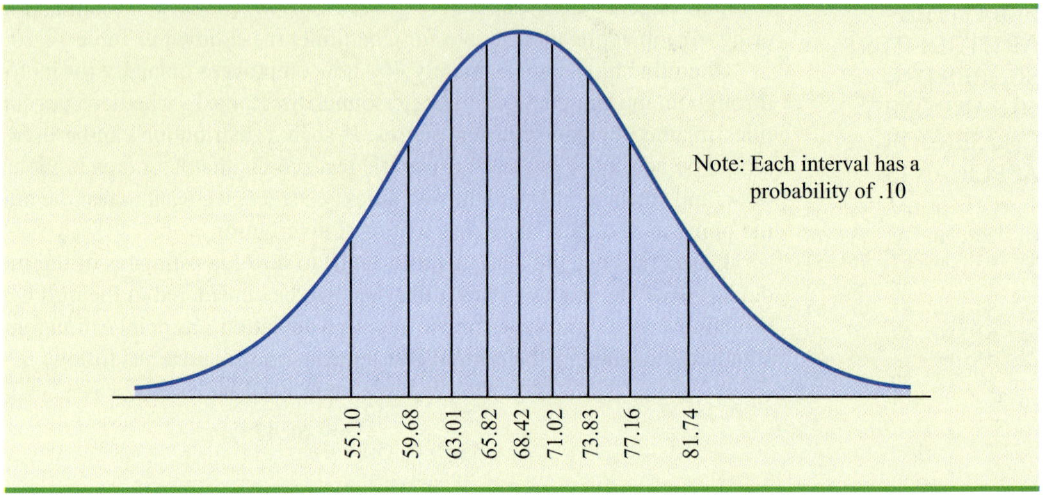

is to divide the normal probability distribution into 10 equal-probability intervals (see Figure 12.4). With a sample size of 50, we would expect five outcomes in each interval or category, and the rule of thumb for expected frequencies would be satisfied.

Let us look more closely at the procedure for calculating the category boundaries. When the normal probability distribution is assumed, the standard normal probability tables can be used to determine these boundaries. First consider the test score cutting off the lowest 10% of the test scores. From the table for the standard normal distribution we find that the z value for this test score is -1.28. Therefore, the test score of $x = 68.42 - 1.28(10.41) = 55.10$ provides this cutoff value for the lowest 10% of the scores. For the lowest 20%, we find $z = -.84$, and thus $x = 68.42 - .84(10.41) = 59.68$. Working through the normal distribution in that way provides the following test score values.

Percentage	z	Test Score
10%	-1.28	$68.42 - 1.28(10.41) = 55.10$
20%	$-.84$	$68.42 - .84(10.41) = 59.68$
30%	$-.52$	$68.42 - .52(10.41) = 63.01$
40%	$-.25$	$68.42 - .25(10.41) = 65.82$
50%	$.00$	$68.42 + 0(10.41) = 68.42$
60%	$+.25$	$68.42 + .25(10.41) = 71.02$
70%	$+.52$	$68.42 + .52(10.41) = 73.83$
80%	$+.84$	$68.42 + .84(10.41) = 77.16$
90%	$+1.28$	$68.42 + 1.28(10.41) = 81.74$

These cutoff or interval boundary points are identified on the graph in Figure 12.4.

With the categories or intervals of test scores now defined and with the known expected frequency of five per category, we can return to the sample data of Table 12.10 and determine the observed frequencies for the categories. Doing so provides the results in Table 12.11.

With the results in Table 12.11, the goodness of fit calculations proceed exactly as before. Namely, we compare the observed and expected results by computing a χ^2 value. The calculations necessary to compute the chi-square test statistic are shown in Table 12.12. We see that the value of the test statistic is $\chi^2 = 7.2$.

To determine whether the computed χ^2 value of 7.2 is large enough to reject H_0, we need to refer to the appropriate chi-square distribution table. Using the rule for computing

TABLE 12.11 OBSERVED AND EXPECTED FREQUENCIES FOR CHEMLINE JOB APPLICANT TEST SCORES

Test Score Interval	Observed Frequency (f_i)	Expected Frequency (e_i)
Less than 55.10	5	5
55.10 to 59.68	5	5
59.68 to 63.01	9	5
63.01 to 65.82	6	5
65.82 to 68.42	2	5
68.42 to 71.02	5	5
71.02 to 73.83	2	5
73.83 to 77.16	5	5
77.16 to 81.74	5	5
81.74 and over	6	5
Total	50	50

TABLE 12.12 COMPUTATION OF THE CHI-SQUARE TEST STATISTIC FOR THE CHEMLINE JOB APPLICANT EXAMPLE

Test Score Interval	Observed Frequency (f_i)	Expected Frequency (e_i)	Difference ($f_i - e_i$)	Squared Difference $(f_i - e_i)^2$	Squared Difference Divided by Expected Frequency $(f_i - e_i)^2/e_i$
Less than 55.10	5	5	0	0	0.0
55.10 to 59.68	5	5	0	0	0.0
59.68 to 63.01	9	5	4	16	3.2
63.01 to 65.82	6	5	1	1	0.2
65.82 to 68.42	2	5	−3	9	1.8
68.42 to 71.02	5	5	0	0	0.0
71.02 to 73.83	2	5	−3	9	1.8
73.83 to 77.16	5	5	0	0	0.0
77.16 to 81.74	5	5	0	0	0.0
81.74 and over	6	5	1	1	0.2
Total	50	50			$\chi^2 = 7.2$

the number of degrees of freedom for the goodness of fit test, we have $k - p - 1 = 10 - 2 - 1 = 7$ degrees of freedom based on $k = 10$ categories and $p = 2$ parameters (mean and standard deviation) estimated from the sample data.

Estimating the two parameters of the normal distribution will cause a loss of two degrees of freedom in the χ^2 test.

Suppose that we test the null hypothesis that the distribution for the test scores is a normal distribution with a .10 level of significance. To test this hypothesis, we need to determine the p-value for the test statistic $\chi^2 = 7.2$ by finding the area in the upper tail of a chi-square distribution with 7 degrees of freedom. Using row seven of Table 12.4, we find that $\chi^2 = 7.2$ provides an area in the upper tail greater than .10. Thus, we know that the p-value is greater than .10. Minitab or Excel procedures in Appendix F can be used to show $\chi^2 = 7.2$ provides a p-value $= .4084$. With p-value $>.10$, the hypothesis that the probability distribution for the Chemline job applicant test scores is a normal probability distribution cannot be rejected. The normal probability distribution may be applied to assist in the interpretation of test scores. A summary of the goodness fit test for a normal probability distribution follows.

NORMAL PROBABILITY DISTRIBUTION GOODNESS OF FIT TEST

1. State the null and alternative hypotheses.

   H_0: The population has a normal probability distribution

   H_a: The population does not have a normal probability distribution

2. Select a random sample and
   a. Compute the sample mean and sample standard deviation.
   b. Define k intervals of values so that the expected frequency is at least five for each interval. Using equal probability intervals is a good approach.
   c. Record the observed frequency of data values f_i in each interval defined.
3. Compute the expected number of occurrences e_i for each interval of values defined in step 2(b). Multiply the sample size by the probability of a normal random variable being in the interval.
4. Compute the value of the test statistic.

$$\chi^2 = \sum_{i=1}^{k} \frac{(f_i - e_i)^2}{e_i}$$

5. Rejection rule:

   p-value approach: Reject H_0 if p-value $\leq \alpha$

   Critical value approach: Reject H_0 if $\chi^2 \geq \chi^2_\alpha$

   where α is the level of significance. The degrees of freedom $= k - p - 1$, where p is the number of parameters of the distribution estimated by the sample. In step 2a, the sample is used to estimate the mean and standard deviation. Thus, $p = 2$ and the degrees of freedom $= k - 2 - 1 = k - 3$.

Exercises

Methods

SELF test

19. Test the following hypotheses by using the χ^2 goodness of fit test.

$$H_0: p_A = .40, p_B = .40, \text{ and } p_C = .20$$

$$H_a: \text{The population proportions are not } p_A = .40, p_B = .40, \text{ and } p_C = .20$$

A sample of size 200 yielded 60 in category A, 120 in category B, and 20 in category C. Use $\alpha = .01$ and test to see whether the proportions are as stated in H_0.

a. Use the p-value approach.
b. Repeat the test using the critical value approach.

SELF test

20. The following data are believed to have come from a normal distribution. Use the goodness of fit test and $\alpha = .05$ to test this claim.

17	23	22	24	19	23	18	22	20	13	11	21	18	20	21
21	18	15	24	23	23	43	29	27	26	30	28	33	23	29

Applications

SELF test

21. During the first 13 weeks of the television season, the Saturday evening 8:00 P.M. to 9:00 P.M. audience proportions were recorded as ABC 29%, CBS 28%, NBC 25%, and independents 18%. A sample of 300 homes two weeks after a Saturday night schedule revision yielded the following viewing audience data: ABC 95 homes, CBS 70 homes, NBC 89 homes, and independents 46 homes. Test with $\alpha = .05$ to determine whether the viewing audience proportions changed.

WEB file

M&M

22. Mars, Inc. manufactures M&M's, one of the most popular candy treats in the world. The milk chocolate candies come in a variety of colors including blue, brown, green, orange, red, and yellow (M&M website, March 2012). The overall proportions for the colors are .24 blue, .13 brown, .20 green, .16 orange, .13 red, and .14 yellow. In a sampling study, several bags of M&M milk chocolates were opened and the following color counts were obtained.

Blue	Brown	Green	Orange	Red	Yellow
105	72	89	84	70	80

Use a .05 level of significance and the sample data to test the hypothesis that the overall proportions for the colors are as stated above. What is your conclusion?

23. *The Wall Street Journal's* Shareholder Scoreboard tracks the performance of 1000 major U.S. companies. The performance of each company is rated based on the annual total return, including stock price changes and the reinvestment of dividends. Ratings are assigned by dividing all 1000 companies into five groups from A (top 20%), B (next 20%), to E (bottom 20%). Shown here are the one-year ratings for a sample of 60 of the largest companies. Do the largest companies differ in performance from the performance of the 1000 companies in the Shareholder Scoreboard? Use $\alpha = .05$.

A	B	C	D	E
5	8	15	20	12

24. The National Highway Traffic Safety Administration reported the percentage of traffic accidents occurring each day of the week (*Time,* March 12, 2012). Assume that a sample of 420 accidents provided the following data.

Sunday	Monday	Tuesday	Wednesday	Thursday	Friday	Saturday
66	50	53	47	55	69	80

a. Conduct a hypothesis test to determine if the proportion of traffic accidents is the same for each day of the week. What is the p-value? Using a .05 level of significance, what is your conclusion?

b. Compute the percentage of traffic accidents occurring on each day of the week. What day has the highest percentage of traffic accidents? Does this seem reasonable? Discuss.

25. Use $\alpha = .01$ and conduct a goodness of fit test to see whether the following sample appears to have been selected from a normal probability distribution.

55	86	94	58	55	95	55	52	69	95	90	65	87	50	56
55	57	98	58	79	92	62	59	88	65					

After you complete the goodness of fit calculations, construct a histogram of the data. Does the histogram representation support the conclusion reached with the goodness of fit test? (*Note:* $\bar{x} = 71$ and $s = 17$.)

WEB file

Demand

26. The weekly demand for a product is believed to be normally distributed. Use a goodness of fit test and the following data to test this assumption. Use $\alpha = .10$. The sample mean is 24.5 and the sample standard deviation is 3.

18	20	22	27	22
25	22	27	25	24
26	23	20	24	26
27	25	19	21	25
26	25	31	29	25
25	28	26	28	24

Summary

In this chapter we have introduced hypothesis tests for the following applications.

1. Testing the equality of population proportions for three or more populations.
2. Testing the independence of two categorical variables.
3. Testing whether a probability distribution for a population follows a specific historical or theoretical probability distribution.

All tests apply to categorical variables and all tests use a chi-square (χ^2) test statistic that is based on the differences between observed frequencies and expected frequencies. In each case, expected frequencies are computed under the assumption that the null hypothesis is true. These chi-square tests are upper tailed tests. Large differences between observed and expected frequencies provide a large value for the chi-square test statistic and indicate that the null hypothesis should be rejected.

The test for the equality of population proportions for three or more populations is based on independent random samples selected from each of the populations. The sample data show the counts for each of two categorical responses for each population. The null hypothesis is that the population proportions are equal. Rejection of the null hypothesis supports the conclusion that the population proportions are not all equal.

The test of independence between two categorical variables uses one sample from a population with the data showing the counts for each combination of two categorical variables. The null hypothesis is that the two variables are independent and the test is referred to as a test of independence. If the null hypothesis is rejected, there is statistical evidence of an association or dependency between the two variables.

The goodness of fit test is used to test the hypothesis that a population has a specific historical or theoretical probability distribution. We showed applications for populations with a multinomial probability distribution and with a normal probability distribution. Since the normal probability distribution applies to continuous data, intervals of data values were established to create the categories for the categorical variable required for the goodness of fit test.

Glossary

Marascuilo procedure A multiple comparison procedure that can be used to test for a significant difference between pairs of population proportions. This test can be helpful in identifying differences between pairs of population proportions whenever the hypothesis of equal population proportions has been rejected.

Test of independence A chi-square test that can be used to test for the independence between two categorical variables. If the hypothesis of independence is rejected, it can be concluded that the categorical variables are associated or dependent.

Goodness of fit test A chi-square test that can be used to test that a population probability distribution has a specific historical or theoretical probability distribution. This test was demonstrated for both a multinomial probability distribution and a normal probability distribution.

Multinomial probability distribution A probability distribution where each outcome belongs to one of three or more categories. The multinomial probability distribution extends the binomial probability from two to three or more outcomes per trial.

Key Formulas

Expected Frequencies Under the Assumption H_0 Is True

$$e_{ij} = \frac{(\text{Row } i \text{ Total})(\text{Column } j \text{ Total})}{\text{Sample Size}} \tag{12.1}$$

Chi-Square Test Statistic

$$\chi^2 = \sum_i \sum_j \frac{(f_{ij} - e_{ij})^2}{e_{ij}} \tag{12.2}$$

Critical Values for the Marascuilo Pairwise Comparison Procedure

$$CV_{ij} = \sqrt{\chi^2_\alpha}\sqrt{\frac{\bar{p}_i(1 - \bar{p}_i)}{n_i} + \frac{\bar{p}_j(1 - \bar{p}_j)}{n_j}} \tag{12.3}$$

Chi-Square Test Statistic for the Goodness of Fit Test

$$\chi^2 = \sum_i \frac{(f_i - e_i)^2}{e_i} \tag{12.6}$$

Supplementary Exercises

27. In a quality control test of parts manufactured at Dabco Corporation, an engineer sampled parts produced on the first, second, and third shifts. The research study was designed to determine if the population proportion of good parts was the same for all three shifts. Sample data follow.

	Production Shift		
Quality	**First**	**Second**	**Third**
Good	285	368	176
Defective	15	32	24

a. Using a .05 level of significance, conduct a hypothesis test to determine if the population proportion of good parts is the same for all three shifts. What is the *p*-value and what is your conclusion?

b. If the conclusion is that the population proportions are not all equal, use a multiple comparison procedure to determine how the shifts differ in terms of quality. What shift or shifts need to improve the quality of parts produced?

28. Phoenix Marketing International identified Bridgeport, Connecticut, Los Alamos, New Mexico, Naples, Florida and Washington D.C. as the four U.S. cities with the highest percentage of

millionaires (*USA Today,* December 7, 2011). Data consistent with that study show the following number of millionaires for samples of individuals from each of the four cities.

	City			
Millionaire	**Bridgeport**	**Los Alamos**	**Naples**	**Washington DC**
Yes	44	35	36	34
No	456	265	364	366

a. What is the estimate of the percentage of millionaires in each of these cities?
b. Using a .05 level of significance, test for the equality of the population proportion of millionaires for these four cities. What is the p-value and what is your conclusion?

WEB file

BothWork

29. Samples taken in three cities, Anchorage, Atlanta, and Minneapolis, were used to learn about the proportion of married couples where both husband and wife are in the workforce (*USA Today,* January 15, 2006).

	City		
In Workforce	**Anchorage**	**Atlanta**	**Minneapolis**
Both Work	57	70	63
Only One	33	50	27

a. Conduct a hypothesis test to determine if the population proportion of married couples with both husband and wife in the workforce is the same for the three cities. Using a .05 level of significance, what is the p-value and what is your conclusion?
b. Using these three samples, what is an estimate of the proportion of married couples with both husband and wife in the workforce?

30. A Pew Research Center survey asked respondents if they would rather live in a place with a slower pace of life or a place with a faster pace of life (*USA Today,* February 13, 2009). The survey also asked the respondent's gender. Consider the following sample data.

	Gender	
Preferred Pace of Life	**Male**	**Female**
Slower	230	218
No Preference	20	24
Faster	90	48

a. Is the preferred pace of life independent of gender? Using a .05 level of significance, what is the p-value and what is your conclusion?
b. Discuss any differences between the preferences of men and women.

31. Bara Research Group conducted a survey about church attendance. The survey respondents were asked about their church attendance and asked to indicate their age. Use the sample data to determine whether church attendance is independent of age. Using a .05 level of significance, what is the p-value and what is your conclusion? What conclusion can you draw about church attendance as individuals grow older?

	Age			
Church Attendance	**20 to 29**	**30 to 39**	**40 to 49**	**50 to 59**
Yes	31	63	94	72
No	69	87	106	78

WEB file Ambulance

32. An ambulance service responds to emergency calls for two counties in Virginia. One county is an urban county and the other is a rural county. A sample of 471 ambulance calls over the past two years showed the county and the day of the week for each emergency call. Data are as follows.

	Day of Week						
County	**Sun**	**Mon**	**Tue**	**Wed**	**Thu**	**Fri**	**Sat**
Urban	61	48	50	55	63	73	43
Rural	7	9	16	13	9	14	10

Test for independence of the county and the day of the week. Using a .05 level of significance, what is the p-value and what is your conclusion?

33. Based on sales over a six-month period, the five top-selling compact cars are Chevy Cruze, Ford Focus, Hyundai Elantra, Honda Civic, and Toyota Corolla (*Motor Trend,* November 2, 2011). Based on total sales, the market shares for these five compact cars were Chevy Cruze 24%, Ford Focus 21%, Hyundai Elantra 19%, Honda Civic 18%, and Toyota Corolla 17%. A sample of 400 compact car sales in Chicago showed the following number of vehicles sold.

Chevy Cruze	108
Ford Focus	92
Hyundai Elantra	64
Honda Civic	84
Toyota Corolla	52

Use a goodness of fit test to determine if the sample data indicate that the market shares for the five compact cars in Chicago are different than the market shares reported by *Motor Trend*. Using a .05 level of significance, what is the p-value and what is your conclusion? What market share differences, if any, exist in Chicago?

WEB file Grades

34. A random sample of final examination grades for a college course follows.

55	85	72	99	48	71	88	70	59	98	80	74	93	85	74
82	90	71	83	60	95	77	84	73	63	72	95	79	51	85
76	81	78	65	75	87	86	70	80	64					

Use $\alpha = .05$ and test to determine whether a normal probability distribution should be rejected as being representative of the population distribution of grades.

35. A salesperson makes four calls per day. A sample of 100 days gives the following frequencies of sales volumes.

Number of Sales	Observed Frequency (days)
0	30
1	32
2	25
3	10
4	3
Total	100

Records show sales are made to 30% of all sales calls. Assuming independent sales calls, the number of sales per day should follow a binomial probability distribution. The binomial probability function presented in Chapter 5 is

$$f(x) = \frac{n!}{x!(n - x)!} p^x(1 - p)^{n-x}$$

For this exercise, assume that the population has a binomial probability distribution with $n = 4$, $p = .30$, and $x = 0, 1, 2, 3$, and 4.

a. Compute the expected frequencies for $x = 0, 1, 2, 3$, and 4 by using the binomial probability function. Combine categories if necessary to satisfy the requirement that the expected frequency is five or more for all categories.
b. Use the goodness of fit test to determine whether the assumption of a binomial probability distribution should be rejected. Use $\alpha = .05$. Because no parameters of the binomial probability distribution were estimated from the sample data, the degrees of freedom are $k - 1$ when k is the number of categories.

Case Problem A Bipartisan Agenda for Change

In a study conducted by Zogby International for the *Democrat and Chronicle,* more than 700 New Yorkers were polled to determine whether the New York state government works. Respondents surveyed were asked questions involving pay cuts for state legislators, restrictions on lobbyists, term limits for legislators, and whether state citizens should be able to put matters directly on the state ballot for a vote. The results regarding several proposed reforms had broad support, crossing all demographic and political lines.

Suppose that a follow-up survey of 100 individuals who live in the western region of New York was conducted. The party affiliation (Democrat, Independent, Republican) of each individual surveyed was recorded, as well as their responses to the following three questions.

1. Should legislative pay be cut for every day the state budget is late?
   Yes ____ No ____
2. Should there be more restrictions on lobbyists?
   Yes ____ No ____
3. Should there be term limits requiring that legislators serve a fixed number of years?
   Yes ____ No ____

WEB file NYReform

The responses were coded using 1 for a Yes response and 2 for a No response. The complete data set is available in the file named NYReform.

Managerial Report

1. Use descriptive statistics to summarize the data from this study. What are your preliminary conclusions about the independence of the response (Yes or No) and party affiliation for each of the three questions in the survey?
2. With regard to question 1, test for the independence of the response (Yes and No) and party affiliation. Use $\alpha = .05$.
3. With regard to question 2, test for the independence of the response (Yes and No) and party affiliation. Use $\alpha = .05$.
4. With regard to question 3, test for the independence of the response (Yes and No) and party affiliation. Use $\alpha = .05$.
5. Does it appear that there is broad support for change across all political lines? Explain.

Appendix 12.1 Chi-Square Tests Using Minitab

Test the Equality of Population Proportions and Test of Independence

The Minitab procedure is identical for both of these applications. We will describe the procedure for the following situations.

1. A data set shows the responses for each element in the sample.
2. A tabular summary of the data shows the observed frequencies for the response categories.

WEB file
AutoLoyalty

We begin with the automobile loyalty example presented in Section 12.1. Responses for a sample of 500 automobile owners is contained in the web file AutoLoyalty. Column C1 shows the population the owner belongs to (Chevrolet Impala, Ford Fusion, or Honda Accord) and column C2 contains the likely to purchase response (Yes or No). The Minitab steps to conduct a chi-square test using the data set follow.

Step 1. Select the **Stat** menu
Step 2. Select **Tables**
Step 3. Choose **Cross Tabulation and Chi-Square**
Step 4. When then Cross Tabulation and Chi-Square dialog box appears:
Enter C2 in the **For Rows** box
Enter C1 in the **For Columns** box
Under the **Display** options, select **Counts**
Select **Chi-Square**
Step 5. When the Cross Tabulation—Chi Square dialog box appears:
Select **Chi-Square analysis**
Click **OK**
Step 6. Click **OK**

The output shows both a tabular summary of the data and the chi-square test results.

This procedure can also be used for a test of independence. Use the web file BeerPreference to conduct the test for the example in Section 12.2.

Next let us show how to conduct this test if a tabular summary of the data showing observed frequencies has already been obtained. We begin with a new Minitab worksheet and label the columns C1 to C3 with the titles of the three populations: Chevrolet Impala, Ford Fusion, and Honda Accord. Then we enter the observed frequencies of the Yes and No responses for each population in its corresponding column. Thus, we enter 69 and 56 in column 1, enter 120 and 80 in column 2, and enter 123 and 52 in column 3. The Minitab steps for this test are as follows.

Step 1. Select the **Stat** menu
Step 2. Select **Tables**
Step 3. Choose **Chi-Square Test (Two-Way Table in Worksheet)**
Step 4. When the Chi-Square Test dialog box appears:
Enter C1-C3 in the **Columns containing the table** box
Click **OK**

Goodness of Fit Test

In order to use Minitab to conduct a goodness of fit test, the user must first obtain a sample from the population and determine the observed frequency for each of k categories. Under the assumption that the hypothesized population distribution is true, the user must also determine the hypothesized or expected proportion for each of the k categories. Using a new

Minitab worksheet, the observed frequencies are entered in column C1 and the corresponding hypothesized proportions are entered in column C2.

Using the Scott Marketing Research example presented in Section 12.3, the sample of 200 customer preferences for products A, B, and C provided observed frequencies of 48, 98, and 54. These frequencies are entered in column C1. Using historical market share data, the hypothesized proportions, .30, .50 and .20, are entered in column C2. The Minitab steps for the goodness of fit test for this multinomial probability distribution follow.

Step 1. Select the **Stat** menu
Step 2. Select **Tables**
Step 3. Choose **Chi-Square Goodness of Fit Test (One Variable)**
Step 4. When the Chi-Square Goodness of Fit Test dialog box appears:
Select **Observed counts**
Enter C1 in the **Observed counts** box
Select **Specific proportions**
Enter C2 in the **Specific proportions** box
Click **OK**

If in any application of the goodness of fit test the null hypothesis is *equal* proportions for the k categories, column C2 is not necessary. In this case, the user can select **Equal proportions** rather than **Specific proportions** in step 4.

Appendix 12.2 Chi-Square Tests Using Excel

The Excel procedure for tests for the equality of population proportions, tests of independence, and goodness of fit tests are basically the same as all make use of the Excel chi-square function CHISQ.TEST. Regardless of the application, the user must do the following before creating an Excel worksheet that will perform the test.

1. Select a sample from the population or populations and record the data
2. Summarize the data to show observed frequencies in a tabular format

Excel's PivotTable can be used to summarize the data in step 2 above. Since this procedure was previously presented in Appendix 2.2, we shall not describe it in this appendix. Rather we will begin the Excel chi-square test procedure with the understanding that the user has already determined the observed frequencies for the study.

WEB file AutoLoyalty

Let us demonstrate the Excel chi-square test by considering the automobile loyalty example presented in Section 12.1. Using the data in the web file AutoLoyalty and the Excel PivotTable procedure, we obtained the observed frequencies shown in the Excel worksheet of Figure 12.5. The user must next insert Excel formulas in the worksheet to compute the expected frequencies. Using equation (12.1), the Excel formulas for expected frequencies are as shown in the background worksheet of Figure 12.5.

The last step is to insert the Excel function CHISQ.TEST. The format of this function is as follows:

=CHISQ.TEST(Observed Frequency Cells, Expected Frequency Cells)

In Figure 12.5, the observed frequency cells are B7 to D8, written B7:D8 and the expected frequency cells are B16 to D17, written B16:D17. The function =CHISQ.TEST(B7:D8,B16:D17) is shown in cell E20 of the background worksheet. This function does all the chi-square test computations and returns the p-value for the test.

FIGURE 12.5 EXCEL WORKSHEET FOR THE AUTOMOBILE LOYALITY STUDY

	A	B	C	D	E	F
1	**Chi Square Test**					
2						
3	**Observed Frequencies**					
4						
5			**Populations**			
6	**Likely Purchase**	Chevrolet Impala	Ford Fusion	Honda Accord	Total	
7	Yes	69	120	123	312	
8	No	56	80	52	188	
9	Total	125	200	175	500	
10						
11						
12	**Expected Frequencies**					
13						
14			**Populations**			
15	**Likely Purchase**	Chevrolet Impala	Ford Fusion	Honda Accord	Total	
16	Yes	78	124.8	109.2	312	
17	No	47	75.2	65.8	188	
18	Total	125	200	175	500	
19						
20				***p*-value**	0.0193	
21						

WEB file

ChiSquare

	A	B	C	D	E	F
1	**Chi Square Test**					
2						
3	**Observed Frequencies**					
4						
5			**Populations**			
6	**Likely Purchase**	Chevrolet Impala	Ford Fusion	Honda Accord	Total	
7	Yes	69	120	123	=SUM(B7:D7)	
8	No	56	80	52	=SUM(B8:D8)	
9	Total	=SUM(B7:B8)	=SUM(C7:C8)	=SUM(D7:D8)	=SUM(E7:E8)	
10						
11						
12	**Expected Frequencies**					
13						
14			**Populations**			
15	**Likely Purchase**	Chevrolet Impala	Ford Fusion	Honda Accord	Total	
16	Yes	=E7*B9/E9	=E7*C9/E9	=E7*D9/E9	=SUM(B16:D16)	
17	No	=E8*B9/E9	=E8*C9/E9	=E8*D9/E9	=SUM(B17:D17)	
18	Total	=SUM(B16:B17)	=SUM(C16:C17)	=SUM(D16:D17)	=SUM(E16:E17)	
19						
20				***p*-value**	=CHISQ.TEST(B7:D8,B16:D17)	
21						

The Excel worksheet shown in Figure 12.5 is available in the webfile ChiSquare.

The test of independence summarizes the observed frequencies in a tabular format very similar to the one shown in Figure 12.5. The formulas to compute expected frequencies are also very similar to the formulas shown in the background worksheet. For the goodness of fit test, the user provides the observed frequencies in a column rather than a table. The user must also provide the associated expected frequencies in another column. Lastly, the CHISQ.TEST function is used to obtain the p-value as described above.

Appendix 12.3 Chi-Square Tests Using StatTools

Test the Equality of Population Proportions and Test of Independence

The StatTools procedure is identical for both of these applications. In each case, the user must do the following before creating an Excel worksheet that can be used to perform the test.

1. Select a sample from the population or populations and record the data
2. Summarize the data to show the observed frequencies in a tabular format

We will begin the StatTools chi-square test procedure with the understanding that the user has already determined the observed frequencies for the study.

WEB file
AutoLoyalty

Let us demonstrate the StatTools chi-square test by considering the automobile loyalty example presented in Section 12.1. Using the data in the web file AutoLoyalty and the Excel PivotTable procedure, we obtained the observed frequencies shown in the Excel worksheet of Figure 12.5. Note that the observed frequencies including the row and column heading are located from cell A6 to cell D8. This is all the information needed to conduct the chi-square test with StatTools. The steps are as follows.

Step 1. Select **Statistical Inference**
Step 2. Select **Chi-Square Independence Test**
Step 3. When the Chi-Square Test for Independence dialog box appears:
Enter A6:D8 in the **Contingency Table Range** box
Click **Table Includes Row and Column Headers**
Click **OK**

A test of independence application would begin with a tabular summary of the observed frequencies for the two categorical variables. The three steps shown above will provide the test of independence results.

Goodness of Fit Test for a Normal Probability Distribution

WEB file
Chemline

StatTools provides a routine for the chi-square goodness of fit test when the population is assumed to have a normal probability distribution. Let us consider the sample of 50 Chemline employee aptitude test scores presented in Section 12.3. The assumption is that the population of test scores has a normal probability distribution. Open the Chemline file and begin by using the Data Set Manager to create a StatTools data set using the procedure described in the appendix in Chapter 1. The remaining steps are as follows.

Step 1. Select **Normality Tests**
Step 2. Select **Chi-square Test**
Step 3. When the Chi-Square Normality Text box appears:
Check the **Name** Score
Click **OK**

The StatTools add-in simplifies the steps required when doing chi-square tests with Excel.

StatTools automatically establishes the data ranges that determine the k categories for the data. Since StatTools may establish the test score categories differently than we did in Section 12.3, the p-values can differ slightly. However, the test conclusion remains the same.

CHAPTER 13

Experimental Design and Analysis of Variance

CONTENTS

STATISTICS *in* PRACTICE

BURKE MARKETING SERVICES, INC.*
CINCINNATI, OHIO

Burke Marketing Services, Inc., is one of the most experienced market research firms in the industry. Burke writes more proposals, on more projects, every day than any other market research company in the world. Supported by state-of-the-art technology, Burke offers a wide variety of research capabilities, providing answers to nearly any marketing question.

In one study, a firm retained Burke to evaluate potential new versions of a children's dry cereal. To maintain confidentiality, we refer to the cereal manufacturer as the Anon Company. The four key factors that Anon's product developers thought would enhance the taste of the cereal were the following:

1. Ratio of wheat to corn in the cereal flake
2. Type of sweetener: sugar, honey, or artificial
3. Presence or absence of flavor bits with a fruit taste
4. Short or long cooking time

Burke designed an experiment to determine what effects these four factors had on cereal taste. For example, one test cereal was made with a specified ratio of wheat to corn, sugar as the sweetener, flavor bits, and a short cooking time; another test cereal was made with a different ratio of wheat to corn and the other three factors the same, and so on. Groups of children then taste-tested the cereals and stated what they thought about the taste of each.

*The authors are indebted to Dr. Ronald Tatham of Burke Marketing Services for providing this Statistics in Practice.

Burke uses taste tests to provide valuable statistical information on what customers want from a product. © Mircea Foto/Shutterstock.com.

Analysis of variance was the statistical method used to study the data obtained from the taste tests. The results of the analysis showed the following:

- The flake composition and sweetener type were highly influential in taste evaluation.
- The flavor bits actually detracted from the taste of the cereal.
- The cooking time had no effect on the taste.

This information helped Anon identify the factors that would lead to the best-tasting cereal.

The experimental design employed by Burke and the subsequent analysis of variance were helpful in making a product design recommendation. In this chapter, we will see how such procedures are carried out.

In Chapter 1 we stated that statistical studies can be classified as either experimental or observational. In an experimental statistical study, an experiment is conducted to generate the data. An experiment begins with identifying a variable of interest. Then one or more other variables, thought to be related, are identified and controlled, and data are collected about how those variables influence the variable of interest.

In an observational study, data are usually obtained through sample surveys and not a controlled experiment. Good design principles are still employed, but the rigorous controls associated with an experimental statistical study are often not possible. For instance, in a study of the relationship between smoking and lung cancer the researcher cannot assign a smoking habit to subjects. The researcher is restricted to simply observing the effects of smoking on people who already smoke and the effects of not smoking on people who do not already smoke.

Sir Ronald Aylmer Fisher (1890–1962) invented the branch of statistics known as experimental design. In addition to being accomplished in statistics, he was a noted scientist in the field of genetics.

In this chapter we introduce three types of experimental designs: a completely randomized design, a randomized block design, and a factorial experiment. For each design we show how a statistical procedure called analysis of variance (ANOVA) can be used to analyze the data available. ANOVA can also be used to analyze the data obtained through an observation a study. For instance, we will see that the ANOVA procedure used for a completely randomized experimental design also works for testing the equality of three or more population means when data are obtained through an observational study. In the following chapters we will see that ANOVA plays a key role in analyzing the results of regression studies involving both experimental and observational data.

In the first section, we introduce the basic principles of an experimental study and show how they are employed in a completely randomized design. In the second section, we then show how ANOVA can be used to analyze the data from a completely randomized experimental design. In later sections we discuss multiple comparison procedures and two other widely used experimental designs, the randomized block design and the factorial experiment.

13.1 An Introduction to Experimental Design and Analysis of Variance

Cause-and-effect relationships can be difficult to establish in observational studies; such relationships are easier to establish in experimental studies.

As an example of an experimental statistical study, let us consider the problem facing Chemitech, Inc. Chemitech developed a new filtration system for municipal water supplies. The components for the new filtration system will be purchased from several suppliers, and Chemitech will assemble the components at its plant in Columbia, South Carolina. The industrial engineering group is responsible for determining the best assembly method for the new filtration system. After considering a variety of possible approaches, the group narrows the alternatives to three: method A, method B, and method C. These methods differ in the sequence of steps used to assemble the system. Managers at Chemitech want to determine which assembly method can produce the greatest number of filtration systems per week.

In the Chemitech experiment, assembly method is the independent variable or **factor**. Because three assembly methods correspond to this factor, we say that three treatments are associated with this experiment; each **treatment** corresponds to one of the three assembly methods. The Chemitech problem is an example of a **single-factor experiment**; it involves one categorical factor (method of assembly). More complex experiments may consist of multiple factors; some factors may be categorical and others may be quantitative.

The three assembly methods or treatments define the three populations of interest for the Chemitech experiment. One population is all Chemitech employees who use assembly method A, another is those who use method B, and the third is those who use method C. Note that for each population the dependent or **response variable** is the number of filtration systems assembled per week, and the primary statistical objective of the experiment is to determine whether the mean number of units produced per week is the same for all three populations (methods).

Randomization is the process of assigning the treatments to the experimental units at random. Prior to the work of Sir R. A. Fisher, treatments were assigned on a systematic or subjective basis.

Suppose a random sample of three employees is selected from all assembly workers at the Chemitech production facility. In experimental design terminology, the three randomly selected workers are the **experimental units**. The experimental design that we will use for the Chemitech problem is called a **completely randomized design**. This type of design requires that each of the three assembly methods or treatments be assigned randomly to one of the experimental units or workers. For example, method A might be randomly assigned to the second worker, method B to the first worker, and method C to the third worker. The concept of *randomization*, as illustrated in this example, is an important principle of all experimental designs.

FIGURE 13.1 COMPLETELY RANDOMIZED DESIGN FOR EVALUATING THE CHEMITECH ASSEMBLY METHOD EXPERIMENT

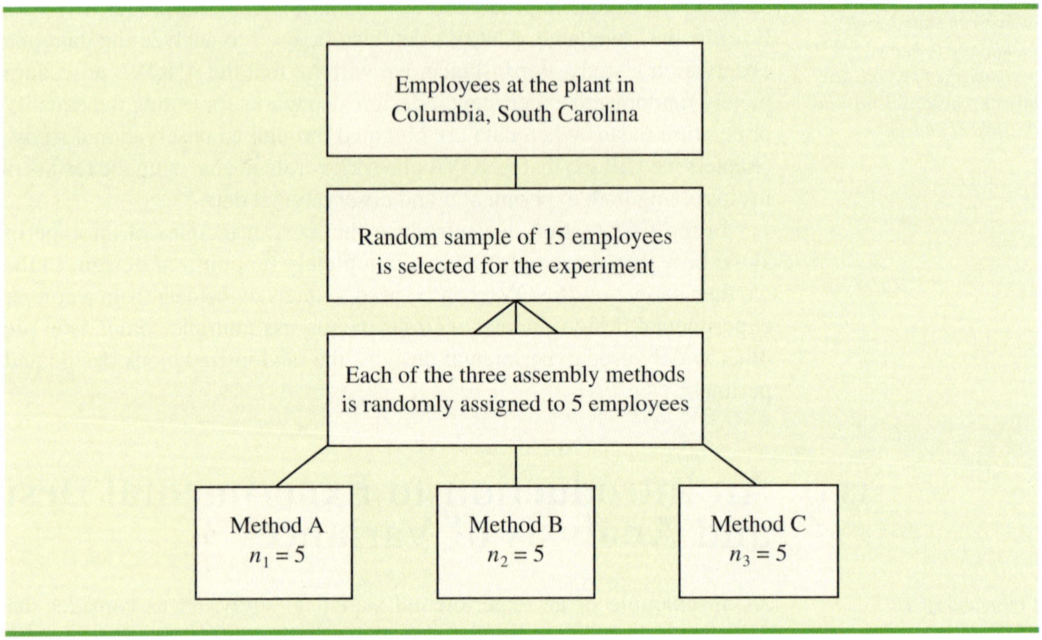

Note that this experiment would result in only one measurement or number of units assembled for each treatment. To obtain additional data for each assembly method, we must repeat or replicate the basic experimental process. Suppose, for example, that instead of selecting just three workers at random we selected 15 workers and then randomly assigned each of the three treatments to 5 of the workers. Because each method of assembly is assigned to 5 workers, we say that five replicates have been obtained. The process of *replication* is another important principle of experimental design. Figure 13.1 shows the completely randomized design for the Chemitech experiment.

Data Collection

Once we are satisfied with the experimental design, we proceed by collecting and analyzing the data. In the Chemitech case, the employees would be instructed in how to perform the assembly method assigned to them and then would begin assembling the new filtration systems using that method. After this assignment and training, the number of units assembled by each employee during one week is as shown in Table 13.1. The sample means, sample variances, and sample standard deviations for each assembly method are also provided. Thus, the sample mean number of units produced using method A is 62; the sample mean using method B is 66; and the sample mean using method C is 52. From these data, method B appears to result in higher production rates than either of the other methods.

The real issue is whether the three sample means observed are different enough for us to conclude that the means of the populations corresponding to the three methods of assembly are different. To write this question in statistical terms, we introduce the following notation.

$$\mu_1 = \text{mean number of units produced per week using method A}$$
$$\mu_2 = \text{mean number of units produced per week using method B}$$
$$\mu_3 = \text{mean number of units produced per week using method C}$$

TABLE 13.1 NUMBER OF UNITS PRODUCED BY 15 WORKERS

WEB file
Chemitech

	Method		
	A	B	C
	58	58	48
	64	69	57
	55	71	59
	66	64	47
	67	68	49
Sample mean	62	66	52
Sample variance	27.5	26.5	31.0
Sample standard deviation	5.244	5.148	5.568

Although we will never know the actual values of μ_1, μ_2, and μ_3, we want to use the sample means to test the following hypotheses.

If H_0 is rejected, we cannot conclude that all population means are different. Rejecting H_0 means that at least two population means have different values.

$$H_0: \mu_1 = \mu_2 = \mu_3$$
$$H_a: \text{Not all population means are equal}$$

As we will demonstrate shortly, analysis of variance (ANOVA) is the statistical procedure used to determine whether the observed differences in the three sample means are large enough to reject H_0.

Assumptions for Analysis of Variance

Three assumptions are required to use analysis of variance.

If the sample sizes are equal, analysis of variance is not sensitive to departures from the assumption of normally distributed populations.

1. **For each population, the response variable is normally distributed.** Implication: In the Chemitech experiment the number of units produced per week (response variable) must be normally distributed for each assembly method.
2. **The variance of the response variable, denoted σ^2, is the same for all of the populations.** Implication: In the Chemitech experiment, the variance of the number of units produced per week must be the same for each assembly method.
3. **The observations must be independent.** Implication: In the Chemitech experiment, the number of units produced per week for each employee must be independent of the number of units produced per week for any other employee.

Analysis of Variance: A Conceptual Overview

If the means for the three populations are equal, we would expect the three sample means to be close together. In fact, the closer the three sample means are to one another, the weaker the evidence we have for the conclusion that the population means differ. Alternatively, the more the sample means differ, the stronger the evidence we have for the conclusion that the population means differ. In other words, if the variability among the sample means is "small," it supports H_0; if the variability among the sample means is "large," it supports H_a.

If the null hypothesis, H_0: $\mu_1 = \mu_2 = \mu_3$, is true, we can use the variability among the sample means to develop an estimate of σ^2. First, note that if the assumptions for analysis

FIGURE 13.2 SAMPLING DISTRIBUTION OF $\bar{x}$ GIVEN H_0 IS TRUE

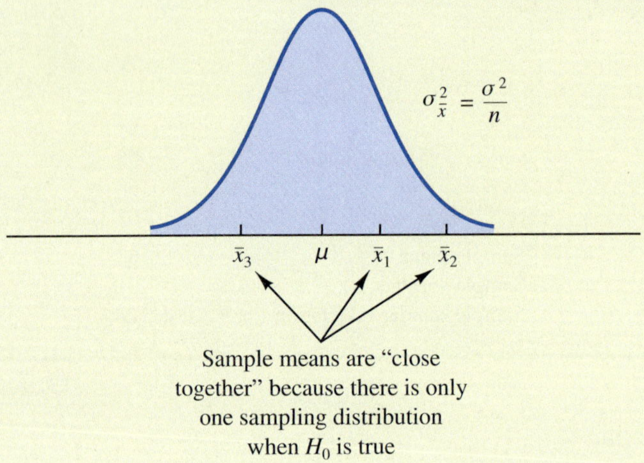

of variance are satisfied and the null hypothesis is true, each sample will have come from the same normal distribution with mean μ and variance σ^2. Recall from Chapter 7 that the sampling distribution of the sample mean $\bar{x}$ for a simple random sample of size n from a normal population will be normally distributed with mean μ and variance σ^2/n. Figure 13.2 illustrates such a sampling distribution.

Thus, if the null hypothesis is true, we can think of each of the three sample means, $\bar{x}_1 = 62$, $\bar{x}_2 = 66$, and $\bar{x}_3 = 52$ from Table 13.1, as values drawn at random from the sampling distribution shown in Figure 13.2. In this case, the mean and variance of the three $\bar{x}$ values can be used to estimate the mean and variance of the sampling distribution. When the sample sizes are equal, as in the Chemitech experiment, the best estimate of the mean of the sampling distribution of $\bar{x}$ is the mean or average of the sample means. In the Chemitech experiment, an estimate of the mean of the sampling distribution of $\bar{x}$ is $(62 + 66 + 52)/3 = 60$. We refer to this estimate as the *overall sample mean.* An estimate of the variance of the sampling distribution of $\bar{x}$, $\sigma_{\bar{x}}^2$, is provided by the variance of the three sample means.

$$s_{\bar{x}}^2 = \frac{(62 - 60)^2 + (66 - 60)^2 + (52 - 60)^2}{3 - 1} = \frac{104}{2} = 52$$

Because $\sigma_{\bar{x}}^2 = \sigma^2/n$, solving for σ^2 gives

$$\sigma^2 = n\sigma_{\bar{x}}^2$$

Hence,

$$\text{Estimate of } \sigma^2 = n\,(\text{Estimate of } \sigma_{\bar{x}}^2) = ns_{\bar{x}}^2 = 5(52) = 260$$

The result, $ns_{\bar{x}}^2 = 260$, is referred to as the *between-treatments* estimate of σ^2.

The between-treatments estimate of σ^2 is based on the assumption that the null hypothesis is true. In this case, each sample comes from the same population, and there is only

FIGURE 13.3 SAMPLING DISTRIBUTIONS OF $\bar{x}$ GIVEN H_0 IS FALSE

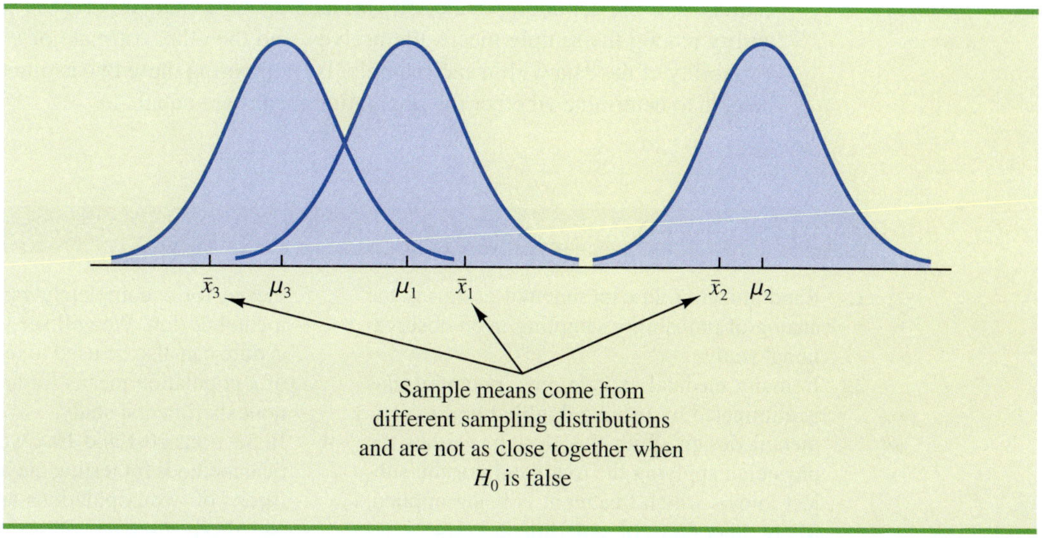

one sampling distribution of $\bar{x}$. To illustrate what happens when H_0 is false, suppose the population means all differ. Note that because the three samples are from normal populations with different means, they will result in three different sampling distributions. Figure 13.3 shows that in this case, the sample means are not as close together as they were when H_0 was true. Thus, $s_{\bar{x}}^2$ will be larger, causing the between-treatments estimate of σ^2 to be larger. In general, when the population means are not equal, the between-treatments estimate will overestimate the population variance σ^2.

The variation within each of the samples also has an effect on the conclusion we reach in analysis of variance. When a simple random sample is selected from each population, each of the sample variances provides an unbiased estimate of σ^2. Hence, we can combine or pool the individual estimates of σ^2 into one overall estimate. The estimate of σ^2 obtained in this way is called the *pooled* or *within-treatments* estimate of σ^2. Because each sample variance provides an estimate of σ^2 based only on the variation within each sample, the within-treatments estimate of σ^2 is not affected by whether the population means are equal. When the sample sizes are equal, the within-treatments estimate of σ^2 can be obtained by computing the average of the individual sample variances. For the Chemitech experiment we obtain

$$\text{Within-treatments estimate of } \sigma^2 = \frac{27.5 + 26.5 + 31.0}{3} = \frac{85}{3} = 28.33$$

In the Chemitech experiment, the between-treatments estimate of σ^2 (260) is much larger than the within-treatments estimate of σ^2 (28.33). In fact, the ratio of these two estimates is 260/28.33 = 9.18. Recall, however, that the between-treatments approach provides a good estimate of σ^2 only if the null hypothesis is true; if the null hypothesis is false, the between-treatments approach overestimates σ^2. The within-treatments approach provides a good estimate of σ^2 in either case. Thus, if the null hypothesis is true, the two estimates will be similar and their ratio will be close to 1. If the null hypothesis is false, the between-treatments estimate will be larger than the within-treatments estimate, and their ratio will be large. In the next section we will show how large this ratio must be to reject H_0.

In summary, the logic behind ANOVA is based on the development of two independent estimates of the common population variance σ^2. One estimate of σ^2 is based on the variability among the sample means themselves, and the other estimate of σ^2 is based on the variability of the data within each sample. By comparing these two estimates of σ^2, we will be able to determine whether the population means are equal.

NOTES AND COMMENTS

1. Randomization in experimental design is the analog of probability sampling in an observational study.
2. In many medical experiments, potential bias is eliminated by using a double-blind experimental design. With this design, neither the physician applying the treatment nor the subject knows which treatment is being applied. Many other types of experiments could benefit from this type of design.
3. In this section we provided a conceptual overview of how analysis of variance can be used to test for the equality of k population means for a completely randomized experimental design. We will see that the same procedure can also be used to test for the equality of k population means for an observational or nonexperimental study.
4. In Sections 10.1 and 10.2 we presented statistical methods for testing the hypothesis that the means of two populations are equal. ANOVA can also be used to test the hypothesis that the means of two populations are equal. In practice, however, analysis of variance is usually not used except when dealing with three or more population means.

13.2 Analysis of Variance and the Completely Randomized Design

In this section we show how analysis of variance can be used to test for the equality of k population means for a completely randomized design. The general form of the hypotheses tested is

$$H_0: \mu_1 = \mu_2 = \cdots = \mu_k$$
$$H_a: \text{Not all population means are equal}$$

where

$$\mu_j = \text{mean of the } j\text{th population}$$

We assume that a simple random sample of size n_j has been selected from each of the k populations or treatments. For the resulting sample data, let

$$\begin{aligned} x_{ij} &= \text{value of observation } i \text{ for treatment } j \\ n_j &= \text{number of observations for treatment } j \\ \bar{x}_j &= \text{sample mean for treatment } j \\ s_j^2 &= \text{sample variance for treatment } j \\ s_j &= \text{sample standard deviation for treatment } j \end{aligned}$$

The formulas for the sample mean and sample variance for treatment j are as follow.

$$\bar{x}_j = \frac{\sum_{i=1}^{n_j} x_{ij}}{n_j} \tag{13.1}$$

$$s_j^2 = \frac{\sum_{i=1}^{n_j} (x_{ij} - \bar{x}_j)^2}{n_j - 1} \tag{13.2}$$

The overall sample mean, denoted $\bar{\bar{x}}$, is the sum of all the observations divided by the total number of observations. That is,

$$\bar{\bar{x}} = \frac{\sum_{j=1}^{k} \sum_{i=1}^{n_j} x_{ij}}{n_T} \tag{13.3}$$

where

$$n_T = n_1 + n_2 + \cdots + n_k \tag{13.4}$$

If the size of each sample is n, $n_T = kn$; in this case equation (13.3) reduces to

$$\bar{\bar{x}} = \frac{\sum_{j=1}^{k} \sum_{i=1}^{n_j} x_{ij}}{kn} = \frac{\sum_{j=1}^{k} \sum_{i=1}^{n_j} x_{ij}/n}{k} = \frac{\sum_{j=1}^{k} \bar{x}_j}{k} \tag{13.5}$$

In other words, whenever the sample sizes are the same, the overall sample mean is just the average of the k sample means.

Because each sample in the Chemitech experiment consists of $n = 5$ observations, the overall sample mean can be computed by using equation (13.5). For the data in Table 13.1 we obtained the following result.

$$\bar{\bar{x}} = \frac{62 + 66 + 52}{3} = 60$$

If the null hypothesis is true ($\mu_1 = \mu_2 = \mu_3 = \mu$), the overall sample mean of 60 is the best estimate of the population mean μ.

Between-Treatments Estimate of Population Variance

In the preceding section, we introduced the concept of a between-treatments estimate of σ^2 and showed how to compute it when the sample sizes were equal. This estimate of σ^2 is called the *mean square due to treatments* and is denoted MSTR. The general formula for computing MSTR is

$$\text{MSTR} = \frac{\sum_{j=1}^{k} n_j(\bar{x}_j - \bar{\bar{x}})^2}{k - 1} \tag{13.6}$$

The numerator in equation (13.6) is called the *sum of squares due to treatments* and is denoted SSTR. The denominator, $k - 1$, represents the degrees of freedom associated with SSTR. Hence, the mean square due to treatments can be computed using the following formula.

MEAN SQUARE DUE TO TREATMENTS

$$\text{MSTR} = \frac{\text{SSTR}}{k - 1} \tag{13.7}$$

where

$$\text{SSTR} = \sum_{j=1}^{k} n_j(\bar{x}_j - \bar{\bar{x}})^2 \tag{13.8}$$

If H_0 is true, MSTR provides an unbiased estimate of σ^2. However, if the means of the k populations are not equal, MSTR is not an unbiased estimate of σ^2; in fact, in that case, MSTR should overestimate σ^2.

For the Chemitech data in Table 13.1, we obtain the following results.

$$\text{SSTR} = \sum_{j=1}^{k} n_j(\bar{x}_j - \bar{\bar{x}})^2 = 5(62 - 60)^2 + 5(66 - 60)^2 + 5(52 - 60)^2 = 520$$

$$\text{MSTR} = \frac{\text{SSTR}}{k - 1} = \frac{520}{2} = 260$$

Within-Treatments Estimate of Population Variance

Earlier, we introduced the concept of a within-treatments estimate of σ^2 and showed how to compute it when the sample sizes were equal. This estimate of σ^2 is called the *mean square due to error* and is denoted MSE. The general formula for computing MSE is

$$\text{MSE} = \frac{\sum_{j=1}^{k}(n_j - 1)s_j^2}{n_T - k} \tag{13.9}$$

The numerator in equation (13.9) is called the *sum of squares due to error* and is denoted SSE. The denominator of MSE is referred to as the degrees of freedom associated with SSE. Hence, the formula for MSE can also be stated as follows.

MEAN SQUARE DUE TO ERROR

$$\text{MSE} = \frac{\text{SSE}}{n_T - k} \tag{13.10}$$

where

$$\text{SSE} = \sum_{j=1}^{k}(n_j - 1)s_j^2 \tag{13.11}$$

Note that MSE is based on the variation within each of the treatments; it is not influenced by whether the null hypothesis is true. Thus, MSE always provides an unbiased estimate of σ^2.

For the Chemitech data in Table 13.1 we obtain the following results.

$$\text{SSE} = \sum_{j=1}^{k}(n_j - 1)s_j^2 = (5 - 1)27.5 + (5 - 1)26.5 + (5 - 1)31 = 340$$

$$\text{MSE} = \frac{\text{SSE}}{n_T - k} = \frac{340}{15 - 3} = \frac{340}{12} = 28.33$$

Comparing the Variance Estimates: The F Test

An introduction to the F distribution and the use of the F distribution table were presented in Section 11.2.

If the null hypothesis is true, MSTR and MSE provide two independent, unbiased estimates of σ^2. Based on the material covered in Chapter 11 we know that for normal populations, the sampling distribution of the ratio of two independent estimates of σ^2 follows an F distribution. Hence, if the null hypothesis is true and the ANOVA assumptions are valid, the sampling distribution of MSTR/MSE is an F distribution with numerator degrees of freedom equal to $k - 1$ and denominator degrees of freedom equal to $n_T - k$. In other words, if the null hypothesis is true, the value of MSTR/MSE should appear to have been selected from this F distribution.

However, if the null hypothesis is false, the value of MSTR/MSE will be inflated because MSTR overestimates σ^2. Hence, we will reject H_0 if the resulting value of MSTR/MSE appears to be too large to have been selected from an F distribution with $k - 1$ numerator degrees of freedom and $n_T - k$ denominator degrees of freedom. Because the decision to reject H_0 is based on the value of MSTR/MSE, the test statistic used to test for the equality of k population means is as follows.

TEST STATISTIC FOR THE EQUALITY OF k POPULATION MEANS

$$F = \frac{\text{MSTR}}{\text{MSE}} \qquad (13.12)$$

The test statistic follows an F distribution with $k - 1$ degrees of freedom in the numerator and $n_T - k$ degrees of freedom in the denominator.

Let us return to the Chemitech experiment and use a level of significance $\alpha = .05$ to conduct the hypothesis test. The value of the test statistic is

$$F = \frac{\text{MSTR}}{\text{MSE}} = \frac{260}{28.33} = 9.18$$

The numerator degrees of freedom is $k - 1 = 3 - 1 = 2$ and the denominator degrees of freedom is $n_T - k = 15 - 3 = 12$. Because we will only reject the null hypothesis for large values of the test statistic, the p-value is the upper tail area of the F distribution to the right of the test statistic $F = 9.18$. Figure 13.4 shows the sampling distribution of F = MSTR/MSE, the value of the test statistic, and the upper tail area that is the p-value for the hypothesis test.

From Table 4 of Appendix B we find the following areas in the upper tail of an F distribution with 2 numerator degrees of freedom and 12 denominator degrees of freedom.

Area in Upper Tail	**.10**	**.05**	**.025**	**.01**
***F* Value ($df_1 = 2, df_2 = 12$)**	2.81	3.89	5.10	6.93

$F = 9.18$

FIGURE 13.4 COMPUTATION OF p-VALUE USING THE SAMPLING DISTRIBUTION OF MSTR/MSE

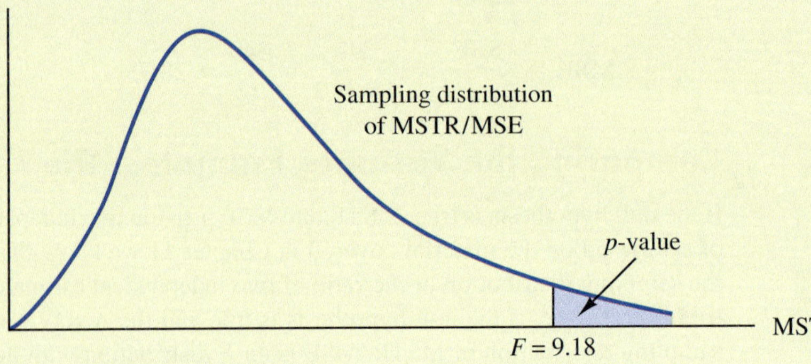

Appendix F shows how to compute p-values using Minitab or Excel.

Because $F = 9.18$ is greater than 6.93, the area in the upper tail at $F = 9.18$ is less than .01. Thus, the p-value is less than .01. Minitab or Excel can be used to show that the exact p-value is .004. With p-value $\leq \alpha = .05$, H_0 is rejected. The test provides sufficient evidence to conclude that the means of the three populations are not equal. In other words, analysis of variance supports the conclusion that the population mean number of units produced per week for the three assembly methods are not equal.

As with other hypothesis testing procedures, the critical value approach may also be used. With $\alpha = .05$, the critical F value occurs with an area of .05 in the upper tail of an F distribution with 2 and 12 degrees of freedom. From the F distribution table, we find $F_{.05} = 3.89$. Hence, the appropriate upper tail rejection rule for the Chemitech experiment is

$$\text{Reject } H_0 \text{ if } F \geq 3.89$$

With $F = 9.18$, we reject H_0 and conclude that the means of the three populations are not equal. A summary of the overall procedure for testing for the equality of k population means follows.

TEST FOR THE EQUALITY OF k POPULATION MEANS

$$H_0\colon \mu_1 = \mu_2 = \cdots = \mu_k$$
$$H_a\colon \text{Not all population means are equal}$$

TEST STATISTIC

$$F = \frac{\text{MSTR}}{\text{MSE}}$$

REJECTION RULE

p-value approach: Reject H_0 if p-value $\leq \alpha$

Critical value approach: Reject H_0 if $F \geq F_\alpha$

where the value of F_α is based on an F distribution with $k - 1$ numerator degrees of freedom and $n_T - k$ denominator degrees of freedom.

TABLE 13.2 ANOVA TABLE FOR A COMPLETELY RANDOMIZED DESIGN

Source of Variation	Sum of Squares	Degrees of Freedom	Mean Square	F	p-value
Treatments	SSTR	$k - 1$	$\text{MSTR} = \dfrac{\text{SSTR}}{k - 1}$	$\dfrac{\text{MSTR}}{\text{MSE}}$	
Error	SSE	$n_T - k$	$\text{MSE} = \dfrac{\text{SSE}}{n_T - k}$		
Total	SST	$n_T - 1$			

ANOVA Table

The results of the preceding calculations can be displayed conveniently in a table referred to as the analysis of variance or **ANOVA table**. The general form of the ANOVA table for a completely randomized design is shown in Table 13.2; Table 13.3 is the corresponding ANOVA table for the Chemitech experiment. The sum of squares associated with the source of variation referred to as "Total" is called the total sum of squares (SST). Note that the results for the Chemitech experiment suggest that SST = SSTR + SSE, and that the degrees of freedom associated with this total sum of squares is the sum of the degrees of freedom associated with the sum of squares due to treatments and the sum of squares due to error.

We point out that SST divided by its degrees of freedom $n_T - 1$ is nothing more than the overall sample variance that would be obtained if we treated the entire set of 15 observations as one data set. With the entire data set as one sample, the formula for computing the total sum of squares, SST, is

$$\text{SST} = \sum_{j=1}^{k} \sum_{i=1}^{n_j} (x_{ij} - \bar{\bar{x}})^2 \tag{13.13}$$

It can be shown that the results we observed for the analysis of variance table for the Chemitech experiment also apply to other problems. That is,

$$\text{SST} = \text{SSTR} + \text{SSE} \tag{13.14}$$

Analysis of variance can be thought of as a statistical procedure for partitioning the total sum of squares into separate components.

In other words, SST can be partitioned into two sums of squares: the sum of squares due to treatments and the sum of squares due to error. Note also that the degrees of freedom corresponding to SST, $n_T - 1$, can be partitioned into the degrees of freedom corresponding to SSTR, $k - 1$, and the degrees of freedom corresponding to SSE, $n_T - k$. The analysis of variance can be viewed as the process of **partitioning** the total sum of squares and the degrees of freedom into their corresponding sources: treatments and error. Dividing the sum of squares by the appropriate degrees of freedom provides the variance estimates, the F value, and the p-value used to test the hypothesis of equal population means.

TABLE 13.3 ANALYSIS OF VARIANCE TABLE FOR THE CHEMITECH EXPERIMENT

Source of Variation	Sum of Squares	Degrees of Freedom	Mean Square	F	p-value
Treatments	520	2	260.00	9.18	.004
Error	340	12	28.33		
Total	860	14			

FIGURE 13.5 MINITAB OUTPUT FOR THE CHEMITECH EXPERIMENT ANALYSIS OF VARIANCE

```
Source     DF      SS       MS       F       P
Factor      2    520.0    260.0    9.18   0.004
Error      12    340.0     28.3
Total      14    860.0

S = 5.323    R-Sq = 60.47%     R-Sq(adj) = 53.88%

                                     Individual 95% CIs For Mean Based on
                                     Pooled StDev
  Level     N     Mean    StDev   ---+---------+---------+---------+------
  A         5   62.000    5.244                (-------*-------)
  B         5   66.000    5.148                         (------*-------)
  C         5   52.000    5.568   (------*-------)
                                  ---+---------+---------+---------+------
Pooled StDev = 5.323                49.0      56.0      63.0      70.0
```

Computer Results for Analysis of Variance

Using statistical computer packages, analysis of variance computations with large sample sizes or a large number of populations can be performed easily. Appendixes 13.1–13.3 show the steps required to use Minitab, Excel, and StatTools to perform the analysis of variance computations. In Figure 13.5 we show output for the Chemitech experiment obtained using Minitab. The first part of the computer output contains the familiar ANOVA table format. Comparing Figure 13.5 with Table 13.3, we see that the same information is available, although some of the headings are slightly different. The heading Source is used for the source of variation column, Factor identifies the treatments row, and the sum of squares and degrees of freedom columns are interchanged.

Note that following the ANOVA table the computer output contains the respective sample sizes, the sample means, and the standard deviations. In addition, Minitab provides a figure that shows individual 95% confidence interval estimates of each population mean. In developing these confidence interval estimates, Minitab uses MSE as the estimate of σ^2. Thus, the square root of MSE provides the best estimate of the population standard deviation σ. This estimate of σ on the computer output is Pooled StDev; it is equal to 5.323. To provide an illustration of how these interval estimates are developed, we will compute a 95% confidence interval estimate of the population mean for method A.

From our study of interval estimation in Chapter 8, we know that the general form of an interval estimate of a population mean is

$$\bar{x} \pm t_{\alpha/2}\frac{s}{\sqrt{n}} \qquad \textbf{(13.15)}$$

where s is the estimate of the population standard deviation σ. Because the best estimate of σ is provided by the Pooled StDev, we use a value of 5.323 for s in expression (13.15). The degrees of freedom for the t value is 12, the degrees of freedom associated with the error sum of squares. Hence, with $t_{.025} = 2.179$ we obtain

$$62 \pm 2.179\frac{5.323}{\sqrt{5}} = 62 \pm 5.19$$

Thus, the individual 95% confidence interval for method A goes from $62 - 5.19 = 56.81$ to $62 + 5.19 = 67.19$. Because the sample sizes are equal for the Chemitech experiment, the individual confidence intervals for methods B and C are also constructed by adding and subtracting 5.19 from each sample mean. Thus, in the figure provided by Minitab we see that the widths of the confidence intervals are the same.

Testing for the Equality of k Population Means: An Observational Study

We have shown how analysis of variance can be used to test for the equality of k population means for a completely randomized experimental design. It is important to understand that ANOVA can also be used to test for the equality of three or more population means using data obtained from an observational study. As an example, let us consider the situation at National Computer Products, Inc. (NCP).

NCP manufactures printers and fax machines at plants located in Atlanta, Dallas, and Seattle. To measure how much employees at these plants know about quality management, a random sample of 6 employees was selected from each plant and the employees selected were given a quality awareness examination. The examination scores for these 18 employees are shown in Table 13.4. The sample means, sample variances, and sample standard deviations for each group are also provided. Managers want to use these data to test the hypothesis that the mean examination score is the same for all three plants.

We define population 1 as all employees at the Atlanta plant, population 2 as all employees at the Dallas plant, and population 3 as all employees at the Seattle plant. Let

$$\mu_1 = \text{mean examination score for population 1}$$
$$\mu_2 = \text{mean examination score for population 2}$$
$$\mu_3 = \text{mean examination score for population 3}$$

Although we will never know the actual values of μ_1, μ_2, and μ_3, we want to use the sample results to test the following hypotheses.

$$H_0: \mu_1 = \mu_2 = \mu_3$$
$$H_a: \text{Not all population means are equal}$$

Note that the hypothesis test for the NCP observational study is exactly the same as the hypothesis test for the Chemitech experiment. Indeed, the same analysis of variance

TABLE 13.4 EXAMINATION SCORES FOR 18 EMPLOYEES

WEB file NCP

	Plant 1 Atlanta	Plant 2 Dallas	Plant 3 Seattle
	85	71	59
	75	75	64
	82	73	62
	76	74	69
	71	69	75
	85	82	67
Sample mean	79	74	66
Sample variance	34	20	32
Sample standard deviation	5.83	4.47	5.66

Exercise 8 will ask you to analyze the NCP data using the analysis of variance procedure.

methodology we used to analyze the Chemitech experiment can also be used to analyze the data from the NCP observational study.

Even though the same ANOVA methodology is used for the analysis, it is worth noting how the NCP observational statistical study differs from the Chemitech experimental statistical study. The individuals who conducted the NCP study had no control over how the plants were assigned to individual employees. That is, the plants were already in operation and a particular employee worked at one of the three plants. All that NCP could do was to select a random sample of 6 employees from each plant and administer the quality awareness examination. To be classified as an experimental study, NCP would have had to be able to randomly select 18 employees and then assign the plants to each employee in a random fashion.

NOTES AND COMMENTS

1. The overall sample mean can also be computed as a weighted average of the k sample means.

$$\bar{\bar{x}} = \frac{n_1\bar{x}_1 + n_2\bar{x}_2 + \cdots + n_k\bar{x}_k}{n_T}$$

In problems where the sample means are provided, this formula is simpler than equation (13.3) for computing the overall mean.

2. If each sample consists of n observations, equation (13.6) can be written as

$$\text{MSTR} = \frac{n\sum_{j=1}^{k}(\bar{x}_j - \bar{\bar{x}})^2}{k-1} = n\left[\frac{\sum_{j=1}^{k}(\bar{x}_j - \bar{\bar{x}})^2}{k-1}\right] = ns_{\bar{x}}^2$$

Note that this result is the same as presented in Section 13.1 when we introduced the concept of the between-treatments estimate of σ^2. Equation (13.6) is simply a generalization of this result to the unequal sample-size case.

3. If each sample has n observations, $n_T = kn$; thus, $n_T - k = k(n-1)$, and equation (13.9) can be rewritten as

$$\text{MSE} = \frac{\sum_{j=1}^{k}(n-1)s_j^2}{k(n-1)} = \frac{(n-1)\sum_{j=1}^{k}s_j^2}{k(n-1)} = \frac{\sum_{j=1}^{k}s_j^2}{k}$$

In other words, if the sample sizes are the same, MSE is the average of the k sample variances. Note that it is the same result we used in Section 13.1 when we introduced the concept of the within-treatments estimate of σ^2.

Exercises

Methods

SELF test

1. The following data are from a completely randomized design.

	Treatment		
	A	B	C
	162	142	126
	142	156	122
	165	124	138
	145	142	140
	148	136	150
	174	152	128
Sample mean	156	142	134
Sample variance	164.4	131.2	110.4

a. Compute the sum of squares between treatments.
b. Compute the mean square between treatments.

c. Compute the sum of squares due to error.
d. Compute the mean square due to error.
e. Set up the ANOVA table for this problem.
f. At the $\alpha = .05$ level of significance, test whether the means for the three treatments are equal.

2. In a completely randomized design, seven experimental units were used for each of the five levels of the factor. Complete the following ANOVA table.

Source of Variation	Sum of Squares	Degrees of Freedom	Mean Square	F	p-value
Treatments	300				
Error					
Total	460				

3. Refer to exercise 2.
   a. What hypotheses are implied in this problem?
   b. At the $\alpha = .05$ level of significance, can we reject the null hypothesis in part (a)? Explain.
4. In an experiment designed to test the output levels of three different treatments, the following results were obtained: SST = 400, SSTR = 150, $n_T = 19$. Set up the ANOVA table and test for any significant difference between the mean output levels of the three treatments. Use $\alpha = .05$.
5. In a completely randomized design, 12 experimental units were used for the first treatment, 15 for the second treatment, and 20 for the third treatment. Complete the following analysis of variance. At a .05 level of significance, is there a significant difference between the treatments?

Source of Variation	Sum of Squares	Degrees of Freedom	Mean Square	F	p-value
Treatments	1200				
Error					
Total	1800				

6. Develop the analysis of variance computations for the following completely randomized design. At $\alpha = .05$, is there a significant difference between the treatment means?

WEB file
Exer6

	Treatment		
	A	B	C
	136	107	92
	120	114	82
	113	125	85
	107	104	101
	131	107	89
	114	109	117
	129	97	110
	102	114	120
		104	98
		89	106
$\bar{x}_j$	119	107	100
s_j^2	146.86	96.44	173.78

Applications

7. Three different methods for assembling a product were proposed by an industrial engineer. To investigate the number of units assembled correctly with each method, 30 employees were randomly selected and randomly assigned to the three proposed methods in such a way that each method was used by 10 workers. The number of units assembled correctly was recorded, and the analysis of variance procedure was applied to the resulting data set. The following results were obtained: SST = 10,800; SSTR = 4560.
   a. Set up the ANOVA table for this problem.
   b. Use $\alpha = .05$ to test for any significant difference in the means for the three assembly methods.
8. Refer to the NCP data in Table 13.4. Set up the ANOVA table and test for any significant difference in the mean examination score for the three plants. Use $\alpha = .05$.
9. To study the effect of temperature on yield in a chemical process, five batches were produced at each of three temperature levels. The results follow. Construct an analysis of variance table. Use a .05 level of significance to test whether the temperature level has an effect on the mean yield of the process.

Temperature		
50° C	**60° C**	**70° C**
34	30	23
24	31	28
36	34	28
39	23	30
32	27	31

10. Auditors must make judgments about various aspects of an audit on the basis of their own direct experience, indirect experience, or a combination of the two. In a study, auditors were asked to make judgments about the frequency of errors to be found in an audit. The judgments by the auditors were then compared to the actual results. Suppose the following data were obtained from a similar study; lower scores indicate better judgments.

WEB file

AudJudg

Direct	Indirect	Combination
17.0	16.6	25.2
18.5	22.2	24.0
15.8	20.5	21.5
18.2	18.3	26.8
20.2	24.2	27.5
16.0	19.8	25.8
13.3	21.2	24.2

Use $\alpha = .05$ to test to see whether the basis for the judgment affects the quality of the judgment. What is your conclusion?

11. Four different paints are advertised as having the same drying time. To check the manufacturer's claims, five samples were tested for each of the paints. The time in minutes until the paint was dry enough for a second coat to be applied was recorded. The following data were obtained.

WEB file
Paint

Paint 1	Paint 2	Paint 3	Paint 4
128	144	133	150
137	133	143	142
135	142	137	135
124	146	136	140
141	130	131	153

At the $\alpha = .05$ level of significance, test to see whether the mean drying time is the same for each type of paint.

12. The *Consumer Reports* Restaurant Customer Satisfaction Survey is based upon 148,599 visits to full-service restaurant chains (*Consumer Reports* website). One of the variables in the study is meal price, the average amount paid per person for dinner and drinks, minus the tip. Suppose a reporter for the *Sun Coast Times* thought that it would be of interest to her readers to conduct a similar study for restaurants located on the Grand Strand section in Myrtle Beach, South Carolina. The reporter selected a sample of 8 seafood restaurants, 8 Italian restaurants, and 8 steakhouses. The following data show the meal prices ($) obtained for the 24 restaurants sampled. Use $\alpha = .05$ to test whether there is a significant difference among the mean meal price for the three types of restaurants.

WEB file
GrandStrand

Italian	Seafood	Steakhouse
$12	$16	$24
13	18	19
15	17	23
17	26	25
18	23	21
20	15	22
17	19	27
24	18	31

13.3 Multiple Comparison Procedures

When we use analysis of variance to test whether the means of k populations are equal, rejection of the null hypothesis allows us to conclude only that the population means are *not all equal.* In some cases we will want to go a step further and determine where the differences among means occur. The purpose of this section is to show how **multiple comparison procedures** can be used to conduct statistical comparisons between pairs of population means.

Fisher's LSD

Suppose that analysis of variance provides statistical evidence to reject the null hypothesis of equal population means. In this case, Fisher's least significant difference (LSD) procedure can be used to determine where the differences occur. To illustrate the use of Fisher's LSD procedure in making pairwise comparisons of population means, recall the Chemitech experiment introduced in Section 13.1. Using analysis of variance, we concluded that the mean number of units produced per week are not the same for the three assembly methods. In this case, the follow-up question is: We believe the assembly methods differ, but where do the differences occur? That is, do the means of populations 1 and 2 differ? Or those of populations 1 and 3? Or those of populations 2 and 3? The following table summarizes Fisher's LSD procedure for comparing pairs of population means.

FISHER'S LSD PROCEDURE

$$H_0: \mu_i = \mu_j$$
$$H_a: \mu_i \neq \mu_j$$

TEST STATISTIC

$$t = \frac{\bar{x}_i - \bar{x}_j}{\sqrt{\text{MSE}\left(\frac{1}{n_i} + \frac{1}{n_j}\right)}} \tag{13.16}$$

REJECTION RULE

p-value approach:	Reject H_0 if p-value $\leq \alpha$
Critical value approach:	Reject H_0 if $t \leq -t_{\alpha/2}$ or $t \geq t_{\alpha/2}$

where the value of $t_{\alpha/2}$ is based on a t distribution with $n_T - k$ degrees of freedom.

Let us now apply this procedure to determine whether there is a significant difference between the means of population 1 (method A) and population 2 (method B) at the $\alpha = .05$ level of significance. Table 13.1 showed that the sample mean is 62 for method A and 66 for method B. Table 13.3 showed that the value of MSE is 28.33; it is the estimate of σ^2 and is based on 12 degrees of freedom. For the Chemitech data the value of the test statistic is

$$t = \frac{62 - 66}{\sqrt{28.33\left(\frac{1}{5} + \frac{1}{5}\right)}} = -1.19$$

Because we have a two-tailed test, the p-value is two times the area under the curve for the t distribution to the left of $t = -1.19$. Using Table 2 in Appendix B, the t distribution table for 12 degrees of freedom provides the following information.

Area in Upper Tail	.20	.10	.05	.025	.01	.005
t Value (12 df)	.873	1.356	1.782	2.179	2.681	3.055

$t = 1.19$

Appendix F shows how to compute p-values using Excel or Minitab.

The t distribution table only contains positive t values. Because the t distribution is symmetric, however, we can find the area under the curve to the right of $t = 1.19$ and double it to find the p-value corresponding to $t = -1.19$. We see that $t = 1.19$ is between .20 and .10. Doubling these amounts, we see that the p-value must be between .40 and .20. Excel or Minitab can be used to show that the exact p-value is .2571. Because the p-value is greater than $\alpha = .05$, we cannot reject the null hypothesis. Hence, we cannot conclude that the population mean number of units produced per week for method A is different from the population mean for method B.

Many practitioners find it easier to determine how large the difference between the sample means must be to reject H_0. In this case the test statistic is $\bar{x}_i - \bar{x}_j$, and the test is conducted by the following procedure.

FISHER'S LSD PROCEDURE BASED ON THE TEST STATISTIC $\bar{x}_i - \bar{x}_j$

$$H_0\colon \mu_i = \mu_j$$
$$H_a\colon \mu_i \neq \mu_j$$

TEST STATISTIC

$$\bar{x}_i - \bar{x}_j$$

REJECTION RULE AT A LEVEL OF SIGNIFICANCE α

$$\text{Reject } H_0 \text{ if } |\bar{x}_i - \bar{x}_j| \geq \text{LSD}$$

where

$$\text{LSD} = t_{\alpha/2}\sqrt{\text{MSE}\left(\frac{1}{n_i} + \frac{1}{n_j}\right)} \tag{13.17}$$

For the Chemitech experiment the value of LSD is

$$\text{LSD} = 2.179\sqrt{28.33\left(\frac{1}{5} + \frac{1}{5}\right)} = 7.34$$

Note that when the sample sizes are equal, only one value for LSD is computed. In such cases we can simply compare the magnitude of the difference between any two sample means with the value of LSD. For example, the difference between the sample means for population 1 (method A) and population 3 (method C) is $62 - 52 = 10$. This difference is greater than LSD $= 7.34$, which means we can reject the null hypothesis that the population mean number of units produced per week for method A is equal to the population mean for method C. Similarly, with the difference between the sample means for populations 2 and 3 of $66 - 52 = 14 > 7.34$, we can also reject the hypothesis that the population mean for method B is equal to the population mean for method C. In effect, our conclusion is that methods A and B both differ from method C.

Fisher's LSD can also be used to develop a confidence interval estimate of the difference between the means of two populations. The general procedure follows.

CONFIDENCE INTERVAL ESTIMATE OF THE DIFFERENCE BETWEEN TWO POPULATION MEANS USING FISHER'S LSD PROCEDURE

$$\bar{x}_i - \bar{x}_j \pm \text{LSD} \tag{13.18}$$

where

$$\text{LSD} = t_{\alpha/2}\sqrt{\text{MSE}\left(\frac{1}{n_i} + \frac{1}{n_j}\right)} \tag{13.19}$$

and $t_{\alpha/2}$ is based on a t distribution with $n_T - k$ degrees of freedom.

If the confidence interval in expression (13.18) includes the value zero, we cannot reject the hypothesis that the two population means are equal. However, if the confidence interval does not include the value zero, we conclude that there is a difference between the population means. For the Chemitech experiment, recall that LSD = 7.34 (corresponding to $t_{.025} = 2.179$). Thus, a 95% confidence interval estimate of the difference between the means of populations 1 and 2 is $62 - 66 \pm 7.34 = -4 \pm 7.34 = -11.34$ to 3.34; because this interval includes zero, we cannot reject the hypothesis that the two population means are equal.

Type I Error Rates

We began the discussion of Fisher's LSD procedure with the premise that analysis of variance gave us statistical evidence to reject the null hypothesis of equal population means. We showed how Fisher's LSD procedure can be used in such cases to determine where the differences occur. Technically, it is referred to as a *protected* or *restricted* LSD test because it is employed only if we first find a significant F value by using analysis of variance. To see why this distinction is important in multiple comparison tests, we need to explain the difference between a *comparisonwise* Type I error rate and an *experimentwise* Type I error rate.

In the Chemitech experiment we used Fisher's LSD procedure to make three pairwise comparisons.

Test 1	Test 2	Test 3
$H_0\colon \mu_1 = \mu_2$	$H_0\colon \mu_1 = \mu_3$	$H_0\colon \mu_2 = \mu_3$
$H_a\colon \mu_1 \neq \mu_2$	$H_a\colon \mu_1 \neq \mu_3$	$H_a\colon \mu_2 \neq \mu_3$

In each case, we used a level of significance of $\alpha = .05$. Therefore, for each test, if the null hypothesis is true, the probability that we will make a Type I error is $\alpha = .05$; hence, the probability that we will not make a Type I error on each test is $1 - .05 = .95$. In discussing multiple comparison procedures we refer to this probability of a Type I error ($\alpha = .05$) as the **comparisonwise Type I error rate**; comparisonwise Type I error rates indicate the level of significance associated with a single pairwise comparison.

Let us now consider a slightly different question. What is the probability that in making three pairwise comparisons, we will commit a Type I error on at least one of the three tests? To answer this question, note that the probability that we will not make a Type I error on any of the three tests is (.95)(.95)(.95) = .8574.[1] Therefore, the probability of making at least one Type I error is $1 - .8574 = .1426$. Thus, when we use Fisher's LSD procedure to make all three pairwise comparisons, the Type I error rate associated with this approach is not .05, but actually .1426; we refer to this error rate as the *overall* or **experimentwise Type I error rate**. To avoid confusion, we denote the experimentwise Type I error rate as α_{EW}.

The experimentwise Type I error rate gets larger for problems with more populations. For example, a problem with five populations has 10 possible pairwise comparisons. If we tested all possible pairwise comparisons by using Fisher's LSD with a comparisonwise error rate of $\alpha = .05$, the experimentwise Type I error rate would be $1 - (1 - .05)^{10} = .40$. In such cases, practitioners look to alternatives that provide better control over the experimentwise error rate.

One alternative for controlling the overall experimentwise error rate, referred to as the Bonferroni adjustment, involves using a smaller comparisonwise error rate for each test. For example, if we want to test C pairwise comparisons and want the maximum probability of

[1]The assumption is that the three tests are independent, and hence the joint probability of the three events can be obtained by simply multiplying the individual probabilities. In fact, the three tests are not independent because MSE is used in each test; therefore, the error involved is even greater than that shown.

making a Type I error for the overall experiment to be α_{EW}, we simply use a comparisonwise error rate equal to α_{EW}/C. In the Chemitech experiment, if we want to use Fisher's LSD procedure to test all three pairwise comparisons with a maximum experimentwise error rate of $\alpha_{EW} = .05$, we set the comparisonwise error rate to be $\alpha = .05/3 = .017$. For a problem with five populations and 10 possible pairwise comparisons, the Bonferroni adjustment would suggest a comparisonwise error rate of $.05/10 = .005$. Recall from our discussion of hypothesis testing in Chapter 9 that for a fixed sample size, any decrease in the probability of making a Type I error will result in an increase in the probability of making a Type II error, which corresponds to accepting the hypothesis that the two population means are equal when in fact they are not equal. As a result, many practitioners are reluctant to perform individual tests with a low comparisonwise Type I error rate because of the increased risk of making a Type II error.

Several other procedures, such as Tukey's procedure and Duncan's multiple range test, have been developed to help in such situations. However, there is considerable controversy in the statistical community as to which procedure is "best." The truth is that no one procedure is best for all types of problems.

Exercises

Methods

SELF test

13. The following data are from a completely randomized design.

	Treatment A	Treatment B	Treatment C
	32	44	33
	30	43	36
	30	44	35
	26	46	36
	32	48	40
Sample mean	30	45	36
Sample variance	6.00	4.00	6.50

a. At the $\alpha = .05$ level of significance, can we reject the null hypothesis that the means of the three treatments are equal?

b. Use Fisher's LSD procedure to test whether there is a significant difference between the means for treatments A and B, treatments A and C, and treatments B and C. Use $\alpha = .05$.

c. Use Fisher's LSD procedure to develop a 95% confidence interval estimate of the difference between the means of treatments A and B.

14. The following data are from a completely randomized design. In the following calculations, use $\alpha = .05$.

	Treatment 1	Treatment 2	Treatment 3
	63	82	69
	47	72	54
	54	88	61
	40	66	48
$\bar{x}_j$	51	77	58
s_j^2	96.67	97.34	81.99

a. Use analysis of variance to test for a significant difference among the means of the three treatments.
b. Use Fisher's LSD procedure to determine which means are different.

Applications

SELF test

15. To test whether the mean time needed to mix a batch of material is the same for machines produced by three manufacturers, the Jacobs Chemical Company obtained the following data on the time (in minutes) needed to mix the material.

Manufacturer		
1	**2**	**3**
20	28	20
26	26	19
24	31	23
22	27	22

a. Use these data to test whether the population mean times for mixing a batch of material differ for the three manufacturers. Use $\alpha = .05$.
b. At the $\alpha = .05$ level of significance, use Fisher's LSD procedure to test for the equality of the means for manufacturers 1 and 3. What conclusion can you draw after carrying out this test?

SELF test

16. Refer to exercise 15. Use Fisher's LSD procedure to develop a 95% confidence interval estimate of the difference between the means for manufacturer 1 and manufacturer 2.
17. The following data are from an experiment designed to investigate the perception of corporate ethical values among individuals specializing in marketing (higher scores indicate higher ethical values).

Marketing Managers	Marketing Research	Advertising
6	5	6
5	5	7
4	4	6
5	4	5
6	5	6
4	4	6

a. Use $\alpha = .05$ to test for significant differences in perception among the three groups.
b. At the $\alpha = .05$ level of significance, we can conclude that there are differences in the perceptions for marketing managers, marketing research specialists, and advertising specialists. Use the procedures in this section to determine where the differences occur. Use $\alpha = .05$.

18. To test for any significant difference in the number of hours between breakdowns for four machines, the following data were obtained.

Machine 1	Machine 2	Machine 3	Machine 4
6.4	8.7	11.1	9.9
7.8	7.4	10.3	12.8
5.3	9.4	9.7	12.1
7.4	10.1	10.3	10.8
8.4	9.2	9.2	11.3
7.3	9.8	8.8	11.5

a. At the $\alpha = .05$ level of significance, what is the difference, if any, in the population mean times among the four machines?
b. Use Fisher's LSD procedure to test for the equality of the means for machines 2 and 4. Use a .05 level of significance.

19. Refer to exercise 18. Use the Bonferroni adjustment to test for a significant difference between all pairs of means. Assume that a maximum overall experimentwise error rate of .05 is desired.

20. The International League of Triple-A minor league baseball consists of 14 teams organized into three divisions: North, South, and West. The following data show the average attendance for the 14 teams in the International League (The Biz of Baseball website, January 2009). Also shown are the teams' records; W denotes the number of games won, L denotes the number of games lost, and PCT is the proportion of games played that were won.

WEB file
Triple-A

Team Name	Division	W	L	PCT	Attendance
Buffalo Bisons	North	66	77	.462	8812
Lehigh Valley IronPigs	North	55	89	.382	8479
Pawtucket Red Sox	North	85	58	.594	9097
Rochester Red Wings	North	74	70	.514	6913
Scranton-Wilkes Barre Yankees	North	88	56	.611	7147
Syracuse Chiefs	North	69	73	.486	5765
Charlotte Knights	South	63	78	.447	4526
Durham Bulls	South	74	70	.514	6995
Norfolk Tides	South	64	78	.451	6286
Richmond Braves	South	63	78	.447	4455
Columbus Clippers	West	69	73	.486	7795
Indianapolis Indians	West	68	76	.472	8538
Louisville Bats	West	88	56	.611	9152
Toledo Mud Hens	West	75	69	.521	8234

a. Use $\alpha = .05$ to test for any difference in the mean attendance for the three divisions.
b. Use Fisher's LSD procedure to determine where the differences occur. Use $\alpha = .05$.

13.4 Randomized Block Design

Thus far we have considered the completely randomized experimental design. Recall that to test for a difference among treatment means, we computed an F value by using the ratio

$$F = \frac{\text{MSTR}}{\text{MSE}} \tag{13.20}$$

A completely randomized design is useful when the experimental units are homogeneous. If the experimental units are heterogeneous, ***blocking*** *is often used to form homogeneous groups.*

A problem can arise whenever differences due to extraneous factors (ones not considered in the experiment) cause the MSE term in this ratio to become large. In such cases, the F value in equation (13.20) can become small, signaling no difference among treatment means when in fact such a difference exists.

In this section we present an experimental design known as a **randomized block design**. Its purpose is to control some of the extraneous sources of variation by removing such variation from the MSE term. This design tends to provide a better estimate of the true error variance and leads to a more powerful hypothesis test in terms of the ability to detect differences among treatment means. To illustrate, let us consider a stress study for air traffic controllers.

Air Traffic Controller Stress Test

A study measuring the fatigue and stress of air traffic controllers resulted in proposals for modification and redesign of the controller's workstation. After consideration of several designs for the workstation, three specific alternatives are selected as having the best potential for reducing controller stress. The key question is: To what extent do the three alternatives differ in terms of their effect on controller stress? To answer this question, we need to design an experiment that will provide measurements of air traffic controller stress under each alternative.

Experimental studies in business often involve experimental units that are highly heterogeneous; as a result, randomized block designs are often employed.

In a completely randomized design, a random sample of controllers would be assigned to each workstation alternative. However, controllers are believed to differ substantially in their ability to handle stressful situations. What is high stress to one controller might be only moderate or even low stress to another. Hence, when considering the within-group source of variation (MSE), we must realize that this variation includes both random error and error due to individual controller differences. In fact, managers expected controller variability to be a major contributor to the MSE term.

Blocking in experimental design is similar to stratification in sampling.

One way to separate the effect of the individual differences is to use a randomized block design. Such a design will identify the variability stemming from individual controller differences and remove it from the MSE term. The randomized block design calls for a single sample of controllers. Each controller in the sample is tested with each of the three workstation alternatives. In experimental design terminology, the workstation is the *factor of interest* and the controllers are the *blocks*. The three treatments or populations associated with the workstation factor correspond to the three workstation alternatives. For simplicity, we refer to the workstation alternatives as system A, system B, and system C.

The *randomized* aspect of the randomized block design is the random order in which the treatments (systems) are assigned to the controllers. If every controller were to test the three systems in the same order, any observed difference in systems might be due to the order of the test rather than to true differences in the systems.

To provide the necessary data, the three workstation alternatives were installed at the Cleveland Control Center in Oberlin, Ohio. Six controllers were selected at random and assigned to operate each of the systems. A follow-up interview and a medical examination of each controller participating in the study provided a measure of the stress for each controller on each system. The data are reported in Table 13.5.

Table 13.6 is a summary of the stress data collected. In this table we include column totals (treatments) and row totals (blocks) as well as some sample means that will be helpful in

TABLE 13.5 A RANDOMIZED BLOCK DESIGN FOR THE AIR TRAFFIC CONTROLLER STRESS TEST

WEB file AirTraffic

		Treatments		
		System A	**System B**	**System C**
Blocks	**Controller 1**	15	15	18
	Controller 2	14	14	14
	Controller 3	10	11	15
	Controller 4	13	12	17
	Controller 5	16	13	16
	Controller 6	13	13	13

TABLE 13.6 SUMMARY OF STRESS DATA FOR THE AIR TRAFFIC CONTROLLER STRESS TEST

		Treatments			Row or Block Totals	Block Means
		System A	System B	System C		
Blocks	Controller 1	15	15	18	48	$\bar{x}_{1\cdot} = 48/3 = 16.0$
	Controller 2	14	14	14	42	$\bar{x}_{2\cdot} = 42/3 = 14.0$
	Controller 3	10	11	15	36	$\bar{x}_{3\cdot} = 36/3 = 12.0$
	Controller 4	13	12	17	42	$\bar{x}_{4\cdot} = 42/3 = 14.0$
	Controller 5	16	13	16	45	$\bar{x}_{5\cdot} = 45/3 = 15.0$
	Controller 6	13	13	13	39	$\bar{x}_{6\cdot} = 39/3 = 13.0$
Column or Treatment Totals		81	78	93	252	$\bar{\bar{x}} = \frac{252}{18} = 14.0$
Treatment Means		$\bar{x}_{\cdot 1} = \frac{81}{6} = 13.5$	$\bar{x}_{\cdot 2} = \frac{78}{6} = 13.0$	$\bar{x}_{\cdot 3} = \frac{93}{6} = 15.5$		

making the sum of squares computations for the ANOVA procedure. Because lower stress values are viewed as better, the sample data seem to favor system B with its mean stress rating of 13. However, the usual question remains: Do the sample results justify the conclusion that the population mean stress levels for the three systems differ? That is, are the differences statistically significant? An analysis of variance computation similar to the one performed for the completely randomized design can be used to answer this statistical question.

ANOVA Procedure

The ANOVA procedure for the randomized block design requires us to partition the sum of squares total (SST) into three groups: sum of squares due to treatments (SSTR), sum of squares due to blocks (SSBL), and sum of squares due to error (SSE). The formula for this partitioning follows.

$$\text{SST} = \text{SSTR} + \text{SSBL} + \text{SSE} \tag{13.21}$$

This sum of squares partition is summarized in the ANOVA table for the randomized block design as shown in Table 13.7. The notation used in the table is

$$k = \text{the number of treatments}$$
$$b = \text{the number of blocks}$$
$$n_T = \text{the total sample size } (n_T = kb)$$

Note that the ANOVA table also shows how the $n_T - 1$ total degrees of freedom are partitioned such that $k - 1$ degrees of freedom go to treatments, $b - 1$ go to blocks, and $(k - 1)(b - 1)$ go to the error term. The mean square column shows the sum of squares divided by the degrees of freedom, and $F = \text{MSTR/MSE}$ is the F ratio used to test for a significant difference among the treatment means. The primary contribution of the randomized block design is that, by including blocks, we remove the individual controller differences from the MSE term and obtain a more powerful test for the stress differences in the three workstation alternatives.

TABLE 13.7 ANOVA TABLE FOR THE RANDOMIZED BLOCK DESIGN WITH k TREATMENTS AND b BLOCKS

Source of Variation	Sum of Squares	Degrees of Freedom	Mean Square	F	p-value
Treatments	SSTR	$k - 1$	$\text{MSTR} = \dfrac{\text{SSTR}}{k - 1}$	$\dfrac{\text{MSTR}}{\text{MSE}}$	
Blocks	SSBL	$b - 1$	$\text{MSBL} = \dfrac{\text{SSBL}}{b - 1}$		
Error	SSE	$(k - 1)(b - 1)$	$\text{MSE} = \dfrac{\text{SSE}}{(k - 1)(b - 1)}$		
Total	SST	$n_T - 1$			

Computations and Conclusions

To compute the F statistic needed to test for a difference among treatment means with a randomized block design, we need to compute MSTR and MSE. To calculate these two mean squares, we must first compute SSTR and SSE; in doing so, we will also compute SSBL and SST. To simplify the presentation, we perform the calculations in four steps. In addition to k, b, and n_T as previously defined, the following notation is used.

x_{ij} = value of the observation corresponding to treatment j in block i
$\bar{x}_{\cdot j}$ = sample mean of the jth treatment
$\bar{x}_{i\cdot}$ = sample mean for the ith block
$\bar{\bar{x}}$ = overall sample mean

Step 1. Compute the total sum of squares (SST).

$$\text{SST} = \sum_{i=1}^{b}\sum_{j=1}^{k}(x_{ij} - \bar{\bar{x}})^2 \quad \textbf{(13.22)}$$

Step 2. Compute the sum of squares due to treatments (SSTR).

$$\text{SSTR} = b\sum_{j=1}^{k}(\bar{x}_{\cdot j} - \bar{\bar{x}})^2 \quad \textbf{(13.23)}$$

Step 3. Compute the sum of squares due to blocks (SSBL).

$$\text{SSBL} = k\sum_{i=1}^{b}(\bar{x}_{i\cdot} - \bar{\bar{x}})^2 \quad \textbf{(13.24)}$$

Step 4. Compute the sum of squares due to error (SSE).

$$\text{SSE} = \text{SST} - \text{SSTR} - \text{SSBL} \quad \textbf{(13.25)}$$

For the air traffic controller data in Table 13.6, these steps lead to the following sums of squares.

Step 1. $\text{SST} = (15 - 14)^2 + (15 - 14)^2 + (18 - 14)^2 + \cdots + (13 - 14)^2 = 70$

Step 2. $\text{SSTR} = 6[(13.5 - 14)^2 + (13.0 - 14)^2 + (15.5 - 14)^2] = 21$

Step 3. $\text{SSBL} = 3[(16 - 14)^2 + (14 - 14)^2 + (12 - 14)^2 + (14 - 14)^2 + (15 - 14)^2 + (13 - 14)^2] = 30$

Step 4. $\text{SSE} = 70 - 21 - 30 = 19$

TABLE 13.8 ANOVA TABLE FOR THE AIR TRAFFIC CONTROLLER STRESS TEST

Source of Variation	Sum of Squares	Degrees of Freedom	Mean Square	F	p-value
Treatments	21	2	10.5	10.5/1.9 = 5.53	.024
Blocks	30	5	6.0		
Error	19	10	1.9		
Total	70	17			

These sums of squares divided by their degrees of freedom provide the corresponding mean square values shown in Table 13.8.

Let us use a level of significance $\alpha = .05$ to conduct the hypothesis test. The value of the test statistic is

$$F = \frac{\text{MSTR}}{\text{MSE}} = \frac{10.5}{1.9} = 5.53$$

The numerator degrees of freedom is $k - 1 = 3 - 1 = 2$ and the denominator degrees of freedom is $(k - 1)(b - 1) = (3 - 1)(6 - 1) = 10$. Because we will only reject the null hypothesis for large values of the test statistic, the p-value is the area under the F distribution to the right of $F = 5.53$. From Table 4 of Appendix B we find that with the degrees of freedom 2 and 10, $F = 5.53$ is between $F_{.025} = 5.46$ and $F_{.01} = 7.56$. As a result, the area in the upper tail, or the p-value, is between .01 and .025. Alternatively, we can use Excel or Minitab to show that the exact p-value for $F = 5.53$ is .024. With $p\text{-value} \leq \alpha = .05$, we reject the null hypothesis $H_0\colon \mu_1 = \mu_2 = \mu_3$ and conclude that the population mean stress levels differ for the three workstation alternatives.

Some general comments can be made about the randomized block design. The experimental design described in this section is a *complete* block design; the word "complete" indicates that each block is subjected to all k treatments. That is, all controllers (blocks) were tested with all three systems (treatments). Experimental designs in which some but not all treatments are applied to each block are referred to as *incomplete* block designs. A discussion of incomplete block designs is beyond the scope of this text.

Because each controller in the air traffic controller stress test was required to use all three systems, this approach guarantees a complete block design. In some cases, however, blocking is carried out with "similar" experimental units in each block. For example, assume that in a pretest of air traffic controllers, the population of controllers was divided into groups ranging from extremely high-stress individuals to extremely low-stress individuals. The blocking could still be accomplished by having three controllers from each of the stress classifications participate in the study. Each block would then consist of three controllers in the same stress group. The randomized aspect of the block design would be the random assignment of the three controllers in each block to the three systems.

Finally, note that the ANOVA table shown in Table 13.7 provides an F value to test for treatment effects but *not* for blocks. The reason is that the experiment was designed to test a single factor—workstation design. The blocking based on individual stress differences was conducted to remove such variation from the MSE term. However, the study was not designed to test specifically for individual differences in stress.

Some analysts compute $F = \text{MSB}/\text{MSE}$ and use that statistic to test for significance of the blocks. Then they use the result as a guide to whether the same type of blocking would be desired in future experiments. However, if individual stress difference is to be a factor in the study, a different experimental design should be used. A test of significance on blocks should not be performed as a basis for a conclusion about a second factor.

NOTES AND COMMENTS

The error degrees of freedom are less for a randomized block design than for a completely randomized design because $b - 1$ degrees of freedom are lost for the b blocks. If n is small, the potential effects due to blocks can be masked because of the loss of error degrees of freedom; for large n, the effects are minimized.

Exercises

Methods

SELF test

21. Consider the experimental results for the following randomized block design. Make the calculations necessary to set up the analysis of variance table.

		Treatments		
		A	B	C
Blocks	1	10	9	8
	2	12	6	5
	3	18	15	14
	4	20	18	18
	5	8	7	8

Use $\alpha = .05$ to test for any significant differences.

22. The following data were obtained for a randomized block design involving five treatments and three blocks: SST = 430, SSTR = 310, SSBL = 85. Set up the ANOVA table and test for any significant differences. Use $\alpha = .05$.

23. An experiment has been conducted for four treatments with eight blocks. Complete the following analysis of variance table.

Source of Variation	Sum of Squares	Degrees of Freedom	Mean Square	*F*
Treatments	900			
Blocks	400			
Error				
Total	1800			

Use $\alpha = .05$ to test for any significant differences.

Applications

24. An automobile dealer conducted a test to determine if the time in minutes needed to complete a minor engine tune-up depends on whether a computerized engine analyzer or an electronic analyzer is used. Because tune-up time varies among compact, intermediate, and full-sized cars, the three types of cars were used as blocks in the experiment. The data obtained follow.

		Analyzer	
		Computerized	**Electronic**
Car	**Compact**	50	42
	Intermediate	55	44
	Full-sized	63	46

Use $\alpha = .05$ to test for any significant differences.

25. The price drivers pay for gasoline often varies a great deal across regions throughout the United States. The following data show the price per gallon for regular gasoline for a random sample of gasoline service stations for three major brands of gasoline (Shell, BP, and Marathon) located in 11 metropolitan areas across the upper Midwest region (OhioGasPrices.com website, March 18, 2012).

WEB file MidwestGas

Metropolitan Area	Shell	BP	Marathon
Akron, Ohio	3.77	3.83	3.78
Cincinnati, Ohio	3.72	3.83	3.87
Cleveland, Ohio	3.87	3.85	3.89
Columbus, Ohio	3.76	3.77	3.79
Ft. Wayne, Indiana	3.83	3.84	3.87
Indianapolis, Indiana	3.85	3.84	3.87
Lansing, Michigan	3.93	4.04	3.99
Lexington, Kentucky	3.79	3.78	3.79
Louisville, Kentucky	3.78	3.84	3.79
Muncie, Indiana	3.81	3.84	3.86
Toledo, Ohio	3.69	3.83	3.86

Use $\alpha = .05$ to test for any significant difference in the mean price of gasoline for the three brands.

26. The Scholastic Aptitude Test (SAT) contains three parts: critical reading, mathematics, and writing. Each part is scored on an 800-point scale. Information on test scores for the 2009 version of the SAT is available at the College Board website. A sample of SAT scores for six students follows.

WEB file SATScores

Student	Critical Reading	Mathematics	Writing
1	526	534	530
2	594	590	586
3	465	464	445
4	561	566	553
5	436	478	430
6	430	458	420

a. Using a .05 level of significance, do students perform differently on the three portions of the SAT?

b. Which portion of the test seems to give the students the most trouble? Explain.

27. A study reported in the *Journal of the American Medical Association* investigated the cardiac demands of heavy snow shoveling. Ten healthy men underwent exercise testing with a treadmill and a cycle ergometer modified for arm cranking. The men then cleared two tracts of heavy, wet snow by using a lightweight plastic snow shovel and an electric snow thrower. Each subject's heart rate, blood pressure, oxygen uptake, and perceived exertion during snow removal were compared with the values obtained during treadmill

and arm-crank ergometer testing. Suppose the following table gives the heart rates in beats per minute for each of the 10 subjects.

WEB file
SnowShoveling

Subject	Treadmill	Arm-Crank Ergometer	Snow Shovel	Snow Thrower
1	177	205	180	98
2	151	177	164	120
3	184	166	167	111
4	161	152	173	122
5	192	142	179	151
6	193	172	205	158
7	164	191	156	117
8	207	170	160	123
9	177	181	175	127
10	174	154	191	109

At the .05 level of significance, test for any significant differences.

13.5 Factorial Experiment

The experimental designs we have considered thus far enable us to draw statistical conclusions about one factor. However, in some experiments we want to draw conclusions about more than one variable or factor. A **factorial experiment** is an experimental design that allows simultaneous conclusions about two or more factors. The term *factorial* is used because the experimental conditions include all possible combinations of the factors. For example, for *a* levels of factor A and *b* levels of factor B, the experiment will involve collecting data on *ab* treatment combinations. In this section we will show the analysis for a two-factor factorial experiment. The basic approach can be extended to experiments involving more than two factors.

As an illustration of a two-factor factorial experiment, we will consider a study involving the Graduate Management Admissions Test (GMAT), a standardized test used by graduate schools of business to evaluate an applicant's ability to pursue a graduate program in that field. Scores on the GMAT range from 200 to 800, with higher scores implying higher aptitude.

In an attempt to improve students' performance on the GMAT, a major Texas university is considering offering the following three GMAT preparation programs.

1. A three-hour review session covering the types of questions generally asked on the GMAT.
2. A one-day program covering relevant exam material, along with the taking and grading of a sample exam.
3. An intensive 10-week course involving the identification of each student's weaknesses and the setting up of individualized programs for improvement.

Hence, one factor in this study is the GMAT preparation program, which has three treatments: three-hour review, one-day program, and 10-week course. Before selecting the preparation program to adopt, further study will be conducted to determine how the proposed programs affect GMAT scores.

The GMAT is usually taken by students from three colleges: the College of Business, the College of Engineering, and the College of Arts and Sciences. Therefore, a second factor of interest in the experiment is whether a student's undergraduate college affects the GMAT score. This second factor, undergraduate college, also has three treatments: business, engineering, and arts and sciences. The factorial design for this experiment with three treatments corresponding to factor A, the preparation program, and three treatments corresponding to

TABLE 13.9 NINE TREATMENT COMBINATIONS FOR THE TWO-FACTOR GMAT EXPERIMENT

		Factor B: College		
		Business	**Engineering**	**Arts and Sciences**
Factor A: Preparation Program	**Three-hour review**	1	2	3
	One-day program	4	5	6
	10-week course	7	8	9

factor B, the undergraduate college, will have a total of $3 \times 3 = 9$ treatment combinations. These treatment combinations or experimental conditions are summarized in Table 13.9.

Assume that a sample of two students will be selected corresponding to each of the nine treatment combinations shown in Table 13.9: Two business students will take the three-hour review, two will take the one-day program, and two will take the 10-week course. In addition, two engineering students and two arts and sciences students will take each of the three preparation programs. In experimental design terminology, the sample size of two for each treatment combination indicates that we have two **replications**. Additional replications and a larger sample size could easily be used, but we elect to minimize the computational aspects for this illustration.

This experimental design requires that 6 students who plan to attend graduate school be randomly selected from *each* of the three undergraduate colleges. Then 2 students from each college should be assigned randomly to each preparation program, resulting in a total of 18 students being used in the study.

Let us assume that the randomly selected students participated in the preparation programs and then took the GMAT. The scores obtained are reported in Table 13.10.

The analysis of variance computations with the data in Table 13.10 will provide answers to the following questions.

- **Main effect (factor A):** Do the preparation programs differ in terms of effect on GMAT scores?
- **Main effect (factor B):** Do the undergraduate colleges differ in terms of effect on GMAT scores?
- **Interaction effect (factors A and B):** Do students in some colleges do better on one type of preparation program whereas others do better on a different type of preparation program?

The term **interaction** refers to a new effect that we can now study because we used a factorial experiment. If the interaction effect has a significant impact on the GMAT scores,

WEB file

GMATStudy

TABLE 13.10 GMAT SCORES FOR THE TWO-FACTOR EXPERIMENT

		Factor B: College		
		Business	**Engineering**	**Arts and Sciences**
Factor A: Preparation Program	**Three-hour review**	500	540	480
		580	460	400
	One-day program	460	560	420
		540	620	480
	10-week course	560	600	480
		600	580	410

TABLE 13.11 ANOVA TABLE FOR THE TWO-FACTOR FACTORIAL EXPERIMENT WITH r REPLICATIONS

Source of Variation	Sum of Squares	Degrees of Freedom	Mean Square	F	p-value
Factor A	SSA	$a - 1$	$\text{MSA} = \dfrac{\text{SSA}}{a - 1}$	$\dfrac{\text{MSA}}{\text{MSE}}$	
Factor B	SSB	$b - 1$	$\text{MSB} = \dfrac{\text{SSB}}{b - 1}$	$\dfrac{\text{MSB}}{\text{MSE}}$	
Interaction	SSAB	$(a - 1)(b - 1)$	$\text{MSAB} = \dfrac{\text{SSAB}}{(a - 1)(b - 1)}$	$\dfrac{\text{MSAB}}{\text{MSE}}$	
Error	SSE	$ab(r - 1)$	$\text{MSE} = \dfrac{\text{SSE}}{ab(r - 1)}$		
Total	SST	$n_T - 1$			

we can conclude that the effect of the type of preparation program depends on the undergraduate college.

ANOVA Procedure

The ANOVA procedure for the two-factor factorial experiment requires us to partition the sum of squares total (SST) into four groups: sum of squares for factor A (SSA), sum of squares for factor B (SSB), sum of squares for interaction (SSAB), and sum of squares due to error (SSE). The formula for this partitioning follows.

$$\text{SST} = \text{SSA} + \text{SSB} + \text{SSAB} + \text{SSE} \tag{13.26}$$

The partitioning of the sum of squares and degrees of freedom is summarized in Table 13.11. The following notation is used.

a = number of levels of factor A
b = number of levels of factor B
r = number of replications
n_T = total number of observations taken in the experiment; $n_T = abr$

Computations and Conclusions

To compute the F statistics needed to test for the significance of factor A, factor B, and interaction, we need to compute MSA, MSB, MSAB, and MSE. To calculate these four mean squares, we must first compute SSA, SSB, SSAB, and SSE; in doing so we will also compute SST. To simplify the presentation, we perform the calculations in five steps. In addition to a, b, r, and n_T as previously defined, the following notation is used.

x_{ijk} = observation corresponding to the kth replicate taken from treatment i of factor A and treatment j of factor B
$\bar{x}_{i\cdot}$ = sample mean for the observations in treatment i (factor A)
$\bar{x}_{\cdot j}$ = sample mean for the observations in treatment j (factor B)
$\bar{x}_{ij}$ = sample mean for the observations corresponding to the combination of treatment i (factor A) and treatment j (factor B)
$\bar{\bar{x}}$ = overall sample mean of all n_T observations

Step 1. Compute the total sum of squares.

$$\text{SST} = \sum_{i=1}^{a}\sum_{j=1}^{b}\sum_{k=1}^{r}(x_{ijk} - \bar{\bar{x}})^2 \qquad \textbf{(13.27)}$$

Step 2. Compute the sum of squares for factor A.

$$\text{SSA} = br\sum_{i=1}^{a}(\bar{x}_{i\cdot} - \bar{\bar{x}})^2 \qquad \textbf{(13.28)}$$

Step 3. Compute the sum of squares for factor B.

$$\text{SSB} = ar\sum_{j=1}^{b}(\bar{x}_{\cdot j} - \bar{\bar{x}})^2 \qquad \textbf{(13.29)}$$

Step 4. Compute the sum of squares for interaction.

$$\text{SSAB} = r\sum_{i=1}^{a}\sum_{j=1}^{b}(\bar{x}_{ij} - \bar{x}_{i\cdot} - \bar{x}_{\cdot j} + \bar{\bar{x}})^2 \qquad \textbf{(13.30)}$$

Step 5. Compute the sum of squares due to error.

$$\text{SSE} = \text{SST} - \text{SSA} - \text{SSB} - \text{SSAB} \qquad \textbf{(13.31)}$$

Table 13.12 reports the data collected in the experiment and the various sums that will help us with the sum of squares computations. Using equations (13.27) through (13.31), we calculate the following sums of squares for the GMAT two-factor factorial experiment.

Step 1. $\text{SST} = (500 - 515)^2 + (580 - 515)^2 + (540 - 515)^2 + \cdots + (410 - 515)^2 = 82{,}450$

Step 2. $\text{SSA} = (3)(2)[(493.33 - 515)^2 + (513.33 - 515)^2 + (538.33 - 515)^2] = 6100$

Step 3. $\text{SSB} = (3)(2)[(540 - 515)^2 + (560 - 515)^2 + (445 - 515)^2] = 45{,}300$

Step 4. $\text{SSAB} = 2[(540 - 493.33 - 540 + 515)^2 + (500 - 493.33 - 560 + 515)^2 + \cdots + (445 - 538.33 - 445 + 515)^2] = 11{,}200$

Step 5. $\text{SSE} = 82{,}450 - 6100 - 45{,}300 - 11{,}200 = 19{,}850$

These sums of squares divided by their corresponding degrees of freedom provide the appropriate mean square values for testing the two main effects (preparation program and undergraduate college) and the interaction effect.

Because of the computational effort involved in any modest- to large-size factorial experiment, the computer usually plays an important role in performing the analysis of variance computations shown above and in the calculation of the p-values used to make the hypothesis testing decisions. Figure 13.6 shows the Minitab output for the analysis of variance for the GMAT two-factor factorial experiment. Let us use the Minitab output and a level of significance $\alpha = .05$ to conduct the hypothesis tests for the two-factor GMAT study. The p-value used to test for significant differences among the three preparation programs (factor A) is .299. Because the p-value $= .299$ is greater than $\alpha = .05$, there is no significant difference in the mean GMAT test scores for the three preparation programs. However, for the undergraduate college effect, the p-value $= .005$ is less than $\alpha = .05$; thus, there is a significant difference in the mean GMAT test scores among the three undergraduate colleges.

TABLE 13.12 GMAT SUMMARY DATA FOR THE TWO-FACTOR EXPERIMENT

	Treatment combination totals	Factor B: College — Business	Factor B: College — Engineering	Factor B: College — Arts and Sciences	Row Totals	Factor A Means
Factor A: Preparation Program	Three-hour review	500 580 1080	540 460 1000	480 400 880	2960	$\bar{x}_{1\cdot} = \frac{2960}{6} = 493.33$
		$\bar{x}_{11} = \frac{1080}{2} = 540$	$\bar{x}_{12} = \frac{1000}{2} = 500$	$\bar{x}_{13} = \frac{880}{2} = 440$		
	One-day program	460 540 1000	560 620 1180	420 480 900	3080	$\bar{x}_{2\cdot} = \frac{3080}{6} = 513.33$
		$\bar{x}_{21} = \frac{1000}{2} = 500$	$\bar{x}_{22} = \frac{1180}{2} = 590$	$\bar{x}_{23} = \frac{900}{2} = 450$		
	10-week course	560 600 1160	600 580 1180	480 410 890	3230	$\bar{x}_{3\cdot} = \frac{3230}{6} = 538.33$
		$\bar{x}_{31} = \frac{1160}{2} = 580$	$\bar{x}_{32} = \frac{1180}{2} = 590$	$\bar{x}_{33} = \frac{890}{2} = 445$		
Column Totals		3240	3360	2670	9270	← Overall total
Factor B Means		$\bar{x}_{\cdot 1} = \frac{3240}{6} = 540$	$\bar{x}_{\cdot 2} = \frac{3360}{6} = 560$	$\bar{x}_{\cdot 3} = \frac{2670}{6} = 445$	$\bar{\bar{x}} = \frac{9270}{18} = 515$	

FIGURE 13.6 MINITAB OUTPUT FOR THE GMAT TWO-FACTOR DESIGN

SOURCE	DF	SS	MS	F	P
Factor A	2	6100	3050	1.38	0.299
Factor B	2	45300	22650	10.27	0.005
Interaction	4	11200	2800	1.27	0.350
Error	9	19850	2206		
Total	17	82450			

Finally, because the p-value of .350 for the interaction effect is greater than $\alpha = .05$, there is no significant interaction effect. Therefore, the study provides no reason to believe that the three preparation programs differ in their ability to prepare students from the different colleges for the GMAT.

Undergraduate college was found to be a significant factor. Checking the calculations in Table 13.12, we see that the sample means are: business students $\bar{x}_{\cdot 1} = 540$, engineering students $\bar{x}_{\cdot 2} = 560$, and arts and sciences students $\bar{x}_{\cdot 3} = 445$. Tests on individual treatment means can be conducted, yet after reviewing the three sample means, we would anticipate no difference in preparation for business and engineering graduates. However, the arts and sciences students appear to be significantly less prepared for the GMAT than students in the other colleges. Perhaps this observation will lead the university to consider other options for assisting these students in preparing for the Graduate Management Admission Test.

Exercises

Methods

SELF test

28. A factorial experiment involving two levels of factor A and three levels of factor B resulted in the following data.

		Factor B		
		Level 1	Level 2	Level 3
Factor A	Level 1	135 165	90 66	75 93
	Level 2	125 95	127 105	120 136

Test for any significant main effects and any interaction. Use $\alpha = .05$.

29. The calculations for a factorial experiment involving four levels of factor A, three levels of factor B, and three replications resulted in the following data: SST = 280, SSA = 26, SSB = 23, SSAB = 175. Set up the ANOVA table and test for any significant main effects and any interaction effect. Use $\alpha = .05$.

Applications

30. A mail-order catalog firm designed a factorial experiment to test the effect of the size of a magazine advertisement and the advertisement design on the number of catalog requests received (data in thousands). Three advertising designs and two different size advertisements were considered. The data obtained follow. Use the ANOVA procedure for

factorial designs to test for any significant effects due to type of design, size of advertisement, or interaction. Use $\alpha = .05$.

		Size of Advertisement	
		Small	**Large**
Design	**A**	8	12
		12	8
	B	22	26
		14	30
	C	10	18
		18	14

31. An amusement park studied methods for decreasing the waiting time (minutes) for rides by loading and unloading riders more efficiently. Two alternative loading/unloading methods have been proposed. To account for potential differences due to the type of ride and the possible interaction between the method of loading and unloading and the type of ride, a factorial experiment was designed. Use the following data to test for any significant effect due to the loading and unloading method, the type of ride, and interaction. Use $\alpha = .05$.

	Type of Ride		
	Roller Coaster	**Screaming Demon**	**Log Flume**
Method 1	41	52	50
	43	44	46
Method 2	49	50	48
	51	46	44

32. As part of a study designed to compare hybrid and similarly equipped conventional vehicles, *Consumer Reports* tested a variety of classes of hybrid and all-gas model cars and sport utility vehicles (SUVs). The following data show the miles-per-gallon rating *Consumer Reports* obtained for two hybrid small cars, two hybrid midsize cars, two hybrid small SUVs, and two hybrid midsize SUVs; also shown are the miles per gallon obtained for eight similarly equipped conventional models (*Consumer Reports,* October 2008).

WEB file
HybridTest

Make/Model	Class	Type	MPG
Honda Civic	Small Car	Hybrid	37
Honda Civic	Small Car	Conventional	28
Toyota Prius	Small Car	Hybrid	44
Toyota Corolla	Small Car	Conventional	32
Chevrolet Malibu	Midsize Car	Hybrid	27
Chevrolet Malibu	Midsize Car	Conventional	23
Nissan Altima	Midsize Car	Hybrid	32
Nissan Altima	Midsize Car	Conventional	25
Ford Escape	Small SUV	Hybrid	27
Ford Escape	Small SUV	Conventional	21
Saturn Vue	Small SUV	Hybrid	28
Saturn Vue	Small SUV	Conventional	22
Lexus RX	Midsize SUV	Hybrid	23
Lexus RX	Midsize SUV	Conventional	19
Toyota Highlander	Midsize SUV	Hybrid	24
Toyota Highlander	Midsize SUV	Conventional	18

At the $\alpha = .05$ level of significance, test for significant effects due to class, type, and interaction.

33. A study reported in *The Accounting Review* examined the separate and joint effects of two levels of time pressure (low and moderate) and three levels of knowledge (naive, declarative, and procedural) on key word selection behavior in tax research. Subjects were given a tax case containing a set of facts, a tax issue, and a key word index consisting of 1336 key words. They were asked to select the key words they believed would refer them to a tax authority relevant to resolving the tax case. Prior to the experiment, a group of tax experts determined that the text contained 19 relevant key words. Subjects in the naive group had little or no declarative or procedural knowledge, subjects in the declarative group had significant declarative knowledge but little or no procedural knowledge, and subjects in the procedural group had significant declarative knowledge and procedural knowledge. Declarative knowledge consists of knowledge of both the applicable tax rules and the technical terms used to describe such rules. Procedural knowledge is knowledge of the rules that guide the tax researcher's search for relevant key words. Subjects in the low time pressure situation were told they had 25 minutes to complete the problem, an amount of time which should be "more than adequate" to complete the case; subjects in the moderate time pressure situation were told they would have "only" 11 minutes to complete the case. Suppose 25 subjects were selected for each of the six treatment combinations and the sample means for each treatment combination are as follows (standard deviations are in parentheses).

		Knowledge		
		Naive	**Declarative**	**Procedural**
Time Pressure	**Low**	1.13 (1.12)	1.56 (1.33)	2.00 (1.54)
	Moderate	0.48 (0.80)	1.68 (1.36)	2.86 (1.80)

Use the ANOVA procedure to test for any significant differences due to time pressure, knowledge, and interaction. Use a .05 level of significance. Assume that the total sum of squares for this experiment is 327.50.

Summary

In this chapter we showed how analysis of variance can be used to test for differences among means of several populations or treatments. We introduced the completely randomized design, the randomized block design, and the two-factor factorial experiment. The completely randomized design and the randomized block design are used to draw conclusions about differences in the means of a single factor. The primary purpose of blocking in the randomized block design is to remove extraneous sources of variation from the error term. Such blocking provides a better estimate of the true error variance and a better test to determine whether the population or treatment means of the factor differ significantly.

We showed that the basis for the statistical tests used in analysis of variance and experimental design is the development of two independent estimates of the population variance σ^2. In the single-factor case, one estimator is based on the variation between the treatments; this estimator provides an unbiased estimate of σ^2 only if the means $\mu_1, \mu_2, \ldots, \mu_k$ are all equal. A second estimator of σ^2 is based on the variation of the observations within each sample; this estimator will always provide an unbiased estimate of σ^2. By computing the ratio of these two estimators (the F statistic) we developed a rejection rule for determining whether to reject the null hypothesis that the population or treatment means are equal. In all the experimental designs considered, the partitioning of the sum of squares and degrees of freedom into their various sources enabled us to compute the appropriate values for the analysis of variance calculations and tests. We also showed how Fisher's LSD procedure and the Bonferroni adjustment can be used to perform pairwise comparisons to determine which means are different.

Glossary

Factor Another word for the independent variable of interest.
Treatments Different levels of a factor.
Single-factor experiment An experiment involving only one factor with k populations or treatments.
Response variable Another word for the dependent variable of interest.
Experimental units The objects of interest in the experiment.
Completely randomized design An experimental design in which the treatments are randomly assigned to the experimental units.
ANOVA table A table used to summarize the analysis of variance computations and results. It contains columns showing the source of variation, the sum of squares, the degrees of freedom, the mean square, and the F value(s).
Partitioning The process of allocating the total sum of squares and degrees of freedom to the various components.
Multiple comparison procedures Statistical procedures that can be used to conduct statistical comparisons between pairs of population means.
Comparisonwise Type I error rate The probability of a Type I error associated with a single pairwise comparison.
Experimentwise Type I error rate The probability of making a Type I error on at least one of several pairwise comparisons.
Blocking The process of using the same or similar experimental units for all treatments. The purpose of blocking is to remove a source of variation from the error term and hence provide a more powerful test for a difference in population or treatment means.
Randomized block design An experimental design employing blocking.
Factorial experiment An experimental design that allows simultaneous conclusions about two or more factors.
Replications The number of times each experimental condition is repeated in an experiment.
Interaction The effect produced when the levels of one factor interact with the levels of another factor in influencing the response variable.

Key Formulas

Completely Randomized Design

Sample Mean for Treatment *j*

$$\bar{x}_j = \frac{\sum_{i=1}^{n_j} x_{ij}}{n_j} \tag{13.1}$$

Sample Variance for Treatment *j*

$$s_j^2 = \frac{\sum_{i=1}^{n_j} (x_{ij} - \bar{x}_j)^2}{n_j - 1} \tag{13.2}$$

Overall Sample Mean

$$\bar{\bar{x}} = \frac{\sum_{j=1}^{k}\sum_{i=1}^{n_j} x_{ij}}{n_T} \tag{13.3}$$

$$n_T = n_1 + n_2 + \cdots + n_k \tag{13.4}$$

Mean Square Due to Treatments

$$\text{MSTR} = \frac{\text{SSTR}}{k - 1} \tag{13.7}$$

Sum of Squares Due to Treatments

$$\text{SSTR} = \sum_{j=1}^{k} n_j(\bar{x}_j - \bar{\bar{x}})^2 \tag{13.8}$$

Mean Square Due to Error

$$\text{MSE} = \frac{\text{SSE}}{n_T - k} \tag{13.10}$$

Sum of Squares Due to Error

$$\text{SSE} = \sum_{j=1}^{k}(n_j - 1)s_j^2 \tag{13.11}$$

Test Statistic for the Equality of *k* Population Means

$$F = \frac{\text{MSTR}}{\text{MSE}} \tag{13.12}$$

Total Sum of Squares

$$\text{SST} = \sum_{j=1}^{k}\sum_{i=1}^{n_j}(x_{ij} - \bar{\bar{x}})^2 \tag{13.13}$$

Partitioning of Sum of Squares

$$\text{SST} = \text{SSTR} + \text{SSE} \tag{13.14}$$

Multiple Comparison Procedures

Test Statistic for Fisher's LSD Procedure

$$t = \frac{\bar{x}_i - \bar{x}_j}{\sqrt{\text{MSE}\left(\frac{1}{n_i} + \frac{1}{n_j}\right)}} \tag{13.16}$$

Fisher's LSD

$$\text{LSD} = t_{\alpha/2}\sqrt{\text{MSE}\left(\frac{1}{n_i} + \frac{1}{n_j}\right)} \tag{13.17}$$

Randomized Block Design

Total Sum of Squares

$$\text{SST} = \sum_{i=1}^{b}\sum_{j=1}^{k}(x_{ij} - \bar{\bar{x}})^2 \tag{13.22}$$

Sum of Squares Due to Treatments

$$\text{SSTR} = b\sum_{j=1}^{k}(\bar{x}_{\cdot j} - \bar{\bar{x}})^2 \tag{13.23}$$

Sum of Squares Due to Blocks

$$\text{SSBL} = k\sum_{i=1}^{b}(\bar{x}_{i\cdot} - \bar{\bar{x}})^2 \tag{13.24}$$

Sum of Squares Due to Error

$$\text{SSE} = \text{SST} - \text{SSTR} - \text{SSBL} \tag{13.25}$$

Factorial Experiment

Total Sum of Squares

$$\text{SST} = \sum_{i=1}^{a}\sum_{j=1}^{b}\sum_{k=1}^{r}(x_{ijk} - \bar{\bar{x}})^2 \tag{13.27}$$

Sum of Squares for Factor A

$$\text{SSA} = br\sum_{i=1}^{a}(\bar{x}_{i\cdot} - \bar{\bar{x}})^2 \tag{13.28}$$

Sum of Squares for Factor B

$$\text{SSB} = ar\sum_{j=1}^{b}(\bar{x}_{\cdot j} - \bar{\bar{x}})^2 \tag{13.29}$$

Sum of Squares for Interaction

$$\text{SSAB} = r\sum_{i=1}^{a}\sum_{j=1}^{b}(\bar{x}_{ij} - \bar{x}_{i\cdot} - \bar{x}_{\cdot j} + \bar{\bar{x}})^2 \tag{13.30}$$

Sum of Squares for Error

$$\text{SSE} = \text{SST} - \text{SSA} - \text{SSB} - \text{SSAB} \tag{13.31}$$

Supplementary Exercises

34. In a completely randomized experimental design, three brands of paper towels were tested for their ability to absorb water. Equal-size towels were used, with four sections of towels tested per brand. The absorbency rating data follow. At a .05 level of significance, does there appear to be a difference in the ability of the brands to absorb water?

	Brand	
x	y	z
91	99	83
100	96	88
88	94	89
89	99	76

35. A study reported in the *Journal of Small Business Management* concluded that self-employed individuals do not experience higher job satisfaction than individuals who are not self-employed. In this study, job satisfaction is measured using 18 items, each of which is rated using a Likert-type scale with 1–5 response options ranging from strong agreement to strong disagreement. A higher score on this scale indicates a higher degree of job satisfaction. The sum of the ratings for the 18 items, ranging from 18–90, is used as the measure of job satisfaction. Suppose that this approach was used to measure the job satisfaction for lawyers, physical therapists, cabinetmakers, and systems analysts. The results obtained for a sample of 10 individuals from each profession follow.

WEB file SatisJob

Lawyer	Physical Therapist	Cabinetmaker	Systems Analyst
44	55	54	44
42	78	65	73
74	80	79	71
42	86	69	60
53	60	79	64
50	59	64	66
45	62	59	41
48	52	78	55
64	55	84	76
38	50	60	62

At the $\alpha = .05$ level of significance, test for any difference in the job satisfaction among the four professions.

36. The U.S. Environmental Protection Agency (EPA) monitors levels of pollutants in the air for cities across the country. Ozone pollution levels are measured using a 500-point scale; lower scores indicate little health risk, and higher scores indicate greater health risk. The following data show the peak levels of ozone pollution in four cities (Birmingham, Alabama; Memphis, Tennessee; Little Rock, Arkansas; and Jackson, Mississippi) for 10 dates in 2012 (U.S. EPA website, March 20, 2012).

WEB file OzoneLevels

	City			
Data	Birmingham AL	Memphis TN	Little Rock AR	Jackson MS
Jan 9	18	20	18	14
Jan17	23	31	22	30
Jan 18	19	25	22	21
Jan 31	29	36	28	35
Feb 1	27	31	28	24
Feb 6	26	31	31	25
Feb 14	31	24	19	25
Feb 17	31	31	28	28
Feb 20	33	35	35	34
Feb 29	20	42	42	21

Use $\alpha = .05$ to test for any significant difference in the mean peak ozone levels among the four cities.

37. The U.S. Census Bureau computes quarterly vacancy and homeownership rates by state and metropolitan statistical area. Each metropolitan statistical area (MSA) has at least one urbanized area of 50,000 or more inhabitants. The following data are the rental vacancy rates (%) for MSAs in four geographic regions of the United States for the first quarter of 2008 (U.S. Census Bureau website, January 2009).

WEB file RentalVacancy

Midwest	Northeast	South	West
16.2	2.7	16.6	7.9
10.1	11.5	8.5	6.6
8.6	6.6	12.1	6.9
12.3	7.9	9.8	5.6
10.0	5.3	9.3	4.3
16.9	10.7	9.1	15.2
16.9	8.6	5.6	5.7
5.4	5.5	9.4	4.0
18.1	12.7	11.6	12.3
11.9	8.3	15.6	3.6
11.0	6.7	18.3	11.0
9.6	14.2	13.4	12.1
7.6	1.7	6.5	8.7
12.9	3.6	11.4	5.0
12.2	11.5	13.1	4.7
13.6	16.3	4.4	3.3
		8.2	3.4
		24.0	5.5
		12.2	
		22.6	
		12.0	
		14.5	
		12.6	
		9.5	
		10.1	

Use $\alpha = .05$ to test whether there the mean vacancy rate is the same for each geographic region.

38. Three different assembly methods have been proposed for a new product. A completely randomized experimental design was chosen to determine which assembly method results in the greatest number of parts produced per hour, and 30 workers were randomly selected and assigned to use one of the proposed methods. The number of units produced by each worker follows.

WEB file Assembly

Method		
A	B	C
97	93	99
73	100	94
93	93	87
100	55	66
73	77	59
91	91	75
100	85	84
86	73	72
92	90	88
95	83	86

Use these data and test to see whether the mean number of parts produced is the same with each method. Use $\alpha = .05$.

39. In a study conducted to investigate browsing activity by shoppers, each shopper was initially classified as a nonbrowser, light browser, or heavy browser. For each shopper, the study obtained a measure to determine how comfortable the shopper was in a store. Higher scores indicated greater comfort. Suppose the following data were collected.

WEB file Browsing

Nonbrowser	Light Browser	Heavy Browser
4	5	5
5	6	7
6	5	5
3	4	7
3	7	4
4	4	6
5	6	5
4	5	7

a. Use $\alpha = .05$ to test for differences among comfort levels for the three types of browsers.
b. Use Fisher's LSD procedure to compare the comfort levels of nonbrowsers and light browsers. Use $\alpha = .05$. What is your conclusion?

40. A research firm tests the miles-per-gallon characteristics of three brands of gasoline. Because of different gasoline performance characteristics in different brands of automobiles, five brands of automobiles are selected and treated as blocks in the experiment; that is, each brand of automobile is tested with each type of gasoline. The results of the experiment (in miles per gallon) follow.

		Gasoline Brands		
		I	II	III
Automobiles	A	18	21	20
	B	24	26	27
	C	30	29	34
	D	22	25	24
	E	20	23	24

a. At $\alpha = .05$, is there a significant difference in the mean miles-per-gallon characteristics of the three brands of gasoline?
b. Analyze the experimental data using the ANOVA procedure for completely randomized designs. Compare your findings with those obtained in part (a). What is the advantage of attempting to remove the block effect?

41. The compact car market in the United States is extremely competitive. Sales for six of the top models for six months in 2011 follow (*Motor Trend,* November 2, 2011).

WEB file CompactCars

Month	Chevy Cruze	Ford Focus	Hyundai Elantra	Honda Civic	Toyota Corolla	VW Jetta
May	22,711	22,303	20,006	18,341	16,985	16,671
June	24,896	21,385	19,992	18,872	17,485	17,105
July	24,468	17,577	15,713	15,181	14,889	14,006
August	21,897	16,420	15,054	14,500	14,093	12,083
September	18,097	16,147	15,023	14,386	13,724	10,309
October	16,244	16,173	14,295	13,058	13,000	12,386

At the .05 level of significance, test for any significant difference in the mean number of cars sold per month for the six models.

42. Major League Baseball franchises rely on attendance for a large share of their total revenue, and weekend games are particularly important. The following table shows the attendance for the Houston Astros for games played during seven weekend series for the first three months (April, May, and June) of the 2011 season (ESPN website, January 12, 2012).

WEB file HoustonAstros

Opponent	Friday	Saturday	Sunday
Florida Marlins	41,042	25,421	22,299
San Diego Padres	23,755	28,100	22,899
Milwaukee Brewers	25,734	26,514	23,908
New York Mets	28,791	31,140	28,406
Arizona Diamondbacks	21,834	31,405	21,882
Atlanta Braves	29,252	32,117	23,765
Tampa Bay Rays	26,682	27,208	23,965

At the .05 level of significance, test whether the mean attendance is the same for these three days. The Houston Astros are considering running a special promotion to increase attendance during one game of each weekend series during the second half of the season. Do these data suggest a particular day on which the Astros should schedule these promotions?

43. A factorial experiment was designed to test for any significant differences in the time needed to perform English to foreign language translations with two computerized language translators. Because the type of language translated was also considered a significant factor, translations were made with both systems for three different languages: Spanish, French, and German. Use the following data for translation time in hours.

	Language		
	Spanish	French	German
System 1	8	10	12
	12	14	16
System 2	6	14	16
	10	16	22

Test for any significant differences due to language translator, type of language, and interaction. Use $\alpha = .05$.

44. A manufacturing company designed a factorial experiment to determine whether the number of defective parts produced by two machines differed and if the number of defective parts produced also depended on whether the raw material needed by each machine was loaded manually or by an automatic feed system. The following data give the numbers of defective parts produced. Use $\alpha = .05$ to test for any significant effect due to machine, loading system, and interaction.

	Loading System	
	Manual	Automatic
Machine 1	30	30
	34	26
Machine 2	20	24
	22	28

Case Problem 1 Wentworth Medical Center

As part of a long-term study of individuals 65 years of age or older, sociologists and physicians at the Wentworth Medical Center in upstate New York investigated the relationship between geographic location and depression. A sample of 60 individuals, all in reasonably good health, was selected; 20 individuals were residents of Florida, 20 were residents of New York, and 20 were residents of North Carolina. Each of the individuals sampled was given a standardized test to measure depression. The data collected follow; higher test scores indicate higher levels of depression. These data are contained in the file Medical1.

A second part of the study considered the relationship between geographic location and depression for individuals 65 years of age or older who had a chronic health condition such as arthritis, hypertension, and/or heart ailment. A sample of 60 individuals with such conditions was identified. Again, 20 were residents of Florida, 20 were residents of New York, and 20 were residents of North Carolina. The levels of depression recorded for this study follow. These data are contained in the file named Medical2.

WEB file Medical1

WEB file Medical2

Data from Medical1			Data from Medical2		
Florida	New York	North Carolina	Florida	New York	North Carolina
3	8	10	13	14	10
7	11	7	12	9	12
7	9	3	17	15	15
3	7	5	17	12	18
8	8	11	20	16	12
8	7	8	21	24	14
8	8	4	16	18	17
5	4	3	14	14	8
5	13	7	13	15	14
2	10	8	17	17	16
6	6	8	12	20	18
2	8	7	9	11	17
6	12	3	12	23	19
6	8	9	15	19	15
9	6	8	16	17	13
7	8	12	15	14	14
5	5	6	13	9	11
4	7	3	10	14	12
7	7	8	11	13	13
3	8	11	17	11	11

Managerial Report

1. Use descriptive statistics to summarize the data from the two studies. What are your preliminary observations about the depression scores?
2. Use analysis of variance on both data sets. State the hypotheses being tested in each case. What are your conclusions?
3. Use inferences about individual treatment means where appropriate. What are your conclusions?

Case Problem 2 Compensation for Sales Professionals

Suppose that a local chapter of sales professionals in the greater San Francisco area conducted a survey of its membership to study the relationship, if any, between the years of experience and salary for individuals employed in inside and outside sales positions. On the survey, respondents were asked to specify one of three levels of years of experience: low (1–10 years), medium (11–20 years), and high (21 or more years). A portion of the data obtained follow. The complete data set, consisting of 120 observations, is contained in the file named SalesSalary.

WEB file
SalesSalary

Observation	Salary $	Position	Experience
1	53,938	Inside	Medium
2	52,694	Inside	Medium
3	70,515	Outside	Low
4	52,031	Inside	Medium
5	62,283	Outside	Low
6	57,718	Inside	Low
7	79,081	Outside	High
8	48,621	Inside	Low
9	72,835	Outside	High
10	54,768	Inside	Medium
.	.	.	.
.	.	.	.
.	.	.	.
115	58,080	Inside	High
116	78,702	Outside	Medium
117	83,131	Outside	Medium
118	57,788	Inside	High
119	53,070	Inside	Medium
120	60,259	Outside	Low

Managerial Report

1. Use descriptive statistics to summarize the data.
2. Develop a 95% confidence interval estimate of the mean annual salary for all salespersons, regardless of years of experience and type of position.
3. Develop a 95% confidence interval estimate of the mean salary for inside salespersons.
4. Develop a 95% confidence interval estimate of the mean salary for outside salespersons.
5. Use analysis of variance to test for any significant differences due to position. Use a .05 level of significance, and for now, ignore the effect of years of experience.
6. Use analysis of variance to test for any significant differences due to years of experience. Use a .05 level of significance, and for now, ignore the effect of position.
7. At the .05 level of significance test for any significant differences due to position, years of experience, and interaction.

Appendix 13.1 Analysis of Variance with Minitab

Completely Randomized Design

In Section 13.2 we showed how analysis of variance could be used to test for the equality of k population means using data from a completely randomized design. To illustrate how Minitab can be used for this type of experimental design, we show how to test whether

WEB file
Chemitech

the mean number of units produced per week is the same for each assembly method in the Chemitech experiment introduced in Section 13.1. The sample data are entered into the first three columns of a Minitab worksheet; column 1 is labeled A, column 2 is labeled B, and column 3 is labeled C. The following steps produce the Minitab output in Figure 13.5.

Step 1. Select the **Stat** menu
Step 2. Choose **ANOVA**
Step 3. Choose **One-way (Unstacked)**
Step 4. When the One-way Analysis of Variance dialog box appears:
Enter C1-C3 in the **Responses (in separate columns)** box
Click **OK**

Randomized Block Design

WEB file
AirTraffic

In Section 13.4 we showed how analysis of variance could be used to test for the equality of k population means using the data from a randomized block design. To illustrate how Minitab can be used for this type of experimental design, we show how to test whether the mean stress levels for air traffic controllers are the same for three workstations using the data in Table 13.5. The blocks (controllers), treatments (system), and stress level scores shown in Table 13.5 are entered into columns C1, C2, and C3 of a Minitab worksheet, respectively. The following steps produce the Minitab output corresponding to the ANOVA table shown in Table 13.8.

The treatments are entered in the Row factor box and the blocks are entered in the Column factor box.

Step 1. Select the **Stat** menu
Step 2. Choose **ANOVA**
Step 3. Choose **Two-way**
Step 4. When the Two-way Analysis of Variance dialog box appears:
Enter C3 in the **Response** box
Enter C2 in the **Row factor** box
Enter C1 in the **Column factor** box
Select **Fit Additive Model**
Click **OK**

Factorial Experiment

WEB file
GMATStudy

In Section 13.5 we showed how analysis of variance could be used to test for the equality of k population means using data from a factorial experiment. To illustrate how Minitab can be used for this type of experimental design, we show how to analyze the data for the two-factor GMAT experiment introduced in that section. The GMAT scores shown in Table 13.10 are entered into column 1 of a Minitab worksheet; column 1 is labeled Score, column 2 is labeled Program, and column 3 is labeled College. The following steps produce the Minitab output corresponding to the ANOVA table shown in Figure 13.6.

Step 1. Select the **Stat** menu
Step 2. Choose **ANOVA**
Step 3. Choose **Two-way**
Step 4. When the Two-way Analysis of Variance dialog box appears:
Enter C1 in the **Response** box
Enter C2 in the **Row factor** box
Enter C3 in the **Column factor** box
Click **OK**

Appendix 13.2 Analysis of Variance with Excel

Completely Randomized Design

In Section 13.2 we showed how analysis of variance could be used to test for the equality of k population means using data from a completely randomized design. To illustrate how Excel can be used to test for the equality of k population means for this type of experimental design, we show how to test whether the mean number of units produced per week is the same for each assembly method in the Chemitech experiment introduced in Section 13.1. The sample data are entered into worksheet rows 2 to 6 of columns A, B, and C as shown in Figure 13.7. The following steps are used to obtain the output shown in cells A8:G22; the ANOVA portion of this output corresponds to the ANOVA table shown in Table 13.3.

WEB file

Chemitech

Step 1. Click the **Data** tab on the Ribbon
Step 2. In the **Analysis** group, click **Data Analysis**
Step 3. Choose **Anova: Single Factor** from the list of Analysis Tools
Step 4. When the Anova: Single Factor dialog box appears:
Enter A1:C6 in **Input Range** box
Select **Columns**
Select **Labels in First Row**
Select **Output Range** and enter A8 in the box
Click **OK**

FIGURE 13.7 EXCEL SOLUTION FOR THE CHEMITECH EXPERIMENT

A1 fx Method A

	A	B	C	D	E	F	G	H
1	**Method A**	**Method B**	**Method C**					
2	58	58	48					
3	64	69	57					
4	55	71	59					
5	66	64	47					
6	67	68	49					
7								
8	Anova: Single Factor							
9								
10	SUMMARY							
11	*Groups*	*Count*	*Sum*	*Average*	*Variance*			
12	Method A	5	310	62	27.5			
13	Method B	5	330	66	26.5			
14	Method C	5	260	52	31			
15								
16								
17	ANOVA							
18	*Source of Variation*	*SS*	*df*	*MS*	*F*	*P-value*	*F crit*	
19	Between Groups	520	2	260	9.1765	0.0038	3.8853	
20	Within Groups	340	12	28.3333				
21								
22	Total	860	14					
23								

FIGURE 13.8 EXCEL SOLUTION FOR THE AIR TRAFFIC CONTROLLER STRESS TEST

A1 | f_x | Controller

	A	B	C	D	E	F	G	H
1	**Controller**	**System A**	**System B**	**System C**				
2	1	15	15	18				
3	2	14	14	14				
4	3	10	11	15				
5	4	13	12	17				
6	5	16	13	16				
7	6	13	13	13				
8								
9	Anova: Two-Factor Without Replication							
10								
11	*SUMMARY*	*Count*	*Sum*	*Average*	*Variance*			
12	1	3	48	16	3			
13	2	3	42	14	0			
14	3	3	36	12	7			
15	4	3	42	14	7			
16	5	3	45	15	3			
17	6	3	39	13	0			
18								
19	System A	6	81	13.5	4.3			
20	System B	6	78	13	2			
21	System C	6	93	15.5	3.5			
22								
23								
24	ANOVA							
25	*Source of Variation*	*SS*	*df*	*MS*	*F*	*P-value*	*F crit*	
26	Rows	30	5	6	3.1579	0.0574	3.3258	
27	Columns	21	2	10.5	5.5263	0.0242	4.1028	
28	Error	19	10	1.9				
29								
30	Total	70	17					
31								

Randomized Block Design

WEB file AirTraffic

In Section 13.4 we showed how analysis of variance could be used to test for the equality of k population means using data from a randomized block design. To illustrate how Excel can be used for this type of experimental design, we show how to test whether the mean stress levels for air traffic controllers are the same for three workstations. The stress level scores shown in Table 13.5 are entered into worksheet rows 2 to 7 of columns B, C, and D as shown in Figure 13.8. The cells in rows 2 to 7 of column A contain the number of each controller (1, 2, 3, 4, 5, 6). The following steps produce the Excel output shown in cells A9:G30. The ANOVA portion of this output corresponds to the ANOVA table shown in Table 13.8.

Step 1. Click the **Data** tab on the Ribbon
Step 2. In the **Analysis** group, click **Data Analysis**
Step 3. Choose **Anova: Two-Factor Without Replication** from the list of Analysis Tools
Step 4. When the Anova: Two-Factor Without Replication dialog box appears:
Enter A1:D7 in **Input Range** box
Select **Labels**
Select **Output Range** and enter A9 in the box
Click **OK**

Factorial Experiment

WEB file
GMATStudy

In Section 13.5 we showed how analysis of variance could be used to test for the equality of k population means using data from a factorial experiment. To illustrate how Excel can be used for this type of experimental design, we show how to analyze the data for the two-factor GMAT experiment introduced in that section. The GMAT scores shown in Table 13.10 are entered into worksheet rows 2 to 7 of columns B, C, and D as shown in Figure 13.9. The following steps are used to obtain the output shown in cells A9:G44; the ANOVA portion of this output corresponds to the Minitab output in Figure 13.6.

Step 1. Click the **Data** tab on the Ribbon
Step 2. In the **Analysis** group, click **Data Analysis**
Step 3. Choose **Anova: Two-Factor With Replication** from the list of Analysis Tools

FIGURE 13.9 EXCEL SOLUTION FOR THE TWO-FACTOR GMAT EXPERIMENT

A1 ▾ f_x

	A	B	C	D	E	F	G	H
1		Business	Engineering	Arts and Sciences				
2	3-hour review	500	540	480				
3		580	460	400				
4	1-day program	460	560	420				
5		540	620	480				
6	10-week course	560	600	480				
7		600	580	410				
8								
9	Anova: Two-Factor With Replication							
10								
11	SUMMARY	Business	Engineering	Arts and Sciences	Total			
12	*3-hour review*							
13	Count	2	2	2	6			
14	Sum	1080	1000	880	2960			
15	Average	540	500	440	493.3333			
16	Variance	3200	3200	3200	3946.667			
17								
18	*1-day program*							
19	Count	2	2	2	6			
20	Sum	1000	1180	900	3080			
21	Average	500	590	450	513.3333			
22	Variance	3200	1800	1800	5386.667			
23								
24	*10-week course*							
25	Count	2	2	2	6			
26	Sum	1160	1180	890	3230			
27	Average	580	590	445	538.3333			
28	Variance	800	200	2450	5936.667			
29								
30	*Total*							
31	Count	6	6	6				
32	Sum	3240	3360	2670				
33	Average	540	560	445				
34	Variance	2720	3200	1510				
35								
36								
37	ANOVA							
38	*Source of Variation*	*SS*	*df*	*MS*	*F*	*P-value*	*F crit*	
39	Sample	6100	2	3050	1.3829	0.2994	4.2565	
40	Columns	45300	2	22650	10.2695	0.0048	4.2565	
41	Interaction	11200	4	2800	1.2695	0.3503	3.6331	
42	Within	19850	9	2205.5556				
43								
44	Total	82450	17					
45								

Step 4. When the Anova: Two-Factor With Replication dialog box appears:
Enter A1:D7 in **Input Range** box
Enter 2 in **Rows per sample** box
Select **Output Range** and enter A9 in the box
Click **OK**

Appendix 13.3 Analysis of a Completely Randomized Design Using StatTools

In this appendix we show how StatTools can be used to test for the equality of k population means for a completely randomized design. We use the Chemitech data in Table 13.1 to illustrate. Begin by using the Data Set Manager to create a StatTools data set for these data using the procedure described in the appendix in Chapter 1. The following steps can be used to test for the equality of the three population means.

WEB file
Chemitech

Step 1. Click the **StatTools** tab on the Ribbon
Step 2. In the **Analyses** group, click **Statistical Inference**
Step 3. Choose the **One-Way ANOVA** option
Step 4. When the StatTools-One-Way ANOVA dialog box appears:
In the **Variables** section:
Click the **Format button** and select **Unstacked**
Select **Method A**
Select **Method B**
Select **Method C**
Select 95% in the **Confidence Level** box
Click **OK**

Note that in step 4 we selected the Unstacked option after clicking the Format button. The Unstacked option means that the data for the three treatments appear in separate columns of the worksheet. In a stacked format, only two columns would be used. For example, the data could have been organized as follows:

	A	B	C
1	**Method**	**Units Produced**	
2	Method A	58	
3	Method A	64	
4	Method A	55	
5	Method A	66	
6	Method A	67	
7	Method B	58	
8	Method B	69	
9	Method B	71	
10	Method B	64	
11	Method B	68	
12	Method C	48	
13	Method C	57	
14	Method C	59	
15	Method C	47	
16	Method C	49	
17			

Data are frequently recorded in a stacked format. For stacked data, simply select the Stacked option after clicking the Format button.

CHAPTER 14

Simple Linear Regression

CONTENTS

STATISTICS *in* PRACTICE

ALLIANCE DATA SYSTEMS*
DALLAS, TEXAS

Alliance Data Systems (ADS) provides transaction processing, credit services, and marketing services for clients in the rapidly growing customer relationship management (CRM) industry. ADS clients are concentrated in four industries: retail, petroleum/convenience stores, utilities, and transportation. In 1983, Alliance began offering end-to-end credit processing services to the retail, petroleum, and casual dining industries; today they employ more than 6500 employees who provide services to clients around the world. Operating more than 140,000 point-of-sale terminals in the United States alone, ADS processes in excess of 2.5 billion transactions annually. The company ranks second in the United States in private label credit services by representing 49 private label programs with nearly 72 million cardholders. In 2001, ADS made an initial public offering and is now listed on the New York Stock Exchange.

As one of its marketing services, ADS designs direct mail campaigns and promotions. With its database containing information on the spending habits of more than 100 million consumers, ADS can target those consumers most likely to benefit from a direct mail promotion. The Analytical Development Group uses regression analysis to build models that measure and predict the responsiveness of consumers to direct market campaigns. Some regression models predict the probability of purchase for individuals receiving a promotion, and others predict the amount spent by those consumers making a purchase.

For one particular campaign, a retail store chain wanted to attract new customers. To predict the effect of the campaign, ADS analysts selected a sample from the consumer database, sent the sampled individuals promotional materials, and then collected transaction data on the consumers' response. Sample data were collected on the amount of purchase made by the consumers responding to the campaign, as well as a variety of consumer-specific variables thought to be useful in predicting sales. The consumer-specific variable that contributed most to predicting the amount purchased was the total amount of credit purchases at related stores over the past 39 months. ADS analysts developed an estimated regression equation relating the amount of purchase to the amount spent at related stores:

Alliance Data Systems analysts discuss use of a regression model to predict sales for a direct marketing campaign. © Courtesy of Alliance Data Systems.

$$\hat{y} = 26.7 + 0.00205x$$

where

$$\hat{y} = \text{amount of purchase}$$
$$x = \text{amount spent at related stores}$$

Using this equation, we could predict that someone spending \$10,000 over the past 39 months at related stores would spend \$47.20 when responding to the direct mail promotion. In this chapter, you will learn how to develop this type of estimated regression equation.

The final model developed by ADS analysts also included several other variables that increased the predictive power of the preceding equation. Some of these variables included the absence/presence of a bank credit card, estimated income, and the average amount spent per trip at a selected store. In the following chapter, we will learn how such additional variables can be incorporated into a multiple regression model.

*The authors are indebted to Philip Clemance, Director of Analytical Development at Alliance Data Systems, for providing this Statistics in Practice.

Managerial decisions often are based on the relationship between two or more variables. For example, after considering the relationship between advertising expenditures and sales, a marketing manager might attempt to predict sales for a given level of advertising expenditures. In another case, a public utility might use the relationship between the daily high temperature and the demand for electricity to predict electricity usage on the basis of next month's anticipated daily high temperatures. Sometimes a manager will rely on intuition to judge how two variables are related. However, if data can be obtained, a statistical procedure called *regression analysis* can be used to develop an equation showing how the variables are related.

The statistical methods used in studying the relationship between two variables were first employed by Sir Francis Galton (1822–1911). Galton was interested in studying the relationship between a father's height and the son's height. Galton's disciple, Karl Pearson (1857–1936), analyzed the relationship between the father's height and the son's height for 1078 pairs of subjects.

In regression terminology, the variable being predicted is called the **dependent variable**. The variable or variables being used to predict the value of the dependent variable are called the **independent variables**. For example, in analyzing the effect of advertising expenditures on sales, a marketing manager's desire to predict sales would suggest making sales the dependent variable. Advertising expenditure would be the independent variable used to help predict sales. In statistical notation, y denotes the dependent variable and x denotes the independent variable.

In this chapter we consider the simplest type of regression analysis involving one independent variable and one dependent variable in which the relationship between the variables is approximated by a straight line. It is called **simple linear regression**. Regression analysis involving two or more independent variables is called multiple regression analysis; multiple regression and cases involving curvilinear relationships are covered in Chapters 15 and 16.

14.1 Simple Linear Regression Model

Armand's Pizza Parlors is a chain of Italian-food restaurants located in a five-state area. Armand's most successful locations are near college campuses. The managers believe that quarterly sales for these restaurants (denoted by y) are related positively to the size of the student population (denoted by x); that is, restaurants near campuses with a large student population tend to generate more sales than those located near campuses with a small student population. Using regression analysis, we can develop an equation showing how the dependent variable y is related to the independent variable x.

Regression Model and Regression Equation

In the Armand's Pizza Parlors example, the population consists of all the Armand's restaurants. For every restaurant in the population, there is a value of x (student population) and a corresponding value of y (quarterly sales). The equation that describes how y is related to x and an error term is called the **regression model**. The regression model used in simple linear regression follows.

SIMPLE LINEAR REGRESSION MODEL

$$y = \beta_0 + \beta_1 x + \epsilon \tag{14.1}$$

β_0 and β_1 are referred to as the parameters of the model, and ϵ (the Greek letter epsilon) is a random variable referred to as the error term. The error term accounts for the variability in y that cannot be explained by the linear relationship between x and y.

The population of all Armand's restaurants can also be viewed as a collection of subpopulations, one for each distinct value of x. For example, one subpopulation consists of all Armand's restaurants located near college campuses with 8000 students; another subpopulation consists of all Armand's restaurants located near college campuses with 9000 students; and so on. Each subpopulation has a corresponding distribution of y values. Thus, a distribution of y values is associated with restaurants located near campuses with 8000 students; a distribution of y values is associated with restaurants located near campuses with 9000 students; and so on. Each distribution of y values has its own mean or expected value. The equation that describes how the expected value of y, denoted $E(y)$, is related to x is called the **regression equation**. The regression equation for simple linear regression follows.

SIMPLE LINEAR REGRESSION EQUATION

$$E(y) = \beta_0 + \beta_1 x \tag{14.2}$$

The graph of the simple linear regression equation is a straight line; β_0 is the y-intercept of the regression line, β_1 is the slope, and $E(y)$ is the mean or expected value of y for a given value of x.

Examples of possible regression lines are shown in Figure 14.1. The regression line in Panel A shows that the mean value of y is related positively to x, with larger values of $E(y)$ associated with larger values of x. The regression line in Panel B shows the mean value of y is related negatively to x, with smaller values of $E(y)$ associated with larger values of x. The regression line in Panel C shows the case in which the mean value of y is not related to x; that is, the mean value of y is the same for every value of x.

Estimated Regression Equation

If the values of the population parameters β_0 and β_1 were known, we could use equation (14.2) to compute the mean value of y for a given value of x. In practice, the parameter values are not known and must be estimated using sample data. Sample statistics (denoted b_0 and b_1) are computed as estimates of the population parameters β_0 and β_1. Substituting the values of the sample statistics b_0 and b_1 for β_0 and β_1 in the regression equation, we obtain the

FIGURE 14.1 POSSIBLE REGRESSION LINES IN SIMPLE LINEAR REGRESSION

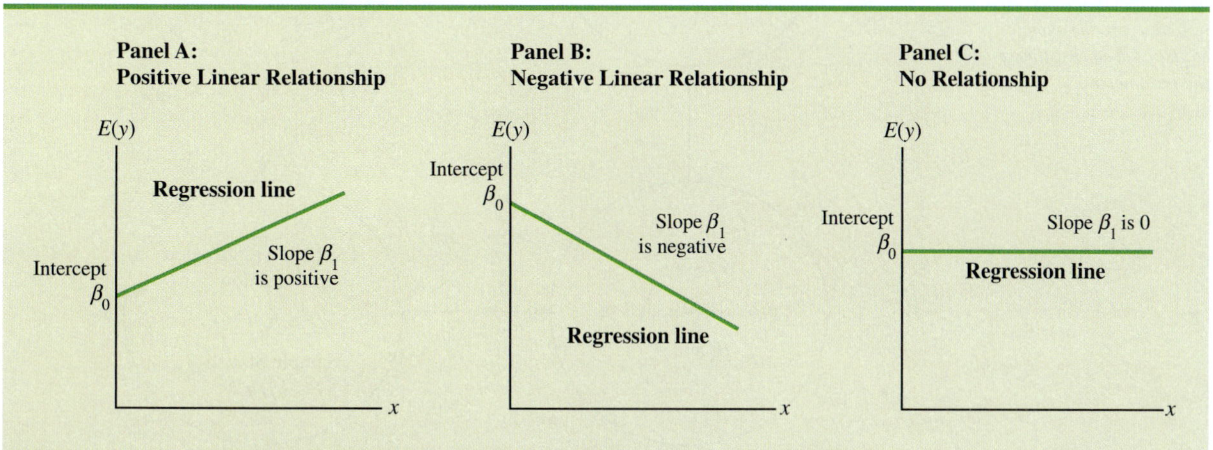

estimated regression equation. The estimated regression equation for simple linear regression follows.

ESTIMATED SIMPLE LINEAR REGRESSION EQUATION

$$\hat{y} = b_0 + b_1 x \tag{14.3}$$

Figure 14.2 provides a summary of the estimation process for simple linear regression.

The graph of the estimated simple linear regression equation is called the *estimated regression line*; b_0 is the y-intercept and b_1 is the slope. In the next section, we show how the least squares method can be used to compute the values of b_0 and b_1 in the estimated regression equation.

The value of $\hat{y}$ provides both a point estimate of $E(y)$ for a given value of x and a prediction of an individual value of y for a given value of x.

In general, $\hat{y}$ is the point estimator of $E(y)$, the mean value of y for a given value of x. Thus, to estimate the mean or expected value of quarterly sales for all restaurants located near campuses with 10,000 students, Armand's would substitute the value of 10,000 for x in equation (14.3). In some cases, however, Armand's may be more interested in predicting sales for one particular restaurant. For example, suppose Armand's would like to predict quarterly sales for the restaurant they are considering building near Talbot College, a school with 10,000 students. As it turns out, the best predictor of y for a given value of x is also provided by $\hat{y}$. Thus, to predict quarterly sales for the restaurant located near Talbot College, Armand's would also substitute the value of 10,000 for x in equation (14.3).

FIGURE 14.2 THE ESTIMATION PROCESS IN SIMPLE LINEAR REGRESSION

The estimation of β_0 and β_1 is a statistical process much like the estimation of μ discussed in Chapter 7. β_0 and β_1 are the unknown parameters of interest, and b_0 and b_1 are the sample statistics used to estimate the parameters.

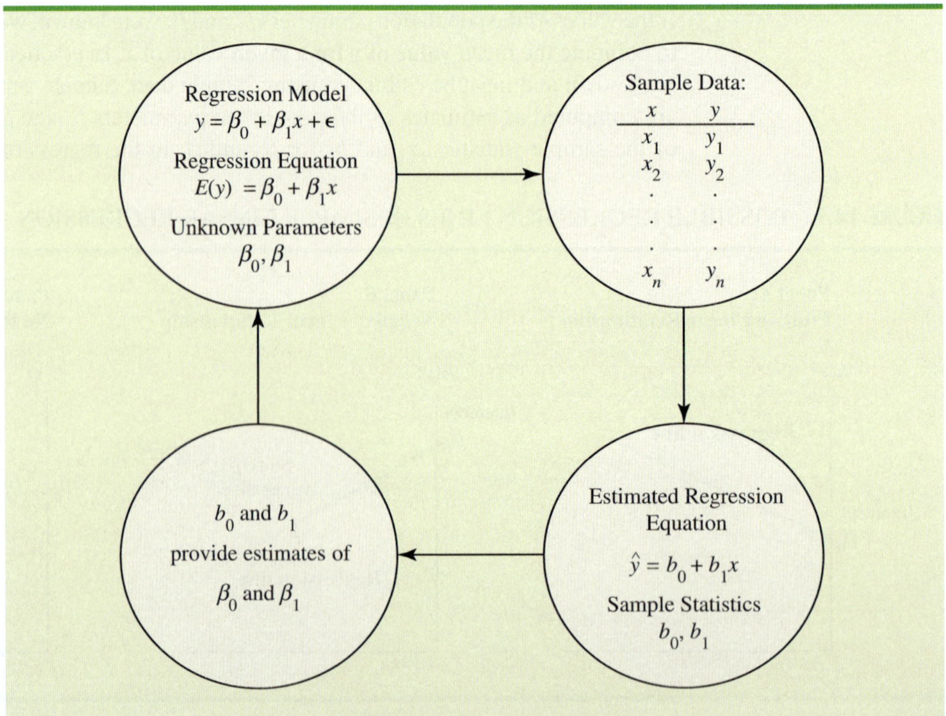

NOTES AND COMMENTS

1. Regression analysis cannot be interpreted as a procedure for establishing a cause-and-effect relationship between variables. It can only indicate how or to what extent variables are associated with each other. Any conclusions about cause and effect must be based upon the judgment of those individuals most knowledgeable about the application.
2. The regression equation in simple linear regression is $E(y) = \beta_0 + \beta_1 x$. More advanced texts in regression analysis often write the regression equation as $E(y|x) = \beta_0 + \beta_1 x$ to emphasize that the regression equation provides the mean value of y for a given value of x.

14.2 Least Squares Method

In simple linear regression, each observation consists of two values: one for the independent variable and one for the dependent variable.

The **least squares method** is a procedure for using sample data to find the estimated regression equation. To illustrate the least squares method, suppose data were collected from a sample of 10 Armand's Pizza Parlor restaurants located near college campuses. For the ith observation or restaurant in the sample, x_i is the size of the student population (in thousands) and y_i is the quarterly sales (in thousands of dollars). The values of x_i and y_i for the 10 restaurants in the sample are summarized in Table 14.1. We see that restaurant 1, with $x_1 = 2$ and $y_1 = 58$, is near a campus with 2000 students and has quarterly sales of \$58,000. Restaurant 2, with $x_2 = 6$ and $y_2 = 105$, is near a campus with 6000 students and has quarterly sales of \$105,000. The largest sales value is for restaurant 10, which is near a campus with 26,000 students and has quarterly sales of \$202,000.

Figure 14.3 is a scatter diagram of the data in Table 14.1. Student population is shown on the horizontal axis and quarterly sales is shown on the vertical axis. **Scatter diagrams** for regression analysis are constructed with the independent variable x on the horizontal axis and the dependent variable y on the vertical axis. The scatter diagram enables us to observe the data graphically and to draw preliminary conclusions about the possible relationship between the variables.

What preliminary conclusions can be drawn from Figure 14.3? Quarterly sales appear to be higher at campuses with larger student populations. In addition, for these data the relationship between the size of the student population and quarterly sales appears to be approximated by a straight line; indeed, a positive linear relationship is indicated between x

TABLE 14.1 STUDENT POPULATION AND QUARTERLY SALES DATA FOR 10 ARMAND'S PIZZA PARLORS

WEB file Armand's

Restaurant i	Student Population (1000s) x_i	Quarterly Sales (\$1000s) y_i
1	2	58
2	6	105
3	8	88
4	8	118
5	12	117
6	16	137
7	20	157
8	20	169
9	22	149
10	26	202

FIGURE 14.3 SCATTER DIAGRAM OF STUDENT POPULATION AND QUARTERLY SALES FOR ARMAND'S PIZZA PARLORS

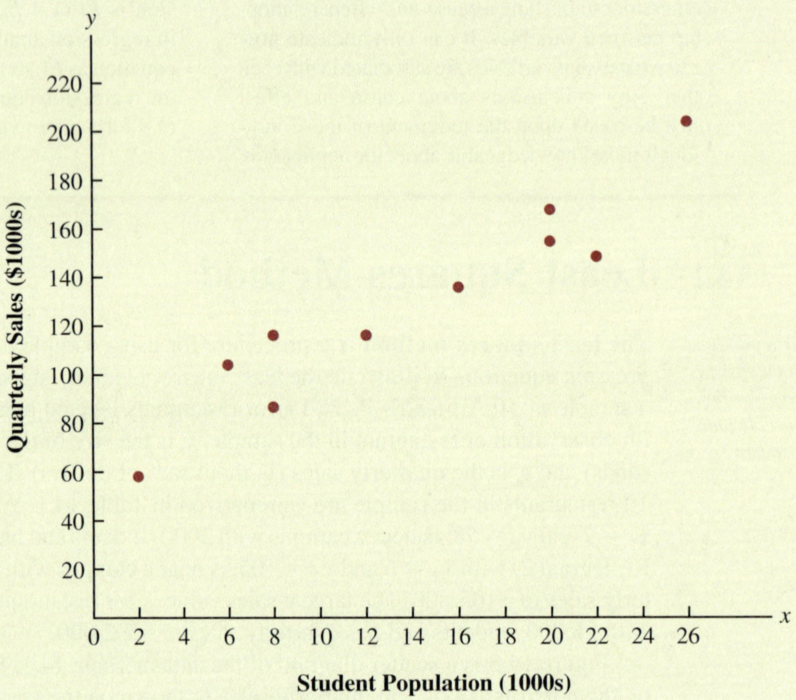

and y. We therefore choose the simple linear regression model to represent the relationship between quarterly sales and student population. Given that choice, our next task is to use the sample data in Table 14.1 to determine the values of b_0 and b_1 in the estimated simple linear regression equation. For the ith restaurant, the estimated regression equation provides

$$\hat{y}_i = b_0 + b_1 x_i \tag{14.4}$$

where

$\hat{y}_i$ = predicted value of quarterly sales ($1000s) for the ith restaurant
b_0 = the y-intercept of the estimated regression line
b_1 = the slope of the estimated regression line
x_i = size of the student population (1000s) for the ith restaurant

With y_i denoting the observed (actual) sales for restaurant i and $\hat{y}_i$ in equation (14.4) representing the predicted value of sales for restaurant i, every restaurant in the sample will have an observed value of sales y_i and a predicted value of sales $\hat{y}_i$. For the estimated regression line to provide a good fit to the data, we want the differences between the observed sales values and the predicted sales values to be small.

The least squares method uses the sample data to provide the values of b_0 and b_1 that minimize the *sum of the squares of the deviations* between the observed values of the dependent variable y_i and the predicted values of the dependent variable $\hat{y}_i$. The criterion for the least squares method is given by expression (14.5).

Carl Friedrich Gauss (1777–1855) proposed the least squares method.

LEAST SQUARES CRITERION

$$\min \Sigma(y_i - \hat{y}_i)^2 \quad \textbf{(14.5)}$$

where

y_i = observed value of the dependent variable for the ith observation
$\hat{y}_i$ = predicted value of the dependent variable for the ith observation

Differential calculus can be used to show (see Appendix 14.1) that the values of b_0 and b_1 that minimize expression (14.5) can be found by using equations (14.6) and (14.7).

In computing b_1 with a calculator, carry as many significant digits as possible in the intermediate calculations. We recommend carrying at least four significant digits.

SLOPE AND y-INTERCEPT FOR THE ESTIMATED REGRESSION EQUATION[1]

$$b_1 = \frac{\Sigma(x_i - \bar{x})(y_i - \bar{y})}{\Sigma(x_i - \bar{x})^2} \quad \textbf{(14.6)}$$

$$b_0 = \bar{y} - b_1\bar{x} \quad \textbf{(14.7)}$$

where

x_i = value of the independent variable for the ith observation
y_i = value of the dependent variable for the ith observation
$\bar{x}$ = mean value for the independent variable
$\bar{y}$ = mean value for the dependent variable
n = total number of observations

Some of the calculations necessary to develop the least squares estimated regression equation for Armand's Pizza Parlors are shown in Table 14.2. With the sample of 10 restaurants, we have $n = 10$ observations. Because equations (14.6) and (14.7) require $\bar{x}$ and $\bar{y}$ we begin the calculations by computing $\bar{x}$ and $\bar{y}$.

$$\bar{x} = \frac{\Sigma x_i}{n} = \frac{140}{10} = 14$$

$$\bar{y} = \frac{\Sigma y_i}{n} = \frac{1300}{10} = 130$$

Using equations (14.6) and (14.7) and the information in Table 14.2, we can compute the slope and intercept of the estimated regression equation for Armand's Pizza Parlors. The calculation of the slope (b_1) proceeds as follows.

[1]An alternate formula for b_1 is

$$b_1 = \frac{\Sigma x_i y_i - (\Sigma x_i \Sigma y_i)/n}{\Sigma x_i^2 - (\Sigma x_i)^2/n}$$

This form of equation (14.6) is often recommended when using a calculator to compute b_1.

TABLE 14.2 CALCULATIONS FOR THE LEAST SQUARES ESTIMATED REGRESSION EQUATION FOR ARMAND'S PIZZA PARLORS

Restaurant i	x_i	y_i	$x_i - \bar{x}$	$y_i - \bar{y}$	$(x_i - \bar{x})(y_i - \bar{y})$	$(x_i - \bar{x})^2$
1	2	58	−12	−72	864	144
2	6	105	−8	−25	200	64
3	8	88	−6	−42	252	36
4	8	118	−6	−12	72	36
5	12	117	−2	−13	26	4
6	16	137	2	7	14	4
7	20	157	6	27	162	36
8	20	169	6	39	234	36
9	22	149	8	19	152	64
10	26	202	12	72	864	144
Totals	140	1300			2840	568
	Σx_i	Σy_i			$\Sigma(x_i - \bar{x})(y_i - \bar{y})$	$\Sigma(x_i - \bar{x})^2$

$$
\begin{aligned}
b_1 &= \frac{\Sigma(x_i - \bar{x})(y_i - \bar{y})}{\Sigma(x_i - \bar{x})^2} \\
&= \frac{2840}{568} \\
&= 5
\end{aligned}
$$

The calculation of the y intercept (b_0) follows.

$$
\begin{aligned}
b_0 &= \bar{y} - b_1\bar{x} \\
&= 130 - 5(14) \\
&= 60
\end{aligned}
$$

Thus, the estimated regression equation is

$$\hat{y} = 60 + 5x$$

Figure 14.4 shows the graph of this equation on the scatter diagram.

The slope of the estimated regression equation ($b_1 = 5$) is positive, implying that as student population increases, sales increase. In fact, we can conclude (based on sales measured in \$1000s and student population in 1000s) that an increase in the student population of 1000 is associated with an increase of \$5000 in expected sales; that is, quarterly sales are expected to increase by \$5 per student.

Using the estimated regression equation to make predictions outside the range of the values of the independent variable should be done with caution because outside that range we cannot be sure that the same relationship is valid.

If we believe the least squares estimated regression equation adequately describes the relationship between x and y, it would seem reasonable to use the estimated regression equation to predict the value of y for a given value of x. For example, if we wanted to predict quarterly sales for a restaurant to be located near a campus with 16,000 students, we would compute

$$\hat{y} = 60 + 5(16) = 140$$

Hence, we would predict quarterly sales of \$140,000 for this restaurant. In the following sections we will discuss methods for assessing the appropriateness of using the estimated regression equation for estimation and prediction.

FIGURE 14.4 GRAPH OF THE ESTIMATED REGRESSION EQUATION FOR ARMAND'S PIZZA PARLORS: $\hat{y} = 60 + 5x$

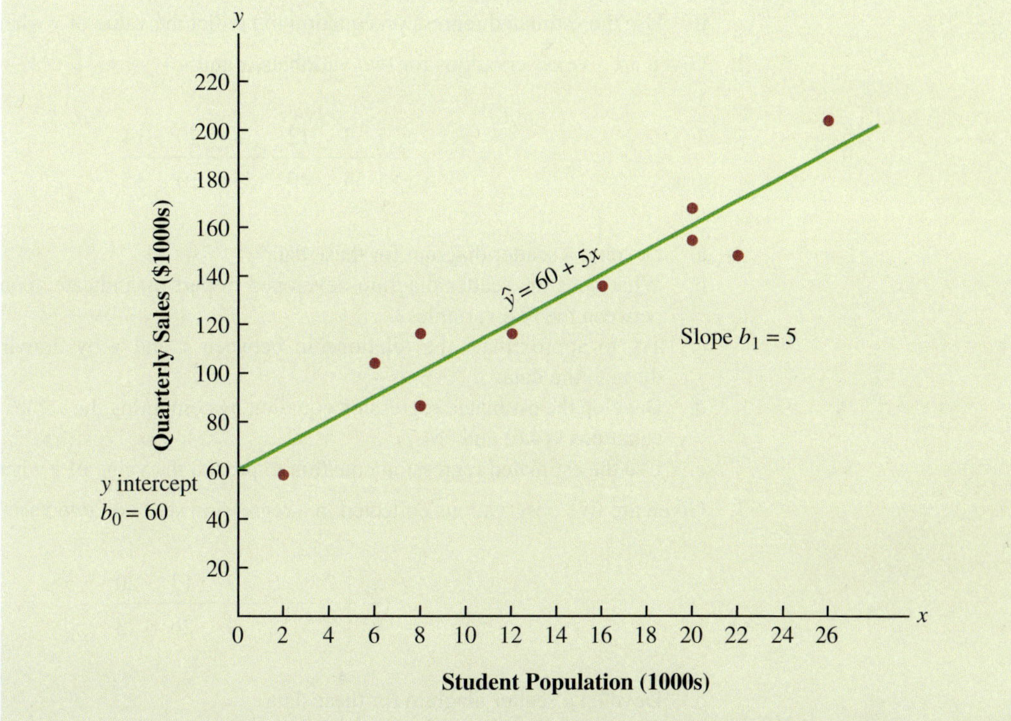

NOTES AND COMMENTS

The least squares method provides an estimated regression equation that minimizes the sum of squared deviations between the observed values of the dependent variable y_i and the predicted values of the dependent variable $\hat{y}_i$. This least squares criterion is used to choose the equation that provides the best fit. If some other criterion were used, such as minimizing the sum of the absolute deviations between y_i and $\hat{y}_i$, a different equation would be obtained. In practice, the least squares method is the most widely used.

Exercises

Methods

SELF test

1. Given are five observations for two variables, x and y.

x_i	1	2	3	4	5
y_i	3	7	5	11	14

a. Develop a scatter diagram for these data.
b. What does the scatter diagram developed in part (a) indicate about the relationship between the two variables?

c. Try to approximate the relationship between x and y by drawing a straight line through the data.
d. Develop the estimated regression equation by computing the values of b_0 and b_1 using equations (14.6) and (14.7).
e. Use the estimated regression equation to predict the value of y when $x = 4$.

2. Given are five observations for two variables, x and y.

x_i	3	12	6	20	14
y_i	55	40	55	10	15

a. Develop a scatter diagram for these data.
b. What does the scatter diagram developed in part (a) indicate about the relationship between the two variables?
c. Try to approximate the relationship between x and y by drawing a straight line through the data.
d. Develop the estimated regression equation by computing the values of b_0 and b_1 using equations (14.6) and (14.7).
e. Use the estimated regression equation to predict the value of y when $x = 10$.

3. Given are five observations collected in a regression study on two variables.

x_i	2	6	9	13	20
y_i	7	18	9	26	23

a. Develop a scatter diagram for these data.
b. Develop the estimated regression equation for these data.
c. Use the estimated regression equation to predict the value of y when $x = 6$.

Applications

SELF test

4. The following data give the percentage of women working in five companies in the retail and trade industry. The percentage of management jobs held by women in each company is also shown.

% Working	67	45	73	54	61
% Management	49	21	65	47	33

a. Develop a scatter diagram for these data with the percentage of women working in the company as the independent variable.
b. What does the scatter diagram developed in part (a) indicate about the relationship between the two variables?
c. Try to approximate the relationship between the percentage of women working in the company and the percentage of management jobs held by women in that company.
d. Develop the estimated regression equation by computing the values of b_0 and b_1.
e. Predict the percentage of management jobs held by women in a company that has 60% women employees.

5. Elliptical trainers are becoming one of the more popular exercise machines. Their smooth and steady low-impact motion makes them a preferred choice for individuals with knee and ankle problems. But selecting the right trainer can be a difficult process. Price and

quality are two important factors in any purchase decision. Are higher prices generally associated with higher quality elliptical trainers? *Consumer Reports* conducted extensive tests to develop an overall rating based on ease of use, ergonomics, construction, and exercise range. The following data show the price and rating for eight elliptical trainers tested (*Consumer Reports,* February 2008).

WEB file
Ellipticals

Brand and Model	Price ($)	Rating
Precor 5.31	3700	87
Keys Fitness CG2	2500	84
Octane Fitness Q37e	2800	82
LifeFitness X1 Basic	1900	74
NordicTrack AudioStrider 990	1000	73
Schwinn 430	800	69
Vision Fitness X6100	1700	68
ProForm XP 520 Razor	600	55

a. Develop a scatter diagram with price as the independent variable.
b. An exercise equipment store that sells primarily higher priced equipment has a sign over the display area that says "Quality: You Get What You Pay For." Based upon your analysis of the data for ellipical trainers, do you think this sign fairly reflects the price-quality relationship for elliptical trainers?
c. Use the least squares method to develop the estimated regression equation.
d. Use the estimated regression equation to predict the rating for an ellipitical trainer with a price of $1500.

6. The National Football League (NFL) records a variety of performance data for individuals and teams. To investigate the importance of passing on the percentage of games won by a team, the following data show the average number of passing yards per attempt (Yds/Att) and the percentage of games won (WinPct) for a random sample of 10 NFL teams for the 2011 season (NFL website, February 12, 2012).

WEB file
NFLPassing

Team	Yds/Att	WinPct
Arizona Cardinals	6.5	50
Atlanta Falcons	7.1	63
Carolina Panthers	7.4	38
Chicago Bears	6.4	50
Dallas Cowboys	7.4	50
New England Patriots	8.3	81
Philadelphia Eagles	7.4	50
Seattle Seahawks	6.1	44
St. Louis Rams	5.2	13
Tampa Bay Buccaneers	6.2	25

a. Develop a scatter diagram with the number of passing yards per attempt on the horizontal axis and the percentage of games won on the vertical axis.
b. What does the scatter diagram developed in part (a) indicate about the relationship between the two variables?
c. Develop the estimated regression equation that could be used to predict the percentage of games won given the average number of passing yards per attempt.
d. Provide an interpretation for the slope of the estimated regression equation.

e. For the 2011 season, the average number of passing yards per attempt for the Kansas City Chiefs was 6.2. Use the estimated regression equation developed in part (c) to predict the percentage of games won by the Kansas City Chiefs. (*Note:* For the 2011 season the Kansas City Chiefs record was 7 wins and 9 losses.) Compare your prediction to the actual percentage of games won by the Kansas City Chiefs.

7. A sales manager collected the following data on annual sales for new customer accounts and the number of years of experience for a sample of 10 salespersons.

WEB file

Sales

Salesperson	Years of Experience	Annual Sales ($1000s)
1	1	80
2	3	97
3	4	92
4	4	102
5	6	103
6	8	111
7	10	119
8	10	123
9	11	117
10	13	136

a. Develop a scatter diagram for these data with years of experience as the independent variable.
b. Develop an estimated regression equation that can be used to predict annual sales given the years of experience.
c. Use the estimated regression equation to predict annual sales for a salesperson with 9 years of experience.

8. The American Association of Individual Investors (AAII) On-Line Discount Broker Survey polls members on their experiences with discount brokers. As part of the survey, members were asked to rate the quality of the speed of execution with their broker as well as provide an overall satisfaction rating for electronic trades. Possible responses (scores) were no opinion (0), unsatisfied (l), somewhat satisfied (2), satisfied (3), and very satisfied (4). For each broker summary scores were computed by calculating a weighted average of the scores provided by each respondent. A portion of the survey results follow (AAII website, February 7, 2012).

WEB file

BrokerRatings

Brokerage	Speed	Satisfaction
Scottrade, Inc.	3.4	3.5
Charles Schwab	3.3	3.4
Fidelity Brokerage Services	3.4	3.9
TD Ameritrade	3.6	3.7
E*Trade Financial	3.2	2.9
Vanguard Brokerage Services	3.8	2.8
USAA Brokerage Services	3.8	3.6
Thinkorswim	2.6	2.6
Wells Fargo Investments	2.7	2.3
Interactive Brokers	4.0	4.0
Zecco.com	2.5	2.5

a. Develop a scatter diagram for these data with the speed of execution as the independent variable.

b. What does the scatter diagram developed in part (a) indicate about the relationship between the two variables?
c. Develop the least squares estimated regression equation.
d. Provide an interpretation for the slope of the estimated regression equation.
e. Suppose Zecco.com developed new software to increase their speed of execution rating. If the new software is able to increase their speed of execution rating from the current value of 2.5 to the average speed of execution rating for the other 10 brokerage firms that were surveyed, what value would you predict for the overall satisfaction rating?

9. Using a global-positioning-system (GPS)-based navigator for your car, you enter a destination and the system will plot a route, give spoken turn-by-turn directions, and show your progress along the route. Today, even budget units include features previously available only on more expensive models. *Consumer Reports* conducted extensive tests of GPS-based navigators and developed an overall rating based on factors such as ease of use, driver information, display, and battery life. The following data show the price and rating for a sample of 20 GPS units with a 4.3-inch screen that *Consumer Reports* tested (*Consumer Reports* website, April 17, 2012).

WEB file
GPS

Brand and Model	Price ($)	Rating
Garmin Nuvi 3490LMT	400	82
Garmin Nuvi 3450	330	80
Garmin Nuvi 3790T	350	77
Garmin Nuvi 3790LMT	400	77
Garmin Nuvi 3750	250	74
Garmin Nuvi 2475LT	230	74
Garmin Nuvi 2455LT	160	73
Garmin Nuvi 2370LT	270	71
Garmin Nuvi 2360LT	250	71
Garmin Nuvi 2360LMT	220	71
Garmin Nuvi 755T	260	70
Motorola Motonab TN565t	200	68
Motorola Motonab TN555	200	67
Garmin Nuvi 1350T	150	65
Garmin Nuvi 1350LMT	180	65
Garmin Nuvi 2300	160	65
Garmin Nuvi 1350	130	64
Tom Tom VIA 1435T	200	62
Garmin Nuvi 1300	140	62
Garmin Nuvi 1300LM	180	62

a. Develop a scatter diagram with price as the independent variable.
b. What does the scatter diagram developed in part (a) indicate about the relationship between the two variables?
c. Use the least squares method to develop the estimated regression equation.
d. Predict the rating for a GPS system with a 4.3-inch screen that has a price of $200.

10. On March 31, 2009, Ford Motor Company's shares were trading at a 26-year low of $2.63. Ford's board of directors gave the CEO a grant of options and restricted shares with an estimated value of $16 million. On April 26, 2011, the price of a share of Ford had increased to $15.58, and the CEO's grant was worth $202.8 million, a gain in value of $186.8 million. The following table shows the share price in 2009 and 2011 for 10 companies, the stock-option and share grants to the CEOs in late 2008 and 2009, and the value of the options and grants in 2011. Also shown are the percentage increases in the stock price and the percentage gains in the options values (*The Wall Street Journal,* April 27, 2011).

WEB file CEOGrants

Company	Stock Price 2009 ($)	Stock Price 2011 ($)	% Increase in Stock Price	Options and Grants Value 2009 ($ millions)	Options and Grants Value 2011 ($ millions)	% Gain in Options Value
Ford Motor	2.63	15.58	492	16.0	202.8	1168
Abercrombie & Fitch	23.80	70.47	196	46.2	196.1	324
Nabors Industries	9.99	32.06	221	37.2	132.2	255
Starbucks	9.99	32.06	221	12.4	75.9	512
Salesforce.com	32.73	137.61	320	7.8	67.0	759
Starwood Hotels	12.70	60.28	375	5.8	57.1	884
Caterpillar	27.96	111.94	300	4.0	47.5	1088
Oracle	18.07	34.97	94	61.9	97.5	58
Capital One	12.24	54.61	346	6.0	40.6	577
Dow Chemical	8.43	39.97	374	5.0	38.8	676

a. Develop a scatter diagram for these data with the percentage increase in the stock price as the independent variable.
b. What does the scatter diagram developed in part (a) indicate about the relationship between the two variables?
c. Develop the least squares estimated regression equation.
d. Provide an interpretation for the slope of the estimated regression equation.
e. Do the rewards for the CEO appear to be based on performance increases as measured by the stock price?

11. Sporty cars are designed to provide better handling, acceleration, and a more responsive driving experience than a typical sedan. But, even within this select group of cars, performance as well as price can vary. *Consumer Reports* provided road-test scores and prices for the following 12 sporty cars (Consumer Reports website, October 2008). Prices are in thousands of dollars and road-test scores are based on a 0–100 rating scale, with higher values indicating better performance.

WEB file SportyCars

Car	Price ($1000s)	Road-Test Score
Chevrolet Cobalt SS	24.5	78
Dodge Caliber SRT4	24.9	56
Ford Mustang GT (V8)	29.0	73
Honda Civic Si	21.7	78
Mazda RX-8	31.3	86
Mini Cooper S	26.4	74
Mitsubishi Lancer Evolution GSR	38.1	83
Nissan Sentra SE-R Spec V	23.3	66
Suburu Impreza WRX	25.2	81
Suburu Impreza WRX Sti	37.6	89
Volkswagen GTI	24.0	83
Volkswagen R32	33.6	83

a. Develop a scatter diagram with price as the independent variable.
b. What does the scatter diagram developed in part (a) indicate about the relationship between the two variables?
c. Use the least squares method to develop the estimated regression equation.
d. Provide an interpretation for the slope of the estimated regression equation.
e. Another sporty car that *Consumer Reports* tested is the BMW 135i; the price for this car was $36,700. Predict the road-test score for the BMW 135i using the estimated regression equation developed in part (c).

12. Concur Technologies, Inc., is a large expense-management company located in Redmond, Washington. *The Wall Street Journal* asked Concur to examine the data from 8.3 million expense reports to provide insights regarding business travel expenses. Their analysis of the data showed that New York was the most expensive city, with an average daily hotel room rate of $198 and an average amount spent on entertainment, including group meals and tickets for shows, sports, and other events, of $172. In comparison, the U.S. averages for these two categories were $89 for the room rate and $99 for entertainment. The following table shows the average daily hotel room rate and the amount spent on entertainment for a random sample of 9 of the 25 most visited U.S. cities (*The Wall Street Journal,* August 18, 2011).

WEB file

BusinessTravel

City	Room Rate ($)	Entertainment ($)
Boston	148	161
Denver	96	105
Nashville	91	101
New Orleans	110	142
Phoenix	90	100
San Diego	102	120
San Francisco	136	167
San Jose	90	140
Tampa	82	98

a. Develop a scatter diagram for these data with the room rate as the independent variable.
b. What does the scatter diagram developed in part (a) indicate about the relationship between the two variables?
c. Develop the least squares estimated regression equation.
d. Provide an interpretation for the slope of the estimated regression equation.
e. The average room rate in Chicago is $128, considerably higher than the U.S. average. Predict the entertainment expense per day for Chicago.

13. To the Internal Revenue Service, the reasonableness of total itemized deductions depends on the taxpayer's adjusted gross income. Large deductions, which include charity and medical deductions, are more reasonable for taxpayers with large adjusted gross incomes. If a taxpayer claims larger than average itemized deductions for a given level of income, the chances of an IRS audit are increased. Data (in thousands of dollars) on adjusted gross income and the average or reasonable amount of itemized deductions follow.

Adjusted Gross Income ($1000s)	Reasonable Amount of Itemized Deductions ($1000s)
22	9.6
27	9.6
32	10.1
48	11.1
65	13.5
85	17.7
120	25.5

a. Develop a scatter diagram for these data with adjusted gross income as the independent variable.
b. Use the least squares method to develop the estimated regression equation.
c. Predict the reasonable level of total itemized deductions for a taxpayer with an adjusted gross income of $52,500. If this taxpayer claimed itemized deductions of $20,400, would the IRS agent's request for an audit appear justified? Explain.

14. *PCWorld* rated four component characteristics for 10 ultraportable laptop computers: features, performance, design, and price. Each characteristic was rated using a 0–100 point scale. An overall rating, referred to as the *PCW World* Rating, was then developed for each laptop. The following table shows the features rating and the *PCW World* Rating for the 10 laptop computers (*PC World* website, February 5, 2009).

WEB file

Laptop

Model	Features Rating	*PCW World* Rating
Thinkpad X200	87	83
VGN-Z598U	85	82
U6V	80	81
Elitebook 2530P	75	78
X360	80	78
Thinkpad X300	76	78
Ideapad U110	81	77
Micro Express JFT2500	73	75
Toughbook W7	79	73
HP Voodoo Envy133	68	72

a. Develop a scatter diagram with the features rating as the independent variable.
b. What does the scatter diagram developed in part (a) indicate about the relationship between the two variables?
c. Use the least squares method to develop the estimated regression equation.
d. Predict the *PCW World* Rating for a new laptop computer that has a features rating of 70.

14.3 Coefficient of Determination

For the Armand's Pizza Parlors example, we developed the estimated regression equation $\hat{y} = 60 + 5x$ to approximate the linear relationship between the size of the student population x and quarterly sales y. A question now is: How well does the estimated regression equation fit the data? In this section, we show that the **coefficient of determination** provides a measure of the goodness of fit for the estimated regression equation.

For the ith observation, the difference between the observed value of the dependent variable, y_i, and the predicted value of the dependent variable, $\hat{y}_i$, is called the **ith residual**. The ith residual represents the error in using $\hat{y}_i$ to estimate y_i. Thus, for the ith observation, the residual is $y_i - \hat{y}_i$. The sum of squares of these residuals or errors is the quantity that is minimized by the least squares method. This quantity, also known as the *sum of squares due to error,* is denoted by SSE.

SUM OF SQUARES DUE TO ERROR

$$\text{SSE} = \Sigma(y_i - \hat{y}_i)^2 \qquad \textbf{(14.8)}$$

The value of SSE is a measure of the error in using the estimated regression equation to predict the values of the dependent variable in the sample.

In Table 14.3 we show the calculations required to compute the sum of squares due to error for the Armand's Pizza Parlors example. For instance, for restaurant 1 the values of the independent and dependent variables are $x_1 = 2$ and $y_1 = 58$. Using the estimated

TABLE 14.3 CALCULATION OF SSE FOR ARMAND'S PIZZA PARLORS

Restaurant i	x_i = Student Population (1000s)	y_i = Quarterly Sales ($1000s)	Predicted Sales $\hat{y}_i = 60 + 5x_i$	Error $y_i - \hat{y}_i$	Squared Error $(y_i - \hat{y}_i)^2$
1	2	58	70	−12	144
2	6	105	90	15	225
3	8	88	100	−12	144
4	8	118	100	18	324
5	12	117	120	−3	9
6	16	137	140	−3	9
7	20	157	160	−3	9
8	20	169	160	9	81
9	22	149	170	−21	441
10	26	202	190	12	144
					SSE = 1530

regression equation, we find that the predicted value of quarterly sales for restaurant 1 is $\hat{y}_1 = 60 + 5(2) = 70$. Thus, the error in using $\hat{y}_1$ to predict y_1 for restaurant 1 is $y_1 - \hat{y}_1 = 58 - 70 = -12$. The squared error, $(-12)^2 = 144$, is shown in the last column of Table 14.3. After computing and squaring the residuals for each restaurant in the sample, we sum them to obtain SSE = 1530. Thus, SSE = 1530 measures the error in using the estimated regression equation $\hat{y} = 60 + 5x$ to predict sales.

Now suppose we are asked to develop an estimate of quarterly sales without knowledge of the size of the student population. Without knowledge of any related variables, we would use the sample mean as an estimate of quarterly sales at any given restaurant. Table 14.2 showed that for the sales data, $\Sigma y_i = 1300$. Hence, the mean value of quarterly sales for the sample of 10 Armand's restaurants is $\bar{y} = \Sigma y_i/n = 1300/10 = 130$. In Table 14.4 we show the sum of squared deviations obtained by using the sample mean $\bar{y} = 130$ to predict the value of quarterly sales for each restaurant in the sample. For the ith restaurant in the sample, the difference $y_i - \bar{y}$ provides a measure of the error involved in using $\bar{y}$ to predict sales. The corresponding sum of squares, called the *total sum of squares,* is denoted SST.

TABLE 14.4 COMPUTATION OF THE TOTAL SUM OF SQUARES FOR ARMAND'S PIZZA PARLORS

Restaurant i	x_i = Student Population (1000s)	y_i = Quarterly Sales ($1000s)	Deviation $y_i - \bar{y}$	Squared Deviation $(y_i - \bar{y})^2$
1	2	58	−72	5184
2	6	105	−25	625
3	8	88	−42	1764
4	8	118	−12	144
5	12	117	−13	169
6	16	137	7	49
7	20	157	27	729
8	20	169	39	1521
9	22	149	19	361
10	26	202	72	5184
				SST = 15,730

TOTAL SUM OF SQUARES

$$SST = \Sigma(y_i - \bar{y})^2 \quad \textbf{(14.9)}$$

The sum at the bottom of the last column in Table 14.4 is the total sum of squares for Armand's Pizza Parlors; it is SST = 15,730.

With SST = 15,730 and SSE = 1530, the estimated regression line provides a much better fit to the data than the line $y = \bar{y}$.

In Figure 14.5 we show the estimated regression line $\hat{y} = 60 + 5x$ and the line corresponding to $\bar{y} = 130$. Note that the points cluster more closely around the estimated regression line than they do about the line $\bar{y} = 130$. For example, for the 10th restaurant in the sample we see that the error is much larger when $\bar{y} = 130$ is used to predict y_{10} than when $\hat{y}_{10} = 60 + 5(26) = 190$ is used. We can think of SST as a measure of how well the observations cluster about the $\bar{y}$ line and SSE as a measure of how well the observations cluster about the $\hat{y}$ line.

To measure how much the $\hat{y}$ values on the estimated regression line deviate from $\bar{y}$, another sum of squares is computed. This sum of squares, called the *sum of squares due to regression,* is denoted SSR.

SUM OF SQUARES DUE TO REGRESSION

$$SSR = \Sigma(\hat{y}_i - \bar{y})^2 \quad \textbf{(14.10)}$$

FIGURE 14.5 DEVIATIONS ABOUT THE ESTIMATED REGRESSION LINE AND THE LINE $y = \bar{y}$ FOR ARMAND'S PIZZA PARLORS

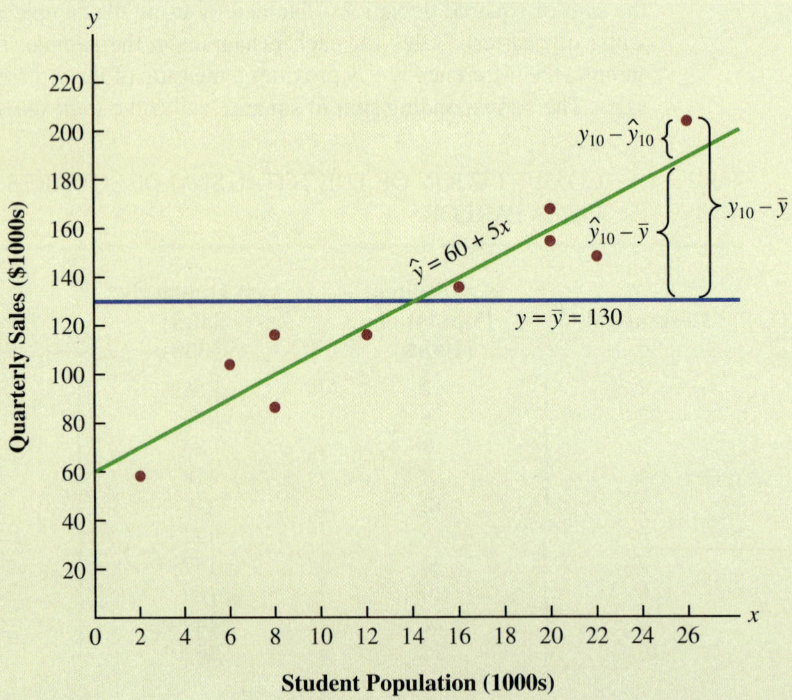

From the preceding discussion, we should expect that SST, SSR, and SSE are related. Indeed, the relationship among these three sums of squares provides one of the most important results in statistics.

SSR can be thought of as the explained portion of SST, and SSE can be thought of as the unexplained portion of SST.

RELATIONSHIP AMONG SST, SSR, AND SSE

$$\text{SST} = \text{SSR} + \text{SSE} \tag{14.11}$$

where

$$\begin{aligned} \text{SST} &= \text{total sum of squares} \\ \text{SSR} &= \text{sum of squares due to regression} \\ \text{SSE} &= \text{sum of squares due to error} \end{aligned}$$

Equation (14.11) shows that the total sum of squares can be partitioned into two components, the sum of squares due to regression and the sum of squares due to error. Hence, if the values of any two of these sum of squares are known, the third sum of squares can be computed easily. For instance, in the Armand's Pizza Parlors example, we already know that SSE = 1530 and SST = 15,730; therefore, solving for SSR in equation (14.11), we find that the sum of squares due to regression is

$$\text{SSR} = \text{SST} - \text{SSE} = 15{,}730 - 1530 = 14{,}200$$

Now let us see how the three sums of squares, SST, SSR, and SSE, can be used to provide a measure of the goodness of fit for the estimated regression equation. The estimated regression equation would provide a perfect fit if every value of the dependent variable y_i happened to lie on the estimated regression line. In this case, $y_i - \hat{y}_i$ would be zero for each observation, resulting in SSE = 0. Because SST = SSR + SSE, we see that for a perfect fit SSR must equal SST, and the ratio (SSR/SST) must equal one. Poorer fits will result in larger values for SSE. Solving for SSE in equation (14.11), we see that SSE = SST − SSR. Hence, the largest value for SSE (and hence the poorest fit) occurs when SSR = 0 and SSE = SST.

The ratio SSR/SST, which will take values between zero and one, is used to evaluate the goodness of fit for the estimated regression equation. This ratio is called the *coefficient of determination* and is denoted by r^2.

COEFFICIENT OF DETERMINATION

$$r^2 = \frac{\text{SSR}}{\text{SST}} \tag{14.12}$$

For the Armand's Pizza Parlors example, the value of the coefficient of determination is

$$r^2 = \frac{\text{SSR}}{\text{SST}} = \frac{14{,}200}{15{,}730} = .9027$$

When we express the coefficient of determination as a percentage, r^2 can be interpreted as the percentage of the total sum of squares that can be explained by using the estimated regression equation. For Armand's Pizza Parlors, we can conclude that 90.27% of the total sum of squares can be explained by using the estimated regression equation $\hat{y} = 60 + 5x$ to predict quarterly sales. In other words, 90.27% of the variability in sales can be explained by the linear relationship between the size of the student population and sales. We should be pleased to find such a good fit for the estimated regression equation.

Correlation Coefficient

In Chapter 3 we introduced the **correlation coefficient** as a descriptive measure of the strength of linear association between two variables, x and y. Values of the correlation coefficient are always between -1 and $+1$. A value of $+1$ indicates that the two variables x and y are perfectly related in a positive linear sense. That is, all data points are on a straight line that has a positive slope. A value of -1 indicates that x and y are perfectly related in a negative linear sense, with all data points on a straight line that has a negative slope. Values of the correlation coefficient close to zero indicate that x and y are not linearly related.

In Section 3.5 we presented the equation for computing the sample correlation coefficient. If a regression analysis has already been performed and the coefficient of determination r^2 computed, the sample correlation coefficient can be computed as follows.

SAMPLE CORRELATION COEFFICIENT

$$\begin{aligned} r_{xy} &= (\text{sign of } b_1)\sqrt{\text{Coefficient of determination}} \\ &= (\text{sign of } b_1)\sqrt{r^2} \end{aligned} \quad \textbf{(14.13)}$$

where

$$b_1 = \text{the slope of the estimated regression equation } \hat{y} = b_0 + b_1 x$$

The sign for the sample correlation coefficient is positive if the estimated regression equation has a positive slope ($b_1 > 0$) and negative if the estimated regression equation has a negative slope ($b_1 < 0$).

For the Armand's Pizza Parlor example, the value of the coefficient of determination corresponding to the estimated regression equation $\hat{y} = 60 + 5x$ is .9027. Because the slope of the estimated regression equation is positive, equation (14.13) shows that the sample correlation coefficient is $+\sqrt{.9027} = +.9501$. With a sample correlation coefficient of $r_{xy} = +.9501$, we would conclude that a strong positive linear association exists between x and y.

In the case of a linear relationship between two variables, both the coefficient of determination and the sample correlation coefficient provide measures of the strength of the relationship. The coefficient of determination provides a measure between zero and one, whereas the sample correlation coefficient provides a measure between -1 and $+1$. Although the sample correlation coefficient is restricted to a linear relationship between two variables, the coefficient of determination can be used for nonlinear relationships and for relationships that have two or more independent variables. Thus, the coefficient of determination provides a wider range of applicability.

NOTES AND COMMENTS

1. In developing the least squares estimated regression equation and computing the coefficient of determination, we made no probabilistic assumptions about the error term ϵ, and no statistical tests for significance of the relationship between x and y were conducted. Larger values of r^2 imply that the least squares line provides a better fit to the data; that is, the observations are more closely grouped about the least squares line. But, using only r^2, we can draw no conclusion about whether the relationship between x and y is statistically significant. Such a conclusion must be based on considerations that involve the sample size and the properties of the appropriate sampling distributions of the least squares estimators.
2. As a practical matter, for typical data found in the social sciences, values of r^2 as low as .25 are often considered useful. For data in the physical and life sciences, r^2 values of .60 or greater are often found; in fact, in some cases, r^2 values greater than .90 can be found. In business applications, r^2 values vary greatly, depending on the unique characteristics of each application.

Exercises

Methods

SELF test

15. The data from exercise 1 follow.

x_i	1	2	3	4	5
y_i	3	7	5	11	14

The estimated regression equation for these data is $\hat{y} = .20 + 2.60x$.

a. Compute SSE, SST, and SSR using equations (14.8), (14.9), and (14.10).
b. Compute the coefficient of determination r^2. Comment on the goodness of fit.
c. Compute the sample correlation coefficient.

16. The data from exercise 2 follow.

x_i	3	12	6	20	14
y_i	55	40	55	10	15

The estimated regression equation for these data is $\hat{y} = 68 - 3x$.

a. Compute SSE, SST, and SSR.
b. Compute the coefficient of determination r^2. Comment on the goodness of fit.
c. Compute the sample correlation coefficient.

17. The data from exercise 3 follow.

x_i	2	6	9	13	20
y_i	7	18	9	26	23

The estimated regression equation for these data is $\hat{y} = 7.6 + .9x$. What percentage of the total sum of squares can be accounted for by the estimated regression equation? What is the value of the sample correlation coefficient?

Applications

SELF test

18. The following data show the brand, price ($), and the overall score for six stereo headphones that were tested by *Consumer Reports* (*Consumer Reports* website, March 5, 2012). The overall score is based on sound quality and effectiveness of ambient noise reduction. Scores range from 0 (lowest) to 100 (highest). The estimated regression equation for these data is $\hat{y} = 23.194 + .318x$, where x = price ($) and y = overall score.

Brand	Price ($)	Score
Bose	180	76
Skullcandy	150	71
Koss	95	61
Phillips/O'Neill	70	56
Denon	70	40
JVC	35	26

a. Compute SST, SSR, and SSE.
b. Compute the coefficient of determination r^2. Comment on the goodness of fit.
c. What is the value of the sample correlation coefficient?

19. In exercise 7 a sales manager collected the following data on x = annual sales and y = years of experience. The estimated regression equation for these data is $\hat{y} = 80 + 4x$.

WEB file Sales

Salesperson	Years of Experience	Annual Sales ($1000s)
1	1	80
2	3	97
3	4	92
4	4	102
5	6	103
6	8	111
7	10	119
8	10	123
9	11	117
10	13	136

a. Compute SST, SSR, and SSE.
b. Compute the coefficient of determination r^2. Comment on the goodness of fit.
c. What is the value of the sample correlation coefficient?

20. *Bicycling,* the world's leading cycling magazine, reviews hundreds of bicycles throughout the year. Their "Road-Race" category contains reviews of bikes used by riders primarily interested in racing. One of the most important factors in selecting a bike for racing is the weight of the bike. The following data show the weight (pounds) and price ($) for 10 racing bikes reviewed by the magazine (*Bicycling* website, March 8, 2012).

WEB file RacingBicycles

Brand	Weight	Price ($)
FELT F5	17.8	2100
PINARELLO Paris	16.1	6250
ORBEA Orca GDR	14.9	8370
EDDY MERCKX EMX-7	15.9	6200
BH RC1 Ultegra	17.2	4000
BH Ultralight 386	13.1	8600
CERVELO S5 Team	16.2	6000
GIANT TCR Advanced 2	17.1	2580
WILIER TRIESTINA Gran Turismo	17.6	3400
SPECIALIZED S-Works Amira SL4	14.1	8000

CUMULATIVE PROBABILITIES FOR THE STANDARD NORMAL DISTRIBUTION

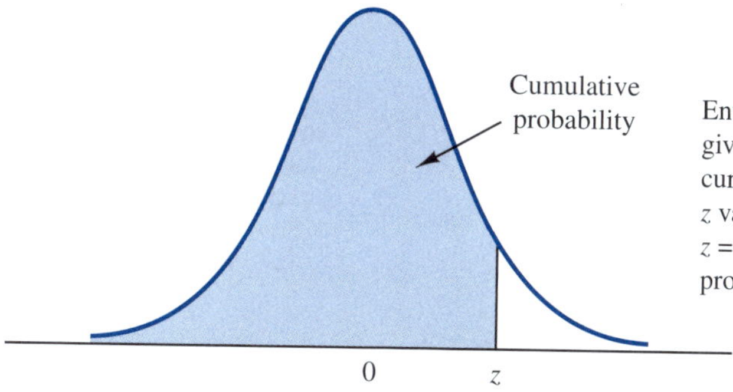

Entries in the table give the area under the curve to the left of the z value. For example, for $z = 1.25$, the cumulative probability is .8944.

z	**.00**	**.01**	**.02**	**.03**	**.04**	**.05**	**.06**	**.07**	**.08**	**.09**
.0	.5000	.5040	.5080	.5120	.5160	.5199	.5239	.5279	.5319	.5359
.1	.5398	.5438	.5478	.5517	.5557	.5596	.5636	.5675	.5714	.5753
.2	.5793	.5832	.5871	.5910	.5948	.5987	.6026	.6064	.6103	.6141
.3	.6179	.6217	.6255	.6293	.6331	.6368	.6406	.6443	.6480	.6517
.4	.6554	.6591	.6628	.6664	.6700	.6736	.6772	.6808	.6844	.6879
.5	.6915	.6950	.6985	.7019	.7054	.7088	.7123	.7157	.7190	.7224
.6	.7257	.7291	.7324	.7357	.7389	.7422	.7454	.7486	.7517	.7549
.7	.7580	.7611	.7642	.7673	.7704	.7734	.7764	.7794	.7823	.7852
.8	.7881	.7910	.7939	.7967	.7995	.8023	.8051	.8078	.8106	.8133
.9	.8159	.8186	.8212	.8238	.8264	.8289	.8315	.8340	.8365	.8389
1.0	.8413	.8438	.8461	.8485	.8508	.8531	.8554	.8577	.8599	.8621
1.1	.8643	.8665	.8686	.8708	.8729	.8749	.8770	.8790	.8810	.8830
1.2	.8849	.8869	.8888	.8907	.8925	.8944	.8962	.8980	.8997	.9015
1.3	.9032	.9049	.9066	.9082	.9099	.9115	.9131	.9147	.9162	.9177
1.4	.9192	.9207	.9222	.9236	.9251	.9265	.9279	.9292	.9306	.9319
1.5	.9332	.9345	.9357	.9370	.9382	.9394	.9406	.9418	.9429	.9441
1.6	.9452	.9463	.9474	.9484	.9495	.9505	.9515	.9525	.9535	.9545
1.7	.9554	.9564	.9573	.9582	.9591	.9599	.9608	.9616	.9625	.9633
1.8	.9641	.9649	.9656	.9664	.9671	.9678	.9686	.9693	.9699	.9706
1.9	.9713	.9719	.9726	.9732	.9738	.9744	.9750	.9756	.9761	.9767
2.0	.9772	.9778	.9783	.9788	.9793	.9798	.9803	.9808	.9812	.9817
2.1	.9821	.9826	.9830	.9834	.9838	.9842	.9846	.9850	.9854	.9857
2.2	.9861	.9864	.9868	.9871	.9875	.9878	.9881	.9884	.9887	.9890
2.3	.9893	.9896	.9898	.9901	.9904	.9906	.9909	.9911	.9913	.9916
2.4	.9918	.9920	.9922	.9925	.9927	.9929	.9931	.9932	.9934	.9936
2.5	.9938	.9940	.9941	.9943	.9945	.9946	.9948	.9949	.9951	.9952
2.6	.9953	.9955	.9956	.9957	.9959	.9960	.9961	.9962	.9963	.9964
2.7	.9965	.9966	.9967	.9968	.9969	.9970	.9971	.9972	.9973	.9974
2.8	.9974	.9975	.9976	.9977	.9977	.9978	.9979	.9979	.9980	.9981
2.9	.9981	.9982	.9982	.9983	.9984	.9984	.9985	.9985	.9986	.9986
3.0	.9987	.9987	.9987	.9988	.9988	.9989	.9989	.9989	.9990	.9990

a. Use the data to develop an estimated regression equation that could be used to estimate the price for a bike given the weight.
b. Compute r^2. Did the estimated regression equation provide a good fit?
c. Predict the price for a bike that weighs 15 pounds.

21. An important application of regression analysis in accounting is in the estimation of cost. By collecting data on volume and cost and using the least squares method to develop an estimated regression equation relating volume and cost, an accountant can estimate the cost associated with a particular manufacturing volume. Consider the following sample of production volumes and total cost data for a manufacturing operation.

Production Volume (units)	Total Cost ($)
400	4000
450	5000
550	5400
600	5900
700	6400
750	7000

a. Use these data to develop an estimated regression equation that could be used to predict the total cost for a given production volume.
b. What is the variable cost per unit produced?
c. Compute the coefficient of determination. What percentage of the variation in total cost can be explained by production volume?
d. The company's production schedule shows 500 units must be produced next month. Predict the total cost for this operation?

22. Refer to exercise 5 where the following data were used to investigate whether higher prices are generally associated with higher ratings for elliptical trainers (*Consumer Reports,* February 2008).

WEB file
Ellipticals

Brand and Model	Price ($)	Rating
Precor 5.31	3700	87
Keys Fitness CG2	2500	84
Octane Fitness Q37e	2800	82
LifeFitness X1 Basic	1900	74
NordicTrack AudioStrider 990	1000	73
Schwinn 430	800	69
Vision Fitness X6100	1700	68
ProForm XP 520 Razor	600	55

With x = price ($) and y = rating, the estimated regression equation is $\hat{y} = 58.158 + .008449x$. For these data, SSE = 173.88.

a. Compute the coefficient of determination r^2.
b. Did the estimated regression equation provide a good fit? Explain.
c. What is the value of the sample correlation coefficient? Does it reflect a strong or weak relationship between price and rating?

14.4 Model Assumptions

In conducting a regression analysis, we begin by making an assumption about the appropriate model for the relationship between the dependent and independent variable(s). For the case of simple linear regression, the assumed regression model is

$$y = \beta_0 + \beta_1 x + \epsilon$$

Then the least squares method is used to develop values for b_0 and b_1, the estimates of the model parameters β_0 and β_1, respectively. The resulting estimated regression equation is

$$\hat{y} = b_0 + b_1 x$$

We saw that the value of the coefficient of determination (r^2) is a measure of the goodness of fit of the estimated regression equation. However, even with a large value of r^2, the estimated regression equation should not be used until further analysis of the appropriateness of the assumed model has been conducted. An important step in determining whether the assumed model is appropriate involves testing for the significance of the relationship. The tests of significance in regression analysis are based on the following assumptions about the error term ϵ.

ASSUMPTIONS ABOUT THE ERROR TERM ϵ IN THE REGRESSION MODEL

$$y = \beta_0 + \beta_1 x + \epsilon$$

1. The error term ϵ is a random variable with a mean or expected value of zero; that is, $E(\epsilon) = 0$.
   Implication: β_0 and β_1 are constants, therefore $E(\beta_0) = \beta_0$ and $E(\beta_1) = \beta_1$; thus, for a given value of x, the expected value of y is

   $$E(y) = \beta_0 + \beta_1 x \qquad \textbf{(14.14)}$$

   As we indicated previously, equation (14.14) is referred to as the regression equation.
2. The variance of ϵ, denoted by σ^2, is the same for all values of x.
   Implication: The variance of y about the regression line equals σ^2 and is the same for all values of x.
3. The values of ϵ are independent.
   Implication: The value of ϵ for a particular value of x is not related to the value of ϵ for any other value of x; thus, the value of y for a particular value of x is not related to the value of y for any other value of x.
4. The error term ϵ is a normally distributed random variable for all values of x.
   Implication: Because y is a linear function of ϵ, y is also a normally distributed random variable for all values of x.

Figure 14.6 illustrates the model assumptions and their implications; note that in this graphical interpretation, the value of $E(y)$ changes according to the specific value of x considered. However, regardless of the x value, the probability distribution of ϵ and hence the probability distributions of y are normally distributed, each with the same variance. The specific value of the error ϵ at any particular point depends on whether the actual value of y is greater than or less than $E(y)$.

FIGURE 14.6 ASSUMPTIONS FOR THE REGRESSION MODEL

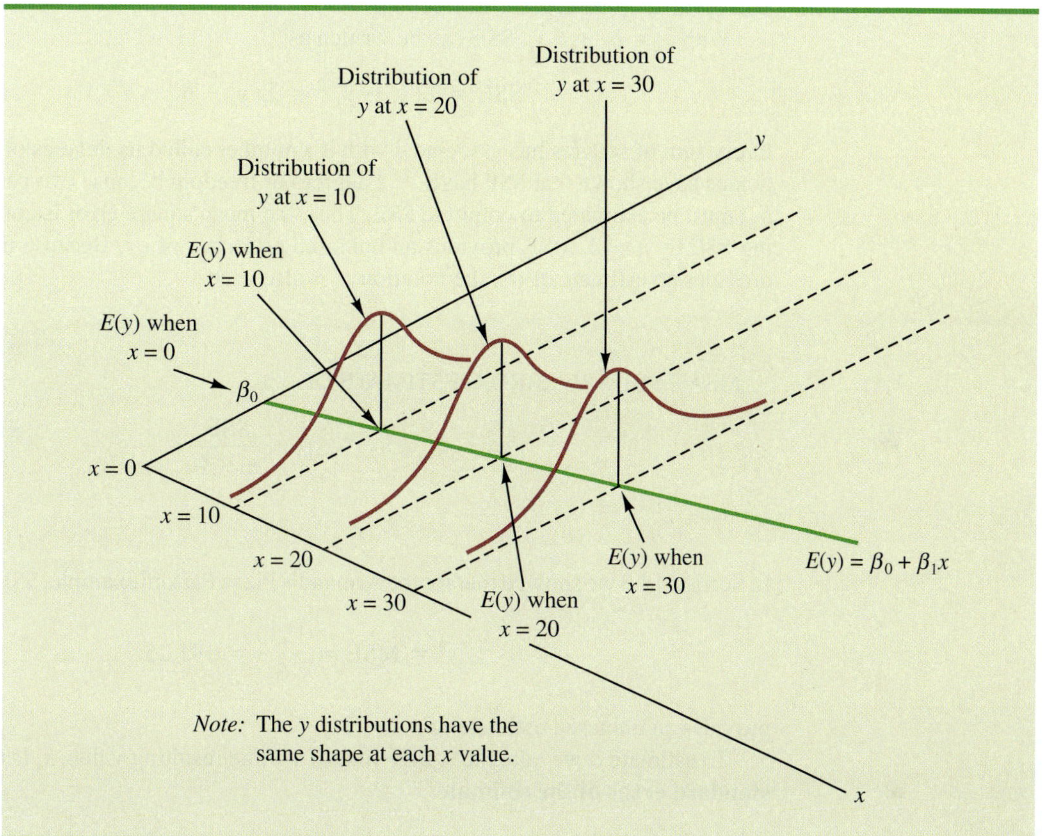

At this point, we must keep in mind that we are also making an assumption or hypothesis about the form of the relationship between x and y. That is, we assume that a straight line represented by $\beta_0 + \beta_1 x$ is the basis for the relationship between the variables. We must not lose sight of the fact that some other model, for instance $y = \beta_0 + \beta_1 x^2 + \epsilon$, may turn out to be a better model for the underlying relationship.

14.5 Testing for Significance

In a simple linear regression equation, the mean or expected value of y is a linear function of x: $E(y) = \beta_0 + \beta_1 x$. If the value of β_1 is zero, $E(y) = \beta_0 + (0)x = \beta_0$. In this case, the mean value of y does not depend on the value of x and hence we would conclude that x and y are not linearly related. Alternatively, if the value of β_1 is not equal to zero, we would conclude that the two variables are related. Thus, to test for a significant regression relationship, we must conduct a hypothesis test to determine whether the value of β_1 is zero. Two tests are commonly used. Both require an estimate of σ^2, the variance of ϵ in the regression model.

Estimate of σ^2

From the regression model and its assumptions we can conclude that σ^2, the variance of ϵ, also represents the variance of the y values about the regression line. Recall that the deviations of the y values about the estimated regression line are called residuals. Thus, SSE, the sum of squared residuals, is a measure of the variability of the actual observations about the estimated regression line. The **mean square error** (MSE) provides the estimate of σ^2; it is SSE divided by its degrees of freedom.

With $\hat{y}_i = b_0 + b_1x_i$, SSE can be written as

$$\text{SSE} = \Sigma(y_i - \hat{y}_i)^2 = \Sigma(y_i - b_0 - b_1x_i)^2$$

Every sum of squares has associated with it a number called its degrees of freedom. Statisticians have shown that SSE has $n - 2$ degrees of freedom because two parameters (β_0 and β_1) must be estimated to compute SSE. Thus, the mean square error is computed by dividing SSE by $n - 2$. MSE provides an unbiased estimator of σ^2. Because the value of MSE provides an estimate of σ^2, the notation s^2 is also used.

MEAN SQUARE ERROR (ESTIMATE OF σ^2)

$$s^2 = \text{MSE} = \frac{\text{SSE}}{n - 2} \tag{14.15}$$

In Section 14.3 we showed that for the Armand's Pizza Parlors example, SSE = 1530; hence,

$$s^2 = \text{MSE} = \frac{1530}{8} = 191.25$$

provides an unbiased estimate of σ^2.

To estimate σ we take the square root of s^2. The resulting value, s, is referred to as the **standard error of the estimate**.

STANDARD ERROR OF THE ESTIMATE

$$s = \sqrt{\text{MSE}} = \sqrt{\frac{\text{SSE}}{n - 2}} \tag{14.16}$$

For the Armand's Pizza Parlors example, $s = \sqrt{\text{MSE}} = \sqrt{191.25} = 13.829$. In the following discussion, we use the standard error of the estimate in the tests for a significant relationship between x and y.

t Test

The simple linear regression model is $y = \beta_0 + \beta_1x + \epsilon$. If x and y are linearly related, we must have $\beta_1 \neq 0$. The purpose of the t test is to see whether we can conclude that $\beta_1 \neq 0$. We will use the sample data to test the following hypotheses about the parameter β_1.

$$H_0\colon \beta_1 = 0$$
$$H_a\colon \beta_1 \neq 0$$

If H_0 is rejected, we will conclude that $\beta_1 \neq 0$ and that a statistically significant relationship exists between the two variables. However, if H_0 cannot be rejected, we will have insufficient evidence to conclude that a significant relationship exists. The properties of the sampling distribution of b_1, the least squares estimator of β_1, provide the basis for the hypothesis test.

First, let us consider what would happen if we used a different random sample for the same regression study. For example, suppose that Armand's Pizza Parlors used the sales records of a different sample of 10 restaurants. A regression analysis of this new sample might result in an estimated regression equation similar to our previous estimated regression equation $\hat{y} = 60 + 5x$. However, it is doubtful that we would obtain exactly the same equation (with an intercept of exactly 60 and a slope of exactly 5). Indeed, b_0 and b_1, the least squares estimators, are sample statistics with their own sampling distributions. The properties of the sampling distribution of b_1 follow.

SAMPLING DISTRIBUTION OF b_1

Expected Value

$$E(b_1) = \beta_1$$

Standard Deviation

$$\sigma_{b_1} = \frac{\sigma}{\sqrt{\Sigma(x_i - \bar{x})^2}} \qquad \textbf{(14.17)}$$

Distribution Form

Normal

Note that the expected value of b_1 is equal to β_1, so b_1 is an unbiased estimator of β_1.

Because we do not know the value of σ, we develop an estimate of σ_{b_1}, denoted s_{b_1}, by estimating σ with s in equation (14.17). Thus, we obtain the following estimate of σ_{b_1}.

The standard deviation of b_1 is also referred to as the standard error of b_1. Thus, s_{b_1} provides an estimate of the standard error of b_1.

ESTIMATED STANDARD DEVIATION OF b_1

$$s_{b_1} = \frac{s}{\sqrt{\Sigma(x_i - \bar{x})^2}} \qquad \textbf{(14.18)}$$

For Armand's Pizza Parlors, $s = 13.829$. Hence, using $\Sigma(x_i - \bar{x})^2 = 568$ as shown in Table 14.2, we have

$$s_{b_1} = \frac{13.829}{\sqrt{568}} = .5803$$

as the estimated standard deviation of b_1.

The t test for a significant relationship is based on the fact that the test statistic

$$\frac{b_1 - \beta_1}{s_{b_1}}$$

follows a t distribution with $n - 2$ degrees of freedom. If the null hypothesis is true, then $\beta_1 = 0$ and $t = b_1/s_{b_1}$.

Let us conduct this test of significance for Armand's Pizza Parlors at the $\alpha = .01$ level of significance. The test statistic is

$$t = \frac{b_1}{s_{b_1}} = \frac{5}{.5803} = 8.62$$

Appendixes 14.3 and 14.4 show how Minitab and Excel can be used to compute the p-value.

The t distribution table (Table 2 of Appendix D) shows that with $n - 2 = 10 - 2 = 8$ degrees of freedom, $t = 3.355$ provides an area of .005 in the upper tail. Thus, the area in the upper tail of the t distribution corresponding to the test statistic $t = 8.62$ must be less than .005. Because this test is a two-tailed test, we double this value to conclude that the p-value associated with $t = 8.62$ must be less than $2(.005) = .01$. Excel or Minitab show the p-value $= .000$. Because the p-value is less than $\alpha = .01$, we reject H_0 and conclude that β_1 is not equal to zero. This evidence is sufficient to conclude that a significant relationship exists between student population and quarterly sales. A summary of the t test for significance in simple linear regression follows.

t TEST FOR SIGNIFICANCE IN SIMPLE LINEAR REGRESSION

$$H_0: \beta_1 = 0$$
$$H_a: \beta_1 \neq 0$$

TEST STATISTIC

$$t = \frac{b_1}{s_{b_1}} \tag{14.19}$$

REJECTION RULE

p-value approach:	Reject H_0 if p-value $\leq \alpha$
Critical value approach:	Reject H_0 if $t \leq -t_{\alpha/2}$ or if $t \geq t_{\alpha/2}$

where $t_{\alpha/2}$ is based on a t distribution with $n - 2$ degrees of freedom.

Confidence Interval for β_1

The form of a confidence interval for β_1 is as follows:

$$b_1 \pm t_{\alpha/2} s_{b_1}$$

The point estimator is b_1 and the margin of error is $t_{\alpha/2} s_{b_1}$. The confidence coefficient associated with this interval is $1 - \alpha$, and $t_{\alpha/2}$ is the t value providing an area of $\alpha/2$ in the upper tail of a t distribution with $n - 2$ degrees of freedom. For example, suppose that we wanted to develop a 99% confidence interval estimate of β_1 for Armand's Pizza Parlors. From Table 2 of Appendix B we find that the t value corresponding to $\alpha = .01$ and $n - 2 = 10 - 2 = 8$ degrees of freedom is $t_{.005} = 3.355$. Thus, the 99% confidence interval estimate of β_1 is

$$b_1 \pm t_{\alpha/2} s_{b_1} = 5 \pm 3.355(.5803) = 5 \pm 1.95$$

or 3.05 to 6.95.

In using the t test for significance, the hypotheses tested were

$$H_0: \beta_1 = 0$$
$$H_a: \beta_1 \neq 0$$

At the $\alpha = .01$ level of significance, we can use the 99% confidence interval as an alternative for drawing the hypothesis testing conclusion for the Armand's data. Because 0, the hypothesized value of β_1, is not included in the confidence interval (3.05 to 6.95), we can reject

H_0 and conclude that a significant statistical relationship exists between the size of the student population and quarterly sales. In general, a confidence interval can be used to test any two-sided hypothesis about β_1. If the hypothesized value of β_1 is contained in the confidence interval, do not reject H_0. Otherwise, reject H_0.

F Test

An F test, based on the F probability distribution, can also be used to test for significance in regression. With only one independent variable, the F test will provide the same conclusion as the t test; that is, if the t test indicates $\beta_1 \neq 0$ and hence a significant relationship, the F test will also indicate a significant relationship. But with more than one independent variable, only the F test can be used to test for an overall significant relationship.

The logic behind the use of the F test for determining whether the regression relationship is statistically significant is based on the development of two independent estimates of σ^2. We explained how MSE provides an estimate of σ^2. If the null hypothesis H_0: $\beta_1 = 0$ is true, the sum of squares due to regression, SSR, divided by its degrees of freedom provides another independent estimate of σ^2. This estimate is called the *mean square due to regression,* or simply the *mean square regression,* and is denoted MSR. In general,

$$\text{MSR} = \frac{\text{SSR}}{\text{Regression degrees of freedom}}$$

For the models we consider in this text, the regression degrees of freedom is always equal to the number of independent variables in the model:

$$\text{MSR} = \frac{\text{SSR}}{\text{Number of independent variables}} \tag{14.20}$$

Because we consider only regression models with one independent variable in this chapter, we have MSR = SSR/1 = SSR. Hence, for Armand's Pizza Parlors, MSR = SSR = 14,200.

If the null hypothesis (H_0: $\beta_1 = 0$) is true, MSR and MSE are two independent estimates of σ^2 and the sampling distribution of MSR/MSE follows an F distribution with numerator degrees of freedom equal to one and denominator degrees of freedom equal to $n - 2$. Therefore, when $\beta_1 = 0$, the value of MSR/MSE should be close to one. However, if the null hypothesis is false ($\beta_1 \neq 0$), MSR will overestimate σ^2 and the value of MSR/MSE will be inflated; thus, large values of MSR/MSE lead to the rejection of H_0 and the conclusion that the relationship between x and y is statistically significant.

Let us conduct the F test for the Armand's Pizza Parlors example. The test statistic is

$$F = \frac{\text{MSR}}{\text{MSE}} = \frac{14{,}200}{191.25} = 74.25$$

The F test and the t test provide identical results for simple linear regression.

The F distribution table (Table 4 of Appendix B) shows that with one degree of freedom in the numerator and $n - 2 = 10 - 2 = 8$ degrees of freedom in the denominator, $F = 11.26$ provides an area of .01 in the upper tail. Thus, the area in the upper tail of the F distribution corresponding to the test statistic $F = 74.25$ must be less than .01. Thus, we conclude that the p-value must be less than .01. Excel or Minitab show the p-value = .000. Because the p-value is less than $\alpha = .01$, we reject H_0 and conclude that a significant relationship exists between the size of the student population and quarterly sales. A summary of the F test for significance in simple linear regression follows.

If H_0 is false, MSE *still provides an unbiased estimate of σ^2 and* MSR *overestimates σ^2. If H_0 is true, both* MSE *and* MSR *provide unbiased estimates of σ^2; in this case the value of* MSR/MSE *should be close to 1.*

F TEST FOR SIGNIFICANCE IN SIMPLE LINEAR REGRESSION

$$H_0\colon \beta_1 = 0$$
$$H_a\colon \beta_1 \neq 0$$

TEST STATISTIC

$$F = \frac{\text{MSR}}{\text{MSE}} \qquad \textbf{(14.21)}$$

REJECTION RULE

p-value approach: Reject H_0 if p-value $\leq \alpha$

Critical value approach: Reject H_0 if $F \geq F_\alpha$

where F_α is based on an F distribution with 1 degree of freedom in the numerator and $n - 2$ degrees of freedom in the denominator.

In Chapter 13 we covered analysis of variance (ANOVA) and showed how an **ANOVA table** could be used to provide a convenient summary of the computational aspects of analysis of variance. A similar ANOVA table can be used to summarize the results of the F test for significance in regression. Table 14.5 is the general form of the ANOVA table for simple linear regression. Table 14.6 is the ANOVA table with the F test computations performed for Armand's Pizza Parlors. Regression, Error, and Total are the labels for the three sources of variation, with SSR, SSE, and SST appearing as the corresponding sum of squares in

In every analysis of variance table the total sum of squares is the sum of the regression sum of squares and the error sum of squares; in addition, the total degrees of freedom is the sum of the regression degrees of freedom and the error degrees of freedom.

TABLE 14.5 GENERAL FORM OF THE ANOVA TABLE FOR SIMPLE LINEAR REGRESSION

Source of Variation	Sum of Squares	Degrees of Freedom	Mean Square	F	p-value
Regression	SSR	1	$\text{MSR} = \frac{\text{SSR}}{1}$	$F = \frac{\text{MSR}}{\text{MSE}}$	
Error	SSE	$n - 2$	$\text{MSE} = \frac{\text{SSE}}{n - 2}$		
Total	SST	$n - 1$			

TABLE 14.6 ANOVA TABLE FOR THE ARMAND'S PIZZA PARLORS PROBLEM

Source of Variation	Sum of Squares	Degrees of Freedom	Mean Square	F	p-value
Regression	14,200	1	$\frac{14{,}200}{1} = 14{,}200$	$\frac{14{,}200}{191.25} = 74.25$	.000
Error	1,530	8	$\frac{1530}{8} = 191.25$		
Total	15,730	9			

column 2. The degrees of freedom, 1 for SSR, $n - 2$ for SSE, and $n - 1$ for SST, are shown in column 3. Column 4 contains the values of MSR and MSE, column 5 contains the value of $F = \text{MSR/MSE}$, and column 6 contains the p-value corresponding to the F value in column 5. Almost all computer printouts of regression analysis include an ANOVA table summary of the F test for significance.

Some Cautions About the Interpretation of Significance Tests

Regression analysis, which can be used to identify how variables are associated with one another, cannot be used as evidence of a cause-and-effect relationship.

Rejecting the null hypothesis H_0: $\beta_1 = 0$ and concluding that the relationship between x and y is significant does not enable us to conclude that a cause-and-effect relationship is present between x and y. Concluding a cause-and-effect relationship is warranted only if the analyst can provide some type of theoretical justification that the relationship is in fact causal. In the Armand's Pizza Parlors example, we can conclude that there is a significant relationship between the size of the student population x and quarterly sales y; moreover, the estimated regression equation $\hat{y} = 60 + 5x$ provides the least squares estimate of the relationship. We cannot, however, conclude that changes in student population x *cause* changes in quarterly sales y just because we identified a statistically significant relationship. The appropriateness of such a cause-and-effect conclusion is left to supporting theoretical justification and to good judgment on the part of the analyst. Armand's managers felt that increases in the student population were a likely cause of increased quarterly sales. Thus, the result of the significance test enabled them to conclude that a cause-and-effect relationship was present.

In addition, just because we are able to reject H_0: $\beta_1 = 0$ and demonstrate statistical significance does not enable us to conclude that the relationship between x and y is linear. We can state only that x and y are related and that a linear relationship explains a significant portion of the variability in y over the range of values for x observed in the sample. Figure 14.7 illustrates this situation. The test for significance calls for the rejection of the null hypothesis H_0: $\beta_1 = 0$ and leads to the conclusion that x and y are significantly related, but the figure shows that the actual relationship between x and y is not linear. Although the

FIGURE 14.7 EXAMPLE OF A LINEAR APPROXIMATION OF A NONLINEAR RELATIONSHIP

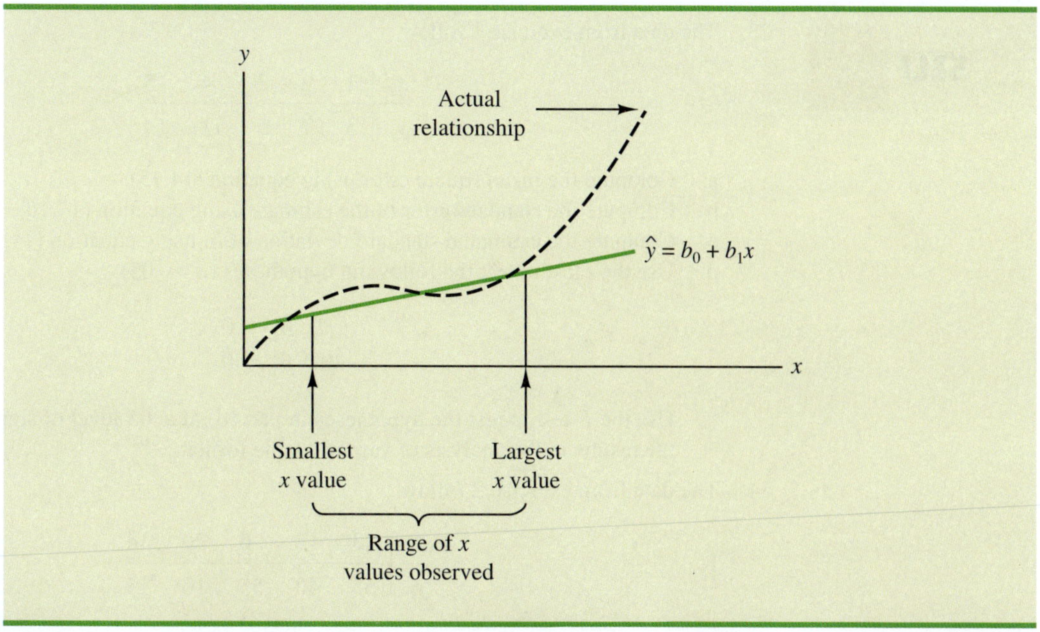

linear approximation provided by $\hat{y} = b_0 + b_1x$ is good over the range of x values observed in the sample, it becomes poor for x values outside that range.

Given a significant relationship, we should feel confident in using the estimated regression equation for predictions corresponding to x values within the range of the x values observed in the sample. For Armand's Pizza Parlors, this range corresponds to values of x between 2 and 26. Unless other reasons indicate that the model is valid beyond this range, predictions outside the range of the independent variable should be made with caution. For Armand's Pizza Parlors, because the regression relationship has been found significant at the .01 level, we should feel confident using it to predict sales for restaurants where the associated student population is between 2000 and 26,000.

NOTES AND COMMENTS

1. The assumptions made about the error term (Section 14.4) are what allow the tests of statistical significance in this section. The properties of the sampling distribution of b_1 and the subsequent t and F tests follow directly from these assumptions.
2. Do not confuse statistical significance with practical significance. With very large sample sizes, statistically significant results can be obtained for small values of b_1; in such cases, one must exercise care in concluding that the relationship has practical significance.
3. A test of significance for a linear relationship between x and y can also be performed by using the sample correlation coefficient r_{xy}. With ρ_{xy} denoting the population correlation coefficient, the hypotheses are as follows.

$$H_0: \rho_{xy} = 0$$
$$H_a: \rho_{xy} \neq 0$$

A significant relationship can be concluded if H_0 is rejected. The details of this test are provided in Appendix 14.2. However, the t and F tests presented previously in this section give the same result as the test for significance using the correlation coefficient. Conducting a test for significance using the correlation coefficient therefore is not necessary if a t or F test has already been conducted.

Exercises

Methods

SELF test

23. The data from exercise 1 follow.

x_i	1	2	3	4	5
y_i	3	7	5	11	14

a. Compute the mean square error using equation (14.15).
b. Compute the standard error of the estimate using equation (14.16).
c. Compute the estimated standard deviation of b_1 using equation (14.18).
d. Use the t test to test the following hypotheses ($\alpha = .05$):

$$H_0: \beta_1 = 0$$
$$H_a: \beta_1 \neq 0$$

e. Use the F test to test the hypotheses in part (d) at a .05 level of significance. Present the results in the analysis of variance table format.

24. The data from exercise 2 follow.

x_i	3	12	6	20	14
y_i	55	40	55	10	15

a. Compute the mean square error using equation (14.15).
b. Compute the standard error of the estimate using equation (14.16).
c. Compute the estimated standard deviation of b_1 using equation (14.18).
d. Use the t test to test the following hypotheses ($\alpha = .05$):

$$H_0: \beta_1 = 0$$
$$H_a: \beta_1 \neq 0$$

e. Use the F test to test the hypotheses in part (d) at a .05 level of significance. Present the results in the analysis of variance table format.

25. The data from exercise 3 follow.

x_i	2	6	9	13	20
y_i	7	18	9	26	23

a. What is the value of the standard error of the estimate?
b. Test for a significant relationship by using the t test. Use $\alpha = .05$.
c. Use the F test to test for a significant relationship. Use $\alpha = .05$. What is your conclusion?

Applications

SELF test

26. In exercise 18 the data on price ($) and the overall score for six stereo headphones tested by *Consumer Reports* were as follows (*Consumer Reports* website, March 5, 2012).

Brand	Price ($)	Score
Bose	180	76
Skullcandy	150	71
Koss	95	61
Phillips/O'Neill	70	56
Denon	70	40
JVC	35	26

a. Does the t test indicate a significant relationship between price and the overall score? What is your conclusion? Use $\alpha = .05$.
b. Test for a significant relationship using the F test. What is your conclusion? Use $\alpha = .05$.
c. Show the ANOVA table for these data.

27. The number of megapixels in a digital camera is one of the most important factors in determining picture quality. But, do digital cameras with more megapixels cost more? The following data show the number of megapixels and the price ($) for 10 digital cameras (*Consumer Reports,* March 2009).

WEB file

DigitalCameras

Brand and Model	Megapixels	Price ($)
Canon PowerShot SD1100 IS	8	180
Casio Exilim Card EX-510	10	200
Sony Cyber-shot DSC-T70	7	230
Pentax Optio M50	8	120
Canon PowerShot G10	15	470
Canon PowerShot A590 IS	8	140
Canon PowerShot E1	10	180
Fujifilm FinePix F00FD	12	310
Sony Cyber-shot DSC-W170	10	250
Canon PowerShot A470	7	110

a. Use these data to develop an estimated regression equation that can be used to predict the price of a digital camera given the number of megapixels.
b. At the .05 level of significance, are the number of megapixels and the price related? Explain.
c. Would you feel comfortable using the estimated regression equation developed in part (a) to predict the price of a digital camera given the number of megapixels? Explain.
d. The Canon Power Shot S95 digital camera has 10 megapixels. Predict the price of this camera using the estimated regression equation developed in part (a).

WEB file BrokerRatings

28. In exercise 8 ratings data on x = the quality of the speed of execution and y = overall satisfaction with electronic trades provided the estimated regression equation $\hat{y} = .2046 + .9077x$. At the .05 level of significance, test whether speed of execution and overall satisfaction are related. Show the ANOVA table. What is your conclusion?

29. Refer to exercise 21, where data on production volume and cost were used to develop an estimated regression equation relating production volume and cost for a particular manufacturing operation. Use $\alpha = .05$ to test whether the production volume is significantly related to the total cost. Show the ANOVA table. What is your conclusion?

30. Refer to excercise 5 where the following data were used to investigate whether higher prices are generally associated with higher ratings for elliptical trainers (*Consumer Reports,* February 2008).

WEB file Ellipticals

Brand and Model	Price ($)	Rating
Precor 5.31	3700	87
Keys Fitness CG2	2500	84
Octane Fitness Q37e	2800	82
LifeFitness X1 Basic	1900	74
NordicTrack AudioStrider 990	1000	73
Schwinn 430	800	69
Vision Fitness X6100	1700	68
ProForm XP 520 Razor	600	55

With x = price ($) and y = rating, the estimated regression equation is $\hat{y} = 58.158 + .008449x$. For these data, SSE = 173.88 and SST = 756. Does the evidence indicate a significant relationship between price and rating?

WEB file RacingBicycles

31. In exercise 20, data on x = weight (pounds) and y = price ($) for 10 road-racing bikes provided the estimated regression equation $\hat{y} = 28{,}574 - 1439x$. (*Bicycling* website, March 8, 2012). For these data SSE = 7,102,922.54 and SST = 52,120,800. Use the F test to determine whether the weight for a bike and the price are related at the .05 level of significance.

14.6 Using the Estimated Regression Equation for Estimation and Prediction

When using the simple linear regression model, we are making an assumption about the relationship between x and y. We then use the least squares method to obtain the estimated simple linear regression equation. If a significant relationship exists between x and y and the coefficient of determination shows that the fit is good, the estimated regression equation should be useful for estimation and prediction.

For the Armand's Pizza Parlors example, the estimated regression equation is $\hat{y} = 60 + 5x$. At the end of Section 14.1 we stated that $\hat{y}$ can be used as a *point estimator* of $E(y)$, the mean or expected value of y for a given value of x, and as a predictor of an individual value of y. For example, suppose Armand's managers want to estimate the mean quarterly sales for *all* restaurants located near college campuses with 10,000 students. Using the estimated regression equation $\hat{y} = 60 + 5x$, we see that for $x = 10$ (10,000 students), $\hat{y} = 60 + 5(10) = 110$. Thus, a *point estimate* of the mean quarterly sales for all restaurant locations near campuses with 10,000 students is \$110,000. In this case we are using $\hat{y}$ as the point estimator of the mean value of y when $x = 10$.

We can also use the estimated regression equation to *predict* an individual value of y for a given value of x. For example, to predict quarterly sales for a new restaurant Armand's is considering building near Talbot College, a campus with 10,000 students, we would compute $\hat{y} = 60 + 5(10) = 110$. Hence, we would predict quarterly sales of \$110,000 for such a new restaurant. In this case, we are using $\hat{y}$ as the *predictor* of y for a new observation when $x = 10$.

When we are using the estimated regression equation to estimate the mean value of y or to predict an individual value of y, it is clear that the estimate or prediction depends on the given value of x. For this reason, as we discuss in more depth the issues concerning estimation and prediction, the following notation will help clarify matters.

x^* = the given value of the independent variable x

y^* = the random variable denoting the possible values of the dependent variable y when $x = x^*$

$E(y^*)$ = the mean or expected value of the dependent variable y when $x = x^*$

$\hat{y}^* = b_0 + b_1x^*$ = the point estimator of $E(y^*)$ and the predictor of an individual value of y^* when $x = x^*$

To illustrate the use of this notation, suppose we want to estimate the mean value of quarterly sales for *all* Armand's restaurants located near a campus with 10,000 students. For this case, $x^* = 10$ and $E(y^*)$ denotes the unknown mean value of quarterly sales for all restaurants where $x^* = 10$. Thus, the point estimate of $E(y^*)$ is provided by $\hat{y}^* = 60 + 5(10) = 110$, or \$110,000. But, using this notation, $\hat{y}^* = 110$ is also the predictor of quarterly sales for the new restaurant located near Talbot College, a school with 10,000 students.

Interval Estimation

Confidence intervals and prediction intervals show the precision of the regression results. Narrower intervals provide a higher degree of precision.

Point estimators and predictors do not provide any information about the precision associated with the estimate and/or prediction. For that we must develop confidence intervals and prediction intervals. A **confidence interval** is an interval estimate of the *mean value of y* for a given value of x. A **prediction interval** is used whenever we want to *predict an individual value of y* for a new observation corresponding to a given value of x. Although the predictor of y for a given value of x is the same as the point estimator of the mean value of y for a given value of x, the interval estimates we obtain for the two cases are different. As we will show, the margin of error is larger for a prediction interval. We begin by showing how to develop an interval estimate of the mean value of y.

Confidence Interval for the Mean Value of y

In general, we cannot expect $\hat{y}^*$ to equal $E(y^*)$ exactly. If we want to make an inference about how close $\hat{y}^*$ is to the true mean value $E(y^*)$, we will have to estimate the variance of $\hat{y}^*$. The formula for estimating the variance of $\hat{y}^*$, denoted by $s^2_{\hat{y}^*}$, is

$$s^2_{\hat{y}^*} = s^2\left[\frac{1}{n} + \frac{(x^* - \bar{x})^2}{\Sigma(x_i - \bar{x})^2}\right] \qquad \textbf{(14.22)}$$

The estimate of the standard deviation of $\hat{y}^*$ is given by the square root of equation (14.22).

$$s_{\hat{y}^*} = s\sqrt{\frac{1}{n} + \frac{(x^* - \bar{x})^2}{\Sigma(x_i - \bar{x})^2}} \qquad \textbf{(14.23)}$$

The computational results for Armand's Pizza Parlors in Section 14.5 provided $s = 13.829$. With $x^* = 10$, $\bar{x} = 14$, and $\Sigma(x_i - \bar{x})^2 = 568$, we can use equation (14.23) to obtain

$$\begin{aligned} s_{\hat{y}^*} &= 13.829\sqrt{\frac{1}{10} + \frac{(10 - 14)^2}{568}} \\ &= 13.829\sqrt{.1282} = 4.95 \end{aligned}$$

The general expression for a confidence interval follows.

The margin of error associated with this confidence interval is $t_{\alpha/2}s_{\hat{y}^*}$.

CONFIDENCE INTERVAL FOR $E(y^*)$

$$\hat{y}^* \pm t_{\alpha/2}s_{\hat{y}^*} \qquad \textbf{(14.24)}$$

where the confidence coefficient is $1 - \alpha$ and $t_{\alpha/2}$ is based on the t distribution with $n - 2$ degrees of freedom.

Using expression (14.24) to develop a 95% confidence interval of the mean quarterly sales for all Armand's restaurants located near campuses with 10,000 students, we need the value of t for $\alpha/2 = .025$ and $n - 2 = 10 - 2 = 8$ degrees of freedom. Using Table 2 of Appendix B, we have $t_{.025} = 2.306$. Thus, with $\hat{y}^* = 110$ and a margin of error of $t_{\alpha/2}s_{\hat{y}^*} = 2.306(4.95) = 11.415$, the 95% confidence interval estimate is

$$110 \pm 11.415$$

In dollars, the 95% confidence interval for the mean quarterly sales of all restaurants near campuses with 10,000 students is \$110,000 ± \$11,415. Therefore, the 95% confidence interval for the mean quarterly sales when the student population is 10,000 is \$98,585 to \$121,415.

Note that the estimated standard deviation of $\hat{y}^*$ given by equation (14.23) is smallest when $x^* - \bar{x} = 0$. In this case the estimated standard deviation of $\hat{y}^*$ becomes

$$s_{\hat{y}^*} = s\sqrt{\frac{1}{n} + \frac{(\bar{x} - \bar{x})^2}{\Sigma(x_i - \bar{x})^2}} = s\sqrt{\frac{1}{n}}$$

This result implies that we can make the best or most precise estimate of the mean value of y whenever $x^* = \bar{x}$. In fact, the further x^* is from $\bar{x}$, the larger $x^* - \bar{x}$ becomes. As a result, the confidence interval for the mean value of y will become wider as x^* deviates more from $\bar{x}$. This pattern is shown graphically in Figure 14.8.

FIGURE 14.8 CONFIDENCE INTERVALS FOR THE MEAN SALES y AT GIVEN VALUES OF STUDENT POPULATION x

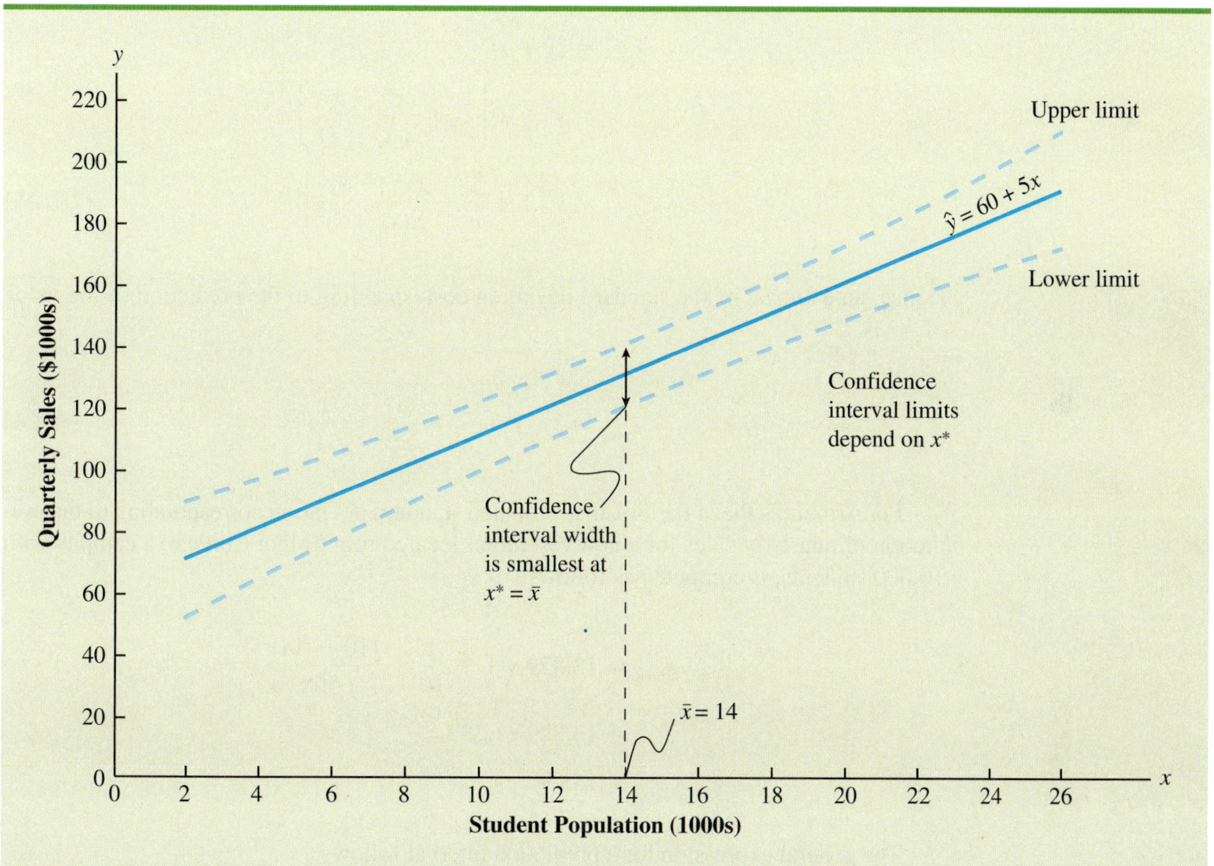

Prediction Interval for an Individual Value of y

Instead of estimating the mean value of quarterly sales for all Armand's restaurants located near campuses with 10,000 students, suppose we want to predict quarterly sales for a new restaurant Armand's is considering building near Talbot College, a campus with 10,000 students. As noted previously, the predictor of y^*, the value of y corresponding to the given x^*, is $\hat{y}^* = b_0 + b_1x^*$. For the new restaurant located near Talbot College, $x^* = 10$ and the prediction of quarterly sales is $\hat{y}^* = 60 + 5(10) = 110$, or \$110,000. Note that the prediction of quarterly sales for the new Armand's restaurant near Talbot College is the same as the point estimate of the mean sales for all Armand's restaurants located near campuses with 10,000 students.

To develop a prediction interval, let us first determine the variance associated with using $\hat{y}^*$ as a predictor of y when $x = x^*$. This variance is made up of the sum of the following two components.

1. The variance of the y^* values about the mean $E(y^*)$, an estimate of which is given by s^2
2. The variance associated with using $\hat{y}^*$ to estimate $E(y^*)$, an estimate of which is given by $s^2_{\hat{y}^*}$

The formula for estimating the variance corresponding to the prediction of the value of y when $x = x^*$, denoted s^2_{pred}, is

$$\begin{aligned} s^2_{\text{pred}} &= s^2 + s^2_{\hat{y}^*} \\ &= s^2 + s^2\left[\frac{1}{n} + \frac{(x^* - \bar{x})^2}{\Sigma(x_i - \bar{x})^2}\right] \\ &= s^2\left[1 + \frac{1}{n} + \frac{(x^* - \bar{x})^2}{\Sigma(x_i - \bar{x})^2}\right] \end{aligned} \tag{14.25}$$

Hence, an estimate of the standard deviation corresponding to the prediction of the value of y^* is

$$s_{\text{pred}} = s\sqrt{1 + \frac{1}{n} + \frac{(x^* - \bar{x})^2}{\Sigma(x_i - \bar{x})^2}} \tag{14.26}$$

For Armand's Pizza Parlors, the estimated standard deviation corresponding to the prediction of quarterly sales for a new restaurant located near Talbot College, a campus with 10,000 students, is computed as follows.

$$\begin{aligned} s_{\text{pred}} &= 13.829\sqrt{1 + \frac{1}{10} + \frac{(10 - 14)^2}{568}} \\ &= 13.829\sqrt{1.282} \\ &= 14.69 \end{aligned}$$

The general expression for a prediction interval follows.

The margin of error associated with this prediction interval is $t_{\alpha/2}s_{\text{pred}}$.

PREDICTION INTERVAL FOR y^*

$$\hat{y}^* \pm t_{\alpha/2}s_{\text{pred}} \tag{14.27}$$

where the confidence coefficient is $1 - \alpha$ and $t_{\alpha/2}$ is based on a t distribution with $n - 2$ degrees of freedom.

The 95% prediction interval for quarterly sales for the new Armand's restaurant located near Talbot College can be found using $t_{\alpha/2} = t_{.025} = 2.306$ and $s_{\text{pred}} = 14.69$. Thus, with $\hat{y}^* = 110$ and a margin of error of $t_{.025}s_{\text{pred}} = 2.306(14.69) = 33.875$, the 95% prediction interval is

$$110 \pm 33.875$$

In dollars, this prediction interval is \$110,000 ± \$33,875 or \$76,125 to \$143,875. Note that the prediction interval for the new restaurant located near Talbot College, a campus with 10,000 students, is wider than the confidence interval for the mean quarterly sales of all restaurants located near campuses with 10,000 students. The difference reflects the fact that we are able to estimate the mean value of y more precisely than we can predict an individual value of y.

FIGURE 14.9 CONFIDENCE AND PREDICTION INTERVALS FOR SALES y AT GIVEN VALUES OF STUDENT POPULATION x

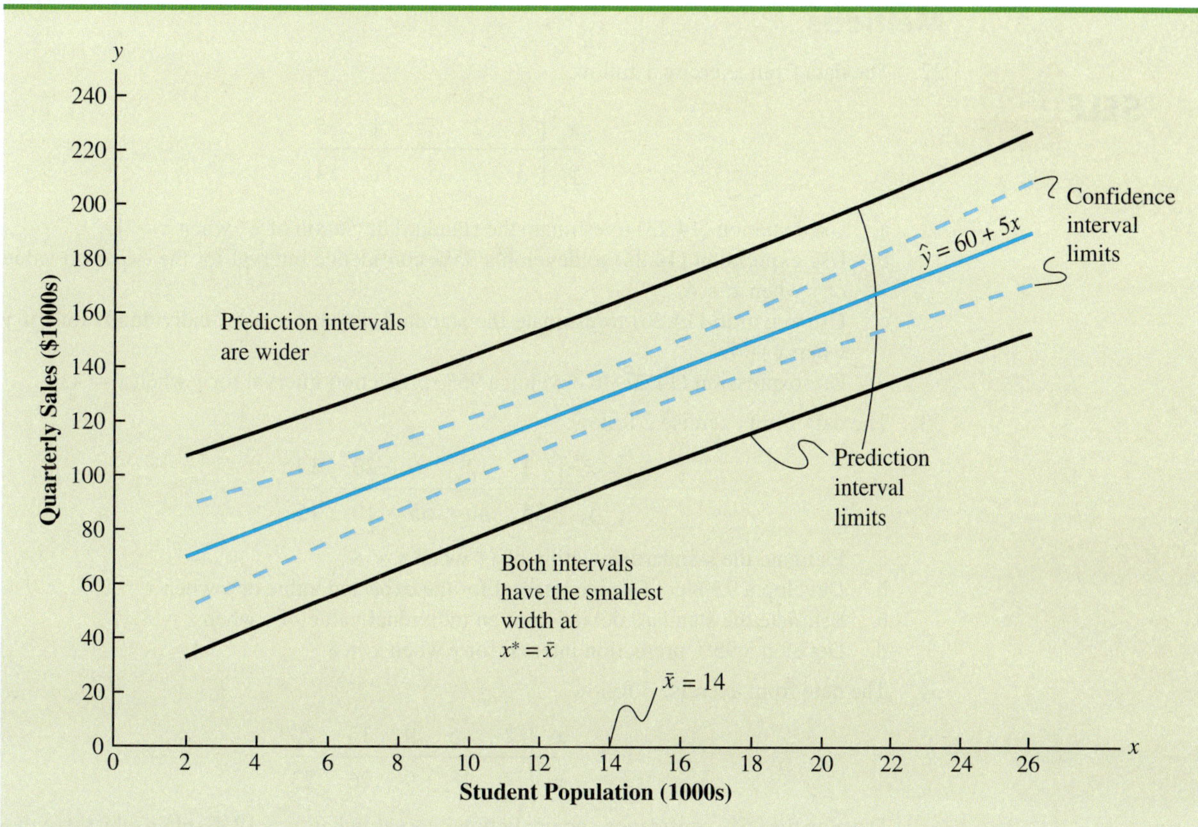

In general, the lines for the confidence interval limits and the prediction interval limits both have curvature.

Confidence intervals and prediction intervals are both more precise when the value of the independent variable x^* is closer to $\bar{x}$. The general shapes of confidence intervals and the wider prediction intervals are shown together in Figure 14.9.

NOTES AND COMMENTS

A prediction interval is used to predict the value of the dependent variable y for a *new observation*. As an illustration, we showed how to develop a prediction interval of quarterly sales for a new restaurant that Armand's is considering building near Talbot College, a campus with 10,000 students. The fact that the value of $x = 10$ is not one of the values of student population for the Armand's sample data in Table 14.1 is not meant to imply that prediction intervals cannot be developed for values of x in the sample data. But, for the ten restaurants that make up the data in Table 14.1, developing a prediction interval for quarterly sales for *one of these restaurants* does not make any sense because we already know the value of quarterly sales for each of these restaurants. In other words, a prediction interval only has meaning for something new, in this case a new observation corresponding to a particular value of x that may or may not equal one of the values of x in the sample.

Exercises

Methods

SELF test

32. The data from exercise 1 follow.

x_i	1	2	3	4	5
y_i	3	7	5	11	14

a. Use equation (14.23) to estimate the standard deviation of $\hat{y}^*$ when $x = 4$.
b. Use expression (14.24) to develop a 95% confidence interval for the expected value of y when $x = 4$.
c. Use equation (14.26) to estimate the standard deviation of an individual value of y when $x = 4$.
d. Use expression (14.27) to develop a 95% prediction interval for y when $x = 4$.

33. The data from exercise 2 follow.

x_i	3	12	6	20	14
y_i	55	40	55	10	15

a. Estimate the standard deviation of $\hat{y}^*$ when $x = 8$.
b. Develop a 95% confidence interval for the expected value of y when $x = 8$.
c. Estimate the standard deviation of an individual value of y when $x = 8$.
d. Develop a 95% prediction interval for y when $x = 8$.

34. The data from exercise 3 follow.

x_i	2	6	9	13	20
y_i	7	18	9	26	23

Develop the 95% confidence and prediction intervals when $x = 12$. Explain why these two intervals are different.

Applications

SELF test

35. The following data are the monthly salaries y and the grade point averages x for students who obtained a bachelor's degree in business administration.

GPA	Monthly Salary ($)
2.6	3600
3.4	3900
3.6	4300
3.2	3800
3.5	4200
2.9	3900

The estimated regression equation for these data is $\hat{y} = 2090.5 + 581.1x$ and MSE = 21,284.

a. Develop a point estimate of the starting salary for a student with a GPA of 3.0.
b. Develop a 95% confidence interval for the mean starting salary for all students with a 3.0 GPA.
c. Develop a 95% prediction interval for Ryan Dailey, a student with a GPA of 3.0.
d. Discuss the differences in your answers to parts (b) and (c).

WEB file

Sales

36. In exercise 7, the data on y = annual sales ($1000s) for new customer accounts and x = number of years of experience for a sample of 10 salespersons provided the estimated regression equation $\hat{y} = 80 + 4x$. For these data $\bar{x} = 7$, $\Sigma(x_i - \bar{x})^2 = 142$, and $s = 4.6098$.
    a. Develop a 95% confidence interval for the mean annual sales for all salespersons with nine years of experience.
    b. The company is considering hiring Tom Smart, a salesperson with nine years of experience. Develop a 95% prediction interval of annual sales for Tom Smart.
    c. Discuss the differences in your answers to parts (a) and (b).
37. In exercise 13, data were given on the adjusted gross income x and the amount of itemized deductions taken by taxpayers. Data were reported in thousands of dollars. With the estimated regression equation $\hat{y} = 4.68 + .16x$, the point estimate of a reasonable level of total itemized deductions for a taxpayer with an adjusted gross income of $52,500 is $13,080.
    a. Develop a 95% confidence interval for the mean amount of total itemized deductions for all taxpayers with an adjusted gross income of $52,500.
    b. Develop a 95% prediction interval estimate for the amount of total itemized deductions for a particular taxpayer with an adjusted gross income of $52,500.
    c. If the particular taxpayer referred to in part (b) claimed total itemized deductions of $20,400, would the IRS agent's request for an audit appear to be justified?
    d. Use your answer to part (b) to give the IRS agent a guideline as to the amount of total itemized deductions a taxpayer with an adjusted gross income of $52,500 should claim before an audit is recommended.
38. Refer to Exercise 21, where data on the production volume x and total cost y for a particular manufacturing operation were used to develop the estimated regression equation $\hat{y} = 1246.67 + 7.6x$.
    a. The company's production schedule shows that 500 units must be produced next month. What is the point estimate of the total cost for next month?
    b. Develop a 99% prediction interval for the total cost for next month.
    c. If an accounting cost report at the end of next month shows that the actual production cost during the month was $6000, should managers be concerned about incurring such a high total cost for the month? Discuss.
39. Almost all U.S. light-rail systems use electric cars that run on tracks built at street level. The Federal Transit Administration claims light-rail is one of the safest modes of travel, with an accident rate of .99 accidents per million passenger miles as compared to 2.29 for buses. The following data show the miles of track and the weekday ridership in thousands of passengers for six light-rail systems (*USA Today,* January 7, 2003).

City	Miles of Track	Ridership (1000s)
Cleveland	15	15
Denver	17	35
Portland	38	81
Sacramento	21	31
San Diego	47	75
San Jose	31	30
St. Louis	34	42

    a. Use these data to develop an estimated regression equation that could be used to predict the ridership given the miles of track.
    b. Did the estimated regression equation provide a good fit? Explain.
    c. Develop a 95% confidence interval for the mean weekday ridership for all light-rail systems with 30 miles of track.

d. Suppose that Charlotte is considering construction of a light-rail system with 30 miles of track. Develop a 95% prediction interval for the weekday ridership for the Charlotte system. Do you think that the prediction interval you developed would be of value to Charlotte planners in anticipating the number of weekday riders for their new light-rail system? Explain.

14.7 Computer Solution

Performing the regression analysis computations without the help of a computer can be quite time consuming. In this section we discuss how the computational burden can be minimized by using a computer software package such as Minitab.

We entered Armand's student population and sales data into a Minitab worksheet. The independent variable was named Pop and the dependent variable was named Sales to assist with interpretation of the computer output. Using Minitab, we obtained the printout for Armand's Pizza Parlors shown in Figure 14.10.[2] The interpretation of this printout follows.

1. Minitab prints the estimated regression equation as Sales = 60.0 + 5.00 Pop.
2. A table is printed that shows the values of the coefficients b_0 and b_1, the standard deviation of each coefficient, the t value obtained by dividing each coefficient value by its standard deviation, and the p-value associated with the t test. Because the p-value is zero (to three decimal places), the sample results indicate that the null hypothesis (H_0: $\beta_1 = 0$) should be rejected. Alternatively, we could compare 8.62 (located in the t-ratio column) to the appropriate critical value. This procedure for the t test was described in Section 14.5.

FIGURE 14.10 MINITAB OUTPUT FOR THE ARMAND'S PIZZA PARLORS PROBLEM

```
The regression equation is
Sales = 60.0 + 5.00 Pop           <---- Estimated regression equation

Predictor      Coef    SE Coef      T       p
Constant     60.000      9.226   6.50   0.000
Pop          5.0000     0.5803   8.62   0.000

S = 13.8293      R-Sq = 90.3%      R-Sq(adj) = 89.1%

Analysis of Variance

SOURCE            DF      SS      MS      F       p
Regression         1   14200   14200  74.25   0.000   <---- ANOVA table
Residual Error     8    1530     191
Total              9   15730

Predicted Values for New Observations

New Obs     Fit   SE Fit        95% C.I.          95% P.I.       <---- Interval estimates
      1  110.00     4.95  (98.58, 121.42)  (76.13, 143.87)
```

[2]The Minitab steps necessary to generate the output are given in Appendix 14.3.

3. Minitab prints the standard error of the estimate, $s = 13.8293$, as well as information about the goodness of fit. Note that "R-sq = 90.3%" is the coefficient of determination expressed as a percentage. The value "R-Sq(adj) = 89.1%" is discussed in Chapter 15.
4. The ANOVA table is printed below the heading Analysis of Variance. Minitab uses the label Residual Error for the error source of variation. Note that DF is an abbreviation for degrees of freedom and that MSR is given as 14,200 and MSE as 191. The ratio of these two values provides the F value of 74.25 and the corresponding p-value of 0.000. Because the p-value is zero (to three decimal places), the relationship between Sales and Pop is judged statistically significant.
5. The 95% confidence interval estimate of the expected sales and the 95% prediction interval estimate of sales for an individual restaurant located near a campus with 10,000 students are printed below the ANOVA table. The confidence interval is (98.58, 121.42) and the prediction interval is (76.13, 143.87) as we showed in Section 14.6.

Exercises

Applications

SELF test

40. The commercial division of a real estate firm is conducting a regression analysis of the relationship between x, annual gross rents (in thousands of dollars), and y, selling price (in thousands of dollars) for apartment buildings. Data were collected on several properties recently sold and the following computer output was obtained.

```
The regression equation is
Y = 20.0 + 7.21 X

Predictor      Coef    SE Coef      T
Constant     20.000     3.2213   6.21
X             7.210     1.3626   5.29

Analysis of Variance

SOURCE            DF         SS
Regression         1    41587.3
Residual Error     7
Total              8    51984.1
```

a. How many apartment buildings were in the sample?
b. Write the estimated regression equation.
c. What is the value of s_{b_1}?
d. Use the F statistic to test the significance of the relationship at a .05 level of significance.
e. Predict the selling price of an apartment building with gross annual rents of $50,000.

41. Following is a portion of the computer output for a regression analysis relating y = maintenance expense (dollars per month) to x = usage (hours per week) of a particular brand of computer terminal.

```
The regression equation is
Y = 6.1092 + .8951 X

Predictor        Coef     SE Coef
Constant       6.1092      0.9361
X              0.8951      0.1490

Analysis of Variance

SOURCE              DF        SS         MS
Regression           1    1575.76    1575.76
Residual Error       8     349.14      43.64
Total                9    1924.90
```

a. Write the estimated regression equation.
b. Use a t test to determine whether monthly maintenance expense is related to usage at the .05 level of significance.
c. Use the estimated regression equation to predict monthly maintenance expense for any terminal that is used 25 hours per week.

42. A regression model relating x, number of salespersons at a branch office, to y, annual sales at the office (in thousands of dollars) provided the following computer output from a regression analysis of the data.

```
The regression equation is
Y = 80.0 + 50.00 X

Predictor        Coef     SE Coef        T
Constant         80.0      11.333     7.06
X                50.0       5.482     9.12

Analysis of Variance

SOURCE              DF        SS         MS
Regression           1    6828.6     6828.6
Residual Error      28    2298.8       82.1
Total               29    9127.4
```

a. Write the estimated regression equation.
b. How many branch offices were involved in the study?
c. Compute the F statistic and test the significance of the relationship at a .05 level of significance.
d. Predict the annual sales at the Memphis branch office. This branch employs 12 salespersons.

43. Out-of-state tuition and fees at the top graduate schools of business can be very expensive, but the starting salary and bonus paid to graduates from many of these schools can be substantial. The following data show the out-of-state tuition and fees (rounded to the nearest \$1000) and the average starting salary and bonus paid to recent graduates (rounded to the nearest \$1000) for a sample of 20 graduate schools of business (*U.S. News & World Report 2009 Edition America's Best Graduate Schools*).

WEB file BusinessSchools

School	Tuition & Fees ($1000s)	Salary & Bonus ($1000s)
Arizona State University	28	98
Babson College	35	94
Cornell University	44	119
Georgetown University	40	109
Georgia Institute of Technology	30	88
Indiana University—Bloomington	35	105
Michigan State University	26	99
Northwestern University	44	123
Ohio State University	35	97
Purdue University—West Lafayette	33	96
Rice University	36	102
Stanford University	46	135
University of California—Davis	35	89
University of Florida	23	71
University of Iowa	25	78
University of Minnesota—Twin Cities	37	100
University of Notre Dame	36	95
University of Rochester	38	99
University of Washington	30	94
University of Wisconsin—Madison	27	93

a. Develop a scatter diagram with salary and bonus as the dependent variable.
b. Does there appear to be any relationship between these variables? Explain.
c. Develop an estimated regression equation that can be used to predict the starting salary and bonus paid to graduates given the cost of out-of-state tuition and fees at the school.
d. Test for a significant relationship at the .05 level of significance. What is your conclusion?
e. Did the estimated regression equation provide a good fit? Explain.
f. Suppose that we randomly select a recent graduate of the University of Virginia graduate school of business. The school has an out-of-state tuition and fees of $43,000. Predict the starting salary and bonus for this graduate.

44. Automobile racing, high-performance driving schools, and driver education programs run by automobile clubs continue to grow in popularity. All these activities require the participant to wear a helmet that is certified by the Snell Memorial Foundation, a not-for-profit organization dedicated to research, education, testing, and development of helmet safety standards. Snell "SA" (Sports Application) rated professional helmets are designed for auto racing and provide extreme impact resistance and high fire protection. One of the key factors in selecting a helmet is weight, since lower weight helmets tend to place less stress on the neck. The following data show the weight and price for 18 SA helmets (SoloRacer website, April 20, 2008).

WEB file RaceHelmets

Helmet	Weight (oz)	Price ($)
Pyrotect Pro Airflow	64	248
Pyrotect Pro Airflow Graphics	64	278
RCi Full Face	64	200
RaceQuip RidgeLine	64	200
HJC AR-10	58	300
HJC Si-12	47	700

(*continued*)

Helmet	Weight (oz)	Price ($)
HJC HX-10	49	900
Impact Racing Super Sport	59	340
Zamp FSA-1	66	199
Zamp RZ-2	58	299
Zamp RZ-2 Ferrari	58	299
Zamp RZ-3 Sport	52	479
Zamp RZ-3 Sport Painted	52	479
Bell M2	63	369
Bell M4	62	369
Bell M4 Pro	54	559
G Force Pro Force 1	63	250
G Force Pro Force 1 Grafx	63	280

a. Develop a scatter diagram with weight as the independent variable.
b. Does there appear to be any relationship between these two variables?
c. Develop the estimated regression equation that could be used to predict the price given the weight.
d. Test for the significance of the relationship at the .05 level of significance.
e. Did the estimated regression equation provide a good fit? Explain.

14.8 Residual Analysis: Validating Model Assumptions

Residual analysis *is the primary tool for determining whether the assumed regression model is appropriate.*

As we noted previously, the *residual* for observation *i* is the difference between the observed value of the dependent variable (y_i) and the predicted value of the dependent variable ($\hat{y}_i$).

RESIDUAL FOR OBSERVATION *i*

$$y_i - \hat{y}_i \qquad \textbf{(14.28)}$$

where

y_i is the observed value of the dependent variable
$\hat{y}_i$ is the predicted value of the dependent variable

In other words, the *i*th residual is the error resulting from using the estimated regression equation to predict the value of the dependent variable. The residuals for the Armand's Pizza Parlors example are computed in Table 14.7. The observed values of the dependent variable are in the second column and the predicted values of the dependent variable, obtained using the estimated regression equation $\hat{y} = 60 + 5x$, are in the third column. An analysis of the corresponding residuals in the fourth column will help determine whether the assumptions made about the regression model are appropriate.

Let us now review the regression assumptions for the Armand's Pizza Parlors example. A simple linear regression model was assumed.

$$y = \beta_0 + \beta_1 x + \epsilon \qquad \textbf{(14.29)}$$

TABLE 14.7 RESIDUALS FOR ARMAND'S PIZZA PARLORS

Student Population x_i	Sales y_i	Predicted Sales $\hat{y}_i = 60 + 5x_i$	Residuals $y_i - \hat{y}_i$
2	58	70	−12
6	105	90	15
8	88	100	−12
8	118	100	18
12	117	120	−3
16	137	140	−3
20	157	160	−3
20	169	160	9
22	149	170	−21
26	202	190	12

This model indicates that we assumed quarterly sales (y) to be a linear function of the size of the student population (x) plus an error term ϵ. In Section 14.4 we made the following assumptions about the error term ϵ.

1. $E(\epsilon) = 0$.
2. The variance of ϵ, denoted by σ^2, is the same for all values of x.
3. The values of ϵ are independent.
4. The error term ϵ has a normal distribution.

These assumptions provide the theoretical basis for the t test and the F test used to determine whether the relationship between x and y is significant, and for the confidence and prediction interval estimates presented in Section 14.6. If the assumptions about the error term ϵ appear questionable, the hypothesis tests about the significance of the regression relationship and the interval estimation results may not be valid.

The residuals provide the best information about ϵ; hence an analysis of the residuals is an important step in determining whether the assumptions for ϵ are appropriate. Much of residual analysis is based on an examination of graphical plots. In this section, we discuss the following residual plots.

1. A plot of the residuals against values of the independent variable x
2. A plot of residuals against the predicted values of the dependent variable y
3. A standardized residual plot
4. A normal probability plot

Residual Plot Against x

A **residual plot** against the independent variable x is a graph in which the values of the independent variable are represented by the horizontal axis and the corresponding residual values are represented by the vertical axis. A point is plotted for each residual. The first coordinate for each point is given by the value of x_i and the second coordinate is given by the corresponding value of the residual $y_i - \hat{y}_i$. For a residual plot against x with the Armand's Pizza Parlors data from Table 14.7, the coordinates of the first point are (2, −12), corresponding to $x_1 = 2$ and $y_1 - \hat{y}_1 = -12$; the coordinates of the second point are (6, 15), corresponding to $x_2 = 6$ and $y_2 - \hat{y}_2 = 15$; and so on. Figure 14.11 shows the resulting residual plot.

Before interpreting the results for this residual plot, let us consider some general patterns that might be observed in any residual plot. Three examples appear in Figure 14.12. If the assumption that the variance of ϵ is the same for all values of x and the assumed regression model is an adequate representation of the relationship between the variables, the

FIGURE 14.11 PLOT OF THE RESIDUALS AGAINST THE INDEPENDENT VARIABLE x FOR ARMAND'S PIZZA PARLORS

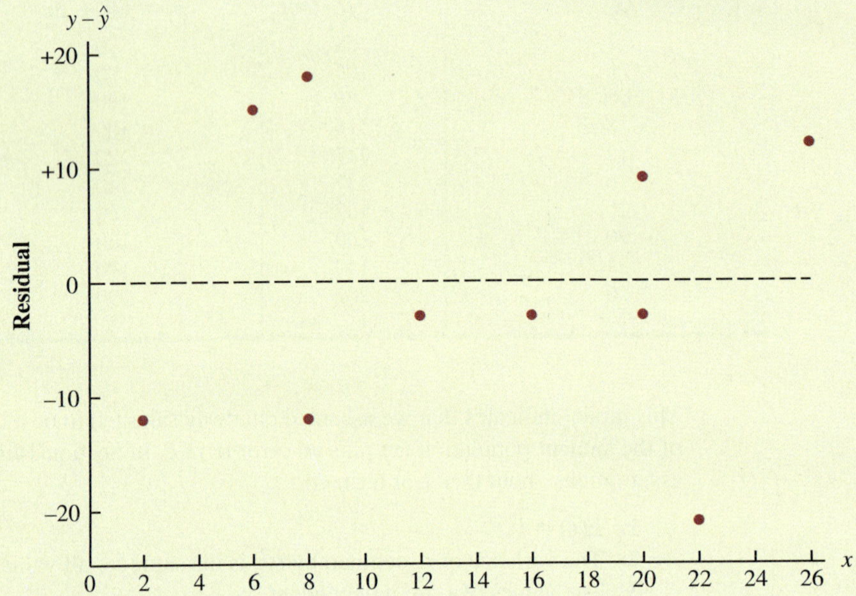

residual plot should give an overall impression of a horizontal band of points such as the one in Panel A of Figure 14.12. However, if the variance of ϵ is not the same for all values of x—for example, if variability about the regression line is greater for larger values of x—a pattern such as the one in Panel B of Figure 14.12 could be observed. In this case, the assumption of a constant variance of ϵ is violated. Another possible residual plot is shown in Panel C. In this case, we would conclude that the assumed regression model is not an adequate representation of the relationship between the variables. A curvilinear regression model or multiple regression model should be considered.

Now let us return to the residual plot for Armand's Pizza Parlors shown in Figure 14.11. The residuals appear to approximate the horizontal pattern in Panel A of Figure 14.12. Hence, we conclude that the residual plot does not provide evidence that the assumptions made for Armand's regression model should be challenged. At this point, we are confident in the conclusion that Armand's simple linear regression model is valid.

Experience and good judgment are always factors in the effective interpretation of residual plots. Seldom does a residual plot conform precisely to one of the patterns in Figure 14.12. Yet analysts who frequently conduct regression studies and frequently review residual plots become adept at understanding the differences between patterns that are reasonable and patterns that indicate the assumptions of the model should be questioned. A residual plot provides one technique to assess the validity of the assumptions for a regression model.

Residual Plot Against $\hat{y}$

Another residual plot represents the predicted value of the dependent variable $\hat{y}$ on the horizontal axis and the residual values on the vertical axis. A point is plotted for each residual. The first coordinate for each point is given by $\hat{y}_i$ and the second coordinate is given by the

FIGURE 14.12 RESIDUAL PLOTS FROM THREE REGRESSION STUDIES

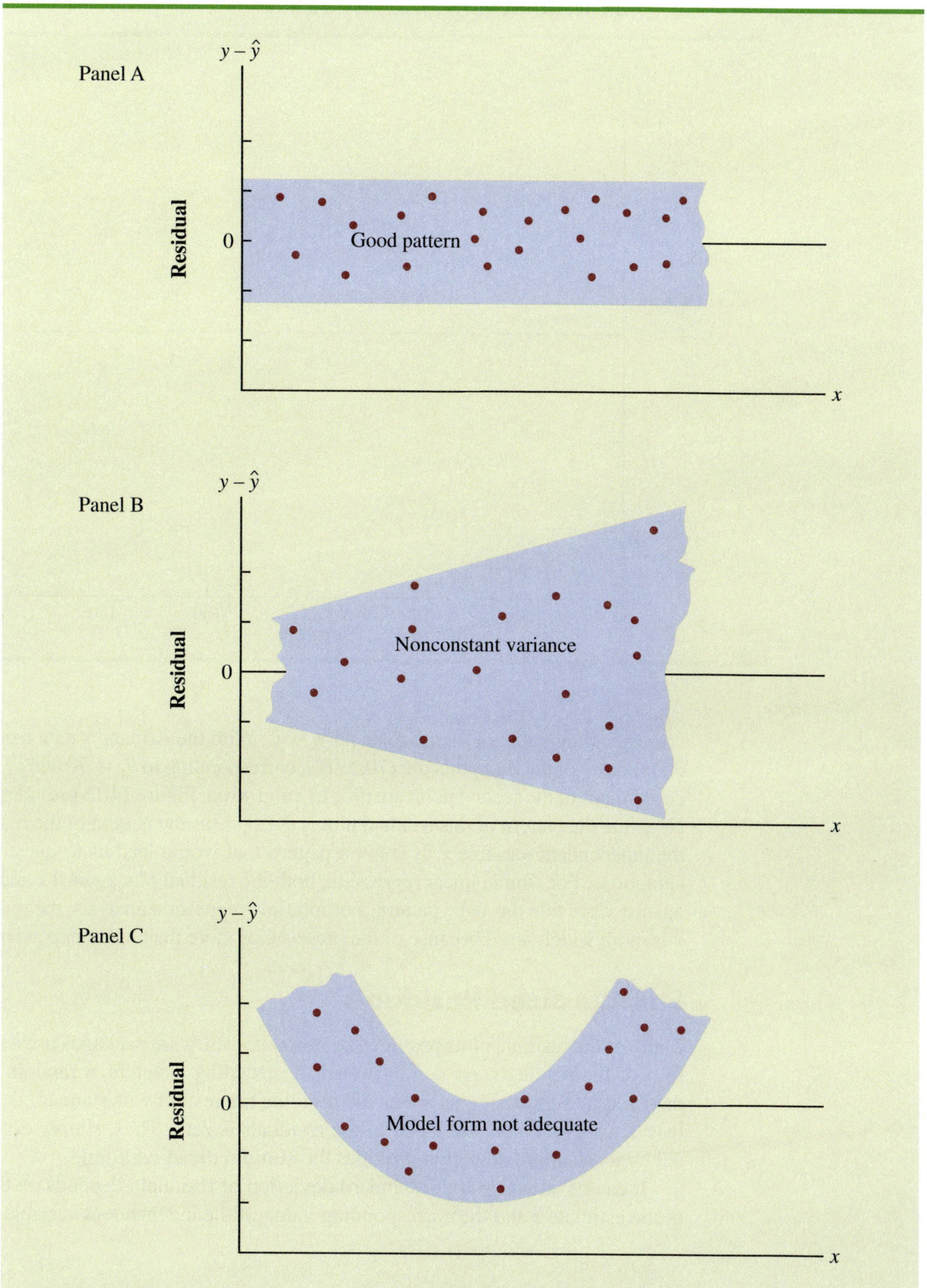

FIGURE 14.13 PLOT OF THE RESIDUALS AGAINST THE PREDICTED VALUES $\hat{y}$ FOR ARMAND'S PIZZA PARLORS

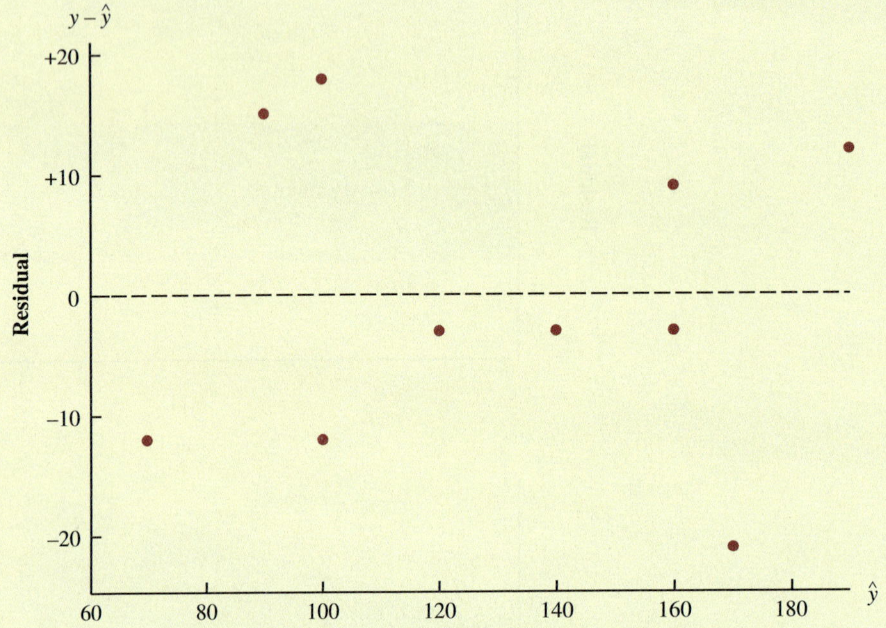

corresponding value of the ith residual $y_i - \hat{y}_i$. With the Armand's data from Table 14.7, the coordinates of the first point are $(70, -12)$, corresponding to $\hat{y}_1 = 70$ and $y_1 - \hat{y}_1 = -12$; the coordinates of the second point are (90, 15); and so on. Figure 14.13 provides the residual plot. Note that the pattern of this residual plot is the same as the pattern of the residual plot against the independent variable x. It is not a pattern that would lead us to question the model assumptions. For simple linear regression, both the residual plot against x and the residual plot against $\hat{y}$ provide the same pattern. For multiple regression analysis, the residual plot against $\hat{y}$ is more widely used because of the presence of more than one independent variable.

Standardized Residuals

Many of the residual plots provided by computer software packages use a standardized version of the residuals. As demonstrated in preceding chapters, a random variable is standardized by subtracting its mean and dividing the result by its standard deviation. With the least squares method, the mean of the residuals is zero. Thus, simply dividing each residual by its standard deviation provides the **standardized residual**.

It can be shown that the standard deviation of residual i depends on the standard error of the estimate s and the corresponding value of the independent variable x_i.

STANDARD DEVIATION OF THE ith RESIDUAL[3]

$$s_{y_i - \hat{y}_i} = s\sqrt{1 - h_i} \qquad \textbf{(14.30)}$$

[3]This equation actually provides an estimate of the standard deviation of the ith residual, because s is used instead of σ.

where

$$s_{y_i - \hat{y}_i} = \text{the standard deviation of residual } i$$
$$s = \text{the standard error of the estimate}$$
$$h_i = \frac{1}{n} + \frac{(x_i - \bar{x})^2}{\Sigma(x_i - \bar{x})^2} \quad \textbf{(14.31)}$$

Note that equation (14.30) shows that the standard deviation of the ith residual depends on x_i because of the presence of h_i in the formula.[4] Once the standard deviation of each residual is calculated, we can compute the standardized residual by dividing each residual by its corresponding standard deviation.

STANDARDIZED RESIDUAL FOR OBSERVATION i

$$\frac{y_i - \hat{y}_i}{s_{y_i - \hat{y}_i}} \quad \textbf{(14.32)}$$

Table 14.8 shows the calculation of the standardized residuals for Armand's Pizza Parlors. Recall that previous calculations showed $s = 13.829$. Figure 14.14 is the plot of the standardized residuals against the independent variable x.

Small departures from normality do not have a great effect on the statistical tests used in regression analysis.

The standardized residual plot can provide insight about the assumption that the error term ϵ has a normal distribution. If this assumption is satisfied, the distribution of the standardized residuals should appear to come from a standard normal probability distribution.[5] Thus, when looking at a standardized residual plot, we should expect to see approximately 95% of the standardized residuals between -2 and $+2$. We see in Figure 14.14 that for the

TABLE 14.8 COMPUTATION OF STANDARDIZED RESIDUALS FOR ARMAND'S PIZZA PARLORS

Restaurant i	x_i	$x_i - \bar{x}$	$(x_i - \bar{x})^2$	$\frac{(x_i - \bar{x})^2}{\Sigma(x_i - \bar{x})^2}$	h_i	$s_{y_i - \hat{y}_i}$	$y_i - \hat{y}_i$	Standardized Residual
1	2	−12	144	.2535	.3535	11.1193	−12	−1.0792
2	6	−8	64	.1127	.2127	12.2709	15	1.2224
3	8	−6	36	.0634	.1634	12.6493	−12	−.9487
4	8	−6	36	.0634	.1634	12.6493	18	1.4230
5	12	−2	4	.0070	.1070	13.0682	−3	−.2296
6	16	2	4	.0070	.1070	13.0682	−3	−.2296
7	20	6	36	.0634	.1634	12.6493	−3	−.2372
8	20	6	36	.0634	.1634	12.6493	9	.7115
9	22	8	64	.1127	.2127	12.2709	−21	−1.7114
10	26	12	144	.2535	.3535	11.1193	12	1.0792
		Total	568					

Note: The values of the residuals were computed in Table 14.7.

[4] h_i is referred to as the *leverage* of observation i. Leverage will be discussed further when we consider influential observations in Section 14.9.

[5] Because s is used instead of σ in equation (14.30), the probability distribution of the standardized residuals is not technically normal. However, in most regression studies, the sample size is large enough that a normal approximation is very good.

FIGURE 14.14 PLOT OF THE STANDARDIZED RESIDUALS AGAINST THE INDEPENDENT VARIABLE x FOR ARMAND'S PIZZA PARLORS

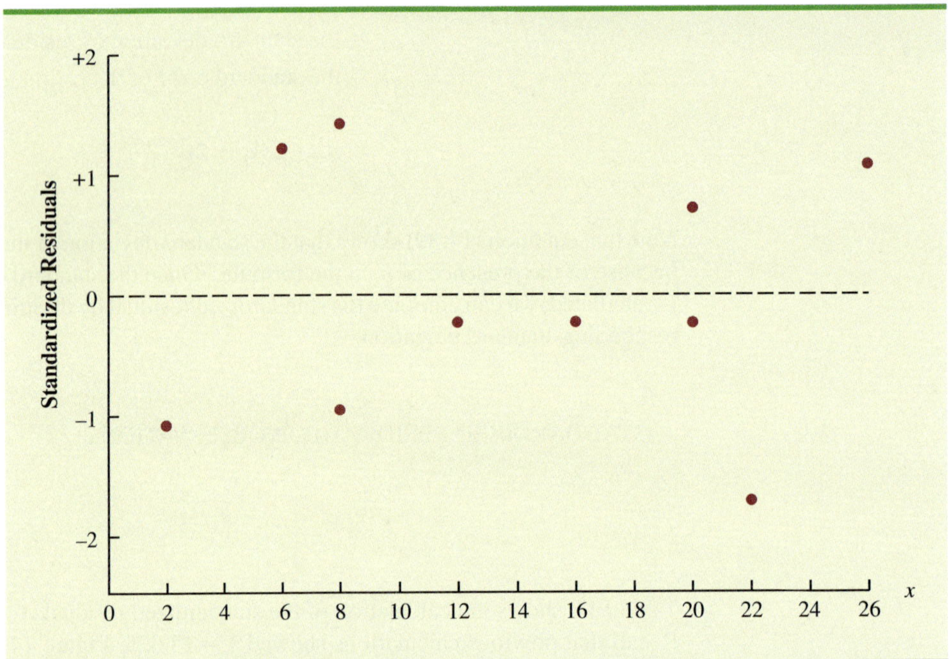

TABLE 14.9

NORMAL SCORES FOR $n = 10$

Order Statistic	Normal Score
1	−1.55
2	−1.00
3	−.65
4	−.37
5	−.12
6	.12
7	.37
8	.65
9	1.00
10	1.55

TABLE 14.10

NORMAL SCORES AND ORDERED STANDARDIZED RESIDUALS FOR ARMAND'S PIZZA PARLORS

Normal Scores	Ordered Standardized Residuals
−1.55	−1.7114
−1.00	−1.0792
−.65	−.9487
−.37	−.2372
−.12	−.2296
.12	−.2296
.37	.7115
.65	1.0792
1.00	1.2224
1.55	1.4230

Armand's example all standardized residuals are between −2 and +2. Therefore, on the basis of the standardized residuals, this plot gives us no reason to question the assumption that ϵ has a normal distribution.

Because of the effort required to compute the estimated values of $\hat{y}$, the residuals, and the standardized residuals, most statistical packages provide these values as optional regression output. Hence, residual plots can be easily obtained. For large problems computer packages are the only practical means for developing the residual plots discussed in this section.

Normal Probability Plot

Another approach for determining the validity of the assumption that the error term has a normal distribution is the **normal probability plot**. To show how a normal probability plot is developed, we introduce the concept of *normal scores*.

Suppose 10 values are selected randomly from a normal probability distribution with a mean of zero and a standard deviation of one, and that the sampling process is repeated over and over with the values in each sample of 10 ordered from smallest to largest. For now, let us consider only the smallest value in each sample. The random variable representing the smallest value obtained in repeated sampling is called the first-order statistic.

Statisticians show that for samples of size 10 from a standard normal probability distribution, the expected value of the first-order statistic is −1.55. This expected value is called a normal score. For the case with a sample of size $n = 10$, there are 10 order statistics and 10 normal scores (see Table 14.9). In general, a data set consisting of n observations will have n order statistics and hence n normal scores.

Let us now show how the 10 normal scores can be used to determine whether the standardized residuals for Armand's Pizza Parlors appear to come from a standard normal probability distribution. We begin by ordering the 10 standardized residuals from Table 14.8. The 10 normal scores and the ordered standardized residuals are shown together in Table 14.10. If the normality assumption is satisfied, the smallest standardized residual should be close to the smallest normal score, the next smallest standardized residual should be close to the next smallest normal

FIGURE 14.15 NORMAL PROBABILITY PLOT FOR ARMAND'S PIZZA PARLORS

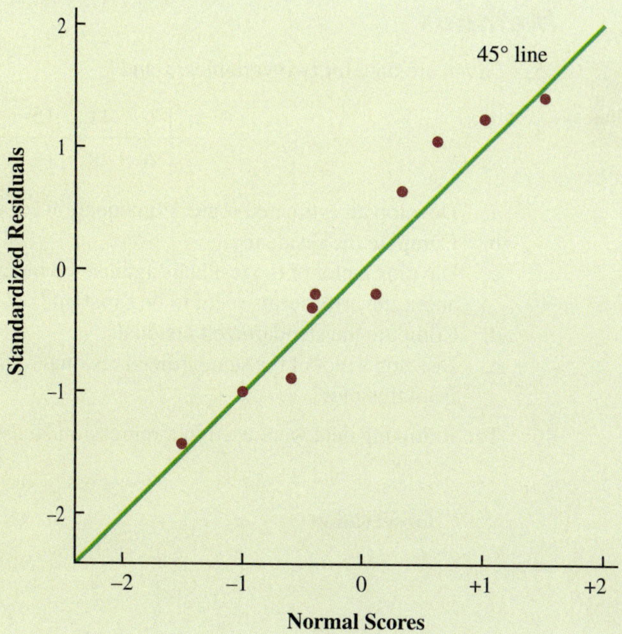

score, and so on. If we were to develop a plot with the normal scores on the horizontal axis and the corresponding standardized residuals on the vertical axis, the plotted points should cluster closely around a 45-degree line passing through the origin if the standardized residuals are approximately normally distributed. Such a plot is referred to as a *normal probability plot.*

Figure 14.15 is the normal probability plot for the Armand's Pizza Parlors example. Judgment is used to determine whether the pattern observed deviates from the line enough to conclude that the standardized residuals are not from a standard normal probability distribution. In Figure 14.15, we see that the points are grouped closely about the line. We therefore conclude that the assumption of the error term having a normal probability distribution is reasonable. In general, the more closely the points are clustered about the 45-degree line, the stronger the evidence supporting the normality assumption. Any substantial curvature in the normal probability plot is evidence that the residuals have not come from a normal distribution. Normal scores and the associated normal probability plot can be obtained easily from statistical packages such as Minitab.

NOTES AND COMMENTS

1. We use residual and normal probability plots to validate the assumptions of a regression model. If our review indicates that one or more assumptions are questionable, a different regression model or a transformation of the data should be considered. The appropriate corrective action when the assumptions are violated must be based on good judgment; recommendations from an experienced statistician can be valuable.
2. Analysis of residuals is the primary method statisticians use to verify that the assumptions associated with a regression model are valid. Even if no violations are found, it does not necessarily follow that the model will yield good predictions. However, if additional statistical tests support the conclusion of significance and the coefficient of determination is large, we should be able to develop good estimates and predictions using the estimated regression equation.

Exercises

Methods

SELF test

45. Given are data for two variables, x and y.

x_i	6	11	15	18	20
y_i	6	8	12	20	30

a. Develop an estimated regression equation for these data.
b. Compute the residuals.
c. Develop a plot of the residuals against the independent variable x. Do the assumptions about the error terms seem to be satisfied?
d. Compute the standardized residuals.
e. Develop a plot of the standardized residuals against $\hat{y}$. What conclusions can you draw from this plot?

46. The following data were used in a regression study.

Observation	x_i	y_i	Observation	x_i	y_i
1	2	4	6	7	6
2	3	5	7	7	9
3	4	4	8	8	5
4	5	6	9	9	11
5	7	4			

a. Develop an estimated regression equation for these data.
b. Construct a plot of the residuals. Do the assumptions about the error term seem to be satisfied?

Applications

SELF test

47. Data on advertising expenditures and revenue (in thousands of dollars) for the Four Seasons Restaurant follow.

Advertising Expenditures	Revenue
1	19
2	32
4	44
6	40
10	52
14	53
20	54

a. Let x equal advertising expenditures and y equal revenue. Use the method of least squares to develop a straight line approximation of the relationship between the two variables.
b. Test whether revenue and advertising expenditures are related at a .05 level of significance.
c. Prepare a residual plot of $y - \hat{y}$ versus $\hat{y}$. Use the result from part (a) to obtain the values of $\hat{y}$.
d. What conclusions can you draw from residual analysis? Should this model be used, or should we look for a better one?

48. Refer to exercise 7, where an estimated regression equation relating years of experience and annual sales was developed.
    a. Compute the residuals and construct a residual plot for this problem.
    b. Do the assumptions about the error terms seem reasonable in light of the residual plot?

49. Recent family home sales in San Antonio provided the following data (San Antonio Realty Watch website, November 2008).

WEB file

HomePrices

Square Footage	Price ($)
1580	142,500
1572	145,000
1352	115,000
2224	155,900
1556	95,000
1435	128,000
1438	100,000
1089	55,000
1941	142,000
1698	115,000
1539	115,000
1364	105,000
1979	155,000
2183	132,000
2096	140,000
1400	85,000
2372	145,000
1752	155,000
1386	80,000
1163	100,000

    a. Develop the estimated regression equation that can be used to predict the sales prices given the square footage.
    b. Construct a residual plot of the standardized residuals against the independent variable.
    c. Do the assumptions about the error term and model form seem reasonable in light of the residual plot?

14.9 Residual Analysis: Outliers and Influential Observations

In Section 14.8 we showed how residual analysis could be used to determine when violations of assumptions about the regression model occur. In this section, we discuss how residual analysis can be used to identify observations that can be classified as outliers or as being especially influential in determining the estimated regression equation. Some steps that should be taken when such observations occur are discussed.

Detecting Outliers

Figure 14.16 is a scatter diagram for a data set that contains an **outlier**, a data point (observation) that does not fit the trend shown by the remaining data. Outliers represent observations that are suspect and warrant careful examination. They may represent erroneous data; if so, the data should be corrected. They may signal a violation of model assumptions; if so, another model should be considered. Finally, they may simply be unusual values that occurred by chance. In this case, they should be retained.

FIGURE 14.16 DATA SET WITH AN OUTLIER

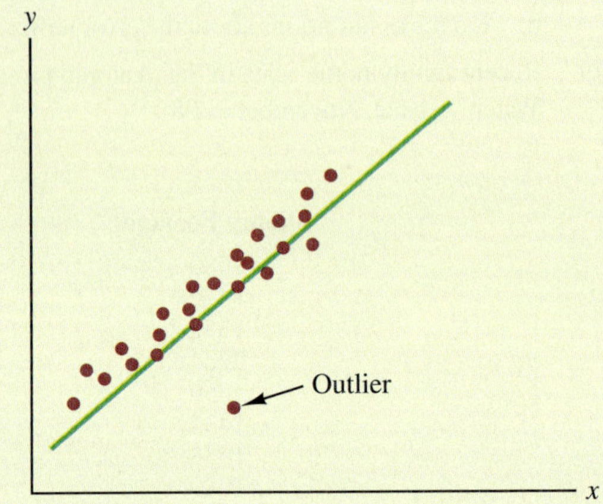

TABLE 14.11

DATA SET ILLUSTRATING THE EFFECT OF AN OUTLIER

x_i	y_i
1	45
1	55
2	50
3	75
3	40
3	45
4	30
4	35
5	25
6	15

To illustrate the process of detecting outliers, consider the data set in Table 14.11; Figure 14.17 is a scatter diagram. Except for observation 4 ($x_4 = 3$, $y_4 = 75$), a pattern suggesting a negative linear relationship is apparent. Indeed, given the pattern of the rest of the data, we would expect y_4 to be much smaller and hence would identify the corresponding observation as an outlier. For the case of simple linear regression, one can often detect outliers by simply examining the scatter diagram.

The standardized residuals can also be used to identify outliers. If an observation deviates greatly from the pattern of the rest of the data (e.g., the outlier in Figure 14.16), the corresponding standardized residual will be large in absolute value. Many computer packages automatically identify observations with standardized residuals that are large in absolute value. In Figure 14.18 we show the Minitab output from a regression analysis of the data in Table 14.11. The next to last line of the output shows that the standardized residual for observation 4 is 2.67. Minitab provides a list of each observation with a standardized residual

FIGURE 14.17 SCATTER DIAGRAM FOR OUTLIER DATA SET

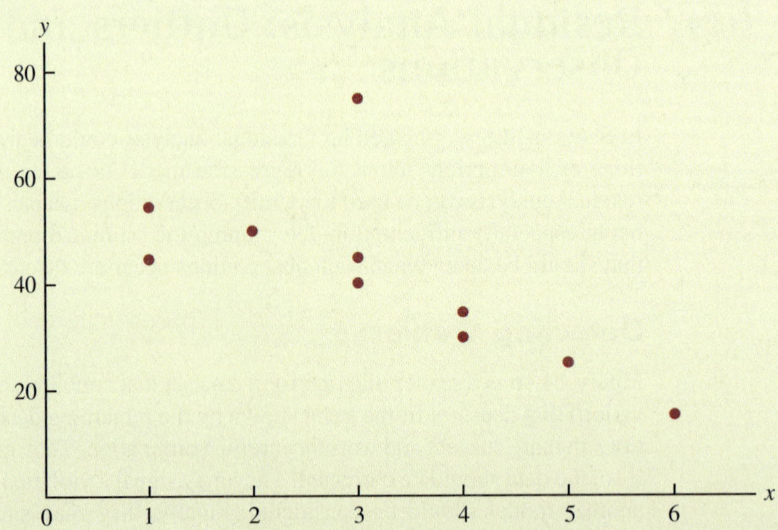

FIGURE 14.18 MINITAB OUTPUT FOR REGRESSION ANALYSIS OF THE OUTLIER DATA SET

```
The regression equation is
y = 65.0 - 7.33 x

Predictor    Coef  SE Coef      T      p
Constant   64.958    9.258   7.02  0.000
X          -7.331    2.608  -2.81  0.023

S = 12.6704   R-Sq = 49.7%   R-Sq(adj) = 43.4%

Analysis of Variance

SOURCE          DF      SS      MS     F      p
Regression       1  1268.2  1268.2  7.90  0.023
Residual Error   8  1284.3   160.5
Total            9  2552.5

Unusual Observations
Obs     x      y    Fit  SE Fit  Residual  St Resid
  4  3.00  75.00  42.97    4.04     32.03     2.67R

R denotes an observation with a large standardized residual.
```

of less than -2 or greater than $+2$ in the Unusual Observation section of the output; in such cases, the observation is printed on a separate line with an R next to the standardized residual, as shown in Figure 14.18. With normally distributed errors, standardized residuals should be outside these limits approximately 5% of the time.

In deciding how to handle an outlier, we should first check to see whether it is a valid observation. Perhaps an error was made in initially recording the data or in entering the data into the computer file. For example, suppose that in checking the data for the outlier in Table 14.17, we find an error; the correct value for observation 4 is $x_4 = 3$, $y_4 = 30$. Figure 14.19 is the Minitab output obtained after correction of the value of y_4. We see that

FIGURE 14.19 MINITAB OUTPUT FOR THE REVISED OUTLIER DATA SET

```
The regression equation is
Y = 59.2 - 6.95 X

Predictor    Coef  SE Coef      T      p
Constant   59.237    3.835  15.45  0.000
X          -6.949    1.080  -6.43  0.000

S = 5.24808   R-Sq = 83.8%   R-Sq(adj) = 81.8%

Analysis of Variance

SOURCE          DF      SS      MS      F      p
Regression       1  1139.7  1139.7  41.38  0.000
Residual Error   8   220.3    27.5
Total            9  1360.0
```

using the incorrect data value substantially affected the goodness of fit. With the correct data, the value of R-sq increased from 49.7% to 83.8% and the value of b_0 decreased from 64.958 to 59.237. The slope of the line changed from −7.331 to −6.949. The identification of the outlier enabled us to correct the data error and improve the regression results.

Detecting Influential Observations

Sometimes one or more observations exert a strong influence on the results obtained. Figure 14.20 shows an example of an **influential observation** in simple linear regression. The estimated regression line has a negative slope. However, if the influential observation were dropped from the data set, the slope of the estimated regression line would change from negative to positive and the y-intercept would be smaller. Clearly, this one observation is much more influential in determining the estimated regression line than any of the others; dropping one of the other observations from the data set would have little effect on the estimated regression equation.

Influential observations can be identified from a scatter diagram when only one independent variable is present. An influential observation may be an outlier (an observation with a y value that deviates substantially from the trend), it may correspond to an x value far away from its mean (e.g., see Figure 14.20), or it may be caused by a combination of the two (a somewhat off-trend y value and a somewhat extreme x value).

Because influential observations may have such a dramatic effect on the estimated regression equation, they must be examined carefully. We should first check to make sure that no error was made in collecting or recording the data. If an error occurred, it can be corrected and a new estimated regression equation can be developed. If the observation is valid, we might consider ourselves fortunate to have it. Such a point, if valid, can contribute to a better understanding of the appropriate model and can lead to a better estimated regression equation. The presence of the influential observation in Figure 14.20, if valid, would suggest trying to obtain data on intermediate values of x to understand better the relationship between x and y.

Observations with extreme values for the independent variables are called **high leverage points**. The influential observation in Figure 14.20 is a point with high leverage. The leverage of an observation is determined by how far the values of the independent variables are from their mean values. For the single-independent-variable case, the leverage of the ith observation, denoted h_i, can be computed by using equation (14.33).

FIGURE 14.20 DATA SET WITH AN INFLUENTIAL OBSERVATION

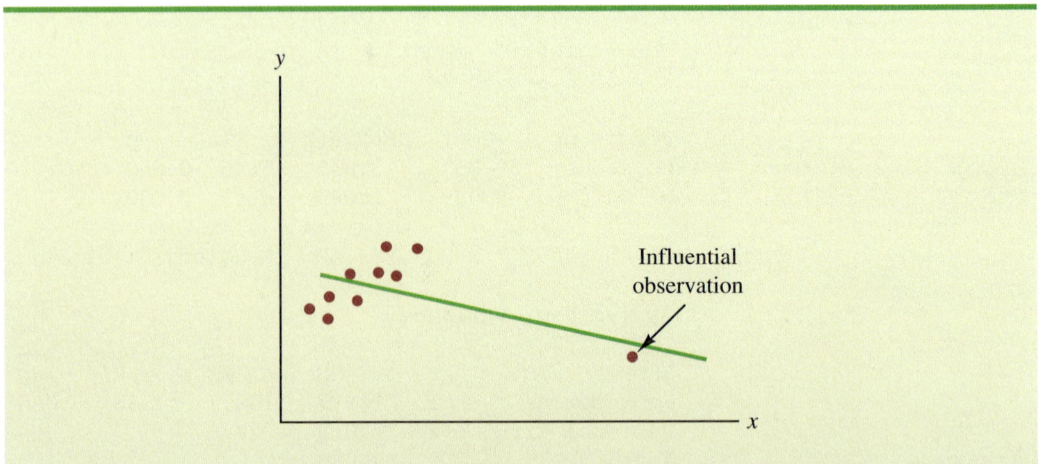

TABLE 14.12

DATA SET WITH A HIGH LEVERAGE OBSERVATION

x_i	y_i
10	125
10	130
15	120
20	115
20	120
25	110
70	100

LEVERAGE OF OBSERVATION *i*

$$h_i = \frac{1}{n} + \frac{(x_i - \bar{x})^2}{\Sigma(x_i - \bar{x})^2} \tag{14.33}$$

From the formula, it is clear that the farther x_i is from its mean $\bar{x}$, the higher the leverage of observation *i*.

Many statistical packages automatically identify observations with high leverage as part of the standard regression output. As an illustration of how the Minitab statistical package identifies points with high leverage, let us consider the data set in Table 14.12.

From Figure 14.21, a scatter diagram for the data set in Table 14.12, it is clear that observation 7 ($x = 70$, $y = 100$) is an observation with an extreme value of x. Hence, we would expect it to be identified as a point with high leverage. For this observation, the leverage is computed by using equation (14.33) as follows.

$$h_7 = \frac{1}{n} + \frac{(x_7 - \bar{x})^2}{\Sigma(x_i - \bar{x})^2} = \frac{1}{7} + \frac{(70 - 24.286)^2}{2621.43} = .94$$

For the case of simple linear regression, Minitab identifies observations as having high leverage if $h_i > 6/n$ or .99, whichever is smaller. For the data set in Table 14.12, $6/n = 6/7 = .86$. Because $h_7 = .94 > .86$, Minitab will identify observation 7 as an observation whose x value gives it large influence. Figure 14.22 shows the Minitab output for a regression analysis of this data set. Observation 7 ($x = 70$, $y = 100$) is identified as having large influence; it is printed on a separate line at the bottom, with an X in the right margin.

Computer software packages are essential for performing the computations to identify influential observations. Minitab's selection rule is discussed here.

Influential observations that are caused by an interaction of large residuals and high leverage can be difficult to detect. Diagnostic procedures are available that take both into account in determining when an observation is influential. One such measure, called Cook's *D* statistic, will be discussed in Chapter 15.

FIGURE 14.21 SCATTER DIAGRAM FOR THE DATA SET WITH A HIGH LEVERAGE OBSERVATION

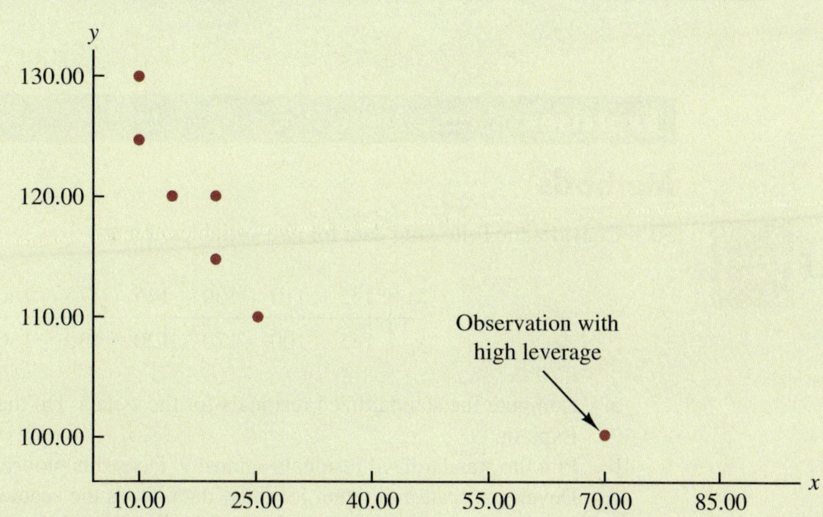

FIGURE 14.22 MINITAB OUTPUT FOR THE DATA SET WITH A HIGH LEVERAGE OBSERVATION

```
The regression equation is
y = 127 - 0.425 x

Predictor      Coef  SE Coef      T      p
Constant    127.466    2.961  43.04  0.000
X          -0.42507  0.09537  -4.46  0.007

S = 4.88282   R-sq = 79.9%   R-sq(adj) = 75.9%

Analysis of Variance

SOURCE          DF      SS      MS      F      p
Regression       1  473.65  473.65  19.87  0.007
Residual Error   5  119.21   23.84
Total            6  592.86

Unusual Observations
Obs     x       y    Fit  SE Fit  Residual  St Resid
  7  70.0  100.00  97.71    4.73      2.29     1.91 X

X denotes an observation whose X value gives it large influence.
```

NOTES AND COMMENTS

Once an observation is identified as potentially influential because of a large residual or high leverage, its impact on the estimated regression equation should be evaluated. More advanced texts discuss diagnostics for doing so. However, if one is not familiar with the more advanced material, a simple procedure is to run the regression analysis with and without the observation. This approach will reveal the influence of the observation on the results.

Exercises

Methods

SELF test

50. Consider the following data for two variables, x and y.

x_i	135	110	130	145	175	160	120
y_i	145	100	120	120	130	130	110

a. Compute the standardized residuals for these data. Do the data include any outliers? Explain.
b. Plot the standardized residuals against $\hat{y}$. Does this plot reveal any outliers?
c. Develop a scatter diagram for these data. Does the scatter diagram indicate any outliers in the data? In general, what implications does this finding have for simple linear regression?

51. Consider the following data for two variables, x and y.

x_i	4	5	7	8	10	12	12	22
y_i	12	14	16	15	18	20	24	19

a. Compute the standardized residuals for these data. Do the data include any outliers? Explain.
b. Compute the leverage values for these data. Do there appear to be any influential observations in these data? Explain.
c. Develop a scatter diagram for these data. Does the scatter diagram indicate any influential observations? Explain.

Applications

52. Charity Navigator is America's leading independent charity evaluator. The following data show the total expenses ($), the percentage of the total budget spent on administrative expenses, the percentage spent on fundraising, and the percentage spent on program expenses for 10 supersized charities (Charity Navigator website, April 12, 2012). Administrative expenses include overhead, administrative staff and associated costs, and organizational meetings. Fundraising expenses are what a charity spends to raise money, and program expenses are what the charity spends on the programs and services it exists to deliver. The sum of the three percentages does not add to 100% because of rounding.

WEB file Charities

Charity	Total Expenses ($)	Administrative Expenses (%)	Fundraising Expenses (%)	Program Expenses (%)
American Red Cross	3,354,177,445	3.9	3.8	92.1
World Vision	1,205,887,020	4.0	7.5	88.3
Smithsonian Institution	1,080,995,083	23.5	2.6	73.7
Food For The Poor	1,050,829,851	.7	2.4	96.8
American Cancer Society	1,003,781,897	6.1	22.2	71.6
Volunteers of America	929,158,968	8.6	1.9	89.4
Dana-Farber Cancer Institute	877,321,613	13.1	1.6	85.2
AmeriCares	854,604,824	.4	.7	98.8
ALSAC—St. Jude Children's Research Hospital	829,662,076	9.6	16.9	73.4
City of Hope	736,176,619	13.7	3.0	83.1

a. Develop a scatter diagram with fundraising expenses (%) on the horizontal axis and program expenses (%) on the vertical axis. Looking at the data, do there appear to be any outliers and/or influential observations?
b. Develop an estimated regression equation that could be used to predict program expenses (%) given fundraising expenses (%).
c. Does the value for the slope of the estimated regression equation make sense in the context of this problem situation?
d. Use residual analysis to determine whether any outliers and/or influential observations are present. Briefly summarize your findings and conclusions.

53. Many countries, especially those in Europe, have significant gold holdings. But, many of these countries also have massive debts. The following data show the total value of gold holdings in billions of U.S. dollars and the debt as a percentage of the gross domestic product for nine countries (WordPress and Trading Economics websites, February 24, 2012).

WEB file
GoldHoldings

Country	Gold Value ($ billions)	Debt (% of GDP)
China	63	17.7
France	146	81.7
Germany	203	83.2
Indonesia	33	69.2
Italy	147	119.0
Netherlands	36	63.7
Russia	50	9.9
Switzerland	62	55.0
United States	487	93.2

a. Develop a scatter diagram for the total value of a country's gold holdings ($ billions) as the independent variable.
b. What does the scatter diagram developed in part (a) indicate about the relationship between the two variables? Do there appear to be any outliers and/or influential observations? Explain.
c. Using the entire data set, develop the estimated regression equation that can be used to predict the debt of a country given the total value of its gold holdings.
d. Use residual analysis to determine whether any outliers or influential observations are present.
e. Suppose that after looking at the scatter diagram in part (a) that you were able to visually identify what appears to be an influential observation. Drop this observation from the data set and fit an estimated regression equation to the remaining data. Compare the estimated slope for the new estimated regression equation to the estimated slope obtained in part (c). Does this approach confirm the conclusion you reached in part (d)? Explain.

54. The following data show the annual revenue ($ millions) and the estimated team value ($ millions) for the 32 teams in the National Football League (*Forbes* website, February 2009).

WEB file
NFLValues

Team	Revenue ($ millions)	Value ($ millions)
Arizona Cardinals	203	914
Atlanta Falcons	203	872
Baltimore Ravens	226	1062
Buffalo Bills	206	885
Carolina Panthers	221	1040
Chicago Bears	226	1064
Cincinnati Bengals	205	941
Cleveland Browns	220	1035
Dallas Cowboys	269	1612
Denver Broncos	226	1061
Detroit Lions	204	917
Green Bay Packers	218	1023
Houston Texans	239	1125
Indianapolis Colts	203	1076
Jacksonville Jaguars	204	876
Kansas City Chiefs	214	1016
Miami Dolphins	232	1044
Minnesota Vikings	195	839
New England Patriots	282	1324
New Orleans Saints	213	937

Team	Revenue ($ millions)	Value ($ millions)
New York Giants	214	1178
New York Jets	213	1170
Oakland Raiders	205	861
Philadelphia Eagles	237	1116
Pittsburgh Steelers	216	1015
San Diego Chargers	207	888
San Francisco 49ers	201	865
Seattle Seahawks	215	1010
St. Louis Rams	206	929
Tampa Bay Buccaneers	224	1053
Tennessee Titans	216	994
Washington Redskins	327	1538

a. Develop a scatter diagram with Revenue on the horizontal axis and Value on the vertical axis. Looking at the scatter diagram, does it appear that there are any outliers and/or influential observations in the data?
b. Develop the estimated regression equation that can be used to predict team value given the value of annual revenue.
c. Use residual analysis to determine whether any outliers and/or influential observations are present. Briefly summarize your findings and conclusions.

Summary

In this chapter we showed how regression analysis can be used to determine how a dependent variable y is related to an independent variable x. In simple linear regression, the regression model is $y = \beta_0 + \beta_1 x + \epsilon$. The simple linear regression equation $E(y) = \beta_0 + \beta_1 x$ describes how the mean or expected value of y is related to x. We used sample data and the least squares method to develop the estimated regression equation $\hat{y} = b_0 + b_1 x$. In effect, b_0 and b_1 are the sample statistics used to estimate the unknown model parameters β_0 and β_1.

The coefficient of determination was presented as a measure of the goodness of fit for the estimated regression equation; it can be interpreted as the proportion of the variation in the dependent variable y that can be explained by the estimated regression equation. We reviewed correlation as a descriptive measure of the strength of a linear relationship between two variables.

The assumptions about the regression model and its associated error term ϵ were discussed, and t and F tests, based on those assumptions, were presented as a means for determining whether the relationship between two variables is statistically significant. We showed how to use the estimated regression equation to develop confidence interval estimates of the mean value of y and prediction interval estimates of individual values of y.

The chapter concluded with a section on the computer solution of regression problems and two sections on the use of residual analysis to validate the model assumptions and to identify outliers and influential observations.

Glossary

Dependent variable The variable that is being predicted or explained. It is denoted by y.
Independent variable The variable that is doing the predicting or explaining. It is denoted by x.
Simple linear regression Regression analysis involving one independent variable and one dependent variable in which the relationship between the variables is approximated by a straight line.

Regression model The equation that describes how y is related to x and an error term; in simple linear regression, the regression model is $y = \beta_0 + \beta_1 x + \epsilon$.

Regression equation The equation that describes how the mean or expected value of the dependent variable is related to the independent variable; in simple linear regression, $E(y) = \beta_0 + \beta_1 x$.

Estimated regression equation The estimate of the regression equation developed from sample data by using the least squares method. For simple linear regression, the estimated regression equation is $\hat{y} = b_0 + b_1 x$.

Least squares method A procedure used to develop the estimated regression equation. The objective is to minimize $\Sigma(y_i - \hat{y}_i)^2$.

Scatter diagram A graph of bivariate data in which the independent variable is on the horizontal axis and the dependent variable is on the vertical axis.

Coefficient of determination A measure of the goodness of fit of the estimated regression equation. It can be interpreted as the proportion of the variability in the dependent variable y that is explained by the estimated regression equation.

***i*th residual** The difference between the observed value of the dependent variable and the value predicted using the estimated regression equation; for the ith observation the ith residual is $y_i - \hat{y}_i$.

Correlation coefficient A measure of the strength of the linear relationship between two variables (previously discussed in Chapter 3).

Mean square error The unbiased estimate of the variance of the error term σ^2. It is denoted by MSE or s^2.

Standard error of the estimate The square root of the mean square error, denoted by s. It is the estimate of σ, the standard deviation of the error term ϵ.

ANOVA table The analysis of variance table used to summarize the computations associated with the F test for significance.

Confidence interval The interval estimate of the mean value of y for a given value of x.

Prediction interval The interval estimate of an individual value of y for a given value of x.

Residual analysis The analysis of the residuals used to determine whether the assumptions made about the regression model appear to be valid. Residual analysis is also used to identify outliers and influential observations.

Residual plot Graphical representation of the residuals that can be used to determine whether the assumptions made about the regression model appear to be valid.

Standardized residual The value obtained by dividing a residual by its standard deviation.

Normal probability plot A graph of the standardized residuals plotted against values of the normal scores. This plot helps determine whether the assumption that the error term has a normal probability distribution appears to be valid.

Outlier A data point or observation that does not fit the trend shown by the remaining data.

Influential observation An observation that has a strong influence or effect on the regression results.

High leverage points Observations with extreme values for the independent variables.

Key Formulas

Simple Linear Regression Model

$$y = \beta_0 + \beta_1 x + \epsilon \quad \textbf{(14.1)}$$

Simple Linear Regression Equation

$$E(y) = \beta_0 + \beta_1 x \quad \textbf{(14.2)}$$

Estimated Simple Linear Regression Equation

$$\hat{y} = b_0 + b_1 x \tag{14.3}$$

Least Squares Criterion

$$\min \Sigma(y_i - \hat{y}_i)^2 \tag{14.5}$$

Slope and y-Intercept for the Estimated Regression Equation

$$b_1 = \frac{\Sigma(x_i - \bar{x})(y_i - \bar{y})}{\Sigma(x_i - \bar{x})^2} \tag{14.6}$$

$$b_0 = \bar{y} - b_1\bar{x} \tag{14.7}$$

Sum of Squares Due to Error

$$\text{SSE} = \Sigma(y_i - \hat{y}_i)^2 \tag{14.8}$$

Total Sum of Squares

$$\text{SST} = \Sigma(y_i - \bar{y})^2 \tag{14.9}$$

Sum of Squares Due to Regression

$$\text{SSR} = \Sigma(\hat{y}_i - \bar{y})^2 \tag{14.10}$$

Relationship Among SST, SSR, and SSE

$$\text{SST} = \text{SSR} + \text{SSE} \tag{14.11}$$

Coefficient of Determination

$$r^2 = \frac{\text{SSR}}{\text{SST}} \tag{14.12}$$

Sample Correlation Coefficient

$$\begin{aligned} r_{xy} &= (\text{sign of } b_1)\sqrt{\text{Coefficient of determination}} \\ &= (\text{sign of } b_1)\sqrt{r^2} \end{aligned} \tag{14.13}$$

Mean Square Error (Estimate of σ^2)

$$s^2 = \text{MSE} = \frac{\text{SSE}}{n - 2} \tag{14.15}$$

Standard Error of the Estimate

$$s = \sqrt{\text{MSE}} = \sqrt{\frac{\text{SSE}}{n - 2}} \tag{14.16}$$

Standard Deviation of b_1

$$\sigma_{b_1} = \frac{\sigma}{\sqrt{\Sigma(x_i - \bar{x})^2}} \tag{14.17}$$

Estimated Standard Deviation of b_1

$$s_{b_1} = \frac{s}{\sqrt{\Sigma(x_i - \bar{x})^2}} \tag{14.18}$$

t Test Statistic

$$t = \frac{b_1}{s_{b_1}} \tag{14.19}$$

Mean Square Regression

$$\text{MSR} = \frac{\text{SSR}}{\text{Number of independent variables}} \tag{14.20}$$

F Test Statistic

$$F = \frac{\text{MSR}}{\text{MSE}} \tag{14.21}$$

Estimated Standard Deviation of $\hat{y}^*$

$$s_{\hat{y}^*} = s\sqrt{\frac{1}{n} + \frac{(x^* - \bar{x})^2}{\Sigma(x_i - \bar{x})^2}} \tag{14.23}$$

Confidence Interval for $E(y^*)$

$$\hat{y}^* \pm t_{\alpha/2} s_{\hat{y}^*} \tag{14.24}$$

Estimated Standard Deviation of an Individual Value

$$s_{\text{pred}} = s\sqrt{1 + \frac{1}{n} + \frac{(x^* - \bar{x})^2}{\Sigma(x_i - \bar{x})^2}} \tag{14.26}$$

Prediction Interval for y^*

$$\hat{y}^* \pm t_{\alpha/2} s_{\text{pred}} \tag{14.27}$$

Residual for Observation *i*

$$y_i - \hat{y}_i \tag{14.28}$$

Standard Deviation of the *i*th Residual

$$s_{y_i - \hat{y}_i} = s\sqrt{1 - h_i} \tag{14.30}$$

Standardized Residual for Observation *i*

$$\frac{y_i - \hat{y}_i}{s_{y_i - \hat{y}_i}} \tag{14.32}$$

Leverage of Observation *i*

$$h_i = \frac{1}{n} + \frac{(x_i - \bar{x})^2}{\Sigma(x_i - \bar{x})^2} \tag{14.33}$$

Supplementary Exercises

55. Does a high value of r^2 imply that two variables are causally related? Explain.
56. In your own words, explain the difference between an interval estimate of the mean value of y for a given x and an interval estimate for an individual value of y for a given x.

57. What is the purpose of testing whether $\beta_1 = 0$? If we reject $\beta_1 = 0$, does it imply a good fit?

58. The Dow Jones Industrial Average (DJIA) and the Standard & Poor's 500 (S&P 500) indexes are used as measures of overall movement in the stock market. The DJIA is based on the price movements of 30 large companies; the S&P 500 is an index composed of 500 stocks. Some say the S&P 500 is a better measure of stock market performance because it is broader based. The closing price for the DJIA and the S&P 500 for 15 weeks, beginning with January 6, 2012, follow (*Barron*'s website, April 17, 2012).

WEB file
DJIAS&P500

Date	DJIA	S&P
January 6	12,360	1278
January 13	12,422	1289
January 20	12,720	1315
January 27	12,660	1316
February 3	12,862	1345
February 10	12,801	1343
February 17	12,950	1362
February 24	12,983	1366
March 2	12,978	1370
March 9	12,922	1371
March 16	13,233	1404
March 23	13,081	1397
March 30	13,212	1408
April 5	13,060	1398
April 13	12,850	1370

a. Develop a scatter diagram with DJIA as the independent variable.
b. Develop the estimated regression equation.
c. Test for a significant relationship. Use $\alpha = .05$.
d. Did the estimated regression equation provide a good fit? Explain.
e. Suppose that the closing price for the DJIA is 13,500. Predict the closing price for the S&P 500.
f. Should we be concerned that the DJIA value of 13,500 used to predict the S&P 500 value in part (e) is beyond the range of the data used to develop the estimated regression equation?

59. The following data show Morningstar's Fair Value estimate and the Share Price for 28 companies. Fair Value is an estimate of a company's value per share that takes into account estimates of the company's growth, profitability, riskiness, and other factors over the next five years (*Morningstar Stocks 500,* 2008 edition).

WEB file
Stocks500

Company	Fair Value ($)	Share Price ($)
Air Products and Chemicals	80	98.63
Allied Waste Industries	17	11.02
America Mobile	83	61.39
AT&T	35	41.56
Bank of America	70	41.26
Barclays PLC	68	40.37
Citigroup	53	29.44
Costco Wholesale Corp.	75	69.76
Covidien, Ltd.	58	44.29
Darden Restaurants	52	27.71
Dun & Bradstreet	87	88.63

(continued)

Company	Fair Value ($)	Share Price ($)
Equifax	42	36.36
Gannett Co.	38	39.00
Genuine Parts	48	46.30
GlaxoSmithKline PLC	57	50.39
Iron Mountain	33	37.02
ITT Corporation	83	66.04
Johnson & Johnson	80	66.70
Las Vegas Sands	98	103.05
Macrovision	23	18.33
Marriott International	39	34.18
Nalco Holding Company	29	24.18
National Interstate	25	33.10
Portugal Telecom	15	13.02
Qualcomm	48	39.35
Royal Dutch Shell Ltd.	87	84.20
SanDisk	60	33.17
Time Warner	42	27.60

a. Develop the estimated regression equation that could be used to estimate the share price given the fair value.
b. At the .05 level of significance, is there a significant relationship between the two variables?
c. Use the estimated regression equation to predict the share price for a company that has a fair value of $50.
d. Do you believe the estimated regression equation would provide a good prediction of the share price? Use r^2 to support your answer.

60. One of the biggest changes in higher education in recent years has been the growth of online universities. The Online Education Database is an independent organization whose mission is to build a comprehensive list of the top accredited online colleges. The following table shows the retention rate (%) and the graduation rate (%) for 29 online colleges (Online Education Database website, January 2009).

WEB file
OnlineEdu

College	Retention Rate (%)	Graduation Rate (%)
Western International University	7	25
South University	51	25
University of Phoenix	4	28
American InterContinental University	29	32
Franklin University	33	33
Devry University	47	33
Tiffin University	63	34
Post University	45	36
Peirce College	60	36
Everest University	62	36
Upper Iowa University	67	36
Dickinson State University	65	37
Western Governors University	78	37
Kaplan University	75	38
Salem International University	54	39
Ashford University	45	41

College	Retention Rate (%)	Graduation Rate (%)
ITT Technical Institute	38	44
Berkeley College	51	45
Grand Canyon University	69	46
Nova Southeastern University	60	47
Westwood College	37	48
Everglades University	63	50
Liberty University	73	51
LeTourneau University	78	52
Rasmussen College	48	53
Keiser University	95	55
Herzing College	68	56
National University	100	57
Florida National College	100	61

a. Develop a scatter diagram with retention rate as the independent variable. What does the scatter diagram indicate about the relationship between the two variables?
b. Develop the estimated regression equation.
c. Test for a significant relationship. Use $\alpha = .05$.
d. Did the estimated regression equation provide a good fit?
e. Suppose you were the president of South University. After reviewing the results, would you have any concerns about the performance of your university as compared to other online universities?
f. Suppose you were the president of the University of Phoenix. After reviewing the results, would you have any concerns about the performance of your university as compared to other online universities?

61. Jensen Tire & Auto is in the process of deciding whether to purchase a maintenance contract for its new computer wheel alignment and balancing machine. Managers feel that maintenance expense should be related to usage, and they collected the following information on weekly usage (hours) and annual maintenance expense (in hundreds of dollars).

WEB file
Jensen

Weekly Usage (hours)	Annual Maintenance Expense
13	17.0
10	22.0
20	30.0
28	37.0
32	47.0
17	30.5
24	32.5
31	39.0
40	51.5
38	40.0

a. Develop the estimated regression equation that relates annual maintenance expense to weekly usage.
b. Test the significance of the relationship in part (a) at a .05 level of significance.
c. Jensen expects to use the new machine 30 hours per week. Develop a 95% prediction interval for the company's annual maintenance expense.
d. If the maintenance contract costs $3000 per year, would you recommend purchasing it? Why or why not?

62. In a manufacturing process the assembly line speed (feet per minute) was thought to affect the number of defective parts found during the inspection process. To test this theory, managers devised a situation in which the same batch of parts was inspected visually at a variety of line speeds. They collected the following data.

Line Speed	Number of Defective Parts Found
20	21
20	19
40	15
30	16
60	14
40	17

a. Develop the estimated regression equation that relates line speed to the number of defective parts found.
b. At a .05 level of significance, determine whether line speed and number of defective parts found are related.
c. Did the estimated regression equation provide a good fit to the data?
d. Develop a 95% confidence interval to predict the mean number of defective parts for a line speed of 50 feet per minute.

63. A sociologist was hired by a large city hospital to investigate the relationship between the number of unauthorized days that employees are absent per year and the distance (miles) between home and work for the employees. A sample of 10 employees was chosen, and the following data were collected.

WEB file
Absent

Distance to Work (miles)	Number of Days Absent
1	8
3	5
4	8
6	7
8	6
10	3
12	5
14	2
14	4
18	2

a. Develop a scatter diagram for these data. Does a linear relationship appear reasonable? Explain.
b. Develop the least squares estimated regression equation.
c. Is there a significant relationship between the two variables? Use $\alpha = .05$.
d. Did the estimated regression equation provide a good fit? Explain.
e. Use the estimated regression equation developed in part (b) to develop a 95% confidence interval for the expected number of days absent for employees living 5 miles from the company.

64. The regional transit authority for a major metropolitan area wants to determine whether there is any relationship between the age of a bus and the annual maintenance cost. A sample of 10 buses resulted in the following data.

Age of Bus (years)	Maintenance Cost ($)
1	350
2	370
2	480
2	520
2	590
3	550
4	750
4	800
5	790
5	950

WEB file AgeCost

a. Develop the least squares estimated regression equation.
b. Test to see whether the two variables are significantly related with $\alpha = .05$.
c. Did the least squares line provide a good fit to the observed data? Explain.
d. Develop a 95% prediction interval for the maintenance cost for a specific bus that is 4 years old.

65. A marketing professor at Givens College is interested in the relationship between hours spent studying and total points earned in a course. Data collected on 10 students who took the course last quarter follow.

Hours Spent Studying	Total Points Earned
45	40
30	35
90	75
60	65
105	90
65	50
90	90
80	80
55	45
75	65

WEB file HoursPts

a. Develop an estimated regression equation showing how total points earned is related to hours spent studying.
b. Test the significance of the model with $\alpha = .05$.
c. Predict the total points earned by Mark Sweeney. He spent 95 hours studying.
d. Develop a 95% prediction interval for the total points earned by Mark Sweeney.

66. Reuters reported the market beta for Xerox was 1.22 (Reuters website, January 30, 2009). Market betas for individual stocks are determined by simple linear regression. For each stock, the dependent variable is its quarterly percentage return (capital appreciation plus dividends) minus the percentage return that could be obtained from a risk-free investment (the Treasury Bill rate is used as the risk-free rate). The independent variable is the quarterly percentage return (capital appreciation plus dividends) for the stock market (S&P 500) minus the percentage return from a risk-free investment. An estimated regression equation is developed with quarterly data; the market beta for the stock is the slope of the estimated regression equation (b_1). The value of the market beta is often interpreted as a measure of the risk associated with the stock. Market betas greater than 1 indicate that the stock is more volatile than the market average; market betas less than 1 indicate that the

stock is less volatile than the market average. Suppose that the following figures are the differences between the percentage return and the risk-free return for 10 quarters for the S&P 500 and Horizon Technology.

WEB file MktBeta

S&P 500	Horizon
1.2	−.7
−2.5	−2.0
−3.0	−5.5
2.0	4.7
5.0	1.8
1.2	4.1
3.0	2.6
−1.0	2.0
.5	−1.3
2.5	5.5

a. Develop an estimated regression equation that can be used to predict the market beta for Horizon Technology. What is Horizon Technology's market beta?
b. Test for a significant relationship at the .05 level of significance.
c. Did the estimated regression equation provide a good fit? Explain.
d. Use the market betas of Xerox and Horizon Technology to compare the risk associated with the two stocks.

67. The Transactional Records Access Clearinghouse at Syracuse University reported data showing the odds of an Internal Revenue Service audit. The following table shows the average adjusted gross income reported and the percent of the returns that were audited for 20 selected IRS districts.

WEB file IRSAudit

District	Adjusted Gross Income ($)	Percent Audited
Los Angeles	36,664	1.3
Sacramento	38,845	1.1
Atlanta	34,886	1.1
Boise	32,512	1.1
Dallas	34,531	1.0
Providence	35,995	1.0
San Jose	37,799	0.9
Cheyenne	33,876	0.9
Fargo	30,513	0.9
New Orleans	30,174	0.9
Oklahoma City	30,060	0.8
Houston	37,153	0.8
Portland	34,918	0.7
Phoenix	33,291	0.7
Augusta	31,504	0.7
Albuquerque	29,199	0.6
Greensboro	33,072	0.6
Columbia	30,859	0.5
Nashville	32,566	0.5
Buffalo	34,296	0.5

a. Develop the estimated regression equation that could be used to predict the percent audited given the average adjusted gross income reported.
b. At the .05 level of significance, determine whether the adjusted gross income and the percent audited are related.

c. Did the estimated regression equation provide a good fit? Explain.
d. Use the estimated regression equation developed in part (a) to calculate a 95% confidence interval for the expected percent audited for districts with an average adjusted gross income of $35,000.

68. The Toyota Camry is one of the best-selling cars in North America. The cost of a previously owned Camry depends upon many factors, including the model year, mileage, and condition. To investigate the relationship between the car's mileage and the sales price for a 2007 model year Camry, the following data show the mileage and sale price for 19 sales (PriceHub website, February 24, 2012).

WEB file

Camry

Miles (1000s)	Price ($1000s)
22	16.2
29	16.0
36	13.8
47	11.5
63	12.5
77	12.9
73	11.2
87	13.0
92	11.8
101	10.8
110	8.3
28	12.5
59	11.1
68	15.0
68	12.2
91	13.0
42	15.6
65	12.7
110	8.3

a. Develop a scatter diagram with the car mileage on the horizontal axis and the price on the vertical axis.
b. What does the scatter diagram developed in part (a) indicate about the relationship between the two variables?
c. Develop the estimated regression equation that could be used to predict the price ($1000s) given the miles (1000s).
d. Test for a significant relationship at the .05 level of significance.
e. Did the estimated regression equation provide a good fit? Explain.
f. Provide an interpretation for the slope of the estimated regression equation.
g. Suppose that you are considering purchasing a previously owned 2007 Camry that has been driven 60,000 miles. Using the estimated regression equation developed in part (c), predict the price for this car. Is this the price you would offer the seller?

Case Problem 1 Measuring Stock Market Risk

One measure of the risk or volatility of an individual stock is the standard deviation of the total return (capital appreciation plus dividends) over several periods of time. Although the standard deviation is easy to compute, it does not take into account the extent to which the price of a given stock varies as a function of a standard market index, such as the S&P 500. As a result, many financial analysts prefer to use another measure of risk referred to as *beta*.

Betas for individual stocks are determined by simple linear regression. The dependent variable is the total return for the stock and the independent variable is the total return for

WEB file

Beta

the stock market.* For this case problem we will use the S&P 500 index as the measure of the total return for the stock market, and an estimated regression equation will be developed using monthly data. The beta for the stock is the slope of the estimated regression equation (b_1). The data contained in the file named Beta provides the total return (capital appreciation plus dividends) over 36 months for eight widely traded common stocks and the S&P 500.

The value of beta for the stock market will always be 1; thus, stocks that tend to rise and fall with the stock market will also have a beta close to 1. Betas greater than 1 indicate that the stock is more volatile than the market, and betas less than 1 indicate that the stock is less volatile than the market. For instance, if a stock has a beta of 1.4, it is 40% *more* volatile than the market, and if a stock has a beta of .4, it is 60% *less* volatile than the market.

Managerial Report

You have been assigned to analyze the risk characteristics of these stocks. Prepare a report that includes but is not limited to the following items.

a. Compute descriptive statistics for each stock and the S&P 500. Comment on your results. Which stocks are the most volatile?

b. Compute the value of beta for each stock. Which of these stocks would you expect to perform best in an up market? Which would you expect to hold their value best in a down market?

c. Comment on how much of the return for the individual stocks is explained by the market.

Case Problem 2 U.S. Department of Transportation

As part of a study on transportation safety, the U.S. Department of Transportation collected data on the number of fatal accidents per 1000 licenses and the percentage of licensed drivers under the age of 21 in a sample of 42 cities. Data collected over a one-year period follow. These data are contained in the file named Safety.

WEB file

Safety

Percent Under 21	Fatal Accidents per 1000 Licenses	Percent Under 21	Fatal Accidents per 1000 Licenses
13	2.962	17	4.100
12	0.708	8	2.190
8	0.885	16	3.623
12	1.652	15	2.623
11	2.091	9	0.835
17	2.627	8	0.820
18	3.830	14	2.890
8	0.368	8	1.267
13	1.142	15	3.224
8	0.645	10	1.014
9	1.028	10	0.493

*Various sources use different approaches for computing betas. For instance, some sources subtract the return that could be obtained from a risk-free investment (e.g., T-bills) from the dependent variable and the independent variable before computing the estimated regression equation. Some also use different indexes for the total return of the stock market; for instance, Value Line computes betas using the New York Stock Exchange composite index.

Percent Under 21	Fatal Accidents per 1000 Licenses	Percent Under 21	Fatal Accidents per 1000 Licenses
16	2.801	14	1.443
12	1.405	18	3.614
9	1.433	10	1.926
10	0.039	14	1.643
9	0.338	16	2.943
11	1.849	12	1.913
12	2.246	15	2.814
14	2.855	13	2.634
14	2.352	9	0.926
11	1.294	17	3.256

Managerial Report

1. Develop numerical and graphical summaries of the data.
2. Use regression analysis to investigate the relationship between the number of fatal accidents and the percentage of drivers under the age of 21. Discuss your findings.
3. What conclusion and recommendations can you derive from your analysis?

Case Problem 3 Selecting a Point-and-Shoot Digital Camera

Consumer Reports tested 166 different point-and-shoot digital cameras. Based upon factors such as the number of megapixels, weight (oz.), image quality, and ease of use, they developed an overall score for each camera tested. The overall score ranges from 0 to 100, with higher scores indicating better overall test results. Selecting a camera with many options can be a difficult process, and price is certainly a key issue for most consumers. By spending more, will a consumer really get a superior camera? And, do cameras that have more megapixels, a factor often considered to be a good measure of picture quality, cost more than cameras with fewer megapixels? Table 14.13 shows the brand, average retail price ($), number of megapixels, weight (oz.), and the overall score for 13 Canon and 15 Nikon subcompact cameras tested by *Consumer Reports* (*Consumer Reports* website, February 7, 2012).

Managerial Report

1. Develop numerical summaries of the data.
2. Using overall score as the dependent variable, develop three scatter diagrams, one using price as the independent variable, one using the number of megapixels as the independent variable, and one using weight as the independent variable. Which of the three independent variables appears to be the best predictor of overall score?
3. Using simple linear regression, develop an estimated regression equation that could be used to predict the overall score given the price of the camera. For this estimated regression equation, perform an analysis of the residuals and discuss your findings and conclusions.
4. Analyze the data using only the observations for the Canon cameras. Discuss the appropriateness of using simple linear regression and make any recommendations regarding the prediction of overall score using just the price of the camera.

TABLE 14.13 DATA FOR 28 POINT-AND-SHOOT DIGITAL CAMERAS

WEB file Cameras

Observation	Brand	Price ($)	Megapixels	Weight (oz.)	Score
1	Canon	330	10	7	66
2	Canon	200	12	5	66
3	Canon	300	12	7	65
4	Canon	200	10	6	62
5	Canon	180	12	5	62
6	Canon	200	12	7	61
7	Canon	200	14	5	60
8	Canon	130	10	7	60
9	Canon	130	12	5	59
10	Canon	110	16	5	55
11	Canon	90	14	5	52
12	Canon	100	10	6	51
13	Canon	90	12	7	46
14	Nikon	270	16	5	65
15	Nikon	300	16	7	63
16	Nikon	200	14	6	61
17	Nikon	400	14	7	59
18	Nikon	120	14	5	57
19	Nikon	170	16	6	56
20	Nikon	150	12	5	56
21	Nikon	230	14	6	55
22	Nikon	180	12	6	53
23	Nikon	130	12	6	53
24	Nikon	80	12	7	52
25	Nikon	80	14	7	50
26	Nikon	100	12	4	46
27	Nikon	110	12	5	45
28	Nikon	130	14	4	42

Case Problem 4 Finding the Best Car Value

When trying to decide what car to buy, real value is not necessarily determined by how much you spend on the initial purchase. Instead, cars that are reliable and don't cost much to own often represent the best values. But, no matter how reliable or inexpensive a car may cost to own, it must also perform well.

To measure value, *Consumer Reports* developed a statistic referred to as a value score. The value score is based upon five-year owner costs, overall road-test scores, and predicted reliability ratings. Five-year owner costs are based on the expenses incurred in the first five years of ownership, including depreciation, fuel, maintenance and repairs, and so on. Using a national average of 12,000 miles per year, an average cost per mile driven is used as the measure of five-year owner costs. Road-test scores are the results of more than 50 tests and evaluations and are based upon a 100-point scale, with higher scores indicating better performance, comfort, convenience, and fuel economy. The highest road-test score obtained in the tests conducted by *Consumer Reports* was a 99 for a Lexus LS 460L. Predicted-reliability ratings (1 = Poor, 2 = Fair, 3 = Good, 4 = Very Good, and 5 = Excellent) are based on data from *Consumer Reports'* Annual Auto Survey.

A car with a value score of 1.0 is considered to be "average-value." A car with a value score of 2.0 is considered to be twice as good a value as a car with a value score of 1.0; a car with a value score of 0.5 is considered half as good as average; and so on. The data for 20 family sedans, including the price ($) of each car tested, follow.

WEB file

FamilySedans

Car	Price ($)	Cost/Mile	Road-Test Score	Predicted Reliability	Value Score
Nissan Altima 2.5 S (4-cyl.)	23,970	0.59	91	4	1.75
Kia Optima LX (2.4)	21,885	0.58	81	4	1.73
Subaru Legacy 2.5i Premium	23,830	0.59	83	4	1.73
Ford Fusion Hybrid	32,360	0.63	84	5	1.70
Honda Accord LX-P (4-cyl.)	23,730	0.56	80	4	1.62
Mazda6 i Sport (4-cyl.)	22,035	0.58	73	4	1.60
Hyundai Sonata GLS (2.4)	21,800	0.56	89	3	1.58
Ford Fusion SE (4-cyl.)	23,625	0.57	76	4	1.55
Chevrolet Malibu LT (4-cyl.)	24,115	0.57	74	3	1.48
Kia Optima SX (2.0T)	29,050	0.72	84	4	1.43
Ford Fusion SEL (V6)	28,400	0.67	80	4	1.42
Nissan Altima 3.5 SR (V6)	30,335	0.69	93	4	1.42
Hyundai Sonata Limited (2.0T)	28,090	0.66	89	3	1.39
Honda Accord EX-L (V6)	28,695	0.67	90	3	1.36
Mazda6 s Grand Touring (V6)	30,790	0.74	81	4	1.34
Ford Fusion SEL (V6, AWD)	30,055	0.71	75	4	1.32
Subaru Legacy 3.6R Limited	30,094	0.71	88	3	1.29
Chevrolet Malibu LTZ (V6)	28,045	0.67	83	3	1.20
Chrysler 200 Limited (V6)	27,825	0.70	52	5	1.20
Chevrolet Impala LT (3.6)	28,995	0.67	63	3	1.05

Managerial Report

1. Develop numerical summaries of the data.
2. Use regression analysis to develop an estimated regression equation that could be used to predict the value score given the price of the car.
3. Use regression analysis to develop an estimated regression equation that could be used to predict the value score given the five-year owner costs (cost/mile).
4. Use regression analysis to develop an estimated regression equation that could be used to predict the value score given the road-test score.
5. Use regression analysis to develop an estimated regression equation that could be used to predict the value score given the predicted-reliability.
6. What conclusions can you derive from your analysis?

Appendix 14.1 Calculus-Based Derivation of Least Squares Formulas

As mentioned in the chapter, the least squares method is a procedure for determining the values of b_0 and b_1 that minimize the sum of squared residuals. The sum of squared residuals is given by

$$\Sigma(y_i - \hat{y}_i)^2$$

Substituting $\hat{y}_i = b_0 + b_1x_i$, we get

$$\Sigma(y_i - b_0 - b_1x_i)^2 \tag{14.34}$$

as the expression that must be minimized.

To minimize expression (14.34), we must take the partial derivatives with respect to b_0 and b_1, set them equal to zero, and solve. Doing so, we get

$$\frac{\partial\Sigma(y_i - b_0 - b_1x_i)^2}{\partial b_0} = -2\Sigma(y_i - b_0 - b_1x_i) = 0 \tag{14.35}$$

$$\frac{\partial\Sigma(y_i - b_0 - b_1x_i)^2}{\partial b_1} = -2\Sigma x_i(y_i - b_0 - b_1x_i) = 0 \tag{14.36}$$

Dividing equation (14.35) by two and summing each term individually yields

$$-\Sigma y_i + \Sigma b_0 + \Sigma b_1x_i = 0$$

Bringing Σy_i to the other side of the equal sign and noting that $\Sigma b_0 = nb_0$, we obtain

$$nb_0 + (\Sigma x_i)b_1 = \Sigma y_i \tag{14.37}$$

Similar algebraic simplification applied to equation (14.36) yields

$$(\Sigma x_i)b_0 + (\Sigma x_i^2)b_1 = \Sigma x_iy_i \tag{14.38}$$

Equations (14.37) and (14.38) are known as the *normal equations*. Solving equation (14.37) for b_0 yields

$$b_0 = \frac{\Sigma y_i}{n} - b_1\frac{\Sigma x_i}{n} \tag{14.39}$$

Using equation (14.39) to substitute for b_0 in equation (14.38) provides

$$\frac{\Sigma x_i\Sigma y_i}{n} - \frac{(\Sigma x_i)^2}{n}b_1 + (\Sigma x_i^2)b_1 = \Sigma x_iy_i \tag{14.40}$$

By rearranging the terms in equation (14.40), we obtain

$$b_1 = \frac{\Sigma x_iy_i - (\Sigma x_i\Sigma y_i)/n}{\Sigma x_i^2 - (\Sigma x_i)^2/n} = \frac{\Sigma(x_i - \bar{x})(y_i - \bar{y})}{\Sigma(x_i - \bar{x})^2} \tag{14.41}$$

Because $\bar{y} = \Sigma y_i/n$ and $\bar{x} = \Sigma x_i/n$, we can rewrite equation (14.39) as

$$b_0 = \bar{y} - b_1\bar{x} \tag{14.42}$$

Equations (14.41) and (14.42) are the formulas (14.6) and (14.7) we used in the chapter to compute the coefficients in the estimated regression equation.

Appendix 14.2 A Test for Significance Using Correlation

Using the sample correlation coefficient r_{xy}, we can determine whether the linear relationship between x and y is significant by testing the following hypotheses about the population correlation coefficient ρ_{xy}.

$$H_0: \rho_{xy} = 0$$
$$H_a: \rho_{xy} \neq 0$$

If H_0 is rejected, we can conclude that the population correlation coefficient is not equal to zero and that the linear relationship between the two variables is significant. This test for significance follows.

A TEST FOR SIGNIFICANCE USING CORRELATION

$$H_0: \rho_{xy} = 0$$
$$H_a: \rho_{xy} \neq 0$$

TEST STATISTIC

$$t = r_{xy}\sqrt{\frac{n-2}{1-r_{xy}^2}} \tag{14.43}$$

REJECTION RULE

p-value approach: Reject H_0 if p-value $\leq \alpha$

Critical value approach: Reject H_0 if $t \leq -t_{\alpha/2}$ or if $t \geq t_{\alpha/2}$

where $t_{\alpha/2}$ is based on a t distribution with $n - 2$ degrees of freedom.

In Section 14.3, we found that the sample with $n = 10$ provided the sample correlation coefficient for student population and quarterly sales of $r_{xy} = .9501$. The test statistic is

$$t = r_{xy}\sqrt{\frac{n-2}{1-r_{xy}^2}} = .9501\sqrt{\frac{10-2}{1-(.9501)^2}} = 8.61$$

The t distribution table shows that with $n - 2 = 10 - 2 = 8$ degrees of freedom, $t = 3.355$ provides an area of .005 in the upper tail. Thus, the area in the upper tail of the t distribution corresponding to the test statistic $t = 8.61$ must be less than .005. Because this test is a two-tailed test, we double this value to conclude that the p-value associated with $t = 8.61$ must be less than $2(.005) = .01$. Excel or Minitab show the p-value $= .000$. Because the p-value is less than $\alpha = .01$, we reject H_0 and conclude that ρ_{xy} is not equal to zero. This evidence is sufficient to conclude that a significant linear relationship exists between student population and quarterly sales.

Note that except for rounding, the test statistic t and the conclusion of a significant relationship are identical to the results obtained in Section 14.5 for the t test conducted using Armand's estimated regression equation $\hat{y} = 60 + 5x$. Performing regression analysis provides the conclusion of a significant relationship between x and y and in addition provides the equation showing how the variables are related. Most analysts therefore use modern computer packages to perform regression analysis and find that using correlation as a test of significance is unnecessary.

Appendix 14.3 Regression Analysis with Minitab

WEB file
Armand's

In Section 14.7 we discussed the computer solution of regression problems by showing Minitab's output for the Armand's Pizza Parlors problem. In this appendix, we describe the steps required to generate the Minitab computer solution. First, the data must be entered in a Minitab worksheet. Student population data are entered in column C1 and quarterly sales data are entered in column C2. The variable names Pop and Sales are entered as the column headings on the worksheet. In subsequent steps, we refer to the data by using the variable names Pop and Sales or the column indicators C1 and C2. The following steps describe how to use Minitab to produce the regression results shown in Figure 14.10.

Step 1. Select the **Stat** menu
Step 2. Select the **Regression** menu
Step 3. Choose **Regression**
Step 4. When the Regression dialog box appears:
Enter Sales in the **Response** box
Enter Pop in the **Predictors** box
Click the **Options** button
When the Regression-Options dialog box appears:
Enter 10 in the **Prediction intervals for new observations** box
Click **OK**
When the Regression dialog box reappears:
Click **OK**

The Minitab regression dialog box provides additional capabilities that can be obtained by selecting the desired options. For instance, to obtain a residual plot that shows the predicted value of the dependent variable $\hat{y}$ on the horizontal axis and the standardized residual values on the vertical axis, step 4 would be as follows:

Step 4. When the Regression dialog box appears:
Enter Sales in the **Response** box
Enter Pop in the **Predictors** box
Click the **Graphs** button
When the Regression-Graphs dialog box appears:
Select **Standardized** under Residuals for Plots
Select **Residuals versus fits** under Residual Plots
Click **OK**
When the Regression dialog box reappears:
Click **OK**

Appendix 14.4 Regression Analysis with Excel

WEB file
Armand's

In this appendix we will illustrate how Excel's Regression tool can be used to perform the regression analysis computations for the Armand's Pizza Parlors problem. Refer to Figure 14.23 as we describe the steps involved. The labels Restaurant, Population, and Sales are entered into cells A1:C1 of the worksheet. To identify each of the 10 observations, we entered the numbers 1 through 10 into cells A2:A11. The sample data are entered into cells B2:C11. The following steps describe how to use Excel to produce the regression results.

Step 1. Click the **Data** tab on the Ribbon
Step 2. In the **Analysis** group, click **Data Analysis**
Step 3. Choose **Regression** from the list of Analysis Tools
Step 4. Click **OK**

FIGURE 14.23 EXCEL SOLUTION TO THE ARMAND'S PIZZA PARLORS PROBLEM

A1 | f_x Restaurant

	A	B	C	D	E	F	G	H	I	J
1	**Restaurant**	**Population**	**Sales**							
2	1	2	58							
3	2	6	105							
4	3	8	88							
5	4	8	118							
6	5	12	117							
7	6	16	137							
8	7	20	157							
9	8	20	169							
10	9	22	149							
11	10	26	202							
12										
13	SUMMARY OUTPUT									
14										
15	*Regression Statistics*									
16	Multiple R	0.9501								
17	R Square	0.9027								
18	Adjusted R Square	0.8906								
19	Standard Error	13.8293								
20	Observations	10								
21										
22	ANOVA									
23		*df*	*SS*	*MS*	*F*	*Significance F*				
24	Regression	1	14200	14200	74.2484	2.55E-05				
25	Residual	8	1530	191.25						
26	Total	9	15730							
27										
28		*Coefficients*	*Standard Error*	*t Stat*	*P-value*	*Lower 95%*	*Upper 95%*	*Lower 99.0%*	*Upper 99.0%*	
29	Intercept	60	9.2260	6.5033	0.0002	38.7247	81.2753	29.0431	90.9569	
30	Population	5	0.5803	8.6167	2.55E-05	3.6619	6.3381	3.0530	6.9470	
31										

Step 5. When the Regression dialog box appears:

Enter C1:C11 in the **Input Y Range** box
Enter B1:B11 in the **Input X Range** box
Select **Labels**
Select **Confidence Level**
Enter 99 in the **Confidence Level** box
Select **Output Range**
Enter A13 in the **Output Range** box
(Any upper left-hand corner cell indicating where the output is to begin may be entered here.)
Click **OK**

The first section of the output, entitled *Regression Statistics,* contains summary statistics such as the coefficient of determination (R Square). The second section of the output, titled ANOVA, contains the analysis of variance table. The last section of the output, which is not titled, contains the estimated regression coefficients and related information. We will begin our discussion of the interpretation of the regression output with the information contained in cells A28:I30.

Interpretation of Estimated Regression Equation Output

The *y* intercept of the estimated regression line, $b_0 = 60$, is shown in cell B29, and the slope of the estimated regression line, $b_1 = 5$, is shown in cell B30. The label Intercept in cell A29 and the label Population in cell A30 are used to identify these two values.

In Section 14.5 we showed that the estimated standard deviation of b_1 is $s_{b_1} = .5803$. Note that the value in cell C30 is .5803. The label Standard Error in cell C28 is Excel's way of indicating that the value in cell C30 is the standard error, or standard deviation, of b_1. Recall that the t test for a significant relationship required the computation of the t statistic, $t = b_1/s_{b_1}$. For the Armand's data, the value of t that we computed was $t = 5/.5803 = 8.62$. The label in cell D28, *t Stat,* reminds us that cell D30 contains the value of the t test statistic.

The value in cell E30 is the p-value associated with the t test for significance. Excel has displayed the p-value in cell E30 using scientific notation. To obtain the decimal value, we move the decimal point 5 places to the left, obtaining a value of .0000255. Because the p-value $= .0000255 < \alpha = .01$, we can reject H_0 and conclude that we have a significant relationship between student population and quarterly sales.

The information in cells F28:I30 can be used to develop confidence interval estimates of the y intercept and slope of the estimated regression equation. Excel always provides the lower and upper limits for a 95% confidence interval. Recall that in step 4 we selected Confidence Level and entered 99 in the Confidence Level box. As a result, Excel's Regression tool also provides the lower and upper limits for a 99% confidence interval. The value in cell H30 is the lower limit for the 99% confidence interval estimate of β_1 and the value in cell I30 is the upper limit. Thus, after rounding, the 99% confidence interval estimate of β_1 is 3.05 to 6.95. The values in cells F30 and G30 provide the lower and upper limits for the 95% confidence interval. Thus, the 95% confidence interval is 3.66 to 6.34.

Interpretation of ANOVA Output

The information in cells A22:F26 is a summary of the analysis of variance computations. The three sources of variation are labeled Regression, Residual, and Total. The label *df* in cell B23 stands for degrees of freedom, the label *SS* in cell C23 stands for sum of squares, and the label *MS* in cell D23 stands for mean square.

In Section 14.5 we stated that the mean square error, obtained by dividing the error or residual sum of squares by its degrees of freedom, provides an estimate of σ^2. The value in cell D25, 191.25, is the mean square error for the Armand's regression output. In Section 14.5 we showed that an F test could also be used to test for significance in regression. The value in cell F24, .0000255, is the p-value associated with the F test for significance. Because the p-value $= .0000255 < \alpha = .01$, we can reject H_0 and conclude that we have a significant relationship between student population and quarterly sales. The label Excel uses to identify the p-value for the F test for significance, shown in cell F23, is *Significance F.*

The label Significance F may be more meaningful if you think of the value in cell F24 as the observed level of significance for the F test.

Interpretation of Regression Statistics Output

The coefficient of determination, .9027, appears in cell B17; the corresponding label, R Square, is shown in cell A17. The square root of the coefficient of determination provides the sample correlation coefficient of .9501 shown in cell B16. Note that Excel uses the label Multiple R (cell A16) to identify this value. In cell A19, the label Standard Error is used to identify the value of the standard error of the estimate shown in cell B19. Thus, the standard error of the estimate is 13.8293. We caution the reader to keep in mind that in the Excel output, the label Standard Error appears in two different places. In the Regression Statistics section of the output, the label Standard Error refers to the estimate of σ. In the Estimated Regression Equation section of the output, the label *Standard Error* refers to s_{b_1}, the standard deviation of the sampling distribution of b_1.

Appendix 14.5 Regression Analysis Using StatTools

WEB file

Armand's

In this appendix we show how StatTools can be used to perform the regression analysis computations for the Armand's Pizza Parlors problem. Begin by using the Data Set Manager to create a StatTools data set for these data using the procedure described in the appendix in Chapter 1. The following steps describe how StatTools can be used to provide the regression results.

Step 1. Click the **StatTools** tab on the Ribbon
Step 2. In the **Analyses** group, click **Regression and Classification**
Step 3. Choose the **Regression** option
Step 4. When the StatTools-Regression dialog box appears:
Select **Multiple** in the **Regression Type** box
In the **Variables** section,
Click the **Format button** and select **Unstacked**
In the column labeled **I** select **Population**
In the column labeled **D** select **Sales**
Click **OK**

The regression analysis output will appear.

Note that in step 4 we selected Multiple in the Regression Type box. In StatTools, the Multiple option is used for both simple linear regression and multiple regression. The StatTools-Regression dialog box contains a number of more advanced options for developing prediction interval estimates and producing residual plots. The StatTools Help facility provides information on using all of these options.

CHAPTER 15

Multiple Regression

CONTENTS

STATISTICS *in* PRACTICE

dunnhumby*
LONDON, ENGLAND

Founded in 1989 by the husband-and-wife team of Clive Humby (a mathematician) and Edwina Dunn (a marketer), dunnhumby combines proven natural abilities with big ideas to find clues and patterns as to what customers are buying and why. The company turns these insights into actionable strategies that create dramatic growth and sustainable loyalty, ultimately improving brand value and the customer experience.

Employing more than 950 people in Europe, Asia, and the Americas, dunnhumby serves a prestigious list of companies, including Kroger, Tesco, Coca-Cola, General Mills, Kimberly-Clark, PepsiCo, Procter & Gamble, and Home Depot. dunnhumbyUSA is a joint venture between the Kroger Company and dunnhumby and has offices in New York, Chicago, Atlanta, Minneapolis, Cincinnati, and Portland.

The company's research begins with data collected about a client's customers. Data come from customer reward or discount card purchase records, electronic point-of-sale transactions, and traditional market research. Analysis of the data often translates billions of data points into detailed insights about the behavior, preferences, and lifestyles of the customers. Such insights allow for more effective merchandising programs to be activated, including strategy recommendations on pricing, promotion, advertising, and product assortment decisions.

Researchers have used a multiple regression technique referred to as logistic regression to help in their analysis of customer-based data. Using logistic regression, an estimated multiple regression equation of the following form is developed.

$$\hat{y} = b_0 + b_1x_1 + b_2x_2 + b_3x_3 + \cdots + b_px_p$$

The dependent variable $\hat{y}$ is a prediction of the probability that a customer belongs to a particular customer group. The independent variables $x_1, x_2, x_3, \ldots, x_p$ are measures of the customer's actual shopping behavior and may include the specific items purchased, number of items purchased, amount purchased, day of the week, hour of the day, and so on. The analysis helps identify the independent variables that are most relevant in predicting the customer's group and provides a better understanding of the customer population, enabling further analysis with far greater confidence. The focus of the analysis is on understanding the customer to the point of developing merchandising, marketing, and direct marketing programs that will maximize the relevancy and service to the customer group.

In this chapter, we will introduce multiple regression and show how the concepts of simple linear regression introduced in Chapter 14 can be extended to the multiple regression case. In addition, we will show how computer software packages are used for multiple regression. In the final section of the chapter we introduce logistic regression using an example that illustrates how the technique is used in a marketing research application.

dunnhumby uses logistic regression to predict customer shopping behavior. © Micro 10x/ Shutterstock.com.

*The authors are indebted to Paul Hunter, Senior Vice President of Solutions for dunnhumby for providing this Statistics in Practice.

In Chapter 14 we presented simple linear regression and demonstrated its use in developing an estimated regression equation that describes the relationship between two variables. Recall that the variable being predicted or explained is called the dependent variable and the variable being used to predict or explain the dependent variable is called the independent variable. In this chapter we continue our study of regression analysis by considering situations involving two or more independent variables. This subject area, called **multiple regression analysis**, enables us to consider more factors and thus obtain better predictions than are possible with simple linear regression.

15.1 Multiple Regression Model

Multiple regression analysis is the study of how a dependent variable y is related to two or more independent variables. In the general case, we will use p to denote the number of independent variables.

Regression Model and Regression Equation

The concepts of a regression model and a regression equation introduced in the preceding chapter are applicable in the multiple regression case. The equation that describes how the dependent variable y is related to the independent variables $x_1, x_2, \ldots, x_p$ and an error term is called the **multiple regression model**. We begin with the assumption that the multiple regression model takes the following form.

MULTIPLE REGRESSION MODEL

$$y = \beta_0 + \beta_1 x_1 + \beta_2 x_2 + \cdots + \beta_p x_p + \epsilon \quad \textbf{(15.1)}$$

In the multiple regression model, $\beta_0, \beta_1, \beta_2, \ldots, \beta_p$ are the parameters and the error term ϵ (the Greek letter epsilon) is a random variable. A close examination of this model reveals that y is a linear function of $x_1, x_2, \ldots, x_p$ (the $\beta_0 + \beta_1 x_1 + \beta_2 x_2 + \cdots + \beta_p x_p$ part) plus the error term ϵ. The error term accounts for the variability in y that cannot be explained by the linear effect of the p independent variables.

In Section 15.4 we will discuss the assumptions for the multiple regression model and ϵ. One of the assumptions is that the mean or expected value of ϵ is zero. A consequence of this assumption is that the mean or expected value of y, denoted $E(y)$, is equal to $\beta_0 + \beta_1 x_1 + \beta_2 x_2 + \cdots + \beta_p x_p$. The equation that describes how the mean value of y is related to $x_1, x_2, \ldots, x_p$ is called the **multiple regression equation**.

MULTIPLE REGRESSION EQUATION

$$E(y) = \beta_0 + \beta_1 x_1 + \beta_2 x_2 + \cdots + \beta_p x_p \quad \textbf{(15.2)}$$

Estimated Multiple Regression Equation

If the values of $\beta_0, \beta_1, \beta_2, \ldots, \beta_p$ were known, equation (15.2) could be used to compute the mean value of y at given values of $x_1, x_2, \ldots, x_p$. Unfortunately, these parameter values will not, in general, be known and must be estimated from sample data. A simple random sample is used to compute sample statistics $b_0, b_1, b_2, \ldots, b_p$ that are used as the point

FIGURE 15.1 THE ESTIMATION PROCESS FOR MULTIPLE REGRESSION

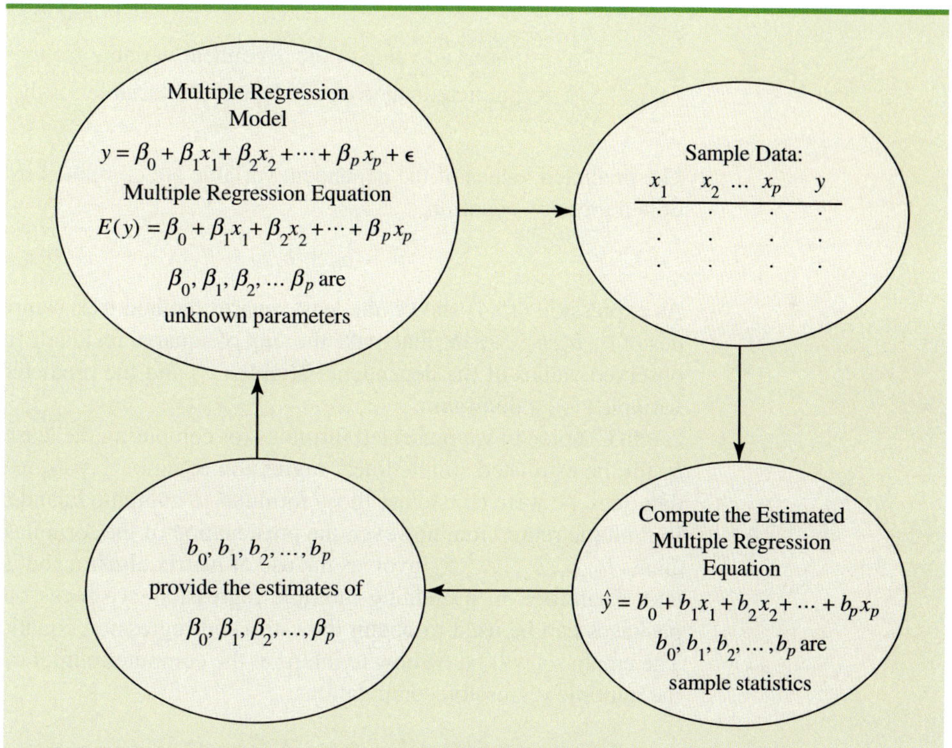

In simple linear regression, b_0 and b_1 were the sample statistics used to estimate the parameters β_0 and β_1. Multiple regression parallels this statistical inference process, with b_0, $b_1, b_2, \ldots, b_p$ denoting the sample statistics used to estimate the parameters $\beta_0, \beta_1, \beta_2, \ldots, \beta_p$.

estimators of the parameters $\beta_0, \beta_1, \beta_2, \ldots, \beta_p$. These sample statistics provide the following **estimated multiple regression equation**.

ESTIMATED MULTIPLE REGRESSION EQUATION

$$\hat{y} = b_0 + b_1 x_1 + b_2 x_2 + \cdots + b_p x_p \quad \textbf{(15.3)}$$

where

$$b_0, b_1, b_2, \ldots, b_p \text{ are the estimates of } \beta_0, \beta_1, \beta_2, \ldots, \beta_p$$
$$\hat{y} = \text{predicted value of the dependent variable}$$

The estimation process for multiple regression is shown in Figure 15.1.

15.2 Least Squares Method

In Chapter 14, we used the **least squares method** to develop the estimated regression equation that best approximated the straight-line relationship between the dependent and independent variables. This same approach is used to develop the estimated multiple regression equation. The least squares criterion is restated as follows.

LEAST SQUARES CRITERION

$$\min \Sigma (y_i - \hat{y}_i)^2 \quad \textbf{(15.4)}$$

where

y_i = observed value of the dependent variable for the ith observation
$\hat{y}_i$ = predicted value of the dependent variable for the ith observation

The predicted values of the dependent variable are computed by using the estimated multiple regression equation,

$$\hat{y} = b_0 + b_1x_1 + b_2x_2 + \cdots + b_px_p$$

As expression (15.4) shows, the least squares method uses sample data to provide the values of $b_0, b_1, b_2, \ldots, b_p$ that make the sum of squared residuals [the deviations between the observed values of the dependent variable (y_i) and the predicted values of the dependent variable ($\hat{y}_i$)] a minimum.

In Chapter 14 we presented formulas for computing the least squares estimators b_0 and b_1 for the estimated simple linear regression equation $\hat{y} = b_0 + b_1x$. With relatively small data sets, we were able to use those formulas to compute b_0 and b_1 by manual calculations. In multiple regression, however, the presentation of the formulas for the regression coefficients $b_0, b_1, b_2, \ldots, b_p$ involves the use of matrix algebra and is beyond the scope of this text. Therefore, in presenting multiple regression, we focus on how computer software packages can be used to obtain the estimated regression equation and other information. The emphasis will be on how to interpret the computer output rather than on how to make the multiple regression computations.

An Example: Butler Trucking Company

As an illustration of multiple regression analysis, we will consider a problem faced by the Butler Trucking Company, an independent trucking company in southern California. A major portion of Butler's business involves deliveries throughout its local area. To develop better work schedules, the managers want to predict the total daily travel time for their drivers.

Initially the managers believed that the total daily travel time would be closely related to the number of miles traveled in making the daily deliveries. A simple random sample of 10 driving assignments provided the data shown in Table 15.1 and the scatter diagram shown in Figure 15.2. After reviewing this scatter diagram, the managers hypothesized that the simple linear regression model $y = \beta_0 + \beta_1x_1 + \epsilon$ could be used to describe the relationship between the total travel time (y) and the number of miles traveled (x_1). To estimate

TABLE 15.1 PRELIMINARY DATA FOR BUTLER TRUCKING

WEB file
Butler

Driving Assignment	x_1 = Miles Traveled	y = Travel Time (hours)
1	100	9.3
2	50	4.8
3	100	8.9
4	100	6.5
5	50	4.2
6	80	6.2
7	75	7.4
8	65	6.0
9	90	7.6
10	90	6.1

FIGURE 15.2 SCATTER DIAGRAM OF PRELIMINARY DATA FOR BUTLER TRUCKING

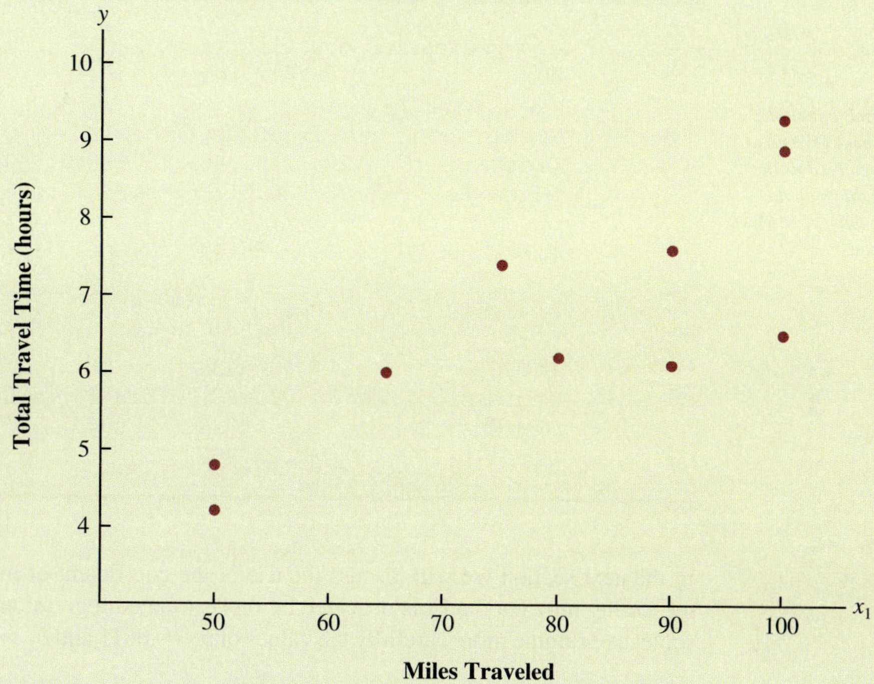

the parameters β_0 and β_1, the least squares method was used to develop the estimated regression equation.

$$\hat{y} = b_0 + b_1x_1 \tag{15.5}$$

In Figure 15.3, we show the Minitab computer output from applying simple linear regression to the data in Table 15.1. The estimated regression equation is

$$\hat{y} = 1.27 + .0678x_1$$

At the .05 level of significance, the F value of 15.81 and its corresponding p-value of .004 indicate that the relationship is significant; that is, we can reject H_0: $\beta_1 = 0$ because the p-value is less than $\alpha = .05$. Note that the same conclusion is obtained from the t value of 3.98 and its associated p-value of .004. Thus, we can conclude that the relationship between the total travel time and the number of miles traveled is significant; longer travel times are associated with more miles traveled. With a coefficient of determination (expressed as a percentage) of R-Sq = 66.4%, we see that 66.4% of the variability in travel time can be explained by the linear effect of the number of miles traveled. This finding is fairly good, but the managers might want to consider adding a second independent variable to explain some of the remaining variability in the dependent variable.

The Minitab steps necessary to generate the output shown in Figure 15.4 are given in Appendix 15.1.

In attempting to identify another independent variable, the managers felt that the number of deliveries could also contribute to the total travel time. The Butler Trucking data, with the number of deliveries added, are shown in Table 15.2. The Minitab computer solution with both miles traveled (x_1) and number of deliveries (x_2) as independent variables is shown in Figure 15.4. The estimated regression equation is

$$\hat{y} = -.869 + .0611x_1 + .923x_2 \tag{15.6}$$

FIGURE 15.3 MINITAB OUTPUT FOR BUTLER TRUCKING WITH ONE INDEPENDENT VARIABLE

```
The regression equation is
Time = 1.27 + 0.0678 Miles

Predictor       Coef   SE Coef     T      p
Constant       1.274     1.401  0.91  0.390
Miles        0.06783   0.01706  3.98  0.004

S = 1.00179    R-Sq = 66.4%    R-Sq(adj) = 62.2%

Analysis of Variance

SOURCE          DF      SS      MS      F      p
Regression       1  15.871  15.871  15.81  0.004
Residual Error   8   8.029   1.004
Total            9  23.900
```

In the Minitab output the variable names Miles *and* Time *were entered as the column headings on the worksheet; thus,* x_1 = Miles *and* y = Time.

In the next section we will discuss the use of the coefficient of multiple determination in measuring how good a fit is provided by this estimated regression equation. Before doing so, let us examine more carefully the values of $b_1 = .0611$ and $b_2 = .923$ in equation (15.6).

Note on Interpretation of Coefficients

One observation can be made at this point about the relationship between the estimated regression equation with only the miles traveled as an independent variable and the equation that includes the number of deliveries as a second independent variable. The value of b_1 is not the same in both cases. In simple linear regression, we interpret b_1 as an estimate of the change in y for a one-unit change in the independent variable. In multiple regression analysis, this interpretation must be modified somewhat. That is, in multiple regression analysis, we interpret each regression coefficient as follows: b_i represents an estimate of the change in y corresponding to a one-unit change in x_i when all other independent variables are held constant. In the Butler Trucking example involving two independent variables, $b_1 = .0611$. Thus,

TABLE 15.2 DATA FOR BUTLER TRUCKING WITH MILES TRAVELED (x_1) AND NUMBER OF DELIVERIES (x_2) AS THE INDEPENDENT VARIABLES

WEB file Butler

Driving Assignment	x_1 = Miles Traveled	x_2 = Number of Deliveries	y = Travel Time (hours)
1	100	4	9.3
2	50	3	4.8
3	100	4	8.9
4	100	2	6.5
5	50	2	4.2
6	80	2	6.2
7	75	3	7.4
8	65	4	6.0
9	90	3	7.6
10	90	2	6.1

FIGURE 15.4 MINITAB OUTPUT FOR BUTLER TRUCKING WITH TWO INDEPENDENT VARIABLES

```
The regression equation is
Time = - 0.869 + 0.0611 Miles + 0.923 Deliveries

Predictor        Coef    SE Coef      T      p
Constant      -0.8687     0.9515  -0.91  0.392
Miles        0.061135   0.009888   6.18  0.000
Deliveries     0.9234     0.2211   4.18  0.004

S = 0.573142   R-Sq = 90.4%   R-Sq(adj) = 87.6%

Analysis of Variance

SOURCE          DF      SS      MS      F      p
Regression       2  21.601  10.800  32.88  0.000
Residual Error   7   2.299   0.328
Total            9  23.900
```

In the Minitab output the variable names Miles, Deliveries, *and* Time *were entered as the column headings on the worksheet; thus,* x_1 = Miles, x_2 = Deliveries, *and* y = Time.

.0611 hours is an estimate of the expected increase in travel time corresponding to an increase of one mile in the distance traveled when the number of deliveries is held constant. Similarly, because $b_2 = .923$, an estimate of the expected increase in travel time corresponding to an increase of one delivery when the number of miles traveled is held constant is .923 hours.

Exercises

Note to student: The exercises involving data in this and subsequent sections were designed to be solved using a computer software package.

Methods

1. The estimated regression equation for a model involving two independent variables and 10 observations follows.

$$\hat{y} = 29.1270 + .5906x_1 + .4980x_2$$

   a. Interpret b_1 and b_2 in this estimated regression equation.
   b. Predict y when $x_1 = 180$ and $x_2 = 310$.

SELF test

2. Consider the following data for a dependent variable y and two independent variables, x_1 and x_2.

WEB file Exer2

x_1	x_2	y
30	12	94
47	10	108
25	17	112
51	16	178
40	5	94
51	19	175
74	7	170
36	12	117
59	13	142
76	16	211

a. Develop an estimated regression equation relating y to x_1. Predict y if $x_1 = 45$.
b. Develop an estimated regression equation relating y to x_2. Predict y if $x_2 = 15$.
c. Develop an estimated regression equation relating y to x_1 and x_2. Predict y if $x_1 = 45$ and $x_2 = 15$.

3. In a regression analysis involving 30 observations, the following estimated regression equation was obtained.

$$\hat{y} = 17.6 + 3.8x_1 - 2.3x_2 + 7.6x_3 + 2.7x_4$$

a. Interpret b_1, b_2, b_3, and b_4 in this estimated regression equation.
b. Predict y when $x_1 = 10$, $x_2 = 5$, $x_3 = 1$, and $x_4 = 2$.

Applications

4. A shoe store developed the following estimated regression equation relating sales to inventory investment and advertising expenditures.

$$\hat{y} = 25 + 10x_1 + 8x_2$$

where

$$x_1 = \text{inventory investment (\$1000s)}$$
$$x_2 = \text{advertising expenditures (\$1000s)}$$
$$y = \text{sales (\$1000s)}$$

a. Predict the sales resulting from a \$15,000 investment in inventory and an advertising budget of \$10,000.
b. Interpret b_1 and b_2 in this estimated regression equation.

SELF test

5. The owner of Showtime Movie Theaters, Inc., would like to predict weekly gross revenue as a function of advertising expenditures. Historical data for a sample of eight weeks follow.

WEB file

Showtime

Weekly Gross Revenue ($1000s)	Television Advertising ($1000s)	Newspaper Advertising ($1000s)
96	5.0	1.5
90	2.0	2.0
95	4.0	1.5
92	2.5	2.5
95	3.0	3.3
94	3.5	2.3
94	2.5	4.2
94	3.0	2.5

a. Develop an estimated regression equation with the amount of television advertising as the independent variable.
b. Develop an estimated regression equation with both television advertising and newspaper advertising as the independent variables.
c. Is the estimated regression equation coefficient for television advertising expenditures the same in part (a) and in part (b)? Interpret the coefficient in each case.
d. Predict weekly gross revenue for a week when \$3500 is spent on television advertising and \$1800 is spent on newspaper advertising?

6. The National Football League (NFL) records a variety of performance data for individuals and teams. To investigate the importance of passing on the percentage of games won by a team, the following data show the conference (Conf), average number of passing yards per

attempt (Yds/Att), the number of interceptions thrown per attempt (Int/Att), and the percentage of games won (Win%) for a random sample of 16 NFL teams for the 2011 season (NFL website, February 12, 2012).

WEB file NFLPassing

Team	Conf	Yds/Att	Int/Att	Win%
Arizona Cardinals	NFC	6.5	.042	50.0
Atlanta Falcons	NFC	7.1	.022	62.5
Carolina Panthers	NFC	7.4	.033	37.5
Cincinnati Bengals	AFC	6.2	.026	56.3
Detroit Lions	NFC	7.2	.024	62.5
Green Bay Packers	NFC	8.9	.014	93.8
Houstan Texans	AFC	7.5	.019	62.5
Indianapolis Colts	AFC	5.6	.026	12.5
Jacksonville Jaguars	AFC	4.6	.032	31.3
Minnesota Vikings	NFC	5.8	.033	18.8
New England Patriots	AFC	8.3	.020	81.3
New Orleans Saints	NFC	8.1	.021	81.3
Oakland Raiders	AFC	7.6	.044	50.0
San Francisco 49ers	NFC	6.5	.011	81.3
Tennessee Titans	AFC	6.7	.024	56.3
Washington Redskins	NFC	6.4	.041	31.3

a. Develop the estimated regression equation that could be used to predict the percentage of games won given the average number of passing yards per attempt.
b. Develop the estimated regression equation that could be used to predict the percentage of games won given the number of interceptions thrown per attempt.
c. Develop the estimated regression equation that could be used to predict the percentage of games won given the average number of passing yards per attempt and the number of interceptions thrown per attempt.
d. The average number of passing yards per attempt for the Kansas City Chiefs was 6.2 and the number of interceptions thrown per attempt was .036. Use the estimated regression equation developed in part (c) to predict the percentage of games won by the Kansas City Chiefs. (*Note:* For the 2011 season the Kansas City Chiefs' record was 7 wins and 9 losses.) Compare your prediction to the actual percentage of games won by the Kansas City Chiefs.

7. *PC World* rated four component characteristics for 10 ultraportable laptop computers: features; performance; design; and price. Each characteristic was rated using a 0–100 point scale. An overall rating, referred to as the *PCW World* Rating, was then developed for each laptop. The following table shows the performance rating, features rating, and the *PCW World* Rating for the 10 laptop computers (*PC World* website, February 5, 2009).

WEB file Laptop

Model	Performance	Features	PCW Rating
Thinkpad X200	77	87	83
VGN-Z598U	97	85	82
U6V	83	80	81
Elitebook 2530P	77	75	78
X360	64	80	78
Thinkpad X300	56	76	78
Ideapad U110	55	81	77
Micro Express JFT2500	76	73	75
Toughbook W7	46	79	73
HP Voodoo Envy133	54	68	72

a. Determine the estimated regression equation that can be used to predict the *PCW World* Rating using the performance rating as the independent variable.
b. Determine the estimated regression equation that can be used to predict the *PCW World* Rating using both the performance rating and the features rating.
c. Predict the *PCW World* Rating for a laptop computer that has a performance rating of 80 and a features rating of 70.

8. The *Condé Nast Traveler* Gold List for 2012 provided ratings for the top 20 small cruise ships (*Condé Nast Traveler* website, March 1, 2012). The data shown below are the scores each ship received based upon the results from *Condé Nast Traveler*'s annual Readers' Choice Survey. Each score represents the percentage of respondents who rated a ship as excellent or very good on several criteria, including Shore Excursions and Food/Dining. An overall score was also reported and used to rank the ships. The highest ranked ship, the *Seabourn Odyssey,* has an overall score of 94.4, the highest component of which is 97.8 for Food/Dining.

WEB file
Ships

Ship	Overall	Shore Excursions	Food/Dining
Seabourn Odyssey	94.4	90.9	97.8
Seabourn Pride	93.0	84.2	96.7
National Geographic Endeavor	92.9	100.0	88.5
Seabourn Sojourn	91.3	94.8	97.1
Paul Gauguin	90.5	87.9	91.2
Seabourn Legend	90.3	82.1	98.8
Seabourn Spirit	90.2	86.3	92.0
Silver Explorer	89.9	92.6	88.9
Silver Spirit	89.4	85.9	90.8
Seven Seas Navigator	89.2	83.3	90.5
Silver Whisperer	89.2	82.0	88.6
National Geographic Explorer	89.1	93.1	89.7
Silver Cloud	88.7	78.3	91.3
Celebrity Xpedition	87.2	91.7	73.6
Silver Shadow	87.2	75.0	89.7
Silver Wind	86.6	78.1	91.6
SeaDream II	86.2	77.4	90.9
Wind Star	86.1	76.5	91.5
Wind Surf	86.1	72.3	89.3
Wind Spirit	85.2	77.4	91.9

a. Determine an estimated regression equation that can be used to predict the overall score given the score for Shore Excursions.
b. Consider the addition of the independent variable Food/Dining. Develop the estimated regression equation that can be used to predict the overall score given the scores for Shore Excursions and Food/Dining.
c. Predict the overall score for a cruise ship with a Shore Excursions score of 80 and a Food/Dining Score of 90.

9. Waterskiing and wakeboarding are two popular water-sports. Finding a model that best suits your intended needs, whether it is waterskiing, wakeboading, or general boating, can be a difficult task. *WaterSki* magazine did extensive testing for 88 boats and provided a wide variety of information to help consumers select the best boat. A portion of the data they reported for 20 boats with a length of between 20 and 22 feet follows (*WaterSki,* January/February 2006). Beam is the maximum width of the boat in inches, HP is the horsepower of the boat's engine, and TopSpeed is the top speed in miles per hour (mph).

WEB file

Boats

Make and Model	Beam	HP	TopSpeed
Calabria Cal Air Pro V-2	100.0	330	45.3
Correct Craft Air Nautique 210	91.0	330	47.3
Correct Craft Air Nautique SV-211	93.0	375	46.9
Correct Craft Ski Nautique 206 Limited	91.0	330	46.7
Gekko GTR 22	96.0	375	50.1
Gekko GTS 20	83.0	375	52.2
Malibu Response LXi	93.5	340	47.2
Malibu Sunsettter LXi	98.0	400	46.0
Malibu Sunsetter 21 XTi	98.0	340	44.0
Malibu Sunscape 21 LSV	98.0	400	47.5
Malibu Wakesetter 21 XTi	98.0	340	44.9
Malibu Wakesetter VLX	98.0	400	47.3
Malibu vRide	93.5	340	44.5
Malibu Ride XTi	93.5	320	44.5
Mastercraft ProStar 209	96.0	350	42.5
Mastercraft X-1	90.0	310	45.8
Mastercraft X-2	94.0	310	42.8
Mastercraft X-9	96.0	350	43.2
MB Sports 190 Plus	92.0	330	45.3
Svfara SVONE	91.0	330	47.7

a. Using these data, develop an estimated regression equation relating the top speed with the boat's beam and horsepower rating.

b. The Svfara SV609 has a beam of 85 inches and an engine with a 330 horsepower rating. Use the estimated regression equation developed in part (a) to predict the top speed for the Svfara SV609.

10. Major League Baseball (MLB) consists of teams that play in the American League and the National League. MLB collects a wide variety of team and player statistics. Some of the statistics often used to evaluate pitching performance are as follows:

ERA: The average number of earned runs given up by the pitcher per nine innings. An earned run is any run that the opponent scores off a particular pitcher except for runs scored as a result of errors.

SO/IP: The average number of strikeouts per inning pitched.

HR/IP: The average number of home runs per inning pitched.

R/IP: The number of runs given up per inning pitched.

The following data show values for these statistics for a random sample of 20 pitchers from the American League for the 2011 season (MLB website, March 1, 2012).

WEB file

MLBPitching

Player	Team	W	L	ERA	SO/IP	HR/IP	R/IP
Verlander, J	DET	24	5	2.40	1.00	.10	.29
Beckett, J	BOS	13	7	2.89	.91	.11	.34
Wilson, C	TEX	16	7	2.94	.92	.07	.40
Sabathia, C	NYY	19	8	3.00	.97	.07	.37
Haren, D	LAA	16	10	3.17	.81	.08	.38
McCarthy, B	OAK	9	9	3.32	.72	.06	.43
Santana, E	LAA	11	12	3.38	.78	.11	.42

(continued)

Player	Team	W	L	ERA	SO/IP	HR/IP	R/IP
Lester, J	BOS	15	9	3.47	.95	.10	.40
Hernandez, F	SEA	14	14	3.47	.95	.08	.42
Buehrle, M	CWS	13	9	3.59	.53	.10	.45
Pineda, M	SEA	9	10	3.74	1.01	.11	.44
Colon, B	NYY	8	10	4.00	.82	.13	.52
Tomlin, J	CLE	12	7	4.25	.54	.15	.48
Pavano, C	MIN	9	13	4.30	.46	.10	.55
Danks, J	CWS	8	12	4.33	.79	.11	.52
Guthrie, J	BAL	9	17	4.33	.63	.13	.54
Lewis, C	TEX	14	10	4.40	.84	.17	.51
Scherzer, M	DET	15	9	4.43	.89	.15	.52
Davis, W	TB	11	10	4.45	.57	.13	.52
Porcello, R	DET	14	9	4.75	.57	.10	.57

a. Develop an estimated regression equation that can be used to predict the average number of runs given up per inning given the average number of strikeouts per inning pitched.
b. Develop an estimated regression equation that can be used to predict the average number of runs given up per inning given the average number of home runs per inning pitched.
c. Develop an estimated regression equation that can be used to predict the average number of runs given up per inning given the average number of strikeouts per inning pitched and the average number of home runs per inning pitched.
d. A. J. Burnett, a pitcher for the New York Yankees, had an average number of strikeouts per inning pitched of .91 and an average number of home runs per inning of .16. Use the estimated regression equation developed in part (c) to predict the average number of runs given up per inning for A. J. Burnett. (*Note:* The actual value for R/IP was .6.)
e. Suppose a suggestion was made to also use the earned run average as another independent variable in part (c). What do you think of this suggestion?

15.3 Multiple Coefficient of Determination

In simple linear regression we showed that the total sum of squares can be partitioned into two components: the sum of squares due to regression and the sum of squares due to error. The same procedure applies to the sum of squares in multiple regression.

RELATIONSHIP AMONG SST, SSR, AND SSE

$$\text{SST} = \text{SSR} + \text{SSE} \tag{15.7}$$

where

$$\text{SST} = \text{total sum of squares} = \Sigma(y_i - \bar{y})^2$$
$$\text{SSR} = \text{sum of squares due to regression} = \Sigma(\hat{y}_i - \bar{y})^2$$
$$\text{SSE} = \text{sum of squares due to error} = \Sigma(y_i - \hat{y}_i)^2$$

Because of the computational difficulty in computing the three sums of squares, we rely on computer packages to determine those values. The analysis of variance part of the Minitab output in Figure 15.4 shows the three values for the Butler Trucking problem with two independent variables: SST = 23.900, SSR = 21.601, and SSE = 2.299. With only one independent variable (number of miles traveled), the Minitab output in Figure 15.3 shows that SST = 23.900, SSR = 15.871, and SSE = 8.029. The value of SST is the same in both cases because it does not depend on $\hat{y}$, but SSR increases and SSE decreases when a second independent variable (number of deliveries) is added. The implication is that the estimated multiple regression equation provides a better fit for the observed data.

In Chapter 14, we used the coefficient of determination, r^2 = SSR/SST, to measure the goodness of fit for the estimated regression equation. The same concept applies to multiple regression. The term **multiple coefficient of determination** indicates that we are measuring the goodness of fit for the estimated multiple regression equation. The multiple coefficient of determination, denoted R^2, is computed as follows.

MULTIPLE COEFFICIENT OF DETERMINATION

$$R^2 = \frac{\text{SSR}}{\text{SST}} \tag{15.8}$$

The multiple coefficient of determination can be interpreted as the proportion of the variability in the dependent variable that can be explained by the estimated multiple regression equation. Hence, when multiplied by 100, it can be interpreted as the percentage of the variability in y that can be explained by the estimated regression equation.

In the two-independent-variable Butler Trucking example, with SSR = 21.601 and SST = 23.900, we have

$$R^2 = \frac{21.601}{23.900} = .904$$

Therefore, 90.4% of the variability in travel time y is explained by the estimated multiple regression equation with miles traveled and number of deliveries as the independent variables. In Figure 15.4, we see that the multiple coefficient of determination (expressed as a percentage) is also provided by the Minitab output; it is denoted by R-Sq = 90.4%.

Adding independent variables causes the prediction errors to become smaller, thus reducing the sum of squares due to error, SSE. *Because* SSR = SST − SSE, *when* SSE *becomes smaller,* SSR *becomes larger, causing* R^2 = SSR/SST *to increase.*

Figure 15.3 shows that the R-Sq value for the estimated regression equation with only one independent variable, number of miles traveled (x_1), is 66.4%. Thus, the percentage of the variability in travel times that is explained by the estimated regression equation increases from 66.4% to 90.4% when number of deliveries is added as a second independent variable. In general, R^2 always increases as independent variables are added to the model.

Many analysts prefer adjusting R^2 for the number of independent variables to avoid overestimating the impact of adding an independent variable on the amount of variability explained by the estimated regression equation. With n denoting the number of observations and p denoting the number of independent variables, the **adjusted multiple coefficient of determination** is computed as follows.

If a variable is added to the model, R^2 becomes larger even if the variable added is not statistically significant. The adjusted multiple coefficient of determination compensates for the number of independent variables in the model.

ADJUSTED MULTIPLE COEFFICIENT OF DETERMINATION

$$R_a^2 = 1 - (1 - R^2)\frac{n - 1}{n - p - 1} \tag{15.9}$$

For the Butler Trucking example with $n = 10$ and $p = 2$, we have

$$R_a^2 = 1 - (1 - .904)\frac{10 - 1}{10 - 2 - 1} = .88$$

Thus, after adjusting for the two independent variables, we have an adjusted multiple coefficient of determination of .88. This value (expressed as a percentage) is provided by the Minitab output in Figure 15.4 as R-Sq(adj) = 87.6%; the value we calculated differs because we used a rounded value of R^2 in the calculation.

NOTES AND COMMENTS

If the value of R^2 is small and the model contains a large number of independent variables, the adjusted coefficient of determination can take a negative value; in such cases, Minitab sets the adjusted coefficient of determination to zero.

Exercises

Methods

11. In exercise 1, the following estimated regression equation based on 10 observations was presented.

$$\hat{y} = 29.1270 + .5906x_1 + .4980x_2$$

The values of SST and SSR are 6724.125 and 6216.375, respectively.

a. Find SSE.
b. Compute R^2.
c. Compute R_a^2.
d. Comment on the goodness of fit.

SELF test

12. In exercise 2, 10 observations were provided for a dependent variable y and two independent variables x_1 and x_2; for these data SST = 15,182.9, and SSR = 14,052.2.

a. Compute R^2.
b. Compute R_a^2.
c. Does the estimated regression equation explain a large amount of the variability in the data? Explain.

13. In exercise 3, the following estimated regression equation based on 30 observations was presented.

$$\hat{y} = 17.6 + 3.8x_1 - 2.3x_2 + 7.6x_3 + 2.7x_4$$

The values of SST and SSR are 1805 and 1760, respectively.

a. Compute R^2.
b. Compute R_a^2.
c. Comment on the goodness of fit.

Applications

14. In exercise 4, the following estimated regression equation relating sales to inventory investment and advertising expenditures was given.

$$\hat{y} = 25 + 10x_1 + 8x_2$$

The data used to develop the model came from a survey of 10 stores; for those data, SST = 16,000 and SSR = 12,000.

a. For the estimated regression equation given, compute R^2.
b. Compute R_a^2.
c. Does the model appear to explain a large amount of variability in the data? Explain.

SELF test

15. In exercise 5, the owner of Showtime Movie Theaters, Inc., used multiple regression analysis to predict gross revenue (y) as a function of television advertising (x_1) and newspaper advertising (x_2). The estimated regression equation was

WEB file Showtime

$$\hat{y} = 83.2 + 2.29x_1 + 1.30x_2$$

The computer solution provided SST = 25.5 and SSR = 23.435.

a. Compute and interpret R^2 and R_a^2.
b. When television advertising was the only independent variable, $R^2 = .653$ and $R_a^2 = .595$. Do you prefer the multiple regression results? Explain.

WEB file NFLPassing

16. In exercise 6, data were given on the average number of passing yards per attempt (Yds/Att), the number of interceptions thrown per attempt (Int/Att), and the percentage of games won (Win%) for a random sample of 16 National Football League (NFL) teams for the 2011 season (NFL website, February 12, 2012).

a. Did the estimated regression equation that uses only the average number of passing yards per attempt as the independent variable to predict the percentage of games won provide a good fit?
b. Discuss the benefit of using both the average number of passing yards per attempt and the number of interceptions thrown per attempt to predict the percentage of games won.

WEB file Boats

17. In exercise 9, an estimated regression equation was developed relating the top speed for a boat to the boat's beam and horsepower rating.

a. Compute and interpret and R^2 and R_a^2.
b. Does the estimated regression equation provide a good fit to the data? Explain.

WEB file MLBPitching

18. Refer to exercise 10, where Major League Baseball (MLB) pitching statistics were reported for a random sample of 20 pitchers from the American League for the 2011 season (MLB website, March 1, 2012).

a. In part (c) of exercise 10, an estimated regression equation was developed relating the average number of runs given up per inning pitched given the average number of strikeouts per inning pitched and the average number of home runs per inning pitched. What are the values of R^2 and R_a^2?
b. Does the estimated regression equation provide a good fit to the data? Explain.
c. Suppose the earned run average (ERA) is used as the dependent variable in part (c) instead of the average number of runs given up per inning pitched. Does the estimated regression equation that uses the ERA provide a good fit to the data? Explain.

15.4 Model Assumptions

In Section 15.1 we introduced the following multiple regression model.

MULTIPLE REGRESSION MODEL

$$y = \beta_0 + \beta_1 x_1 + \beta_2 x_2 + \cdots + \beta_p x_p + \epsilon \qquad \textbf{(15.10)}$$

The assumptions about the error term ϵ in the multiple regression model parallel those for the simple linear regression model.

ASSUMPTIONS ABOUT THE ERROR TERM ϵ IN THE MULTIPLE REGRESSION MODEL $y = \beta_0 + \beta_1 x_1 + \cdots + \beta_p x_p + \epsilon$

1. The error term ϵ is a random variable with mean or expected value of zero; that is, $E(\epsilon) = 0$.
   Implication: For given values of $x_1, x_2, \ldots, x_p$, the expected, or average, value of y is given by

   $$E(y) = \beta_0 + \beta_1 x_1 + \beta_2 x_2 + \cdots + \beta_p x_p \qquad \textbf{(15.11)}$$

   Equation (15.11) is the multiple regression equation we introduced in Section 15.1. In this equation, $E(y)$ represents the average of all possible values of y that might occur for the given values of $x_1, x_2, \ldots, x_p$.
2. The variance of ϵ is denoted by σ^2 and is the same for all values of the independent variables $x_1, x_2, \ldots, x_p$.
   Implication: The variance of y about the regression line equals σ^2 and is the same for all values of $x_1, x_2, \ldots, x_p$.
3. The values of ϵ are independent.
   Implication: The value of ϵ for a particular set of values for the independent variables is not related to the value of ϵ for any other set of values.
4. The error term ϵ is a normally distributed random variable reflecting the deviation between the y value and the expected value of y given by $\beta_0 + \beta_1 x_1 + \beta_2 x_2 + \cdots + \beta_p x_p$.
   Implication: Because $\beta_0, \beta_1, \ldots, \beta_p$ are constants for the given values of $x_1, x_2, \ldots, x_p$, the dependent variable y is also a normally distributed random variable.

To obtain more insight about the form of the relationship given by equation (15.11), consider the following two-independent-variable multiple regression equation.

$$E(y) = \beta_0 + \beta_1 x_1 + \beta_2 x_2$$

The graph of this equation is a plane in three-dimensional space. Figure 15.5 provides an example of such a graph. Note that the value of ϵ shown is the difference between the actual y value and the expected value of y, $E(y)$, when $x_1 = x_1^*$ and $x_2 = x_2^*$.

FIGURE 15.5 GRAPH OF THE REGRESSION EQUATION FOR MULTIPLE REGRESSION ANALYSIS WITH TWO INDEPENDENT VARIABLES

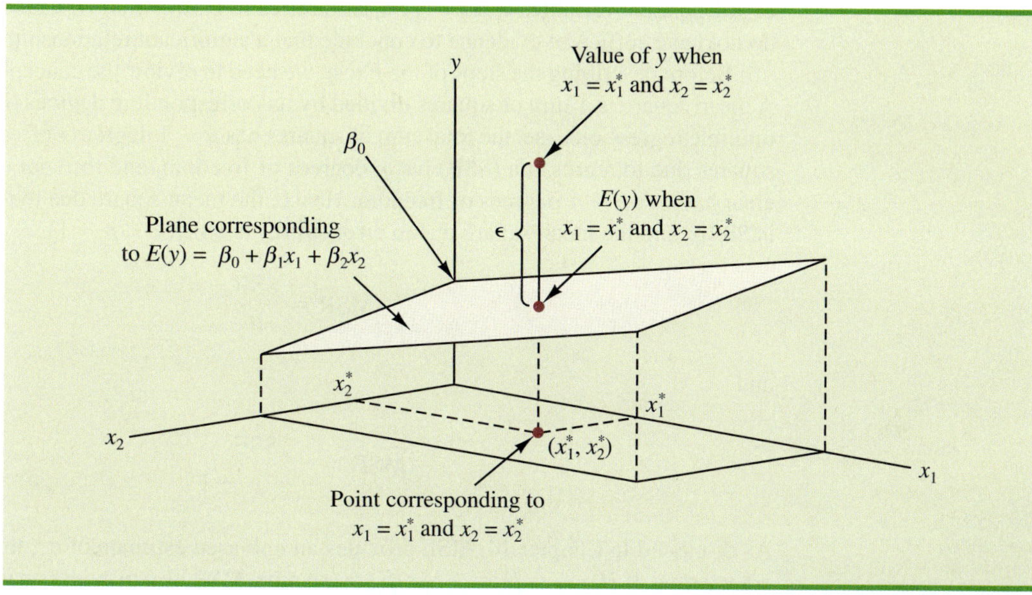

In regression analysis, the term *response variable* is often used in place of the term *dependent variable.* Furthermore, since the multiple regression equation generates a plane or surface, its graph is called a *response surface.*

15.5 Testing for Significance

In this section we show how to conduct significance tests for a multiple regression relationship. The significance tests we used in simple linear regression were a t test and an F test. In simple linear regression, both tests provide the same conclusion; that is, if the null hypothesis is rejected, we conclude that $\beta_1 \neq 0$. In multiple regression, the t test and the F test have different purposes.

1. The F test is used to determine whether a significant relationship exists between the dependent variable and the set of all the independent variables; we will refer to the F test as the test for *overall significance.*
2. If the F test shows an overall significance, the t test is used to determine whether each of the individual independent variables is significant. A separate t test is conducted for each of the independent variables in the model; we refer to each of these t tests as a test for *individual significance.*

In the material that follows, we will explain the F test and the t test and apply each to the Butler Trucking Company example.

F Test

The multiple regression model as defined in Section 15.4 is

$$y = \beta_0 + \beta_1 x_1 + \beta_2 x_2 + \cdots + \beta_p x_p + \epsilon$$

The hypotheses for the F test involve the parameters of the multiple regression model.

$$H_0: \beta_1 = \beta_2 = \cdots = \beta_p = 0$$
$$H_a: \text{One or more of the parameters is not equal to zero}$$

If H_0 is rejected, the test gives us sufficient statistical evidence to conclude that one or more of the parameters is not equal to zero and that the overall relationship between y and the set of independent variables $x_1, x_2, \ldots, x_p$ is significant. However, if H_0 cannot be rejected, we do not have sufficient evidence to conclude that a significant relationship is present.

Before describing the steps of the F test, we need to review the concept of *mean square*. A mean square is a sum of squares divided by its corresponding degrees of freedom. In the multiple regression case, the total sum of squares has $n - 1$ degrees of freedom, the sum of squares due to regression (SSR) has p degrees of freedom, and the sum of squares due to error has $n - p - 1$ degrees of freedom. Hence, the mean square due to regression (MSR) is SSR/p and the mean square due to error (MSE) is SSE/$(n - p - 1)$.

$$\text{MSR} = \frac{\text{SSR}}{p} \tag{15.12}$$

and

$$\text{MSE} = \frac{\text{SSE}}{n - p - 1} \tag{15.13}$$

As discussed in Chapter 14, MSE provides an unbiased estimate of σ^2, the variance of the error term ϵ. If H_0: $\beta_1 = \beta_2 = \cdots = \beta_p = 0$ is true, MSR also provides an unbiased estimate of σ^2, and the value of MSR/MSE should be close to 1. However, if H_0 is false, MSR overestimates σ^2 and the value of MSR/MSE becomes larger. To determine how large the value of MSR/MSE must be to reject H_0, we make use of the fact that if H_0 is true and the assumptions about the multiple regression model are valid, the sampling distribution of MSR/MSE is an F distribution with p degrees of freedom in the numerator and $n - p - 1$ in the denominator. A summary of the F test for significance in multiple regression follows.

F TEST FOR OVERALL SIGNIFICANCE

$$H_0\colon \beta_1 = \beta_2 = \cdots = \beta_p = 0$$
$$H_a\colon \text{One or more of the parameters is not equal to zero}$$

TEST STATISTIC

$$F = \frac{\text{MSR}}{\text{MSE}} \tag{15.14}$$

REJECTION RULE

p-value approach:	Reject H_0 if p-value $\leq \alpha$
Critical value approach:	Reject H_0 if $F \geq F_\alpha$

where F_α is based on an F distribution with p degrees of freedom in the numerator and $n - p - 1$ degrees of freedom in the denominator.

Let us apply the F test to the Butler Trucking Company multiple regression problem. With two independent variables, the hypotheses are written as follows.

$$H_0\colon \beta_1 = \beta_2 = 0$$
$$H_a\colon \beta_1 \text{ and/or } \beta_2 \text{ is not equal to zero}$$

FIGURE 15.6 MINITAB OUTPUT FOR BUTLER TRUCKING WITH TWO INDEPENDENT VARIABLES, MILES TRAVELED (x_1) AND NUMBER OF DELIVERIES (x_2)

```
The regression equation is
Time = - 0.869 + 0.0611 Miles + 0.923 Deliveries

Predictor         Coef    SE Coef      T      p
Constant       -0.8687     0.9515  -0.91  0.392
Miles         0.061135   0.009888   6.18  0.000
Deliveries      0.9234     0.2211   4.18  0.004

S = 0.573142   R-Sq = 90.4%   R-Sq(adj) = 87.6%

Analysis of Variance

SOURCE          DF      SS      MS      F      p
Regression       2  21.601  10.800  32.88  0.000
Residual Error   7   2.299   0.328
Total            9  23.900
```

Figure 15.6 is the Minitab output for the multiple regression model with miles traveled (x_1) and number of deliveries (x_2) as the two independent variables. In the analysis of variance part of the output, we see that MSR = 10.8 and MSE = .328. Using equation (15.14), we obtain the test statistic.

$$F = \frac{10.8}{.328} = 32.9$$

Note that the F value on the Minitab output is $F = 32.88$; the value we calculated differs because we used rounded values for MSR and MSE in the calculation. Using $\alpha = .01$, the p-value $= 0.000$ in the last column of the analysis of variance table (Figure 15.6) indicates that we can reject H_0: $\beta_1 = \beta_2 = 0$ because the p-value is less than $\alpha = .01$. Alternatively, Table 4 of Appendix B shows that with two degrees of freedom in the numerator and seven degrees of freedom in the denominator, $F_{.01} = 9.55$. With $32.9 > 9.55$, we reject H_0: $\beta_1 = \beta_2 = 0$ and conclude that a significant relationship is present between travel time y and the two independent variables, miles traveled and number of deliveries.

As noted previously, the mean square error provides an unbiased estimate of σ^2, the variance of the error term ϵ. Referring to Figure 15.6, we see that the estimate of σ^2 is MSE = .328. The square root of MSE is the estimate of the standard deviation of the error term. As defined in Section 14.5, this standard deviation is called the standard error of the estimate and is denoted s. Hence, we have $s = \sqrt{\text{MSE}} = \sqrt{.328} = .573$. Note that the value of the standard error of the estimate appears in the Minitab output in Figure 15.6.

Table 15.3 is the general analysis of variance (ANOVA) table that provides the F test results for a multiple regression model. The value of the F test statistic appears in the last column and can be compared to F_α with p degrees of freedom in the numerator and $n - p - 1$ degrees of freedom in the denominator to make the hypothesis test conclusion. By reviewing the Minitab output for Butler Trucking Company in Figure 15.6, we see that Minitab's analysis of variance table contains this information. Moreover, Minitab also provides the p-value corresponding to the F test statistic.

TABLE 15.3 ANOVA TABLE FOR A MULTIPLE REGRESSION MODEL WITH p INDEPENDENT VARIABLES

Source	Sum of Squares	Degrees of Freedom	Mean Square	F
Regression	SSR	p	$\text{MSR} = \dfrac{\text{SSR}}{p}$	$F = \dfrac{\text{MSR}}{\text{MSE}}$
Error	SSE	$n - p - 1$	$\text{MSE} = \dfrac{\text{SSE}}{n - p - 1}$	
Total	SST	$n - 1$		

t Test

If the F test shows that the multiple regression relationship is significant, a t test can be conducted to determine the significance of each of the individual parameters. The t test for individual significance follows.

t TEST FOR INDIVIDUAL SIGNIFICANCE

For any parameter β_i

$$H_0\colon \beta_i = 0$$
$$H_a\colon \beta_i \neq 0$$

TEST STATISTIC

$$t = \frac{b_i}{s_{b_i}} \tag{15.15}$$

REJECTION RULE

p-value approach: Reject H_0 if p-value $\leq \alpha$

Critical value approach: Reject H_0 if $t \leq -t_{\alpha/2}$ or if $t \geq t_{\alpha/2}$

where $t_{\alpha/2}$ is based on a t distribution with $n - p - 1$ degrees of freedom.

In the test statistic, s_{b_i} is the estimate of the standard deviation of b_i. The value of s_{b_i} will be provided by the computer software package.

Let us conduct the t test for the Butler Trucking regression problem. Refer to the section of Figure 15.6 that shows the Minitab output for the t-ratio calculations. Values of b_1, b_2, s_{b_1}, and s_{b_2} are as follows.

$$b_1 = .061135 \quad s_{b_1} = .009888$$
$$b_2 = .9234 \quad s_{b_2} = .2211$$

Using equation (15.15), we obtain the test statistic for the hypotheses involving parameters β_1 and β_2.

$$t = .061135/.009888 = 6.18$$
$$t = .9234/.2211 = 4.18$$

Note that both of these t-ratio values and the corresponding p-values are provided by the Minitab output in Figure 15.6. Using $\alpha = .01$, the p-values of .000 and .004 on the Minitab output indicate that we can reject H_0: $\beta_1 = 0$ and H_0: $\beta_2 = 0$. Hence, both parameters are statistically significant. Alternatively, Table 2 of Appendix B shows that with $n - p - 1 = 10 - 2 - 1 = 7$ degrees of freedom, $t_{.005} = 3.499$. With $6.18 > 3.499$, we reject H_0: $\beta_1 = 0$. Similarly, with $4.18 > 3.499$, we reject H_0: $\beta_2 = 0$.

Multicollinearity

We use the term *independent variable* in regression analysis to refer to any variable being used to predict or explain the value of the dependent variable. The term does not mean, however, that the independent variables themselves are independent in any statistical sense. On the contrary, most independent variables in a multiple regression problem are correlated to some degree with one another. For example, in the Butler Trucking example involving the two independent variables x_1 (miles traveled) and x_2 (number of deliveries), we could treat the miles traveled as the dependent variable and the number of deliveries as the independent variable to determine whether those two variables are themselves related. We could then compute the sample correlation coefficient $r_{x_1x_2}$ to determine the extent to which the variables are related. Doing so yields $r_{x_1x_2} = .16$. Thus, we find some degree of linear association between the two independent variables. In multiple regression analysis, **multicollinearity** refers to the correlation among the independent variables.

To provide a better perspective of the potential problems of multicollinearity, let us consider a modification of the Butler Trucking example. Instead of x_2 being the number of deliveries, let x_2 denote the number of gallons of gasoline consumed. Clearly, x_1 (the miles traveled) and x_2 are related; that is, we know that the number of gallons of gasoline used depends on the number of miles traveled. Hence, we would conclude logically that x_1 and x_2 are highly correlated independent variables.

Assume that we obtain the equation $\hat{y} = b_0 + b_1x_1 + b_2x_2$ and find that the F test shows the relationship to be significant. Then suppose we conduct a t test on β_1 to determine whether $\beta_1 \neq 0$, and we cannot reject H_0: $\beta_1 = 0$. Does this result mean that travel time is not related to miles traveled? Not necessarily. What it probably means is that with x_2 already in the model, x_1 does not make a significant contribution to determining the value of y. This interpretation makes sense in our example; if we know the amount of gasoline consumed, we do not gain much additional information useful in predicting y by knowing the miles traveled. Similarly, a t test might lead us to conclude $\beta_2 = 0$ on the grounds that, with x_1 in the model, knowledge of the amount of gasoline consumed does not add much.

A sample correlation coefficient greater than +.7 or less than −.7 for two independent variables is a rule of thumb warning of potential problems with multicollinearity.

To summarize, in t tests for the significance of individual parameters, the difficulty caused by multicollinearity is that it is possible to conclude that none of the individual parameters are significantly different from zero when an F test on the overall multiple regression equation indicates a significant relationship. This problem is avoided when there is little correlation among the independent variables.

Statisticians have developed several tests for determining whether multicollinearity is high enough to cause problems. According to the rule of thumb test, multicollinearity is a potential problem if the absolute value of the sample correlation coefficient exceeds .7 for any two of the independent variables. The other types of tests are more advanced and beyond the scope of this text.

When the independent variables are highly correlated, it is not possible to determine the separate effect of any particular independent variable on the dependent variable.

If possible, every attempt should be made to avoid including independent variables that are highly correlated. In practice, however, strict adherence to this policy is rarely possible. When decision makers have reason to believe substantial multicollinearity is present, they must realize that separating the effects of the individual independent variables on the dependent variable is difficult.

NOTES AND COMMENTS

Ordinarily, multicollinearity does not affect the way in which we perform our regression analysis or interpret the output from a study. However, when multicollinearity is severe—that is, when two or more of the independent variables are highly correlated with one another—we can have difficulty interpreting the results of t tests on the individual parameters. In addition to the type of problem illustrated in this section, severe cases of multicollinearity have been shown to result in least squares estimates that have the wrong sign. That is, in simulated studies where researchers created the underlying regression model and then applied the least squares technique to develop estimates of β_0, β_1, β_2, and so on, it has been shown that under conditions of high multicollinearity the least squares estimates can have a sign opposite that of the parameter being estimated. For example, β_2 might actually be $+10$ and b_2, its estimate, might turn out to be -2. Thus, little faith can be placed in the individual coefficients if multicollinearity is present to a high degree.

Exercises

Methods

SELF test

19. In exercise 1, the following estimated regression equation based on 10 observations was presented.

$$\hat{y} = 29.1270 + .5906x_1 + .4980x_2$$

Here SST = 6724.125, SSR = 6216.375, $s_{b_1} = .0813$, and $s_{b_2} = .0567$.

a. Compute MSR and MSE.
b. Compute F and perform the appropriate F test. Use $\alpha = .05$.
c. Perform a t test for the significance of β_1. Use $\alpha = .05$.
d. Perform a t test for the significance of β_2. Use $\alpha = .05$.

20. Refer to the data presented in exercise 2. The estimated regression equation for these data is

$$\hat{y} = -18.37 + 2.01x_1 + 4.74x_2$$

Here SST = 15,182.9, SSR = 14,052.2, $s_{b_1} = .2471$, and $s_{b_2} = .9484$.

a. Test for a significant relationship among x_1, x_2, and y. Use $\alpha = .05$.
b. Is β_1 significant? Use $\alpha = .05$.
c. Is β_2 significant? Use $\alpha = .05$.

21. The following estimated regression equation was developed for a model involving two independent variables.

$$\hat{y} = 40.7 + 8.63x_1 + 2.71x_2$$

After x_2 was dropped from the model, the least squares method was used to obtain an estimated regression equation involving only x_1 as an independent variable.

$$\hat{y} = 42.0 + 9.01x_1$$

a. Give an interpretation of the coefficient of x_1 in both models.
b. Could multicollinearity explain why the coefficient of x_1 differs in the two models? If so, how?

Applications

22. In exercise 4, the following estimated regression equation relating sales to inventory investment and advertising expenditures was given.

$$\hat{y} = 25 + 10x_1 + 8x_2$$

The data used to develop the model came from a survey of 10 stores; for these data SST = 16,000 and SSR = 12,000.

a. Compute SSE, MSE, and MSR.
b. Use an F test and a .05 level of significance to determine whether there is a relationship among the variables.

SELF test

23. Refer to exercise 5.
    a. Use $\alpha = .01$ to test the hypotheses

$$H_0: \beta_1 = \beta_2 = 0$$
$$H_a: \beta_1 \text{ and/or } \beta_2 \text{ is not equal to zero}$$

for the model $y = \beta_0 + \beta_1 x_1 + \beta_2 x_2 + \epsilon$, where

$$x_1 = \text{television advertising (\$1000s)}$$
$$x_2 = \text{newspaper advertising (\$1000s)}$$

    b. Use $\alpha = .05$ to test the significance of β_1. Should x_1 be dropped from the model?
    c. Use $\alpha = .05$ to test the significance of β_2. Should x_2 be dropped from the model?

24. *The Wall Street Journal* conducted a study of basketball spending at top colleges. A portion of the data showing the revenue ($ millions), percentage of wins, and the coach's salary ($ millions) for 39 of the country's top basketball programs follows (*The Wall Street Journal,* March 11–12, 2006).

WEB file
Basketball

School	Revenue	% Wins	Salary
Alabama	6.5	61	1.00
Arizona	16.6	63	.70
Arkansas	11.1	72	.80
Boston College	3.4	80	.53
⋮	⋮	⋮	⋮
Washington	5.0	83	.89
West Virginia	4.9	67	.70
Wichita State	3.1	75	.41
Wisconsin	12.0	66	.70

    a. Develop the estimated regression equation that can be used to predict the coach's salary given the revenue generated by the program and the percentage of wins.
    b. Use the F test to determine the overall significance of the relationship. What is your conclusion at the .05 level of significance?
    c. Use the t test to determine the significance of each independent variable. What is your conclusion at the .05 level of significance?

25. The *Condé Nast Traveler* Gold List for 2012 provided ratings for the top 20 small cruise ships (*Condé Nast Traveler* website, March 1, 2012). The data shown below are the scores each ship received based upon the results from *Condé Nast Traveler's* annual Readers' Choice Survey. Each score represents the percentage of respondents who rated a ship as excellent or very good on several criteria, including Itineraries/Schedule, Shore Excursions, and Food/Dining. An overall score was also reported and used to rank the ships. The highest ranked ship, the *Seabourn Odyssey,* has an overall score of 94.4, the highest component of which is 97.8 for Food/Dining.

WEB file CruiseShips

Ship	Overall	Itineraries/ Schedule	Shore Excursions	Food/ Dining
Seabourn Odyssey	94.4	94.6	90.9	97.8
Seabourn Pride	93.0	96.7	84.2	96.7
National Geographic Endeavor	92.9	100.0	100.0	88.5
Seabourn Sojourn	91.3	88.6	94.8	97.1
Paul Gauguin	90.5	95.1	87.9	91.2
Seabourn Legend	90.3	92.5	82.1	98.8
Seabourn Spirit	90.2	96.0	86.3	92.0
Silver Explorer	89.9	92.6	92.6	88.9
Silver Spirit	89.4	94.7	85.9	90.8
Seven Seas Navigator	89.2	90.6	83.3	90.5
Silver Whisperer	89.2	90.9	82.0	88.6
National Geographic Explorer	89.1	93.1	93.1	89.7
Silver Cloud	88.7	92.6	78.3	91.3
Celebrity Xpedition	87.2	93.1	91.7	73.6
Silver Shadow	87.2	91.0	75.0	89.7
Silver Wind	86.6	94.4	78.1	91.6
SeaDream II	86.2	95.5	77.4	90.9
Wind Star	86.1	94.9	76.5	91.5
Wind Surf	86.1	92.1	72.3	89.3
Wind Spirit	85.2	93.5	77.4	91.9

a. Determine the estimated regression equation that can be used to predict the overall score given the scores for Itineraries/Schedule, Shore Excursions, and Food/Dining.
b. Use the F test to determine the overall significance of the relationship. What is your conclusion at the .05 level of significance?
c. Use the t test to determine the significance of each independent variable. What is your conclusion at the .05 level of significance?
d. Remove any independent variable that is not significant from the estimated regression equation. What is your recommended estimated regression equation?

WEB file MLBPitching

26. In exercise 10, data showing the values of several pitching statistics for a random sample of 20 pitchers from the American League of Major League Baseball were provided. In part (c) of this exercise an estimated regression equation was developed to predict the average number of runs given up per inning pitched (R/IP) given the average number of strikeouts per inning pitched (SO/IP) and the average number of home runs per inning pitched (HR/IP).
    a. Use the F test to determine the overall significance of the relationship. What is your conclusion at the .05 level of significance?
    b. Use the t test to determine the significance of each independent variable. What is your conclusion at the .05 level of significance?

15.6 Using the Estimated Regression Equation for Estimation and Prediction

The procedures for estimating the mean value of y and predicting an individual value of y in multiple regression are similar to those in regression analysis involving one independent variable. First, recall that in Chapter 14 we showed that the point estimate of the expected value of y for a given value of x was the same as the point estimate of an individual value of y. In both cases, we used $\hat{y} = b_0 + b_1x$ as the point estimate.

In multiple regression we use the same procedure. That is, we substitute the given values of $x_1, x_2, \ldots, x_p$ into the estimated regression equation and use the corresponding value of $\hat{y}$ as the point estimate. Suppose that for the Butler Trucking example we want to use the

TABLE 15.4 THE 95% CONFIDENCE AND PREDICTION INTERVALS FOR BUTLER TRUCKING

Value of x_1	Value of x_2	Confidence Interval Lower Limit	Confidence Interval Upper Limit	Prediction Interval Lower Limit	Prediction Interval Upper Limit
50	2	3.146	4.924	2.414	5.656
50	3	4.127	5.789	3.368	6.548
50	4	4.815	6.948	4.157	7.607
100	2	6.258	7.926	5.500	8.683
100	3	7.385	8.645	6.520	9.510
100	4	8.135	9.742	7.362	10.515

estimated regression equation involving x_1 (miles traveled) and x_2 (number of deliveries) to develop two interval estimates:

1. A *confidence interval* of the mean travel time for all trucks that travel 100 miles and make two deliveries
2. A *prediction interval* of the travel time for *one specific* truck that travels 100 miles and makes two deliveries

Using the estimated regression equation $\hat{y} = -.869 + .0611x_1 + .923x_2$ with $x_1 = 100$ and $x_2 = 2$, we obtain the following value of $\hat{y}$.

$$\hat{y} = -.869 + .0611(100) + .923(2) = 7.09$$

Hence, the point estimate of travel time in both cases is approximately seven hours.

To develop interval estimates for the mean value of y and for an individual value of y, we use a procedure similar to that for regression analysis involving one independent variable. The formulas required are beyond the scope of the text, but computer packages for multiple regression analysis will often provide confidence intervals once the values of x_1, $x_2, \ldots, x_p$ are specified by the user. In Table 15.4 we show the 95% confidence and prediction intervals for the Butler Trucking example for selected values of x_1 and x_2; these values were obtained using Minitab. Note that the interval estimate for an individual value of y is wider than the interval estimate for the expected value of y. This difference simply reflects the fact that for given values of x_1 and x_2 we can estimate the mean travel time for all trucks with more precision than we can predict the travel time for one specific truck.

Exercises

Methods

27. In exercise 1, the following estimated regression equation based on 10 observations was presented.

$$\hat{y} = 29.1270 + .5906x_1 + .4980x_2$$

a. Develop a point estimate of the mean value of y when $x_1 = 180$ and $x_2 = 310$.
b. Develop a point estimate for an individual value of y when $x_1 = 180$ and $x_2 = 310$.

SELF test

28. Refer to the data in exercise 2. The estimated regression equation for those data is

$$\hat{y} = -18.4 + 2.01x_1 + 4.74x_2$$

a. Develop a 95% confidence interval for the mean value of y when $x_1 = 45$ and $x_2 = 15$.
b. Develop a 95% prediction interval for y when $x_1 = 45$ and $x_2 = 15$.

Applications

SELF test

29. In exercise 5, the owner of Showtime Movie Theaters, Inc., used multiple regression analysis to predict gross revenue (y) as a function of television advertising (x_1) and newspaper advertising (x_2). The estimated regression equation was

$$\hat{y} = 83.2 + 2.29x_1 + 1.30x_2$$

   a. What is the gross revenue expected for a week when \$3500 is spent on television advertising ($x_1 = 3.5$) and \$1800 is spent on newspaper advertising ($x_2 = 1.8$)?
   b. Provide a 95% confidence interval for the mean revenue of all weeks with the expenditures listed in part (a).
   c. Provide a 95% prediction interval for next week's revenue, assuming that the advertising expenditures will be allocated as in part (a).

WEB file Boats

30. In exercise 9 an estimated regression equation was developed relating the top speed for a boat to the boat's beam and horsepower rating.
   a. Develop a 95% confidence interval for the mean top speed of a boat with a beam of 85 inches and an engine with a 330 horsepower rating.
   b. The Svfara SV609 has a beam of 85 inches and an engine with a 330 horsepower rating. Develop a 95% prediction interval for the mean top speed for the Svfara SV609.

31. The American Association of Individual Investors (AAII) On-Line Discount Broker Survey polls members on their experiences with electronic trades handled by discount brokers. As part of the survey, members were asked to rate their satisfaction with the trade price and the speed of execution, as well as provide an overall satisfaction rating. Possible responses (scores) were no opinion (0), unsatisfied (1), somewhat satisfied (2), satisfied (3), and very satisfied (4). For each broker, summary scores were computed by computing a weighted average of the scores provided by each respondent. A portion of the survey results follows (AAII website, February 7, 2012).

WEB file Broker

Brokerage	Trade Price	Speed of Execution	Satisfaction Electronic Trades
Scottrade, Inc.	3.4	3.4	3.5
Charles Schwab	3.2	3.3	3.4
Fidelity Brokerage Services	3.1	3.4	3.9
TD Ameritrade	2.9	3.6	3.7
E*Trade Financial	2.9	3.2	2.9
(Not listed)	2.5	3.2	2.7
Vanguard Brokerage Services	2.6	3.8	2.8
USAA Brokerage Services	2.4	3.8	3.6
Thinkorswim	2.6	2.6	2.6
Wells Fargo Investments	2.3	2.7	2.3
Interactive Brokers	3.7	4.0	4.0
Zecco.com	2.5	2.5	2.5
Firstrade Securities	3.0	3.0	4.0
Banc of America Investment Services	4.0	1.0	2.0

   a. Develop an estimated regression equation using trade price and speed of execution to predict overall satisfaction with the broker.
   b. Finger Lakes Investments has developed a new electronic trading system and would like to predict overall customer satisfaction assuming they can provide satisfactory levels of service levels (3) for both trade price and speed of execution. Use the estimated repression equation developed in part (a) to predict overall satisfaction level for Finger Lakes Investments if they can achieve these performance levels.

c. Develop a 95% confidence interval estimate of the overall satisfaction of electronic trades for all brokers that provide satisfactory levels of service for both trade price and speed of execution.

d. Develop a 95% prediction interval of overall satisfaction for Finger Lakes Investments assuming they achieve service levels of 3 for both trade price and speed of execution.

15.7 Categorical Independent Variables

The independent variables may be categorical or quantitative.

Thus far, the examples we have considered involved quantitative independent variables such as student population, distance traveled, and number of deliveries. In many situations, however, we must work with **categorical independent variables** such as gender (male, female), method of payment (cash, credit card, check), and so on. The purpose of this section is to show how categorical variables are handled in regression analysis. To illustrate the use and interpretation of a categorical independent variable, we will consider a problem facing the managers of Johnson Filtration, Inc.

An Example: Johnson Filtration, Inc.

Johnson Filtration, Inc., provides maintenance service for water-filtration systems throughout southern Florida. Customers contact Johnson with requests for maintenance service on their water-filtration systems. To estimate the service time and the service cost, Johnson's managers want to predict the repair time necessary for each maintenance request. Hence, repair time in hours is the dependent variable. Repair time is believed to be related to two factors, the number of months since the last maintenance service and the type of repair problem (mechanical or electrical). Data for a sample of 10 service calls are reported in Table 15.5.

Let y denote the repair time in hours and x_1 denote the number of months since the last maintenance service. The regression model that uses only x_1 to predict y is

$$y = \beta_0 + \beta_1 x_1 + \epsilon$$

Using Minitab to develop the estimated regression equation, we obtained the output shown in Figure 15.7. The estimated regression equation is

$$\hat{y} = 2.15 + .304x_1 \qquad (15.16)$$

At the .05 level of significance, the p-value of .016 for the t (or F) test indicates that the number of months since the last service is significantly related to repair time. R-sq = 53.4% indicates that x_1 alone explains 53.4% of the variability in repair time.

TABLE 15.5 DATA FOR THE JOHNSON FILTRATION EXAMPLE

Service Call	Months Since Last Service	Type of Repair	Repair Time in Hours
1	2	electrical	2.9
2	6	mechanical	3.0
3	8	electrical	4.8
4	3	mechanical	1.8
5	2	electrical	2.9
6	7	electrical	4.9
7	9	mechanical	4.2
8	8	mechanical	4.8
9	4	electrical	4.4
10	6	electrical	4.5

FIGURE 15.7 MINITAB OUTPUT FOR JOHNSON FILTRATION WITH MONTHS SINCE LAST SERVICE (x_1) AS THE INDEPENDENT VARIABLE

In the Minitab output the variable names Months *and* Time *were entered as the column headings on the worksheet; thus,* x_1 = Months *and* y = Time.

```
The regression equation is
Time = 2.15 + 0.304 Months

Predictor    Coef   SE Coef     T      p
Constant   2.1473    0.6050  3.55  0.008
Months     0.3041    0.1004  3.03  0.016

S = 0.781022   R-Sq = 53.4%   R-Sq(adj) = 47.6%

Analysis of Variance

SOURCE          DF       SS      MS     F      p
Regression       1   5.5960  5.5960  9.17  0.016
Residual Error   8   4.8800  0.6100
Total            9  10.4760
```

To incorporate the type of repair into the regression model, we define the following variable.

$$x_2 = \begin{cases} 0 \text{ if the type of repair is mechanical} \\ 1 \text{ if the type of repair is electrical} \end{cases}$$

In regression analysis x_2 is called a **dummy** or *indicator* **variable**. Using this dummy variable, we can write the multiple regression model as

$$y = \beta_0 + \beta_1 x_1 + \beta_2 x_2 + \epsilon$$

Table 15.6 is the revised data set that includes the values of the dummy variable. Using Minitab and the data in Table 15.6, we can develop estimates of the model parameters. The Minitab output in Figure 15.8 shows that the estimated multiple regression equation is

$$\hat{y} = .93 + .388x_1 + 1.26x_2 \qquad \textbf{(15.17)}$$

TABLE 15.6 DATA FOR THE JOHNSON FILTRATION EXAMPLE WITH TYPE OF REPAIR INDICATED BY A DUMMY VARIABLE (x_2 = 0 FOR MECHANICAL; x_2 = 1 FOR ELECTRICAL)

WEB file
Johnson

Customer	Months Since Last Service (x_1)	Type of Repair (x_2)	Repair Time in Hours (y)
1	2	1	2.9
2	6	0	3.0
3	8	1	4.8
4	3	0	1.8
5	2	1	2.9
6	7	1	4.9
7	9	0	4.2
8	8	0	4.8
9	4	1	4.4
10	6	1	4.5

FIGURE 15.8 MINITAB OUTPUT FOR JOHNSON FILTRATION WITH MONTHS SINCE LAST SERVICE (x_1) AND TYPE OF REPAIR (x_2) AS THE INDEPENDENT VARIABLES

In the Minitab output the variable names Months, Type, *and* Time *were entered as the column headings on the worksheet; thus,* x_1 = Months, x_2 = Type, *and* y = Time.

```
The regression equation is
Time = 0.930 + 0.388 Months + 1.26 Type

Predictor       Coef   SE Coef     T      p
Constant      0.9305    0.4670  1.99  0.087
Months       0.38762   0.06257  6.20  0.000
Type          1.2627    0.3141  4.02  0.005

S = 0.459048    R-Sq = 85.9%    R-Sq(adj) = 81.9%

Analysis of Variance

SOURCE          DF       SS      MS      F      p
Regression       2   9.0009  4.5005  21.36  0.001
Residual Error   7   1.4751  0.2107
Total            9  10.4760
```

At the .05 level of significance, the p-value of .001 associated with the F test ($F = 21.36$) indicates that the regression relationship is significant. The t test part of the printout in Figure 15.8 shows that both months since last service (p-value = .000) and type of repair (p-value = .005) are statistically significant. In addition, R-Sq = 85.9% and R-Sq (adj) = 81.9% indicate that the estimated regression equation does a good job of explaining the variability in repair times. Thus, equation (15.17) should prove helpful in predicting the repair time necessary for the various service calls.

Interpreting the Parameters

The multiple regression equation for the Johnson Filtration example is

$$E(y) = \beta_0 + \beta_1 x_1 + \beta_2 x_2 \tag{15.18}$$

To understand how to interpret the parameters β_0, β_1, and β_2 when a categorical variable is present, consider the case when $x_2 = 0$ (mechanical repair). Using $E(y \mid \text{mechanical})$ to denote the mean or expected value of repair time *given* a mechanical repair, we have

$$E(y \mid \text{mechanical}) = \beta_0 + \beta_1 x_1 + \beta_2(0) = \beta_0 + \beta_1 x_1 \tag{15.19}$$

Similarly, for an electrical repair ($x_2 = 1$), we have

$$\begin{aligned} E(y \mid \text{electrical}) &= \beta_0 + \beta_1 x_1 + \beta_2(1) = \beta_0 + \beta_1 x_1 + \beta_2 \\ &= (\beta_0 + \beta_2) + \beta_1 x_1 \end{aligned} \tag{15.20}$$

Comparing equations (15.19) and (15.20), we see that the mean repair time is a linear function of x_1 for both mechanical and electrical repairs. The slope of both equations is β_1, but the y-intercept differs. The y-intercept is β_0 in equation (15.19) for mechanical repairs and $(\beta_0 + \beta_2)$ in equation (15.20) for electrical repairs. The interpretation of β_2 is that it indicates the difference between the mean repair time for an electrical repair and the mean repair time for a mechanical repair.

If β_2 is positive, the mean repair time for an electrical repair will be greater than that for a mechanical repair; if β_2 is negative, the mean repair time for an electrical repair will be less than that for a mechanical repair. Finally, if $\beta_2 = 0$, there is no difference in the mean repair time between electrical and mechanical repairs and the type of repair is not related to the repair time.

Using the estimated multiple regression equation $\hat{y} = .93 + .388x_1 + 1.26x_2$, we see that .93 is the estimate of β_0 and 1.26 is the estimate of β_2. Thus, when $x_2 = 0$ (mechanical repair)

$$\hat{y} = .93 + .388x_1 \tag{15.21}$$

and when $x_2 = 1$ (electrical repair)

$$\begin{aligned}\hat{y} &= .93 + .388x_1 + 1.26(1) \\ &= 2.19 + .388x_1\end{aligned} \tag{15.22}$$

In effect, the use of a dummy variable for type of repair provides two estimated regression equations that can be used to predict the repair time, one corresponding to mechanical repairs and one corresponding to electrical repairs. In addition, with $b_2 = 1.26$, we learn that, on average, electrical repairs require 1.26 hours longer than mechanical repairs.

Figure 15.9 is the plot of the Johnson data from Table 15.6. Repair time in hours (y) is represented by the vertical axis and months since last service (x_1) is represented by the horizontal axis. A data point for a mechanical repair is indicated by an M and a data point for an electrical repair is indicated by an E. Equations (15.21) and (15.22) are plotted on the graph to show graphically the two equations that can be used to predict the repair time, one corresponding to mechanical repairs and one corresponding to electrical repairs.

FIGURE 15.9 SCATTER DIAGRAM FOR THE JOHNSON FILTRATION REPAIR DATA FROM TABLE 15.6

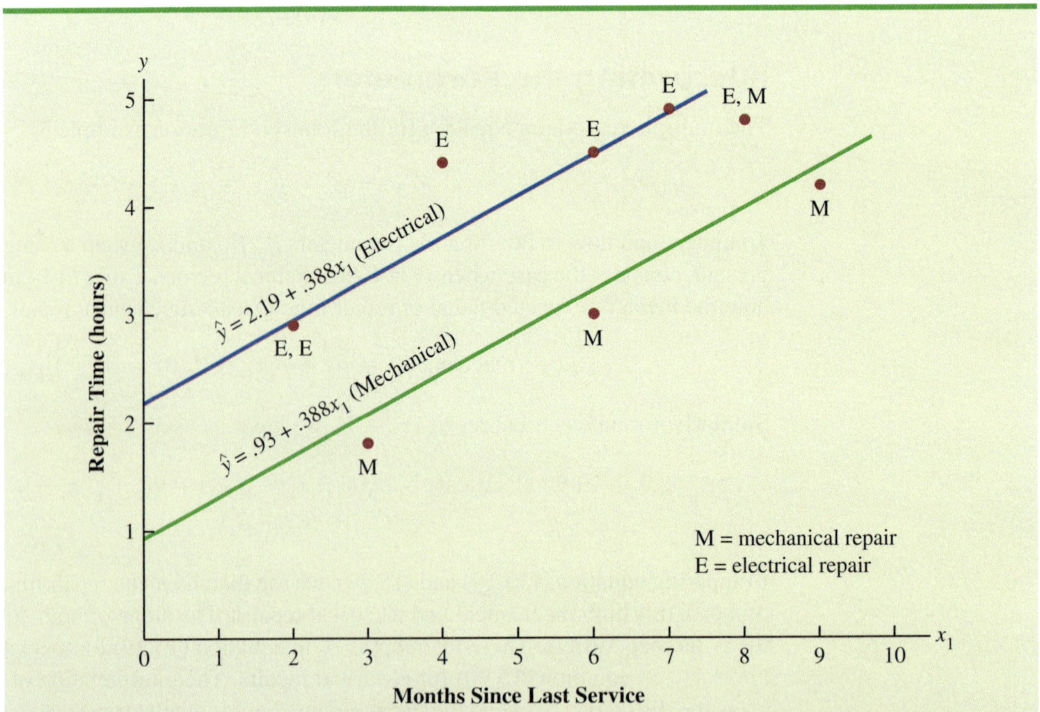

More Complex Categorical Variables

A categorical variable with k levels must be modeled using k − 1 dummy variables. Care must be taken in defining and interpreting the dummy variables.

Because the categorical variable for the Johnson Filtration example had two levels (mechanical and electrical), defining a dummy variable with zero indicating a mechanical repair and one indicating an electrical repair was easy. However, when a categorical variable has more than two levels, care must be taken in both defining and interpreting the dummy variables. As we will show, if a categorical variable has k levels, $k - 1$ dummy variables are required, with each dummy variable being coded as 0 or 1.

For example, suppose a manufacturer of copy machines organized the sales territories for a particular state into three regions: A, B, and C. The managers want to use regression analysis to help predict the number of copiers sold per week. With the number of units sold as the dependent variable, they are considering several independent variables (the number of sales personnel, advertising expenditures, and so on). Suppose the managers believe sales region is also an important factor in predicting the number of copiers sold. Because sales region is a categorical variable with three levels, A, B and C, we will need $3 - 1 = 2$ dummy variables to represent the sales region. Each variable can be coded 0 or 1 as follows.

$$x_1 = \begin{cases} 1 \text{ if sales region B} \\ 0 \text{ otherwise} \end{cases}$$

$$x_2 = \begin{cases} 1 \text{ if sales region C} \\ 0 \text{ otherwise} \end{cases}$$

With this definition, we have the following values of x_1 and x_2.

Region	x_1	x_2
A	0	0
B	1	0
C	0	1

Observations corresponding to region A would be coded $x_1 = 0, x_2 = 0$; observations corresponding to region B would be coded $x_1 = 1, x_2 = 0$; and observations corresponding to region C would be coded $x_1 = 0, x_2 = 1$.

The regression equation relating the expected value of the number of units sold, $E(y)$, to the dummy variables would be written as

$$E(y) = \beta_0 + \beta_1 x_1 + \beta_2 x_2$$

To help us interpret the parameters β_0, β_1, and β_2, consider the following three variations of the regression equation.

$$E(y \mid \text{region A}) = \beta_0 + \beta_1(0) + \beta_2(0) = \beta_0$$
$$E(y \mid \text{region B}) = \beta_0 + \beta_1(1) + \beta_2(0) = \beta_0 + \beta_1$$
$$E(y \mid \text{region C}) = \beta_0 + \beta_1(0) + \beta_2(1) = \beta_0 + \beta_2$$

Thus, β_0 is the mean or expected value of sales for region A; β_1 is the difference between the mean number of units sold in region B and the mean number of units sold in region A; and β_2 is the difference between the mean number of units sold in region C and the mean number of units sold in region A.

Two dummy variables were required because sales region is a categorical variable with three levels. But the assignment of $x_1 = 0, x_2 = 0$ to indicate region A, $x_1 = 1, x_2 = 0$ to indicate region B, and $x_1 = 0, x_2 = 1$ to indicate region C was arbitrary. For example, we could have chosen $x_1 = 1, x_2 = 0$ to indicate region A, $x_1 = 0, x_2 = 0$ to indicate region B, and $x_1 = 0, x_2 = 1$ to indicate region C. In that case, β_1 would have been interpreted as the mean difference between regions A and B and β_2 as the mean difference between regions C and B.

The important point to remember is that when a categorical variable has k levels, $k - 1$ dummy variables are required in the multiple regression analysis. Thus, if the sales region example had a fourth region, labeled D, three dummy variables would be necessary. For example, the three dummy variables can be coded as follows.

$$x_1 = \begin{cases} 1 \text{ if sales region B} \\ 0 \text{ otherwise} \end{cases} \qquad x_2 = \begin{cases} 1 \text{ if sales region C} \\ 0 \text{ otherwise} \end{cases} \qquad x_3 = \begin{cases} 1 \text{ if sales region D} \\ 0 \text{ otherwise} \end{cases}$$

Exercises

Methods

SELF test

32. Consider a regression study involving a dependent variable y, a quantitative independent variable x_1, and a categorical independent variable with two levels (level 1 and level 2).
    a. Write a multiple regression equation relating x_1 and the categorical variable to y.
    b. What is the expected value of y corresponding to level 1 of the categorical variable?
    c. What is the expected value of y corresponding to level 2 of the categorical variable?
    d. Interpret the parameters in your regression equation.
33. Consider a regression study involving a dependent variable y, a quantitative independent variable x_1, and a categorical independent variable with three possible levels (level 1, level 2, and level 3).
    a. How many dummy variables are required to represent the categorical variable?
    b. Write a multiple regression equation relating x_1 and the categorical variable to y.
    c. Interpret the parameters in your regression equation.

Applications

SELF test

34. Management proposed the following regression model to predict sales at a fast-food outlet.

$$y = \beta_0 + \beta_1 x_1 + \beta_2 x_2 + \beta_3 x_3 + \epsilon$$

where

$$\begin{aligned} x_1 &= \text{number of competitors within one mile} \\ x_2 &= \text{population within one mile (1000s)} \\ x_3 &= \begin{cases} 1 \text{ if drive-up window present} \\ 0 \text{ otherwise} \end{cases} \\ y &= \text{sales (\$1000s)} \end{aligned}$$

The following estimated regression equation was developed after 20 outlets were surveyed.

$$\hat{y} = 10.1 - 4.2x_1 + 6.8x_2 + 15.3x_3$$

a. What is the expected amount of sales attributable to the drive-up window?
b. Predict sales for a store with two competitors, a population of 8000 within one mile, and no drive-up window.
c. Predict sales for a store with one competitor, a population of 3000 within one mile, and a drive-up window.

35. Refer to the Johnson Filtration problem introduced in this section. Suppose that in addition to information on the number of months since the machine was serviced and whether a mechanical or an electrical repair was necessary, the managers obtained a list showing which repairperson performed the service. The revised data follow.

WEB file
Repair

Repair Time in Hours	Months Since Last Service	Type of Repair	Repairperson
2.9	2	Electrical	Dave Newton
3.0	6	Mechanical	Dave Newton
4.8	8	Electrical	Bob Jones
1.8	3	Mechanical	Dave Newton
2.9	2	Electrical	Dave Newton
4.9	7	Electrical	Bob Jones
4.2	9	Mechanical	Bob Jones
4.8	8	Mechanical	Bob Jones
4.4	4	Electrical	Bob Jones
4.5	6	Electrical	Dave Newton

a. Ignore for now the months since the last maintenance service (x_1) and the repairperson who performed the service. Develop the estimated simple linear regression equation to predict the repair time (y) given the type of repair (x_2). Recall that $x_2 = 0$ if the type of repair is mechanical and 1 if the type of repair is electrical.
b. Does the equation that you developed in part (a) provide a good fit for the observed data? Explain.
c. Ignore for now the months since the last maintenance service and the type of repair associated with the machine. Develop the estimated simple linear regression equation to predict the repair time given the repairperson who performed the service. Let $x_3 = 0$ if Bob Jones performed the service and $x_3 = 1$ if Dave Newton performed the service.
d. Does the equation that you developed in part (c) provide a good fit for the observed data? Explain.

36. This problem is an extension of the situation described in exercise 35.
a. Develop the estimated regression equation to predict the repair time given the number of months since the last maintenance service, the type of repair, and the repairperson who performed the service.
b. At the .05 level of significance, test whether the estimated regression equation developed in part (a) represents a significant relationship between the independent variables and the dependent variable.
c. Is the addition of the independent variable x_3, the repairperson who performed the service, statistically significant? Use $\alpha = .05$. What explanation can you give for the results observed?

37. The *Consumer Reports* Restaurant Customer Satisfaction Survey is based upon 148,599 visits to full-service restaurant chains (*Consumer Reports* website, February 11, 2009). Assume the following data are representative of the results reported. The variable type indicates whether the restaurant is an Italian restaurant or a seafood/steakhouse. Price indicates the average amount paid per person for dinner and drinks, minus the tip. Score reflects diners' overall satisfaction, with higher values indicating greater overall satisfaction. A score of 80 can be interpreted as very satisfied.

WEB file
RestaurantRatings

Restaurant	Type	Price ($)	Score
Bertucci's	Italian	16	77
Black Angus Steakhouse	Seafood/Steakhouse	24	79
Bonefish Grill	Seafood/Steakhouse	26	85

(*continued*)

Restaurant	Type	Price ($)	Score
Bravo! Cucina Italiana	Italian	18	84
Buca di Beppo	Italian	17	81
Bugaboo Creek Steak House	Seafood/Steakhouse	18	77
Carrabba's Italian Grill	Italian	23	86
Charlie Brown's Steakhouse	Seafood/Steakhouse	17	75
Il Fornaio	Italian	28	83
Joe's Crab Shack	Seafood/Steakhouse	15	71
Johnny Carino's Italian	Italian	17	81
Lone Star Steakhouse & Saloon	Seafood/Steakhouse	17	76
LongHorn Steakhouse	Seafood/Steakhouse	19	81
Maggiano's Little Italy	Italian	22	83
McGrath's Fish House	Seafood/Steakhouse	16	81
Olive Garden	Italian	19	81
Outback Steakhouse	Seafood/Steakhouse	20	80
Red Lobster	Seafood/Steakhouse	18	78
Romano's Macaroni Grill	Italian	18	82
The Old Spaghetti Factory	Italian	12	79
Uno Chicago Grill	Italian	16	76

a. Develop the estimated regression equation to show how overall customer satisfaction is related to the independent variable average meal price.
b. At the .05 level of significance, test whether the estimated regression equation developed in part (a) indicates a significant relationship between overall customer satisfaction and average meal price.
c. Develop a dummy variable that will account for the type of restaurant (Italian or seafood/steakhouse).
d. Develop the estimated regression equation to show how overall customer satisfaction is related to the average meal price and the type of restaurant.
e. Is type of restaurant a significant factor in overall customer satisfaction?
f. Predict the *Consumer Reports* customer satisfaction score for a seafood/steakhouse that has an average meal price of $20. How much would the predicted score have changed for an Italian restaurant?

38. A 10-year study conducted by the American Heart Association provided data on how age, blood pressure, and smoking relate to the risk of strokes. Assume that the following data are from a portion of this study. Risk is interpreted as the probability (times 100) that the patient will have a stroke over the next 10-year period. For the smoking variable, define a dummy variable with 1 indicating a smoker and 0 indicating a nonsmoker.

WEB file Stroke

Risk	Age	Pressure	Smoker
12	57	152	No
24	67	163	No
13	58	155	No
56	86	177	Yes
28	59	196	No
51	76	189	Yes
18	56	155	Yes
31	78	120	No
37	80	135	Yes
15	78	98	No
22	71	152	No
36	70	173	Yes

Risk	Age	Pressure	Smoker
15	67	135	Yes
48	77	209	Yes
15	60	199	No
36	82	119	Yes
8	66	166	No
34	80	125	Yes
3	62	117	No
37	59	207	Yes

a. Develop an estimated regression equation that relates risk of a stroke to the person's age, blood pressure, and whether the person is a smoker.
b. Is smoking a significant factor in the risk of a stroke? Explain. Use $\alpha = .05$.
c. What is the probability of a stroke over the next 10 years for Art Speen, a 68-year-old smoker who has blood pressure of 175? What action might the physician recommend for this patient?

15.8 Residual Analysis

In Chapter 14 we pointed out that standardized residuals are frequently used in residual plots and in the identification of outliers. The general formula for the standardized residual for observation i follows.

STANDARDIZED RESIDUAL FOR OBSERVATION i

$$\frac{y_i - \hat{y}_i}{s_{y_i - \hat{y}_i}} \tag{15.23}$$

where

$$s_{y_i - \hat{y}_i} = \text{the standard deviation of residual } i$$

The general formula for the standard deviation of residual i is defined as follows.

STANDARD DEVIATION OF RESIDUAL i

$$s_{y_i - \hat{y}_i} = s\sqrt{1 - h_i} \tag{15.24}$$

where

$$s = \text{standard error of the estimate}$$
$$h_i = \text{leverage of observation } i$$

As we stated in Chapter 14, the **leverage** of an observation is determined by how far the values of the independent variables are from their means. The computation of h_i, $s_{y_i - \hat{y}_i}$, and hence the standardized residual for observation i in multiple regression analysis is too complex to be

TABLE 15.7 RESIDUALS AND STANDARDIZED RESIDUALS FOR THE BUTLER TRUCKING REGRESSION ANALYSIS

Miles Traveled (x_1)	Deliveries (x_2)	Travel Time (y)	Predicted Value ($\hat{y}$)	Residual ($y - \hat{y}$)	Standardized Residual
100	4	9.3	8.93846	.361541	.78344
50	3	4.8	4.95830	−.158304	−.34962
100	4	8.9	8.93846	−.038460	−.08334
100	2	6.5	7.09161	−.591609	−1.30929
50	2	4.2	4.03488	.165121	.38167
80	2	6.2	5.86892	.331083	.65431
75	3	7.4	6.48667	.913331	1.68917
65	4	6.0	6.79875	−.798749	−1.77372
90	3	7.6	7.40369	.196311	.36703
90	2	6.1	6.48026	−.380263	−.77639

done by hand. However, the standardized residuals can be easily obtained as part of the output from statistical software packages. Table 15.7 lists the predicted values, the residuals, and the standardized residuals for the Butler Trucking example presented previously in this chapter; we obtained these values by using the Minitab statistical software package. The predicted values in the table are based on the estimated regression equation $\hat{y} = -.869 + .0611x_1 + .923x_2$.

The standardized residuals and the predicted values of y from Table 15.7 are used in Figure 15.10, the standardized residual plot for the Butler Trucking multiple regression example. This standardized residual plot does not indicate any unusual abnormalities. Also, all the standardized residuals are between −2 and +2; hence, we have no reason to question the assumption that the error term ϵ is normally distributed. We conclude that the model assumptions are reasonable.

FIGURE 15.10 STANDARDIZED RESIDUAL PLOT FOR BUTLER TRUCKING

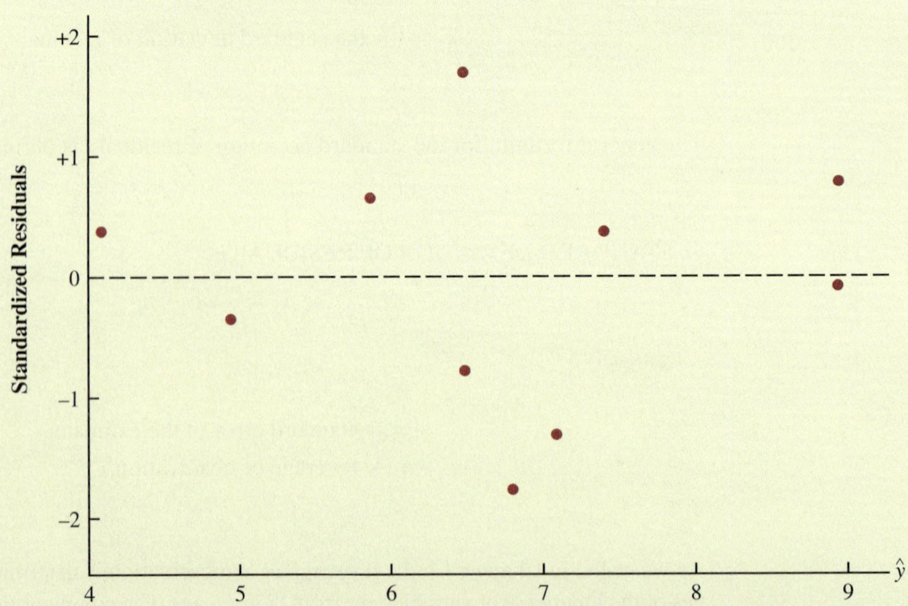

A normal probability plot also can be used to determine whether the distribution of ϵ appears to be normal. The procedure and interpretation for a normal probability plot were discussed in Section 14.8. The same procedure is appropriate for multiple regression. Again, we would use a statistical software package to perform the computations and provide the normal probability plot.

Detecting Outliers

An **outlier** is an observation that is unusual in comparison with the other data; in other words, an outlier does not fit the pattern of the other data. In Chapter 14 we showed an example of an outlier and discussed how standardized residuals can be used to detect outliers. Minitab classifies an observation as an outlier if the value of its standardized residual is less than -2 or greater than $+2$. Applying this rule to the standardized residuals for the Butler Trucking example (see Table 15.7), we do not detect any outliers in the data set.

In general, the presence of one or more outliers in a data set tends to increase s, the standard error of the estimate, and hence increase $s_{y-\hat{y}_i}$, the standard deviation of residual i. Because $s_{y_i-\hat{y}_i}$ appears in the denominator of the formula for the standardized residual (15.23), the size of the standardized residual will decrease as s increases. As a result, even though a residual may be unusually large, the large denominator in expression (15.23) may cause the standardized residual rule to fail to identify the observation as being an outlier. We can circumvent this difficulty by using a form of the standardized residuals called **studentized deleted residuals**.

Studentized Deleted Residuals and Outliers

Suppose the ith observation is deleted from the data set and a new estimated regression equation is developed with the remaining $n - 1$ observations. Let $s_{(i)}$ denote the standard error of the estimate based on the data set with the ith observation deleted. If we compute the standard deviation of residual i using $s_{(i)}$ instead of s, and then compute the standardized residual for observation i using the revised $s_{y_i-\hat{y}_i}$ value, the resulting standardized residual is called a studentized deleted residual. If the ith observation is an outlier, $s_{(i)}$ will be less than s. The absolute value of the ith studentized deleted residual therefore will be larger than the absolute value of the standardized residual. In this sense, studentized deleted residuals may detect outliers that standardized residuals do not detect.

Many statistical software packages provide an option for obtaining studentized deleted residuals. Using Minitab, we obtained the studentized deleted residuals for the Butler Trucking example; the results are reported in Table 15.8. The t distribution can be used to

TABLE 15.8 STUDENTIZED DELETED RESIDUALS FOR BUTLER TRUCKING

Miles Traveled (x_1)	Deliveries (x_2)	Travel Time (y)	Standardized Residual	Studentized Deleted Residual
100	4	9.3	.78344	.75939
50	3	4.8	−.34962	−.32654
100	4	8.9	−.08334	−.07720
100	2	6.5	−1.30929	−1.39494
50	2	4.2	.38167	.35709
80	2	6.2	.65431	.62519
75	3	7.4	1.68917	2.03187
65	4	6.0	−1.77372	−2.21314
90	3	7.6	.36703	.34312
90	2	6.1	−.77639	−.75190

TABLE 15.9 LEVERAGE AND COOK'S DISTANCE MEASURES FOR BUTLER TRUCKING

Miles Traveled (x_1)	Deliveries (x_2)	Travel Time (y)	Leverage (h_i)	Cook's D (D_i)
100	4	9.3	.351704	.110994
50	3	4.8	.375863	.024536
100	4	8.9	.351704	.001256
100	2	6.5	.378451	.347923
50	2	4.2	.430220	.036663
80	2	6.2	.220557	.040381
75	3	7.4	.110009	.117562
65	4	6.0	.382657	.650029
90	3	7.6	.129098	.006656
90	2	6.1	.269737	.074217

determine whether the studentized deleted residuals indicate the presence of outliers. Recall that p denotes the number of independent variables and n denotes the number of observations. Hence, if we delete the ith observation, the number of observations in the reduced data set is $n - 1$; in this case the error sum of squares has $(n - 1) - p - 1$ degrees of freedom. For the Butler Trucking example with $n = 10$ and $p = 2$, the degrees of freedom for the error sum of squares with the ith observation deleted is $9 - 2 - 1 = 6$. At a .05 level of significance, the t distribution (Table 2 of Appendix B) shows that with six degrees of freedom, $t_{.025} = 2.447$. If the value of the ith studentized deleted residual is less than -2.447 or greater than $+2.447$, we can conclude that the ith observation is an outlier. The studentized deleted residuals in Table 15.8 do not exceed those limits; therefore, we conclude that outliers are not present in the data set.

Influential Observations

In Section 14.9 we discussed how the leverage of an observation can be used to identify observations for which the value of the independent variable may have a strong influence on the regression results. As we indicated in the discussion of standardized residuals, the leverage of an observation, denoted h_i, measures how far the values of the independent variables are from their mean values. The leverage values are easily obtained as part of the output from statistical software packages. Minitab computes the leverage values and uses the rule of thumb $h_i > 3(p + 1)/n$ to identify **influential observations**. For the Butler Trucking example with $p = 2$ independent variables and $n = 10$ observations, the critical value for leverage is $3(2 + 1)/10 = .9$. The leverage values for the Butler Trucking example obtained by using Minitab are reported in Table 15.9. Because h_i does not exceed .9, we do not detect influential observations in the data set.

TABLE 15.10 DATA SET ILLUSTRATING POTENTIAL PROBLEM USING THE LEVERAGE CRITERION

x_i	y_i	Leverage h_i
1	18	.204170
1	21	.204170
2	22	.164205
3	21	.138141
4	23	.125977
4	24	.125977
5	26	.127715
15	39	.909644

Using Cook's Distance Measure to Identify Influential Observations

A problem that can arise in using leverage to identify influential observations is that an observation can be identified as having high leverage and not necessarily be influential in terms of the resulting estimated regression equation. For example, Table 15.10 is a data set consisting of eight observations and their corresponding leverage values (obtained by using Minitab). Because the leverage for the eighth observation is $.91 > .75$ (the critical leverage value), this observation is identified as influential. Before reaching any final conclusions, however, let us consider the situation from a different perspective.

FIGURE 15.11 SCATTER DIAGRAM FOR THE DATA SET IN TABLE 15.10

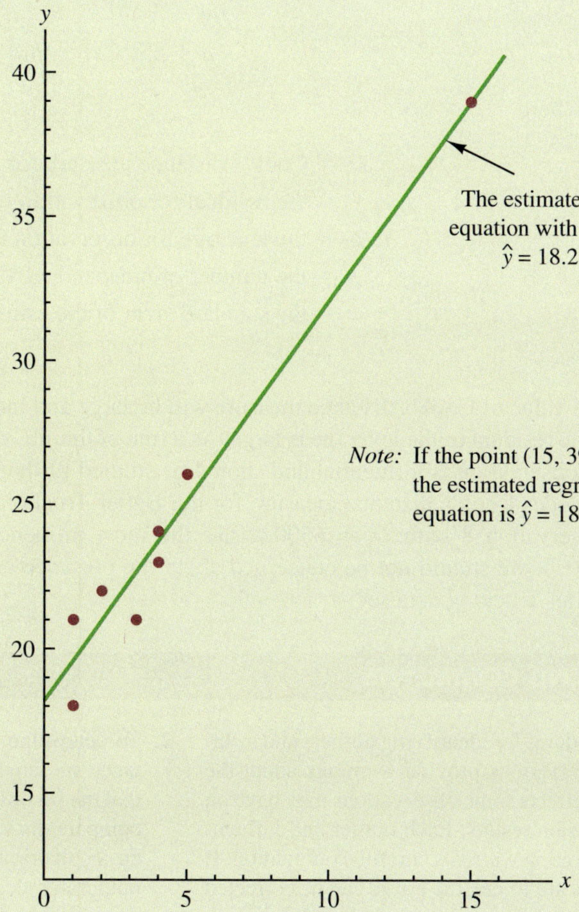

Figure 15.11 shows the scatter diagram corresponding to the data set in Table 15.10. We used Minitab to develop the following estimated regression equation for these data.

$$\hat{y} = 18.2 + 1.39x$$

The straight line in Figure 15.11 is the graph of this equation. Now, let us delete the observation $x = 15$, $y = 39$ from the data set and fit a new estimated regression equation to the remaining seven observations; the new estimated regression equation is

$$\hat{y} = 18.1 + 1.42x$$

We note that the y-intercept and slope of the new estimated regression equation are very close to the values obtained using all the data. Although the leverage criterion identified the eighth observation as influential, this observation clearly had little influence on the results obtained. Thus, in some situations using only leverage to identify influential observations can lead to wrong conclusions.

Cook's distance measure uses both the leverage of observation i, h_i, and the residual for observation i, $(y_i - \hat{y}_i)$, to determine whether the observation is influential.

COOK'S DISTANCE MEASURE

$$D_i = \frac{(y_i - \hat{y}_i)^2}{(p + 1)s^2}\left[\frac{h_i}{(1 - h_i)^2}\right] \tag{15.25}$$

where

D_i = Cook's distance measure for observation i
$y_i - \hat{y}_i$ = the residual for observation i
h_i = the leverage for observation i
p = the number of independent variables
s = the standard error of the estimate

The value of Cook's distance measure will be large and indicate an influential observation if the residual or the leverage is large. As a rule of thumb, values of $D_i > 1$ indicate that the ith observation is influential and should be studied further. The last column of Table 15.9 provides Cook's distance measure for the Butler Trucking problem as given by Minitab. Observation 8 with $D_i = .650029$ has the most influence. However, applying the rule $D_i > 1$, we should not be concerned about the presence of influential observations in the Butler Trucking data set.

NOTES AND COMMENTS

1. The procedures for identifying outliers and influential observations provide warnings about the potential effects some observations may have on the regression results. Each outlier and influential observation warrants careful examination. If data errors are found, the errors can be corrected and the regression analysis repeated. In general, outliers and influential observations should not be removed from the data set unless clear evidence shows that they are not based on elements of the population being studied and should not have been included in the original data set.
2. To determine whether the value of Cook's distance measure D_i is large enough to conclude that the ith observation is influential, we can also compare the value of D_i to the 50th percentile of an F distribution (denoted $F_{.50}$) with $p + 1$ numerator degrees of freedom and $n - p - 1$ denominator degrees of freedom. F tables corresponding to a .50 level of significance must be available to carry out the test. The rule of thumb we provided ($D_i > 1$) is based on the fact that the table value is close to one for a wide variety of cases.

Exercises

Methods

SELF test

39. Data for two variables, x and y, follow.

x_i	1	2	3	4	5
y_i	3	7	5	11	14

a. Develop the estimated regression equation for these data.
b. Plot the standardized residuals versus $\hat{y}$. Do there appear to be any outliers in these data? Explain.
c. Compute the studentized deleted residuals for these data. At the .05 level of significance, can any of these observations be classified as an outlier? Explain.

40. Data for two variables, x and y, follow.

x_i	22	24	26	28	40
y_i	12	21	31	35	70

a. Develop the estimated regression equation for these data.
b. Compute the studentized deleted residuals for these data. At the .05 level of significance, can any of these observations be classified as an outlier? Explain.
c. Compute the leverage values for these data. Do there appear to be any influential observations in these data? Explain.
d. Compute Cook's distance measure for these data. Are any observations influential? Explain.

Applications

SELF test

41. Exercise 5 gave the following data on weekly gross revenue, television advertising, and newspaper advertising for Showtime Movie Theaters.

WEB file Showtime

Weekly Gross Revenue ($1000s)	Television Advertising ($1000s)	Newspaper Advertising ($1000s)
96	5.0	1.5
90	2.0	2.0
95	4.0	1.5
92	2.5	2.5
95	3.0	3.3
94	3.5	2.3
94	2.5	4.2
94	3.0	2.5

a. Find an estimated regression equation relating weekly gross revenue to television and newspaper advertising.
b. Plot the standardized residuals against $\hat{y}$. Does the residual plot support the assumptions about ϵ? Explain.
c. Check for any outliers in these data. What are your conclusions?
d. Are there any influential observations? Explain.

42. The following data show the curb weight, horsepower, and ¼-mile speed for 16 popular sports and GT cars. Suppose that the price of each sports and GT car is also available. The complete data set is as follows:

WEB file Auto2

Sports & GT Car	Price ($1000s)	Curb Weight (lb.)	Horsepower	Speed at ¼ Mile (mph)
Acura Integra Type R	25.035	2577	195	90.7
Acura NSX-T	93.758	3066	290	108.0
BMW Z3 2.8	40.900	2844	189	93.2
Chevrolet Camaro Z28	24.865	3439	305	103.2
Chevrolet Corvette Convertible	50.144	3246	345	102.1
Dodge Viper RT/10	69.742	3319	450	116.2
Ford Mustang GT	23.200	3227	225	91.7
Honda Prelude Type SH	26.382	3042	195	89.7
Mercedes-Benz CLK320	44.988	3240	215	93.0
Mercedes-Benz SLK230	42.762	3025	185	92.3
Mitsubishi 3000GT VR-4	47.518	3737	320	99.0

(continued)

Sports & GT Car	Price ($1000s)	Curb Weight (lb.)	Horsepower	Speed at ¼ Mile (mph)
Nissan 240SX SE	25.066	2862	155	84.6
Pontiac Firebird Trans Am	27.770	3455	305	103.2
Porsche Boxster	45.560	2822	201	93.2
Toyota Supra Turbo	40.989	3505	320	105.0
Volvo C70	41.120	3285	236	97.0

a. Find the estimated regression equation that uses price and horsepower to predict ¼-mile speed.
b. Plot the standardized residuals against $\hat{y}$. Does the residual plot support the assumption about ϵ? Explain.
c. Check for any outliers. What are your conclusions?
d. Are there any influential observations? Explain.

WEB file LPGA

43. The Ladies Professional Golfers Association (LPGA) maintains statistics on performance and earnings for members of the LPGA Tour. Year-end performance statistics for the 30 players who had the highest total earnings in LPGA Tour events for 2005 appear in the file named LPGA (LPGA website, 2006). Earnings ($1000s) is the total earnings in thousands of dollars; Scoring Avg. is the average score for all events; Greens in Reg. is the percentage of time a player is able to hit the green in regulation; and Putting Avg. is the average number of putts taken on greens hit in regulation. A green is considered hit in regulation if any part of the ball is touching the putting surface and the difference between the value of par for the hole and the number of strokes taken to hit the green is at least 2.
a. Develop an estimated regression equation that can be used to predict the average score for all events given the percentage of time a player is able to hit the green in regulation and the average number of putts taken on greens hit in regulation.
b. Plot the standardized residuals against $\hat{y}$. Does the residual plot support the assumption about ϵ? Explain.
c. Check for any outliers. What are your conclusions?
d. Are there any influential observations? Explain.

15.9 Logistic Regression

In many regression applications the dependent variable may only assume two discrete values. For instance, a bank might like to develop an estimated regression equation for predicting whether a person will be approved for a credit card. The dependent variable can be coded as $y = 1$ if the bank approves the request for a credit card and $y = 0$ if the bank rejects the request for a credit card. Using logistic regression we can estimate the probability that the bank will approve the request for a credit card given a particular set of values for the chosen independent variables.

Let us consider an application of logistic regression involving a direct mail promotion being used by Simmons Stores. Simmons owns and operates a national chain of women's apparel stores. Five thousand copies of an expensive four-color sales catalog have been printed, and each catalog includes a coupon that provides a $50 discount on purchases of $200 or more. The catalogs are expensive and Simmons would like to send them to only those customers who have the highest probability of using the coupon.

Management thinks that annual spending at Simmons Stores and whether a customer has a Simmons credit card are two variables that might be helpful in predicting whether a customer who receives the catalog will use the coupon. Simmons conducted a pilot study using a random sample of 50 Simmons credit card customers and 50 other customers who do not have a Simmons credit card. Simmons sent the catalog to each of the 100 customers selected. At the end of a test period, Simmons noted whether the customer used the coupon. The sample data for the first 10 catalog recipients are shown in Table 15.11. The amount each customer spent last year at Simmons is shown in thousands of dollars and the credit card information has been coded as 1 if the customer has a Simmons credit card and 0 if not. In the Coupon column, a 1 is recorded if the sampled customer used the coupon and 0 if not.

We might think of building a multiple regression model using the data in Table 15.11 to help Simmons estimate whether a catalog recipient will use the coupon. We would use Annual Spending ($1000) and Simmons Card as independent variables and Coupon as the dependent variable. Because the dependent variable may only assume the values of 0 or 1, however, the ordinary multiple regression model is not applicable. This example shows the type of situation for which logistic regression was developed. Let us see how logistic regression can be used to help Simmons estimate which type of customer is most likely to take advantage of their promotion.

Logistic Regression Equation

In many ways logistic regression is like ordinary regression. It requires a dependent variable, y, and one or more independent variables. In multiple regression analysis, the mean or expected value of y is referred to as the multiple regression equation.

$$E(y) = \beta_0 + \beta_1 x_1 + \beta_2 x_2 + \cdots + \beta_p x_p \qquad \textbf{(15.26)}$$

In logistic regression, statistical theory as well as practice has shown that the relationship between $E(y)$ and $x_1, x_2, \ldots, x_p$ is better described by the following nonlinear equation.

LOGISTIC REGRESSION EQUATION

$$E(y) = \frac{e^{\beta_0 + \beta_1 x_1 + \beta_2 x_2 + \cdots + \beta_p x_p}}{1 + e^{\beta_0 + \beta_1 x_1 + \beta_2 x_2 + \cdots + \beta_p x_p}} \qquad \textbf{(15.27)}$$

If the two values of the dependent variable y are coded as 0 or 1, the value of $E(y)$ in equation (15.27) provides the *probability* that $y = 1$ given a particular set of values for the

WEB file
Simmons

TABLE 15.11 PARTIAL SAMPLE DATA FOR THE SIMMONS STORES EXAMPLE

Customer	Annual Spending ($1000)	Simmons Card	Coupon
1	2.291	1	0
2	3.215	1	0
3	2.135	1	0
4	3.924	0	0
5	2.528	1	0
6	2.473	0	1
7	2.384	0	0
8	7.076	0	0
9	1.182	1	1
10	3.345	0	0

independent variables $x_1, x_2, \ldots, x_p$. Because of the interpretation of $E(y)$ as a probability, the **logistic regression equation** is often written as follows.

INTERPRETATION OF $E(y)$ AS A PROBABILITY IN LOGISTIC REGRESSION

$$E(y) = P(y = 1|x_1, x_2, \ldots, x_p) \quad \textbf{(15.28)}$$

To provide a better understanding of the characteristics of the logistic regression equation, suppose the model involves only one independent variable x and the values of the model parameters are $\beta_0 = -7$ and $\beta_1 = 3$. The logistic regression equation corresponding to these parameter values is

$$E(y) = P(y = 1|x) = \frac{e^{\beta_0+\beta_1 x}}{1 + e^{\beta_0+\beta_1 x}} = \frac{e^{-7+3x}}{1 + e^{-7+3x}} \quad \textbf{(15.29)}$$

Figure 15.12 shows a graph of equation (15.29). Note that the graph is S-shaped. The value of $E(y)$ ranges from 0 to 1, with the value of $E(y)$ gradually approaching 1 as the value of x becomes larger and the value of $E(y)$ approaching 0 as the value of x becomes smaller. Note also that the values of $E(y)$, representing probability, increase fairly rapidly as x increases from 2 to 3. The fact that the values of $E(y)$ range from 0 to 1 and that the curve is S-shaped makes equation (15.29) ideally suited to model the probability the dependent variable is equal to 1.

Estimating the Logistic Regression Equation

In simple linear and multiple regression the least squares method is used to compute $b_0, b_1, \ldots, b_p$ as estimates of the model parameters $(\beta_0, \beta_1, \ldots, \beta_p)$. The nonlinear form of the logistic regression equation makes the method of computing estimates more complex and beyond the scope of this text. We will use computer software to provide the estimates. The **estimated logistic regression equation** is

FIGURE 15.12 LOGISTIC REGRESSION EQUATION FOR $\beta_0 = -7$ AND $\beta_1 = 3$

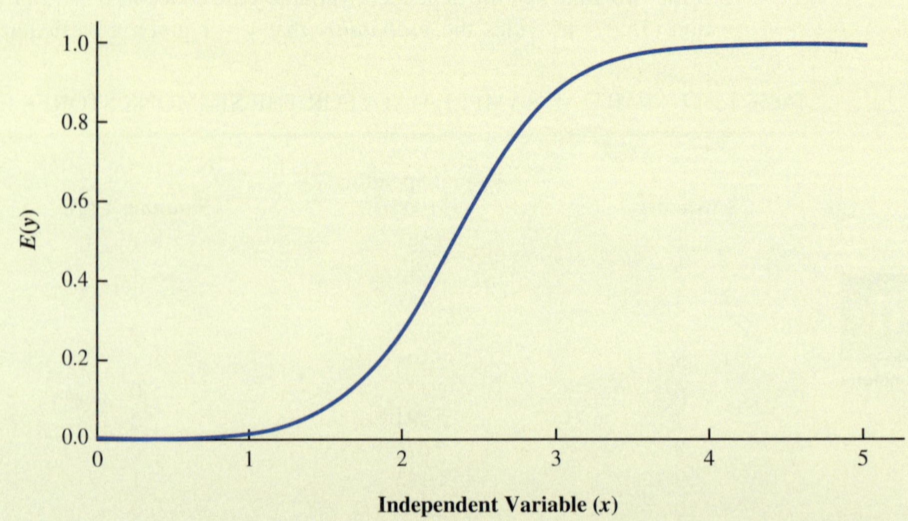

ESTIMATED LOGISTIC REGRESSION EQUATION

$$\hat{y} = \text{estimate of } P(y = 1|x_1, x_2, \ldots, x_p) = \frac{e^{b_0 + b_1x_1 + b_2x_2 + \cdots + b_px_p}}{1 + e^{b_0 + b_1x_1 + b_2x_2 + \cdots + b_px_p}} \tag{15.30}$$

Here, $\hat{y}$ provides an estimate of the probability that $y = 1$ given a particular set of values for the independent variables.

Let us now return to the Simmons Stores example. The variables in the study are defined as follows:

$$y = \begin{cases} 0 \text{ if the customer did not use the coupon} \\ 1 \text{ if the customer used the coupon} \end{cases}$$

$$x_1 = \text{annual spending at Simmons Stores (\$1000s)}$$

$$x_2 = \begin{cases} 0 \text{ if the customer does not have a Simmons credit card} \\ 1 \text{ if the customer has a Simmons credit card} \end{cases}$$

Thus, we choose a logistic regression equation with two independent variables.

$$E(y) = \frac{e^{\beta_0 + \beta_1x_1 + \beta_2x_2}}{1 + e^{\beta_0 + \beta_1x_1 + \beta_2x_2}} \tag{15.31}$$

In Appendix 15.3 we show how Minitab is used to generate the output in Figure 15.13.

Using the sample data (see Table 15.11), Minitab's binary logistic regression procedure was used to compute estimates of the model parameters β_0, β_1, and β_2. A portion of the output obtained is shown in Figure 15.13. We see that $b_0 = -2.14637$, $b_1 = .341643$, and $b_2 = 1.09873$. Thus, the estimated logistic regression equation is

$$\hat{y} = \frac{e^{b_0 + b_1x_1 + b_2x_2}}{1 + e^{b_0 + b_1x_1 + b_2x_2}} = \frac{e^{-2.14637 + .341643x_1 + 1.09873x_2}}{1 + e^{-2.14637 + .341643x_1 + 1.09873x_2}} \tag{15.32}$$

We can now use equation (15.32) to estimate the probability of using the coupon for a particular type of customer. For example, to estimate the probability of using the coupon for customers who spend \$2000 annually and do not have a Simmons credit card, we substitute $x_1 = 2$ and $x_2 = 0$ into equation (15.32).

FIGURE 15.13 PARTIAL LOGISTIC REGRESSION OUTPUT FOR THE SIMMONS STORES EXAMPLE

In the Minitab output, x_1 = Spending and x_2 = Card.

```
Logistic Regression Table
                                                    Odds     95%    CI
Predictor       Coef    SE Coef      Z       p     Ratio   Lower  Upper
Constant    -2.14637   0.577245  -3.72   0.000
Spending    0.341643   0.128672   2.66   0.008     1.41    1.09   1.81
Card         1.09873   0.444696   2.47   0.013     3.00    1.25   7.17

Log-Likelihood = -60.487
Test that all slopes are zero: G = 13.628, DF = 2, P-Value = 0.001
```

$$\hat{y} = \frac{e^{-2.14637+.341643(2)+1.09873(0)}}{1 + e^{-2.14637+.341643(2)+1.09873(0)}} = \frac{e^{-1.4631}}{1 + e^{-1.4631}} = \frac{.2315}{1.2315} = .1880$$

Thus, an estimate of the probability of using the coupon for this particular group of customers is approximately 0.19. Similarly, to estimate the probability of using the coupon for customers who spent \$2000 last year and have a Simmons credit card, we substitute $x_1 = 2$ and $x_2 = 1$ into equation (15.32).

$$\hat{y} = \frac{e^{-2.14637+.341643(2)+1.09873(1)}}{1 + e^{-2.14637+.341643(2)+1.09873(1)}} = \frac{e^{-.3644}}{1 + e^{-.3644}} = \frac{.6946}{1.6946} = .4099$$

Thus, for this group of customers, the probability of using the coupon is approximately 0.41. It appears that the probability of using the coupon is much higher for customers with a Simmons credit card. Before reaching any conclusions, however, we need to assess the statistical significance of our model.

Testing for Significance

Testing for significance in logistic regression is similar to testing for significance in multiple regression. First we conduct a test for overall significance. For the Simmons Stores example, the hypotheses for the test of overall significance follow:

$$H_0\colon \beta_1 = \beta_2 = 0$$
$$H_a\colon \text{One or both of the parameters is not equal to zero}$$

The test for overall significance is based upon the value of a G test statistic. If the null hypothesis is true, the sampling distribution of G follows a chi-square distribution with degrees of freedom equal to the number of independent variables in the model. Although the computation of G is beyond the scope of the book, the value of G and its corresponding p-value are provided as part of Minitab's binary logistic regression output. Referring to the last line in Figure 15.13, we see that the value of G is 13.628, its degrees of freedom are 2, and its p-value is .001. Thus, at any level of significance $\alpha \geq .001$, we would reject the null hypothesis and conclude that the overall model is significant.

If the G test shows an overall significance, a z test can be used to determine whether each of the individual independent variables is making a significant contribution to the overall model. For the independent variables x_i, the hypotheses are

$$H_0\colon \beta_i = 0$$
$$H_a\colon \beta_i \neq 0$$

If the null hypothesis is true, the value of the estimated coefficient divided by its standard error follows a standard normal probability distribution. The column labeled Z in the Minitab output contains the values of $z_i = b_i/s_{b_i}$ for each of the estimated coefficients and the column labeled p contains the corresponding p-values. Suppose we use $\alpha = .05$ to test for the significance of the independent variables in the Simmons model. For the independent variable x_1 the z value is 2.66 and the corresponding p-value is .008. Thus, at the .05 level of significance we can reject $H_0\colon \beta_1 = 0$. In a similar fashion we can also reject $H_0\colon \beta_2 = 0$ because the p-value corresponding to $z = 2.47$ is .013. Hence, at the .05 level of significance, both independent variables are statistically significant.

Managerial Use

We described how to develop the estimated logistic regression equation and how to test it for significance. Let us now use it to make a decision recommendation concerning the Simmons Stores catalog promotion. For Simmons Stores, we already computed $P(y = 1|x_1 = 2, x_2 = 1) = .4099$ and $P(y = 1|x_1 = 2, x_2 = 0) = .1880$. These probabilities indicate that for customers with annual spending of \$2000 the presence of a Simmons credit card increases the probability of using the coupon. In Table 15.12 we show estimated probabilities for values of annual spending ranging from \$1000 to \$7000 for both customers who have a Simmons credit card and customers who do not have a Simmons credit card. How can Simmons use this information to better target customers for the new promotion? Suppose Simmons wants to send the promotional catalog only to customers who have a 0.40 or higher probability of using the coupon. Using the estimated probabilities in Table 15.12, Simmons promotion strategy would be:

Customers who have a Simmons credit card: Send the catalog to every customer who spent \$2000 or more last year.

Customers who do not have a Simmons credit card: Send the catalog to every customer who spent \$6000 or more last year.

Looking at the estimated probabilities further, we see that the probability of using the coupon for customers who do not have a Simmons credit card but spend \$5000 annually is .3922. Thus, Simmons may want to consider revising this strategy by including those customers who do not have a credit card, as long as they spent \$5000 or more last year.

Interpreting the Logistic Regression Equation

Interpreting a regression equation involves relating the independent variables to the business question that the equation was developed to answer. With logistic regression, it is difficult to interpret the relation between the independent variables and the probability that $y = 1$ directly because the logistic regression equation is nonlinear. However, statisticians have shown that the relationship can be interpreted indirectly using a concept called the odds ratio.

The **odds in favor of an event occurring** is defined as the probability the event will occur divided by the probability the event will not occur. In logistic regression the event of interest is always $y = 1$. Given a particular set of values for the independent variables, the odds in favor of $y = 1$ can be calculated as follows:

$$\text{odds} = \frac{P(y = 1|x_1, x_2, \ldots, x_p)}{P(y = 0|x_1, x_2, \ldots, x_p)} = \frac{P(y = 1|x_1, x_2, \ldots, x_p)}{1 - P(y = 1|x_1, x_2, \ldots, x_p)} \quad \textbf{(15.33)}$$

The **odds ratio** measures the impact on the odds of a one-unit increase in only one of the independent variables. The odds ratio is the odds that $y = 1$ given that one of the

TABLE 15.12 ESTIMATED PROBABILITIES FOR SIMMONS STORES

		Annual Spending						
		\$1000	**\$2000**	**\$3000**	**\$4000**	**\$5000**	**\$6000**	**\$7000**
Credit Card	**Yes**	.3305	.4099	.4943	.5791	.6594	.7315	.7931
	No	.1413	.1880	.2457	.3144	.3922	.4759	.5610

independent variables has been increased by one unit (odds_1) divided by the odds that $y = 1$ given no change in the values for the independent variables (odds_0).

ODDS RATIO

$$\text{Odds Ratio} = \frac{\text{odds}_1}{\text{odds}_0} \tag{15.34}$$

For example, suppose we want to compare the odds of using the coupon for customers who spend \$2000 annually and have a Simmons credit card ($x_1 = 2$ and $x_2 = 1$) to the odds of using the coupon for customers who spend \$2000 annually and do not have a Simmons credit card ($x_1 = 2$ and $x_2 = 0$). We are interested in interpreting the effect of a one-unit increase in the independent variable x_2. In this case

$$\text{odds}_1 = \frac{P(y = 1|x_1 = 2, x_2 = 1)}{1 - P(y = 1|x_1 = 2, x_2 = 1)}$$

and

$$\text{odds}_0 = \frac{P(y = 1|x_1 = 2, x_2 = 0)}{1 - P(y = 1|x_1 = 2, x_2 = 0)}$$

Previously we showed that an estimate of the probability that $y = 1$ given $x_1 = 2$ and $x_2 = 1$ is .4099, and an estimate of the probability that $y = 1$ given $x_1 = 2$ and $x_2 = 0$ is .1880. Thus,

$$\text{estimate of odds}_1 = \frac{.4099}{1 - .4099} = .6946$$

and

$$\text{estimate of odds}_0 = \frac{.1880}{1 - .1880} = .2315$$

The estimated odds ratio is

$$\text{Estimated odds ratio} = \frac{.6946}{.2315} = 3.00$$

Thus, we can conclude that the estimated odds in favor of using the coupon for customers who spent \$2000 last year and have a Simmons credit card are 3 times greater than the estimated odds in favor of using the coupon for customers who spent \$2000 last year and do not have a Simmons credit card.

The odds ratio for each independent variable is computed while holding all the other independent variables constant. But it does not matter what constant values are used for the other independent variables. For instance, if we computed the odds ratio for the Simmons credit card variable (x_2) using \$3000, instead of \$2000, as the value for the annual spending variable (x_1), we would still obtain the same value for the estimated odds ratio (3.00). Thus, we can conclude that the estimated odds of using the coupon for customers who have a Simmons credit card are 3 times greater than the estimated odds of using the coupon for customers who do not have a Simmons credit card.

The odds ratio is standard output for logistic regression software packages. Refer to the Minitab output in Figure 15.13. The column with the heading Odds Ratio contains the estimated odds ratios for each of the independent variables. The estimated odds ratio for x_1 is 1.41 and the estimated odds ratio for x_2 is 3.00. We already showed how to interpret the estimated odds ratio for the binary independent variable x_2. Let us now consider the interpretation of the estimated odds ratio for the continuous independent variable x_1.

The value of 1.41 in the Odds Ratio column of the Minitab output tells us that the estimated odds in favor of using the coupon for customers who spent \$3000 last year is 1.41 times greater than the estimated odds in favor of using the coupon for customers who spent \$2000 last year. Moreover, this interpretation is true for any one-unit change in x_1. For instance, the estimated odds in favor of using the coupon for someone who spent \$5000 last year is 1.41 times greater than the odds in favor of using the coupon for a customer who spent \$4000 last year. But suppose we are interested in the change in the odds for an increase of more than one unit for an independent variable. Note that x_1 can range from 1 to 7. The odds ratio given by the Minitab output does not answer this question. To answer this question we must explore the relationship between the odds ratio and the regression coefficients.

A unique relationship exists between the odds ratio for a variable and its corresponding regression coefficient. For each independent variable in a logistic regression equation it can be shown that

$$\text{Odds ratio} = e^{\beta_i}$$

To illustrate this relationship, consider the independent variable x_1 in the Simmons example. The estimated odds ratio for x_1 is

$$\text{Estimated odds ratio} = e^{b_1} = e^{.341643} = 1.41$$

Similarly, the estimated odds ratio for x_2 is

$$\text{Estimated odds ratio} = e^{b_2} = e^{1.09873} = 3.00$$

This relationship between the odds ratio and the coefficients of the independent variables makes it easy to compute estimated odds ratios once we develop estimates of the model parameters. Moreover, it also provides us with the ability to investigate changes in the odds ratio of more than or less than one unit for a continuous independent variable.

The odds ratio for an independent variable represents the change in the odds for a one-unit change in the independent variable holding all the other independent variables constant. Suppose that we want to consider the effect of a change of more than one unit, say c units. For instance, suppose in the Simmons example that we want to compare the odds of using the coupon for customers who spend \$5000 annually ($x_1 = 5$) to the odds of using the coupon for customers who spend \$2000 annually ($x_1 = 2$). In this case $c = 5 - 2 = 3$ and the corresponding estimated odds ratio is

$$e^{cb_1} = e^{3(.341643)} = e^{1.0249} = 2.79$$

This result indicates that the estimated odds of using the coupon for customers who spend \$5000 annually is 2.79 times greater than the estimated odds of using the coupon for customers who spend \$2000 annually. In other words, the estimated odds ratio for an increase of \$3000 in annual spending is 2.79.

In general, the odds ratio enables us to compare the odds for two different events. If the value of the odds ratio is 1, the odds for both events are the same. Thus, if the independent variable we are considering (such as Simmons credit card status) has a positive impact on the probability of the event occurring, the corresponding odds ratio will be greater than 1. Most logistic regression software packages provide a confidence interval for the odds ratio. The Minitab output in Figure 15.13 provides a 95% confidence interval for each of the odds ratios. For example, the point estimate of the odds ratio for x_1 is 1.41 and the 95% confidence interval is 1.09 to 1.81. Because the confidence interval does not contain the value of 1, we can conclude that x_1, has a significant effect on the estimated odds ratio. Similarly, the 95% confidence interval for the odds ratio for x_2 is 1.25 to 7.17. Because this interval does not contain the value of 1, we can also conclude that x_2 has a significant effect on the odds ratio.

Logit Transformation

An interesting relationship can be observed between the odds in favor of $y = 1$ and the exponent for e in the logistic regression equation. It can be shown that

$$\ln(\text{odds}) = \beta_0 + \beta_1 x_1 + \beta_2 x_2 + \cdots + \beta_p x_p$$

This equation shows that the natural logarithm of the odds in favor of $y = 1$ is a linear function of the independent variables. This linear function is called the **logit**. We will use the notation $g(x_1, x_2, \ldots, x_p)$ to denote the logit.

LOGIT

$$g(x_1, x_2, \ldots, x_p) = \beta_0 + \beta_1 x_1 + \beta_2 x_2 + \cdots + \beta_p x_p \tag{15.35}$$

Substituting $g(x_1, x_2, \ldots, x_p)$ for $\beta_1 + \beta_1 x_1 + \beta_2 x_2 + \cdots + \beta_p x_p$ in equation (15.27), we can write the logistic regression equation as

$$E(y) = \frac{e^{g(x_1, x_2, \ldots, x_p)}}{1 + e^{g(x_1, x_2, \ldots, x_p)}} \tag{15.36}$$

Once we estimate the parameters in the logistic regression equation, we can compute an estimate of the logit. Using $\hat{g}(x_1, x_2, \ldots, x_p)$ to denote the **estimated logit**, we obtain

ESTIMATED LOGIT

$$\hat{g}(x_1, x_2, \ldots, x_p) = b_0 + b_1 x_1 + b_2 x_2 + \cdots + b_p x_p \tag{15.37}$$

Thus, in terms of the estimated logit, the estimated regression equation is

$$\hat{y} = \frac{e^{b_0 + b_1 x_1 + b_2 x_2 + \cdots + b_p x_p}}{1 + e^{b_0 + b_1 x_1 + b_2 x_2 + \cdots + b_p x_p}} = \frac{e^{\hat{g}(x_1, x_2, \ldots, x_p)}}{1 + e^{\hat{g}(x_1, x_2, \ldots, x_p)}} \tag{15.38}$$

For the Simmons Stores example, the estimated logit is

$$\hat{g}(x_1, x_2) = -2.14637 + .341643x_1 + 1.09873x_2$$

and the estimated regression equation is

$$\hat{y} = \frac{e^{\hat{g}(x_1, x_2)}}{1 + e^{\hat{g}(x_1, x_2)}} = \frac{e^{-2.14637 + .341643x_1 + 1.09873x_2}}{1 + e^{-2.14637 + .341643x_1 + 1.09873x_2}}$$

Thus, because of the unique relationship between the estimated logit and the estimated logistic regression equation, we can compute the estimated probabilities for Simmons Stores by dividing $e^{\hat{g}(x_1, x_2)}$ by $1 + e^{\hat{g}(x_1, x_2)}$.

NOTES AND COMMENTS

1. Because of the unique relationship between the estimated coefficients in the model and the corresponding odds ratios, the overall test for significance based upon the G statistic is also a test of overall significance for the odds ratios. In addition, the z test for the individual significance of a model parameter also provides a statistical test of significance for the corresponding odds ratio.
2. In simple and multiple regression, the coefficient of determination is used to measure the goodness of fit. In logistic regression, no single measure provides a similar interpretation. A discussion of goodness of fit is beyond the scope of our introductory treatment of logistic regression.

Exercises

Applications

WEB file Simmons

44. Refer to the Simmons Stores example introduced in this section. The dependent variable is coded as $y = 1$ if the customer used the coupon and 0 if not. Suppose that the only information available to help predict whether the customer will use the coupon is the customer's credit card status, coded as $x = 1$ if the customer has a Simmons credit card and $x = 0$ if not.
    a. Write the logistic regression equation relating x to y.
    b. What is the interpretation of $E(y)$ when $x = 0$?
    c. For the Simmons data in Table 15.11, use Minitab to compute the estimated logit.
    d. Use the estimated logit computed in part (c) to estimate the probability of using the coupon for customers who do not have a Simmons credit card and to estimate the probability of using the coupon for customers who have a Simmons credit card.
    e. What is the estimated odds ratio? What is its interpretation?
45. In Table 15.12 we provided estimates of the probability of using the coupon in the Simmons Stores catalog promotion. A different value is obtained for each combination of values for the independent variables.
    a. Compute the odds in favor of using the coupon for a customer with annual spending of \$4000 who does not have a Simmons credit card ($x_1 = 4, x_2 = 0$).
    b. Use the information in Table 15.12 and part (a) to compute the odds ratio for the Simmons credit card variable $x_2 = 0$, holding annual spending constant at $x_1 = 4$.
    c. In the text, the odds ratio for the credit card variable was computed using the information in the \$2000 column of Table 15.12. Did you get the same value for the odds ratio in part (b)?
46. Community Bank would like to increase the number of customers who use payroll direct deposit. Management is considering a new sales campaign that will require each branch manager to call each customer who does not currently use payroll direct deposit. As an incentive to sign up for payroll direct deposit, each customer contacted will be offered free checking for two years. Because of the time and cost associated with the new campaign, management would like to focus their efforts on customers who have the highest probability of signing up for payroll direct deposit. Management believes that the average monthly balance in a customer's checking account may be a useful predictor of whether the customer will sign up for direct payroll deposit. To investigate the relationship between these two variables, Community Bank tried the new campaign using a sample of 50 checking account customers who do not currently use payroll direct deposit. The sample data show the average monthly checking account balance (in hundreds of dollars) and whether the customer contacted signed up for payroll direct deposit (coded 1 if the customer signed up for payroll direct deposit and 0 if not). The data are contained in the data set named Bank; a portion of the data follows.

WEB file Bank

Customer	x = Monthly Balance	y = Direct Deposit
1	1.22	0
2	1.56	0
3	2.10	0
4	2.25	0
5	2.89	0
6	3.55	0
7	3.56	0
8	3.65	1
.	.	.
.	.	.
.	.	.
48	18.45	1
49	24.98	0
50	26.05	1

a. Write the logistic regression equation relating x to y.
b. For the Community Bank data, use Minitab to compute the estimated logistic regression equation.
c. Conduct a test of significance using the G test statistic. Use $\alpha = .05$.
d. Estimate the probability that customers with an average monthly balance of \$1000 will sign up for direct payroll deposit.
e. Suppose Community Bank only wants to contact customers who have a .50 or higher probability of signing up for direct payroll deposit. What is the average monthly balance required to achieve this level of probability?
f. What is the estimated odds ratio? What is its interpretation?

47. Over the past few years the percentage of students who leave Lakeland College at the end of the first year has increased. Last year Lakeland started a voluntary one-week orientation program to help first-year students adjust to campus life. If Lakeland is able to show that the orientation program has a positive effect on retention, they will consider making the program a requirement for all first-year students. Lakeland's administration also suspects that students with lower GPAs have a higher probability of leaving Lakeland at the end of the first year. In order to investigate the relation of these variables to retention, Lakeland selected a random sample of 100 students from last year's entering class. The data are contained in the data set named Lakeland; a portion of the data follows.

WEB file Lakeland

Student	GPA	Program	Return
1	3.78	1	1
2	2.38	0	1
3	1.30	0	0
4	2.19	1	0
5	3.22	1	1
6	2.68	1	1
.	.	.	.
.	.	.	.
.	.	.	.
98	2.57	1	1
99	1.70	1	1
100	3.85	1	1

The dependent variable was coded as $y = 1$ if the student returned to Lakeland for the sophomore year and $y = 0$ if not. The two independent variables are:

$$x_1 = \text{GPA at the end of the first semester}$$

$$x_2 = \begin{cases} 0 \text{ if the student did not attend the orientation program} \\ 1 \text{ if the student attended the orientation program} \end{cases}$$

a. Write the logistic regression equation relating x_1 and x_2 to y.
b. What is the interpretation of $E(y)$ when $x_2 = 0$?
c. Use both independent variables and Minitab to compute the estimated logit.
d. Conduct a test for overall significance using $\alpha = .05$.
e. Use $\alpha = .05$ to determine whether each of the independent variables is significant.
f. Use the estimated logit computed in part (c) to estimate the probability that students with a 2.5 grade point average who did not attend the orientation program will return to Lakeland for their sophomore year. What is the estimated probability for students with a 2.5 grade point average who attended the orientation program?
g. What is the estimated odds ratio for the orientation program? Interpret it.
h. Would you recommend making the orientation program a required activity? Why or why not?

WEB file

TireRatings

48. The Tire Rack maintains an independent consumer survey to help drivers help each other by sharing their long-term tire experiences. The data contained in the file named TireRatings show survey results for 68 all-season tires (Tire Rack website, March 21, 2012). Performance traits are rated using the following 10-point scale.

Superior		Excellent		Good		Fair		Unacceptable	
10	9	8	7	6	5	4	3	2	1

The values for the variable labeled Wet are the average of the ratings for each tire's wet traction performance and the values for the variable labeled Noise are the average of the ratings for the noise level generated by each tire. Respondents were also asked whether they would buy the tire again using the following 10-point scale:

Definitely		Probably		Possibly		Probably Not		Definitely Not	
10	9	8	7	6	5	4	3	2	1

The values for the variable labeled Buy Again are the average of the buy-again responses. For the purposes of this exercise, we created the following binary dependent variable:

$$\text{Purchase} = \begin{cases} 1 \text{ if the value of the Buy-Again variable is 7 or greater} \\ 0 \text{ if the value of the Buy-Again variable is less than 7} \end{cases}$$

Thus, if Purchase = 1, the respondent would probably or definitely buy the tire again.

a. Write the logistic regression equation relating x_1 = Wet performance rating and x_2 = Noise performance rating to y = Purchase.
b. Use Minitab to compute the estimated logit.
c. Use the estimated logit to compute an estimate of the probability that a customer will probably or definitely purchase a particular tire again with a Wet performance rating of 8 and a Noise performance rating of 8.
d. Suppose that the Wet and Noise performance ratings were 7. How does that affect the probability that a customer will probably or definitely purchase a particular tire again with these performance ratings?
e. If you were the CEO of a tire company, what do the results for parts (c) and (d) tell you?

Summary

In this chapter, we introduced multiple regression analysis as an extension of simple linear regression analysis presented in Chapter 14. Multiple regression analysis enables us to understand how a dependent variable is related to two or more independent variables. The mulitple regression equation $E(y) = \beta_0 + \beta_1x_1 + \beta_2x_2 + \cdots + \beta_px_p$ shows that the mean or expected value of the dependent variable y, denoted $E(y)$, is related to the values of the independent variables $x_1, x_2, \ldots, x_p$. Sample data and the least squares method are used to develop the estimated multiple regression equation $\hat{y} = b_0 + b_1x_1 + b_2x_2 + \cdots + b_px_p$. In effect $b_0, b_1, b_2, \ldots, b_p$ are sample statistics used to estimate the unknown model parameters $\beta_0, \beta_1, \beta_2, \ldots, \beta_p$. Computer printouts were used throughout the chapter to emphasize the fact that statistical software packages are the only realistic means of performing the numerous computations required in multiple regression analysis.

The multiple coefficient of determination was presented as a measure of the goodness of fit of the estimated regression equation. It determines the proportion of the variation of y that can be explained by the estimated regression equation. The adjusted multiple coefficient of determination is a similar measure of goodness of fit that adjusts for the number of independent variables and thus avoids overestimating the impact of adding more independent variables.

An F test and a t test were presented as ways to determine statistically whether the relationship among the variables is significant. The F test is used to determine whether there is a significant overall relationship between the dependent variable and the set of all independent variables. The t test is used to determine whether there is a significant relationship between the dependent variable and an individual independent variable given the other independent variables in the regression model. Correlation among the independent variables, known as multicollinearity, was discussed.

The section on categorical independent variables showed how dummy variables can be used to incorporate categorical data into multiple regression analysis. The section on residual analysis showed how residual analysis can be used to validate the model assumptions, detect outliers, and identify influential observations. Standardized residuals, leverage, studentized deleted residuals, and Cook's distance measure were discussed. The chapter concluded with a section on how logistic regression can be used to model situations in which the dependent variable may only assume two values.

Glossary

Multiple regression analysis Regression analysis involving two or more independent variables.
Multiple regression model The mathematical equation that describes how the dependent variable y is related to the independent variables $x_1, x_2, \ldots, x_p$ and an error term ϵ.
Multiple regression equation The mathematical equation relating the expected value or mean value of the dependent variable to the values of the independent variables; that is, $E(y) = \beta_0 + \beta_1x_1 + \beta_2x_2 + \cdots + \beta_px_p$.
Estimated multiple regression equation The estimate of the multiple regression equation based on sample data and the least squares method; it is $\hat{y} = b_0 + b_1x_1 + b_2x_2 + \cdots + b_px_p$.
Least squares method The method used to develop the estimated regression equation. It minimizes the sum of squared residuals (the deviations between the observed values of the dependent variable, y_i, and the predicted values of the dependent variable, $\hat{y}_i$).
Multiple coefficient of determination A measure of the goodness of fit of the estimated multiple regression equation. It can be interpreted as the proportion of the variability in the dependent variable that is explained by the estimated regression equation.

Adjusted multiple coefficient of determination A measure of the goodness of fit of the estimated multiple regression equation that adjusts for the number of independent variables in the model and thus avoids overestimating the impact of adding more independent variables.

Multicollinearity The term used to describe the correlation among the independent variables.

Categorical independent variable An independent variable with categorical data.

Dummy variable A variable used to model the effect of categorical independent variables. A dummy variable may take only the value zero or one.

Leverage A measure of how far the values of the independent variables are from their mean values.

Outlier An observation that does not fit the pattern of the other data.

Studentized deleted residuals Standardized residuals that are based on a revised standard error of the estimate obtained by deleting observation i from the data set and then performing the regression analysis and computations.

Influential observation An observation that has a strong influence on the regression results.

Cook's distance measure A measure of the influence of an observation based on both the leverage of observation i and the residual for observation i.

Logistic regression equation The mathematical equation relating $E(y)$, the probability that $y = 1$, to the values of the independent variables; that is, $E(y) = P(y = 1|x_1, x_2, \ldots, x_p) = \dfrac{e^{\beta_0+\beta_1x_1+\beta_2x_2+\cdots+\beta_px_p}}{1 + e^{\beta_0+\beta_1x_1+\beta_2x_2+\cdots+\beta_px_p}}$.

Estimated logistic regression equation The estimate of the logistic regression equation based on sample data; that is, $\hat{y}$ = estimate of $P(y = 1|x_1, x_2, \ldots, x_p) = \dfrac{e^{b_0+b_1x_1+b_2x_2+\cdots+b_px_p}}{1 + e^{b_0+b_1x_1+b_2x_2+\cdots+b_px_p}}$.

Odds in favor of an event occurring The probability the event will occur divided by the probability the event will not occur.

Odds ratio The odds that $y = 1$ given that one of the independent variables increased by one unit (odds_1) divided by the odds that $y = 1$ given no change in the values for the independent variables (odds_0); that is, Odds ratio $= \text{odds}_1/\text{odds}_0$.

Logit The natural logarithm of the odds in favor of $y = 1$; that is, $g(x_1, x_2, \ldots, x_p) = \beta_0 + \beta_1x_1 + \beta_2x_2 + \cdots + \beta_px_p$.

Estimated logit An estimate of the logit based on sample data; that is, $\hat{g}(x_1, x_2, \ldots, x_p) = b_0 + b_1x_1 + b_2x_2 + \cdots + b_px_p$.

Key Formulas

Multiple Regression Model

$$y = \beta_0 + \beta_1x_1 + \beta_2x_2 + \cdots + \beta_px_p + \epsilon \tag{15.1}$$

Multiple Regression Equation

$$E(y) = \beta_0 + \beta_1x_1 + \beta_2x_2 + \cdots + \beta_px_p \tag{15.2}$$

Estimated Multiple Regression Equation

$$\hat{y} = b_0 + b_1x_1 + b_2x_2 + \cdots + b_px_p \tag{15.3}$$

Least Squares Criterion

$$\min \Sigma(y_i - \hat{y}_i)^2 \tag{15.4}$$

Relationship Among SST, SSR, and SSE

$$\text{SST} = \text{SSR} + \text{SSE} \tag{15.7}$$

Multiple Coefficient of Determination

$$R^2 = \frac{\text{SSR}}{\text{SST}} \tag{15.8}$$

Adjusted Multiple Coefficient of Determination

$$R_{\text{a}}^2 = 1 - (1 - R^2)\frac{n - 1}{n - p - 1} \tag{15.9}$$

Mean Square Due to Regression

$$\text{MSR} = \frac{\text{SSR}}{p} \tag{15.12}$$

Mean Square Due to Error

$$\text{MSE} = \frac{\text{SSE}}{n - p - 1} \tag{15.13}$$

***F* Test Statistic**

$$F = \frac{\text{MSR}}{\text{MSE}} \tag{15.14}$$

***t* Test Statistic**

$$t = \frac{b_i}{s_{b_i}} \tag{15.15}$$

Standardized Residual for Observation *i*

$$\frac{y_i - \hat{y}_i}{s_{y_i - \hat{y}_i}} \tag{15.23}$$

Standard Deviation of Residual *i*

$$s_{y_i - \hat{y}_i} = s\sqrt{1 - h_i} \tag{15.24}$$

Cook's Distance Measure

$$D_i = \frac{(y_i - \hat{y}_i)^2}{(p + 1)s^2}\left[\frac{h_i}{(1 - h_i)^2}\right] \tag{15.25}$$

Logistic Regression Equation

$$E(y) = \frac{e^{\beta_0 + \beta_1 x_1 + \beta_2 x_2 + \cdots + \beta_p x_p}}{1 + e^{\beta_0 + \beta_1 x_1 + \beta_2 x_2 + \cdots + \beta_p x_p}} \tag{15.27}$$

Estimated Logistic Regression Equation

$$\hat{y} = \text{estimate of } P(y = 1|x_1, x_2, \ldots, x_p) = \frac{e^{b_0+b_1x_1+b_2x_2+\cdots+b_px_p}}{1 + e^{b_0+b_1x_1+b_2x_2+\cdots+b_px_p}} \quad \textbf{(15.30)}$$

Odds Ratio

$$\text{Odds ratio} = \frac{\text{odds}_1}{\text{odds}_0} \quad \textbf{(15.34)}$$

Logit

$$g(x_1, x_2, \ldots, x_p) = \beta_0 + \beta_1x_1 + \beta_2x_2 + \cdots + \beta_px_p \quad \textbf{(15.35)}$$

Estimated Logit

$$\hat{g}(x_1, x_2, \ldots, x_p) = b_0 + b_1x_1 + b_2x_2 + \cdots + b_px_p \quad \textbf{(15.37)}$$

Supplementary Exercises

49. The admissions officer for Clearwater College developed the following estimated regression equation relating the final college GPA to the student's SAT mathematics score and high-school GPA.

$$\hat{y} = -1.41 + .0235x_1 + .00486x_2$$

where

$$\begin{aligned} x_1 &= \text{high-school grade point average} \\ x_2 &= \text{SAT mathematics score} \\ y &= \text{final college grade point average} \end{aligned}$$

a. Interpret the coefficients in this estimated regression equation.
b. Predict the final college GPA for a student who has a high-school average of 84 and a score of 540 on the SAT mathematics test.

50. The personnel director for Electronics Associates developed the following estimated regression equation relating an employee's score on a job satisfaction test to his or her length of service and wage rate.

$$\hat{y} = 14.4 - 8.69x_1 + 13.5x_2$$

where

$$\begin{aligned} x_1 &= \text{length of service (years)} \\ x_2 &= \text{wage rate (dollars)} \\ y &= \text{job satisfaction test score (higher scores indicate greater job satisfaction)} \end{aligned}$$

a. Interpret the coefficients in this estimated regression equation.
b. Predict the job satisfaction test score for an employee who has four years of service and makes \$6.50 per hour.

51. A partial computer output from a regression analysis follows.

```
The regression equation is
Y = 8.103 + 7.602 X1 + 3.111 X2

Predictor          Coef         SE Coef          T
Constant         ______          2.667        _____
X1               ______          2.105        _____
X2               ______          0.613        _____

S = 3.335       R-Sq = 92.3%      R-Sq(adj) = _____%

Analysis of Variance

SOURCE               DF          SS          MS         F
Regression         _____        1612       _____      _____
Residual Error       12        _____       _____
Total              _____       _____
```

a. Compute the missing entries in this output.
b. Use the F test and $\alpha = .05$ to see whether a significant relationship is present.
c. Use the t test and $\alpha = .05$ to test H_0: $\beta_1 = 0$ and H_0: $\beta_2 = 0$.
d. Compute R_a^2.

52. Recall that in exercise 49, the admissions officer for Clearwater College developed the following estimated regression equation relating final college GPA to the student's SAT mathematics score and high-school GPA.

$$\hat{y} = -1.41 + .0235x_1 + .00486x_2$$

where

x_1 = high-school grade point average
x_2 = SAT mathematics score
y = final college grade point average

A portion of the Minitab computer output follows.

```
The regression equation is
Y = -1.41 + .0235 X1 + .00486 X2

Predictor          Coef         SE Coef          T
Constant         -1.4053        0.4848        _____
X1               0.023467       0.008666      _____
X2               ______         0.001077      _____

S = 0.1298      R-Sq = _____      R-Sq(adj) = _____

Analysis of Variance

SOURCE               DF          SS          MS         F
Regression         _____       1.76209     _____      _____
Residual Error     _____       _______     _____
Total                9         1.88000
```

a. Complete the missing entries in this output.
b. Use the F test and a .05 level of significance to see whether a significant relationship is present.
c. Use the t test and $\alpha = .05$ to test H_0: $\beta_1 = 0$ and H_0: $\beta_2 = 0$.
d. Did the estimated regression equation provide a good fit to the data? Explain.

53. Recall that in exercise 50 the personnel director for Electronics Associates developed the following estimated regression equation relating an employee's score on a job satisfaction test to length of service and wage rate.

$$\hat{y} = 14.4 - 8.69x_1 + 13.5x_2$$

where

x_1 = length of service (years)
x_2 = wage rate (dollars)
y = job satisfaction test score (higher scores indicate greater job satisfaction)

A portion of the Minitab computer output follows.

```
The regression equation is
Y = 14.4 - 8.69 X1 + 13.52 X2

Predictor        Coef      SE Coef        T
Constant       14.448        8.191     1.76
X1             ______        1.555    _____
X2             13.517        2.085    _____

S = 3.773     R-Sq = ______%  R-Sq(adj) = ______%

Analysis of Variance
```

SOURCE	DF	SS	MS	F
Regression	2	_____	_____	_____
Residual Error	_____	71.17	_____	
Total	7	720.0		

a. Complete the missing entries in this output.
b. Compute F and test using $\alpha = .05$ to see whether a significant relationship is present.
c. Did the estimated regression equation provide a good fit to the data? Explain.
d. Use the t test and $\alpha = .05$ to test H_0: $\beta_1 = 0$ and H_0: $\beta_2 = 0$.

54. The Tire Rack, America's leading online distributor of tires and wheels, conducts extensive testing to provide customers with products that are right for their vehicle, driving style, and driving conditions. In addition, the Tire Rack maintains an independent consumer survey to help drivers help each other by sharing their long-term tire experiences. The following data show survey ratings (1 to 10 scale with 10 the highest rating) for 18 maximum performance summer tires (Tire Rack website, February 3, 2009). The variable Steering rates the tire's steering responsiveness, Tread Wear rates quickness of wear based on the driver's expectations, and Buy Again rates the driver's overall tire satisfaction and desire to purchase the same tire again.

WEB file TireRack

Tire	Steering	Tread Wear	Buy Again
Goodyear Assurance TripleTred	8.9	8.5	8.1
Michelin HydroEdge	8.9	9.0	8.3
Michelin Harmony	8.3	8.8	8.2
Dunlop SP 60	8.2	8.5	7.9
Goodyear Assurance ComforTred	7.9	7.7	7.1
Yokohama Y372	8.4	8.2	8.9
Yokohama Aegis LS4	7.9	7.0	7.1
Kumho Power Star 758	7.9	7.9	8.3
Goodyear Assurance	7.6	5.8	4.5
Hankook H406	7.8	6.8	6.2
Michelin Energy LX4	7.4	5.7	4.8
Michelin MX4	7.0	6.5	5.3
Michelin Symmetry	6.9	5.7	4.2
Kumho 722	7.2	6.6	5.0
Dunlop SP 40 A/S	6.2	4.2	3.4
Bridgestone Insignia SE200	5.7	5.5	3.6
Goodyear Integrity	5.7	5.4	2.9
Dunlop SP20 FE	5.7	5.0	3.3

a. Develop an estimated regression equation that can be used to predict the Buy Again rating given based on the Steering rating. At the .05 level of significance, test for a significant relationship.
b. Did the estimated regression equation developed in part (a) provide a good fit to the data? Explain.
c. Develop an estimated regression equation that can be used to predict the Buy Again rating given the Steering rating and the Tread Wear rating.
d. Is the addition of the Tread Wear independent variable significant? Use $\alpha = .05$.

WEB file 2012FuelEcon

55. The Department of Energy and the U.S. Environmental Protection Agency's *2012 Fuel Economy Guide* provides fuel efficiency data for 2012 model year cars and trucks (Department of Energy website, April 16, 2012). The file named 2012FuelEcon provides a portion of the data for 309 cars. The column labeled Manufacturer shows the name of the company that manufactured the car; the column labeled Displacement shows the engine's displacement in liters; the column labeled Fuel shows the required or recommended type of fuel (regular or premium gasoline); the column labeled Drive identifies the type of drive (F for front wheel, R for rear wheel, and A for all wheel); and the column labeled Hwy MPG shows the fuel efficiency rating for highway driving in terms of miles per gallon.
   a. Develop an estimated regression equation that can be used to predict the fuel efficiency for highway driving given the engine's displacement. Test for significance using $\alpha = .05$.
   b. Consider the addition of the dummy variable FuelPremium, where the value of FuelPremium is 1 if the required or recommended type of fuel is premium gasoline and 0 if the type of fuel is regular gasoline. Develop the estimated regression equation that can be used to predict the fuel efficiency for highway driving given the engine's displacement and the dummy variable FuelPremium.
   c. Use $\alpha = .05$ to determine whether the dummy variable added in part (b) is significant.
   d. Consider the addition of the dummy variables FrontWheel and RearWheel. The value of FrontWheel is 1 if the car has front wheel drive and 0 otherwise; the value of RearWheel is 1 if the car has rear wheel drive and 0 otherwise. Thus, for a car that has all-wheel drive, the value of FrontWheel and the value of RearWheel is 0. Develop the estimated regression equation that can be used to predict the fuel efficiency for

highway driving given the engine's displacement, the dummy variable FuelPremium, and the dummy variables FrontWheel and RearWheel.

e. For the estimated regression equation developed in part (d), test for overall significance and individual significance using $\alpha = .05$.

56. A portion of a data set containing information for 45 mutual funds that are part of the *Morningstar Funds 500* for 2008 follows. The complete data set is available in the file named MutualFunds. The data set includes the following five variables:

Fund Type: The type of fund, labeled DE (Domestic Equity), IE (International Equity), and FI (Fixed Income).

Net Asset Value ($): The closing price per share on December 31, 2007.

5-Year Average Return (%): The average annual return for the fund over the past five years.

Expense Ratio (%): The percentage of assets deducted each fiscal year for fund expenses.

Morningstar Rank: The risk adjusted star rating for each fund; Morningstar ranks go from a low of 1-Star to a high of 5-Stars.

WEB file
MutualFunds

Fund Name	Fund Type	Net Asset Value ($)	5-Year Average Return (%)	Expense Ratio (%)	Morningstar Rank
Amer Cent Inc & Growth Inv	DE	28.88	12.39	.67	2-Star
American Century Intl. Disc	IE	14.37	30.53	1.41	3-Star
American Century Tax-Free Bond	FI	10.73	3.34	.49	4-Star
American Century Ultra	DE	24.94	10.88	.99	3-Star
Ariel	DE	46.39	11.32	1.03	2-Star
Artisan Intl Val	IE	25.52	24.95	1.23	3-Star
Artisan Small Cap	DE	16.92	15.67	1.18	3-Star
Baron Asset	DE	50.67	16.77	1.31	5-Star
Brandywine	DE	36.58	18.14	1.08	4-Star
⋮	⋮	⋮	⋮	⋮	⋮

a. Develop an estimated regression equation that can be used to predict the 5-year average return given the type of fund. At the .05 level of significance, test for a significant relationship.

b. Did the estimated regression equation developed in part (a) provide a good fit to the data? Explain.

c. Develop the estimated regression equation that can be used to predict the 5-year average return given the type of fund, the net asset value, and the expense ratio. At the .05 level of significance, test for a significant relationship. Do you think any variables should be deleted from the estimated regression equation? Explain.

d. Morningstar Rank is a categorical variable. Because the data set contains only funds with four ranks (2-Star through 5-Star), use the following dummy variables: 3StarRank = 1 for a 3-Star fund, 0 otherwise; 4StarRank = 1 for a 4-Star fund, 0 otherwise; and 5StarRank = 1 for a 5-Star fund, 0 otherwise. Develop an estimated regression equation that can be used to predict the 5-year average return given the type of fund, the expense ratio, and the Morningstar Rank. Using $\alpha = .05$, remove any independent variables that are not significant.

e. Use the estimated regression equation developed in part (d) to predict the 5-year average return for a domestic equity fund with an expense ratio of 1.05% and a 3-Star Morningstar Rank.

57. *Fortune* magazine publishes an annual list of the 100 best companies to work for. The data in the file named FortuneBest shows a portion of the data for a random sample of 30 of the companies that made the top 100 list for 2012 (*Fortune,* February 6, 2012). The column labeled Rank shows the rank of the company in the Fortune 100 list; the column labeled Size indicates whether the company is a small, midsize, or large company; the column labeled Salaried ($1000s) shows the average annual salary for salaried employees rounded to the nearest $1000; and the column labeled Hourly ($1000s) shows the average annual salary for hourly employees rounded to the nearest $1000. *Fortune* defines large companies as having more than 10,000 employees, midsize companies as having between 2500 and 10,000 employees, and small companies as having fewer than 2500 employees.

WEB file
FortuneBest

Rank	Company	Size	Salaried ($1000s)	Hourly ($1000s)
4	Wegmans Food Markets	Large	56	29
6	NetApp	Midsize	143	76
7	Camden Property Trust	Small	71	37
8	Recreational Equipment (REI)	Large	103	28
10	Quicken Loans	Midsize	78	54
11	Zappos.com	Midsize	48	25
12	Mercedes-Benz USA	Small	118	50
20	USAA	Large	96	47
22	The Container Store	Midsize	71	45
25	Ultimate Software	Small	166	56
37	Plante Moran	Small	73	45
42	Baptist Health South Florida	Large	126	80
50	World Wide Technology	Small	129	31
53	Methodist Hospital	Large	100	83
58	Perkins Coie	Small	189	63
60	American Express	Large	114	35
64	TDIndustries	Small	93	47
66	QuikTrip	Large	69	44
72	EOG Resources	Small	189	81
75	FactSet Research Systems	Small	103	51
80	Stryker	Large	71	43
81	SRC	Small	84	33
84	Booz Allen Hamilton	Large	105	77
91	CarMax	Large	57	34
93	GoDaddy.com	Midsize	105	71
94	KPMG	Large	79	59
95	Navy Federal Credit Union	Midsize	77	39
97	Schweitzer Engineering Labs	Small	99	28
99	Darden Restaurants	Large	57	24
100	Intercontinental Hotels Group	Large	63	26

a. Use these data to develop an estimated regression equation that could be used to predict the average annual salary for salaried employees given the average annual salary for hourly employees.

b. Use $\alpha = .05$ to test for overall significance.

c. To incorporate the effect of size, a categorical variable with three levels, we used two dummy variables: Size-Midsize and Size-Small. The value of Size-Midsize = 1 if the company is a midsize company and 0 otherwise. And, the value of Size-Small = 1 if the company is a small company and 0 otherwise. Develop an estimated regression equation that could be used to predict the average annual salary for salaried employees given the average annual salary for hourly employees and the size of the company.

d. For the estimated regression equation developed in part (c), use the t test to determine the significance of the independent variables. Use $\alpha = .05$.

e. Based upon your findings in part (d), develop an estimated regression equation that can be used to predict the average annual salary for salaried employees given the average annual salary for hourly employees and the size of the company.

Case Problem 1 Consumer Research, Inc.

Consumer Research, Inc., is an independent agency that conducts research on consumer attitudes and behaviors for a variety of firms. In one study, a client asked for an investigation of consumer characteristics that can be used to predict the amount charged by credit card users. Data were collected on annual income, household size, and annual credit card charges for a sample of 50 consumers. The following data are contained in the file named Consumer.

WEB file

Consumer

Income ($1000s)	Household Size	Amount Charged ($)	Income ($1000s)	Household Size	Amount Charged ($)
54	3	4016	54	6	5573
30	2	3159	30	1	2583
32	4	5100	48	2	3866
50	5	4742	34	5	3586
31	2	1864	67	4	5037
55	2	4070	50	2	3605
37	1	2731	67	5	5345
40	2	3348	55	6	5370
66	4	4764	52	2	3890
51	3	4110	62	3	4705
25	3	4208	64	2	4157
48	4	4219	22	3	3579
27	1	2477	29	4	3890
33	2	2514	39	2	2972
65	3	4214	35	1	3121
63	4	4965	39	4	4183
42	6	4412	54	3	3730
21	2	2448	23	6	4127
44	1	2995	27	2	2921
37	5	4171	26	7	4603
62	6	5678	61	2	4273
21	3	3623	30	2	3067
55	7	5301	22	4	3074
42	2	3020	46	5	4820
41	7	4828	66	4	5149

Managerial Report

1. Use methods of descriptive statistics to summarize the data. Comment on the findings.
2. Develop estimated regression equations, first using annual income as the independent variable and then using household size as the independent variable. Which variable is the better predictor of annual credit card charges? Discuss your findings.
3. Develop an estimated regression equation with annual income and household size as the independent variables. Discuss your findings.
4. What is the predicted annual credit card charge for a three-person household with an annual income of $40,000?
5. Discuss the need for other independent variables that could be added to the model. What additional variables might be helpful?

Case Problem 2 Predicting Winnings for NASCAR Drivers

Matt Kenseth won the 2012 Daytona 500, the most important race of the NASCAR season. His win was no surprise because for the 2011 season he finished fourth in the point standings with 2330 points, behind Tony Stewart (2403 points), Carl Edwards (2403 points), and Kevin Harvick (2345 points). In 2011 he earned $6,183,580 by winning three Poles (fastest driver in qualifying), winning three races, finishing in the top five 12 times, and finishing in the top ten 20 times. NASCAR's point system in 2011 allocated 43 points to the driver who finished first, 42 points to the driver who finished second, and so on down to 1 point for the driver who finished in the 43rd position. In addition any driver who led a lap received 1 bonus point, the driver who led the most laps received an additional bonus point, and the race winner was awarded 3 bonus points. But, the maximum number of points a driver could earn in any race was 48. Table 15.13 shows data for the 2011 season for the top 35 drivers (NASCAR website, February 28, 2011).

TABLE 15.13 NASCAR RESULTS FOR THE 2011 SEASON

WEB file NASCAR

Driver	Points	Poles	Wins	Top 5	Top 10	Winnings ($)
Tony Stewart	2403	1	5	9	19	6,529,870
Carl Edwards	2403	3	1	19	26	8,485,990
Kevin Harvick	2345	0	4	9	19	6,197,140
Matt Kenseth	2330	3	3	12	20	6,183,580
Brad Keselowski	2319	1	3	10	14	5,087,740
Jimmie Johnson	2304	0	2	14	21	6,296,360
Dale Earnhardt Jr.	2290	1	0	4	12	4,163,690
Jeff Gordon	2287	1	3	13	18	5,912,830
Denny Hamlin	2284	0	1	5	14	5,401,190
Ryan Newman	2284	3	1	9	17	5,303,020
Kurt Busch	2262	3	2	8	16	5,936,470
Kyle Busch	2246	1	4	14	18	6,161,020
Clint Bowyer	1047	0	1	4	16	5,633,950
Kasey Kahne	1041	2	1	8	15	4,775,160
A. J. Allmendinger	1013	0	0	1	10	4,825,560
Greg Biffle	997	3	0	3	10	4,318,050
Paul Menard	947	0	1	4	8	3,853,690
Martin Truex Jr.	937	1	0	3	12	3,955,560
Marcos Ambrose	936	0	1	5	12	4,750,390
Jeff Burton	935	0	0	2	5	3,807,780
Juan Montoya	932	2	0	2	8	5,020,780
Mark Martin	930	2	0	2	10	3,830,910
David Ragan	906	2	1	4	8	4,203,660
Joey Logano	902	2	0	4	6	3,856,010
Brian Vickers	846	0	0	3	7	4,301,880
Regan Smith	820	0	1	2	5	4,579,860
Jamie McMurray	795	1	0	2	4	4,794,770
David Reutimann	757	1	0	1	3	4,374,770
Bobby Labonte	670	0	0	1	2	4,505,650
David Gilliland	572	0	0	1	2	3,878,390
Casey Mears	541	0	0	0	0	2,838,320
Dave Blaney	508	0	0	1	1	3,229,210
Andy Lally	398	0	0	0	0	2,868,220
Robby Gordon	268	0	0	0	0	2,271,890
J. J. Yeley	192	0	0	0	0	2,559,500

Managerial Report

1. Suppose you wanted to predict Winnings ($) using only the number of poles won (Poles), the number of wins (Wins), the number of top five finishes (Top 5), or the number of top ten finishes (Top 10). Which of these four variables provides the best single predictor of winnings?
2. Develop an estimated regression equation that can be used to predict Winnings ($) given the number of poles won (Poles), the number of wins (Wins), the number of top five finishes (Top 5), and the number of top ten (Top 10) finishes. Test for individual significance and discuss your findings and conclusions.
3. Create two new independent variables: Top 2–5 and Top 6–10. Top 2–5 represents the number of times the driver finished between second and fifth place and Top 6–10 represents the number of times the driver finished between sixth and tenth place. Develop an estimated regression equation that can be used to predict Winnings ($) using Poles, Wins, Top 2–5, and Top 6–10. Test for individual significance and discuss your findings and conclusions.
4. Based upon the results of your analysis, what estimated regression equation would you recommend using to predict Winnings ($)? Provide an interpretation of the estimated regression coefficients for this equation.

Case Problem 3 Finding the Best Car Value

When trying to decide what car to buy, real value is not necessarily determined by how much you spend on the initial purchase. Instead, cars that are reliable and don't cost much to own often represent the best values. But no matter how reliable or inexpensive a car may cost to own, it must also perform well.

To measure value, *Consumer Reports* developed a statistic referred to as a value score. The value score is based upon five-year owner costs, overall road-test scores, and predicted-reliability ratings. Five-year owner costs are based upon the expenses incurred in the first five years of ownership, including depreciation, fuel, maintenance and repairs, and so on. Using a national average of 12,000 miles per year, an average cost per mile driven is used as the measure of five-year owner costs. Road-test scores are the results of more than 50 tests and evaluations and are based on a 100-point scale, with higher scores indicating better performance, comfort, convenience, and fuel economy. The highest road-test score obtained in the tests conducted by *Consumer Reports* was a 99 for a Lexus LS 460L. Predicted-reliability ratings (1 = Poor, 2 = Fair, 3 = Good, 4 = Very Good, and 5 = Excellent) are based upon data from *Consumer Reports*' Annual Auto Survey.

WEB file CarValues

A car with a value score of 1.0 is considered to be an "average-value" car. A car with a value score of 2.0 is considered to be twice as good a value as a car with a value score of 1.0; a car with a value score of 0.5 is considered half as good as average; and so on. The data for three sizes of cars (13 small sedans, 20 family sedans, and 21 upscale sedans), including the price ($) of each car tested, are contained in the file named CarValues (*Consumer Reports* website, April 18, 2012). To incorporate the effect of size of car, a categorical variable with three values (small sedan, family sedan, and upscale sedan), use the following dummy variables:

$$\text{Family-Sedan} = \begin{cases} 1 \text{ if the car is a Family Sedan} \\ 0 \text{ otherwise} \end{cases}$$

$$\text{Upscale-Sedan} = \begin{cases} 1 \text{ if the car is an Upscale Sedan} \\ 0 \text{ otherwise} \end{cases}$$

Managerial Report

1. Treating Cost/Mile as the dependent variable, develop an estimated regression with Family-Sedan and Upscale-Sedan as the independent variables. Discuss your findings.
2. Treating Value Score as the dependent variable, develop an estimated regression equation using Cost/Mile, Road-Test Score, Predicted Reliability, Family-Sedan, and Upscale-Sedan as the independent variables.
3. Delete any independent variables that are not significant from the estimated regression equation developed in part 2 using a .05 level of significance. After deleting any independent variables that are not significant, develop a new estimated regression equation.
4. Suppose someone claims that "smaller cars provide better values than larger cars." For the data in this case, the Small Sedans represent the smallest type of car and the Upscale Sedans represent the largest type of car. Does your analysis support this claim?
5. Use regression analysis to develop an estimated regression equation that could be used to predict the value score given the value of the Road-Test Score.
6. Use regression analysis to develop an estimated regression equation that could be used to predict the value score given the Predicted Reliability.
7. What conclusions can you derive from your analysis?

Appendix 15.1 Multiple Regression with Minitab

WEB file

Butler

In Section 15.2 we discussed the computer solution of multiple regression problems by showing Minitab's output for the Butler Trucking Company problem. In this appendix we describe the steps required to generate the Minitab computer solution. First, the data must be entered in a Minitab worksheet. The miles traveled are entered in column C1, the number of deliveries are entered in column C2, and the travel times (hours) are entered in column C3. The variable names Miles, Deliveries, and Time were entered as the column headings on the worksheet. In subsequent steps, we refer to the data by using the variable names Miles, Deliveries, and Time or the column indicators C1, C2, and C3. The following steps describe how to use Minitab to produce the regression results shown in Figure 15.4.

Step 1. Select the **Stat** menu
Step 2. Select the **Regression** menu
Step 3. Choose **Regression**
Step 4. When the **Regression** dialog box appears:
Enter Time in the **Response** box
Enter Miles and Deliveries in the **Predictors** box
Click **OK**

Appendix 15.2 Multiple Regression with Excel

WEB file

Butler

In Section 15.2 we discussed the computer solution of multiple regression problems by showing Minitab's output for the Butler Trucking Company problem. In this appendix we describe how to use Excel's Regression tool to develop the estimated multiple regression equation for the Butler Trucking problem. Refer to Figure 15.14 as we describe the tasks involved. First, the labels Assignment, Miles, Deliveries, and Time are entered into cells A1:D1 of the worksheet, and the sample data into cells B2:D11. The numbers 1–10 in cells A2:A11 identify each observation.

FIGURE 15.14 EXCEL OUTPUT FOR BUTLER TRUCKING WITH TWO INDEPENDENT VARIABLES

	A	B	C	D	E	F	G	H	I	J
1	**Assignment**	**Miles**	**Deliveries**	**Time**						
2	1	100	4	9.3						
3	2	50	3	4.8						
4	3	100	4	8.9						
5	4	100	2	6.5						
6	5	50	2	4.2						
7	6	80	2	6.2						
8	7	75	3	7.4						
9	8	65	4	6						
10	9	90	3	7.6						
11	10	90	2	6.1						
12										
13	SUMMARY OUTPUT									
14										
15	*Regression Statistics*									
16	Multiple R	0.9507								
17	R Square	0.9038								
18	Adjusted R Square	0.8763								
19	Standard Error	0.5731								
20	Observations	10								
21										
22	ANOVA									
23		*df*	*SS*	*MS*	*F*	*Significance F*				
24	Regression	2	21.6006	10.8003	32.8784	0.0003				
25	Residual	7	2.2994	0.3285						
26	Total	9	23.9							
27										
28		*Coefficients*	*Standard Error*	*t Stat*	*P-value*	*Lower 95%*	*Upper 95%*	*Lower 99.0%*	*Upper 99.0%*	
29	Intercept	-0.8687	0.9515	-0.9129	0.3916	-3.1188	1.3813	-4.1986	2.4612	
30	Miles	0.0611	0.0099	6.1824	0.0005	0.0378	0.0845	0.0265	0.0957	
31	Deliveries	0.9234	0.2211	4.1763	0.0042	0.4006	1.4463	0.1496	1.6972	
32										

The following steps describe how to use the Regression tool for the multiple regression analysis.

Step 1. Click the **Data** tab on the Ribbon
Step 2. In the **Analysis** group, click **Data Analysis**
Step 3. Choose **Regression** from the list of Analysis Tools
Step 4. When the Regression dialog box appears:
Enter D1:D11 in the **Input Y Range** box
Enter B1:C11 in the **Input X Range** box
Select **Labels**
Select **Confidence Level**
Enter 99 in the **Confidence Level** box
Select **Output Range**
Enter A13 in the **Output Range** box (to identify the upper left corner of the section of the worksheet where the output will appear)
Click **OK**

In the Excel output shown in Figure 15.14 the label for the independent variable x_1 is Miles (see cell A30), and the label for the independent variable x_2 is Deliveries (see cell A31). The estimated regression equation is

$$\hat{y} = -.8687 + .0611x_1 + .9234x_2$$

Note that using Excel's Regression tool for multiple regression is almost the same as using it for simple linear regression. The major difference is that in the multiple regression case a larger range of cells is required in order to identify the independent variables.

Appendix 15.3 Logistic Regression with Minitab

WEB file Simmons

Minitab calls logistic regression with a dependent variable that can only assume the values 0 and 1 Binary Logistic Regression. In this appendix we describe the steps required to use Minitab's Binary Logistic Regression procedure to generate the computer output for the Simmons Stores problem shown in Figure 15.13. First, the data must be entered in a Minitab worksheet. The amounts customers spent last year at Simmons (in thousands of dollars) are entered into column C2, the credit card data (1 if a Simmons card; 0 otherwise) are entered into column C3, and the coupon use data (1 if the customer used the coupon; 0 otherwise) are entered in column C4. The variable names Spending, Card, and Coupon are entered as the column headings on the worksheet. In subsequent steps, we refer to the data by using the variable names Spending, Card, and Coupon or the column indicators C2, C3, and C4. The following steps will generate the logistic regression output.

Step 1. Select the **Stat** menu
Step 2. Select the **Regression** menu
Step 3. Choose **Binary Logistic Regression**
Step 4. When the **Binary Logistic Regression** dialog box appears:
Enter Coupon in the **Response** box
Enter Spending and Card in the **Model** box
Click **OK**

The information in Figure 15.13 will now appear as a portion of the output.

Appendix 15.4 Multiple Regression Analysis Using StatTools

WEB file Butler

In this appendix we show how StatTools can be used to perform the regression analysis computations for the Butler Trucking problem. Begin by using the Data Set Manager to create a StatTools data set for these data using the procedure described in the appendix in Chapter 1. The following steps describe how StatTools can be used to provide the regression results.

Step 1. Click the **StatTools** tab on the Ribbon
Step 2. In the **Analyses** group, click **Regression and Classification**
Step 3. Choose the **Regression** option
Step 4. When the StatTools-Regression dialog box appears:
Select **Multiple** in the **Regression Type** box
In the **Variables** section:
Click the **Format** button and select **Unstacked**
In the column labeled **I** select **Miles**
In the column labeled **I** select **Deliveries**
In the column labeled **D** select **Time**
Click **OK**

The regression analysis output will appear.

The StatTools-Regression dialog box contains a number of more advanced options for developing prediction interval estimates and producing residual plots. The StatTools Help facility provides information on using all of these options.

APPENDIXES

Appendix A: References and Bibliography

General

Freedman, D., R. Pisani, and R. Purves. *Statistics*, 4th ed. W. W. Norton, 2007.

Hogg, R. V., and E. A. Tanis. *Probability and Statistical Inference,* 8th ed. Prentice Hall, 2009.

McKean, J. W., R. V. Hogg, and A. T. Craig. *Introduction to Mathematical Statistics,* 7th ed. Prentice Hall, 2012.

Miller, I., and M. Miller. *John E. Freund's Mathematical Statistics,* 7th ed. Pearson, 2003.

Moore, D. S., G. P. McCabe, and B. Craig. *Introduction to the Practice of Statistics,* 7th ed. Freeman, 2010.

Wackerly, D. D., W. Mendenhall, and R. L. Scheaffer. *Mathematical Statistics with Applications,* 7th ed. Cengage Learning, 2007.

Experimental Design

Cochran, W. G., and G. M. Cox. *Experimental Designs,* 2nd ed. Wiley, 1992.

Hicks, C. R., and K. V. Turner. *Fundamental Concepts in the Design of Experiments,* 5th ed. Oxford University Press, 1999.

Montgomery, D. C. *Design and Analysis of Experiments,* 8th ed. Wiley, 2012.

Winer, B. J., K. M. Michels, and D. R. Brown. *Statistical Principles in Experimental Design,* 3rd ed. McGraw-Hill, 1991.

Wu, C. F. Jeff, and M. Hamada. *Experiments: Planning, Analysis, and Optimization,* 2nd ed. Wiley, 2009.

Time Series and Forecasting

Bowerman, B. L., and R. T. O'Connell. *Forecasting and Time Series: An Applied Approach,* 3rd ed. Brooks/Cole, 2000.

Box, G. E. P., G. M. Jenkins, and G. C. Reinsel. *Time Series Analysis: Forecasting and Control,* 4th ed. Wiley, 2008.

Makridakis, S. G., S. C. Wheelwright, and R. J. Hyndman. *Forecasting Methods and Applications,* 3rd ed. Wiley, 1997.

Wilson, J. H., B. Keating, and John Galt Solutions, Inc. *Business Forecasting with Accompanying Excel-Based Forecast X*™*,* 5th ed. McGraw-Hill/Irwin, 2007.

Index Numbers

U.S. Department of Commerce. *Survey of Current Business.*

U.S. Department of Labor, Bureau of Labor Statistics. *CPI Detailed Report.*

U.S. Department of Labor. *Producer Price Indexes.*

Nonparametric Methods

Conover, W. J. *Practical Nonparametric Statistics,* 3rd ed. Wiley, 1999.

Gibbons, J. D., and S. Chakraborti. *Nonparametric Statistical Inference,* 5th ed. CRC Press, 2010.

Higgins, J. J. *Introduction to Modern Nonparametric Statistics*. Thomson-Brooks/Cole, 2004.

Hollander, M., and D. A. Wolfe. *Non-Parametric Statistical Methods,* 2nd ed. Wiley, 1999.

Probability

Hogg, R. V., and E. A. Tanis. *Probability and Statistical Inference,* 8th ed. Prentice Hall, 2009.

Ross, S. M. *Introduction to Probability Models,* 10th ed. Academic Press, 2009.

Wackerly, D. D., W. Mendenhall, and R. L. Scheaffer. *Mathematical Statistics with Applications,* 7th ed. Cengage Learning, 2007.

Quality Control

DeFeo, J. A., and J. M. Juran, *Juran's Quality Handbook,* 6th ed. McGraw-Hill, 2010.

Evans, J. R., and W. M. Lindsay. *The Management and Control of Quality,* 6th ed. South-Western, 2006.

Montgomery, D. C. *Introduction to Statistical Quality Control,* 6th ed. Wiley, 2008.

Regression Analysis

Chatterjee, S., and A. S. Hadi. *Regression Analysis by Example,* 4th ed. Wiley, 2006.

Draper, N. R., and H. Smith. *Applied Regression Analysis,* 3rd ed. Wiley, 1998.

Graybill, F. A., and H. K. Iyer. *Regression Analysis: Concepts and Applications.* Wadsworth, 1994.

Hosmer, D. W., and S. Lemeshow. *Applied Logistic Regression,* 2nd ed. Wiley, 2000.

Kleinbaum, D. G., L. L. Kupper, and K. E. Muller. *Applied Regression Analysis and Multivariate Methods,* 4th ed. Cengage Learning, 2007.

Neter, J., W. Wasserman, M. H. Kutner, and C. Nashtsheim. *Applied Linear Statistical Models,* 5th ed. McGraw-Hill, 2004.

Mendenhall, M., T. Sincich., and T. R. Dye. *A Second Course in Statistics: Regression Analysis,* 7th ed. Prentice Hall, 2011.

Decision Analysis

Clemen, R. T., and T. Reilly. *Making Hard Decisions with Decision Tools.* Cengage Learning, 2004.

Goodwin, P., and G. Wright. *Decision Analysis for Management Judgment,* 4th ed. Wiley, 2010.

Pratt, J. W., H. Raiffa, and R. Schlaifer. *Introduction to Statistical Decision Theory.* MIT Press, 1995.

Sampling

Cochran, W. G. *Sampling Techniques,* 3rd ed. Wiley, 1977.

Hansen, M. H., W. N. Hurwitz, W. G. Madow, and M. N. Hanson. *Sample Survey Methods and Theory.* Wiley, 1993.

Kish, L. *Survey Sampling.* Wiley, 2008.

Levy, P. S., and S. Lemeshow. *Sampling of Populations: Methods and Applications,* 4th ed. Wiley, 2009.

Scheaffer, R. L., W. Mendenhall, and L. Ott. *Elementary Survey Sampling,* 7th ed. Duxbury Press, 2011.

Data Visualization

Cleveland, W. S. *Visualizing Data.* Hobart Press, 1993.

Cleveland, W. S. *The Elements of Graphing Data,* 2nd ed. Hobart Press, 1994.

Few, S. *Show Me the Numbers: Designing Tables and Graphs to Enlighten.* Analytics Press, 2004.

Few, S. *Information Dashboard Design: The Effective Visual Communication of Data.* O'Reilly Media, 2006.

Few, S. *Now You See It: Simple Visualization Techniques for Quantitative Analysis.* Analytics Press, 2009.

Fry, B. *Visualizing Data: Exploring and Explaining Data with the Processing Environment.* O'Reilly Media, 2008.

Robbins, N. B. *Creating More Effective Graphs.* Wiley, 2004.

Telea, A. C. *Data Visualization Principles and Practice.* A.K. Peters Ltd., 2008.

Tufte, E. R. *Envisioning Information.* Graphics Press, 1990.

Tufte, E. R. *The Visual Display of Quantitative Information,* 2nd ed. Graphics Press, 1990.

Tufte, E. R. *Visual Explanations: Images and Quantities, Evidence and Narrative.* Graphics Press, 1997.

Tufte, E. R. *Visual and Statistical Thinking: Displays of Evidence for Making Decisions.* Graphics Press, 1997.

Tufte, E. R. *Beautiful Evidence.* Graphics Press, 2006.

Wong, D. M. *The Wall Street Journal Guide to Information Graphics.* W. W. Norton & Company, 2010.

Young, F. W., P. M. Valero-Mora, and M. Friendly. *Visual Statistics: Seeing Data with Dynamic Interactive Graphics.* Wiley, 2006.

Appendix B: Tables

TABLE 1 CUMULATIVE PROBABILITIES FOR THE STANDARD NORMAL DISTRIBUTION

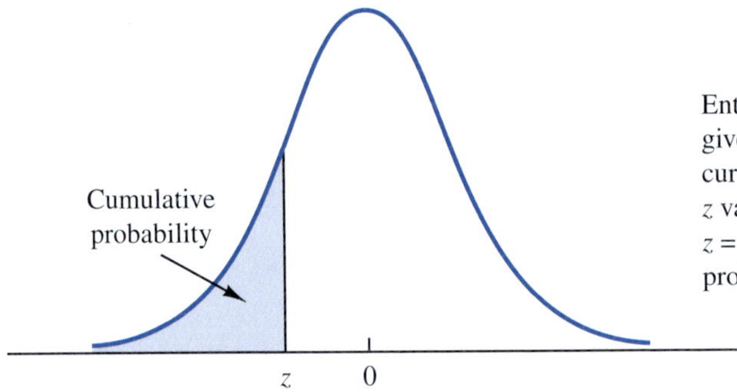

Entries in the table give the area under the curve to the left of the z value. For example, for $z = -.85$, the cumulative probability is .1977.

z	.00	.01	.02	.03	.04	.05	.06	.07	.08	.09
−3.0	.0013	.0013	.0013	.0012	.0012	.0011	.0011	.0011	.0010	.0010
−2.9	.0019	.0018	.0018	.0017	.0016	.0016	.0015	.0015	.0014	.0014
−2.8	.0026	.0025	.0024	.0023	.0023	.0022	.0021	.0021	.0020	.0019
−2.7	.0035	.0034	.0033	.0032	.0031	.0030	.0029	.0028	.0027	.0026
−2.6	.0047	.0045	.0044	.0043	.0041	.0040	.0039	.0038	.0037	.0036
−2.5	.0062	.0060	.0059	.0057	.0055	.0054	.0052	.0051	.0049	.0048
−2.4	.0082	.0080	.0078	.0075	.0073	.0071	.0069	.0068	.0066	.0064
−2.3	.0107	.0104	.0102	.0099	.0096	.0094	.0091	.0089	.0087	.0084
−2.2	.0139	.0136	.0132	.0129	.0125	.0122	.0119	.0116	.0113	.0110
−2.1	.0179	.0174	.0170	.0166	.0162	.0158	.0154	.0150	.0146	.0143
−2.0	.0228	.0222	.0217	.0212	.0207	.0202	.0197	.0192	.0188	.0183
−1.9	.0287	.0281	.0274	.0268	.0262	.0256	.0250	.0244	.0239	.0233
−1.8	.0359	.0351	.0344	.0336	.0329	.0322	.0314	.0307	.0301	.0294
−1.7	.0446	.0436	.0427	.0418	.0409	.0401	.0392	.0384	.0375	.0367
−1.6	.0548	.0537	.0526	.0516	.0505	.0495	.0485	.0475	.0465	.0455
−1.5	.0668	.0655	.0643	.0630	.0618	.0606	.0594	.0582	.0571	.0559
−1.4	.0808	.0793	.0778	.0764	.0749	.0735	.0721	.0708	.0694	.0681
−1.3	.0968	.0951	.0934	.0918	.0901	.0885	.0869	.0853	.0838	.0823
−1.2	.1151	.1131	.1112	.1093	.1075	.1056	.1038	.1020	.1003	.0985
−1.1	.1357	.1335	.1314	.1292	.1271	.1251	.1230	.1210	.1190	.1170
−1.0	.1587	.1562	.1539	.1515	.1492	.1469	.1446	.1423	.1401	.1379
−.9	.1841	.1814	.1788	.1762	.1736	.1711	.1685	.1660	.1635	.1611
−.8	.2119	.2090	.2061	.2033	.2005	.1977	.1949	.1922	.1894	.1867
−.7	.2420	.2389	.2358	.2327	.2296	.2266	.2236	.2206	.2177	.2148
−.6	.2743	.2709	.2676	.2643	.2611	.2578	.2546	.2514	.2483	.2451
−.5	.3085	.3050	.3015	.2981	.2946	.2912	.2877	.2843	.2810	.2776
−.4	.3446	.3409	.3372	.3336	.3300	.3264	.3228	.3192	.3156	.3121
−.3	.3821	.3783	.3745	.3707	.3669	.3632	.3594	.3557	.3520	.3483
−.2	.4207	.4168	.4129	.4090	.4052	.4013	.3974	.3936	.3897	.3859
−.1	.4602	.4562	.4522	.4483	.4443	.4404	.4364	.4325	.4286	.4247
−.0	.5000	.4960	.4920	.4880	.4840	.4801	.4761	.4721	.4681	.4641

TABLE 1 CUMULATIVE PROBABILITIES FOR THE STANDARD NORMAL DISTRIBUTION (*Continued*)

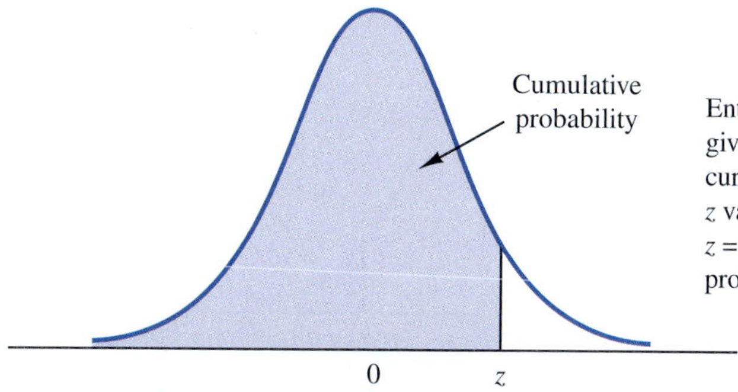

Entries in the table give the area under the curve to the left of the z value. For example, for $z = 1.25$, the cumulative probability is .8944.

z	.00	.01	.02	.03	.04	.05	.06	.07	.08	.09
.0	.5000	.5040	.5080	.5120	.5160	.5199	.5239	.5279	.5319	.5359
.1	.5398	.5438	.5478	.5517	.5557	.5596	.5636	.5675	.5714	.5753
.2	.5793	.5832	.5871	.5910	.5948	.5987	.6026	.6064	.6103	.6141
.3	.6179	.6217	.6255	.6293	.6331	.6368	.6406	.6443	.6480	.6517
.4	.6554	.6591	.6628	.6664	.6700	.6736	.6772	.6808	.6844	.6879
.5	.6915	.6950	.6985	.7019	.7054	.7088	.7123	.7157	.7190	.7224
.6	.7257	.7291	.7324	.7357	.7389	.7422	.7454	.7486	.7517	.7549
.7	.7580	.7611	.7642	.7673	.7704	.7734	.7764	.7794	.7823	.7852
.8	.7881	.7910	.7939	.7967	.7995	.8023	.8051	.8078	.8106	.8133
.9	.8159	.8186	.8212	.8238	.8264	.8289	.8315	.8340	.8365	.8389
1.0	.8413	.8438	.8461	.8485	.8508	.8531	.8554	.8577	.8599	.8621
1.1	.8643	.8665	.8686	.8708	.8729	.8749	.8770	.8790	.8810	.8830
1.2	.8849	.8869	.8888	.8907	.8925	.8944	.8962	.8980	.8997	.9015
1.3	.9032	.9049	.9066	.9082	.9099	.9115	.9131	.9147	.9162	.9177
1.4	.9192	.9207	.9222	.9236	.9251	.9265	.9279	.9292	.9306	.9319
1.5	.9332	.9345	.9357	.9370	.9382	.9394	.9406	.9418	.9429	.9441
1.6	.9452	.9463	.9474	.9484	.9495	.9505	.9515	.9525	.9535	.9545
1.7	.9554	.9564	.9573	.9582	.9591	.9599	.9608	.9616	.9625	.9633
1.8	.9641	.9649	.9656	.9664	.9671	.9678	.9686	.9693	.9699	.9706
1.9	.9713	.9719	.9726	.9732	.9738	.9744	.9750	.9756	.9761	.9767
2.0	.9772	.9778	.9783	.9788	.9793	.9798	.9803	.9808	.9812	.9817
2.1	.9821	.9826	.9830	.9834	.9838	.9842	.9846	.9850	.9854	.9857
2.2	.9861	.9864	.9868	.9871	.9875	.9878	.9881	.9884	.9887	.9890
2.3	.9893	.9896	.9898	.9901	.9904	.9906	.9909	.9911	.9913	.9916
2.4	.9918	.9920	.9922	.9925	.9927	.9929	.9931	.9932	.9934	.9936
2.5	.9938	.9940	.9941	.9943	.9945	.9946	.9948	.9949	.9951	.9952
2.6	.9953	.9955	.9956	.9957	.9959	.9960	.9961	.9962	.9963	.9964
2.7	.9965	.9966	.9967	.9968	.9969	.9970	.9971	.9972	.9973	.9974
2.8	.9974	.9975	.9976	.9977	.9977	.9978	.9979	.9979	.9980	.9981
2.9	.9981	.9982	.9982	.9983	.9984	.9984	.9985	.9985	.9986	.9986
3.0	.9987	.9987	.9987	.9988	.9988	.9989	.9989	.9989	.9990	.9990

TABLE 2 *t* DISTRIBUTION

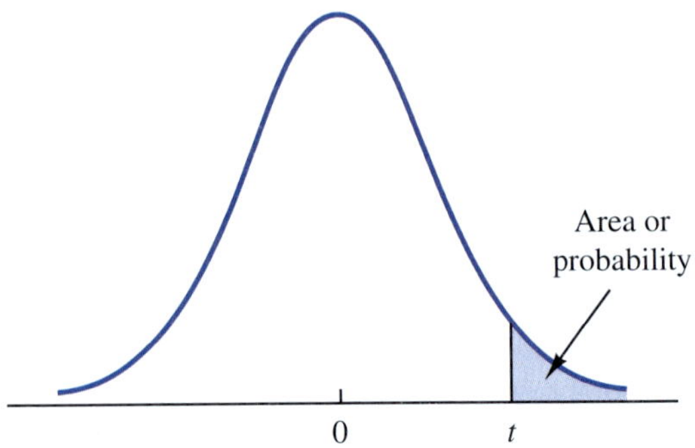

Entries in the table give t values for an area or probability in the upper tail of the t distribution. For example, with 10 degrees of freedom and a .05 area in the upper tail, $t_{.05} = 1.812$.

Degrees of Freedom	Area in Upper Tail					
	.20	.10	.05	.025	.01	.005
1	1.376	3.078	6.314	12.706	31.821	63.656
2	1.061	1.886	2.920	4.303	6.965	9.925
3	.978	1.638	2.353	3.182	4.541	5.841
4	.941	1.533	2.132	2.776	3.747	4.604
5	.920	1.476	2.015	2.571	3.365	4.032
6	.906	1.440	1.943	2.447	3.143	3.707
7	.896	1.415	1.895	2.365	2.998	3.499
8	.889	1.397	1.860	2.306	2.896	3.355
9	.883	1.383	1.833	2.262	2.821	3.250
10	.879	1.372	1.812	2.228	2.764	3.169
11	.876	1.363	1.796	2.201	2.718	3.106
12	.873	1.356	1.782	2.179	2.681	3.055
13	.870	1.350	1.771	2.160	2.650	3.012
14	.868	1.345	1.761	2.145	2.624	2.977
15	.866	1.341	1.753	2.131	2.602	2.947
16	.865	1.337	1.746	2.120	2.583	2.921
17	.863	1.333	1.740	2.110	2.567	2.898
18	.862	1.330	1.734	2.101	2.552	2.878
19	.861	1.328	1.729	2.093	2.539	2.861
20	.860	1.325	1.725	2.086	2.528	2.845
21	.859	1.323	1.721	2.080	2.518	2.831
22	.858	1.321	1.717	2.074	2.508	2.819
23	.858	1.319	1.714	2.069	2.500	2.807
24	.857	1.318	1.711	2.064	2.492	2.797
25	.856	1.316	1.708	2.060	2.485	2.787
26	.856	1.315	1.706	2.056	2.479	2.779
27	.855	1.314	1.703	2.052	2.473	2.771
28	.855	1.313	1.701	2.048	2.467	2.763
29	.854	1.311	1.699	2.045	2.462	2.756
30	.854	1.310	1.697	2.042	2.457	2.750
31	.853	1.309	1.696	2.040	2.453	2.744
32	.853	1.309	1.694	2.037	2.449	2.738
33	.853	1.308	1.692	2.035	2.445	2.733
34	.852	1.307	1.691	2.032	2.441	2.728

TABLE 2 *t* DISTRIBUTION (*Continued*)

Degrees of Freedom	Area in Upper Tail					
	.20	.10	.05	.025	.01	.005
35	.852	1.306	1.690	2.030	2.438	2.724
36	.852	1.306	1.688	2.028	2.434	2.719
37	.851	1.305	1.687	2.026	2.431	2.715
38	.851	1.304	1.686	2.024	2.429	2.712
39	.851	1.304	1.685	2.023	2.426	2.708
40	.851	1.303	1.684	2.021	2.423	2.704
41	.850	1.303	1.683	2.020	2.421	2.701
42	.850	1.302	1.682	2.018	2.418	2.698
43	.850	1.302	1.681	2.017	2.416	2.695
44	.850	1.301	1.680	2.015	2.414	2.692
45	.850	1.301	1.679	2.014	2.412	2.690
46	.850	1.300	1.679	2.013	2.410	2.687
47	.849	1.300	1.678	2.012	2.408	2.685
48	.849	1.299	1.677	2.011	2.407	2.682
49	.849	1.299	1.677	2.010	2.405	2.680
50	.849	1.299	1.676	2.009	2.403	2.678
51	.849	1.298	1.675	2.008	2.402	2.676
52	.849	1.298	1.675	2.007	2.400	2.674
53	.848	1.298	1.674	2.006	2.399	2.672
54	.848	1.297	1.674	2.005	2.397	2.670
55	.848	1.297	1.673	2.004	2.396	2.668
56	.848	1.297	1.673	2.003	2.395	2.667
57	.848	1.297	1.672	2.002	2.394	2.665
58	.848	1.296	1.672	2.002	2.392	2.663
59	.848	1.296	1.671	2.001	2.391	2.662
60	.848	1.296	1.671	2.000	2.390	2.660
61	.848	1.296	1.670	2.000	2.389	2.659
62	.847	1.295	1.670	1.999	2.388	2.657
63	.847	1.295	1.669	1.998	2.387	2.656
64	.847	1.295	1.669	1.998	2.386	2.655
65	.847	1.295	1.669	1.997	2.385	2.654
66	.847	1.295	1.668	1.997	2.384	2.652
67	.847	1.294	1.668	1.996	2.383	2.651
68	.847	1.294	1.668	1.995	2.382	2.650
69	.847	1.294	1.667	1.995	2.382	2.649
70	.847	1.294	1.667	1.994	2.381	2.648
71	.847	1.294	1.667	1.994	2.380	2.647
72	.847	1.293	1.666	1.993	2.379	2.646
73	.847	1.293	1.666	1.993	2.379	2.645
74	.847	1.293	1.666	1.993	2.378	2.644
75	.846	1.293	1.665	1.992	2.377	2.643
76	.846	1.293	1.665	1.992	2.376	2.642
77	.846	1.293	1.665	1.991	2.376	2.641
78	.846	1.292	1.665	1.991	2.375	2.640
79	.846	1.292	1.664	1.990	2.374	2.639

TABLE 2 *t* DISTRIBUTION (*Continued*)

Degrees of Freedom	Area in Upper Tail .20	.10	.05	.025	.01	.005
80	.846	1.292	1.664	1.990	2.374	2.639
81	.846	1.292	1.664	1.990	2.373	2.638
82	.846	1.292	1.664	1.989	2.373	2.637
83	.846	1.292	1.663	1.989	2.372	2.636
84	.846	1.292	1.663	1.989	2.372	2.636
85	.846	1.292	1.663	1.988	2.371	2.635
86	.846	1.291	1.663	1.988	2.370	2.634
87	.846	1.291	1.663	1.988	2.370	2.634
88	.846	1.291	1.662	1.987	2.369	2.633
89	.846	1.291	1.662	1.987	2.369	2.632
90	.846	1.291	1.662	1.987	2.368	2.632
91	.846	1.291	1.662	1.986	2.368	2.631
92	.846	1.291	1.662	1.986	2.368	2.630
93	.846	1.291	1.661	1.986	2.367	2.630
94	.845	1.291	1.661	1.986	2.367	2.629
95	.845	1.291	1.661	1.985	2.366	2.629
96	.845	1.290	1.661	1.985	2.366	2.628
97	.845	1.290	1.661	1.985	2.365	2.627
98	.845	1.290	1.661	1.984	2.365	2.627
99	.845	1.290	1.660	1.984	2.364	2.626
100	.845	1.290	1.660	1.984	2.364	2.626
∞	.842	1.282	1.645	1.960	2.326	2.576

TABLE 3 CHI-SQUARE DISTRIBUTION

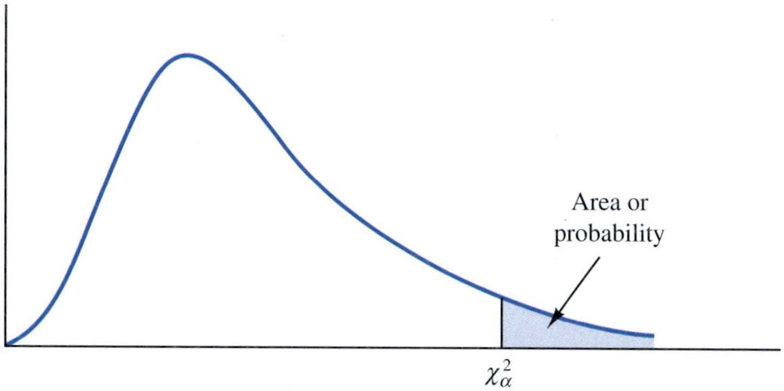

Entries in the table give χ^2_α values, where α is the area or probability in the upper tail of the chi-square distribution. For example, with 10 degrees of freedom and a .01 area in the upper tail, $\chi^2_{.01} = 23.209$.

Degrees of Freedom	Area in Upper Tail									
	.995	.99	.975	.95	.90	.10	.05	.025	.01	.005
1	.000	.000	.001	.004	.016	2.706	3.841	5.024	6.635	7.879
2	.010	.020	.051	.103	.211	4.605	5.991	7.378	9.210	10.597
3	.072	.115	.216	.352	.584	6.251	7.815	9.348	11.345	12.838
4	.207	.297	.484	.711	1.064	7.779	9.488	11.143	13.277	14.860
5	.412	.554	.831	1.145	1.610	9.236	11.070	12.832	15.086	16.750
6	.676	.872	1.237	1.635	2.204	10.645	12.592	14.449	16.812	18.548
7	.989	1.239	1.690	2.167	2.833	12.017	14.067	16.013	18.475	20.278
8	1.344	1.647	2.180	2.733	3.490	13.362	15.507	17.535	20.090	21.955
9	1.735	2.088	2.700	3.325	4.168	14.684	16.919	19.023	21.666	23.589
10	2.156	2.558	3.247	3.940	4.865	15.987	18.307	20.483	23.209	25.188
11	2.603	3.053	3.816	4.575	5.578	17.275	19.675	21.920	24.725	26.757
12	3.074	3.571	4.404	5.226	6.304	18.549	21.026	23.337	26.217	28.300
13	3.565	4.107	5.009	5.892	7.041	19.812	22.362	24.736	27.688	29.819
14	4.075	4.660	5.629	6.571	7.790	21.064	23.685	26.119	29.141	31.319
15	4.601	5.229	6.262	7.261	8.547	22.307	24.996	27.488	30.578	32.801
16	5.142	5.812	6.908	7.962	9.312	23.542	26.296	28.845	32.000	34.267
17	5.697	6.408	7.564	8.672	10.085	24.769	27.587	30.191	33.409	35.718
18	6.265	7.015	8.231	9.390	10.865	25.989	28.869	31.526	34.805	37.156
19	6.844	7.633	8.907	10.117	11.651	27.204	30.144	32.852	36.191	38.582
20	7.434	8.260	9.591	10.851	12.443	28.412	31.410	34.170	37.566	39.997
21	8.034	8.897	10.283	11.591	13.240	29.615	32.671	35.479	38.932	41.401
22	8.643	9.542	10.982	12.338	14.041	30.813	33.924	36.781	40.289	42.796
23	9.260	10.196	11.689	13.091	14.848	32.007	35.172	38.076	41.638	44.181
24	9.886	10.856	12.401	13.848	15.659	33.196	36.415	39.364	42.980	45.558
25	10.520	11.524	13.120	14.611	16.473	34.382	37.652	40.646	44.314	46.928
26	11.160	12.198	13.844	15.379	17.292	35.563	38.885	41.923	45.642	48.290
27	11.808	12.878	14.573	16.151	18.114	36.741	40.113	43.195	46.963	49.645
28	12.461	13.565	15.308	16.928	18.939	37.916	41.337	44.461	48.278	50.994
29	13.121	14.256	16.047	17.708	19.768	39.087	42.557	45.722	49.588	52.335

TABLE 3 CHI-SQUARE DISTRIBUTION (*Continued*)

Degrees of Freedom	Area in Upper Tail .995	.99	.975	.95	.90	.10	.05	.025	.01	.005
30	13.787	14.953	16.791	18.493	20.599	40.256	43.773	46.979	50.892	53.672
35	17.192	18.509	20.569	22.465	24.797	46.059	49.802	53.203	57.342	60.275
40	20.707	22.164	24.433	26.509	29.051	51.805	55.758	59.342	63.691	66.766
45	24.311	25.901	28.366	30.612	33.350	57.505	61.656	65.410	69.957	73.166
50	27.991	29.707	32.357	34.764	37.689	63.167	67.505	71.420	76.154	79.490
55	31.735	33.571	36.398	38.958	42.060	68.796	73.311	77.380	82.292	85.749
60	35.534	37.485	40.482	43.188	46.459	74.397	79.082	83.298	88.379	91.952
65	39.383	41.444	44.603	47.450	50.883	79.973	84.821	89.177	94.422	98.105
70	43.275	45.442	48.758	51.739	55.329	85.527	90.531	95.023	100.425	104.215
75	47.206	49.475	52.942	56.054	59.795	91.061	96.217	100.839	106.393	110.285
80	51.172	53.540	57.153	60.391	64.278	96.578	101.879	106.629	112.329	116.321
85	55.170	57.634	61.389	64.749	68.777	102.079	107.522	112.393	118.236	122.324
90	59.196	61.754	65.647	69.126	73.291	107.565	113.145	118.136	124.116	128.299
95	63.250	65.898	69.925	73.520	77.818	113.038	118.752	123.858	129.973	134.247
100	67.328	70.065	74.222	77.929	82.358	118.498	124.342	129.561	135.807	140.170

TABLE 4 *F* DISTRIBUTION

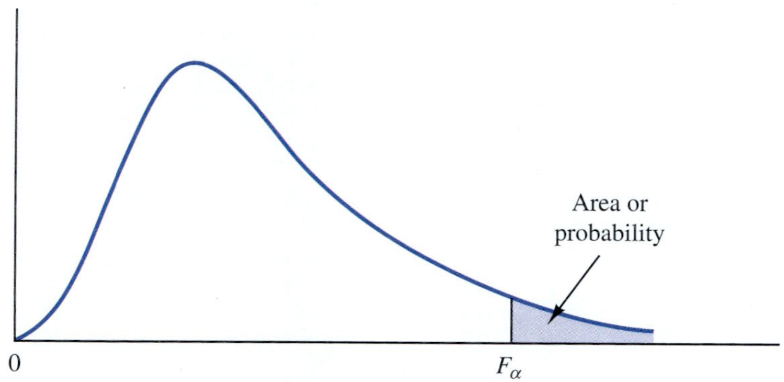

Entries in the table give F_α values, where α is the area or probability in the upper tail of the *F* distribution. For example, with 4 numerator degrees of freedom, 8 denominator degrees of freedom, and a .05 area in the upper tail, $F_{.05} = 3.84$.

Denominator Degrees of Freedom	Area in Upper Tail	Numerator Degrees of Freedom 1	2	3	4	5	6	7	8	9	10	15	20	25	30	40	60	100	1000
1	.10	39.86	49.50	53.59	55.83	57.24	58.20	58.91	59.44	59.86	60.19	61.22	61.74	62.05	62.26	62.53	62.79	63.01	63.30
	.05	161.45	199.50	215.71	224.58	230.16	233.99	236.77	238.88	240.54	241.88	245.95	248.02	249.26	250.10	251.14	252.20	253.04	254.19
	.025	647.79	799.48	864.15	899.60	921.83	937.11	948.20	956.64	963.28	968.63	984.87	993.08	998.09	1001.40	1005.60	1009.79	1013.16	1017.76
	.01	4052.18	4999.34	5403.53	5624.26	5763.96	5858.95	5928.33	5980.95	6022.40	6055.93	6156.97	6208.66	6239.86	6260.35	6286.43	6312.97	6333.92	6362.80
2	.10	8.53	9.00	9.16	9.24	9.29	9.33	9.35	9.37	9.38	9.39	9.42	9.44	9.45	9.46	9.47	9.47	9.48	9.49
	.05	18.51	19.00	19.16	19.25	19.30	19.33	19.35	19.37	19.38	19.40	19.43	19.45	19.46	19.46	19.47	19.48	19.49	19.49
	.025	38.51	39.00	39.17	39.25	39.30	39.33	39.36	39.37	39.39	39.40	39.43	39.45	39.46	39.46	39.47	39.48	39.49	39.50
	.01	98.50	99.00	99.16	99.25	99.30	99.33	99.36	99.38	99.39	99.40	99.43	99.45	99.46	99.47	99.48	99.48	99.49	99.50
3	.10	5.54	5.46	5.39	5.34	5.31	5.28	5.27	5.25	5.24	5.23	5.20	5.18	5.17	5.17	5.16	5.15	5.14	5.13
	.05	10.13	9.55	9.28	9.12	9.01	8.94	8.89	8.85	8.81	8.79	8.70	8.66	8.63	8.62	8.59	8.57	8.55	8.53
	.025	17.44	16.04	15.44	15.10	14.88	14.73	14.62	14.54	14.47	14.42	14.25	14.17	14.12	14.08	14.04	13.99	13.96	13.91
	.01	34.12	30.82	29.46	28.71	28.24	27.91	27.67	27.49	27.34	27.23	26.87	26.69	26.58	26.50	26.41	26.32	26.24	26.14
4	.10	4.54	4.32	4.19	4.11	4.05	4.01	3.98	3.95	3.94	3.92	3.87	3.84	3.83	3.82	3.80	3.79	3.78	3.76
	.05	7.71	6.94	6.59	6.39	6.26	6.16	6.09	6.04	6.00	5.96	5.86	5.80	5.77	5.75	5.72	5.69	5.66	5.63
	.025	12.22	10.65	9.98	9.60	9.36	9.20	9.07	8.98	8.90	8.84	8.66	8.56	8.50	8.46	8.41	8.36	8.32	8.26
	.01	21.20	18.00	16.69	15.98	15.52	15.21	14.98	14.80	14.66	14.55	14.20	14.02	13.91	13.84	13.75	13.65	13.58	13.47
5	.10	4.06	3.78	3.62	3.52	3.45	3.40	3.37	3.34	3.32	3.30	3.324	3.21	3.19	3.17	3.16	3.14	3.13	3.11
	.05	6.61.	5.79	5.41	5.19	5.05	4.95	4.88	4.82	4.77	4.74	4.62	4.56	4.52	4.50	4.46	4.43	4.41	4.37
	.025	10.01	8.43	7.76	7.39	7.15	6.98	6.85	6.76	6.68	6.62	6.43	6.33	6.27	6.23	6.18	6.12	6.08	6.02
	.01	16.26	13.27	12.06	11.39	10.97	10.67	10.46	10.29	10.16	10.05	9.72	9.55	9.45	9.38	9.29	9.20	9.13	9.03

TABLE 4 *F* DISTRIBUTION (*Continued*)

Denominator Degrees of Freedom	Area in Upper Tail	Numerator Degrees of Freedom																	
		1	2	3	4	5	6	7	8	9	10	15	20	25	30	40	60	100	1000
6	.10	3.78	3.46	3.29	3.18	3.11	3.05	3.01	2.98	2.96	2.94	2.87	2.84	2.81	2.80	2.78	2.76	2.75	2.72
	.05	5.99	5.14	4.76	4.53	4.39	4.28	4.21	4.15	4.10	4.06	3.94	3.87	3.83	3.81	3.77	3.74	3.71	3.67
	.025	8.81	7.26	6.60	6.23	5.99	5.82	5.70	5.60	5.52	5.46	5.27	5.17	5.11	5.07	5.01	4.96	4.92	4.86
	.01	13.75	10.92	9.78	9.15	8.75	8.47	8.26	8.10	7.98	7.87	7.56	7.40	7.30	7.23	7.14	7.06	6.99	6.89
7	.10	3.59	3.26	3.07	2.96	2.88	2.83	2.78	2.75	2.72	2.70	2.63	2.59	2.57	2.56	2.54	2.51	2.50	2.47
	.05	5.59	4.74	4.35	4.12	3.97	3.87	3.79	3.73	3.68	3.64	3.51	3.44	3.40	3.38	3.34	3.30	3.27	3.23
	.025	8.07	6.54	5.89	5.52	5.29	5.12	4.99	4.90	4.82	4.76	4.57	4.47	4.40	4.36	4.31	4.25	4.21	4.15
	.01	12.25	9.55	8.45	7.85	7.46	7.19	6.99	6.84	6.72	6.62	6.31	6.16	6.06	5.99	5.91	5.82	5.75	5.66
8	.10	3.46	3.11	2.92	2.81	2.73	2.67	2.62	2.59	2.56	2.54	2.46	2.42	2.40	2.38	2.36	2.34	2.32	2.30
	.05	5.32	4.46	4.07	3.84	3.69	3.58	3.50	3.44	3.39	3.35	3.22	3.15	3.11	3.08	3.04	3.01	2.97	2.93
	.025	7.57	6.06	5.42	5.05	4.82	4.65	4.53	4.43	4.36	4.30	4.10	4.00	3.94	3.89	3.84	3.78	3.74	3.68
	.01	11.26	8.65	7.59	7.01	6.63	6.37	6.18	6.03	5.91	5.81	5.52	5.36	5.26	5.20	5.12	5.03	4.96	4.87
9	.10	3.36	3.01	2.81	2.69	2.61	2.55	2.51	2.47	2.44	2.42	2.34	2.30	2.27	2.25	2.23	2.21	2.19	2.16
	.05	5.12	4.26	3.86	3.63	3.48	3.37	3.29	3.23	3.18	3.14	3.01	2.94	2.89	2.86	2.83	2.79	2.76	2.71
	.025	7.21	5.71	5.08	4.72	4.48	4.32	4.20	4.10	4.03	3.96	3.77	3.67	3.60	3.56	3.51	3.45	3.40	3.34
	.01	10.56	8.02	6.99	6.42	6.06	5.80	5.61	5.47	5.35	5.26	4.96	4.81	4.71	4.65	4.57	4.48	4.41	4.32
10	.10	3.29	2.92	2.73	2.61	2.52	2.46	2.41	2.38	2.35	2.32	2.24	2.20	2.17	2.16	2.13	2.11	2.09	2.06
	.05	4.96	4.10	3.71	3.48	3.33	3.22	3.14	3.07	3.02	2.98	2.85	2.77	2.73	2.70	2.66	2.62	2.59	2.54
	.025	6.94	5.46	4.83	4.47	4.24	4.07	3.95	3.85	3.78	3.72	3.52	3.42	3.35	3.31	3.26	3.20	3.15	3.09
	.01	10.04	7.56	6.55	5.99	5.64	5.39	5.20	5.06	4.94	4.85	4.56	4.41	4.31	4.25	4.17	4.08	4.01	3.92
11	.10	3.23	2.86	2.66	2.54	2.45	2.39	2.34	2.30	2.27	2.25	2.17	2.12	2.10	2.08	2.05	2.03	2.01	1.98
	.05	4.84	3.98	3.59	3.36	3.20	3.09	3.01	2.95	2.90	2.85	2.72	2.65	2.60	2.57	2.53	2.49	2.46	2.41
	.025	6.72	5.26	4.63	4.28	4.04	3.88	3.76	3.66	3.59	3.53	3.33	3.23	3.16	3.12	3.06	3.00	2.96	2.89
	.01	9.65	7.21	6.22	5.67	5.32	5.07	4.89	4.74	4.63	4.54	4.25	4.10	4.01	3.94	3.86	3.78	3.71	3.61
12	.10	3.18	2.81	2.61	2.48	2.39	2.33	2.28	2.24	2.21	2.19	2.10	2.06	2.03	2.01	1.99	1.96	1.94	1.91
	.05	4.75	3.89	3.49	3.26	3.11	3.00	2.91	2.85	2.80	2.75	2.62	2.54	2.50	2.47	2.43	2.38	2.35	2.30
	.025	6.55	5.10	4.47	4.12	3.89	3.73	3.61	3.51	3.44	3.37	3.18	3.07	3.01	2.96	2.91	2.85	2.80	2.73
	.01	9.33	6.93	5.95	5.41	5.06	4.82	4.64	4.50	4.39	4.30	4.01	3.86	3.76	3.70	3.62	3.54	3.47	3.37
13	.10	3.14	2.76	2.56	2.43	2.35	2.28	2.23	2.20	2.16	2.14	2.05	2.01	1.98	1.96	1.93	1.90	1.88	1.85
	.05	4.67	3.81	3.41	3.18	3.03	2.92	2.83	2.77	2.71	2.67	2.53	2.46	2.41	2.38	2.34	2.30	2.26	2.21
	.025	6.41	4.97	4.35	4.00	3.77	3.60	3.48	3.39	3.31	3.25	3.05	2.95	2.88	2.84	2.78	2.72	2.67	2.60
	.01	9.07	6.70	5.74	5.21	4.86	4.62	4.44	4.30	4.19	4.10	3.82	3.66	3.57	3.51	3.43	3.34	3.27	3.18
14	.10	3.10	2.73	2.52	2.39	2.31	2.24	2.19	2.15	2.12	2.10	2.01	1.96	1.93	1.99	1.89	1.86	1.83	1.80
	.05	4.60	3.74	3.34	3.11	2.96	2.85	2.76	2.70	2.65	2.60	2.46	2.39	2.34	2.31	2.27	2.22	2.19	2.14
	.025	6.30	4.86	4.24	3.89	3.66	3.50	3.38	3.29	3.21	3.15	2.95	2.84	2.78	2.73	2.67	2.61	2.56	2.50
	.01	8.86	6.51	5.56	5.04	4.69	4.46	4.28	4.14	4.03	3.94	3.66	3.51	3.41	3.35	3.27	3.18	3.11	3.02
15	.10	3.07	2.70	2.49	2.36	2.27	2.21	2.16	2.12	2.09	2.06	1.97	1.92	1.89	1.87	1.85	1.82	1.79	1.76
	.05	4.54	3.68	3.29	3.06	2.90	2.79	2.71	2.64	2.59	2.54	2.40	2.33	2.28	2.25	2.20	2.16	2.12	2.07
	.025	6.20	4.77	4.15	3.80	3.58	3.41	3.29	3.20	3.12	3.06	2.86	2.76	2.69	2.64	2.59	2.52	2.47	2.40
	.01	8.68	6.36	5.42	4.89	4.56	4.32	4.14	4.00	3.89	3.80	3.52	3.37	3.28	3.21	3.13	3.05	2.98	2.88

Denominator Degrees of Freedom	Area in Upper Tail	Numerator Degrees of Freedom																	
		1	2	3	4	5	6	7	8	9	10	15	20	25	30	40	60	100	1000
16	.10	3.05	2.67	2.46	2.33	2.24	2.18	2.13	2.09	2.06	2.03	1.94	1.89	1.86	1.84	1.81	1.78	1.76	1.72
	.05	4.49	3.63	3.24	3.01	2.85	2.74	2.66	2.59	2.54	2.49	2.35	2.28	2.23	2.19	2.15	2.11	2.07	2.02
	.025	6.12	4.69	4.08	3.73	3.50	3.34	3.22	3.12	3.05	2.99	2.79	2.68	2.61	2.57	2.51	2.45	2.40	2.32
	.01	8.53	6.23	5.29	4.77	4.44	4.20	4.03	3.89	3.78	3.69	3.41	3.26	3.16	3.10	3.02	2.93	2.86	2.76
17	.10	3.03	2.64	2.44	2.31	2.22	2.15	2.10	2.06	2.03	2.00	1.91	1.86	1.83	1.81	1.78	1.75	1.73	1.69
	.05	4.45	3.59	3.20	2.96	2.81	2.70	2.61	2.55	2.49	2.45	2.31	2.23	2.18	2.15	2.10	2.06	2.02	1.97
	.025	6.04	4.62	4.01	3.66	3.44	3.28	3.16	3.06	2.98	2.92	2.72	2.62	2.55	2.50	2.44	2.38	2.33	2.26
	.01	8.40	6.11	5.19	4.67	4.34	4.10	3.93	3.79	3.68	3.59	3.31	3.16	3.07	3.00	2.92	2.83	2.76	2.66
18	.10	3.01	2.62	2.42	2.29	2.20	2.13	2.08	2.04	2.00	1.98	1.89	1.84	1.80	1.78	1.75	1.72	1.70	1.66
	.05	4.41	3.55	3.16	2.93	2.77	2.66	2.58	2.51	2.46	2.41	2.27	2.19	2.14	2.11	2.06	2.02	1.98	1.92
	.025	5.98	4.56	3.95	3.61	3.38	3.22	3.10	3.01	2.93	2.87	2.67	2.56	2.49	2.44	2.38	2.32	2.27	2.20
	.01	8.29	6.01	5.09	4.58	4.25	4.01	3.84	3.71	3.60	3.51	3.23	3.08	2.98	2.92	2.84	2.75	2.68	2.58
19	.10	2.99	2.61	2.40	2.27	2.18	2.11	2.06	2.02	1.98	1.96	1.86	1.81	1.78	1.76	1.73	1.70	1.67	1.64
	.05	4.38	3.52	3.13	2.90	2.74	2.63	2.54	2.48	2.42	2.38	2.23	2.16	2.11	2.07	2.03	1.98	1.94	1.88
	.025	5.92	4.51	3.90	3.56	3.33	3.17	3.05	2.96	2.88	2.82	2.62	2.51	2.44	2.39	2.33	2.27	2.22	2.14
	.01	8.18	5.93	5.01	4.50	4.17	3.94	3.77	3.63	3.52	3.43	3.15	3.00	2.91	2.84	2.76	2.67	2.60	2.50
20	.10	2.97	2.59	2.38	2.25	2.16	2.09	2.04	2.00	1.96	1.94	1.84	1.79	1.76	1.74	1.71	1.68	1.65	1.61
	.05	4.35	3.49	3.10	2.87	2.71	2.60	2.51	2.45	2.39	2.35	2.20	2.12	2.07	2.04	1.99	1.95	1.91	1.85
	.025	5.87	4.46	3.86	3.51	3.29	3.13	3.01	2.91	2.84	2.77	2.57	2.46	2.40	2.35	2.29	2.22	2.17	2.09
	.01	8.10	5.85	4.94	4.43	4.10	3.87	3.70	3.56	3.46	3.37	3.09	2.94	2.84	2.78	2.69	2.61	2.54	2.43
21	.10	2.96	2.57	2.36	2.23	2.14	2.08	2.02	1.98	1.95	1.92	1.83	1.78	1.74	1.72	1.69	1.66	1.63	1.59
	.05	4.32	3.47	3.07	2.84	2.68	2.57	2.49	2.42	2.37	2.32	2.18	2.10	2.05	2.01	1.96	1.92	1.88	1.82
	.025	5.83	4.42	3.82	3.48	3.25	3.09	2.97	2.87	2.80	2.73	2.53	2.42	2.36	2.31	2.25	2.18	2.13	2.05
	.01	8.02	5.78	4.87	4.37	4.04	3.81	3.64	3.51	3.40	3.31	3.03	2.88	2.79	2.72	2.64	2.55	2.48	2.37
22	.10	2.95	2.56	2.35	2.22	2.13	2.06	2.01	1.97	1.93	1.90	1.81	1.76	1.73	1.70	1.67	1.64	1.61	1.57
	.05	4.30	3.44	3.05	2.82	2.66	2.55	2.46	2.40	2.34	2.30	2.15	2.07	2.02	1.98	1.94	1.89	1.85	1.79
	.025	5.79	4.38	3.78	3.44	3.22	3.05	2.93	2.84	2.76	2.70	2.50	2.39	2.32	2.27	2.21	2.14	2.09	2.01
	.01	7.95	5.72	4.82	4.31	3.99	3.76	3.59	3.45	3.35	3.26	2.98	2.83	2.73	2.67	2.58	2.50	2.42	2.32
23	.10	2.94	2.55	2.34	2.21	2.11	2.05	1.99	1.95	1.92	1.89	1.80	1.74	1.71	1.69	1.66	1.62	1.59	1.55
	.05	4.28	3.42	3.03	2.80	2.64	2.53	2.44	2.37	2.32	2.27	2.13	2.05	2.00	1.96	1.91	1.86	1.82	1.76
	.025	5.75	4.35	3.75	3.41	3.18	3.02	2.90	2.81	2.73	2.67	2.47	2.36	2.29	2.24	2.18	2.11	2.06	1.98
	.01	7.88	5.66	4.76	4.26	3.94	3.71	3.54	3.41	3.30	3.21	2.93	2.78	2.69	2.62	2.54	2.45	2.37	2.27
24	.10	2.93	2.54	2.33	2.19	2.10	2.04	1.98	1.94	1.91	1.88	1.78	1.73	1.70	1.67	1.64	1.61	1.58	1.54
	.05	4.26	3.40	3.01	2.78	2.62	2.51	2.42	2.36	2.30	2.25	2.11	2.03	1.97	1.94	1.89	1.84	1.80	1.74
	.025	5.72	4.32	3.72	3.38	3.15	2.99	2.87	2.78	2.70	2.64	2.44	2.33	2.26	2.21	2.15	2.08	2.02	1.94
	.01	7.82	5.61	4.72	4.22	3.90	3.67	3.50	3.36	3.26	3.17	2.89	2.74	2.64	2.58	2.49	2.40	2.33	2.22

TABLE 4 *F* DISTRIBUTION (*Continued*)

Denominator Degrees of Freedom	Area in Upper Tail	Numerator Degrees of Freedom																	
		1	2	3	4	5	6	7	8	9	10	15	20	25	30	40	60	100	1000
25	.10	2.92	2.53	2.32	2.18	2.09	2.02	1.97	1.93	1.89	1.87	1.77	1.72	1.68	1.66	1.63	1.59	1.56	1.52
	.05	4.24	3.39	2.99	2.76	2.60	2.49	2.40	2.34	2.28	2.24	2.09	2.01	1.96	1.92	1.87	1.82	1.78	1.72
	.025	5.69	4.29	3.69	3.35	3.13	2.97	2.85	2.75	2.68	2.61	2.41	2.30	2.23	2.18	2.12	2.05	2.00	1.91
	.01	7.77	5.57	4.68	4.18	3.85	3.63	3.46	3.32	3.22	3.13	2.85	2.70	2.60	2.54	2.45	2.36	2.29	2.18
26	.10	2.91	2.52	2.31	2.17	2.08	2.01	1.96	1.92	1.88	1.86	1.76	1.71	1.67	1.65	1.61	1.58	1.55	1.51
	.05	4.23	3.37	2.98	2.74	2.59	2.47	2.39	2.32	2.27	2.22	2.07	1.99	1.94	1.90	1.85	1.80	1.76	1.70
	.025	5.66	4.27	3.67	3.33	3.10	2.94	2.82	2.73	2.65	2.59	2.39	2.28	2.21	2.16	2.09	2.03	1.97	1.89
	.01	7.72	5.53	4.64	4.14	3.82	3.59	3.42	3.29	3.18	3.09	2.81	2.66	2.57	2.50	2.42	2.33	2.25	2.14
27	.10	2.90	2.51	2.30	2.17	2.07	2.00	1.95	1.91	1.37	1.85	1.75	1.70	1.66	1.64	1.60	1.57	1.54	1.50
	.05	4.21	3.35	2.96	2.73	2.57	2.46	2.37	2.31	2.25	2.20	2.06	1.97	1.92	1.88	1.84	1.79	1.74	1.68
	.025	5.63	4.24	3.65	3.31	3.08	2.92	2.80	2.71	2.53	2.57	2.36	2.25	2.18	2.13	2.07	2.00	1.94	1.86
	.01	7.68	5.49	4.60	4.11	3.78	3.56	3.39	3.26	3.15	3.06	2.78	2.63	2.54	2.47	2.38	2.29	2.22	2.11
28	.10	2.89	2.50	2.29	2.16	2.06	2.00	1.94	1.90	1.37	1.84	1.74	1.69	1.65	1.63	1.59	1.56	1.53	1.48
	.05	4.20	3.34	2.95	2.71	2.56	2.45	2.36	2.29	2.24	2.19	2.04	1.96	1.91	1.87	1.82	1.77	1.73	1.66
	.025	5.61	4.22	3.63	3.29	3.06	2.90	2.78	2.69	2.51	2.55	2.34	2.23	2.16	2.11	2.05	1.98	1.92	1.84
	.01	7.64	5.45	4.57	4.07	3.75	3.53	3.36	3.23	3.12	3.03	2.75	2.60	2.51	2.44	2.35	2.26	2.19	2.08
29	.10	2.89	2.50	2.28	2.15	2.06	1.99	1.93	1.89	1.86	1.83	1.73	1.68	1.64	1.62	1.58	1.55	1.52	1.47
	.05	4.18	3.33	2.93	2.70	2.55	2.43	2.35	2.28	2.22	2.18	2.03	1.94	1.89	1.85	1.81	1.75	1.71	1.65
	.025	5.59	4.20	3.61	3.27	3.04	2.88	2.76	2.67	2.59	2.53	2.32	2.21	2.14	2.09	2.03	1.96	1.90	1.82
	.01	7.60	5.42	4.54	4.04	3.73	3.50	3.33	3.20	3.09	3.00	2.73	2.57	2.48	2.41	2.33	2.23	2.16	2.05
30	.10	2.88	2.49	2.28	2.14	2.05	1.98	1.93	1.88	1.85	1.82	1.72	1.67	1.63	1.61	1.57	1.54	1.51	1.46
	.05	4.17	3.32	2.92	2.69	2.53	2.42	2.33	2.27	2.21	2.16	2.01	1.93	1.88	1.84	1.79	1.74	1.70	1.63
	.025	5.57	4.18	3.59	3.25	3.03	2.87	2.75	2.65	2.57	2.51	2.31	2.20	2.12	2.07	2.01	1.94	1.88	1.80
	.01	7.56	5.39	4.51	4.02	3.70	3.47	3.30	3.17	3.07	2.98	2.70	2.55	2.45	2.39	2.30	2.21	2.13	2.02
40	.10	2.84	2.44	2.23	2.09	2.00	1.93	1.87	1.83	1.79	1.76	1.66	1.61	1.57	1.54	1.51	1.47	1.43	1.38
	.05	4.08	3.23	2.84	2.61	2.45	2.34	2.25	2.18	2.12	2.08	1.92	1.84	1.78	1.74	1.69	1.64	1.59	1.52
	.025	5.42	4.05	3.46	3.13	2.90	2.74	2.62	2.53	2.45	2.39	2.18	2.07	1.99	1.94	1.88	1.80	1.74	1.65
	.01	7.31	5.18	4.31	3.83	3.51	3.29	3.12	2.99	2.89	2.80	2.52	2.37	2.27	2.20	2.11	2.02	1.94	1.82
60	.10	2.79	2.39	2.18	2.04	1.95	1.87	1.82	1.77	1.74	1.71	1.60	1.54	1.50	1.48	1.44	1.40	1.36	1.30
	.05	4.00	3.15	2.76	2.53	2.37	2.25	2.17	2.10	2.04	1.99	1.84	1.75	1.69	1.65	1.59	1.53	1.48	1.40
	.025	5.29	3.93	3.34	3.01	2.79	2.63	2.51	2.41	2.33	2.27	2.06	1.94	1.87	1.82	1.74	1.67	1.60	1.49
	.01	7.08	4.98	4.13	3.65	3.34	3.12	2.95	2.82	2.72	2.63	2.35	2.20	2.10	2.03	1.94	1.84	1.75	1.62
100	.10	2.76	2.36	2.14	2.00	1.91	1.83	1.78	1.73	1.69	1.66	1.56	1.49	1.45	1.42	1.38	1.34	1.29	1.22
	.05	3.94	3.09	2.70	2.46	2.31	2.19	2.10	2.03	1.97	1.93	1.77	1.68	1.62	1.57	1.52	1.45	1.39	1.30
	.025	5.18	3.83	3.25	2.92	2.70	2.54	2.42	2.32	2.24	2.18	1.97	1.85	1.77	1.71	1.64	1.56	1.48	1.36
	.01	6.90	4.82	3.98	3.51	3.21	2.99	2.82	2.69	2.59	2.50	2.22	2.07	1.97	1.89	1.80	1.69	1.60	1.45
1000	.10	2.71	2.31	2.09	1.95	1.85	1.78	1.72	1.68	1.64	1.61	1.49	1.43	1.38	1.35	1.30	1.25	1.20	1.08
	.05	3.85	3.00	2.61	2.38	2.22	2.11	2.02	1.95	1.89	1.84	1.68	1.58	1.52	1.47	1.41	1.33	1.26	1.11
	.025	5.04	3.70	3.13	2.80	2.58	2.42	2.30	2.20	2.13	2.06	1.85	1.72	1.64	1.58	1.50	1.41	1.32	1.13
	.01	6.66	4.63	3.80	3.34	3.04	2.82	2.66	2.53	2.43	2.34	2.06	1.90	1.79	1.72	1.61	1.50	1.38	1.16

TABLE 5 BINOMIAL PROBABILITIES

Entries in the table give the probability of x successes in n trials of a binomial experiment, where p is the probability of a success on one trial. For example, with six trials and $p = .05$, the probability of two successes is .0305.

		p								
n	*x*	**.01**	**.02**	**.03**	**.04**	**.05**	**.06**	**.07**	**.08**	**.09**
2	0	.9801	.9604	.9409	.9216	.9025	.8836	.8649	.8464	.8281
	1	.0198	.0392	.0582	.0768	.0950	.1128	.1302	.1472	.1638
	2	.0001	.0004	.0009	.0016	.0025	.0036	.0049	.0064	.0081
3	0	.9703	.9412	.9127	.8847	.8574	.8306	.8044	.7787	.7536
	1	.0294	.0576	.0847	.1106	.1354	.1590	.1816	.2031	.2236
	2	.0003	.0012	.0026	.0046	.0071	.0102	.0137	.0177	.0221
	3	.0000	.0000	.0000	.0001	.0001	.0002	.0003	.0005	.0007
4	0	.9606	.9224	.8853	.8493	.8145	.7807	.7481	.7164	.6857
	1	.0388	.0753	.1095	.1416	.1715	.1993	.2252	.2492	.2713
	2	.0006	.0023	.0051	.0088	.0135	.0191	.0254	.0325	.0402
	3	.0000	.0000	.0001	.0002	.0005	.0008	.0013	.0019	.0027
	4	.0000	.0000	.0000	.0000	.0000	.0000	.0000	.0000	.0001
5	0	.9510	.9039	.8587	.8154	.7738	.7339	.6957	.6591	.6240
	1	.0480	.0922	.1328	.1699	.2036	.2342	.2618	.2866	.3086
	2	.0010	.0038	.0082	.0142	.0214	.0299	.0394	.0498	.0610
	3	.0000	.0001	.0003	.0006	.0011	.0019	.0030	.0043	.0060
	4	.0000	.0000	.0000	.0000	.0000	.0001	.0001	.0002	.0003
	5	.0000	.0000	.0000	.0000	.0000	.0000	.0000	.0000	.0000
6	0	.9415	.8858	.8330	.7828	.7351	.6899	.6470	.6064	.5679
	1	.0571	.1085	.1546	.1957	.2321	.2642	.2922	.3164	.3370
	2	.0014	.0055	.0120	.0204	.0305	.0422	.0550	.0688	.0833
	3	.0000	.0002	.0005	.0011	.0021	.0036	.0055	.0080	.0110
	4	.0000	.0000	.0000	.0000	.0001	.0002	.0003	.0005	.0008
	5	.0000	.0000	.0000	.0000	.0000	.0000	.0000	.0000	.0000
	6	.0000	.0000	.0000	.0000	.0000	.0000	.0000	.0000	.0000
7	0	.9321	.8681	.8080	.7514	.6983	.6485	.6017	.5578	.5168
	1	.0659	.1240	.1749	.2192	.2573	.2897	.3170	.3396	.3578
	2	.0020	.0076	.0162	.0274	.0406	.0555	.0716	.0886	.1061
	3	.0000	.0003	.0008	.0019	.0036	.0059	.0090	.0128	.0175
	4	.0000	.0000	.0000	.0001	.0002	.0004	.0007	.0011	.0017
	5	.0000	.0000	.0000	.0000	.0000	.0000	.0000	.0001	.0001
	6	.0000	.0000	.0000	.0000	.0000	.0000	.0000	.0000	.0000
	7	.0000	.0000	.0000	.0000	.0000	.0000	.0000	.0000	.0000
8	0	.9227	.8508	.7837	.7214	.6634	.6096	.5596	.5132	.4703
	1	.0746	.1389	.1939	.2405	.2793	.3113	.3370	.3570	.3721
	2	.0026	.0099	.0210	.0351	.0515	.0695	.0888	.1087	.1288
	3	.0001	.0004	.0013	.0029	.0054	.0089	.0134	.0189	.0255
	4	.0000	.0000	.0001	.0002	.0004	.0007	.0013	.0021	.0031
	5	.0000	.0000	.0000	.0000	.0000	.0000	.0001	.0001	.0002
	6	.0000	.0000	.0000	.0000	.0000	.0000	.0000	.0000	.0000
	7	.0000	.0000	.0000	.0000	.0000	.0000	.0000	.0000	.0000
	8	.0000	.0000	.0000	.0000	.0000	.0000	.0000	.0000	.0000

TABLE 5 BINOMIAL PROBABILITIES (*Continued*)

		p								
n	*x*	.01	.02	.03	.04	.05	.06	.07	.08	.09
9	0	.9135	.8337	.7602	.6925	.6302	.5730	.5204	.4722	.4279
	1	.0830	.1531	.2116	.2597	.2985	.3292	.3525	.3695	.3809
	2	.0034	.0125	.0262	.0433	.0629	.0840	.1061	.1285	.1507
	3	.0001	.0006	.0019	.0042	.0077	.0125	.0186	.0261	.0348
	4	.0000	.0000	.0001	.0003	.0006	.0012	.0021	.0034	.0052
	5	.0000	.0000	.0000	.0000	.0000	.0001	.0002	.0003	.0005
	6	.0000	.0000	.0000	.0000	.0000	.0000	.0000	.0000	.0000
	7	.0000	.0000	.0000	.0000	.0000	.0000	.0000	.0000	.0000
	8	.0000	.0000	.0000	.0000	.0000	.0000	.0000	.0000	.0000
	9	.0000	.0000	.0000	.0000	.0000	.0000	.0000	.0000	.0000
10	0	.9044	.8171	.7374	.6648	.5987	.5386	.4840	.4344	.3894
	1	.0914	.1667	.2281	.2770	.3151	.3438	.3643	.3777	.3851
	2	.0042	.0153	.0317	.0519	.0746	.0988	.1234	.1478	.1714
	3	.0001	.0008	.0026	.0058	.0105	.0168	.0248	.0343	.0452
	4	.0000	.0000	.0001	.0004	.0010	.0019	.0033	.0052	.0078
	5	.0000	.0000	.0000	.0000	.0001	.0001	.0003	.0005	.0009
	6	.0000	.0000	.0000	.0000	.0000	.0000	.0000	.0000	.0001
	7	.0000	.0000	.0000	.0000	.0000	.0000	.0000	.0000	.0000
	8	.0000	.0000	.0000	.0000	.0000	.0000	.0000	.0000	.0000
	9	.0000	.0000	.0000	.0000	.0000	.0000	.0000	.0000	.0000
	10	.0000	.0000	.0000	.0000	.0000	.0000	.0000	.0000	.0000
12	0	.8864	.7847	.6938	.6127	.5404	.4759	.4186	.3677	.3225
	1	.1074	.1922	.2575	.3064	.3413	.3645	.3781	.3837	.3827
	2	.0060	.0216	.0438	.0702	.0988	.1280	.1565	.1835	.2082
	3	.0002	.0015	.0045	.0098	.0173	.0272	.0393	.0532	.0686
	4	.0000	.0001	.0003	.0009	.0021	.0039	.0067	.0104	.0153
	5	.0000	.0000	.0000	.0001	.0002	.0004	.0008	.0014	.0024
	6	.0000	.0000	.0000	.0000	.0000	.0000	.0001	.0001	.0003
	7	.0000	.0000	.0000	.0000	.0000	.0000	.0000	.0000	.0000
	8	.0000	.0000	.0000	.0000	.0000	.0000	.0000	.0000	.0000
	9	.0000	.0000	.0000	.0000	.0000	.0000	.0000	.0000	.0000
	10	.0000	.0000	.0000	.0000	.0000	.0000	.0000	.0000	.0000
	11	.0000	.0000	.0000	.0000	.0000	.0000	.0000	.0000	.0000
	12	.0000	.0000	.0000	.0000	.0000	.0000	.0000	.0000	.0000
15	0	.8601	.7386	.6333	.5421	.4633	.3953	.3367	.2863	.2430
	1	.1303	.2261	.2938	.3388	.3658	.3785	.3801	.3734	.3605
	2	.0092	.0323	.0636	.0988	.1348	.1691	.2003	.2273	.2496
	3	.0004	.0029	.0085	.0178	.0307	.0468	.0653	.0857	.1070
	4	.0000	.0002	.0008	.0022	.0049	.0090	.0148	.0223	.0317
	5	.0000	.0000	.0001	.0002	.0006	.0013	.0024	.0043	.0069
	6	.0000	.0000	.0000	.0000	.0000	.0001	.0003	.0006	.0011
	7	.0000	.0000	.0000	.0000	.0000	.0000	.0000	.0001	.0001
	8	.0000	.0000	.0000	.0000	.0000	.0000	.0000	.0000	.0000
	9	.0000	.0000	.0000	.0000	.0000	.0000	.0000	.0000	.0000
	10	.0000	.0000	.0000	.0000	.0000	.0000	.0000	.0000	.0000
	11	.0000	.0000	.0000	.0000	.0000	.0000	.0000	.0000	.0000
	12	.0000	.0000	.0000	.0000	.0000	.0000	.0000	.0000	.0000
	13	.0000	.0000	.0000	.0000	.0000	.0000	.0000	.0000	.0000
	14	.0000	.0000	.0000	.0000	.0000	.0000	.0000	.0000	.0000
	15	.0000	.0000	.0000	.0000	.0000	.0000	.0000	.0000	.0000

TABLE 5 BINOMIAL PROBABILITIES (*Continued*)

		p								
n	*x*	**.01**	**.02**	**.03**	**.04**	**.05**	**.06**	**.07**	**.08**	**.09**
18	0	.8345	.6951	.5780	.4796	.3972	.3283	.2708	.2229	.1831
	1	.1517	.2554	.3217	.3597	.3763	.3772	.3669	.3489	.3260
	2	.0130	.0443	.0846	.1274	.1683	.2047	.2348	.2579	.2741
	3	.0007	.0048	.0140	.0283	.0473	.0697	.0942	.1196	.1446
	4	.0000	.0004	.0016	.0044	.0093	.0167	.0266	.0390	.0536
	5	.0000	.0000	.0001	.0005	.0014	.0030	.0056	.0095	.0148
	6	.0000	.0000	.0000	.0000	.0002	.0004	.0009	.0018	.0032
	7	.0000	.0000	.0000	.0000	.0000	.0000	.0001	.0003	.0005
	8	.0000	.0000	.0000	.0000	.0000	.0000	.0000	.0000	.0001
	9	.0000	.0000	.0000	.0000	.0000	.0000	.0000	.0000	.0000
	10	.0000	.0000	.0000	.0000	.0000	.0000	.0000	.0000	.0000
	11	.0000	.0000	.0000	.0000	.0000	.0000	.0000	.0000	.0000
	12	.0000	.0000	.0000	.0000	.0000	.0000	.0000	.0000	.0000
	13	.0000	.0000	.0000	.0000	.0000	.0000	.0000	.0000	.0000
	14	.0000	.0000	.0000	.0000	.0000	.0000	.0000	.0000	.0000
	15	.0000	.0000	.0000	.0000	.0000	.0000	.0000	.0000	.0000
	16	.0000	.0000	.0000	.0000	.0000	.0000	.0000	.0000	.0000
	17	.0000	.0000	.0000	.0000	.0000	.0000	.0000	.0000	.0000
	18	.0000	.0000	.0000	.0000	.0000	.0000	.0000	.0000	.0000
20	0	.8179	.6676	.5438	.4420	.3585	.2901	.2342	.1887	.1516
	1	.1652	.2725	.3364	.3683	.3774	.3703	.3526	.3282	.3000
	2	.0159	.0528	.0988	.1458	.1887	.2246	.2521	.2711	.2818
	3	.0010	.0065	.0183	.0364	.0596	.0860	.1139	.1414	.1672
	4	.0000	.0006	.0024	.0065	.0133	.0233	.0364	.0523	.0703
	5	.0000	.0000	.0002	.0009	.0022	.0048	.0088	.0145	.0222
	6	.0000	.0000	.0000	.0001	.0003	.0008	.0017	.0032	.0055
	7	.0000	.0000	.0000	.0000	.0000	.0001	.0002	.0005	.0011
	8	.0000	.0000	.0000	.0000	.0000	.0000	.0000	.0001	.0002
	9	.0000	.0000	.0000	.0000	.0000	.0000	.0000	.0000	.0000
	10	.0000	.0000	.0000	.0000	.0000	.0000	.0000	.0000	.0000
	11	.0000	.0000	.0000	.0000	.0000	.0000	.0000	.0000	.0000
	12	.0000	.0000	.0000	.0000	.0000	.0000	.0000	.0000	.0000
	13	.0000	.0000	.0000	.0000	.0000	.0000	.0000	.0000	.0000
	14	.0000	.0000	.0000	.0000	.0000	.0000	.0000	.0000	.0000
	15	.0000	.0000	.0000	.0000	.0000	.0000	.0000	.0000	.0000
	16	.0000	.0000	.0000	.0000	.0000	.0000	.0000	.0000	.0000
	17	.0000	.0000	.0000	.0000	.0000	.0000	.0000	.0000	.0000
	18	.0000	.0000	.0000	.0000	.0000	.0000	.0000	.0000	.0000
	19	.0000	.0000	.0000	.0000	.0000	.0000	.0000	.0000	.0000
	20	.0000	.0000	.0000	.0000	.0000	.0000	.0000	.0000	.0000

TABLE 5 BINOMIAL PROBABILITIES (*Continued*)

		p								
n	*x*	**.10**	**.15**	**.20**	**.25**	**.30**	**.35**	**.40**	**.45**	**.50**
2	0	.8100	.7225	.6400	.5625	.4900	.4225	.3600	.3025	.2500
	1	.1800	.2550	.3200	.3750	.4200	.4550	.4800	.4950	.5000
	2	.0100	.0225	.0400	.0625	.0900	.1225	.1600	.2025	.2500
3	0	.7290	.6141	.5120	.4219	.3430	.2746	.2160	.1664	.1250
	1	.2430	.3251	.3840	.4219	.4410	.4436	.4320	.4084	.3750
	2	.0270	.0574	.0960	.1406	.1890	.2389	.2880	.3341	.3750
	3	.0010	.0034	.0080	.0156	.0270	.0429	.0640	.0911	.1250
4	0	.6561	.5220	.4096	.3164	.2401	.1785	.1296	.0915	.0625
	1	.2916	.3685	.4096	.4219	.4116	.3845	.3456	.2995	.2500
	2	.0486	.0975	.1536	.2109	.2646	.3105	.3456	.3675	.3750
	3	.0036	.0115	.0256	.0469	.0756	.1115	.1536	.2005	.2500
	4	.0001	.0005	.0016	.0039	.0081	.0150	.0256	.0410	.0625
5	0	.5905	.4437	.3277	.2373	.1681	.1160	.0778	.0503	.0312
	1	.3280	.3915	.4096	.3955	.3602	.3124	.2592	.2059	.1562
	2	.0729	.1382	.2048	.2637	.3087	.3364	.3456	.3369	.3125
	3	.0081	.0244	.0512	.0879	.1323	.1811	.2304	.2757	.3125
	4	.0004	.0022	.0064	.0146	.0284	.0488	.0768	.1128	.1562
	5	.0000	.0001	.0003	.0010	.0024	.0053	.0102	.0185	.0312
6	0	.5314	.3771	.2621	.1780	.1176	.0754	.0467	.0277	.0156
	1	.3543	.3993	.3932	.3560	.3025	.2437	.1866	.1359	.0938
	2	.0984	.1762	.2458	.2966	.3241	.3280	.3110	.2780	.2344
	3	.0146	.0415	.0819	.1318	.1852	.2355	.2765	.3032	.3125
	4	.0012	.0055	.0154	.0330	.0595	.0951	.1382	.1861	.2344
	5	.0001	.0004	.0015	.0044	.0102	.0205	.0369	.0609	.0938
	6	.0000	.0000	.0001	.0002	.0007	.0018	.0041	.0083	.0156
7	0	.4783	.3206	.2097	.1335	.0824	.0490	.0280	.0152	.0078
	1	.3720	.3960	.3670	.3115	.2471	.1848	.1306	.0872	.0547
	2	.1240	.2097	.2753	.3115	.3177	.2985	.2613	.2140	.1641
	3	.0230	.0617	.1147	.1730	.2269	.2679	.2903	.2918	.2734
	4	.0026	.0109	.0287	.0577	.0972	.1442	.1935	.2388	.2734
	5	.0002	.0012	.0043	.0115	.0250	.0466	.0774	.1172	.1641
	6	.0000	.0001	.0004	.0013	.0036	.0084	.0172	.0320	.0547
	7	.0000	.0000	.0000	.0001	.0002	.0006	.0016	.0037	.0078
8	0	.4305	.2725	.1678	.1001	.0576	.0319	.0168	.0084	.0039
	1	.3826	.3847	.3355	.2670	.1977	.1373	.0896	.0548	.0312
	2	.1488	.2376	.2936	.3115	.2965	.2587	.2090	.1569	.1094
	3	.0331	.0839	.1468	.2076	.2541	.2786	.2787	.2568	.2188
	4	.0046	.0185	.0459	.0865	.1361	.1875	.2322	.2627	.2734
	5	.0004	.0026	.0092	.0231	.0467	.0808	.1239	.1719	.2188
	6	.0000	.0002	.0011	.0038	.0100	.0217	.0413	.0703	.1094
	7	.0000	.0000	.0001	.0004	.0012	.0033	.0079	.0164	.0313
	8	.0000	.0000	.0000	.0000	.0001	.0002	.0007	.0017	.0039

TABLE 5 BINOMIAL PROBABILITIES (*Continued*)

		p								
n	*x*	.10	.15	.20	.25	.30	.35	.40	.45	.50
9	0	.3874	.2316	.1342	.0751	.0404	.0207	.0101	.0046	.0020
	1	.3874	.3679	.3020	.2253	.1556	.1004	.0605	.0339	.0176
	2	.1722	.2597	.3020	.3003	.2668	.2162	.1612	.1110	.0703
	3	.0446	.1069	.1762	.2336	.2668	.2716	.2508	.2119	.1641
	4	.0074	.0283	.0661	.1168	.1715	.2194	.2508	.2600	.2461
	5	.0008	.0050	.0165	.0389	.0735	.1181	.1672	.2128	.2461
	6	.0001	.0006	.0028	.0087	.0210	.0424	.0743	.1160	.1641
	7	.0000	.0000	.0003	.0012	.0039	.0098	.0212	.0407	.0703
	8	.0000	.0000	.0000	.0001	.0004	.0013	.0035	.0083	.0176
	9	.0000	.0000	.0000	.0000	.0000	.0001	.0003	.0008	.0020
10	0	.3487	.1969	.1074	.0563	.0282	.0135	.0060	.0025	.0010
	1	.3874	.3474	.2684	.1877	.1211	.0725	.0403	.0207	.0098
	2	.1937	.2759	.3020	.2816	.2335	.1757	.1209	.0763	.0439
	3	.0574	.1298	.2013	.2503	.2668	.2522	.2150	.1665	.1172
	4	.0112	.0401	.0881	.1460	.2001	.2377	.2508	.2384	.2051
	5	.0015	.0085	.0264	.0584	.1029	.1536	.2007	.2340	.2461
	6	.0001	.0012	.0055	.0162	.0368	.0689	.1115	.1596	.2051
	7	.0000	.0001	.0008	.0031	.0090	.0212	.0425	.0746	.1172
	8	.0000	.0000	.0001	.0004	.0014	.0043	.0106	.0229	.0439
	9	.0000	.0000	.0000	.0000	.0001	.0005	.0016	.0042	.0098
	10	.0000	.0000	.0000	.0000	.0000	.0000	.0001	.0003	.0010
12	0	.2824	.1422	.0687	.0317	.0138	.0057	.0022	.0008	.0002
	1	.3766	.3012	.2062	.1267	.0712	.0368	.0174	.0075	.0029
	2	.2301	.2924	.2835	.2323	.1678	.1088	.0639	.0339	.0161
	3	.0853	.1720	.2362	.2581	.2397	.1954	.1419	.0923	.0537
	4	.0213	.0683	.1329	.1936	.2311	.2367	.2128	.1700	.1208
	5	.0038	.0193	.0532	.1032	.1585	.2039	.2270	.2225	.1934
	6	.0005	.0040	.0155	.0401	.0792	.1281	.1766	.2124	.2256
	7	.0000	.0006	.0033	.0115	.0291	.0591	.1009	.1489	.1934
	8	.0000	.0001	.0005	.0024	.0078	.0199	.0420	.0762	.1208
	9	.0000	.0000	.0001	.0004	.0015	.0048	.0125	.0277	.0537
	10	.0000	.0000	.0000	.0000	.0002	.0008	.0025	.0068	.0161
	11	.0000	.0000	.0000	.0000	.0000	.0001	.0003	.0010	.0029
	12	.0000	.0000	.0000	.0000	.0000	.0000	.0000	.0001	.0002
15	0	.2059	.0874	.0352	.0134	.0047	.0016	.0005	.0001	.0000
	1	.3432	.2312	.1319	.0668	.0305	.0126	.0047	.0016	.0005
	2	.2669	.2856	.2309	.1559	.0916	.0476	.0219	.0090	.0032
	3	.1285	.2184	.2501	.2252	.1700	.1110	.0634	.0318	.0139
	4	.0428	.1156	.1876	.2252	.2186	.1792	.1268	.0780	.0417
	5	.0105	.0449	.1032	.1651	.2061	.2123	.1859	.1404	.0916
	6	.0019	.0132	.0430	.0917	.1472	.1906	.2066	.1914	.1527
	7	.0003	.0030	.0138	.0393	.0811	.1319	.1771	.2013	.1964
	8	.0000	.0005	.0035	.0131	.0348	.0710	.1181	.1647	.1964
	9	.0000	.0001	.0007	.0034	.0016	.0298	.0612	.1048	.1527
	10	.0000	.0000	.0001	.0007	.0030	.0096	.0245	.0515	.0916
	11	.0000	.0000	.0000	.0001	.0006	.0024	.0074	.0191	.0417
	12	.0000	.0000	.0000	.0000	.0001	.0004	.0016	.0052	.0139
	13	.0000	.0000	.0000	.0000	.0000	.0001	.0003	.0010	.0032
	14	.0000	.0000	.0000	.0000	.0000	.0000	.0000	.0001	.0005
	15	.0000	.0000	.0000	.0000	.0000	.0000	.0000	.0000	.0000

TABLE 5 BINOMIAL PROBABILITIES (*Continued*)

		p								
n	*x*	.10	.15	.20	.25	.30	.35	.40	.45	.50
18	0	.1501	.0536	.0180	.0056	.0016	.0004	.0001	.0000	.0000
	1	.3002	.1704	.0811	.0338	.0126	.0042	.0012	.0003	.0001
	2	.2835	.2556	.1723	.0958	.0458	.0190	.0069	.0022	.0006
	3	.1680	.2406	.2297	.1704	.1046	.0547	.0246	.0095	.0031
	4	.0700	.1592	.2153	.2130	.1681	.1104	.0614	.0291	.0117
	5	.0218	.0787	.1507	.1988	.2017	.1664	.1146	.0666	.0327
	6	.0052	.0301	.0816	.1436	.1873	.1941	.1655	.1181	.0708
	7	.0010	.0091	.0350	.0820	.1376	.1792	.1892	.1657	.1214
	8	.0002	.0022	.0120	.0376	.0811	.1327	.1734	.1864	.1669
	9	.0000	.0004	.0033	.0139	.0386	.0794	.1284	.1694	.1855
	10	.0000	.0001	.0008	.0042	.0149	.0385	.0771	.1248	.1669
	11	.0000	.0000	.0001	.0010	.0046	.0151	.0374	.0742	.1214
	12	.0000	.0000	.0000	.0002	.0012	.0047	.0145	.0354	.0708
	13	.0000	.0000	.0000	.0000	.0002	.0012	.0045	.0134	.0327
	14	.0000	.0000	.0000	.0000	.0000	.0002	.0011	.0039	.0117
	15	.0000	.0000	.0000	.0000	.0000	.0000	.0002	.0009	.0031
	16	.0000	.0000	.0000	.0000	.0000	.0000	.0000	.0001	.0006
	17	.0000	.0000	.0000	.0000	.0000	.0000	.0000	.0000	.0001
	18	.0000	.0000	.0000	.0000	.0000	.0000	.0000	.0000	.0000
20	0	.1216	.0388	.0115	.0032	.0008	.0002	.0000	.0000	.0000
	1	.2702	.1368	.0576	.0211	.0068	.0020	.0005	.0001	.0000
	2	.2852	.2293	.1369	.0669	.0278	.0100	.0031	.0008	.0002
	3	.1901	.2428	.2054	.1339	.0716	.0323	.0123	.0040	.0011
	4	.0898	.1821	.2182	.1897	.1304	.0738	.0350	.0139	.0046
	5	.0319	.1028	.1746	.2023	.1789	.1272	.0746	.0365	.0148
	6	.0089	.0454	.1091	.1686	.1916	.1712	.1244	.0746	.0370
	7	.0020	.0160	.0545	.1124	.1643	.1844	.1659	.1221	.0739
	8	.0004	.0046	.0222	.0609	.1144	.1614	.1797	.1623	.1201
	9	.0001	.0011	.0074	.0271	.0654	.1158	.1597	.1771	.1602
	10	.0000	.0002	.0020	.0099	.0308	.0686	.1171	.1593	.1762
	11	.0000	.0000	.0005	.0030	.0120	.0336	.0710	.1185	.1602
	12	.0000	.0000	.0001	.0008	.0039	.0136	.0355	.0727	.1201
	13	.0000	.0000	.0000	.0002	.0010	.0045	.0146	.0366	.0739
	14	.0000	.0000	.0000	.0000	.0002	.0012	.0049	.0150	.0370
	15	.0000	.0000	.0000	.0000	.0000	.0003	.0013	.0049	.0148
	16	.0000	.0000	.0000	.0000	.0000	.0000	.0003	.0013	.0046
	17	.0000	.0000	.0000	.0000	.0000	.0000	.0000	.0002	.0011
	18	.0000	.0000	.0000	.0000	.0000	.0000	.0000	.0000	.0002
	19	.0000	.0000	.0000	.0000	.0000	.0000	.0000	.0000	.0000
	20	.0000	.0000	.0000	.0000	.0000	.0000	.0000	.0000	.0000

TABLE 5 BINOMIAL PROBABILITIES (*Continued*)

		p								
n	*x*	**.55**	**.60**	**.65**	**.70**	**.75**	**.80**	**.85**	**.90**	**.95**
2	0	.2025	.1600	.1225	.0900	.0625	.0400	.0225	.0100	.0025
	1	.4950	.4800	.4550	.4200	.3750	.3200	.2550	.1800	.0950
	2	.3025	.3600	.4225	.4900	.5625	.6400	.7225	.8100	.9025
3	0	.0911	.0640	.0429	.0270	.0156	.0080	.0034	.0010	.0001
	1	.3341	.2880	.2389	.1890	.1406	.0960	.0574	.0270	.0071
	2	.4084	.4320	.4436	.4410	.4219	.3840	.3251	.2430	.1354
	3	.1664	.2160	.2746	.3430	.4219	.5120	.6141	.7290	.8574
4	0	.0410	.0256	.0150	.0081	.0039	.0016	.0005	.0001	.0000
	1	.2005	.1536	.1115	.0756	.0469	.0256	.0115	.0036	.0005
	2	.3675	.3456	.3105	.2646	.2109	.1536	.0975	.0486	.0135
	3	.2995	.3456	.3845	.4116	.4219	.4096	.3685	.2916	.1715
	4	.0915	.1296	.1785	.2401	.3164	.4096	.5220	.6561	.8145
5	0	.0185	.0102	.0053	.0024	.0010	.0003	.0001	.0000	.0000
	1	.1128	.0768	.0488	.0284	.0146	.0064	.0022	.0005	.0000
	2	.2757	.2304	.1811	.1323	.0879	.0512	.0244	.0081	.0011
	3	.3369	.3456	.3364	.3087	.2637	.2048	.1382	.0729	.0214
	4	.2059	.2592	.3124	.3601	.3955	.4096	.3915	.3281	.2036
	5	.0503	.0778	.1160	.1681	.2373	.3277	.4437	.5905	.7738
6	0	.0083	.0041	.0018	.0007	.0002	.0001	.0000	.0000	.0000
	1	.0609	.0369	.0205	.0102	.0044	.0015	.0004	.0001	.0000
	2	.1861	.1382	.0951	.0595	.0330	.0154	.0055	.0012	.0001
	3	.3032	.2765	.2355	.1852	.1318	.0819	.0415	.0146	.0021
	4	.2780	.3110	.3280	.3241	.2966	.2458	.1762	.0984	.0305
	5	.1359	.1866	.2437	.3025	.3560	.3932	.3993	.3543	.2321
	6	.0277	.0467	.0754	.1176	.1780	.2621	.3771	.5314	.7351
7	0	.0037	.0016	.0006	.0002	.0001	.0000	.0000	.0000	.0000
	1	.0320	.0172	.0084	.0036	.0013	.0004	.0001	.0000	.0000
	2	.1172	.0774	.0466	.0250	.0115	.0043	.0012	.0002	.0000
	3	.2388	.1935	.1442	.0972	.0577	.0287	.0109	.0026	.0002
	4	.2918	.2903	.2679	.2269	.1730	.1147	.0617	.0230	.0036
	5	.2140	.2613	.2985	.3177	.3115	.2753	.2097	.1240	.0406
	6	.0872	.1306	.1848	.2471	.3115	.3670	.3960	.3720	.2573
	7	.0152	.0280	.0490	.0824	.1335	.2097	.3206	.4783	.6983
8	0	.0017	.0007	.0002	.0001	.0000	.0000	.0000	.0000	.0000
	1	.0164	.0079	.0033	.0012	.0004	.0001	.0000	.0000	.0000
	2	.0703	.0413	.0217	.0100	.0038	.0011	.0002	.0000	.0000
	3	.1719	.1239	.0808	.0467	.0231	.0092	.0026	.0004	.0000
	4	.2627	.2322	.1875	.1361	.0865	.0459	.0185	.0046	.0004
	5	.2568	.2787	.2786	.2541	.2076	.1468	.0839	.0331	.0054
	6	.1569	.2090	.2587	.2965	.3115	.2936	.2376	.1488	.0515
	7	.0548	.0896	.1373	.1977	.2670	.3355	.3847	.3826	.2793
	8	.0084	.0168	.0319	.0576	.1001	.1678	.2725	.4305	.6634

TABLE 5 BINOMIAL PROBABILITIES (*Continued*)

		p								
n	*x*	.55	.60	.65	.70	.75	.80	.85	.90	.95
9	0	.0008	.0003	.0001	.0000	.0000	.0000	.0000	.0000	.0000
	1	.0083	.0035	.0013	.0004	.0001	.0000	.0000	.0000	.0000
	2	.0407	.0212	.0098	.0039	.0012	.0003	.0000	.0000	.0000
	3	.1160	.0743	.0424	.0210	.0087	.0028	.0006	.0001	.0000
	4	.2128	.1672	.1181	.0735	.0389	.0165	.0050	.0008	.0000
	5	.2600	.2508	.2194	.1715	.1168	.0661	.0283	.0074	.0006
	6	.2119	.2508	.2716	.2668	.2336	.1762	.1069	.0446	.0077
	7	.1110	.1612	.2162	.2668	.3003	.3020	.2597	.1722	.0629
	8	.0339	.0605	.1004	.1556	.2253	.3020	.3679	.3874	.2985
	9	.0046	.0101	.0207	.0404	.0751	.1342	.2316	.3874	.6302
10	0	.0003	.0001	.0000	.0000	.0000	.0000	.0000	.0000	.0000
	1	.0042	.0016	.0005	.0001	.0000	.0000	.0000	.0000	.0000
	2	.0229	.0106	.0043	.0014	.0004	.0001	.0000	.0000	.0000
	3	.0746	.0425	.0212	.0090	.0031	.0008	.0001	.0000	.0000
	4	.1596	.1115	.0689	.0368	.0162	.0055	.0012	.0001	.0000
	5	.2340	.2007	.1536	.1029	.0584	.0264	.0085	.0015	.0001
	6	.2384	.2508	.2377	.2001	.1460	.0881	.0401	.0112	.0010
	7	.1665	.2150	.2522	.2668	.2503	.2013	.1298	.0574	.0105
	8	.0763	.1209	.1757	.2335	.2816	.3020	.2759	.1937	.0746
	9	.0207	.0403	.0725	.1211	.1877	.2684	.3474	.3874	.3151
	10	.0025	.0060	.0135	.0282	.0563	.1074	.1969	.3487	.5987
12	0	.0001	.0000	.0000	.0000	.0000	.0000	.0000	.0000	.0000
	1	.0010	.0003	.0001	.0000	.0000	.0000	.0000	.0000	.0000
	2	.0068	.0025	.0008	.0002	.0000	.0000	.0000	.0000	.0000
	3	.0277	.0125	.0048	.0015	.0004	.0001	.0000	.0000	.0000
	4	.0762	.0420	.0199	.0078	.0024	.0005	.0001	.0000	.0000
	5	.1489	.1009	.0591	.0291	.0115	.0033	.0006	.0000	.0000
	6	.2124	.1766	.1281	.0792	.0401	.0155	.0040	.0005	.0000
	7	.2225	.2270	.2039	.1585	.1032	.0532	.0193	.0038	.0002
	8	.1700	.2128	.2367	.2311	.1936	.1329	.0683	.0213	.0021
	9	.0923	.1419	.1954	.2397	.2581	.2362	.1720	.0852	.0173
	10	.0339	.0639	.1088	.1678	.2323	.2835	.2924	.2301	.0988
	11	.0075	.0174	.0368	.0712	.1267	.2062	.3012	.3766	.3413
	12	.0008	.0022	.0057	.0138	.0317	.0687	.1422	.2824	.5404
15	0	.0000	.0000	.0000	.0000	.0000	.0000	.0000	.0000	.0000
	1	.0001	.0000	.0000	.0000	.0000	.0000	.0000	.0000	.0000
	2	.0010	.0003	.0001	.0000	.0000	.0000	.0000	.0000	.0000
	3	.0052	.0016	.0004	.0001	.0000	.0000	.0000	.0000	.0000
	4	.0191	.0074	.0024	.0006	.0001	.0000	.0000	.0000	.0000
	5	.0515	.0245	.0096	.0030	.0007	.0001	.0000	.0000	.0000
	6	.1048	.0612	.0298	.0116	.0034	.0007	.0001	.0000	.0000
	7	.1647	.1181	.0710	.0348	.0131	.0035	.0005	.0000	.0000
	8	.2013	.1771	.1319	.0811	.0393	.0138	.0030	.0003	.0000
	9	.1914	.2066	.1906	.1472	.0917	.0430	.0132	.0019	.0000
	10	.1404	.1859	.2123	.2061	.1651	.1032	.0449	.0105	.0006
	11	.0780	.1268	.1792	.2186	.2252	.1876	.1156	.0428	.0049

TABLE 5 BINOMIAL PROBABILITIES (*Continued*)

		p								
n	x	.55	.60	.65	.70	.75	.80	.85	.90	.95
	12	.0318	.0634	.1110	.1700	.2252	.2501	.2184	.1285	.0307
	13	.0090	.0219	.0476	.0916	.1559	.2309	.2856	.2669	.1348
	14	.0016	.0047	.0126	.0305	.0668	.1319	.2312	.3432	.3658
	15	.0001	.0005	.0016	.0047	.0134	.0352	.0874	.2059	.4633
18	0	.0000	.0000	.0000	.0000	.0000	.0000	.0000	.0000	.0000
	1	.0000	.0000	.0000	.0000	.0000	.0000	.0000	.0000	.0000
	2	.0001	.0000	.0000	.0000	.0000	.0000	.0000	.0000	.0000
	3	.0009	.0002	.0000	.0000	.0000	.0000	.0000	.0000	.0000
	4	.0039	.0011	.0002	.0000	.0000	.0000	.0000	.0000	.0000
	5	.0134	.0045	.0012	.0002	.0000	.0000	.0000	.0000	.0000
	6	.0354	.0145	.0047	.0012	.0002	.0000	.0000	.0000	.0000
	7	.0742	.0374	.0151	.0046	.0010	.0001	.0000	.0000	.0000
	8	.1248	.0771	.0385	.0149	.0042	.0008	.0001	.0000	.0000
	9	.1694	.1284	.0794	.0386	.0139	.0033	.0004	.0000	.0000
	10	.1864	.1734	.1327	.0811	.0376	.0120	.0022	.0002	.0000
	11	.1657	.1892	.1792	.1376	.0820	.0350	.0091	.0010	.0000
	12	.1181	.1655	.1941	.1873	.1436	.0816	.0301	.0052	.0002
	13	.0666	.1146	.1664	.2017	.1988	.1507	.0787	.0218	.0014
	14	.0291	.0614	.1104	.1681	.2130	.2153	.1592	.0700	.0093
	15	.0095	.0246	.0547	.1046	.1704	.2297	.2406	.1680	.0473
	16	.0022	.0069	.0190	.0458	.0958	.1723	.2556	.2835	.1683
	17	.0003	.0012	.0042	.0126	.0338	.0811	.1704	.3002	.3763
	18	.0000	.0001	.0004	.0016	.0056	.0180	.0536	.1501	.3972
20	0	.0000	.0000	.0000	.0000	.0000	.0000	.0000	.0000	.0000
	1	.0000	.0000	.0000	.0000	.0000	.0000	.0000	.0000	.0000
	2	.0000	.0000	.0000	.0000	.0000	.0000	.0000	.0000	.0000
	3	.0002	.0000	.0000	.0000	.0000	.0000	.0000	.0000	.0000
	4	.0013	.0003	.0000	.0000	.0000	.0000	.0000	.0000	.0000
	5	.0049	.0013	.0003	.0000	.0000	.0000	.0000	.0000	.0000
	6	.0150	.0049	.0012	.0002	.0000	.0000	.0000	.0000	.0000
	7	.0366	.0146	.0045	.0010	.0002	.0000	.0000	.0000	.0000
	8	.0727	.0355	.0136	.0039	.0008	.0001	.0000	.0000	.0000
	9	.1185	.0710	.0336	.0120	.0030	.0005	.0000	.0000	.0000
	10	.1593	.1171	.0686	.0308	.0099	.0020	.0002	.0000	.0000
	11	.1771	.1597	.1158	.0654	.0271	.0074	.0011	.0001	.0000
	12	.1623	.1797	.1614	.1144	.0609	.0222	.0046	.0004	.0000
	13	.1221	.1659	.1844	.1643	.1124	.0545	.0160	.0020	.0000
	14	.0746	.1244	.1712	.1916	.1686	.1091	.0454	.0089	.0003
	15	.0365	.0746	.1272	.1789	.2023	.1746	.1028	.0319	.0022
	16	.0139	.0350	.0738	.1304	.1897	.2182	.1821	.0898	.0133
	17	.0040	.0123	.0323	.0716	.1339	.2054	.2428	.1901	.0596
	18	.0008	.0031	.0100	.0278	.0669	.1369	.2293	.2852	.1887
	19	.0001	.0005	.0020	.0068	.0211	.0576	.1368	.2702	.3774
	20	.0000	.0000	.0002	.0008	.0032	.0115	.0388	.1216	.3585

TABLE 6 VALUES OF $e^{-\mu}$

μ	$e^{-\mu}$	μ	$e^{-\mu}$	μ	$e^{-\mu}$
.00	1.0000	2.00	.1353	4.00	.0183
.05	.9512	2.05	.1287	4.05	.0174
.10	.9048	2.10	.1225	4.10	.0166
.15	.8607	2.15	.1165	4.15	.0158
.20	.8187	2.20	.1108	4.20	.0150
.25	.7788	2.25	.1054	4.25	.0143
.30	.7408	2.30	.1003	4.30	.0136
.35	.7047	2.35	.0954	4.35	.0129
.40	.6703	2.40	.0907	4.40	.0123
.45	.6376	2.45	.0863	4.45	.0117
.50	.6065	2.50	.0821	4.50	.0111
.55	.5769	2.55	.0781	4.55	.0106
.60	.5488	2.60	.0743	4.60	.0101
.65	.5220	2.65	.0707	4.65	.0096
.70	.4966	2.70	.0672	4.70	.0091
.75	.4724	2.75	.0639	4.75	.0087
.80	.4493	2.80	.0608	4.80	.0082
.85	.4274	2.85	.0578	4.85	.0078
.90	.4066	2.90	.0550	4.90	.0074
.95	.3867	2.95	.0523	4.95	.0071
1.00	.3679	3.00	.0498	5.00	.0067
1.05	.3499	3.05	.0474	6.00	.0025
1.10	.3329	3.10	.0450	7.00	.0009
1.15	.3166	3.15	.0429	8.00	.000335
1.20	.3012	3.20	.0408	9.00	.000123
				10.00	.000045
1.25	.2865	3.25	.0388		
1.30	.2725	3.30	.0369		
1.35	.2592	3.35	.0351		
1.40	.2466	3.40	.0334		
1.45	.2346	3.45	.0317		
1.50	.2231	3.50	.0302		
1.55	.2122	3.55	.0287		
1.60	.2019	3.60	.0273		
1.65	.1920	3.65	.0260		
1.70	.1827	3.70	.0247		
1.75	.1738	3.75	.0235		
1.80	.1653	3.80	.0224		
1.85	.1572	3.85	.0213		
1.90	.1496	3.90	.0202		
1.95	.1423	3.95	.0193		

TABLE 7 POISSON PROBABILITIES

Entries in the table give the probability of x occurrences for a Poisson process with a mean μ. For example, when $\mu = 2.5$, the probability of four occurrences is .1336.

	μ									
x	0.1	0.2	0.3	0.4	0.5	0.6	0.7	0.8	0.9	1.0
0	.9048	.8187	.7408	.6703	.6065	.5488	.4966	.4493	.4066	.3679
1	.0905	.1637	.2222	.2681	.3033	.3293	.3476	.3595	.3659	.3679
2	.0045	.0164	.0333	.0536	.0758	.0988	.1217	.1438	.1647	.1839
3	.0002	.0011	.0033	.0072	.0126	.0198	.0284	.0383	.0494	.0613
4	.0000	.0001	.0002	.0007	.0016	.0030	.0050	.0077	.0111	.0153
5	.0000	.0000	.0000	.0001	.0002	.0004	.0007	.0012	.0020	.0031
6	.0000	.0000	.0000	.0000	.0000	.0000	.0001	.0002	.0003	.0005
7	.0000	.0000	.0000	.0000	.0000	.0000	.0000	.0000	.0000	.0001

	μ									
x	1.1	1.2	1.3	1.4	1.5	1.6	1.7	1.8	1.9	2.0
0	.3329	.3012	.2725	.2466	.2231	.2019	.1827	.1653	.1496	.1353
1	.3662	.3614	.3543	.3452	.3347	.3230	.3106	.2975	.2842	.2707
2	.2014	.2169	.2303	.2417	.2510	.2584	.2640	.2678	.2700	.2707
3	.0738	.0867	.0998	.1128	.1255	.1378	.1496	.1607	.1710	.1804
4	.0203	.0260	.0324	.0395	.0471	.0551	.0636	.0723	.0812	.0902
5	.0045	.0062	.0084	.0111	.0141	.0176	.0216	.0260	.0309	.0361
6	.0008	.0012	.0018	.0026	.0035	.0047	.0061	.0078	.0098	.0120
7	.0001	.0002	.0003	.0005	.0008	.0011	.0015	.0020	.0027	.0034
8	.0000	.0000	.0001	.0001	.0001	.0002	.0003	.0005	.0006	.0009
9	.0000	.0000	.0000	.0000	.0000	.0000	.0001	.0001	.0001	.0002

	μ									
x	2.1	2.2	2.3	2.4	2.5	2.6	2.7	2.8	2.9	3.0
0	.1225	.1108	.1003	.0907	.0821	.0743	.0672	.0608	.0550	.0498
1	.2572	.2438	.2306	.2177	.2052	.1931	.1815	.1703	.1596	.1494
2	.2700	.2681	.2652	.2613	.2565	.2510	.2450	.2384	.2314	.2240
3	.1890	.1966	.2033	.2090	.2138	.2176	.2205	.2225	.2237	.2240
4	.0992	.1082	.1169	.1254	.1336	.1414	.1488	.1557	.1622	.1680
5	.0417	.0476	.0538	.0602	.0668	.0735	.0804	.0872	.0940	.1008
6	.0146	.0174	.0206	.0241	.0278	.0319	.0362	.0407	.0455	.0504
7	.0044	.0055	.0068	.0083	.0099	.0118	.0139	.0163	.0188	.0216
8	.0011	.0015	.0019	.0025	.0031	.0038	.0047	.0057	.0068	.0081
9	.0003	.0004	.0005	.0007	.0009	.0011	.0014	.0018	.0022	.0027
10	.0001	.0001	.0001	.0002	.0002	.0003	.0004	.0005	.0006	.0008
11	.0000	.0000	.0000	.0000	.0000	.0001	.0001	.0001	.0002	.0002
12	.0000	.0000	.0000	.0000	.0000	.0000	.0000	.0000	.0000	.0001

TABLE 7 POISSON PROBABILITIES (*Continued*)

	μ									
x	**3.1**	**3.2**	**3.3**	**3.4**	**3.5**	**3.6**	**3.7**	**3.8**	**3.9**	**4.0**
0	.0450	.0408	.0369	.0344	.0302	.0273	.0247	.0224	.0202	.0183
1	.1397	.1304	.1217	.1135	.1057	.0984	.0915	.0850	.0789	.0733
2	.2165	.2087	.2008	.1929	.1850	.1771	.1692	.1615	.1539	.1465
3	.2237	.2226	.2209	.2186	.2158	.2125	.2087	.2046	.2001	.1954
4	.1734	.1781	.1823	.1858	.1888	.1912	.1931	.1944	.1951	.1954
5	.1075	.1140	.1203	.1264	.1322	.1377	.1429	.1477	.1522	.1563
6	.0555	.0608	.0662	.0716	.0771	.0826	.0881	.0936	.0989	.1042
7	.0246	.0278	.0312	.0348	.0385	.0425	.0466	.0508	.0551	.0595
8	.0095	.0111	.0129	.0148	.0169	.0191	.0215	.0241	.0269	.0298
9	.0033	.0040	.0047	.0056	.0066	.0076	.0089	.0102	.0116	.0132
10	.0010	.0013	.0016	.0019	.0023	.0028	.0033	.0039	.0045	.0053
11	.0003	.0004	.0005	.0006	.0007	.0009	.0011	.0013	.0016	.0019
12	.0001	.0001	.0001	.0002	.0002	.0003	.0003	.0004	.0005	.0006
13	.0000	.0000	.0000	.0000	.0001	.0001	.0001	.0001	.0002	.0002
14	.0000	.0000	.0000	.0000	.0000	.0000	.0000	.0000	.0000	.0001

	μ									
x	**4.1**	**4.2**	**4.3**	**4.4**	**4.5**	**4.6**	**4.7**	**4.8**	**4.9**	**5.0**
0	.0166	.0150	.0136	.0123	.0111	.0101	.0091	.0082	.0074	.0067
1	.0679	.0630	.0583	.0540	.0500	.0462	.0427	.0395	.0365	.0337
2	.1393	.1323	.1254	.1188	.1125	.1063	.1005	.0948	.0894	.0842
3	.1904	.1852	.1798	.1743	.1687	.1631	.1574	.1517	.1460	.1404
4	.1951	.1944	.1933	.1917	.1898	.1875	.1849	.1820	.1789	.1755
5	.1600	.1633	.1662	.1687	.1708	.1725	.1738	.1747	.1753	.1755
6	.1093	.1143	.1191	.1237	.1281	.1323	.1362	.1398	.1432	.1462
7	.0640	.0686	.0732	.0778	.0824	.0869	.0914	.0959	.1002	.1044
8	.0328	.0360	.0393	.0428	.0463	.0500	.0537	.0575	.0614	.0653
9	.0150	.0168	.0188	.0209	.0232	.0255	.0280	.0307	.0334	.0363
10	.0061	.0071	.0081	.0092	.0104	.0118	.0132	.0147	.0164	.0181
11	.0023	.0027	.0032	.0037	.0043	.0049	.0056	.0064	.0073	.0082
12	.0008	.0009	.0011	.0014	.0016	.0019	.0022	.0026	.0030	.0034
13	.0002	.0003	.0004	.0005	.0006	.0007	.0008	.0009	.0011	.0013
14	.0001	.0001	.0001	.0001	.0002	.0002	.0003	.0003	.0004	.0005
15	.0000	.0000	.0000	.0000	.0001	.0001	.0001	.0001	.0001	.0002

	μ									
x	**5.1**	**5.2**	**5.3**	**5.4**	**5.5**	**5.6**	**5.7**	**5.8**	**5.9**	**6.0**
0	.0061	.0055	.0050	.0045	.0041	.0037	.0033	.0030	.0027	.0025
1	.0311	.0287	.0265	.0244	.0225	.0207	.0191	.0176	.0162	.0149
2	.0793	.0746	.0701	.0659	.0618	.0580	.0544	.0509	.0477	.0446
3	.1348	.1293	.1239	.1185	.1133	.1082	.1033	.0985	.0938	.0892
4	.1719	.1681	.1641	.1600	.1558	.1515	.1472	.1428	.1383	.1339

TABLE 7 POISSON PROBABILITIES (*Continued*)

	μ									
x	**5.1**	**5.2**	**5.3**	**5.4**	**5.5**	**5.6**	**5.7**	**5.8**	**5.9**	**6.0**
5	.1753	.1748	.1740	.1728	.1714	.1697	.1678	.1656	.1632	.1606
6	.1490	.1515	.1537	.1555	.1571	.1587	.1594	.1601	.1605	.1606
7	.1086	.1125	.1163	.1200	.1234	.1267	.1298	.1326	.1353	.1377
8	.0692	.0731	.0771	.0810	.0849	.0887	.0925	.0962	.0998	.1033
9	.0392	.0423	.0454	.0486	.0519	.0552	.0586	.0620	.0654	.0688
10	.0200	.0220	.0241	.0262	.0285	.0309	.0334	.0359	.0386	.0413
11	.0093	.0104	.0116	.0129	.0143	.0157	.0173	.0190	.0207	.0225
12	.0039	.0045	.0051	.0058	.0065	.0073	.0082	.0092	.0102	.0113
13	.0015	.0018	.0021	.0024	.0028	.0032	.0036	.0041	.0046	.0052
14	.0006	.0007	.0008	.0009	.0011	.0013	.0015	.0017	.0019	.0022
15	.0002	.0002	.0003	.0003	.0004	.0005	.0006	.0007	.0008	.0009
16	.0001	.0001	.0001	.0001	.0001	.0002	.0002	.0002	.0003	.0003
17	.0000	.0000	.0000	.0000	.0000	.0001	.0001	.0001	.0001	.0001

	μ									
x	**6.1**	**6.2**	**6.3**	**6.4**	**6.5**	**6.6**	**6.7**	**6.8**	**6.9**	**7.0**
0	.0022	.0020	.0018	.0017	.0015	.0014	.0012	.0011	.0010	.0009
1	.0137	.0126	.0116	.0106	.0098	.0090	.0082	.0076	.0070	.0064
2	.0417	.0390	.0364	.0340	.0318	.0296	.0276	.0258	.0240	.0223
3	.0848	.0806	.0765	.0726	.0688	.0652	.0617	.0584	.0552	.0521
4	.1294	.1249	.1205	.1162	.1118	.1076	.1034	.0992	.0952	.0912
5	.1579	.1549	.1519	.1487	.1454	.1420	.1385	.1349	.1314	.1277
6	.1605	.1601	.1595	.1586	.1575	.1562	.1546	.1529	.1511	.1490
7	.1399	.1418	.1435	.1450	.1462	.1472	.1480	.1486	.1489	.1490
8	.1066	.1099	.1130	.1160	.1188	.1215	.1240	.1263	.1284	.1304
9	.0723	.0757	.0791	.0825	.0858	.0891	.0923	.0954	.0985	.1014
10	.0441	.0469	.0498	.0528	.0558	.0588	.0618	.0649	.0679	.0710
11	.0245	.0265	.0285	.0307	.0330	.0353	.0377	.0401	.0426	.0452
12	.0124	.0137	.0150	.0164	.0179	.0194	.0210	.0227	.0245	.0264
13	.0058	.0065	.0073	.0081	.0089	.0098	.0108	.0119	.0130	.0142
14	.0025	.0029	.0033	.0037	.0041	.0046	.0052	.0058	.0064	.0071
15	.0010	.0012	.0014	.0016	.0018	.0020	.0023	.0026	.0029	.0033
16	.0004	.0005	.0005	.0006	.0007	.0008	.0010	.0011	.0013	.0014
17	.0001	.0002	.0002	.0002	.0003	.0003	.0004	.0004	.0005	.0006
18	.0000	.0001	.0001	.0001	.0001	.0001	.0001	.0002	.0002	.0002
19	.0000	.0000	.0000	.0000	.0000	.0000	.0000	.0001	.0001	.0001

	μ									
x	**7.1**	**7.2**	**7.3**	**7.4**	**7.5**	**7.6**	**7.7**	**7.8**	**7.9**	**8.0**
0	.0008	.0007	.0007	.0006	.0006	.0005	.0005	.0004	.0004	.0003
1	.0059	.0054	.0049	.0045	.0041	.0038	.0035	.0032	.0029	.0027
2	.0208	.0194	.0180	.0167	.0156	.0145	.0134	.0125	.0116	.0107
3	.0492	.0464	.0438	.0413	.0389	.0366	.0345	.0324	.0305	.0286
4	.0874	.0836	.0799	.0764	.0729	.0696	.0663	.0632	.0602	.0573

TABLE 7 POISSON PROBABILITIES (*Continued*)

	μ									
x	**7.1**	**7.2**	**7.3**	**7.4**	**7.5**	**7.6**	**7.7**	**7.8**	**7.9**	**8.0**
5	.1241	.1204	.1167	.1130	.1094	.1057	.1021	.0986	.0951	.0916
6	.1468	.1445	.1420	.1394	.1367	.1339	.1311	.1282	.1252	.1221
7	.1489	.1486	.1481	.1474	.1465	.1454	.1442	.1428	.1413	.1396
8	.1321	.1337	.1351	.1363	.1373	.1382	.1388	.1392	.1395	.1396
9	.1042	.1070	.1096	.1121	.1144	.1167	.1187	.1207	.1224	.1241
10	.0740	.0770	.0800	.0829	.0858	.0887	.0914	.0941	.0967	.0993
11	.0478	.0504	.0531	.0558	.0585	.0613	.0640	.0667	.0695	.0722
12	.0283	.0303	.0323	.0344	.0366	.0388	.0411	.0434	.0457	.0481
13	.0154	.0168	.0181	.0196	.0211	.0227	.0243	.0260	.0278	.0296
14	.0078	.0086	.0095	.0104	.0113	.0123	.0134	.0145	.0157	.0169
15	.0037	.0041	.0046	.0051	.0057	.0062	.0069	.0075	.0083	.0090
16	.0016	.0019	.0021	.0024	.0026	.0030	.0033	.0037	.0041	.0045
17	.0007	.0008	.0009	.0010	.0012	.0013	.0015	.0017	.0019	.0021
18	.0003	.0003	.0004	.0004	.0005	.0006	.0006	.0007	.0008	.0009
19	.0001	.0001	.0001	.0002	.0002	.0002	.0003	.0003	.0003	.0004
20	.0000	.0000	.0001	.0001	.0001	.0001	.0001	.0001	.0001	.0002
21	.0000	.0000	.0000	.0000	.0000	.0000	.0000	.0000	.0001	.0001

	μ									
x	**8.1**	**8.2**	**8.3**	**8.4**	**8.5**	**8.6**	**8.7**	**8.8**	**8.9**	**9.0**
0	.0003	.0003	.0002	.0002	.0002	.0002	.0002	.0002	.0001	.0001
1	.0025	.0023	.0021	.0019	.0017	.0016	.0014	.0013	.0012	.0011
2	.0100	.0092	.0086	.0079	.0074	.0068	.0063	.0058	.0054	.0050
3	.0269	.0252	.0237	.0222	.0208	.0195	.0183	.0171	.0160	.0150
4	.0544	.0517	.0491	.0466	.0443	.0420	.0398	.0377	.0357	.0337
5	.0882	.0849	.0816	.0784	.0752	.0722	.0692	.0663	.0635	.0607
6	.1191	.1160	.1128	.1097	.1066	.1034	.1003	.0972	.0941	.0911
7	.1378	.1358	.1338	.1317	.1294	.1271	.1247	.1222	.1197	.1171
8	.1395	.1392	.1388	.1382	.1375	.1366	.1356	.1344	.1332	.1318
9	.1256	.1269	.1280	.1290	.1299	.1306	.1311	.1315	.1317	.1318
10	.1017	.1040	.1063	.1084	.1104	.1123	.1140	.1157	.1172	.1186
11	.0749	.0776	.0802	.0828	.0853	.0878	.0902	.0925	.0948	.0970
12	.0505	.0530	.0555	.0579	.0604	.0629	.0654	.0679	.0703	.0728
13	.0315	.0334	.0354	.0374	.0395	.0416	.0438	.0459	.0481	.0504
14	.0182	.0196	.0210	.0225	.0240	.0256	.0272	.0289	.0306	.0324
15	.0098	.0107	.0116	.0126	.0136	.0147	.0158	.0169	.0182	.1094
16	.0050	.0055	.0060	.0066	.0072	.0079	.0086	.0093	.0101	.0109
17	.0024	.0026	.0029	.0033	.0036	.0040	.0044	.0048	.0053	.0058
18	.0011	.0012	.0014	.0015	.0017	.0019	.0021	.0024	.0026	.0029
19	.0005	.0005	.0006	.0007	.0008	.0009	.0010	.0011	.0012	.0014
20	.0002	.0002	.0002	.0003	.0003	.0004	.0004	.0005	.0005	.0006
21	.0001	.0001	.0001	.0001	.0001	.0002	.0002	.0002	.0002	.0003
22	.0000	.0000	.0000	.0000	.0001	.0001	.0001	.0001	.0001	.0001

TABLE 7 POISSON PROBABILITIES (*Continued*)

	μ									
x	9.1	9.2	9.3	9.4	9.5	9.6	9.7	9.8	9.9	10
0	.0001	.0001	.0001	.0001	.0001	.0001	.0001	.0001	.0001	.0000
1	.0010	.0009	.0009	.0008	.0007	.0007	.0006	.0005	.0005	.0005
2	.0046	.0043	.0040	.0037	.0034	.0031	.0029	.0027	.0025	.0023
3	.0140	.0131	.0123	.0115	.0107	.0100	.0093	.0087	.0081	.0076
4	.0319	.0302	.0285	.0269	.0254	.0240	.0226	.0213	.0201	.0189
5	.0581	.0555	.0530	.0506	.0483	.0460	.0439	.0418	.0398	.0378
6	.0881	.0851	.0822	.0793	.0764	.0736	.0709	.0682	.0656	.0631
7	.1145	.1118	.1091	.1064	.1037	.1010	.0982	.0955	.0928	.0901
8	.1302	.1286	.1269	.1251	.1232	.1212	.1191	.1170	.1148	.1126
9	.1317	.1315	.1311	.1306	.1300	.1293	.1284	.1274	.1263	.1251
10	.1198	.1210	.1219	.1228	.1235	.1241	.1245	.1249	.1250	.1251
11	.0991	.1012	.1031	.1049	.1067	.1083	.1098	.1112	.1125	.1137
12	.0752	.0776	.0799	.0822	.0844	.0866	.0888	.0908	.0928	.0948
13	.0526	.0549	.0572	.0594	.0617	.0640	.0662	.0685	.0707	.0729
14	.0342	.0361	.0380	.0399	.0419	.0439	.0459	.0479	.0500	.0521
15	.0208	.0221	.0235	.0250	.0265	.0281	.0297	.0313	.0330	.0347
16	.0118	.0127	.0137	.0147	.0157	.0168	.0180	.0192	.0204	.0217
17	.0063	.0069	.0075	.0081	.0088	.0095	.0103	.0111	.0119	.0128
18	.0032	.0035	.0039	.0042	.0046	.0051	.0055	.0060	.0065	.0071
19	.0015	.0017	.0019	.0021	.0023	.0026	.0028	.0031	.0034	.0037
20	.0007	.0008	.0009	.0010	.0011	.0012	.0014	.0015	.0017	.0019
21	.0003	.0003	.0004	.0004	.0005	.0006	.0006	.0007	.0008	.0009
22	.0001	.0001	.0002	.0002	.0002	.0002	.0003	.0003	.0004	.0004
23	.0000	.0001	.0001	.0001	.0001	.0001	.0001	.0001	.0002	.0002
24	.0000	.0000	.0000	.0000	.0000	.0000	.0000	.0001	.0001	.0001

	μ									
x	11	12	13	14	15	16	17	18	19	20
0	.0000	.0000	.0000	.0000	.0000	.0000	.0000	.0000	.0000	.0000
1	.0002	.0001	.0000	.0000	.0000	.0000	.0000	.0000	.0000	.0000
2	.0010	.0004	.0002	.0001	.0000	.0000	.0000	.0000	.0000	.0000
3	.0037	.0018	.0008	.0004	.0002	.0001	.0000	.0000	.0000	.0000
4	.0102	.0053	.0027	.0013	.0006	.0003	.0001	.0001	.0000	.0000
5	.0224	.0127	.0070	.0037	.0019	.0010	.0005	.0002	.0001	.0001
6	.0411	.0255	.0152	.0087	.0048	.0026	.0014	.0007	.0004	.0002
7	.0646	.0437	.0281	.0174	.0104	.0060	.0034	.0018	.0010	.0005
8	.0888	.0655	.0457	.0304	.0194	.0120	.0072	.0042	.0024	.0013
9	.1085	.0874	.0661	.0473	.0324	.0213	.0135	.0083	.0050	.0029
10	.1194	.1048	.0859	.0663	.0486	.0341	.0230	.0150	.0095	.0058
11	.1194	.1144	.1015	.0844	.0663	.0496	.0355	.0245	.0164	.0106
12	.1094	.1144	.1099	.0984	.0829	.0661	.0504	.0368	.0259	.0176
13	.0926	.1056	.1099	.1060	.0956	.0814	.0658	.0509	.0378	.0271
14	.0728	.0905	.1021	.1060	.1024	.0930	.0800	.0655	.0514	.0387

TABLE 7 POISSON PROBABILITIES (*Continued*)

	μ									
x	**11**	**12**	**13**	**14**	**15**	**16**	**17**	**18**	**19**	**20**
15	.0534	.0724	.0885	.0989	.1024	.0992	.0906	.0786	.0650	.0516
16	.0367	.0543	.0719	.0866	.0960	.0992	.0963	.0884	.0772	.0646
17	.0237	.0383	.0550	.0713	.0847	.0934	.0963	.0936	.0863	.0760
18	.0145	.0256	.0397	.0554	.0706	.0830	.0909	.0936	.0911	.0844
19	.0084	.0161	.0272	.0409	.0557	.0699	.0814	.0887	.0911	.0888
20	.0046	.0097	.0177	.0286	.0418	.0559	.0692	.0798	.0866	.0888
21	.0024	.0055	.0109	.0191	.0299	.0426	.0560	.0684	.0783	.0846
22	.0012	.0030	.0065	.0121	.0204	.0310	.0433	.0560	.0676	.0769
23	.0006	.0016	.0037	.0074	.0133	.0216	.0320	.0438	.0559	.0669
24	.0003	.0008	.0020	.0043	.0083	.0144	.0226	.0328	.0442	.0557
25	.0001	.0004	.0010	.0024	.0050	.0092	.0154	.0237	.0336	.0446
26	.0000	.0002	.0005	.0013	.0029	.0057	.0101	.0164	.0246	.0343
27	.0000	.0001	.0002	.0007	.0016	.0034	.0063	.0109	.0173	.0254
28	.0000	.0000	.0001	.0003	.0009	.0019	.0038	.0070	.0117	.0181
29	.0000	.0000	.0001	.0002	.0004	.0011	.0023	.0044	.0077	.0125
30	.0000	.0000	.0000	.0001	.0002	.0006	.0013	.0026	.0049	.0083
31	.0000	.0000	.0000	.0000	.0001	.0003	.0007	.0015	.0030	.0054
32	.0000	.0000	.0000	.0000	.0001	.0001	.0004	.0009	.0018	.0034
33	.0000	.0000	.0000	.0000	.0000	.0001	.0002	.0005	.0010	.0020
34	.0000	.0000	.0000	.0000	.0000	.0000	.0001	.0002	.0006	.0012
35	.0000	.0000	.0000	.0000	.0000	.0000	.0000	.0001	.0003	.0007
36	.0000	.0000	.0000	.0000	.0000	.0000	.0000	.0001	.0002	.0004
37	.0000	.0000	.0000	.0000	.0000	.0000	.0000	.0000	.0001	.0002
38	.0000	.0000	.0000	.0000	.0000	.0000	.0000	.0000	.0000	.0001
39	.0000	.0000	.0000	.0000	.0000	.0000	.0000	.0000	.0000	.0001

Appendix C: Summation Notation

Summations

Definition

$$\sum_{i=1}^{n} x_i = x_1 + x_2 + \cdots + x_n \tag{C.1}$$

Example for $x_1 = 5, x_2 = 8, x_3 = 14$:

$$\begin{aligned}\sum_{i=1}^{3} x_i &= x_1 + x_2 + x_3 \\ &= 5 + 8 + 14 \\ &= 27\end{aligned}$$

Result 1

For a constant c:

$$\sum_{i=1}^{n} c = \underbrace{(c + c + \cdots + c)}_{n \text{ times}} = nc \tag{C.2}$$

Example for $c = 5, n = 10$:

$$\sum_{i=1}^{10} 5 = 10(5) = 50$$

Example for $c = \bar{x}$:

$$\sum_{i=1}^{n} \bar{x} = n\bar{x}$$

Result 2

$$\begin{aligned}\sum_{i=1}^{n} cx_i &= cx_1 + cx_2 + \cdots + cx_n \\ &= c(x_1 + x_2 + \cdots + x_n) = c\sum_{i=1}^{n} x_i\end{aligned} \tag{C.3}$$

Example for $x_1 = 5, x_2 = 8, x_3 = 14, c = 2$:

$$\sum_{i=1}^{3} 2x_i = 2\sum_{i=1}^{3} x_i = 2(27) = 54$$

Result 3

$$\sum_{i=1}^{n} (ax_i + by_i) = a\sum_{i=1}^{n} x_i + b\sum_{i=1}^{n} y_i \tag{C.4}$$

Example for $x_1 = 5, x_2 = 8, x_3 = 14, a = 2, y_1 = 7, y_2 = 3, y_3 = 8, b = 4$:

$$\begin{aligned}\sum_{i=1}^{3}(2x_i + 4y_i) &= 2\sum_{i=1}^{3}x_i + 4\sum_{i=1}^{3}y_i \\ &= 2(27) + 4(18) \\ &= 54 + 72 \\ &= 126\end{aligned}$$

Double Summations

Consider the following data involving the variable x_{ij}, where i is the subscript denoting the row position and j is the subscript denoting the column position:

		Column		
		1	**2**	**3**
Row	**1**	$x_{11} = 10$	$x_{12} = 8$	$x_{13} = 6$
	2	$x_{21} = 7$	$x_{22} = 4$	$x_{23} = 12$

Definition

$$\begin{aligned}\sum_{i=1}^{n}\sum_{j=1}^{m}x_{ij} = &(x_{11} + x_{12} + \cdots + x_{1m}) + (x_{21} + x_{22} + \cdots + x_{2m}) \\ &+ (x_{31} + x_{32} + \cdots + x_{3m}) + \cdots + (x_{n1} + x_{n2} + \cdots + x_{nm})\end{aligned} \tag{C.5}$$

Example:

$$\begin{aligned}\sum_{i=1}^{2}\sum_{j=1}^{3}x_{ij} &= x_{11} + x_{12} + x_{13} + x_{21} + x_{22} + x_{23} \\ &= 10 + 8 + 6 + 7 + 4 + 12 \\ &= 47\end{aligned}$$

Definition

$$\sum_{i=1}^{n}x_{ij} = x_{1j} + x_{2j} + \cdots + x_{nj} \tag{C.6}$$

Example:

$$\begin{aligned}\sum_{i=1}^{2}x_{i2} &= x_{12} + x_{22} \\ &= 8 + 4 \\ &= 12\end{aligned}$$

Shorthand Notation

Sometimes when a summation is for all values of the subscript, we use the following shorthand notations:

$$\sum_{i=1}^{n}x_i = \sum x_i \tag{C.7}$$

$$\sum_{i=1}^{n}\sum_{j=1}^{m}x_{ij} = \sum\sum x_{ij} \tag{C.8}$$

$$\sum_{i=1}^{n}x_{ij} = \sum_{i}x_{ij} \tag{C.9}$$

Appendix D: Self-Test Solutions and Answers to Even-Numbered Exercises

Chapter 1

2. a. 10
b. 5
c. Categorical variables: Size and Fuel
Quantitiative variables: Cylinders, City MPG, and Highway MPG
d.

Variable	Measurement Scale
Size	Ordinal
Cylinders	Ratio
City MPG	Ratio
Highway MPG	Ratio
Fuel	Nominal

3. a. Average for city driving = 182/10 = 18.2 mpg
b. Average for highway driving = 261/10 = 26.1 mpg
On average, the miles per gallon for highway driving is 7.9 mpg greater than for city driving
c. 3 of 10 or 30% have four-cyclinder engines
d. 6 of 10 or 60% use regular fuel

4. a. 7
b. 5
c. Categorical variables: State, Campus Setting, and NCAA Division
d. Quantitiative variables: Endowment and Applicants Admitted

6. a. Quantitative
b. Categorical
c. Categorical
d. Quantitative
e. Categorical

8. a. 1015
b. Categorical
c. Percentages
d. .10(1015) = 101.5; 101 or 102 respondents

10. a. Categorical
b. Percentages
c. 15%
d. Support against

12. a. All visitors to Hawaii
b. Yes
c. First and fourth questions provide quantitative data
Second and third questions provide categorical data

13. a. Federal spending ($ trillions)
b. Quantitative
c. Time series
d. Federal spending has increased over time

14. a. Graph with time series line for each company
b. Hertz leader in 2007–2008; Avis increasing and now similar to Hertz; Dollar declining
c. A bar chart of cross-sectional data
Bar heights: Hertz 290, Dollar 108, Avis 270

18. a. 67%
b. 612
c. Categorical

20. a. 43% of managers were bullish or very bullish, and 21% of managers expected health care to be the leading industry over the next 12 months
b. The average 12-month return estimate is 11.2% for the population of investment managers
c. The sample average of 2.5 years is an estimate of how long the population of investment managers think it will take to resume sustainable growth

22. a. The population consists of all customers of the chain stores in Charlotte, North Carolina
b. Some of the ways the grocery store chain could use to collect the data are
- Customers entering or leaving the store could be surveyed
- A survey could be mailed to customers who have a shopper's club card
- Customers could be given a printed survey when they check out
- Customers could be given a coupon that asks them to complete a brief online survey; if they do, they will receive a 5% discount on their next shopping trip

24. a. Correct
b. Incorrect
c. Correct
d. Incorrect
e. Incorrect

Chapter 2

2. a. .20
b. 40
c/d.

Class	Frequency	Percent Frequency
A	44	22
B	36	18
C	80	40
D	40	20
Total	200	100

3. a. $360° \times 58/120 = 174°$

b. $360° \times 42/120 = 126°$

c.

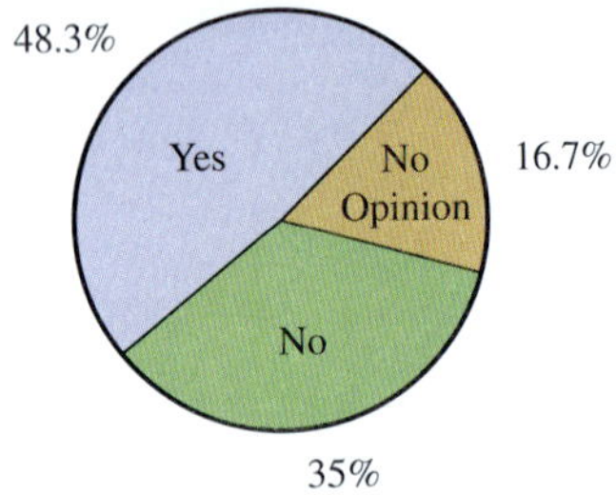

d.

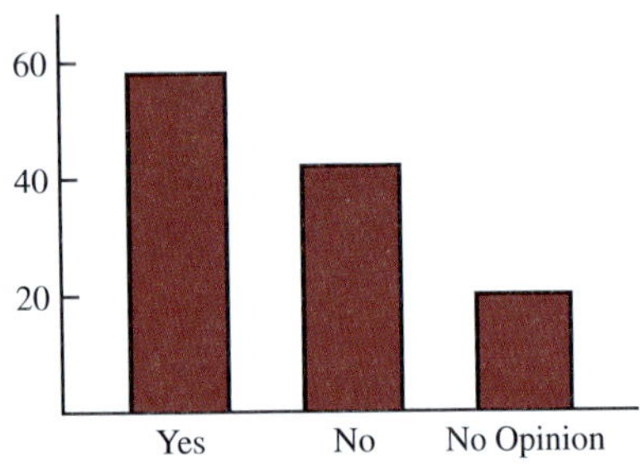

4. a. These data are categorical

b.

Show	Relative Frequency	Percent Frequency
Jep	10	20
JJ	8	16
OWS	7	14
THM	12	24
WoF	13	26
Total	50	100

c.

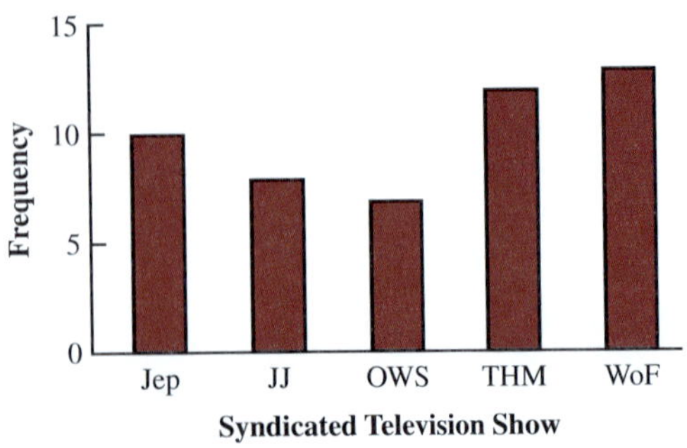

Syndicated Television Show

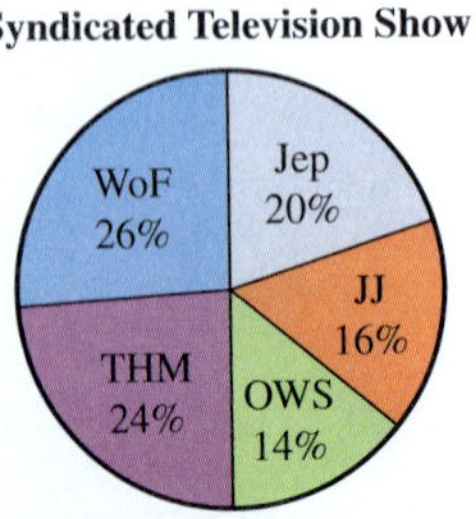

d. The largest viewing audience is for *Wheel of Fortune* and the second largest is for *Two and a Half Men*

6. a.

Network	Relative Frequency	Percent Frequency
ABC	6	24
CBS	9	36
FOX	1	4
NBC	9	36
Total	25	100

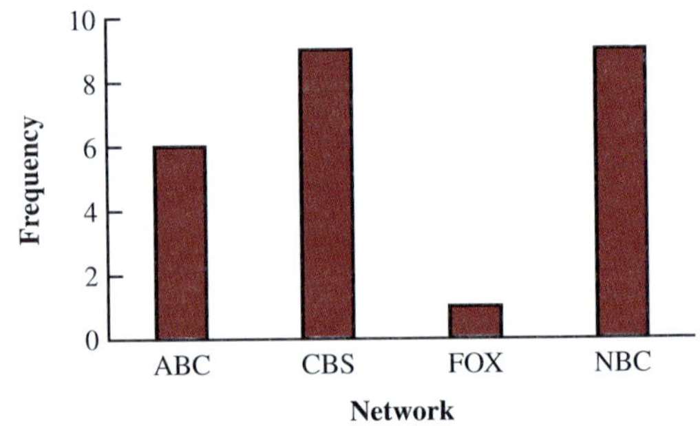

b. For these data, NBC and CBS tie for the number of top-rated shows; each has 9 (36%) of the top 25; ABC is third with 6 (24%) and the much younger FOX network has 1 (4%)

7. a.

Rating	Frequency	Percent Frequency
Excellent	20	40
Very Good	23	46
Good	4	8
Fair	1	2
Poor	2	4
Total	50	100

Management should be very pleased; 86% of the ratings are very good or excellent.

b. Review explanations from the three with Fair or Poor ratings to identify reasons for the low ratings

8. a.

Position	Frequency	Relative Frequency
P	17	.309
H	4	.073
1	5	.091
2	4	.073
3	2	.036
S	5	.091
L	6	.109
C	5	.091
R	7	.127
Totals	55	1.000

b. Pitcher
c. 3rd base
d. Right field
e. Infielders 16 to outfielders 18

10. a/b.

Rating	Frequency	Percent Frequency
Excellent	20	2
Good	101	10
Fair	528	52
Bad	244	24
Terrible	122	12
Total	1015	100

c.

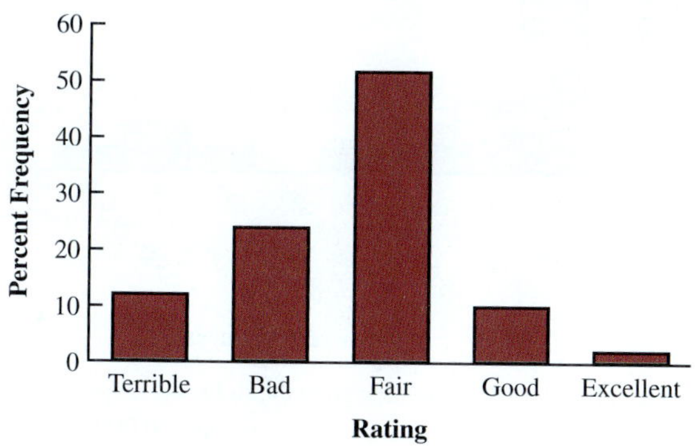

d. 36% a bad or a terrible job
12% a good or excellent job
e. 50% a bad or a terrible job
4% a good or excellent job
More pessimism in Spain

12.

Class	Cumulative Frequency	Cumulative Relative Frequency
≤19	10	.20
≤29	24	.48
≤39	41	.82
≤49	48	.96
≤59	50	1.00

14. b/c.

Class	Frequency	Percent Frequency
6.0–7.9	4	20
8.0–9.9	2	10
10.0–11.9	8	40
12.0–13.9	3	15
14.0–15.9	3	15
Totals	20	100

15. Leaf unit = .1

```
 6 | 3
 7 | 5 5 7
 8 | 1 3 4 8
 9 | 3 6
10 | 0 4 5
11 | 3
```

16. Leaf unit = 10

```
11 | 6
12 | 0 2
13 | 0 6 7
14 | 2 2 7
15 | 5
16 | 0 2 8
17 | 0 2 3
```

17. a/b.

Waiting Time	Frequency	Relative Frequency
0–4	4	.20
5–9	8	.40
10–14	5	.25
15–19	2	.10
20–24	1	.05
Totals	20	1.00

c/d.

Waiting Time	Cumulative Frequency	Cumulative Relative Frequency
≤4	4	.20
≤9	12	.60
≤14	17	.85
≤19	19	.95
≤24	20	1.00

e. 12/20 = .60

18. a.

Salary	Frequency
150–159	1
160–169	3
170–179	7
180–189	5
190–199	1
200–209	2
210–219	1
Total	20

b.

Salary	Percent Frequency
150–159	5
160–169	15
170–179	35
180–189	25
190–199	5
200–209	10
210–219	5
Total	100

c.

Salary	Cumulative Percent Frequency
Less than or equal to 159	5
Less than or equal to 169	20
Less than or equal to 179	55
Less than or equal to 189	80
Less than or equal to 199	85
Less than or equal to 209	95
Less than or equal to 219	100
Total	100

e. There is skewness to the right

f. 15%

20. a. Lowest = 12, Highest = 23

b.

Hours in Meetings per Week	Frequency	Percent Frequency
11–12	1	4
13–14	2	8
15–16	6	24
17–18	3	12
19–20	5	20
21–22	4	16
23–24	4	16
	25	100

c.

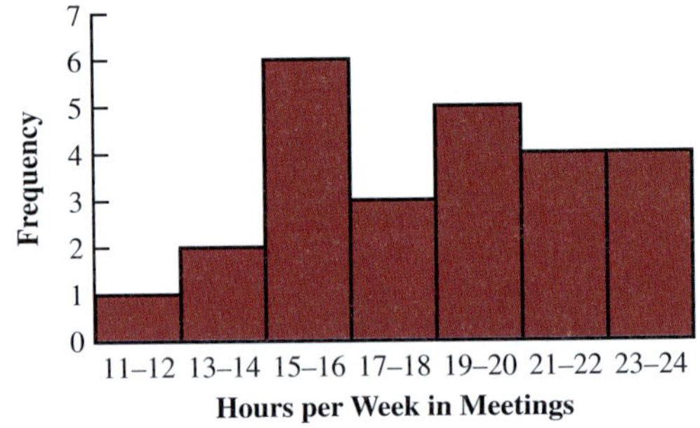

d. The distribution is slightly skewed to the left

22. a.

# U.S. Locations	Frequency	Percent Frequency
0–4999	10	50
5000–9999	3	15
10000–14999	2	10
15000–19999	1	5
20000–24999	0	0
25000–29999	1	5
30000–34999	2	10
35000–39999	1	5
Total:	20	100

b.

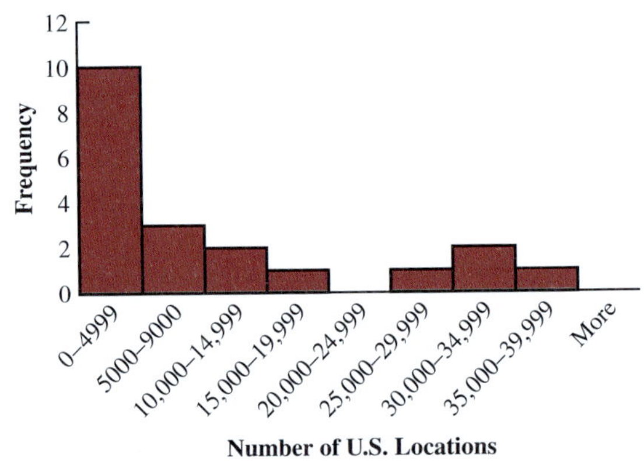

c. The distribution is skewed to the right; the majority of the franchises in this list have fewer than 20,000 locations (50% + 15% + 15% = 80%); McDonald's, Subway, and 7-Eleven have the highest number of locations

24. Median Pay

6	6 7 7
7	2 4 6 7 7 8 9
8	0 0 1 3 7
9	9
10	0 6
11	0
12	1

Top Pay

10	0 6 9
11	1 6 9
12	2 5 6
13	0 5 8 8
14	0 6
15	2 5 7
16	
17	
18	
19	
20	
21	4
22	1

The median pay for these careers is generally in the $70 and $80 thousands. The top pay is rather evenly distributed between $100 and $160 thousand.

26. a.

```
2 | 14
2 | 67
3 | 011123
3 | 5677
4 | 003333344
4 | 6679
5 | 00022
5 | 5679
6 | 14
6 | 6
7 | 2
```

b. 40–44 with 9
c. 43 with 5

27. a.

x		y: 1	2	Total
	A	5	0	5
	B	11	2	13
	C	2	10	12
	Total	18	12	30

b.

x		y: 1	2	Total
	A	100.0	0.0	100.0
	B	84.6	15.4	100.0
	C	16.7	83.3	100.0

c.

x		y: 1	2
	A	27.8	0.0
	B	61.1	16.7
	C	11.1	83.3
	Total	100.0	100.0

d. *A* values are always in $y = 1$
B values are most often in $y = 1$
C values are most often in $y = 2$

28. a.

x	y: 20–39	40–59	60–79	80–100	Grand Total
10–29			1	4	5
30–49	2		4		6
50–69	1	3	1		5
70–90	4				4
Grand Total	7	3	6	4	20

b.

x	y: 20–39	40–59	60–79	80–100	Grand Total
10–29			20.0	80.0	100
30–49	33.3		66.7		100
50–69	20.0	60.0	20.0		100
70–90	100.0				100

c.

x	y: 20–39	40–59	60–79	80–100
10–29	0.0	0.0	16.7	100.0
30–49	28.6	0.0	66.7	0.0
50–69	14.3	100.0	16.7	0.0
70–90	57.1	0.0	0.0	0.0
Grand Total	100	100	100	100

d. Higher values of *x* are associated with lower values of *y* and vice versa

30. a.

Education Level	Household Income ($1000s): Under 25	25.0–49.9	50.0–74.9	75.0–99.9	100 or more	Total
Not H.S. Graduate	32.10	18.71	9.13	5.26	2.20	13.51
H.S. Graduate	37.52	37.05	33.04	25.73	16.00	29.97
Some College	21.42	28.44	30.74	31.71	24.43	27.21
Bachelor's Degree	6.75	11.33	18.72	25.19	32.26	18.70
Beyond Bach. Deg.	2.21	4.48	8.37	12.11	25.11	10.61
Total	100.00	100.00	100.00	100.00	100.00	100.00

13.51% of the heads of households did not graduate from high school

b. 25.11%, 53.54%

c. Positive relationship between income and education level

32. a.

Fund Type	5-Year Average Return 0–9.99	10–19.99	20–29.99	30–39.99	40–49.99	50–59.99	Total
DE	1	25	1	0	0	0	27
FI	9	1	0	0	0	0	10
IE	0	2	3	2	0	1	8
Total	10	28	4	2	0	1	45

b.

5-Year Average Return	Frequency
0–9.99	10
10–19.99	28
20–29.99	4
30–39.99	2
40–49.99	0
50–59.99	1
Total	45

c.

Fund Type	Frequency
DE	27
FI	10
IE	8
Total	45

d. The margin of the crosstabulation shows these frequency distributions

e. Higher returns—International Equity funds
Lower returns—Fixed Income funds

34. b. Higher 5-year returns are associated with higher net asset values.

36. a.

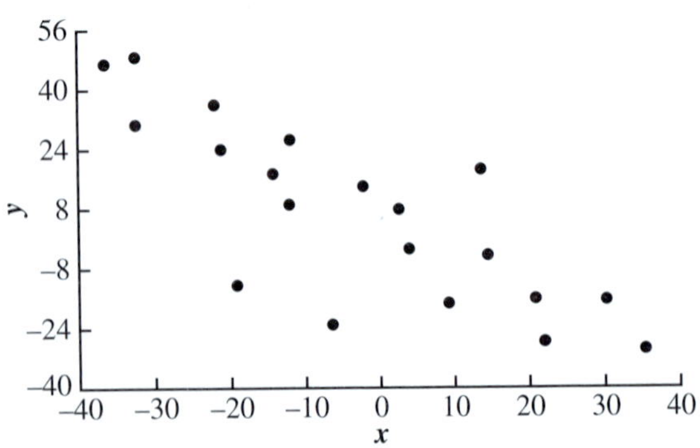

b. A negative relationship between x and y; y decreases as x increases

38. a.

		y Yes	No	
x	Low	66.667	33.333	100
	Medium	30.000	70.000	100
	High	80.000	20.000	100

b.

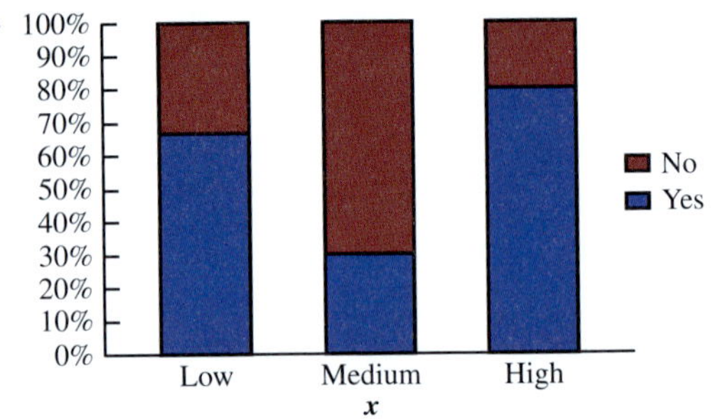

40. a.

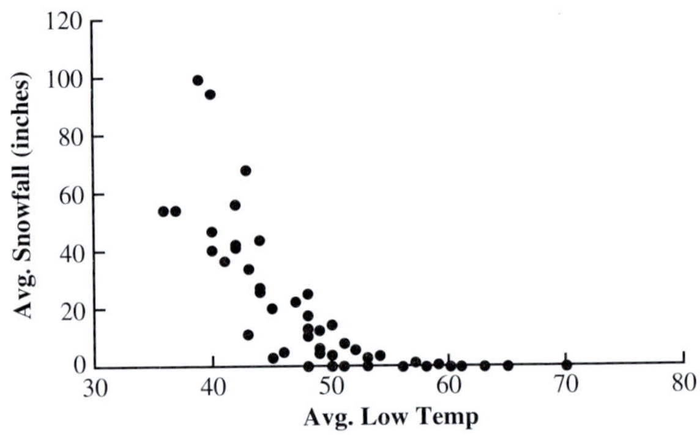

b. Colder average low temperature seems to lead to higher amounts of snowfall

c. Two cities have an average snowfall of nearly 100 inches of snowfall: Buffalo, New York and Rochester, New York; both are located near large lakes in New York

42. a.

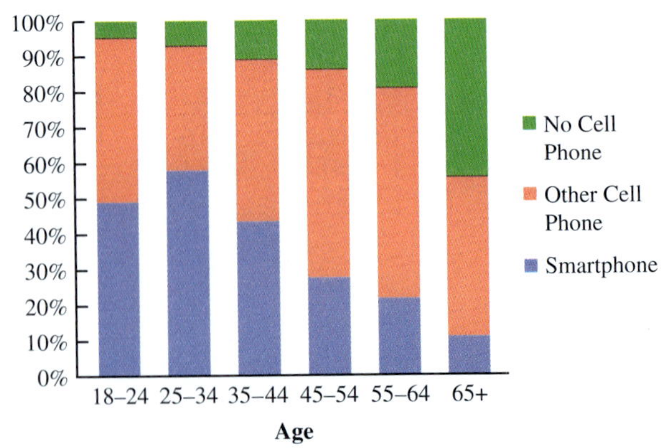

b. After an increase in age 25–34, smartphone ownership decreases as age increases; the percentage of people with no cell phone increases with age; there is less variation across age groups in the percentage who own other cell phones

c. Unless a newer device replaces the smartphone, we would expect smartphone ownership would become less sensitive to age; this would be true because current users will become older and because the device will become to be seen more as a necessity than a luxury

44. a.

SAT Score	Frequency
800–999	1
1000–1199	3
1200–1399	6
1400–1599	10
1600–1799	7
1800–1999	2
2000–2199	1
Total	30

b. Nearly symmetrical

c. 33% of the scores fall between 1400 and 1599
A score below 800 or above 2200 is unusual
The average is near or slightly above 1500

46. a.

Population in Millions	Frequency	Percent Frequency
0.0–2.4	15	30.0
2.5–4.9	13	26.0
5.0–7.4	10	20.0
7.5–9.9	5	10.0
10.0–12.4	1	2.0
12.5–14.9	2	4.0
15.0–17.4	0	0.0
17.5–19.9	2	4.0
20.0–22.4	0	0.0
22.5–24.9	0	0.0
25.0–27.4	1	2.0
27.5–29.9	0	0.0
30.0–32.4	0	0.0
32.5–34.9	0	0.0
35.0–37.4	1	2.0
37.5–39.9	0	0.0
More	0	0.0

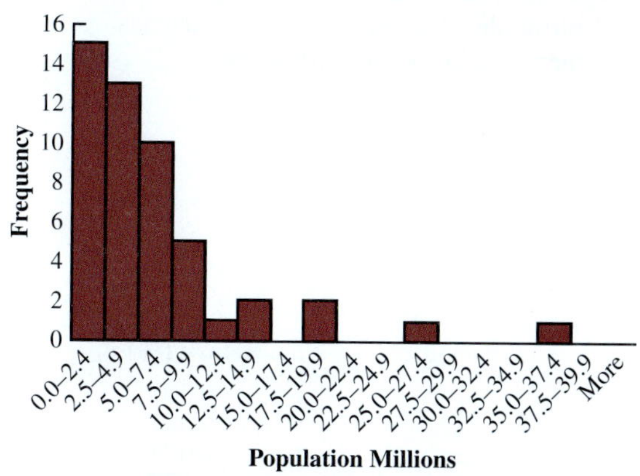

b. The distribution is skewed to the right

c. Fifteen states (30%) have a population less than 2.5 million; over half the states have population less than 5 million (28 states—56%); only seven states have a population greater than 10 million (California, Florida, Illinois, New York, Ohio, Pennsylvania, and Texas); the largest state is California (37.3 million) and the smallest states are Vermont and Wyoming (600 thousand)

48. a.

Industry	Frequency	Percent Frequency
Bank	26	13
Cable	44	22
Car	42	21
Cell	60	30
Collection	28	14
Total	200	100

b.

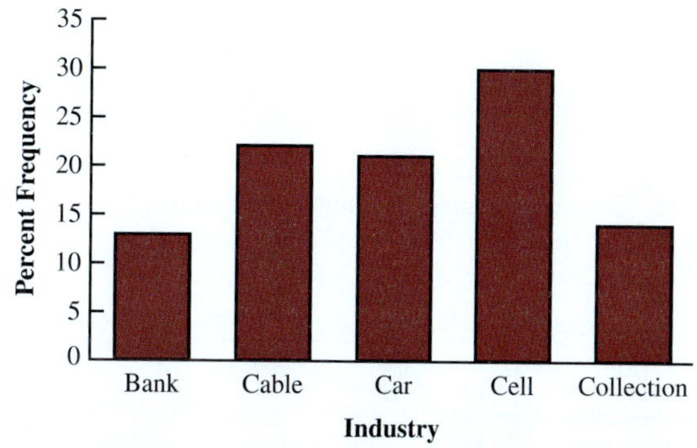

c. The cellular phone providers had the highest number of complaints

d. The percentage frequency distribution shows that the two financial industries (banks and collection agencies) had about the same number of complaints; new car dealers and cable and satellite television companies also had about the same number of complaints

50. a.

Level of Support	Percent Frequency
Strongly favor	30.10
Favor more than oppose	34.83
Oppose more than favor	21.13
Strongly oppose	13.94
Total	100.00

Overall favor higher tax $= 30.10\% + 34.83\%$
$= 64.93\%$

b. 20.2, 19.5, 20.6, 20.7, 19.0
Roughly 20% per country

c. The crosstabulation with column percentages:

	Country				
Support	Great Britain	Italy	Spain	Germany	United States
Strongly favor	31.00	31.96	45.99	19.98	20.98
Favor more than oppose	34.04	39.04	32.01	36.99	32.06
Oppose more than favor	23.00	17.99	13.98	24.03	26.96
Strongly oppose	11.96	11.01	8.03	18.99	20.00
Total	100.00	100.00	100.00	100.00	100.00

Considering the percentage of respondents who favor the higher tax by either saying "strongly favor" or "favor more than oppose," 65.04%, 71.00%, 78.00%, 56.97%, and 53.04% for the five countries; all show more than 50% support, but all European countries show more support for the tax than the United States; Italy and Spain show the highest level of support

52. a. Row totals: 247; 54; 82; 121
Column totals: 149; 317; 17; 7; 14

b.

Year	Freq.
1973 or before	247
1974–79	54
1980–86	82
1987–91	121
Total	504

Fuel	Freq.
Elect.	149
Nat. Gas	317
Oil	17
Propane	7
Other	14
Total	504

c. Crosstabulation of column percentages

Year Constructed	Fuel Type: Elect.	Nat. Gas	Oil	Propane	Other
1973 or before	26.9	57.7	70.5	71.4	50.0
1974–1979	16.1	8.2	11.8	28.6	0.0
1980–1986	24.8	12.0	5.9	0.0	42.9
1987–1991	32.2	22.1	11.8	0.0	7.1
Total	100.0	100.0	100.0	100.0	100.0

d. Crosstabulation of row percentages

Year Constructed	Fuel Type: Elect.	Nat. Gas	Oil	Propane	Other	Total
1973 or before	16.2	74.1	4.9	2.0	2.8	100.0
1974–1979	44.5	48.1	3.7	3.7	0.0	100.0
1980–1986	45.1	46.4	1.2	0.0	7.3	100.0
1987–1991	39.7	57.8	1.7	0.0	0.8	100.0

54. c. Older colleges and universities tend to have higher graduation rates.

56. a.

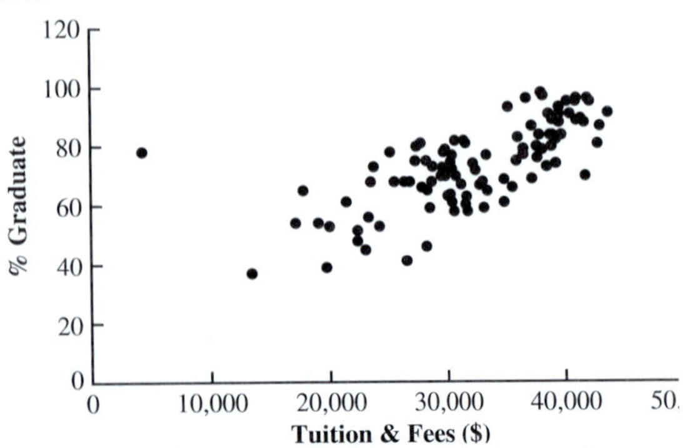

b. There appears to be a strong positive relationship between Tuition & Fees and % Graduation.

58. a.

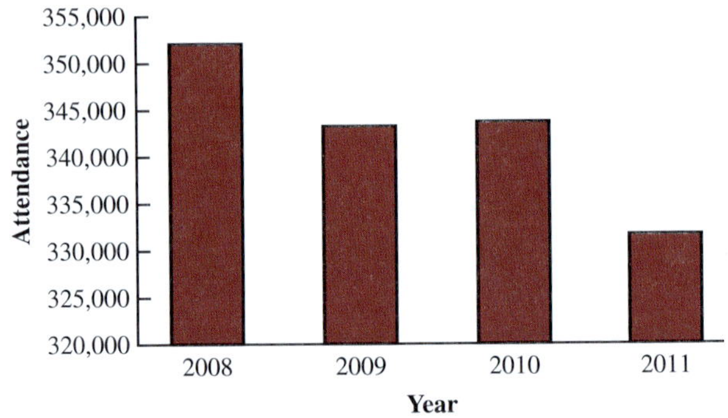

Zoo attendance appears to be dropping over time

b.

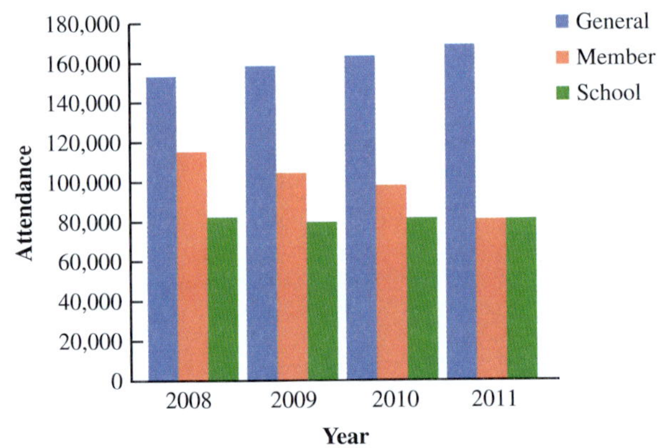

c. General attendance is increasing, but not enough to offset the decrease in member attendance; school membership appears fairly stable

Chapter 3

2. 16, 16.5

4.

Period	Return (%)
1	−0.060
2	−0.080
3	−0.040
4	0.020
5	0.054

The mean growth factor over the five periods is

$$\bar{x}_g = \sqrt[n]{(x_1)(x_2)\cdots(x_5)}$$
$$= \sqrt[5]{(0.940)(0.920)(0.960)(1.020)(1.054)}$$
$$= \sqrt[5]{(0.8925)} = 0.9775$$

So the mean growth rate $(0.9775 - 1)100\% = -2.25\%$

5. Arrange data in order: 15, 20, 25, 25, 27, 28, 30, 34

$i = \frac{20}{100}(8) = 1.6$; round up to position 2

20th percentile = 20

$i = \frac{25}{100}(8) = 2$; use positions 2 and 3

25th percentile $= \frac{20 + 25}{2} = 22.5$

$i = \frac{65}{100}(8) = 5.2$; round up to position 6

65th percentile = 28

$i = \frac{75}{100}(8) = 6$; use positions 6 and 7

75th percentile $= \frac{28 + 30}{2} = 29$

6. 59.73, 57, 53

8. a. 18.42
b. 6.32
c. 34.3%
d. Reductions of only .65 shots and .9% made shots per game
Yes, agree but not dramatically

10. a. $\bar{x} = \frac{\Sigma x_i}{n} = \frac{3200}{20} = 160$

Order the data from low 100 to high 360

Median: $i = \left(\frac{50}{100}\right)20 = 10$; use 10th and 11th positions

$\text{Median} = \left(\frac{130 + 140}{2}\right) = 135$

Mode = 120 (occur 3 times)

b. $i = \left(\frac{25}{100}\right) 20 = 5$; use 5th and 6th positions

$Q_1 = \left(\frac{115 + 115}{2}\right) = 115$

$i = \left(\frac{75}{100}\right)20 = 15$; use 15th and 16th positions

$Q_3 = \left(\frac{180 + 195}{2}\right) = 187.5$

c. $i = \left(\frac{90}{100}\right) 20 = 18$; use 18th and 19th positions

90th percentile $= \left(\frac{235 + 255}{2}\right) = 245$

90% of the tax returns cost \$245 or less

12. a. The minimum number of viewers who watched a new episode is 13.3 million, and the maximum number is 16.5 million

b. The mean number of viewers who watched a new episode is 15.04 million or approximately 15.0 million; the median is also 15.0 million; the data are multimodal (13.6, 14.0, 16.1, and 16.2 million); in such cases the mode is usually not reported

c. The data are first arranged in ascending order. The index for the first quartile is $i = \left(\frac{25}{100}\right)21 = 5.25$, so the first quartile is the value of the 6th observation in the sorted data, or 14.1; the index for the third quartile is $i = \left(\frac{75}{100}\right)21 = 15.75$, so the third quartile is the value of the 16th observation in the sorted data, or 16.0

d. A graph showing the viewership data over the air dates follows: Period 1 corresponds to the first episode of the season, period 2 corresponds to the second episode, and so on

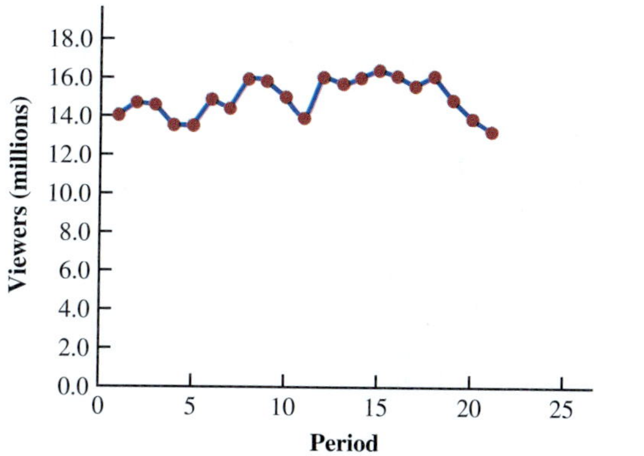

This graph shows that viewership of *The Big Bang Theory* has been relatively stable over the 2011–2012 television season

14. For March 2011

The index for the first quartile is $i = \left(\frac{25}{100}\right)50 = 12.50$, so the first quartile is the value of the 13th observation in the sorted data, or 6.8

The index for the median quartile is $i = \left(\frac{50}{100}\right)50 = 25.0$, so the median (or second quartile) is the average of the values of the 25th and 26th observations in the sorted data, or 8.0

The index for the third quartile is $i = \left(\frac{75}{100}\right)50 = 37.50$, so the third quartile is the value of the 38th observation in the sorted data, or 9.4

For March 2012

The minimum is 3.0

The index for the first quartile is $i = \left(\frac{25}{100}\right)50 = 12.50$, so the first quartile is the value of the 13th observation in the sorted data, or 6.8

The index for the median quartile is $i = \left(\frac{50}{100}\right)50 = 25.0$, so the median (or second quartile) is the average of the values of the 25th and 26th observations in the sorted data, or 7.35

The index for the third quartile is $i = \left(\frac{75}{100}\right)50 = 37.50$, so the third quartile is the value of the 38th observation in the sorted data, or 8.6

It may be easier to compare these results if we place them in a table

	March 2011	March 2012
First Quartile	6.8	6.8
Median	8.0	7.35
Third Quartile	9.4	8.6

The results show that in March 2012 approximately 25% of the states had an unemployment rate of 6.8% or less, the same as in March 2011; however, the median of 7.35% and the third quartile of 8.6% in March 2012 are both less than the corresponding values in March 2011, indicating that unemployment rates across the states are decreasing

16. a.

Grade x_i	Weight w_i
4 (A)	9
3 (B)	15
2 (C)	33
1 (D)	3
0 (F)	0
	60 credit hours

$$\bar{x} = \frac{\Sigma w_i x_i}{\Sigma w_i} = \frac{9(4) + 15(3) + 33(2) + 3(1)}{9 + 15 + 33 + 3} = \frac{150}{60} = 2.5$$

b. Yes

18. 3.8, 3.7

20.

	Stivers		Trippi	
Year	End of Year Value ($)	Growth Factor	End of Year Value ($)	Growth Factor
2004	11,000	1.100	5,600	1.120
2005	12,000	1.091	6,300	1.125
2006	13,000	1.083	6,900	1.095
2007	14,000	1.077	7,600	1.101
2008	15,000	1.071	8,500	1.118
2009	16,000	1.067	9,200	1.082
2010	17,000	1.063	9,900	1.076
2011	18,000	1.059	10,600	1.071

For the Stivers mutual fund we have $18000 = 10000[(x_1)(x_2) \cdots (x_8)]$, so $[(x_1)(x_2) \cdots (x_8)]$ $= 1.8$ and

$$\bar{x}_g = \sqrt[n]{(x_1)(x_2) \cdots (x_8)} = \sqrt[8]{1.80} = 1.07624$$

So the mean annual return for the Stivers mutual fund is $(1.07624 - 1)100 = 7.624\%$

For the Trippi mutual fund we have $10600 = 5000\,[(x_1)(x_2) \cdots (x_8)]$, so $[(x_1)(x_2) \cdots (x_8)]$ $= 2.12$ and

$$\bar{x}_g = \sqrt[n]{(x_1)(x_2) \cdots (x_8)} = \sqrt[8]{2.12} = 1.09848$$

So the mean annual return for the Trippi mutual fund is $(1.09848 - 1)100 = 9.848\%$

While the Stivers mutual fund has generated a nice annual return of 7.6%, the annual return of 9.8% earned by the Trippi mutual fund is far superior

22. $25{,}000{,}000 = 10{,}000{,}000[(x_1)(x_2) \cdots (x_6)]$,

so $[(x_1)(x_2) \cdots (x_6)] = 2.50$

so $\bar{x}_g = \sqrt[n]{(x_1)(x_2) \cdots (x_6)} = \sqrt[6]{2.50} = 1.165$

So the mean annual growth rate is $(1.165 - 1)100 = 16.5\%$

24. 16, 4

25. Range $= 34 - 15 = 19$

Arrange data in order: 15, 20, 25, 25, 27, 28, 30, 34

$$i = \frac{25}{100}(8) = 2;\ Q_1 = \frac{20 + 25}{2} = 22.5$$

$$i = \frac{75}{100}(8) = 6;\ Q_3 = \frac{28 + 30}{2} = 29$$

$$\text{IQR} = Q_3 - Q_1 = 29 - 22.5 = 6.5$$

$$\bar{x} = \frac{\Sigma x_i}{n} = \frac{204}{8} = 25.5$$

x_i	$(x_i - \bar{x})$	$(x_i - \bar{x})^2$
27	1.5	2.25
25	−.5	.25
20	−5.5	30.25
15	−10.5	110.25
30	4.5	20.25
34	8.5	72.25
28	2.5	6.25
25	−.5	.25
		242.00

$$s^2 = \frac{\Sigma(x_i - \bar{x})^2}{n - 1} = \frac{242}{8 - 1} = 34.57$$

$$s = \sqrt{34.57} = 5.88$$

26. a. Range $= 190 - 168 = 22$

b. $\bar{x} = \frac{\Sigma x_i}{n} = \frac{1068}{6} = 178$

$$s^2 = \frac{\Sigma(x_i - \bar{x})^2}{n - 1} = \frac{4^2 + (-10)^2 + 6^2 + 12^2 + (-8)^2 + (-4)^2}{6 - 1} = \frac{376}{5} = 75.2$$

c. $s = \sqrt{75.2} = 8.67$

d. $\frac{s}{\bar{x}}(100) = \frac{8.67}{178}(100\%) = 4.87\%$

28. a. The mean serve speed is 180.95, the variance is 21.42, and the standard deviation is 4.63

b. Although the mean serve speed for the 20 Women's Singles serve speed leaders for the 2011 Wimbledon tournament is slightly higher, the difference is very small; furthermore, given the variation in the 20 Women's Singles serve speed leaders from the 2012 Australian Open and the 20 Women's Singles serve speed leaders from the 2011 Wimbledon tournament, the difference in the mean serve speeds is most likely due to random variation in the players' performances

30. *Dawson:* range = 2, s = .67
Clark: range = 8, s = 2.58

32. **a.** 1285, 433 Freshmen spend more
b. 1720, 352
c. 404, 131.5
d. 367.04, 96.96
e. Freshmen have more variability

34. *Quarter-milers:* s = .0564, Coef. of Var. = 5.8%
Milers: s = .1295, Coef. of Var. = 2.9%

36. .20, 1.50, 0, −.50, −2.20

37. **a.** $z = \dfrac{20-30}{5} = -2,\ z = \dfrac{40-30}{5} = 2 \quad 1 - \dfrac{1}{2^2} = .75$
At least 75%

b. $z = \dfrac{15-30}{5} = -3,\ z = \dfrac{45-30}{5} = 3 \quad 1 - \dfrac{1}{3^2} = .89$
At least 89%

c. $z = \dfrac{22-30}{5} = -1.6,\ z = \dfrac{38-30}{5} = 1.6 \quad 1 - \dfrac{1}{1.6^2} = .61$
At least 61%

d. $z = \dfrac{18-30}{5} = -2.4,\ z = \dfrac{42-30}{5} = 2.4 \quad 1 - \dfrac{1}{2.4^2} = .83$
At least 83%

e. $z = \dfrac{12-30}{5} = -3.6,\ z = \dfrac{48-30}{5} = 3.6 \quad 1 - \dfrac{1}{3.6^2} = .92$
At least 92%

38. **a.** 95%
b. Almost all
c. 68%

39. **a.** z = 2 standard deviations

$$1 - \frac{1}{z^2} = 1 - \frac{1}{2^2} = \frac{3}{4};\ \text{at least } 75\%$$

b. z = 2.5 standard deviations

$$1 - \frac{1}{z^2} = 1 - \frac{1}{2.5^2} = .84;\ \text{at least } 84\%$$

c. z = 2 standard deviations
Empirical rule: 95%

40. **a.** 68%
b. 81.5%
c. 2.5%

42. **a.** −.67
b. 1.50
c. Neither is an outlier
d. Yes; z = 8.25

44. **a.** 76.5, 7
b. 16%, 2.5%
c. 12.2, 7.89; no outliers

46. 15, 22.5, 26, 29, 34

48. Arrange data in order: 5, 6, 8, 10, 10, 12, 15, 16, 18

$i = \dfrac{25}{100}(9) = 2.25$; round up to position 3

$Q_1 = 8$
Median (5th position) = 10

$i = \dfrac{75}{100}(9) = 6.75$; round up to position 7

$Q_3 = 15$
5-number summary: 5, 8, 10, 15, 18

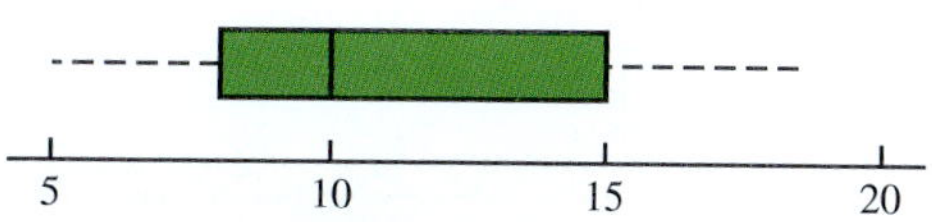

50. **a.** Men's 1st place 43.73 minutes faster
b. Medians: 109.64, 131.67
Men's median time 22.03 minutes faster
c. 65.30, 87.18, 109.64, 128.40, 148.70
109.03, 122.08, 131.67, 147.18, 189.28
d. Men's Limits: 25.35 to 190.23; no outliers
Women's Limits: 84.43 to 184.83; 2 outliers
e. Women runners show less variation

51. **a.** Arrange data in order low to high

$i = \dfrac{25}{100}(21) = 5.25$; round up to 6th position

$Q_1 = 1872$
Median (11th position) = 4019

$i = \dfrac{75}{100}(21) = 15.75$; round up to 16th position

$Q_3 = 8305$
5-number summary: 608, 1872, 4019, 8305, 14,138

b. IQR = $Q_3 - Q_1$ = 8305 − 1872 = 6433
Lower limit: 1872 − 1.5(6433) = −7777.5
Upper limit: 8305 + 1.5(6433) = 17,955
c. No; data are within limits
d. 41,138 > 27,604; 41,138 would be an outlier; data value would be reviewed and corrected

e.

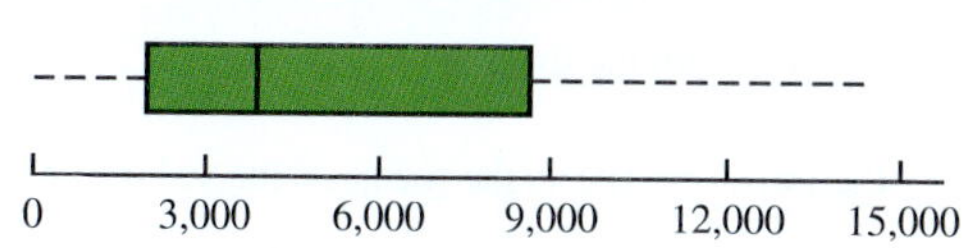

52. **a.** 73.5
b. 68, 71.5, 73.5, 74.5, 77
c. Limits: 67 and 79; no outliers
d. 66, 68, 71, 73, 75; 60.5 and 80.5
63, 65, 66, 67.6, 69; 61.25 and 71.25
75, 77, 78.5, 79.5, 81; 73.25 and 83.25
No outliers for any of the services
e. Verizon is highest rated
Sprint is lowest rated

54. **a.** 18.2, 15.35
b. 11.7, 23.5

c. 3.4, 11.7, 15.35, 23.5, 41.3

d. Yes; Alger Small Cap 41.3

55. b. There appears to be a negative linear relationship between x and y

c.

x_i	y_i	$x_i - \bar{x}$	$y_i - \bar{y}$	$(x_i - \bar{x})(y_i - \bar{y})$
4	50	−4	4	−16
6	50	−2	4	−8
11	40	3	−6	−18
3	60	−5	14	−70
16	30	8	−16	−128
40	230	0	0	−240

$\bar{x} = 8$; $\bar{y} = 46$

$$s_{xy} = \frac{\Sigma(x_i - \bar{x})(y_i - \bar{y})}{n - 1} = \frac{-240}{4} = -60$$

The sample covariance indicates a negative linear association between x and y

d. $r_{xy} = \dfrac{s_{xy}}{s_x s_y} = \dfrac{-60}{(5.43)(11.40)} = -.969$

The sample correlation coefficient of −.969 is indicative of a strong negative linear relationship

56. b. There appears to be a positive linear relationship between x and y

c. $s_{xy} = 26.5$

d. $r_{xy} = .693$

58. −.91; negative relationship

60. b. .910

c. Strong positive linear relationship; no

62. a. The mean is 2.95 and the median is 3.0

b. The index for the first quartile is $i = \left(\frac{25}{100}\right)20 = 5$, so the first quartile is the mean of the values of the 5th and 6th observations in the sorted data, or $\frac{1 + 1}{2} = 1$

The index for the third quartile is $i = \left(\frac{75}{100}\right)20 = 15$, so the third quartile is the mean of the values of the 15th and 16th observations in the sorted data, or $\frac{4 + 5}{2} = 4.5$

c. The range is 7 and the interquartile range is 4.5 – 1 = 3.5

d. The variance is 4.37 and standard deviation is 2.09

e. Because most people dine out relatively few times per week and a few families dine out very frequently, we would expect the data to be positively skewed; the skewness measure of 0.34 indicates the data are somewhat skewed to the right

f. The lower limit is −4.25 and the upper limit is 9.75; no values in the data are less than the lower limit or greater than the upper limit, so the Minitab boxplot indicates there are no outliers

Boxplot of Dining Out

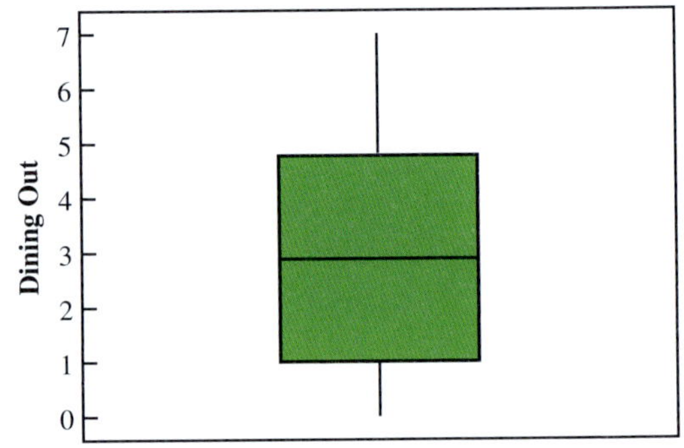

64. a. The mean and median patient wait times for offices with a wait-tracking system are 17.2 and 13.5, respectively; the mean and median patient wait times for offices without a wait-tracking system are 29.1 and 23.5, respectively

b. The variance and standard deviation of patient wait times for offices with a wait-tracking system are 86.2 and 9.3, respectively; the variance and standard deviation of patient wait times for offices without a wait-tracking system are 275.7 and 16.6, respectively

c. Offices with a wait-tracking system have substantially shorter patient wait times than offices without a wait-tracking system

d. $z = \dfrac{37 - 29.1}{16.6} = 0.48$

e. $z = \dfrac{37 - 17.2}{9.3} = 2.13$

As indicated by the positive z-scores, both patients had wait times that exceeded the means of their respective samples; even though the patients had the same wait time, the z-score for the sixth patient in the sample who visited an office with a wait-tracking system is much larger because that patient is part of a sample with a smaller mean and a smaller standard deviation

f. The z-scores for all patients follow

Without Wait-Tracking System	With Wait-Tracking System
−0.31	1.49
2.28	−0.67
−0.73	−0.34
−0.55	0.09
0.11	−0.56
0.90	2.13
−1.03	−0.88
−0.37	−0.45
−0.79	−0.56
0.48	−0.24

The z-scores do not indicate the existence of any outliers in either sample

66. a. \$670
b. \$456
c. $z = 3$; yes
d. Save time and prevent a penalty cost

68. a. 215.9
b. 55%
c. 175.0, 628.3
d. 48.8, 175.0, 215.9, 628.3, 2325.0
e. Yes, any price over 1308.25
f. 482.1; prefer median

70. a. 364 rooms
b. \$457
c. −.293; slight negative correlation
Higher cost per night tends to be associated with smaller hotels

72. a. .268, low or weak positive correlation
b. Very poor predictor; spring training is practice and does not count toward standings or playoffs

74. a. 60.68
b. $s^2 = 31.23$; $s = 5.59$

Chapter 4

2. $\binom{6}{3} = \frac{6!}{3!3!} = \frac{6 \cdot 5 \cdot 4 \cdot 3 \cdot 2 \cdot 1}{(3 \cdot 2 \cdot 1)(3 \cdot 2 \cdot 1)} = 20$

ABC	ACE	BCD	BEF
ABD	ACF	BCE	CDE
ABE	ADE	BCF	CDF
ABF	ADF	BDE	CEF
ACD	AEF	BDF	DEF

4. b. (H,H,H), (H,H,T), (H,T,H), (H,T,T), (T,H,H), (T,H,T), (T,T,H), (T,T,T)
c. ⅛

6. $P(E_1) = .40$, $P(E_2) = .26$, $P(E_3) = .34$
The relative frequency method was used

8. a. 4: Commission Positive—Council Approves
Commission Positive—Council Disapproves
Commission Negative—Council Approves
Commission Negative—Council Disapproves

9. $\binom{50}{4} = \frac{50!}{4!46!} = \frac{50 \cdot 49 \cdot 48 \cdot 47}{4 \cdot 3 \cdot 2 \cdot 1} = 230{,}300$

10. a. Using the table, P(Debt) = .94
b. Five of the 8 institutions, P(over 60%) = 5/8 = .625
c. Two of the 8 institutions, P(more than \$30,000) = 2/8 = .25
d. P(No debt) = 1 − P(debt) = 1 − .72 = .28
e. A weighted average with 72% having average debt of \$32,980 and 28% having no debt

$$\text{Average debt per graduate} = \frac{.72(\$32{,}980) + .28(\$0)}{.72 + .28} = \$23{,}746$$

12. a. 3,478,761
b. 1/3,478,761
c. 1/146,107,962

14. a. ¼
b. ½
c. ¾

15. a. S = {ace of clubs, ace of diamonds, ace of hearts, ace of spades}
b. S = {2 of clubs, 3 of clubs, . . . , 10 of clubs, J of clubs, Q of clubs, K of clubs, A of clubs}
c. There are 12; jack, queen, or king in each of the four suits
d. For (a): 4/52 = 1/13 = .08
For (b): 13/52 = 1/4 = .25
For (c): 12/52 = .23

16. a. 36
c. ⅙
d. $\frac{5}{18}$
e. No; P(odd) = P(even) = $\frac{1}{2}$
f. Classical

17. a. (4, 6), (4, 7), (4, 8)
b. .05 + .10 + .15 = .30
c. (2, 8), (3, 8), (4, 8)
d. .05 + .05 + .15 = .25
e. .15

18. a. .0222
b. .8226
c. .1048

20. a. .108
b. .096
c. .434

22. a. .40, .40, .60
b. .80, yes
c. $A^c = \{E_3, E_4, E_5\}$; $C^c = \{E_1, E_4\}$;
$P(A^c) = .60$; $P(C^c) = .40$
d. (E_1, E_2, E_5); .60
e. .80

23. a. $P(A) = P(E_1) + P(E_4) + P(E_6)$
$= .05 + .25 + .10 = .40$
$P(B) = P(E_2) + P(E_4) + P(E_7)$
$= .20 + .25 + .05 = .50$
$P(C) = P(E_2) + P(E_3) + P(E_5) + P(E_7)$
$= .20 + .20 + .15 + .05 = .60$
b. $A \cup B = \{E_1, E_2, E_4, E_6, E_7\}$;
$P(A \cup B) = P(E_1) + P(E_2) + P(E_4) + P(E_6) + P(E_7)$
$= .05 + .20 + .25 + .10 + .05$
$= .65$
c. $A \cap B = \{E_4\}$; $P(A \cap B) = P(E_4) = .25$
d. Yes, they are mutually exclusive
e. $B^c = \{E_1, E_3, E_5, E_6\}$;
$P(B^c) = P(E_1) + P(E_3) + P(E_5) + P(E_6)$
$= .05 + .20 + .15 + .10$
$= .50$

24. a. .05
b. .70

26. a. .64
b. .48
c. .36
d. .76

28. Let B = rented a car for business reasons
P = rented a car for personal reasons

a. $P(B \cup P) = P(B) + P(P) - P(B \cap P)$
$= .540 + .458 - .300$
$= .698$

b. $P(\text{Neither}) = 1 - .698 = .302$

30. a. $P(A \mid B) = \dfrac{P(A \cap B)}{P(B)} = \dfrac{.40}{.60} = .6667$

b. $P(B \mid A) = \dfrac{P(A \cap B)}{P(A)} = \dfrac{.40}{.50} = .80$

c. No, because $P(A \mid B) \neq P(A)$

32. a.

	Car	Light Truck	Total
U.S.	.1330	.2939	.4269
Non-U.S.	.3478	.2253	.5731
Total	.4808	.5192	1.0000

b. .4269, .5731 Non-U.S. higher
.4808, .5192 Light Truck slightly higher
c. .3115, .6885 Light Truck higher
d. .6909, .3931 Car higher
e. .5661, U.S. higher for Light Trucks

33. a.

		Undergraduate Major			
		Business	Engineering	Other	Totals
Intended Enrollment Status	Full-Time	0.270	0.151	0.192	0.613
	Part-Time	0.115	0.123	0.149	0.387
	Totals	0.385	0.274	0.341	1.000

b. $P(\text{Business}) = 0.385$, $P(\text{Engineering}) = 0.274$, and $P(\text{Other}) = 0.341$, so Business is the undergraduate major that produces the most potential MBA students

c. $P(\text{Engineering} \mid \text{Full-Time})$
$= \dfrac{P(\text{Engineering} \cap \text{Full-Time})}{P(\text{Full-Time})} = \dfrac{0.151}{0.613} = 0.246$

d. $P(\text{Full-Time} \mid \text{Business})$
$= \dfrac{P(\text{Full-Time} \cap \text{Business})}{P(\text{Business})} = \dfrac{0.270}{0.385} = 0.701$

e. For independence, we must have that $P(A)P(B) = P(A \cap B)$; from the joint probability table in part (a) of this problem, we have

$P(A) = 0.613$
$P(B) = 0.385$

So $P(A)\,P(B) = (0.387)(0.385) = 0.236$
But

$P(A \cap B) = (0.270)$

Because $P(A)P(B) \neq P(A \cap B)$, the events are not independent

34. a.

	On Time	Late	Total
Southwest	.3336	.0664	.40
US Airways	.2629	.0871	.35
JetBlue	.1753	.0747	.25
Total	.7718	.2282	1.00

b. Southwest (.40)
c. .7718
d. US Airways (.3817); Southwest (.2910)

36. a. We have that $P(\text{Make the Shot}) = .93$ for each foul shot, so the probability that Jamal Crawford will make two consecutive foul shots is $P(\text{Make the Shot})\,P(\text{Make the Shot}) = (.93)(.93) = .8649$

b. There are three unique ways that Jamal Crawford can make at least one shot—he can make the first shot and miss the second shot, miss the first shot and make the second shot, or make both shots; since the event "Miss the Shot" is the complement of the event "Make the Shot," $P(\text{Miss the Shot}) = 1 - P(\text{Make the Shot}) = 1 - .93 = .07$; thus

$P(\text{Make the Shot})\,P(\text{Miss the Shot}) = (.93)(.07) = .0651$
$P(\text{Miss the Shot})\,P(\text{Make the Shot}) = (.07)(.93) = .0651$
$P(\text{Make the Shot})\,P(\text{Make the Shot}) = (.93)(.93) = \underline{.8649}$
.9951

c. We can find this probability in two ways; we can calculate the probability directly

$P(\text{Miss the Shot})\,P(\text{Miss the Shot}) = (.07)(.07) = .0049$

Or we can recognize that the event "Miss both Shots" is the complement of the event "Make at Least One of the Two Shots," so

$P(\text{Miss the Shot})\,P(\text{Miss the Shot}) = 1 - .9951 = .0049$

d. For the Portland Trail Blazers' center, we have $P(\text{Make the Shot}) = .58$ for each foul shot, so the probability that the Portland Trail Blazers' center will make two consecutive foul shots is $P(\text{Make the Shot})\,P(\text{Make the Shot}) = (.58)(.58) = .3364$

Again, there are three unique ways that the Portland Trail Blazers' center can make at least one shot—he can make the first shot and miss the second shot, miss the first shot and make the second shot, or make both shots; since the event "Miss the Shot" is the complement of the event "Make the Shot," $P(\text{Miss the Shot}) = 1 - P(\text{Make the Shot}) = 1 - .58 = .42$; thus

$P(\text{Make the Shot})\,P(\text{Miss the Shot}) = (.58)(.42) = .2436$
$P(\text{Miss the Shot})\,P(\text{Make the Shot}) = (.42)(.58) = .2436$
$P(\text{Make the Shot})\,P(\text{Make the Shot}) = (.58)(.58) = \underline{.3364}$
.8236

We can again find the probability the Portland Trail Blazers' center will miss both shots in two ways; we can calculate the probability directly

$P(\text{Miss the Shot})\,P(\text{Miss the Shot}) = (.42)(.42) = .1764$

Or we can recognize that the event "Miss both Shots" is the complement of the event "Make at Least One of the Two Shots," so

P(Miss the Shot) P(Miss the Shot) $= 1 - .9951 = .1764$

Intentionally fouling the Portland Trail Blazers' center is a better strategy than intentionally fouling Jamal Crawford

38. a.

Grade	Met Proficiency Standards Yes	No	Total
3	.11196	.05663	0.16858
4	.08271	.08205	0.16476
5	.08517	.07922	0.16439
6	.08588	.07777	0.16365
7	.09671	.07031	0.16702
8	.09618	.07542	0.17159
Total	.55861	.44139	1.00000

b. The column marginal probabilities are .55861 and .44139; the row marginal probabilities are .16858, .16476, and so on

c. .6641; .5020

d. .2004; .1481

39. a. Yes, because $P(A_1 \cap A_2) = 0$

b. $P(A_1 \cap B) = P(A_1)P(B \mid A_1) = .40(.20) = .08$

$P(A_2 \cap B) = P(A_2)P(B \mid A_2) = .60(.05) = .03$

c. $P(B) = P(A_1 \cap B) + P(A_2 \cap B) = .08 + .03 = .11$

d. $P(A_1 \mid B) = \dfrac{.08}{.11} = .7273$

$P(A_2 \mid B) = \dfrac{.03}{.11} = .2727$

40. a. .10, .20, .09

b. .51

c. .26, .51, .23

42. M = missed payment

D_1 = customer defaults

D_2 = customer does not default

$P(D_1) = .05, P(D_2) = .95, P(M \mid D_2) = .2, P(M \mid D_1) = 1$

a. $P(D_1 \mid M) = \dfrac{P(D_1)P(M \mid D_1)}{P(D_1)P(M \mid D_1) + P(D_2)P(M \mid D_2)}$

$= \dfrac{(.05)(1)}{(.05)(1) + (.95)(.2)}$

$= \dfrac{.05}{.24} = .21$

b. Yes, the probability of default is greater than .20

44. a. $P(A_1) = .095$

$P(A_2) = .905$

$P(W \mid A_1) = .60$

$P(W \mid A_2) = .49$

b.

Events	$P(A_i)$	$P(W \mid A_i)$	$P(A_i \cap W)$	$P(A_i \mid W)$
A_1	0.095	0.60	0.05700	0.1139
A_2	0.905	0.49	0.44345	0.8861
		$P(W) =$	0.50045	1.0000

$P(A_1 \mid W) = .1139$

c.

Events	$P(A_i)$	$P(M \mid A_i)$	$P(A_i \cap M)$	$P(A_i \mid M)$
A_1	0.095	0.40	0.03800	0.0761
A_2	0.905	0.51	0.46155	0.9239
		$P(M) =$	0.49995	1.0000

$P(A_1 \mid M) = .0761$

d. $P(W) = .50045$

$P(M) = .49965$

46. a. .60

b. .26

c. .40

d. .74

48. a. 0.5029

b. 0.5758

c. No, from part (a) we have $P(F) = 0.5029$ and from part (b) we have $P(A \mid F) = 0.5758$; since $P(F) \neq P(A \mid F)$, events A and F are not independent

50. a. .76

b. .24

52. b. .2022

c. .4618

d. .4005

54. a. .7766

b. $P(\text{OKAY} \mid 30\text{–}49)$

$= \dfrac{P(\text{OKAY} \cap 30\text{–}49)}{P(30\text{–}49)} = \dfrac{0.0907}{0.3180} = 0.2852$

c. $P(50+ \mid \text{NOT OKAY})$

$= \dfrac{P(50+ \cap \text{NOT OKAY})}{P(\text{NOT OKAY})} = \dfrac{0.4008}{0.7766} = 0.5161$

d. The attitude about this practice is not independent of the age of the respondent; we can show this in several ways: One example is to use the result from part (b); We have

$P(\text{OKAY} \mid 30\text{–}49) = 0.2852$

and

$P(\text{OKAY}) = 0.2234$

If the attitude about this practice were independent of the age of the respondent, we would expect these probabilities to be equal; since these probabilities are not equal, the data suggest the attitude about this practice is not independent of the age of the respondent

e. Respondents in the 50+ age category are far more likely to say this practice is NOT OKAY than are respondents in the 18–29 age category:

$P(\text{NOT OKAY} \mid 50+)$

$$= \frac{P(\text{NOT OKAY} \cap 50+)}{P(50+)} = \frac{0.4008}{0.4731} = 0.8472$$

$P(\text{NOT OKAY} \mid 18\text{–}29)$

$$= \frac{P(\text{NOT OKAY} \cap 18\text{–}29)}{P(18\text{–}29)} = \frac{0.1485}{0.2089} = 0.7109$$

56. a. .25
b. .125
c. .0125
d. .10
e. No

58. a.

	Young Adult	Older Adult	Total
Blogger	.0432	.0368	.08
Nonblogger	.2208	.6992	.92
Total	.2640	.7360	1.00

b. .2640
c. .0432
d. .1636

60. a. $P(\text{spam} \mid \textit{shipping!})$

$$= \frac{P(\text{spam})P(\textit{shipping!} \mid \text{spam})}{P(\text{spam})P(\textit{shipping!} \mid \text{spam}) + P(\text{ham})P(\textit{shipping!} \mid \text{ham})}$$

$$= \frac{(0.10)(0.051)}{(0.10)(0.051) + (0.90)(0.0015)} = 0.791$$

$P(\text{ham} \mid \textit{shipping!})$

$$= \frac{P(\text{ham})P(\textit{shipping!} \mid \text{ham})}{P(\text{ham})P(\textit{shipping!} \mid \text{ham}) + P(\text{spam})P(\textit{shipping!} \mid \text{spam})}$$

$$= \frac{(0.90)(0.0015)}{(0.90)(0.0015) + (0.10)(0.051)} = 0.209$$

If a message includes the word *shipping!*, the probability the message is spam is high (0.7910), and so the message should be flagged as spam

b. $P(\text{spam} \mid \textit{today!})$

$$= \frac{P(\text{spam})P(\textit{today!} \mid \text{spam})}{P(\text{spam})P(\textit{today!} \mid \text{spam}) + P(\text{ham})P(\textit{today!} \mid \text{ham})}$$

$$= \frac{(0.10)(0.045)}{(0.10)(0.045) + (0.90)(0.0022)} = 0.694$$

$P(\text{spam} \mid \textit{here!})$

$$= \frac{P(\text{spam})P(\textit{here!} \mid \text{spam})}{P(\text{spam})P(\textit{here!} \mid \text{spam}) + P(\text{ham})P(\textit{here!} \mid \text{ham})}$$

$$= \frac{(0.10)(0.034)}{(0.10)(0.034) + (0.90)(0.0022)} = 0.632$$

A message that includes the word *today!* is more likely to be spam because $P(\textit{today!} \mid \text{spam})$ is larger than $P(\textit{here!} \mid \text{spam})$; because *today!* occurs more often in unwanted messages (spam), it is easier to distinguish spam from ham in messages that include *today!*

c. $P(\text{spam} \mid \textit{available})$

$$= \frac{P(\text{spam})P(\textit{available} \mid \text{spam})}{P(\text{spam})P(\textit{available} \mid \text{spam}) + P(\text{ham})P(\textit{available} \mid \text{ham})}$$

$$= \frac{(0.10)(0.014)}{(0.10)(0.014) + (0.90)(0.0041)} = 0.275$$

$P(\text{spam} \mid \textit{fingertips!})$

$$= \frac{P(\text{spam})P(\textit{fingertips!} \mid \text{spam})}{P(\text{spam})P(\textit{fingertips!} \mid \text{spam}) + P(\text{ham})P(\textit{fingertips!} \mid \text{ham})}$$

$$= \frac{(0.10)(0.014)}{(0.10)(0.014) + (0.90)(0.0011)} = 0.586$$

A message that includes the word *fingertips!* is more likely to be spam; because $P(\textit{fingertips!} \mid \text{ham})$ is smaller than $P(\textit{available} \mid \text{ham})$; because *available* occurs more often in legitimate messages (ham), it is more difficult to distinguish spam from ham in messages that include *available*

d. It is easier to distinguish spam from ham when a word occurs more often in unwanted messages (spam) and/or less often in legitimate messages (ham)

Chapter 5

1. a. Head, Head (H, H)
Head, Tail (H, T)
Tail, Head (T, H)
Tail, Tail (T, T)

b. x = number of heads on two coin tosses

c.

Outcome	Values of x
(H, H)	2
(H, T)	1
(T, H)	1
(T, T)	0

d. Discrete; 0, 1, and 2

2. a. x = time in minutes to assemble product
b. Any positive value: $x > 0$
c. Continuous

3. Let Y = position is offered
N = position is not offered

a. $S = \{(Y, Y, Y), (Y, Y, N), (Y, N, Y), (Y, N, N), (N, Y, Y), (N, Y, N), (N, N, Y), (N, N, N)\}$

b. Let N = number of offers made; N is a discrete random variable

c.

Experimental Outcome	(Y, Y, Y)	(Y, Y, N)	(Y, N, Y)	(Y, N, N)	(N, Y, Y)	(N, Y, N)	(N, N, Y)	(N, N, N)
Value of N	3	2	2	1	2	1	1	0

4. $x = 0, 1, 2, \ldots, 9$

6. a. $0, 1, 2, \ldots, 20$; discrete
b. $0, 1, 2, \ldots$; discrete
c. $0, 1, 2, \ldots, 50$; discrete
d. $0 \le x \le 8$; continuous
e. $x > 0$; continuous

7. a. $f(x) \geq 0$ for all values of x
$\Sigma f(x) = 1$; therefore, it is a valid probability distribution

b. Probability $x = 30$ is $f(30) = .25$

c. Probability $x \leq 25$ is $f(20) + f(25) = .20 + .15 = .35$

d. Probability $x > 30$ is $f(35) = .40$

8. a.

x	$f(x)$
1	3/20 = .15
2	5/20 = .25
3	8/20 = .40
4	4/20 = .20
	Total 1.00

b.

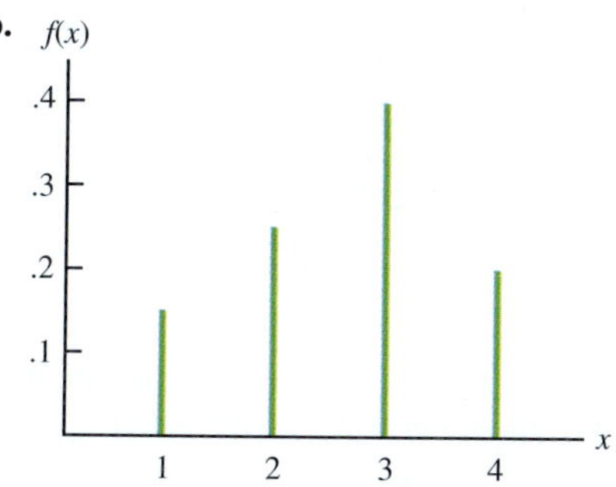

c. $f(x) \geq 0$ for $x = 1, 2, 3, 4$
$\Sigma f(x) = 1$

10. a.

x	1	2	3	4	5
$f(x)$	.05	.09	.03	.42	.41

b.

x	1	2	3	4	5
$f(x)$	.04	.10	.12	.46	.28

c. .83

d. .28

e. Senior executives are more satisfied

12. a. Yes

b. .15

c. .10

14. a. .05

b. .70

c. .40

16. a.

y	$f(y)$	$yf(y)$
2	.20	.4
4	.30	1.2
7	.40	2.8
8	.10	.8
Totals	1.00	5.2

$E(y) = \mu = 5.2$

b.

y	$y - \mu$	$(y - \mu)^2$	$f(y)$	$(y - \mu)^2 f(y)$
2	−3.20	10.24	.20	2.048
4	−1.20	1.44	.30	.432
7	1.80	3.24	.40	1.296
8	2.80	7.84	.10	.784
			Total	4.560

$Var(y) = 4.56$

$\sigma = \sqrt{4.56} = 2.14$

18. a/b.

x	$f(x)$	$xf(x)$	$x - \mu$	$(x - \mu)^2$	$(x - \mu)^2 f(x)$
0	0.04	0.00	−1.84	3.39	0.12
1	0.34	0.34	−0.84	0.71	0.24
2	0.41	0.82	0.16	0.02	0.01
3	0.18	0.53	1.16	1.34	0.24
4	0.04	0.15	2.16	4.66	0.17
Total	1.00	1.84			0.79
		↑ $E(x)$			↑ $Var(x)$

c/d.

y	$f(y)$	$yf(y)$	$y - \mu$	$(y - \mu)^2$	$y - \mu^2 f(y)$
0	0.00	0.00	−2.93	8.58	0.01
1	0.03	0.03	−1.93	3.72	0.12
2	0.23	0.45	−0.93	0.86	0.20
3	0.52	1.55	0.07	0.01	0.00
4	0.22	0.90	1.07	1.15	0.26
Total	1.00	2.93			0.59
		↑ $E(y)$			↑ $Var(y)$

e. The number of bedrooms in owner-occupied houses is greater than in renter-occupied houses; the expected number of bedrooms is $2.93 - 1.84 = 1.09$ greater, and the variability in the number of bedrooms is less for the owner-occupied houses

20. a. 430

b. −90; concern is to protect against the expense of a large loss

22. a. 445

b. $1250 loss

24. a. Medium: 145; large: 140

b. Medium: 2725; large: 12,400

25. a.

$E(x) = .2(50) + .5(30) + .3(40) = 37$

$E(y) = .2(80) + .5(50) + .3(60) = 59$

$Var(x) = .2(50-37)^2 + .5(30-37)^2 + .3(40-37)^2 = 61$

$Var(y) = .2(80-59)^2 + .5(50-59)^2 + .3(60-59)^2 = 129$

b.

$x + y$	$f(x + y)$
130	.2
80	.5
100	.3

c.

$x + y$	$f(x + y)$	$(x + y)f(x + y)$	$x + y - E(x + y)$
130	.2	26	34
80	.5	40	−16
100	.3	30	4
		$E(x + y) = 96$	

$[x + y - E(x + y)]^2$	$[x + y - E(x + y)]^2 f(x + y)$
1156	231.2
256	128.0
16	4.8
	$Var(x + y) = 364$

d.

$\sigma_{xy} = [Var(x + y) - Var(x) - Var(y)]/2 = (364-61-129)/2 = 87$

$Var(x) = 61$ and $Var(y) = 129$ were computed in part (a), so

$$\sigma_x = \sqrt{61} = 7.8102 \qquad \sigma_y = \sqrt{129} = 11.3578$$

$$\rho_{xy} = \frac{\sigma_{xy}}{\sigma_x \sigma_y} = \frac{87}{(7.8102)(11.3578)} = .98$$

The random variables x and y are positively related; both the covariance and correlation coefficient are positive; indeed, they are very highly correlated; the correlation coefficient is almost equal to 1

e. $Var(x + y) = Var(x) + Var(y) + 2\sigma_{xy}$
$= 61 + 129 + 2(87) = 364$

$Var(x) + Var(y) = 61 + 129 = 190$

The variance of the sum of x and y is greater than the sum of the variances by two times the covariance: $2(87) = 174$; the reason it is positive is that, in this case, the variables are positively related; whenever two random variables are positively related, the variance of the sum of the random variables will be greater than the sum of the variances of the individual random variables

26. a. 5%, 1%, stock 1 is riskier
b. \$42.25, \$25.00
c. 5.825, 2.236
d. 6.875%, 3.329%
e. −.6, strong negative relationship

27. a. Dividing each of the frequencies in the table by the total number of restaurants provides the joint probability table below; the bivariate probability for each pair of quality and meal price is shown in the body of the table; this is the bivariate probability distribution; for instance, the probability of a rating of 2 on quality and a rating of 3 on meal price is given by $f(2, 3) = .18$; the marginal probability distribution for quality, x, is in the rightmost column; the marginal probability for meal price, y, is in the bottom row

	Meal Price y			
Quality x	**1**	**2**	**3**	**Total**
1	0.14	0.13	0.01	0.28
2	0.11	0.21	0.18	0.50
3	0.01	0.05	0.16	0.22
Total	0.26	0.39	0.35	1

b. $E(x) = 1(.28) + 2(.50) + 3(.22) = 1.94$
$Var(x) = .28(1 - 1.94)^2 + .50(2 - 1.94)^2 + .22(3 - 1.94)^2 = .4964$

c. $E(y) = 1(.26) + 2(.39) + 3(.35) = 2.09$
$Var(y) = .26(1 - 2.09)^2 + .39(2 - 2.09)^2 + .35(3 - 2.09)^2 = .6019$

d. $\sigma_{xy} = [Var(x + y) = Var(x) - Var(y)]/2$
$= [1.6691 - .4964 - .6019]/2 = .2854$

Since the covariance $\sigma_{xy} = .2854$ is positive, we can conclude that as the quality rating goes up, the meal price goes up; this is as we would expect

e. $$\rho_{xy} = \frac{\sigma_{xy}}{\sigma_x \sigma_y} = \frac{.2854}{\sqrt{.4964}\sqrt{.6019}} = .5221$$

With a correlation coefficient of .5221, we would call this a moderately positive relationship; it is not likely to find a low-cost restaurant that is also high quality, but, it is possible; there are 3 of them leading to $f(3,1) = .01$

28. a. $E(y) = \$45.30$, $Var(y) = 3.81$, $\sigma_y = \$1.95$
b. $E(x) = \$90.50$, $Var(x) = 24.75$, $\sigma_x = \$4.97$
c.

z	$f(z)$
128	.05
130	.20
133	.20
138	.25
140	.20
143	.10
	1.00

d. \$135.8, 21.26, \$4.61
e. No, $\sigma_{xy} = -3.65$
f. No, they are less

30. a. 333.486, −1.974
b. 9.055%, 19.89%
c. 9.425%, 11.63%
d. 7.238%, 4.94%
e. Aggresive: 50% Core Bonds, 50% REITS
Conservative: 80% Core Bonds, 20% REITS

31. a.

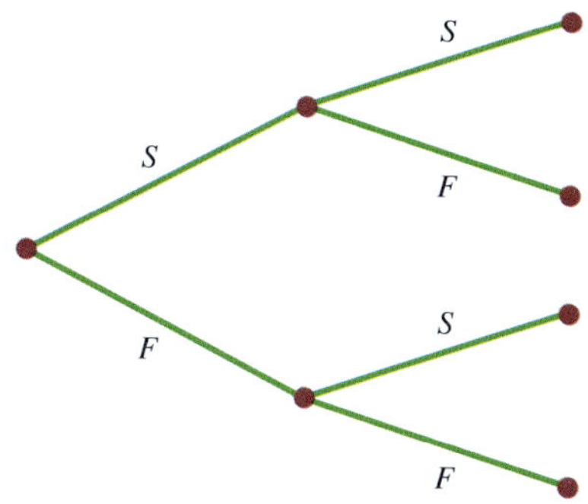

b. $f(1) = \binom{2}{1}(.4)^1(.6)^1 = \frac{2!}{1!1!}(.4)(.6) = .48$

c. $f(0) = \binom{2}{0}(.4)^0(.6)^2 = \frac{2!}{0!2!}(1)(.36) = .36$

d. $f(2) = \binom{2}{2}(.4)^2(.6)^0 = \frac{2!}{2!0!}(.16)(.1) = .16$

e. $P(x \geq 1) = f(1) + f(2) = .48 + .16 = .64$

f. $E(x) = np = 2(.4) = .8$

$Var(x) = np(1 - p) = 2(.4)(.6) = .48$

$\sigma = \sqrt{.48} = .6928$

32. a. .3487
b. .1937
c. .9298
d. .6513
e. 1
f. .9, .95

34. a. .2789
b. .4181
c. .0733

36. a. Probability of a defective part being produced must be .03 for each part selected; parts must be selected independently

b. Let D = defective
G = not defective

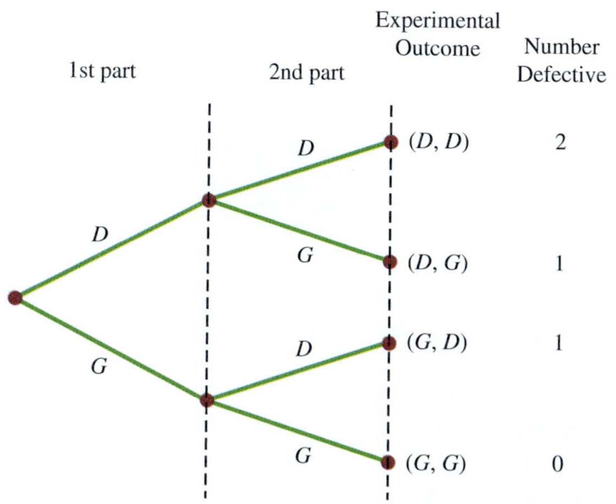

c. Two outcomes result in exactly one defect

d. $P(\text{no defects}) = (.97)(.97) = .9409$
$P(\text{1 defect}) = 2(.03)(.97) = .0582$
$P(\text{2 defects}) = (.03)(.03) = .0009$

38. a. .90
b. .99
c. .999
d. Yes

40. a. .2262
b. .8355

42. a. .1897
b. .9757
c. $f(12) = .0008$; yes
d. 5

44. a. $f(x) = \frac{3^x e^{-3}}{x!}$
b. .2241
c. .1494
d. .8008

45. a. $f(x) = \frac{2^x e^{-2}}{x!}$

b. $\mu = 6$ for 3 time periods

c. $f(x) = \frac{6^x e^{-6}}{x!}$

d. $f(2) = \frac{2^2 e^{-2}}{2!} = \frac{4(.1353)}{2} = .2706$

e. $f(6) = \frac{6^6 e^{-6}}{6!} = .1606$

f. $f(5) = \frac{4^5 e^{-4}}{5!} = .1563$

46. a. .1952
b. .1048
c. .0183
d. .0907

48. a. $f(0) = \frac{7^0 e^{-7}}{0!} = e^{-7} = .0009$

b. probability $= 1 - [f(0) + f(1)]$

$f(1) = \frac{7^1 e^{-7}}{1!} = 7e^{-7} = .0064$

probability $= 1 - [.0009 + .0064] = .9927$

c. $\mu = 3.5$

$f(0) = \frac{3.5^0 e^{-3.5}}{0!} = e^{-3.5} = .0302$

probability $= 1 - f(0) = 1 - .0302 = .9698$

d.
probability $= 1 - [f(0) + f(1) + f(2) + f(3) + f(4)]$
$= 1 - [.0009 + .0064 + .0223 + .0521 + .0912]$
$= .8271$

50. a. $\mu = 1.25$
b. .2865
c. .3581
d. .3554

52. a. $f(1) = \dfrac{\binom{3}{1}\binom{10-3}{4-1}}{\binom{10}{4}} = \dfrac{\left(\frac{3!}{1!2!}\right)\left(\frac{7!}{3!4!}\right)}{\frac{10!}{4!6!}}$

$= \dfrac{(3)(35)}{210} = .50$

b. $f(2) = \dfrac{\binom{3}{2}\binom{10-3}{2-2}}{\binom{10}{2}} = \dfrac{(3)(1)}{45} = .067$

c. $f(0) = \dfrac{\binom{3}{0}\binom{10-3}{2-0}}{\binom{10}{2}} = \dfrac{(1)(21)}{45} = .4667$

d. $f(2) = \dfrac{\binom{3}{2}\binom{10-3}{4-2}}{\binom{10}{4}} = \dfrac{(3)(21)}{210} = .30$

e. $x = 4$ is *greater than* $r = 3$; thus, $f(4) = 0$

54. a. .5250
b. .8167

56. $N = 60$, $n = 10$

a. $r = 20$, $x = 0$

$f(0) = \dfrac{\binom{20}{0}\binom{40}{10}}{\binom{60}{10}} = \dfrac{(1)\left(\frac{40!}{10!30!}\right)}{\frac{60!}{10!50!}}$

$= \left(\dfrac{40!}{10!30!}\right)\left(\dfrac{10!50!}{60!}\right)$

$= \dfrac{40 \cdot 39 \cdot 38 \cdot 37 \cdot 36 \cdot 35 \cdot 34 \cdot 33 \cdot 32 \cdot 31}{60 \cdot 59 \cdot 58 \cdot 57 \cdot 56 \cdot 55 \cdot 54 \cdot 53 \cdot 52 \cdot 51}$

$= .0112$

b. $r = 20$, $x = 1$

$f(1) = \dfrac{\binom{20}{1}\binom{40}{9}}{\binom{60}{10}} = 20\left(\dfrac{40!}{9!31!}\right)\left(\dfrac{10!50!}{60!}\right)$

$= .0725$

c. $1 - f(0) - f(1) = 1 - .0112 - .0725 = .9163$

d. Same as the probability one will be from Hawaii; .0725

58. a. .2917
b. .0083
c. .5250, .1750; 1 bank
d. .7083
e. .90, .49, .70

60. a.

x	1	2	3	4	5
$f(x)$	.24	.21	.10	.21	.24

b. 3.00, 2.34
c. Bonds: $E(x) = 1.36$, $Var(x) = .23$
Stocks: $E(x) = 4$, $Var(x) = 1$

62. a. .05, .40, 0 terminal only used when a purchase is made

b.

x	$f(x)$	$E(x) = 1.14$	$Var(x) = .3804$
0	.13		
1	.60		
2	.27		
	1.00		

c. .5, .45
d.

t	$f(t)$	$E(t) = 1.64$	$Var(t) = .5504$
1	.50		
2	.38		
3	.10		
4	.02		
	1.00		

e. $\sigma_{xy} = -.14$, $\rho_{xy} = -.3384$, negative relationship

64. a. .0596
b. .3585
c. 100
d. 95, 9.75

66. a. .9510
b. .0480
c. .0490

68. a. 240
b. 12.96
c. 12.96

70. .1912

72. a. .2240
b. .5767

74. a. .4667
b. .4667
c. .0667

Chapter 6

1. a.

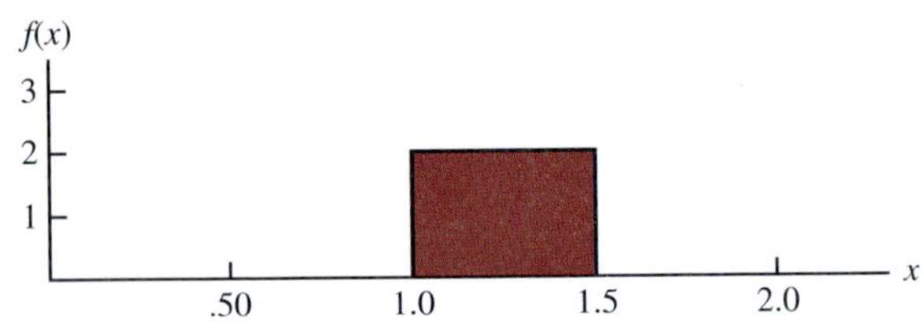

b. $P(x = 1.25) = 0$; the probability of any single point is zero because the area under the curve above any single point is zero
c. $P(1.0 \le x \le 1.25) = 2(.25) = .50$
d. $P(1.20 < x < 1.5) = 2(.30) = .60$

2. b. .50
c. .60
d. 15
e. 8.33

4. a.

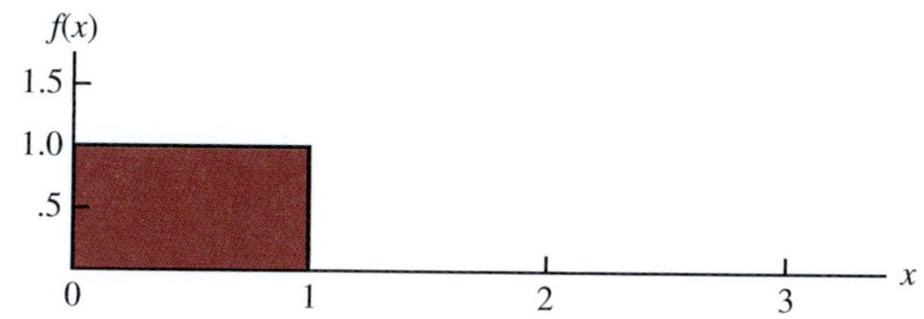

b. $P(.25 < x < .75) = 1(.50) = .50$
c. $P(x \le .30) = 1(.30) = .30$
d. $P(x > .60) = 1(.40) = .40$

6. a. .125
b. .50
c. .25

10. a. .9332
b. .8413
c. .0919
d. .4938

12. a. .2967
b. .4418
c. .3300
d. .5910
e. .8849
f. .2389

13. a. $P(-1.98 \le z \le .49) = P(z \le .49) - P(z < -1.98)$ $= .6879 - .0239 = .6640$
b. $P(.52 \le z \le 1.22) = P(z \le 1.22) - P(z < .52)$ $= .8888 - .6985 = .1903$
c. $P(-1.75 \le z \le -1.04) = P(z \le -1.04) - P(z < -1.75) = .1492 - .0401 = .1091$

14. a. $z = 1.96$
b. $z = 1.96$
c. $z = .61$
d. $z = 1.12$
e. $z = .44$
f. $z = .44$

15. a. The z value corresponding to a cumulative probability of .2119 is $z = -.80$
b. Compute $.9030/2 = .4515$; the cumulative probability of $.5000 + .4515 = .9515$ corresponds to $z = 1.66$
c. Compute $.2052/2 = .1026$; z corresponds to a cumulative probability of $.5000 + .1026 = .6026$, so $z = .26$
d. The z value corresponding to a cumulative probability of .9948 is $z = 2.56$
e. The area to the left of z is $1 - .6915 = .3085$, so $z = -.50$

16. a. $z = 2.33$
b. $z = 1.96$
c. $z = 1.645$
d. $z = 1.28$

18. $\mu = 14.4$ and $\sigma = 4.4$

a. At $x = 20$, $z = \dfrac{20 - 14.4}{4.4} = 1.27$

$P(z \le 1.27) = .8980$
$P(x \ge 20) = 1 - .8980 = .1020$

b. At $x = 10$, $z = \dfrac{10 - 14.4}{4.4} = -1.00$

$P(z \le -1.00) = .1587$
So, $P(x \le 10) = .1587$

c. A z-value of 1.28 cuts off an area of approximately 10% in the upper tail

$x = 14.4 + 4.4(1.28) = 20.03$

A return of $20.03% or higher will put a domestic stock fund in the top 10%

20. a. .1788
b. 69.15%
c. .0495

22. a. .6553
b. 13.05 hours
c. .9838

24. a. 200, 26.04
b. .2206
c. .1251
d. 242.84 million

26. a. $\mu = np = 100(.20) = 20$
$\sigma^2 = np(1 - p) = 100(.20)(.80) = 16$
$\sigma = \sqrt{16} = 4$

b. Yes, because $np = 20$ and $n(1 - p) = 80$
c. $P(23.5 \le x \le 24.5)$

$z = \dfrac{24.5 - 20}{4} = 1.13 \qquad P(z \le 1.13) = .8708$

$z = \dfrac{23.5 - 20}{4} = .88 \qquad P(z \le .88) = .8106$

$P(23.5 \le x \le 24.5) = P(.88 \le z \le 1.13)$
$= .8708 - .8106 = .0602$

d. $P(17.5 \le x \le 22.5)$

$z = \dfrac{22.5 - 20}{4} = .63 \qquad P(z \le .63) = .7357$

$z = \dfrac{17.5 - 20}{4} = -.63 \qquad P(z \le -.63) = .2643$

$P(17.5 \le x \le 22.5) = P(-.63 \le z \le .63)$
$= .7357 - .2643 = .4714$

e. $P(x \le 15.5)$

$z = \dfrac{15.5 - 20}{4} = -1.13 \qquad P(z \le -1.13) = .1292$

$P(x \le 15.5) = P(z \le -1.13) = .1292$

28. a. $\mu = np = 250(.20) = 50$
b. $\sigma^2 = np(1 - p) = 250(.20)(1 - 20) = 40$
$\sigma = \sqrt{40} = 6.3246$

$P(x < 40) = P(x \le 39.5)$

$z = \dfrac{x - \mu}{\sigma} = \dfrac{39.5 - 50}{6.3246} = -1.66 \qquad \text{Area} = .0485$

$P(x \le 39.5) = .0485$

c. $P(55 \le x \le 60) = P(54.5 \le x \le 60.5)$

$z = \dfrac{x - \mu}{\sigma} = \dfrac{54.5 - 50}{6.3246} = .71 \qquad \text{Area} = .7611$

$z = \frac{x - \mu}{\sigma} = \frac{60.5 - 50}{6.3246} = 1.66$ Area $= .9515$

$P(54.5 \le x \le 60.5) = .9515 - .7611 = .1904$

d. $P(x \ge 70) = P(x \ge 69.5)$

$z = \frac{x - \mu}{\sigma} = \frac{69.5 - 50}{6.3246} = 3.08$ Area $= .9990$

$P(x \ge 69.5) = 1 - .9990 = .0010$

30. a. 144
b. .1841
c. .9943

32. a. .5276
b. .3935
c. .4724
d. .1341

33. a. $P(x \le x_0) = 1 - e^{-x_0/3}$
b. $P(x \le 2) = 1 - e^{-2/3} = 1 - .5134 = .4866$
c. $P(x \ge 3) = 1 - P(x \le 3) = 1 - (1 - e^{-3/3})$
$= e^{-1} = .3679$
d. $P(x \le 5) = 1 - e^{-5/3} = 1 - .1889 = .8111$
e. $P(2 \le x \le 5) = P(x \le 5) - P(x \le 2)$
$= .8111 - .4866 = .3245$

34. a. $f(x) = \frac{1}{20}e^{-x/20}$
b. .5276
c. .3679
d. .5105

35. a.

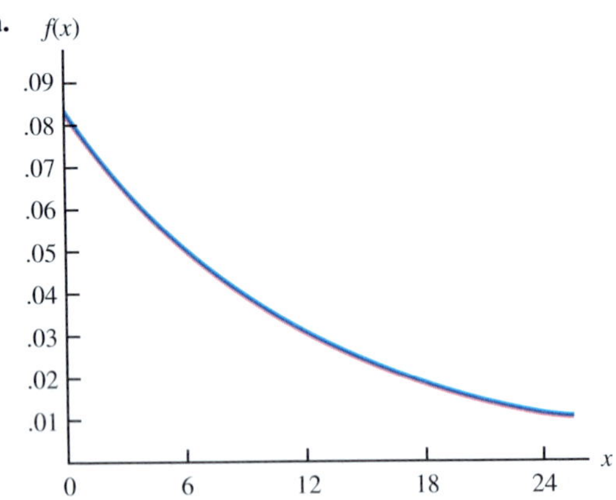

b. $P(x \le 12) = 1 - e^{-12/12} = 1 - .3679 = .6321$
c. $P(x \le 6) = 1 - e^{-6/12} = 1 - .6065 = .3935$
d. $P(x \ge 30) = 1 - P(x < 30)$
$= 1 - (1 - e^{-30/12})$
$= .0821$

36. a. .3935
b. .2386
c. .1353

38. a. $f(x) = 5.5e^{-5.5x}$
b. .2528
c. .6002

40. a. \$16,312
b. 7.64%
c. \$22,948

42. a. $\sigma = 25.5319$
b. .9401
c. 706 or more

44. a. .0228
b. \$50

46. a. 38.3%
b. 3.59% better, 96.41% worse
c. 38.21%

48. $\mu = 19.23$ ounces

50. a. Lose \$240
b. .1788
c. .3557
d. .0594

52. a. $\frac{1}{7}$ minute
b. $7e^{-7x}$
c. .0009
d. .2466

54. a. 2 minutes
b. .2212
c. .3935
d. .0821

Chapter 7

1. a. AB, AC, AD, AE, BC, BD, BE, CD, CE, DE
b. With 10 samples, each has a $\frac{1}{10}$ probability
c. E and C because 8 and 0 do not apply; 5 identifies E; 7 does not apply; 5 is skipped because E is already in the sample; 3 identifies C; 2 is not needed because the sample of size 2 is complete

2. 22, 147, 229, 289

3. 459, 147, 385, 113, 340, 401, 215, 2, 33, 348

4. a. Bell South, LSI Logic, General Electric
b. 120

6. 2782, 493, 825, 1807, 289

8. ExxonMobil, Chevron, Travelers, Microsoft, Pfizer, and Intel

10. a. finite; **b.** infinite; **c.** infinite; **d.** finite; **e.** infinite

11. a. $\bar{x} = \frac{\Sigma x_i}{n} = \frac{54}{6} = 9$

b. $s = \sqrt{\frac{\Sigma(x_i - \bar{x})^2}{n - 1}}$

$\Sigma(x_i - \bar{x})^2 = (-4)^2 + (-1)^2 + 1^2 + (-2)^2 + 1^2 + 5^2$
$= 48$

$s = \sqrt{\frac{48}{6 - 1}} = 3.1$

12. a. .50
b. .3667

13. a. $\bar{x} = \frac{\Sigma x_i}{n} = \frac{465}{5} = 93$

b.

x_i	$(x_i - \bar{x})$	$(x_i - \bar{x})^2$
94	+1	1
100	+7	49
85	−8	64
94	+1	1
92	−1	1
Totals 465	0	116

$$s = \sqrt{\frac{\Sigma(x_i - \bar{x})^2}{n - 1}} = \sqrt{\frac{116}{4}} = 5.39$$

14. a. .45
b. .15
c. .45

16. a. All U.S. adults age 50 and older
b. .8216
c. 315
d. .8310
e. Target population is same as sampled population; if restricted to AARP members, inferences are questionable

18. a. 200
b. 5
c. Normal with $E(\bar{x}) = 200$ and $\sigma_{\bar{x}} = 5$
d. The probability distribution of $\bar{x}$

19. a. The sampling distribution is normal with
$E(\bar{x}) = \mu = 200$
$\sigma_{\bar{x}} = \sigma/\sqrt{n} = 50/\sqrt{100} = 5$
For ±5, $195 \leq \bar{x} \leq 205$
Using the standard normal probability table:

$$\text{At } \bar{x} = 205, z = \frac{\bar{x} - \mu}{\sigma_{\bar{x}}} = \frac{5}{5} = 1$$

$P(z \leq 1) = .8413$

$$\text{At } \bar{x} = 195, z = \frac{\bar{x} - \mu}{\sigma_{\bar{x}}} = \frac{-5}{5} = -1$$

$P(z < -1) = .1587$
$P(195 \leq \bar{x} \leq 205) = .8413 - .1587 = .6826$

b. For ±10, $190 \leq \bar{x} \leq 210$
Using the standard normal probability table:

$$\text{At } \bar{x} = 210, z = \frac{\bar{x} - \mu}{\sigma_{\bar{x}}} = \frac{10}{5} = 2$$

$P(z \leq 2) = .9772$

$$\text{At } \bar{x} = 190, z = \frac{\bar{x} - \mu}{\sigma_{\bar{x}}} = \frac{-10}{5} = -2$$

$P(z < -2) = .0228$
$P(190 \leq \bar{x} \leq 210) = .9722 - .0228 = .9544$

20. 3.54, 2.50, 2.04, 1.77
$\sigma_{\bar{x}}$ decreases as n increases

22. a. Normal with $E(\bar{x}) = 51{,}800$ and $\sigma_{\bar{x}} = 516.40$
b. $\sigma_{\bar{x}}$ decreases to 365.15
c. $\sigma_{\bar{x}}$ decreases as n increases

23. a.

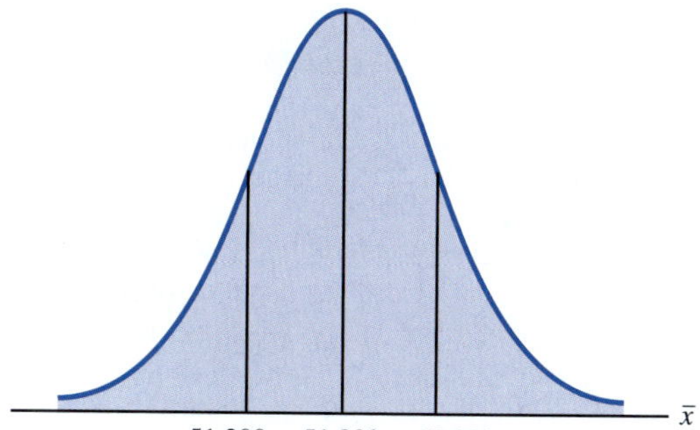

$$\sigma_{\bar{x}} = \frac{\sigma}{\sqrt{n}} = \frac{4000}{\sqrt{60}} = 516.40$$

$$\text{At } \bar{x} = 52{,}300, z = \frac{52{,}300 - 51{,}800}{516.40} = .97$$

$P(\bar{x} \leq 52{,}300) = P(z \leq .97) = .8340$

$$\text{At } \bar{x} = 51{,}300, z = \frac{51{,}300 - 51{,}800}{516.40} = -.97$$

$P(\bar{x} < 51{,}300) = P(z < -.97) = .1660$
$P(51{,}300 \leq \bar{x} \leq 52{,}300) = .8340 - .1660 = .6680$

b. $\sigma_{\bar{x}} = \frac{\sigma}{\sqrt{n}} = \frac{4000}{\sqrt{120}} = 365.15$

$$\text{At } \bar{x} = 52{,}300, z = \frac{52{,}300 - 51{,}800}{365.15} = 1.37$$

$P(\bar{x} \leq 52{,}300) = P(z \leq 1.37) = .9147$

$$\text{At } \bar{x} = 51{,}300, z = \frac{51{,}300 - 51{,}800}{365.15} = -1.37$$

$P(\bar{x} < 51{,}300) = P(z < -1.37) = .0853$
$P(51{,}300 \leq \bar{x} \leq 52{,}300) = .9147 - .0853 = .8294$

24. a. Normal with $E(\bar{x}) = 17.5$ and $\sigma_{\bar{x}} = .57$
b. .9198
c. .6212

26. a. .4246, .5284, .6922, .9586
b. Higher probability the sample mean will be close to population mean

28. a. Normal with $E(\bar{x}) = 95$ and $\sigma_{\bar{x}} = 2.56$
b. .7580
c. .8502
d. Part (c), larger sample size

30. a. $n/N = .01$; no
b. 1.29, 1.30; little difference
c. .8764

32. a. $E(\bar{p}) = .40$

$$\sigma_{\bar{p}} = \sqrt{\frac{p(1 - p)}{n}} = \sqrt{\frac{(.40)(.60)}{200}} = .0346$$

Within ±.03 means $.37 \leq \bar{p} \leq .43$

$$z = \frac{\bar{p} - p}{\sigma_{\bar{p}}} = \frac{.03}{.0346} = .87$$

$$P(.37 \le \bar{p} \le .43) = P(-.87 \le z \le .87) = .8078 - .1922 = .6156$$

b. $z = \dfrac{\bar{p} - p}{\sigma_{\bar{p}}} = \dfrac{.05}{.0346} = 1.44$

$$P(.35 \le \bar{p} \le .45) = P(-1.44 \le z \le 1.44) = .9251 - .0749 = .8502$$

34. a. .6156
b. .7814
c. .9488
d. .9942
e. Higher probability with larger n

35. a.

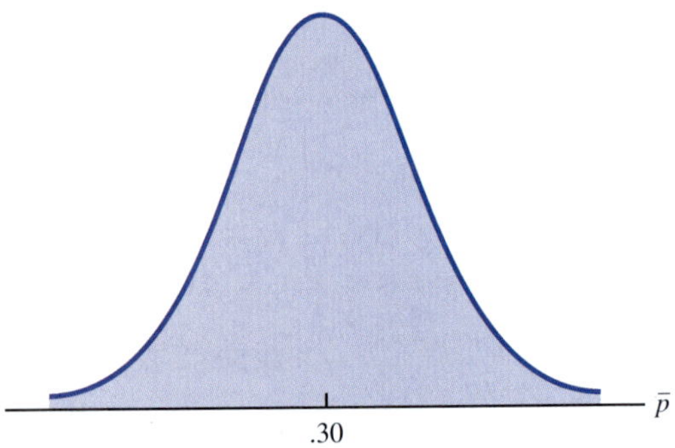

$$\sigma_{\bar{p}} = \sqrt{\frac{p(1-p)}{n}} = \sqrt{\frac{.30(.70)}{100}} = .0458$$

The normal distribution is appropriate because $np = 100(.30) = 30$ and $n(1 - p) = 100(.70) = 70$ are both greater than 5

b. $P(.20 \le \bar{p} \le .40) = ?$

$$z = \frac{.40 - .30}{.0458} = 2.18$$

$$P(.20 \le \bar{p} \le .40) = P(-2.18 \le z \le 2.18) = .9854 - .0146 = .9708$$

c. $P(.25 \le \bar{p} \le .35) = ?$

$$z = \frac{.35 - .30}{.0458} = 1.09$$

$$P(.25 \le \bar{p} \le .35) = P(-1.09 \le z \le 1.09) = .8621 - .1379 = .7242$$

36. a. Normal with $E(\bar{p}) = .55$ and $\sigma_{\bar{p}} = .0352$
b. .8444
c. Normal with $E(\bar{p}) = .45$ and $\sigma_{\bar{p}} = .0352$
d. .8444
e. No, standard error is the same in both parts
f. .9556, the probability is larger because the increased sample size reduces the standard error

38. a. Normal with $E(\bar{p}) = .42$ and $\sigma_{\bar{p}} = .0285$
b. .7062
c. .9198
d. Probabilities would increase

40. a. Normal with $E(\bar{p}) = .76$ and $\sigma_{\bar{p}} = .0214$
b. .8384
c. .9452

42. 122, 99, 25, 55, 115, 102, 61

44. a. Normal with $E(\bar{x}) = 406$ and $\sigma_{\bar{x}} = 10$
b. .8664
c. $z = -2.60$, .0047, Yes

46. a. 955
b. .50
c. .7062
d. .8230

48. a. 625
b. .7888

50. a. Normal with $E(\bar{p}) = .28$ and $\sigma_{\bar{p}} = .0290$
b. .8324
c. .5098

52. a. .8882
b. .0233

54. a. 48
b. Normal, $E(\bar{p}) = .25$, $\sigma_{\bar{p}} = .0625$
c. .2119

Chapter 8

2. Use $\bar{x} \pm z_{\alpha/2}(\sigma/\sqrt{n})$
a. $32 \pm 1.645(6/\sqrt{50})$
32 ± 1.4; 30.6 to 33.4
b. $32 \pm 1.96(6/\sqrt{50})$
32 ± 1.66; 30.34 to 33.66
c. $32 \pm 2.576(6/\sqrt{50})$
32 ± 2.19; 29.81 to 34.19

4. 54

5. a. With 99% confidence $z_{\alpha/2} = z_{.005} = 2.576$
Margin of Error $= 2.576\,\sigma/\sqrt{n} = 2.576\,(6/\sqrt{64}) = 1.93$
b. Confidence Interval: 21.52 ± 1.93 or 19.59 to 23.45

6. 8.1 to 8.9

8. a. Population is at least approximately normal
b. 3.41
c. 4.48

10. a. \$113,638 to \$124,672
b. \$112,581 to \$125,729
c. \$110,515 to \$127,795
d. Width increases as confidence level increases

12. a. 2.179
b. −1.676
c. 2.457
d. −1.708 and 1.708
e. −2.014 and 2.014

13. a. $\bar{x} = \dfrac{\Sigma x_i}{n} = \dfrac{80}{8} = 10$

b. $s = \sqrt{\dfrac{\Sigma(x_i - \bar{x})^2}{n - 1}} = \sqrt{\dfrac{84}{7}} = 3.464$

c. $t_{.025}\left(\frac{s}{\sqrt{n}}\right) = 2.365\left(\frac{3.46}{\sqrt{8}}\right) = 2.9$

d. $\bar{x} \pm t_{.025}\left(\frac{s}{\sqrt{n}}\right)$

10 ± 2.9 (7.1 to 12.9)

14. a. 21.5 to 23.5
b. 21.3 to 23.7
c. 20.9 to 24.1
d. A larger margin of error and a wider interval

15. $\bar{x} \pm t_{\alpha/2}(s/\sqrt{n})$

90% confidence: $df = 64$ and $t_{.05} = 1.669$

$19.5 \pm 1.669\left(\frac{5.2}{\sqrt{65}}\right)$

19.5 ± 1.08 or (18.42 to 20.58)

95% confidence: $df = 64$ and $t_{.025} = 1.998$

$19.5 \pm 1.998\left(\frac{5.2}{\sqrt{65}}\right)$

19.5 ± 1.29 or (18.21 to 20.79)

16. a. 9.7063, 7.9805
b. 7.1536 to 12.2590
c. 3.8854, 1.6194
d. 3.3674 to 4.4034

18. a. 22 weeks
b. 3.8020
c. 18.20 to 25.80
d. Larger n next time

20. $\bar{x} = 22$; 21.48 to 22.52

22. a. \$9,269 to \$12,541
b. 1523
c. 4,748,714, \$34 million

24. a. Planning value of $\sigma = \frac{\text{Range}}{4} = \frac{36}{4} = 9$

b. $n = \frac{z_{.025}^2\sigma^2}{E^2} = \frac{(1.96)^2(9)^2}{(3)^2} = 34.57$; use $n = 35$

c. $n = \frac{(1.96)^2(9)^2}{(2)^2} = 77.79$; use $n = 78$

25. a. Use $n = \frac{z_{\alpha/2}^2\sigma^2}{E^2}$

$n = \frac{(1.96)^2(6.84)^2}{(1.5)^2} = 79.88$; use $n = 80$

b. $n = \frac{(1.645)^2(6.84)^2}{(2)^2} = 31.65$; use $n = 32$

26. a. 25
b. 49
c. 97

28. a. 328
b. 465
c. 803
d. n gets larger; no to 99% confidence

30. 1537

31. a. $\bar{p} = \frac{100}{400} = .25$

b. $\sqrt{\frac{\bar{p}(1 - \bar{p})}{n}} = \sqrt{\frac{.25(.75)}{400}} = .0217$

c. $\bar{p} \pm z_{.025}\sqrt{\frac{\bar{p}(1 - \bar{p})}{n}}$

$.25 \pm 1.96(.0217)$

$.25 \pm .0424$; .2076 to .2924

32. a. .6733 to .7267
b. .6682 to .7318

34. 1068

35. a. $\bar{p} = \frac{1760}{2000} = .88$

b. Margin of error

$z_{.05} = \sqrt{\frac{\bar{p}(1 - \bar{p})}{n}} = 1.645\sqrt{\frac{.88(1 - .88)}{2000}} = .0120$

c. Confidence interval

$.88 \pm .0120$ or .868 to .892

d. Margin of error

$z_{.05} = \sqrt{\frac{\bar{p}(1 - \bar{p})}{n}} = 1.96\sqrt{\frac{.88(1 - .88)}{2000}} = .0142$

95% confidence interval

$.88 \pm .0142$ or .8658 to .8942

36. a. .23
b. .1716 to .2884

38. a. .1790
b. .0738, .5682 to .7158
c. 354

39. a. $n = \frac{z_{.025}^2 p^*(1 - p^*)}{E^2} = \frac{(1.96)^2(.156)(1 - .156)}{(.03)^2}$

$= 562$

b. $n = \frac{z_{.005}^2 p^*(1 - p^*)}{E^2} = \frac{(2.576)^2(.156)(1 - .156)}{(.03)^2}$

$= 970.77$; use 971

40. .0346 (.4854 to .5546)

42. a. .0442
b. 601, 1068, 2401, 9604

44. a. 4.00
b. \$29.77 to \$37.77

46. a. 122
b. \$1751 to \$1995
c. \$172, 316 million
d. Less than \$1873

48. a. 14 minutes
b. 13.38 to 14.62
c. 32 per day
d. Staff reduction

50. 37

52. 176

54. a. .5420
b. .0508
c. .4912 to .5928

56. a. .8273
b. .7957 to .8589

58. a. 1267
b. 1509

60. a. .3101
b. .2898 to .3304
c. 8219; no, this sample size is unnecessarily large

Chapter 9

2. a. H_0: $\mu \leq 14$
H_a: $\mu > 14$
b. No evidence that the new plan increases sales
c. The research hypothesis $\mu > 14$ is supported; the new plan increases sales

4. a. H_0: $\mu \geq 220$
H_a: $\mu < 220$
b. Cannot conclude proposed method reduces cost.
c. Can conclude proposed method reduces cost.

5. a. Conclude that the population mean monthly cost of electricity in the Chicago neighborhood is greater than \$104 and hence higher than in the comparable neighborhood in Cincinnati
b. The Type I error is rejecting H_0 when it is true; this error occurs if the researcher concludes that the population mean monthly cost of electricity is greater than \$104 in the Chicago neighborhood when the population mean cost is actually less than or equal to \$104
c. The Type II error is accepting H_0 when it is false; this error occurs if the researcher concludes that the population mean monthly cost for the Chicago neighborhood is less than or equal to \$104 when it is not

6. a. H_0: $\mu \leq 1$
H_a: $\mu > 1$
b. Claiming $\mu > 1$ when it is not true
c. Claiming $\mu \leq 1$ when it is not true

8. a. H_0: $\mu \geq 220$
H_a: $\mu < 220$
b. Claiming $\mu < 220$ when it is not true
c. Claiming $\mu \geq 220$ when it is not true

10. a. $z = \dfrac{\bar{x} - \mu_0}{\sigma/\sqrt{n}} = \dfrac{26.4 - 25}{6/\sqrt{40}} = 1.48$
b. Using normal table with $z = 1.48$: p-value $=$ $1.0000 - .9306 = .0694$
c. p-value $> .01$, do not reject H_0
d. Reject H_0 if $z \geq 2.33$
$1.48 < 2.33$, do not reject H_0

11. a. $z = \dfrac{\bar{x} - \mu_0}{\sigma/\sqrt{n}} = \dfrac{14.15 - 15}{3/\sqrt{50}} = -2.00$
b. p-value $= 2(.0228) = .0456$
c. p-value $\leq .05$, reject H_0
d. Reject H_0 if $z \leq -1.96$ or $z \geq 1.96$
$-2.00 \leq -1.96$, reject H_0

12. a. .1056; do not reject H_0
b. .0062; reject H_0
c. ≈ 0; reject H_0
d. .7967; do not reject H_0

14. a. .3844; do not reject H_0
b. .0074; reject H_0
c. .0836; do not reject H_0

15. a. H_0: $\mu \geq 1056$
H_a: $\mu < 1056$
b. $z = \dfrac{\bar{x} - \mu_0}{\sigma/\sqrt{n}} = \dfrac{910 - 1056}{1600/\sqrt{400}} = -1.83$
p-value $= .0336$
c. p-value $\leq .05$, reject H_0; the mean refund of "last-minute" filers is less than \$1056
d. Reject H_0 if $z \leq -1.645$
$-1.83 \leq -1.645$; reject H_0

16. a. H_0: $\mu \leq 3173$
H_a: $\mu > 3173$
b. .0207
c. Reject H_0, conclude mean credit card balance for undergraduate student has increased

18. a. H_0: $\mu = 4.1$
H_a: $\mu \neq 4.1$
b. -2.21, .0272
c. Reject H_0; return for Mid-Cap Growth Funds differs from that for U.S. Diversified Funds

20. a. H_0: $\mu \geq 32.79$
H_a: $\mu < 32.79$
b. -2.73
c. .0032
d. Reject H_0; conclude the mean monthly Internet bill is less in the southern state

22. a. H_0: $\mu = 8$
H_a: $\mu \neq 8$
b. .1706
c. Do not reject H_0; we cannot conclude the mean waiting time differs from 8 minutes
d. 7.83 to 8.97; yes

24. a. $t = \dfrac{\bar{x} - \mu_0}{s/\sqrt{n}} = \dfrac{17 - 18}{4.5/\sqrt{48}} = -1.54$
b. Degrees of freedom $= n - 1 = 47$
Area in lower tail is between .05 and .10
p-value (two-tail) is between .10 and .20
Exact p-value $= .1303$
c. p-value $> .05$; do not reject H_0
d. With $df = 47$, $t_{.025} = 2.012$
Reject H_0 if $t \leq -2.012$ or $t \geq 2.012$
$t = -1.54$; do not reject H_0

26. a. Between .02 and .05; exact p-value $= .0397$; reject H_0
b. Between .01 and .02; exact p-value $= .0125$; reject H_0
c. Between .10 and .20; exact p-value $= .1285$; do not reject H_0

27. a. H_0: $\mu \geq 238$
H_a: $\mu < 238$

b. $t = \dfrac{\bar{x} - \mu_0}{s/\sqrt{n}} = \dfrac{231 - 238}{80/\sqrt{100}} = -.88$

Degrees of freedom $= n - 1 = 99$
p-value is between .10 and .20
Exact p-value = .1905

c. p-value > .05; do not reject H_0
Cannot conclude mean weekly benefit in Virginia is less than the national mean

d. $df = 99$, $t_{.05} = -1.66$
Reject H_0 if $t \leq -1.66$
$-.88 > -1.66$; do not reject H_0

28. a. H_0: $\mu \geq 9$
H_a: $\mu < 9$

b. Between .005 and .01
Exact p-value = .0072

c. Reject H_0; mean tenure of a CEO is less than 9 years

30. a. H_0: $\mu = 6.4$
H_a: $\mu \neq 6.4$

b. Between .10 and .20
Exact p-value = .1268

c. Do not reject H_0; cannot conclude that the group consensus is wrong

32. a. H_0: $\mu = 10{,}192$
H_a: $\mu \neq 10{,}192$

b. Between .02 and .05
Exact p-value = .0304

c. Reject H_0; mean price at dealership differs from national mean price

34. a. H_0: $\mu = 2$
H_a: $\mu \neq 2$

b. 2.2

c. .516

d. Between .20 and .40
Exact p-value = .2535

e. Do not reject H_0; no reason to change from 2 hours for cost estimating

36. a. $z = \dfrac{\bar{p} - p_0}{\sqrt{\dfrac{p_0(1 - p_0)}{n}}} = \dfrac{.68 - .75}{\sqrt{\dfrac{.75(1 - .75)}{300}}} = -2.80$

p-value = .0026
p-value $\leq$ .05; reject H_0

b. $z = \dfrac{.72 - .75}{\sqrt{\dfrac{.75(1 - .75)}{300}}} = -1.20$

p-value = .1151
p-value > .05; do not reject H_0

c. $z = \dfrac{.70 - .75}{\sqrt{\dfrac{.75(1 - .75)}{300}}} = -2.00$

p-value = .0228
p-value $\leq$ .05; reject H_0

d. $z = \dfrac{.77 - .75}{\sqrt{\dfrac{.75(1 - .75)}{300}}} = .80$

p-value = .7881
p-value > .05; do not reject H_0

38. a. H_0: $p = .64$
H_a: $p \neq .64$

b. $\bar{p} = 52/100 = .52$

$z = \dfrac{\bar{p} - p_0}{\sqrt{\dfrac{p_0(1 - p_0)}{n}}} = \dfrac{.52 - .64}{\sqrt{\dfrac{.64(1 - .64)}{100}}} = -2.50$

p-value = 2(.0062) = .0124

c. p-value $\leq$ .05; reject H_0
Proportion differs from the reported .64

d. Yes, because $\bar{p} = .52$ indicates that fewer believe the supermarket brand is as good as the name brand

40. a. 21

b. H_0: $p \geq .46$
H_a: $p < .46$
p-value $\approx$.0436

c. Yes, .0436

42. a. $\bar{p} = .15$

b. .0718 to .2282

c. The return rate for the Houston store is different than the national average

44. a. H_0: $p \leq .51$
H_a: $p > .51$

b. $\bar{p} = .58$, p-value = .0026

c. Reject H_0; people working the night shift get drowsy more often

46.

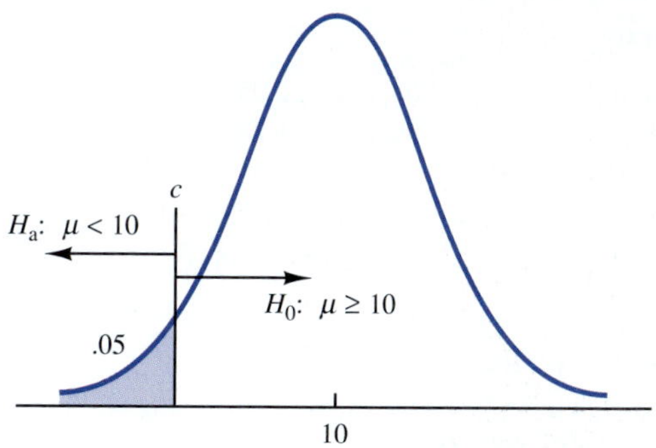

$c = 10 - 1.645(5/\sqrt{120}) = 9.25$
Reject H_0 if $\bar{x} \leq 9.25$

a. When $\mu = 9$,

$z = \dfrac{9.25 - 9}{5/\sqrt{120}} = .55$

$P(\text{Reject } H_0) = (1.0000 - .7088) = .2912$

b. Type II error

c. When $\mu = 8$,

$$z = \frac{9.25 - 8}{5/\sqrt{120}} = 2.74$$

$$\beta = (1.0000 - .9969) = .0031$$

48. a. Concluding $\mu \leq 15$ when it is not true
b. .2676
c. .0179

49. a. H_0: $\mu \geq 25$
H_a: $\mu < 25$
Reject H_0 if $z \leq -2.05$

$$z = \frac{\bar{x} - \mu_0}{\sigma/\sqrt{n}} = \frac{\bar{x} - 25}{3/\sqrt{30}} = -2.05$$

Solve for $\bar{x} = 23.88$
Decision Rule: Accept H_0 if $\bar{x} > 23.88$
Reject H_0 if $\bar{x} \leq 23.88$

b. For $\mu = 23$,

$$z = \frac{23.88 - 23}{3/\sqrt{30}} = 1.61$$

$$\beta = 1.0000 - .9463 = .0537$$

c. For $\mu = 24$,

$$z = \frac{23.88 - 24}{3/\sqrt{30}} = -.22$$

$$\beta = 1.0000 - .4129 = .5871$$

d. The Type II error cannot be made in this case; note that when $\mu = 25.5$, H_0 is true; the Type II error can only be made when H_0 is false

50. a. Concluding $\mu = 28$ when it is not true
b. .0853, .6179, .6179, .0853
c. .9147

52. .1151, .0015
Increasing n reduces β

54. $n = \dfrac{(z_\alpha + z_\beta)^2\sigma^2}{(\mu_0 - \mu_a)^2} = \dfrac{(1.645 + 1.28)^2(5)^2}{(10 - 9)^2} = 214$

56. 109

57. At $\mu_0 = 400$, $\alpha = .02$; $z_{.02} = 2.05$
At $\mu_a = 385$, $\beta = .10$; $z_{.10} = 1.28$
With $\sigma = 30$,

$$n = \frac{(z_\alpha + z_\beta)^2\sigma^2}{(\mu_0 - \mu_a)^2} = \frac{(2.05 + 1.28)^2(30)^2}{(400 - 385)^2} = 44.4 \text{ or } 45$$

58. 324

60. a. H_0: $\mu = 16$
H_a: $\mu \neq 16$
b. .0286; reject H_0
Readjust line
c. .2186; do not reject H_0
Continue operation
d. $z = 2.19$; reject H_0
$z = -1.23$; do not reject H_0
Yes, same conclusion

62. a. H_0: $\mu \leq 119{,}155$
H_a: $\mu > 119{,}155$
b. .0047
c. Reject H_0; mean annual income for theatergoers in Bay Area is higher

64. $t = -1.05$
p-value between .20 and .40
Exact p-value = .2999
Do not reject H_0; there is no evidence to conclude that the age at which women had their first child has changed

66. $t = 2.26$
p-value between .01 and .025
Exact p-value = .0155
Reject H_0; mean cost is greater than \$125,000

68. a. H_0: $p \leq .80$
H_a: $p > .80$
Conclude that airline travelers feel security will be improved
b. Cannot reject H_0; mandatory use is not recommended

70. a. H_0: $p \leq .80$
H_a: $p > .80$
b. .84
c. .0418
d. Reject H_0; more than 80% of customers are satisfied with service of home agents

72. H_0: $p \geq .90$
H_a: $p < .90$
p-value = .0808
Do not reject H_0; claim of at least 90% cannot be rejected

74. a. H_0: $\mu \leq 72$
H_a: $\mu > 72$
b. .2912
c. .7939
d. 0, because H_0 is true

76. a. 45
b. .0192, .2358, .7291, .7291, .2358, .0192

Chapter 10

1. a. $\bar{x}_1 - \bar{x}_2 = 13.6 - 11.6 = 2$
b. $z_{\alpha/2} = z_{.05} = 1.645$

$$\bar{x}_1 - \bar{x}_2 \pm 1.645\sqrt{\frac{\sigma_1^2}{n_1} + \frac{\sigma_2^2}{n_2}}$$

$$2 \pm 1.645\sqrt{\frac{(2.2)^2}{50} + \frac{(3)^2}{35}}$$

$2 \pm .98$ (1.02 to 2.98)

c. $z_{\alpha/2} = z_{.05} = 1.96$

$$2 \pm 1.96\sqrt{\frac{(2.2)^2}{50} + \frac{(3)^2}{35}}$$

2 ± 1.17 (.83 to 3.17)

2. a. $z = \dfrac{(\bar{x}_1 - \bar{x}_2) - D_0}{\sqrt{\dfrac{\sigma_1^2}{n_1} + \dfrac{\sigma_2^2}{n_2}}} = \dfrac{(25.2 - 22.8) - 0}{\sqrt{\dfrac{(5.2)^2}{40} + \dfrac{(6)^2}{50}}} = 2.03$

b. p-value = 1.0000 − .9788 = .0212
c. p-value ≤ .05; reject H_0

4. a. $\bar{x}_1 - \bar{x}_2 = 85.36 - 81.40 = 3.96$

b. $z_{.025}\sqrt{\frac{\sigma_1^2}{n_1} + \frac{\sigma_2^2}{n_2}} = 1.96\sqrt{\frac{(4.55)^2}{37} + \frac{(3.97)^2}{44}} = 1.88$

c. 3.96 ± 1.88 (2.08 to 5.84)

6. p-value = .0351
Reject H_0; mean price in Atlanta lower than mean price in Houston

8. a. Reject H_0; customer service has improved for Rite Aid

b. Do not reject H_0; the difference is not statistically significant

c. p-value = .0336; reject H_0; customer service has improved for Expedia

d. 1.80

e. The increase for J.C. Penney is not statistically significant

9. a. $\bar{x}_1 - \bar{x}_2 = 22.5 - 20.1 = 2.4$

b. $$df = \frac{\left(\frac{s_1^2}{n_1} + \frac{s_2^2}{n_2}\right)^2}{\frac{1}{n_1 - 1}\left(\frac{s_1^2}{n_1}\right)^2 + \frac{1}{n_2 - 1}\left(\frac{s_2^2}{n_2}\right)^2}$$

$$= \frac{\left(\frac{2.5^2}{20} + \frac{4.8^2}{30}\right)^2}{\frac{1}{19}\left(\frac{2.5^2}{20}\right)^2 + \frac{1}{29}\left(\frac{4.8^2}{30}\right)^2} = 45.8$$

c. $df = 45$, $t_{.025} = 2.014$

$$t_{.025}\sqrt{\frac{s_1^2}{n_1} + \frac{s_2^2}{n_2}} = 2.014\sqrt{\frac{2.5^2}{20} + \frac{4.8^2}{30}} = 2.1$$

d. 2.4 ± 2.1 (.3 to 4.5)

10. a. $$t = \frac{(\bar{x}_1 - \bar{x}_2) - 0}{\sqrt{\frac{s_1^2}{n_1} + \frac{s_2^2}{n_2}}} = \frac{(13.6 - 10.1) - 0}{\sqrt{\frac{5.2^2}{35} + \frac{8.5^2}{40}}} = 2.18$$

b. $$df = \frac{\left(\frac{s_1^2}{n_1} + \frac{s_2^2}{n_2}\right)^2}{\frac{1}{n_1 - 1}\left(\frac{s_1^2}{n_1}\right)^2 + \frac{1}{n_2 - 1}\left(\frac{s_2^2}{n_2}\right)^2}$$

$$= \frac{\left(\frac{5.2^2}{35} + \frac{8.5^2}{40}\right)^2}{\frac{1}{34}\left(\frac{5.2^2}{35}\right)^2 + \frac{1}{39}\left(\frac{8.5^2}{40}\right)^2} = 65.7$$

Use $df = 65$

c. $df = 65$, area in tail is between .01 and .025; two-tailed p-value is between .02 and .05
Exact p-value = .0329

d. p-value $\leq .05$; reject H_0

12. a. $\bar{x}_1 - \bar{x}_2 = 22.5 - 18.6 = 3.9$ miles

b. $$df = \frac{\left(\frac{s_1^2}{n_1} + \frac{s_2^2}{n_2}\right)^2}{\frac{1}{n_1 - 1}\left(\frac{s_1^2}{n_1}\right)^2 + \frac{1}{n_2 - 1}\left(\frac{s_2^2}{n_2}\right)^2}$$

$$= \frac{\left(\frac{8.4^2}{50} + \frac{7.4^2}{40}\right)^2}{\frac{1}{49}\left(\frac{8.4^2}{50}\right)^2 + \frac{1}{39}\left(\frac{7.4^2}{40}\right)^2} = 87.1$$

Use $df = 87$, $t_{.025} = 1.988$

$$3.9 \pm 1.988\sqrt{\frac{8.4^2}{50} + \frac{7.4^2}{40}}$$

3.9 ± 3.3 (.6 to 7.2)

14. a. $H_0: \mu_1 - \mu_2 \geq 0$
$H_a: \mu_1 - \mu_2 < 0$

b. -2.41

c. Using t table, p-value is between .005 and .01
Exact p-value = .009

d. Reject H_0; nursing salaries are lower in Tampa

16. a. $H_0: \mu_1 - \mu_2 \leq 0$
$H_a: \mu_1 - \mu_2 > 0$

b. 38

c. $t = 1.80$, $df = 25$
Using t table, p-value is between .025 and .05
Exact p-value = .0420

d. Reject H_0; conclude higher mean score if college grad

18. a. $H_0: \mu_1 - \mu_2 = 0$
$H_a: \mu_1 - \mu_2 \neq 0$

b. 50.6 and 52.8 minutes

c. p-value greater than .40
Do not reject H_0; cannot conclude population mean delay times differ

19. a. 1, 2, 0, 0, 2

b. $\bar{d} = \Sigma d_i/n = 5/5 = 1$

c. $$s_d = \sqrt{\frac{\Sigma(d_i - \bar{d})^2}{n - 1}} = \sqrt{\frac{4}{5 - 1}} = 1$$

d. $$t = \frac{\bar{d} - \mu}{s_d/\sqrt{n}} = \frac{1 - 0}{1/\sqrt{5}} = 2.24$$

$df = n - 1 = 4$
Using t table, p-value is between .025 and .05
Exact p-value = .0443
p-value $\leq .05$; reject H_0

20. a. 3, −1, 3, 5, 3, 0, 1

b. 2

c. 2.08

d. 2

e. .07 to 3.93

21. $H_0: \mu_d \leq 0$
$H_a: \mu_d > 0$
$\bar{d} = .625$
$s_d = 1.30$

$$t = \frac{\bar{d} - \mu_d}{s_d/\sqrt{n}} = \frac{.625 - 0}{1.30/\sqrt{8}} = 1.36$$

$df = n - 1 = 7$
Using t table, p-value is between .10 and .20
Exact p-value = .1080
p-value > .05; do not reject H_0; cannot conclude commercial improves mean potential to purchase

22. a. \$3.41
b. \$1.67 to \$5.15
Very nice increase

24. a. H_0: $\mu_d \leq 0$
H_a: $\mu_d > 0$
$\bar{d} = 23$, $t = 2.05$
p-value between .05 and .025
Reject H_0; conclude airfares have increased
b. \$487, \$464
c. 5% increase in airfares

26. a. $t = -1.42$
Using t table, p-value is between .10 and .20
Exact p-value = .1718
Do not reject H_0; no difference in mean scores
b. −1.05
c. 1.28; yes

28. a. $\bar{p}_1 - \bar{p}_2 = .48 - .36 = .12$

b. $\bar{p}_1 - \bar{p}_2 \pm z_{.05}\sqrt{\dfrac{\bar{p}_1(1-\bar{p}_1)}{n_1} + \dfrac{\bar{p}_2(1-\bar{p}_2)}{n_2}}$

$$.12 \pm 1.645\sqrt{\frac{.48(1-.48)}{400} + \frac{.36(1-.36)}{300}}$$

.12 ± .0614 (.0586 to .1814)

c. $.12 \pm 1.96\sqrt{\dfrac{.48(1-.48)}{400} + \dfrac{.36(1-.36)}{300}}$

.12 ± .0731 (.0469 to .1931)

29. a. $\bar{p} = \dfrac{n_1\bar{p}_1 + n_2\bar{p}_2}{n_1 + n_2} = \dfrac{200(.22) + 300(.16)}{200 + 300} = .1840$

$$z = \frac{\bar{p}_1 - \bar{p}_2}{\sqrt{\bar{p}(1-\bar{p})\left(\frac{1}{n_1} + \frac{1}{n_2}\right)}}$$

$$= \frac{.22 - .16}{\sqrt{.1840(1-.1840)\left(\frac{1}{200} + \frac{1}{300}\right)}} = 1.70$$

p-value = 1.0000 − .9554 = .0446
b. p-value ≤ .05; reject H_0

30. $\bar{p}_1 = 220/400 = .55$ $\bar{p}_2 = 192/400 = .48$

$$\bar{p}_1 - \bar{p}_2 \pm z_{.025}\sqrt{\frac{\bar{p}_1(1-\bar{p}_1)}{n_1} + \frac{\bar{p}_2(1-\bar{p}_2)}{n_2}}$$

$$.55 - .48 \pm 1.96\sqrt{\frac{.55(1-.55)}{400} + \frac{.48(1-.48)}{400}}$$

.07 ± .0691 (.0009 to .1391)

32. a. H_0: $p_w \leq p_m$
H_a: $p_w > p_m$
b. $\bar{p}_w = .3699$
c. $\bar{p}_m = .3400$
d. p-value = .1093
Do not reject H_0; cannot conclude women are more likely to ask directions

34. a. .64
b. .45
c. .19 ± .0813 (.1087 to .2713)

36. a. H_0: $p_1 - p_2 \leq 0$
H_a: $p_1 - p_2 > 0$
b. .84, .81
c. p-value = .0094
Reject H_0; conclude an increase
d. .005 to .055; yes due to increase

38. a. H_0: $\mu_1 - \mu_2 = 0$
H_a: $\mu_1 - \mu_2 \neq 0$
$z = 2.79$
p-value = .0052
Reject H_0; a significant difference between systems exists

40. a. H_0: $\mu_1 - \mu_2 \leq 0$
H_a: $\mu_1 - \mu_2 > 0$
b. $t = .60$, $df = 57$
Using t table, p-value is greater than .20
Exact p-value = .2754
Do not reject H_0; cannot conclude that funds with loads have a higher mean rate of return

42. a. A decline of \$2.45
b. 2.45 ± 2.15 (.30 to 4.60)
c. 8% decrease
d. \$23.93

44. a. p-value ≈ 0, reject H_0
b. .0468 to .1332

46. a. .35 and .47
b. .12 ± .1037 (.0163 to .2237)
c. Yes, we would expect occupancy rates to be higher

Chapter 11

2. $s^2 = 25$
a. With 19 degrees of freedom, $\chi^2_{.05} = 30.144$ and $\chi^2_{.95} = 10.117$

$$\frac{19(25)}{30.144} \leq \sigma^2 \leq \frac{19(25)}{10.117}$$

$$15.76 \leq \sigma^2 \leq 46.95$$

b. With 19 degrees of freedom, $\chi^2_{.025} = 32.852$ and $\chi^2_{.975} = 8.907$

$$\frac{19(25)}{32.852} \leq \sigma^2 \leq \frac{19(25)}{8.907}$$

$$14.46 \leq \sigma^2 \leq 53.33$$

c. $3.8 \leq \sigma \leq 7.3$

4. a. .22 to .71
b. .47 to .84

6. a. \$41
b. 23.52
c. 17.37 to 36.40

8. a. .4748
b. .6891

c. .2383 to 1.3687
.4882 to 1.1699

9. H_0: $\sigma^2 \leq .0004$
H_a: $\sigma^2 > .0004$

$$\chi^2 = \frac{(n-1)s^2}{\sigma_0^2} = \frac{(30-1)(.0005)}{.0004} = 36.25$$

From table with 29 degrees of freedom, p-value is greater than .10
p-value $> .05$; do not reject H_0
The product specification does not appear to be violated

10. a. 84
b. 118.71
c. 10.90
d. $\chi^2 = 11.54$; p-value $> .20$
Do not reject hypothesis $\sigma = 12$

12. a. .8106
b. $\chi^2 = 9.49$
p-value greater than .20
Do not reject H_0; cannot conclude the variance for the other magazine is different

14. a. $F = 2.4$
p-value between .025 and .05
Reject H_0
b. $F_{.05} = 2.2$; reject H_0

15. a. Larger sample variance is s_1^2

$$F = \frac{s_1^2}{s_2^2} = \frac{8.2}{4} = 2.05$$

Degrees of freedom: 20, 25
From table, area in tail is between .025 and .05
p-value for two-tailed test is between .05 and .10
p-value $> .05$; do not reject H_0
b. For a two-tailed test:
$F_{\alpha/2} = F_{.025} = 2.30$
Reject H_0 if $F \geq 2.30$
$2.05 < 2.30$; do not reject H_0

16. $F = 1.59$
p-value is between .05 and .025
Reject H_0; the Fidelity Fund has greater variance

17. a. Population 1 is 4-year-old automobiles
H_0: $\sigma_1^2 \leq \sigma_2^2$
H_a: $\sigma_1^2 > \sigma_2^2$

b. $$F = \frac{s_1^2}{s_2^2} = \frac{170^2}{100^2} = 2.89$$

Degrees of freedom: 25, 24
From tables, p-value is less than .01
p-value $\leq .01$; reject H_0
Conclude that 4-year-old automobiles have a larger variance in annual repair costs compared to 2-year-old automobiles, which is expected because older automobiles are more likely to have more expensive repairs that lead to greater variance in the annual repair costs

18. $F = 1.44$
p-value greater than .20
Do not reject H_0; the difference between the variances is not statistically significant

20. $F = 5.29$
p-value ≈ 0
Reject H_0; population variances are not equal for seniors and managers

22. a. $F = 4$
p-value less than .01
Reject H_0; greater variability in stopping distance on wet pavement

24. 10.72 to 24.68

26. a. $\chi^2 = 27.44$
p-value between .01 and .025
Reject H_0; variance exceeds maximum requirements
b. .00012 to .00042

28. $\chi^2 = 31.50$
p-value between .05 and .10
Reject H_0; conclude that population variance is greater than 1

30. a. $n = 15$
b. 6.25 to 11.13

32. $F = 1.39$
Do not reject H_0; cannot conclude the variances of grade point averages are different

34. $F = 2.08$
p-value between .05 and .10
Reject H_0; conclude the population variances are not equal

Chapter 12

1. H_0: $p_1 = p_2 = p_3$
H_a: Not all population proportions are equal
Expected frequencies (e_{ij}):

	1	2	3	Total
Yes	132.0	158.4	105.6	396
No	118.0	141.6	94.4	354
Total	250	300	200	750

Chi-square calculations $(f_{ij} - e_{ij})^2/e_{ij}$:

	1	2	3	Total
Yes	2.45	.45	.87	3.77
No	2.75	.50	.98	4.22
				$\chi^2 = 7.99$

$df = k - 1 = (3 - 1) = 2$
χ^2 table with $\chi^2 = 7.99$ shows p-value between .025 and .01
p-value $\leq .05$, reject H_0; not all population proportions are equal

2. a. $\bar{p}_1 = 150/250 = .60$
$\bar{p}_2 = 150/300 = .50$
$\bar{p}_3 = 96/200 = .48$

b. For 1 vs. 2

$$CV_{12} = \sqrt{\chi^2_{\alpha;\,k-1}}\sqrt{\frac{\bar{p}_1(1-\bar{p}_1)}{n_1} + \frac{\bar{p}_2(1-\bar{p}_2)}{n_2}}$$

$$= \sqrt{5.991}\sqrt{\frac{.60(1-.60)}{250} + \frac{.50(1-.50)}{300}} = .1037$$

p_i	p_j	Difference	n_i	n_j	Critical Value	Significant Diff > CV
.60	.50	.10	250	300	.1037	
.60	.48	.12	250	200	.1150	Yes
.50	.48	.02	300	200	.1117	

One comparison is significant, 1 vs. 3

4. a. H_0: $p_1 = p_2 = p_3$
H_a: Not all population proportions are equal

b. Expected frequencies (e_{ij}):

Component	A	B	C	Total
Defective	25	25	25	75
Good	475	475	475	1425
Total	500	500	500	1500

Chi-square calculations $(f_{ij} - e_{ij})^2/e_{ij}$:

Component	A	B	C	Total
Defective	4.00	1.00	9.00	14.00
Good	.21	.05	.47	0.74
				$\chi^2 = 14.74$

$df = k - 1 = (3 - 1) = 2$
χ^2 table, $\chi^2 = 14.74$, p-value is less than .01
p-value $\leq .05$, reject H_0; three suppliers do not provide equal proportions of defective components

c. $\bar{p}_1 = 15/500 = .03$
$\bar{p}_2 = 20/500 = .04$
$\bar{p}_3 = 40/500 = .08$
For supplier A vs. supplier B

$$CV_{ij} = \sqrt{\chi^2_{\alpha;\,k-1}}\sqrt{\frac{\bar{p}_i(1-\bar{p}_i)}{n_i} + \frac{\bar{p}_j(1-\bar{p}_j)}{n_j}}$$

$$= \sqrt{5.991}\sqrt{\frac{.03(1-.03)}{500} + \frac{.04(1-.04)}{500}} = .0284$$

Comparison	p_i	p_j	Difference	n_i	n_j	Critical Value	Significant Diff > CV
A vs. B	.03	.04	.01	500	500	.0284	
A vs. C	.03	.08	.05	500	500	.0351	Yes
B vs. C	.04	.08	.04	500	500	.0366	Yes

Supplier A and supplier B are both significantly different from supplier C

6. a. .14, .09

b. $\chi^2 = 3.41$, $df = 1$
p-value between .10 and .05
Reject H_0; conclude two offices do not have equal error rates

c. z provides options for one-tailed tests

8. $\chi^2 = 5.70$, $df = 4$
p-value greater than .10
Do no reject H_0; no evidence suppliers differ in quality

9. H_0: The column variable is independent of the row variable
H_a: The column variable is not independent of the row variable
Expected frequencies (e_{ij}):

	A	B	C	Total
P	28.5	39.9	45.6	114
Q	21.5	30.1	34.4	86
Total	50	70	80	200

Chi-square calculations $(f_{ij} - e_{ij})^2 / e_{ij}$:

	A	B	C	Total
P	2.54	.42	.42	3.38
Q	3.36	.56	.56	4.48
				$\chi^2 = 7.86$

$df = (2 - 1)(3 - 1) = 2$
Using the χ^2 table, p-value between .01 and .025
p-value $\leq .05$, reject H_0; conclude variables are not independent

10. $\chi^2 = 19.77$, $df = 4$
p-value less than .005
Reject H_0; conclude variables are not independent

11. a. H_0: Ticket purchased is independent of flight
H_a: Ticket purchased is not independent of flight
Expected frequencies:

$e_{11} = 35.59$ $\quad e_{12} = 15.41$
$e_{21} = 150.73$ $\quad e_{22} = 65.27$
$e_{31} = 455.68$ $\quad e_{32} = 197.32$

Observed Frequency (f_i)	Expected Frequency (e_i)	Chi-square $(f_i - e_i)^2 / e_i$
29	35.59	1.22
22	15.41	2.82
95	150.73	20.61
121	65.27	47.59
518	455.68	8.52
135	197.32	19.68
920		$\chi^2 = 100.43$

$df = (r - 1)(c - 1) = (3 - 1)(2 - 1) = 2$
Using the χ^2 table, p-value is less than .005
p-value $\leq .05$, reject H_0; conclude ticket purchased is not independent of the type of flight

b. Column Percentages

	Type of Flight	
Type of Ticket	**Domestic**	**International**
First Class	4.5%	7.9%
Business Class	14.8%	43.5%
Economy Class	80.7%	48.6%

A higher percentage of first-class and business-class tickets are purchased for international flights

12. a. $\chi^2 = 9.44$, $df = 2$
p-value is less than .01
Reject H_0; plan not independent of type of company

b.

Employment Plan	Private	Public
Add Employees	.5139	.2963
No Change	.2639	.3148
Lay Off Employees	.2222	.3889

Employment opportunities better for private companies

14. a. $\chi^2 = 6.57$, $df = 6$
p-value greater than .10
Do not reject H_0; cannot reject assumption of independence

b. 29%, 46%, and 25%
Outstanding is most frequent owner rating

16. a. 6446

b. $\chi^2 = 425.4$, $df = 15$
p-value = 0
Reject H_0; attitude not independent of country

c. Italy (58%), Spain (32%)

18. $\chi^2 = 45.36$, $df = 4$
p-value less than .005
Reject H_0; conclude that the ratings of the hosts are not independent

19. a. Expected frequencies:
$e_1 = 200(.40) = 80$, $e_2 = 200(.40) = 80$
$e_3 = 200(.20) = 40$
Observed frequencies: $f_1 = 60, f_2 = 120, f_3 = 20$

$$\chi^2 = \frac{(60-80)^2}{80} + \frac{(120-80)^2}{80} + \frac{(20-40)^2}{40}$$

$$= \frac{400}{80} + \frac{1600}{80} + \frac{400}{40} = 35$$

$df = k - 1 = 3 - 1 = 2$
$\chi^2 = 35$ shows p-value less than .005
p-value $\leq .01$; reject H_0
Conclude proportions differ from .40, .40, and .20

b. Reject H_0 if $\chi^2 \geq 9.210$; reject H_0

20. With $n = 30$, use six classes, each probability = .1667
$\bar{x} = 22.8$, $s = 6.27$

z	Cutoff value of x
−.98	22.8 − .98 (6.27) = 16.66
−.43	22.8 − .43 (6.27) = 20.11
0	22.8 + 0 (6.27) = 22.80
.43	22.8 + .43 (6.27) = 25.49
.98	22.8 + .98 (6.27) = 28.94

Interval	Observed Frequency	Expected Frequency	Difference
less than 16.66	3	5	−2
16.66–20.11	7	5	2
20.11–22.80	5	5	0
22.80–25.49	7	5	2
25.49–28.94	3	5	−2
28.94 and up	5	5	0

$$\chi^2 = \frac{(-2)^2}{5} + \frac{(2)^2}{5} + \frac{(0)^2}{5} + \frac{(2)^2}{5} + \frac{(-2)^2}{5} + \frac{(0)^2}{5} + \frac{16}{5}$$

$$= 3.20$$

$df = k - 2 - 1 = 6 - 2 - 1 = 3$
$\chi^2 = 3.20$ shows p-value greater than .10
p-value $> .05$; do not reject H_0; normal distribution cannot be rejected

21. H_0: The population proportions are .29, .28, .25, and .18
H_a: The proportions are not as shown above
Expected frequencies: $300(.29) = 87$, $300(.28) = 84$
$300(.25) = 75$, $300(.18) = 54$
Observed frequencies: $f_1 = 95, f_2 = 70, f_3 = 89, f_4 = 46$

$$\chi^2 = \frac{(95-87)^2}{87} + \frac{(70-84)^2}{84} + \frac{(89-75)^2}{75}$$

$$+ \frac{(46-54)^2}{54} = 6.87$$

$df = k - 1 = 4 - 1 = 3$
$\chi^2 = 6.87$ shows p-value between .05 and .10
p-value $> .05$; do not reject H_0; no significant change in viewing audience proportions

22. $\chi^2 = 5.85$, $df = 5$
p-value greater than .10
Do not reject H_0; cannot reject the hypothesis that percentages are as stated

24. a. $\chi^2 = 14.33$, $df = 6$
p-value between .05 and .025
Reject H_0; conclude proportion not the same for each day of the week

b. 15.17, 11.90, 12.62, 11.19, 13.10, 16.43, 19.05
Saturday and Friday have the highest percentage

26. $\chi^2 = 2.8$, $df = 3$
p-value greater than .10
Do not reject H_0; assumption of a normal distribution cannot be rejected

28. a. 8.8%, 11.7%, 9.0%, 8.5%

b. $\chi^2 = 2.48$, $df = 3$
p-value greater than .10
Do not reject H_0; cannot reject assumption that the population proportions are equal

30. a. $\chi^2 = 9.56$, $df = 2$
p-value is less than .01
Reject H_0; conclude preferred pace is not independent of gender

b. Women slower 75.17% to 67.65%
Men faster 26.47% to 16.55%

32. $\chi^2 = 6.17$, $df = 6$
p-value greater than .10
Do not reject H_0; assumption county and day of week are independent is not rejected

34. $\chi^2 = 2.00$, $df = 5$
p-value greater than .10
Do not reject H_0; assumption of normal distribution cannot be rejected

Chapter 13

1. a. $\bar{\bar{x}} = (156 + 142 + 134)/3 = 144$

$$\text{SSTR} = \sum_{j=1}^{k} n_j(\bar{x}_j - \bar{\bar{x}})^2$$
$$= 6(156 - 144)^2 + 6(142 - 144)^2 + 6(134 - 144)^2$$
$$= 1488$$

b. $\text{MSTR} = \dfrac{\text{SSTR}}{k - 1} = \dfrac{1488}{2} = 744$

c. $s_1^2 = 164.4, \quad s_2^2 = 131.2, \quad s_3^2 = 110.4$

$$\text{SSE} = \sum_{j=1}^{k} (n_j - 1)s_j^2$$
$$= 5(164.4) + 5(131.2) + 5(110.4)$$
$$= 2030$$

d. $\text{MSE} = \dfrac{\text{SSE}}{n_T - k} = \dfrac{2030}{18 - 3} = 135.3$

e.

Source of Variation	Sum of Squares	Degrees of Freedom	Mean Square	F	p-value
Treatments	1488	2	744	5.50	.0162
Error	2030	15	135.3		
Total	3518	17			

f. $F = \dfrac{\text{MSTR}}{\text{MSE}} = \dfrac{744}{135.3} = 5.50$

From the F table (2 numerator degrees of freedom and 15 denominator), p-value is between .01 and .025
Using Excel or Minitab, the p-value corresponding to $F = 5.50$ is .0162
Because p-value $\le \alpha = .05$, we reject the hypothesis that the means for the three treatments are equal

2.

Source of Variation	Sum of Squares	Degrees of Freedom	Mean Square	F	p-value
Treatments	300	4	75	14.07	.0000
Error	160	30	5.33		
Total	460	34			

4.

Source of Variation	Sum of Squares	Degrees of Freedom	Mean Square	F	p-value
Treatments	150	2	75	4.80	.0233
Error	250	16	15.63		
Total	400	18			

Reject H_0 because p-value $\le \alpha = .05$

6. Because p-value $= .0082$ is less than $\alpha = .05$, we reject the null hypothesis that the means of the three treatments are equal

8. $\bar{\bar{x}} = (79 + 74 + 66)/3 = 73$

$$\text{SSTR} = \sum_{j=1}^{k} n_j(\bar{x}_j - \bar{\bar{x}})^2 = 6(79 - 73)^2 + 6(74 - 73)^2 + 6(66 - 73)^2 = 516$$

$$\text{MSTR} = \frac{\text{SSTR}}{k - 1} = \frac{516}{2} = 258$$

$s_1^2 = 34 \qquad s_2^2 = 20 \qquad s_3^2 = 32$

$$\text{SSE} = \sum_{j=1}^{k} (n_j - 1)s_j^2 = 5(34) + 5(20) + 5(32) = 430$$

$$\text{MSE} = \frac{\text{SSE}}{n_T - k} = \frac{430}{18 - 3} = 28.67$$

$$F = \frac{\text{MSTR}}{\text{MSE}} = \frac{258}{28.67} = 9.00$$

Source of Variation	Sum of Squares	Degrees of Freedom	Mean Square	F	p-value
Treatments	516	2	258	9.00	.003
Error	430	15	28.67		
Total	946	17			

Using F table (2 numerator degrees of freedom and 15 denominator), p-value is less than .01
Using Excel or Minitab, the p-value corresponding to $F = 9.00$ is .003
Because p-value $\le \alpha = .05$, we reject the null hypothesis that the means for the three plants are equal; in other words, analysis of variance supports the conclusion that the population mean examination scores at the three NCP plants are not equal

10. p-value $= .0000$
Because p-value $\le \alpha = .05$, we reject the null hypothesis that the means for the three groups are equal

12. p-value = .0038
Because p-value $\leq \alpha = .05$, we reject the null hypothesis that the mean meal prices are the same for the three types of restaurants

13. a. $\bar{\bar{x}} = (30 + 45 + 36)/3 = 37$

$$\text{SSTR} = \sum_{j=1}^{k} n_j(\bar{x}_j - \bar{\bar{x}})^2 = 5(30 - 37)^2 + 5(45 - 37)^2 + 5(36 - 37)^2 = 570$$

$$\text{MSTR} = \frac{\text{SSTR}}{k - 1} = \frac{570}{2} = 285$$

$$\text{SSE} = \sum_{j=1}^{k} (n_j - 1)s_j^2 = 4(6) + 4(4) + 4(6.5) = 66$$

$$\text{MSE} = \frac{\text{SSE}}{n_T - k} = \frac{66}{15 - 3} = 5.5$$

$$F = \frac{\text{MSTR}}{\text{MSE}} = \frac{285}{5.5} = 51.82$$

Using F table (2 numerator degrees of freedom and 12 denominator), p-value is less than .01

Using Excel or Minitab, the p-value corresponding to $F = 51.82$ is .0000

Because p-value $\leq \alpha = .05$, we reject the null hypothesis that the means of the three populations are equal

b. $\text{LSD} = t_{\alpha/2}\sqrt{\text{MSE}\left(\frac{1}{n_i} + \frac{1}{n_j}\right)}$

$$= t_{.025}\sqrt{5.5\left(\frac{1}{5} + \frac{1}{5}\right)}$$

$$= 2.179\sqrt{2.2} = 3.23$$

$|\bar{x}_1 - \bar{x}_2| = |30 - 45| = 15 >$ LSD; significant difference
$|\bar{x}_1 - \bar{x}_3| = |30 - 36| = 6 >$ LSD; significant difference
$|\bar{x}_2 - \bar{x}_3| = |45 - 36| = 9 >$ LSD; significant difference

c. $\bar{x}_1 - \bar{x}_2 \pm t_{\alpha/2}\sqrt{\text{MSE}\left(\frac{1}{n_1} + \frac{1}{n_2}\right)}$

$$(30 - 45) \pm 2.179\sqrt{5.5\left(\frac{1}{5} + \frac{1}{5}\right)}$$

$$-15 \pm 3.23 = -18.23 \text{ to } -11.77$$

14. a. Significant; p-value = .0106
b. LSD = 15.34
1 and 2; significant
1 and 3; not significant
2 and 3; significant

15. a.

	Manufacturer 1	Manufacturer 2	Manufacturer 3
Sample Mean	23	28	21
Sample Variance	6.67	4.67	3.33

$\bar{\bar{x}} = (23 + 28 + 21)/3 = 24$

$$\text{SSTR} = \sum_{j=1}^{k} n_j(\bar{x}_j - \bar{\bar{x}})^2$$
$$= 4(23 - 24)^2 + 4(28 - 24)^2 + 4(21 - 24)^2$$
$$= 104$$

$$\text{MSTR} = \frac{\text{SSTR}}{k - 1} = \frac{104}{2} = 52$$

$$\text{SSE} = \sum_{j=1}^{k} (n_j - 1)s_j^2$$
$$= 3(6.67) + 3(4.67) + 3(3.33) = 44.01$$

$$\text{MSE} = \frac{\text{SSE}}{n_T - k} = \frac{44.01}{12 - 3} = 4.89$$

$$F = \frac{\text{MSTR}}{\text{MSE}} = \frac{52}{4.89} = 10.63$$

Using F table (2 numerator degrees of freedom and 9 denominator), p-value is less than .01

Using Excel or Minitab, the p-value corresponding to $F = 10.63$ is .0043

Because p-value $\leq \alpha = .05$, we reject the null hypothesis that the mean time needed to mix a batch of material is the same for each manufacturer

b. $\text{LSD} = t_{\alpha/2}\sqrt{\text{MSE}\left(\frac{1}{n_1} + \frac{1}{n_3}\right)}$

$$= t_{.025}\sqrt{4.89\left(\frac{1}{4} + \frac{1}{4}\right)}$$

$$= 2.262\sqrt{2.45} = 3.54$$

Since $|\bar{x}_1 - \bar{x}_3| = |23 - 21| = 2 < 3.54$, there does not appear to be any significant difference between the means for manufacturer 1 and manufacturer 3

16. $\bar{x}_1 - \bar{x}_2 \pm$ LSD
$23 - 28 \pm 3.54$
$-5 \pm 3.54 = -8.54$ to -1.46

18. a. Significant; p-value = .0000
b. Significant; $2.3 >$ LSD $= 1.19$

20. a. Significant; p-value = .011
b. Comparing North and South
$|7702 - 5566| = 2136 >$ LSD $= 1620.76$
significant difference

Comparing North and West
$|7702 - 8430| = 728 >$ LSD $= 1620.76$
no significant difference

Comparing South and West
$|5566 - 8430| = 2864 >$ LSD $= 1775.45$
significant difference

21. ***Treatment Means***
$\bar{x}_{\cdot 1} = 13.6, \quad \bar{x}_{\cdot 2} = 11.0, \quad \bar{x}_{\cdot 3} = 10.6$

Block Means
$\bar{x}_{1\cdot} = 9, \bar{x}_{2\cdot} = 7.67, \bar{x}_{3\cdot} = 15.67, \bar{x}_{4\cdot} = 18.67, \bar{x}_{5\cdot} = 7.67$

Overall Mean
$\bar{\bar{x}} = 176/15 = 11.73$

Step 1

$$\text{SST} = \sum_i \sum_j (x_{ij} - \bar{\bar{x}})^2$$
$$= (10 - 11.73)^2 + (9 - 11.73)^2 + \cdots + (8 - 11.73)^2$$
$$= 354.93$$

Step 2

$$\text{SSTR} = b \sum_j (\bar{x}_{\cdot j} - \bar{\bar{x}})^2$$
$$= 5[(13.6 - 11.73)^2 + (11.0 - 11.73)^2 + (10.6 - 11.73)^2] = 26.53$$

Step 3

$$\text{SSBL} = k \sum_j (\bar{x}_{i\cdot} - \bar{\bar{x}})^2$$
$$= 3[(9 - 11.73)^2 + (7.67 - 11.73)^2 + (15.67 - 11.73)^2 + (18.67 - 11.73)^2 + (7.67 - 11.73)^2] = 312.32$$

Step 4

$$\text{SSE} = \text{SST} - \text{SSTR} - \text{SSBL}$$
$$= 354.93 - 26.53 - 312.32 = 16.08$$

Source of Variation	Sum of Squares	Degrees of Freedom	Mean Square	F	p-value
Treatments	26.53	2	13.27	6.60	.0203
Blocks	312.32	4	78.08		
Error	16.08	8	2.01		
Total	354.93	14			

From the F table (2 numerator degrees of freedom and 8 denominator), p-value is between .01 and .025

Actual p-value = .0203

Because p-value $\leq \alpha = .05$, we reject the null hypothesis that the means of the three treatments are equal

22.

Source of Variation	Sum of Squares	Degrees of Freedom	Mean Square	F	p-value
Treatments	310	4	77.5	17.69	.0005
Blocks	85	2	42.5		
Error	35	8	4.38		
Total	430	14			

Significant; p-value $\leq \alpha = .05$

24. p-value = .0453

Because p-value $\leq \alpha = .05$, we reject the null hypothesis that the mean tune-up times are the same for both analyzers

26. a. Significant; p-value = .0231

b. Writing section

28. *Step 1*

$$\text{SST} = \sum_i \sum_j \sum_k (x_{ijk} - \bar{\bar{x}})^2$$
$$= (135 - 111)^2 + (165 - 111)^2 + \cdots + (136 - 111)^2 = 9028$$

Step 2

$$\text{SSA} = br \sum_i (\bar{x}_{j\cdot} - \bar{\bar{x}})^2$$
$$= 3(2)[(104 - 111)^2 + (118 - 111)^2] = 588$$

Step 3

$$\text{SSB} = ar \sum_j (\bar{x}_{\cdot j} - \bar{\bar{x}})^2$$
$$= 2(2)[(130 - 111)^2 + (97 - 111)^2 + (106 - 111)^2]$$
$$= 2328$$

Step 4

$$\text{SSAB} = r \sum_i \sum_j (\bar{x}_{ij} - \bar{x}_{i\cdot} - \bar{x}_{\cdot j} + \bar{\bar{x}})^2$$
$$= 2[(150 - 104 - 130 + 111)^2 + (78 - 104 - 97 + 111)^2 + \cdots + (128 - 118 - 106 + 111)^2] = 4392$$

Step 5

$$\text{SSE} = \text{SST} - \text{SSA} - \text{SSB} - \text{SSAB}$$
$$= 9028 - 588 - 2328 - 4392 = 1720$$

Source of Variation	Sum of Squares	Degrees of Freedom	Mean Square	F	p-value
Factor A	588	1	588	2.05	.2022
Factor B	2328	2	1164	4.06	.0767
Interaction	4392	2	2196	7.66	.0223
Error	1720	6	286.67		
Total	9028	11			

Factor A: $F = 2.05$

Using F table (1 numerator degree of freedom and 6 denominator), p-value is greater than .10

Using Excel or Minitab, the p-value corresponding to $F = 2.05$ is .2022

Because p-value $> \alpha = .05$, Factor A is not significant

Factor B: $F = 4.06$

Using F table (2 numerator degrees of freedom and 6 denominator), p-value is between .05 and .10

Using Excel or Minitab, the p-value corresponding to $F = 4.06$ is .0767

Because p-value $> \alpha = .05$, Factor B is not significant

Interaction: $F = 7.66$

Using F table (2 numerator degrees of freedom and 6 denominator), p-value is between .01 and .025

Using Excel or Minitab, the p-value corresponding to $F = 7.66$ is .0223

Because p-value $\leq \alpha = .05$, interaction is significant

30. Design: p-value = .0104; significant
Size: p-value = .1340; not significant
Interaction: p-value = .2519; not significant

32. Class: p-value = .0002; significant
Type: p-value = .0006; significant
Interaction: p-value = .4229; not significant

34. Significant; p-value = .0134

36. Not significant; p-value = .088

38. Not significant; p-value $= .2455$

40. a. Significant; p-value $= .0175$

42. The blocks correspond to the 7 weekend series (Opponent) and the treatments correspond to the days for the series (Day)

The Minitab two-way output is

Source	DF	SS	MS	F	P
Day	2	101469683	50734841	2.69	0.109
Opponent	6	79329936	13221656	0.70	0.655
Error	12	226577122	18881427		
Total	20	407376741			

Because the p-value for Day (.109) is greater than $\alpha = .05$, there is no significant difference in the mean attendance per game for games played on Friday, Saturday, and Sunday; these data do not suggest a particular day on which the Astros should schedule these promotions

44. Type of machine (p-value $= .0226$) is significant; type of loading system (p-value $= .7913$) and interaction (p-value $= .0671$) are not significant

Chapter 14

1. a.

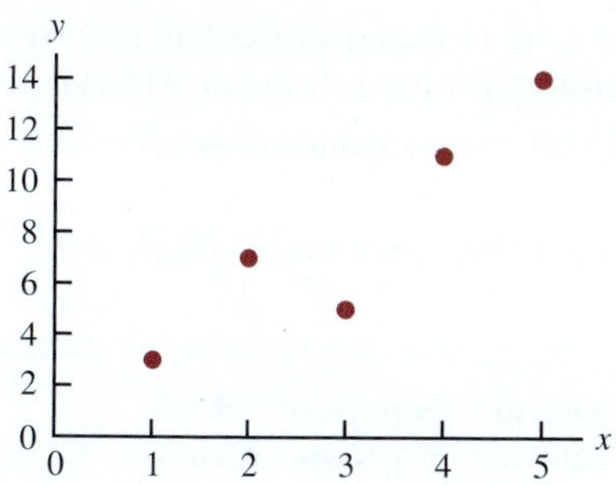

b. There appears to be a positive linear relationship between x and y

c. Many different straight lines can be drawn to provide a linear approximation of the relationship between x and y; in part (d) we will determine the equation of a straight line that "best" represents the relationship according to the least squares criterion

d. Summations needed to compute the slope and y-intercept:

$$\bar{x} = \frac{\Sigma x_i}{n} = \frac{15}{5} = 3, \quad \bar{y} = \frac{\Sigma y_i}{n} = \frac{40}{5} = 8,$$

$$\Sigma(x_i - \bar{x})(y_i - \bar{y}) = 26, \quad \Sigma(x_i - \bar{x})^2 = 10$$

$$b_1 = \frac{\Sigma(x_i - \bar{x})(y_i - \bar{y})}{\Sigma(x_i - \bar{x})^2} = \frac{26}{10} = 2.6$$

$$b_0 = \bar{y} - b_1\bar{x} = 8 - (2.6)(3) = 0.2$$

$$\hat{y} = 0.2 - 2.6x$$

e. $\hat{y} = .2 + 2.6x = .2 + 2.6(4) = 10.6$

2. b. There appears to be a negative linear relationship between x and y

d. $\hat{y} = 68 - 3x$

e. 38

4. a.

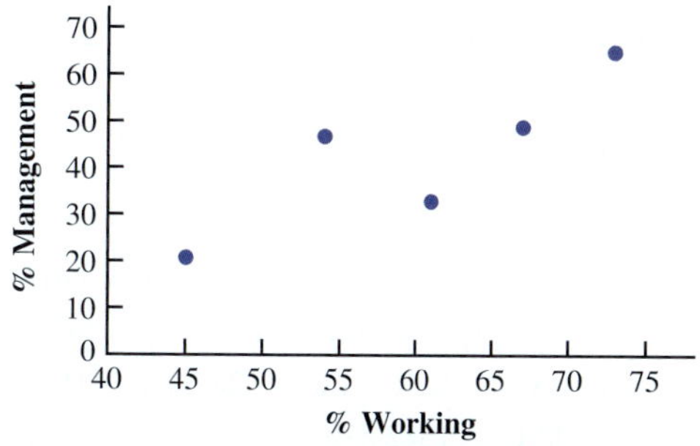

b. There appears to be a positive linear relationship between the percentage of women working in the five companies (x) and the percentage of management jobs held by women in that company (y)

c. Many different straight lines can be drawn to provide a linear approximation of the relationship between x and y; in part (d) we will determine the equation of a straight line that "best" represents the relationship according to the least squares criterion

d. $$\bar{x} = \frac{\Sigma x_i}{n} = \frac{300}{5} = 60 \quad \bar{y} = \frac{\Sigma y_i}{n} = \frac{215}{5} = 43$$

$$\Sigma(x_i - \bar{x})(y_i - \bar{y}) = 624 \quad \Sigma(x_i - \bar{x})^2 = 480$$

$$b_1 = \frac{\Sigma(x_i - \bar{x})(y_i - \bar{y})}{\Sigma(x_i - \bar{x})^2} = \frac{624}{480} = 1.3$$

$$b_0 = \bar{y} - b_1\bar{x} = 43 - 1.3(60) = -35$$

$$\hat{y} = -35 + 1.3x$$

e. $\hat{y} = -35 + 1.3x = -35 + 1.3(60) = 43\%$

6. c. $\hat{y} = -70.391 + 17.175x$

e. 43.8 or approximately 44%

8. c. $\hat{y} = .2046 + .9077x$

e. 3.29 or approximately 3.3

10. c. $\hat{y} = -167.81 + 2.7149x$

e. Yes

12. c. $\hat{y} = 17.49 + 1.0334x$

d. \$150

14. c. $\hat{y} = 37.1217 + .51758x$

d. 73

15. a. $\hat{y}_i = .2 + 2.6x_i$ and $\bar{y} = 8$

x_i	y_i	$\hat{y}_i$	$y_i - \hat{y}_i$	$(y_i - \hat{y}_i)^2$	$y_i - \bar{y}$	$(y_i - \bar{y})^2$
1	3	2.8	.2	.04	−5	25
2	7	5.4	1.6	2.56	−1	1
3	5	8.0	−3.0	9.00	−3	9
4	11	10.6	.4	.16	3	9
5	14	13.2	.8	.64	6	36
				SSE = 12.40		SST = 80

SSR = SST − SSE = 80 − 12.4 = 67.6

b. $r^2 = \frac{\text{SSR}}{\text{SST}} = \frac{67.6}{80} = .845$

The least squares line provided a good fit; 84.5% of the variability in y has been explained by the least squares line

c. $r_{xy} = \sqrt{.845} = +.9192$

16. a. SSE = 230, SST = 1850, SSR = 1620

b. $r^2 = .876$

c. $r_{xy} = -.936$

18. a. $\bar{x} = \Sigma x_i/n = 600/6 = 100$ $\bar{y} = \Sigma y_i/n = 330/6 = 55$

$\text{SST} = \Sigma(y_i - \bar{y})^2 = 1800$ $\text{SSE} = \Sigma(y_i - \hat{y}_i)^2 = 287.624$

SSR = SST − SSR = 1800 − 287.624 = 1512.376

b. $r^2 = \frac{\text{SSR}}{\text{SST}} = \frac{1512.376}{1800} = .84$

c. $r = \sqrt{r^2} = \sqrt{.84} = .917$

20. a. $\hat{y} = 28{,}574 - 1439x$

b. $r^2 = .864$

c. $6989

22. a. .77

b. Yes

c. $r_{xy} = +.88$, strong

23. a. $s^2 = \text{MSE} = \frac{\text{SSE}}{n-2} = \frac{12.4}{3} = 4.133$

b. $s = \sqrt{\text{MSE}} = \sqrt{4.133} = 2.033$

c. $\Sigma(x_i - \bar{x})^2 = 10$

$$s_{b_1} = \frac{s}{\sqrt{\Sigma(x_i - \bar{x})^2}} = \frac{2.033}{\sqrt{10}} = .643$$

d. $t = \frac{b_1 - \beta_1}{s_{b_1}} = \frac{2.6 - 0}{.643} = 4.044$

From the t table (3 degrees of freedom), area in tail is between .01 and .025

p-value is between .02 and .05

Using Excel or Minitab, the p-value corresponding to $t = 4.04$ is .0272

Because p-value $\leq \alpha$, we reject H_0: $\beta_1 = 0$

e. $\text{MSR} = \frac{\text{SSR}}{1} = 67.6$

$$F = \frac{\text{MSR}}{\text{MSE}} = \frac{67.6}{4.133} = 16.36$$

From the F table (1 numerator degree of freedom and 3 denominator), p-value is between .025 and .05

Using Excel or Minitab, the p-value corresponding to $F = 16.36$ is .0272

Because p-value $\leq \alpha$, we reject H_0: $\beta_1 = 0$

Source of Variation	Sum of Squares	Degrees of Freedom	Mean Square	*F*	*p*-value
Regression	67.6	1	67.6	16.36	.0272
Error	12.4	3	4.133		
Total	80	4			

24. a. 76.6667

b. 8.7560

c. .6526

d. Significant; p-value = .0193

e. Significant; p-value = .0193

26. a. In the statement of exercise 18, $\hat{y} = 23.194 + .318x$

In solving exercise 18, we found SSE = 287.624

$s^2 = \text{MSE} = \text{SSE}/(n-2) = 287.624/4 = 71.906$

$s = \sqrt{\text{MSE}} = \sqrt{71.906} = 8.4797$

$\Sigma(x - \bar{x})^2 = 14{,}950$

$$s_{b_1} = \frac{s}{\sqrt{\Sigma(x - \bar{x})^2}} = \frac{8.4797}{\sqrt{14{,}950}} = .0694$$

$$t = \frac{b_1}{s_{b_1}} = \frac{.318}{.0694} = 4.58$$

Using t table (4 degrees of freedom), area in tail is between .005 and .01

p-value is between .01 and .02

Using Excel, the p-value corresponding to $t = 4.58$ is .010

Because p-value $\leq \alpha$, we reject H_0: $\beta_1 = 0$; there is a significant relationship between price and overall score

b. In exercise 18 we found SSR = 1512.376

MSR = SSR/1 = 1512.376/1 = 1512.376

F = MSR/MSE = 1512.376/71.906 = 21.03

Using F table (1 degree of freedom numerator and 4 denominator), p-value is between .025 and .01

Using Excel, the p-value corresponding to $F = 11.74$ is .010

Because p-value $\leq \alpha$, we reject H_0: $\beta_1 = 0$

c.

Source of Variation	Sum of Squares	Degrees of Freedom	Mean Square	*F*	*p*-value
Regression	1512.376	1	1512.376	21.03	.010
Error	287.624	4	71.906		
Total	1800	5			

28. They are related; p-value = .000

30. Significant; p-value = .0042

32. a. $s = 2.033$

$\bar{x} = 3$, $\Sigma(x_i - \bar{x})^2 = 10$

$$s_{\hat{y}^*} = s\sqrt{\frac{1}{n} + \frac{(x^* - \bar{x})^2}{\Sigma(x_i - \bar{x})^2}}$$

$$= 2.033\sqrt{\frac{1}{5} + \frac{(4-3)^2}{10}} = 1.11$$

b. $\hat{y}^* = .2 + 2.6x^* = .2 + 2.6(4) = 10.6$

$\hat{y}^* \pm t_{\alpha/2}s_{\hat{y}^*}$

$10.6 \pm 3.182(1.11)$

10.6 ± 3.53, or 7.07 to 14.13

c. $s_{\text{pred}} = s\sqrt{1 + \frac{1}{n} + \frac{(x^* - \bar{x})^2}{\Sigma(x_i - \bar{x})^2}}$

$= 2.033\sqrt{1 + \frac{1}{5} + \frac{(4-3)^2}{10}} = 2.32$

d. $\hat{y}^* \pm t_{\alpha/2}s_{\text{pred}}$

$10.6 \pm 3.182(2.32)$

10.6 ± 7.38, or 3.22 to 17.98

34. Confidence interval: 8.65 to 21.15

Prediction interval: −4.50 to 41.30

35. a. $\hat{y}^* = 2090.5 + 581.1x^* = 2090.5 + 581.1(3) = 3833.8$

b. $s = \sqrt{\text{MSE}} = \sqrt{21{,}284} = 145.89$

$\bar{x} = 3.2,\ \Sigma(x_i - \bar{x})^2 = 0.74$

$s_{\hat{y}^*} = s\sqrt{\frac{1}{n} + \frac{(x^* - \bar{x})^2}{\Sigma(x_i - \bar{x})^2}}$

$= 145.89\sqrt{\frac{1}{6} + \frac{(3-3.2)^2}{0.74}} = 68.54$

$\hat{y}^* \pm t_{\alpha/2}s_{\hat{y}^*}$

$3833.8 \pm 2.776(68.54) = 3833.8 \pm 190.27$

or \$3643.53 to \$4024.07

c. $s_{\text{pred}} = s\sqrt{1 + \frac{1}{n} + \frac{(x^* - \bar{x})^2}{\Sigma(x_i - \bar{x})^2}}$

$= 145.89\sqrt{1 + \frac{1}{6} + \frac{(3-3.2)^2}{0.74}} = 161.19$

$\hat{y}^* \pm t_{\alpha/2}s_{\text{pred}}$

$3833.8 \pm 2.776(161.19) = 3833.8 \pm 447.46$

or \$3386.34 to \$4281.26

d. As expected, the prediction interval is much wider than the confidence interval. This is due to the fact that it is more difficult to predict the starting salary for one new student with a GPA of 3.0 than it is to estimate the mean for all students with a GPA of 3.0.

36. a. \$112,190 to \$119,810

b. \$104,710 to \$127,290

38. a. \$5046.67

b. \$3815.10 to \$6278.24

c. Not out of line

40. a. 9

b. $\hat{y} = 20.0 + 7.21x$

c. 1.3626

d. SSE = SST − SSR = 51,984.1 − 41,587.3 = 10,396.8

MSE = 10,396.8/7 = 1485.3

$F = \frac{\text{MSR}}{\text{MSE}} = \frac{41{,}587.3}{1485.3} = 28.0$

From the F table (1 numerator degree of freedom and 7 denominator), p-value is less than .01

Using Excel or Minitab, the p-value corresponding to $F = 28.0$ is .0011

Because p-value $\le \alpha = .05$, we reject H_0: $\beta_1 = 0$

e. $\hat{y} = 20.0 + 7.21(50) = 380.5$, or \$380,500

42. a. $\hat{y} = 80.0 + 50.0x$

b. 30

c. Significant; p-value = .000

d. \$680,000

44. b. Yes

c. $\hat{y} = 2044.38 - 28.35$ weight

d. Significant; p-value = .000

e. .774; a good fit

45. a. $\bar{x} = \frac{\Sigma x_i}{n} = \frac{70}{5} = 14,\ \bar{y} = \frac{\Sigma y_i}{n} = \frac{76}{5} = 15.2,$

$\Sigma(x_i - \bar{x})(y_i - \bar{y}) = 200,\ \Sigma(x_i - \bar{x})^2 = 126$

$b_1 = \frac{\Sigma(x_i - \bar{x})(y_i - \bar{y})}{\Sigma(x_i - \bar{x})^2} = \frac{200}{126} = 1.5873$

$b_0 = \bar{y} - b_1\bar{x} = 15.2 - (1.5873)(14) = -7.0222$

$\hat{y} = -7.02 + 1.59x$

b.

x_i	y_i	$\hat{y}_i$	$y_i - \hat{y}_i$
6	6	2.52	3.48
11	8	10.47	−2.47
15	12	16.83	−4.83
18	20	21.60	−1.60
20	30	24.78	5.22

c.

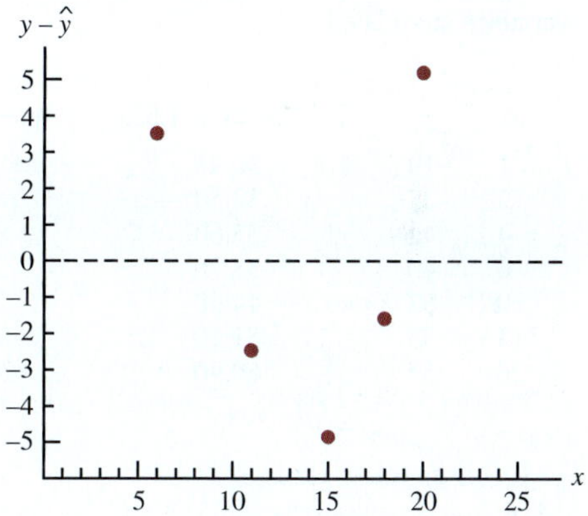

With only five observations, it is difficult to determine whether the assumptions are satisfied; however, the plot does suggest curvature in the residuals, which would indicate that the error term assumptions are not satisfied; the scatter diagram for these data also indicates that the underlying relationship between x and y may be curvilinear

d. $s^2 = 23.78$

$h_i = \frac{1}{n} + \frac{(x_i - \bar{x})^2}{\Sigma(x_i - \bar{x})^2} = \frac{1}{5} + \frac{(x_i - 14)^2}{126}$

x_i	h_i	$s_{y_i - \hat{y}_i}$	$y_i - \hat{y}_i$	Standardized Residuals
6	.7079	2.64	3.48	1.32
11	.2714	4.16	−2.47	−.59
15	.2079	4.34	−4.83	−1.11
18	.3270	4.00	−1.60	−.40
20	.4857	3.50	5.22	1.49

e. The plot of the standardized residuals against $\hat{y}$ has the same shape as the original residual plot; as stated in part (c), the curvature observed indicates that the assumptions regarding the error term may not be satisfied

46. a. $\hat{y} = 2.32 + .64x$

b. No; the variance appears to increase for larger values of x

47. a. Let x = advertising expenditures and y = revenue

$\hat{y} = 29.4 + 1.55x$

b. SST = 1002, SSE = 310.28, SSR = 691.72

$$\text{MSR} = \frac{\text{SSR}}{1} = 691.72$$

$$\text{MSE} = \frac{\text{SSE}}{n-2} = \frac{310.28}{5} = 62.0554$$

$$F = \frac{\text{MSR}}{\text{MSE}} = \frac{691.72}{62.0554} = 11.15$$

From the F table (1 numerator degree of freedom and 5 denominator), p-value is between .01 and .025

Using Excel or Minitab, p-value = .0206

Because p-value $\leq \alpha = .05$, we conclude that the two variables are related

c.

x_i	y_i	$\hat{y}_i = 29.40 + 1.55x_i$	$y_i - \hat{y}_i$
1	19	30.95	−11.95
2	32	32.50	−.50
4	44	35.60	8.40
6	40	38.70	1.30
10	52	44.90	7.10
14	53	51.10	1.90
20	54	60.40	−6.40

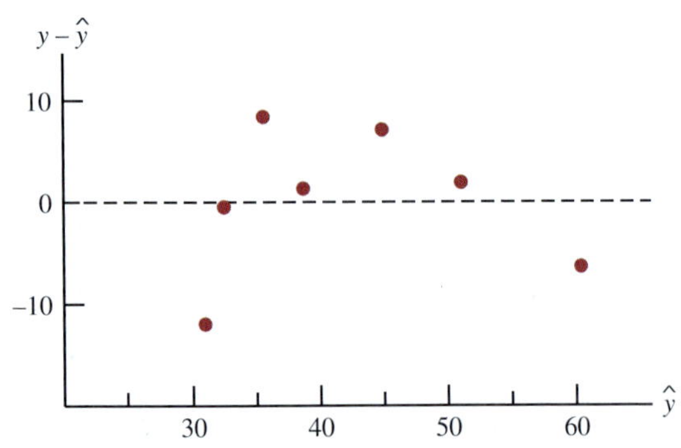

d. The residual plot leads us to question the assumption of a linear relationship between x and y; even though the relationship is significant at the $\alpha = .05$ level, it would be extremely dangerous to extrapolate beyond the range of the data

48. b. Yes

50. a. Using Minitab, we obtained the estimated regression equation $\hat{y} = 66.1 + .402x$; a portion of the Minitab output is shown in Figure D14.50; the fitted values and standardized residuals are shown:

x_i	y_i	$\hat{y}_i$	Standardized Residuals
135	145	120.41	2.11
110	100	110.35	−1.08
130	120	118.40	.14
145	120	124.43	−.38
175	130	136.50	−.78
160	130	130.47	−.04
120	110	114.38	−.41

b.

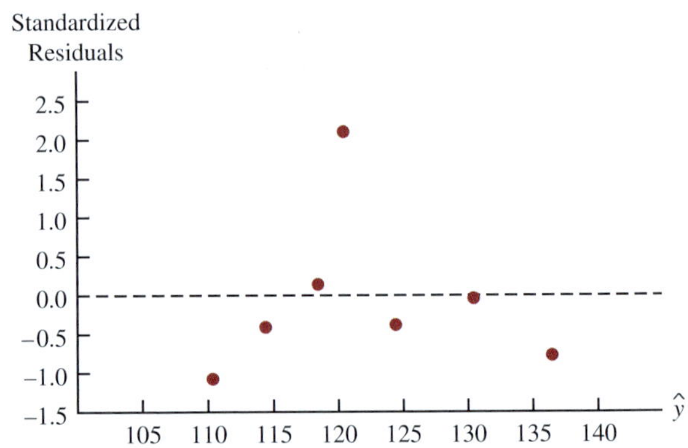

The standardized residual plot indicates that the observation $x = 135$, $y = 145$ may be an outlier; note that this observation has a standardized residual of 2.11

c. The scatter diagram is shown:

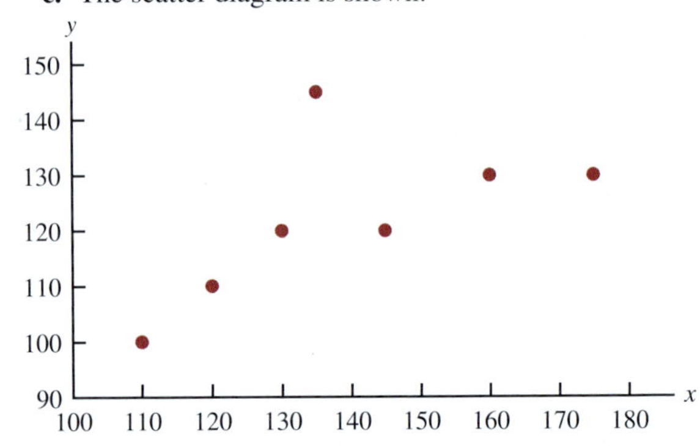

The scatter diagram also indicates that the observation $x = 135$, $y = 145$ may be an outlier; the implication is that for simple linear regression outliers can be identified by looking at the scatter diagram

52. b. $\hat{y} = 91.0 - 0.917x$

b. Smithsonian Institution: outlier

American Cancer Society: influential observation

54. b. Value = −252 + 5.83 Revenue

c. There are five unusual observations (9, 19, 21, 22, and 32).

58. b. $\hat{y} = -669 + .157$ DJIA
c. Significant; p-value = .001
d. $r^2 = .949$; excellent fit

60. b. GR(%) = 25.4 + .285 RR(%)
c. Significant; p-value = .000
d. No; $r^2 = .449$
e. Yes
f. Yes

62. a. $\hat{y} = 22.2 - .148x$
b. Significant relationship; p-value = .028
c. Good fit; $r^2 = .739$
d. 12.294 to 17.271

64. a. $\hat{y} = 220 + 132x$
b. Significant; p-value = .000
c. $r^2 = .873$; very good fit
d. \$559.50 to \$933.90

66. a. Market beta = .95
b. Significant; p-value = .029
c. $r^2 = .470$; not a good fit
d. Xerox has a higher risk

68. b. There appears to be a negative linear relationship between the two variables
c. $\hat{y} = 16.5 - .0588$ Miles
d. Significant; p-value = .000
e. $r^2 = .539$; reasonably good fit
g. approximately \$13,000; no

FIGURE D14.50

```
The regression equation is
Y = 66.1 + 0.402 X

Predictor       Coef    SE Coef       T        p
Constant       66.10      32.06    2.06    0.094
X             0.4023     0.2276    1.77    0.137

S = 12.62       R-sq = 38.5%       R-sq(adj) = 26.1%

Analysis of Variance

SOURCE            DF        SS       MS       F        p
Regression         1     497.2    497.2    3.12    0.137
Residual Error     5     795.7    159.1
Total              6    1292.9

Unusual Observations
Obs     X          Y       Fit    SE Fit    Residual    St Resid
  1   135     145.00    120.42      4.87       24.58       2.11R

 R denotes an observation with a large standardized residual
```

Chapter 15

2. a. The estimated regression equation is
$\hat{y} = 45.06 + 1.94x_1$
An estimate of y when $x_1 = 45$ is
$\hat{y} = 45.06 + 1.94(45) = 132.36$
b. The estimated regression equation is
$\hat{y} = 85.22 + 4.32x_2$
An estimate of y when $x_2 = 15$ is
$\hat{y} = 85.22 + 4.32(15) = 150.02$
c. The estimated regression equation is
$\hat{y} = -18.37 + 2.01x_1 + 4.74x_2$
An estimate of y when $x_1 = 45$ and $x_2 = 15$ is
$\hat{y} = -18.37 + 2.01(45) + 4.74(15) = 143.18$

4. a. \$255,000

5. a. The Minitab output is shown in Figure D15.5a
b. The Minitab output is shown in Figure D15.5b
c. It is 1.60 in part (a) and 2.29 in part (b); in part (a) the coefficient is an estimate of the change in revenue due to a one-unit change in television advertising expenditures; in part (b) it represents an estimate of the change in revenue due to a one-unit change in television advertising expenditures when the amount of newspaper advertising is held constant
d. Revenue = 83.2 + 2.29(3.5) + 1.30(1.8) = 93.56 or \$93,560

FIGURE D15.5a

```
The regression equation is
Revenue = 88.6 + 1.60 TVAdv

Predictor      Coef    SE Coef       T        p
Constant     88.638      1.582   56.02    0.000
TVAdv        1.6039     0.4778    3.36    0.015

S = 1.215     R-sq = 65.3%     R-sq(adj) = 59.5%

Analysis of Variance

SOURCE            DF       SS       MS       F        p
Regression         1   16.640   16.640   11.27    0.015
Residual Error     6    8.860    1.477
Total              7   25.500
```

FIGURE D15.5b

```
The regression equation is
Revenue = 83.2 + 2.29 TVAdv + 1.30 NewsAdv

Predictor      Coef    SE Coef       T        p
Constant     83.230      1.574   52.88    0.000
TVAdv        2.2902     0.3041    7.53    0.001
NewsAdv      1.3010     0.3207    4.06    0.010

S = 0.6426     R-sq = 91.9%     R-sq(adj) = 88.7%

Analysis of Variance

SOURCE            DF       SS       MS       F        p
Regression         2   23.435   11.718   28.38    0.002
Residual Error     5    2.065    0.413
Total              7   25.500
```

6. a. Win% = −58.8 + 16.4 Yds/Att
b. Win% = 97.5 − 1600 Int/Att
c. Win% = −5.8 + 12.9 Yds/Att − 1084 Int/Att
d. 35%

8. a. Overall = 69.3 + .235 Shore Excursions
b. Overall = 45.2 + .253 Shore Excursions + .248 Food/Dining
c. 87.76 or approximately 88.

10. a. R/IP = .676 − .284 SO/IP
b. R/IP = .308 + 1.35 HR/IP
c. R/IP = .537 − .248 SO/IP + 1.03 HR/IP
d. .48
e. Suggestion does not make sense

12. a. $R^2 = \frac{\text{SSR}}{\text{SST}} = \frac{14{,}052.2}{15{,}182.9} = .926$

b. $R_a^2 = 1 - (1 - R^2)\frac{n - 1}{n - p - 1}$

$= 1 - (1 - .926)\frac{10 - 1}{10 - 2 - 1} = .905$

c. Yes; after adjusting for the number of independent variables in the model, we see that 90.5% of the variability in y has been accounted for

14. a. .75
b. .68

15. a. $R^2 = \frac{\text{SSR}}{\text{SST}} = \frac{23.435}{25.5} = .919$

$R_a^2 = 1 - (1 - R^2)\frac{n - 1}{n - p - 1}$

$= 1 - (1 - .919)\frac{8 - 1}{8 - 2 - 1} = .887$

b. Multiple regression analysis is preferred because both R^2 and R_a^2 show an increased percentage of the variability of y explained when both independent variables are used

16. a. No, $R^2 = .577$

b. Better fit with multiple regression

18. a. $R^2 = .563, R_a^2 = .512$

b. The fit is not very good

19. a. $\text{MSR} = \dfrac{\text{SSR}}{p} = \dfrac{6216.375}{2} = 3108.188$

$\text{MSE} = \dfrac{\text{SSE}}{n - p - 1} = \dfrac{507.75}{10 - 2 - 1} = 72.536$

b. $F = \dfrac{\text{MSR}}{\text{MSE}} = \dfrac{3108.188}{72.536} = 42.85$

From the F table (2 numerator degrees of freedom and 7 denominator), p-value is less than .01

Using Excel or Minitab the p-value corresponding to $F = 42.85$ is .0001

Because p-value $\leq \alpha$, the overall model is significant

c. $t = \dfrac{b_1}{s_{b_1}} = \dfrac{.5906}{.0813} = 7.26$

p-value = .0002

Because p-value $\leq \alpha$, β_1 is significant

d. $t = \dfrac{b_2}{s_{b_2}} = \dfrac{.4980}{.0567} = 8.78$

p-value = .0001

Because p-value $\leq \alpha$, β_2 is significant

20. a. Significant; p-value = .000

b. Significant; p-value = .000

c. Significant; p-value = .002

22. a. SSE = 4000, $s^2 = 571.43$, MSR = 6000

b. Significant; p-value = .008

23. a. $F = 28.38$

p-value = .002

Because p-value $\leq \alpha$, there is a significant relationship

b. $t = 7.53$

p-value = .001

Because p-value $\leq \alpha$, β_1 is significant and x_1 should not be dropped from the model

c. $t = 4.06$

p-value = .010

Because p-value $\leq \alpha$, β_2 is significant and x_2 should not be dropped from the model

24. a. $\hat{y} = -.682 + .0498$ Revenue $+ .0147$ % Wins

b. Significant; p-value = .001

c. Revenue is significant; p-value = .001

%Wins is significant; p-value = .025

26. a. Significant; p-value = .001

b. All significant; p-values are all $< \alpha = .05$

28. a. Using Minitab, the 95% confidence interval is 132.16 to 154.16

b. Using Minitab, the 95% prediction interval is 111.13 at 175.18

29. a. See Minitab output in Figure D15.5b.

$\hat{y} = 83.23 + 2.29(3.5) + 1.30(1.8) = 93.555$ or \$93,555

b. Minitab results: 92.840 to 94.335, or \$92,840 to \$94,335

c. Minitab results: 91.774 to 95.401, or \$91,774 to \$95,401

30. a. 46.758 to 50.646

b. 44.815 to 52.589

32. a. $E(y) = \beta_0 + \beta_1 x_1 + \beta_2 x_2$

$$\text{where } x_2 = \begin{cases} 0 \text{ if level 1} \\ 1 \text{ if level 2} \end{cases}$$

b. $E(y) = \beta_0 + \beta_1 x_1 + \beta_2(0) = \beta_0 + \beta_1 x_1$

c. $E(y) = \beta_0 + \beta_1 x_1 + \beta_2(1) = \beta_0 + \beta_1 x_1 + \beta_2$

d. $\beta_2 = E(y \mid \text{level 2}) - E(y \mid \text{level 1})$

β_1 is the change in $E(y)$ for a 1-unit change in x_1 holding x_2 constant

34. a. \$15,300

b. $\hat{y} = 10.1 - 4.2(2) + 6.8(8) + 15.3(0) = 56.1$

Sales prediction: \$56,100

c. $\hat{y} = 10.1 - 4.2(1) + 6.8(3) + 15.3(1) = 41.6$

Sales prediction: \$41,600

36. a. $\hat{y} = 1.86 + 0.291$ Months $+ 1.10$ Type $- 0.609$ Person

b. Significant; p-value = .002

c. Person is not significant; p-value = .167

38. a. $\hat{y} = -91.8 + 1.08$ Age $+ .252$ Pressure $+ 8.74$ Smoker

b. Significant; p-value = .01

c. 95% prediction interval is 21.35 to 47.18 or a probability of .2135 to .4718; quit smoking and begin some type of treatment to reduce his blood pressure

39. a. The Minitab output is shown in Figure D15.39

b. Minitab provides the following values:

x_i	y_i	$\hat{y}_i$	Standardized Residual
1	3	2.8	.16
2	7	5.4	.94
3	5	8.0	−1.65
4	11	10.6	.24
5	14	13.2	.62

FIGURE D15.39

```
The regression equation is
Y = 0.20 + 2.60 X

Predictor       Coef     SE Coef       T        p
Constant       0.200       2.132    0.09    0.931
X             2.6000      0.6429    4.04    0.027

S = 2.033       R-sq = 84.5%       R-sq(adj) = 79.3%

Analysis of Variance
SOURCE            DF         SS          MS          F          p
Regression         1     67.600      67.600      16.35      0.027
Residual Error     3     12.400       4.133
Total              4     80.000
```

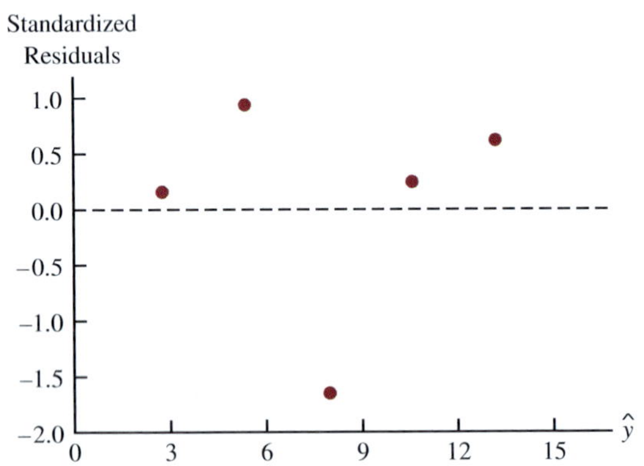

The point (3, 5) does not appear to follow the trend of the remaining data; however, the value of the standardized residual for this point, −1.65, is not large enough for us to conclude that (3, 5) is an outlier

c. Minitab provides the following values:

x_i	y_i	Studentized Deleted Residual
1	3	.13
2	7	.91
3	5	−4.42
4	11	.19
5	14	.54

$t_{.025} = 4.303$ ($n - p - 2 = 5 - 1 - 2 = 2$ degrees of freedom)

Because the studentized deleted residual for (3, 5) is $-4.42 < -4.303$, we conclude that the 3rd observation is an outlier

40. a. $\hat{y} = -53.3 + 3.11x$

b. −1.94, −.12, 1.79, .40, −1.90; no

c. .38, .28, .22, .20, .92; no

d. .60, .00, .26, .03, 11.09; yes, the fifth observation

41. a. The Minitab output appears in Figure D15.5b; the estimated regression equation is

$$\text{Revenue} = 83.2 + 2.29\ \text{TVAdv} + 1.30\ \text{NewsAdv}$$

b. Minitab provides the following values:

$\hat{y}_i$	Standardized Residual	$\hat{y}_i$	Standardized Residual
96.63	−1.62	94.39	1.10
90.41	−1.08	94.24	−.40
94.34	1.22	94.42	−1.12
92.21	−.37	93.35	1.08

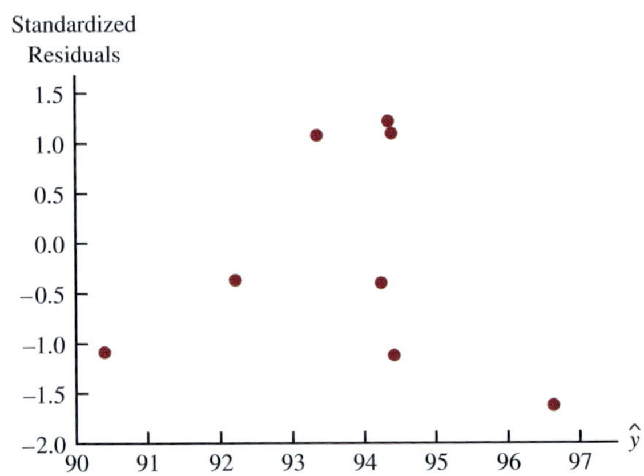

With relatively few observations, it is difficult to determine whether any of the assumptions regarding ϵ have been violated; for instance, an argument could be made that there does not appear to be any pattern in the plot; alternatively, an argument could be made that there is a curvilinear pattern in the plot

c. The values of the standardized residuals are greater than −2 and less than +2; thus, using this test, there are no outliers

As a further check for outliers, we used Minitab to compute the following studentized deleted residuals:

Observation	Studentized Deleted Residual	Observation	Studentized Deleted Residual
1	−2.11	5	1.13
2	−1.10	6	−.36
3	1.31	7	−1.16
4	−.33	8	1.10

$t_{.025} = 2.776$ ($n - p - 2 = 8 - 2 - 2 = 4$ degrees of freedom)

Because none of the studentized deleted residuals are less than -2.776 or greater than 2.776, we conclude that there are no outliers in the data

d. Minitab provides the following values:

Observation	h_i	D_i
1	.63	1.52
2	.65	.70
3	.30	.22
4	.23	.01
5	.26	.14
6	.14	.01
7	.66	.81
8	.13	.06

The critical leverage value is

$$\frac{3(p+1)}{n} = \frac{3(2+1)}{8} = 1.125$$

Because none of the values exceed 1.125, we conclude that there are no influential observations; however, using Cook's distance measure, we see that $D_1 > 1$ (rule of thumb critical value); thus, we conclude that the first observation is influential

Final conclusion: observation 1 is an influential observation

42. b. Unusual trend
c. No outliers
d. Observation 2 is an influential observation

44. a. $E(y) = \dfrac{e^{\beta_0+\beta_1 x}}{1 + e^{\beta_0+\beta_1 x}}$
b. Estimate of the probability that a customer who does not have a Simmons credit card will make a purchase
c. $\hat{g}(x) = -0.9445 + 1.0245x$
d. .28 for customers who do not have a Simmons credit card
.52 for customers who have a Simmons credit card
e. Estimated odds ratio = 2.79

46. a. $E(y) = \dfrac{e^{\beta_0+\beta_1 x}}{1 + e^{\beta_0+\beta_1 x}}$
b. $E(y) = \dfrac{e^{-2.6355+0.22018x}}{1 + e^{-2.6355+0.22018x}}$
c. Significant; p-value = .0002
d. .39
e. $1200
f. Estimated odds ratio = 1.25

48. a. $E(y) = \dfrac{e^{\beta_0+\beta_1 x_1+\beta_2 x_2}}{1 + e^{\beta_0+\beta_1 x_1+\beta_2 x_2}}$
b. $\hat{g}(x) = -39.4982 + 3.37449$ Wet $+ 1.81628$ Noise
c. .88
d. Probability is .04

50. b. 67.39

52. a. $\hat{y} = -1.41 + .0235x_1 + .00486x_2$
b. Significant; p-value = .0001
c. Both significant
d. $R^2 = .937$; $R^2_{\text{a}} = 9.19$; good fit

54. a. Buy Again = −7.522 + 1.8151 Steering
b. Yes
c. Buy Again = −5.388 + .6899 Steering + .9113 Treadwear
d. Significant; p-value = .001

56. a. $\hat{y} = 4.9090 + 10.4658$ FundDE $+ 21.6823$ FundIE
b. $R^2 = .6144$; reasonably good fit
c. $\hat{y} = 1.1899 + 6.8969$ FundDE $+ 17.6800$ FundIE
$+ 0.0265$ Net Asset Value ($)
$+ 6.4564$ Expense Ratio (%)
Net Asset Value ($) is not significant and can be deleted
d. $\hat{y} = -4.6074 + 8.1713$ FundDE $+ 19.5194$ FundIE
$+ 5.5197$ Expense Ratio (%) $+ 5.9237$ 3StarRank
$+ 8.2367$ 4StarRank $+ 6.6241$ 5StarRank
e. 15.28%

Chapter 16

1. a. The Minitab output is shown in Figure D16.1a
b. Because the p-value corresponding to $F = 6.85$ is $.059 > \alpha = .05$, the relationship is not significant
c.

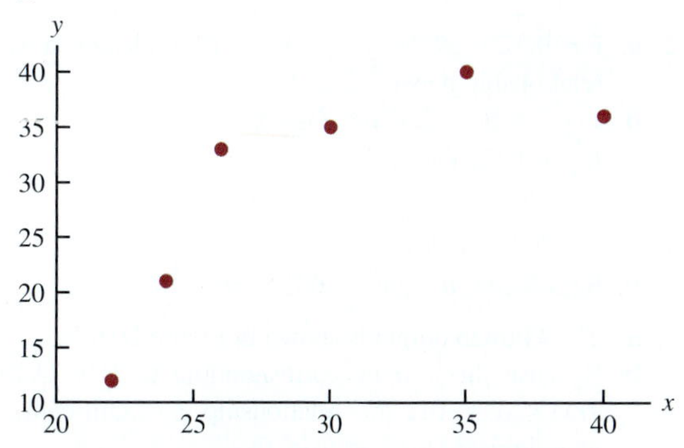

The scatter diagram suggests that a curvilinear relationship may be appropriate
d. The Minitab output is shown in Figure D16.1d
e. Because the p-value corresponding to $F = 25.68$ is $.013 < \alpha = .05$, the relationship is significant
f. $\hat{y} = -168.88 + 12.187(25) - .17704(25)^2 = 25.145$

FIGURE D16.1a

```
The regression equation is
Y = - 6.8 + 1.23 X

Predictor        Coef    SE Coef        T        p
Constant        -6.77      14.17    -0.48    0.658
X              1.2296     0.4697     2.62    0.059

S = 7.269     R-sq = 63.1%      R-sq(adj) = 53.9%

Analysis of Variance

SOURCE             DF        SS        MS        F        p
Regression          1    362.13    362.13     6.85    0.059
Residual Error      4    211.37     52.84
Total               5    573.50
```

FIGURE D16.1d

```
The regression equation is
Y = - 169 + 12.2 X - 0.177 XSQ

Predictor         Coef    SE Coef        T        p
Constant       -168.88      39.79    -4.74    0.024
X               12.187      2.663     4.58    0.020
XSQ           -0.17704    0.04290    -4.13    0.026

S = 3.248     R-sq = 94.5%      R-sq(adj) = 90.8%

Analysis of Variance

SOURCE             DF        SS        MS        F        p
Regression          2    541.85    270.92    25.68    0.013
Residual Error      3     31.65     10.55
Total               5    573.50
```

2. a. $\hat{y} = 9.32 + .424x$; p-value $= .117$ indicates a weak relationship between x and y

b. $\hat{y} = -8.10 + 2.41x - .0480x^2$

$R_a^2 = .932$; a good fit

c. 20.965

4. a. $\hat{y} = 943 + 8.71x$

b. Significant; p-value $= .005 < \alpha = .01$

5. a. The Minitab output is shown in Figure D16.5a

b. Because the p-value corresponding to $F = 73.15$ is $.003 < \alpha = .01$, the relationship is significant; we would reject H_0: $\beta_1 = \beta_2 = 0$

c. See Figure D16.5c

6. b. No, the relationship appears to be curvilinear

c. Several possible models; e.g.,

$\hat{y} = 2.90 - .185x + .00351x^2$

8. a. It appears that a simple linear regression model is not appropriate

b. Price $= 33829 - 4571$ Rating $+ 154$ RatingSq

c. logPrice $= -10.2 + 10.4$ logRating

d. Part (c); higher percentage of variability is explained

10. a. Significant; p-value $= .000$

b. Significant; p-value $= .000$

11. a. SSE $= 1805 - 1760 = 45$

$$F = \frac{\text{MSR}}{\text{MSE}} = \left(\frac{1760/4}{45/25}\right) = 244.44$$

Because p-value $= .000$, the relationship is significant

b. $\text{SSE}(x_1, x_2, x_3, x_4) = 45$

c. $\text{SSE}(x_2, x_3) = 1805 - 1705 = 100$

d. $$F = \frac{(100 - 45)/2}{1.8} = 15.28$$

Because p-value $= .000$, x_1 and x_2 are significant

FIGURE D16.5a

```
The regression equation is
Y = 433 + 37.4 X -0.383 XSQ

Predictor        Coef     SE Coef        T        p
Constant        432.6       141.2     3.06    0.055
X              37.429       7.807     4.79    0.017
XSQ           -0.3829      0.1036    -3.70    0.034

S = 15.83     R-sq = 98.0%     R-sq(adj) = 96.7%

Analysis of Variance

SOURCE            DF        SS        MS        F        p
Regression         2     36643     18322    73.15    0.003
Residual Error     3       751       250
Total              5     37395
```

FIGURE D16.5c

```
    Fit     Stdev.Fit              95% C.I.              95% P.I.
1302.01       9.93       (1270.41, 1333.61)    (1242.55, 1361.47)
```

12. a. The Minitab output is shown in Figure D16.12a

b. The Minitab output is shown in Figure D16.12b

c. $$F = \frac{[\text{SSE(reduced)} - \text{SSE(full)}]/(\#\text{ extra terms})}{\text{MSE(full)}}$$

$$= \frac{(7.2998 - 4.3240)/2}{.1663} = 8.95$$

The p-value associated with $F = 8.95$ (2 numerator degrees of freedom and 26 denominator) is .001; with a p-value $< \alpha = .05$, the addition of the two independent variables is significant

14. a. $\hat{y} = -111 + 1.32\text{ Age} + .296\text{ Pressure}$

b. $\hat{y} = -123 + 1.51\text{ Age} + .448\text{ Pressure} + 8.87\text{ Smoker} - .00276\text{ AgePress}$

c. Significant; p-value $= .000$

16. a. Weeks $= -8.9 + 1.51$ Age

b. Weeks $= -.07 + 1.73$ Age $- 2.7$ Manager $- 15.1$ Head $- 17.4$ Sales

c. Same as part (b)

d. Same as part (b)

e. Weeks $= 13.1 + 1.64$ Age $- 9.76$ Married $- 19.4$ Head $- 29.0$ Manager $- 19.0$ Sales

FIGURE D16.12a

```
The regression equation is
Scoring Avg. = 46.3 + 14.1 Putting Avg.

Predictor          Coef     SE Coef       T        p
Constant         46.277       6.026    7.68    0.000
Putting Avg.     14.103       3.356    4.20    0.000

S = 0.510596     R-Sq = 38.7%     R-Sq(adj) = 36.5%

Analysis of Variance

SOURCE            DF         SS         MS        F         p
Regression         1     4.6036     4.6036    17.66    0.0000
Residual Error    28     7.2998     0.2607
Total             29    11.9035
```

FIGURE D16.12b

```
The regression equation is
Scoring Avg. = 59.0 - 10.3 Greens in Reg.
  + 11.4 Putting Avg - 1.81 Sand Saves

Predictor           Coef    SE Coef        T       p
Constant          59.022      5.774    10.22   0.000
Greens in Reg.   -10.281      2.877    -3.57   0.001
Putting Avg.      11.413      2.760     4.14   0.000
Sand Saves       -1.8130     0.9210    -1.97   0.060

S = 0.407808     R-Sq = 63.7%     R-Sq(adj) = 59.5%

Analysis of Variance

Source           DF        SS        MS        F       p
Regression        3    7.5795    2.5265    15.19   0.000
Residual Error   26    4.3240    0.1663
Total            29   11.9035
```

18. a. RPG = −4.05 + 27.6 OBP

b. A variety of models will provide a good fit; the five-variable model identified using Minitab's Stepwise Regression procedure with Alpha-to-Enter = .10 and Alpha-to-Remove = .10 follows:

RPG = −.0909 + 32.2 OBP + .109 HR − 21.5 AVG + .244 3B − .0223 BB

20.

x_1	x_2	x_3	**Treatment**
0	0	0	A
1	0	0	B
0	1	0	C
0	0	1	D

$$E(y) = \beta_0 + \beta_1 x_1 + \beta_2 x_2 + \beta_3 x_3$$

22. Factor A: $x_1 = 0$ if level 1 and 1 if level 2

Factor B:

x_2	x_3	**Level**
0	0	1
1	0	2
0	1	3

$$E(y) = \beta_0 + \beta_1 x_1 + \beta_2 x_2 + \beta_3 x_1 x_2 + \beta_4 x_1 x_3$$

23. a. The dummy variables are defined as follows:

D1	**D2**	**Mfg.**
0	0	1
1	0	2
0	1	3

$$E(y) = \beta_0 + \beta_1 \text{D1} + \beta_2 \text{D2}$$

b. The Minitab output is shown below:

```
The regression equation is
TIME = 23.0 + 5.00 D1 - 2.00 D2

Predictor      Coef   SE Coef       T       p
Constant     23.000     1.106   20.80   0.000
D1            5.000     1.563    3.20   0.011
D2           -2.000     1.563   -1.28   0.233

S = 2.211      R-Sq = 70.3%   R-Sq(adj) = 63.7%

Analysis of Variance

SOURCE           DF        SS        MS       F       p
Regression        2   104.000    52.000    1064   0.004
Residual Error    9    44.000     4.889
Total            11   148.000
```

c. H_0: $\beta_1 = \beta_2 = 0$

d. The p-value of .004 is less than $\alpha = .05$; therefore, we can reject H_0 and conclude that the mean time to mix a batch of material is not the same for each manufacturer

24. a. Not significant at the .05 level of significance; p-value = .093

b. 139

26. Overall significant; p-value = .029
Individually, none of the variables are significant at the .05 level of significance; a larger sample size would be helpful

28. $d = 1.60$; test is inconclusive

30. a.

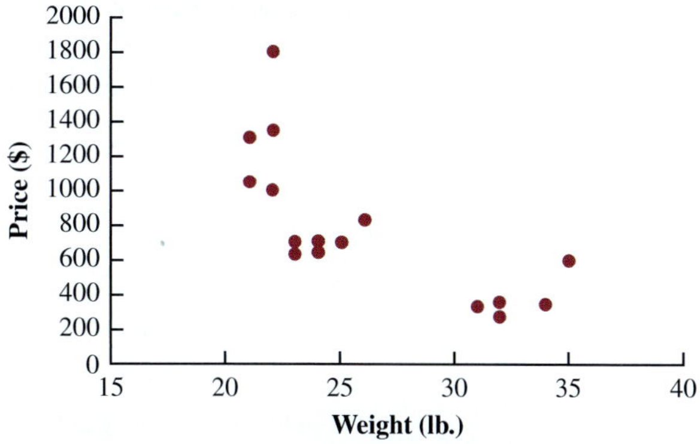

There appears to be a curvilinear relationship between weight and price

b. A portion of the Minitab output follows:

```
The regression equation is
Price = 11376 - 728 Weight + 12.0 WeightSq

Predictor      Coef    SE Coef       T       p
Constant      11376       2565    4.43   0.000
Weight       -728.3      193.7   -3.76   0.002
WeightSq     11.974      3.539    3.38   0.004

S = 242.804    R-Sq = 77.0%    R-Sq(adj) = 74.1%

Analysis of Variance

SOURCE            DF        SS        MS       F       p
Regression         2   3161747   1580874   26.82   0.000
Residual Error    16    943263     58954
Total             18   4105011
```

The results obtained support the conclusion that there is a curvilinear relationship between weight and price

c. A portion of the Minitab output follows:

```
The regression equation is
Price = 1284 - 572 Type_Fitness - 907 Type_Comfort

Predictor          Coef    SE Coef       T       p
Constant        1283.75      95.22   13.48   0.000
Type_Fitness     -571.8      153.5   -3.72   0.002
Type_Comfort     -907.1      145.5   -6.24   0.000

S = 269.328    R-Sq = 71.7%    R-Sq(adj) = 68.2%

Analysis of Variance

SOURCE            DF        SS        MS       F       p
Regression         2   2944410   1472205   20.30   0.000
Residual Error    16   1160601     72538
Total             18   4105011
```

Type of bike appears to be a significant factor in predicting price, but the estimated regression equation developed in part (b) appears to provide a slightly better fit

d. A portion of the Minitab output follows; in this output WxF denotes the interaction between the weight of the bike and the dummy variable Type_Fitness and WxC denotes the interaction between the weight of the bike and the dummy variable Type_Comfort

```
The regression equation is
Price = 5924 - 215 Weight - 6343 Type_Fitness - 7232
        Type_Comfort + 261 WxF + 266 WxC

Predictor          Coef   SE Coef       T       p
Constant           5924      1547    3.83   0.002
Weight          -214.56     71.42   -3.00   0.010
Type_Fitness      -6343      2596   -2.44   0.030
Type_Comfort      -7232      2518   -2.87   0.013
WxF               261.3     111.8    2.34   0.036
WxC              266.41     93.98    2.83   0.014

S = 224.438    R-Sq = 84.0%    R-Sq(adj) = 77.9%

Analysis of Variance

SOURCE           DF        SS       MS       F       p
Regression        5   3450170   690034   13.70   0.000
Residual Error   13    654841    50372
Total            18   4105011
```

By taking into account the type of bike, the weight, and the interaction between these two factors, this estimated regression equation provides an excellent fit

32. a. Delay = 63.0 + 11.1 Industry; no significant positive autocorrelation

34. Significant differences between comfort levels for the three types of browsers; p-value = .034

Chapter 17

1. The following table shows the calculations for parts (a), (b), and (c):

Week	Time Series Value	Forecast	Forecast Error	Absolute Value of Forecast Error	Squared Forecast Error	Percentage Error	Absolute Value of Percentage Error
1	18						
2	13	18	−5	5	25	−38.46	38.46
3	16	13	3	3	9	18.75	18.75
4	11	16	−5	5	25	−45.45	45.45
5	17	11	6	6	36	35.29	35.29
6	14	17	−3	3	9	−21.43	21.43
			Totals	22	104	−51.30	159.38

a. $\text{MAE} = \frac{22}{5} = 4.4$

b. $\text{MSE} = \frac{104}{5} = 20.8$

c. $\text{MAPE} = \frac{159.38}{5} = 31.88$

d. Forecast for week 7 is 14

2. The following table shows the calculations for parts (a), (b), and (c):

Week	Time Series Value	Forecast	Forecast Error	Absolute Value of Forecast Error	Squared Forecast Error	Percentage Error	Absolute Value of Percentage Error
1	18						
2	13	18.00	−5.00	5.00	25.00	−38.46	38.46
3	16	15.50	0.50	0.50	0.25	3.13	3.13
4	11	15.67	−4.67	4.67	21.81	−42.45	42.45
5	17	14.50	2.50	2.50	6.25	14.71	14.71
6	14	15.00	−1.00	1.00	1.00	−7.14	7.14
			Totals	13.67	54.31	−70.21	105.86

a. $\text{MAE} = \frac{13.67}{5} = 2.73$

b. $\text{MSE} = \frac{54.31}{5} = 10.86$

c. $\text{MAPE} = \frac{105.89}{5} = 21.18$

d. Forecast for week 7 is

$$\frac{18 + 13 + 16 + 11 + 17 + 14}{6} = 14.83$$

4. a. $\text{MSE} = \frac{363}{6} = 60.5$

Forecast for month 8 is 15

b. $\text{MSE} = \frac{216.72}{6} = 36.12$

Forecast for month 8 is 18

c. The average of all the previous values is better because MSE is smaller

5. a. The data appear to follow a horizontal pattern

b. Three-week moving average

Week	Time Series Value	Forecast	Forecast Error	Squared Forecast Error
1	18			
2	13			
3	16			
4	11	15.67	−4.67	21.78
5	17	13.33	3.67	13.44
6	14	14.67	−0.67	0.44
			Total	35.67

$$\text{MSE} = \frac{35.67}{3} = 11.89$$

The forecast for week 7 $= \frac{(11 + 17 + 14)}{3} = 14$

c. Smoothing constant = .2

Week	Time Series Value	Forecast	Forecast Error	Squared Forecast Error
1	18			
2	13	18.00	−5.00	25.00
3	16	17.00	−1.00	1.00
4	11	16.80	−5.80	33.64
5	17	15.64	1.36	1.85
6	14	15.91	−1.91	3.66
			Total	65.15

$$\text{MSE} = \frac{65.15}{5} = 13.03$$

The forecast for week 7 is .2(14) + (1 − .2)15.91 = 15.53

d. The three-week moving average provides a better forecast since it has a smaller MSE

e. Smoothing constant = .4

Week	Time Series Value	Forecast	Forecast Error	Squared Forecast Error
1	18			
2	13	18.00	−5.00	25.00
3	16	16.00	0.00	0.00
4	11	16.00	−5.00	25.00
5	17	14.00	3.00	9.00
6	14	15.20	−1.20	1.44
			Total	60.44

$$\text{MSE} = \frac{60.44}{5} = 12.09$$

The exponential smoothing forecast using $\alpha = .4$ provides a better forecast than the exponential smoothing forecast using $\alpha = .2$ since it has a smaller MSE

6. a. The data appear to follow a horizontal pattern

b. $\text{MSE} = \frac{110}{4} = 27.5$

The forecast for week 8 is 19

c. $\text{MSE} = \frac{252.87}{6} = 42.15$

The forecast for week 7 is 19.12

d. The three-week moving average provides a better forecast since it has a smaller MSE

e. MSE = 39.79

The exponential smoothing forecast using $\alpha = .4$ provides a better forecast than the exponential smoothing forecast using $\alpha = .2$ since it has a smaller MSE

8. a.

Week	4	5	6	7	8	9	10	11	12
Forecast	19.33	21.33	19.83	17.83	18.33	18.33	20.33	20.33	17.83

b. MSE = 11.49

Prefer the unweighted moving average here; it has a smaller MSE

c. You could always find a weighted moving average at least as good as the unweighted one; actually the unweighted moving average is a special case of the weighted ones where the weights are equal

10. b. The more recent data receive the greater weight or importance in determining the forecast; the moving averages method weights the last n data values equally in determining the forecast

12. a. The data appear to follow a horizontal pattern

b. MSE(3-Month) = .12
MSE(4-Month) = .14
Use 3-Month moving averages

c. 9.63

13. a. The data appear to follow a horizontal pattern

b.

Month	Time-Series Value	3-Month Moving Average Forecast	(Error)^2	$\alpha = .2$ Forecast	(Error)^2
1	240				
2	350			240.00	12100.00
3	230			262.00	1024.00
4	260	273.33	177.69	255.60	19.36
5	280	280.00	0.00	256.48	553.19
6	320	256.67	4010.69	261.18	3459.79
7	220	286.67	4444.89	272.95	2803.70
8	310	273.33	1344.69	262.36	2269.57
9	240	283.33	1877.49	271.89	1016.97
10	310	256.67	2844.09	265.51	1979.36
11	240	286.67	2178.09	274.41	1184.05
12	230	263.33	1110.89	267.53	1408.50
		Totals	17,988.52		27,818.49

MSE (3-Month) = 17,988.52/9 = 1998.72

MSE ($\alpha = .2$) = 27,818.49/11 = 2528.95

Based on the preceding MSE values, the 3-Month moving averages appear better; however, exponential smoothing was penalized by including month 2, which was difficult for any method to forecast; using only the errors for months 4 to 12, the MSE for exponential smoothing is

$$\text{MSE}(\alpha = .2) = 14{,}694.49/9 = 1632.72$$

Thus, exponential smoothing was better considering months 4 to 12

c. Using exponential smoothing,

$$F_{13} = \alpha Y_{12} + (1 - \alpha)F_{12}$$
$$= .20(230) + .80(267.53) = 260$$

14. a. The data appear to follow a horizontal pattern

b. Values for months 2–12 are as follows:

105.00 114.00 115.80 112.56 105.79 110.05
120.54 126.38 118.46 106.92 104.85

MSE = 510.29

c. Values for months 2–12 are as follows:

105.00 120.00 120.00 112.50 101.25 110.63
127.81 133.91 116.95 98.48 99.24

MSE = 540.55

Conclusion: A smoothing constant of .3 is better than a smoothing constant of .5 since the MSE is less for 0.3

16. a.

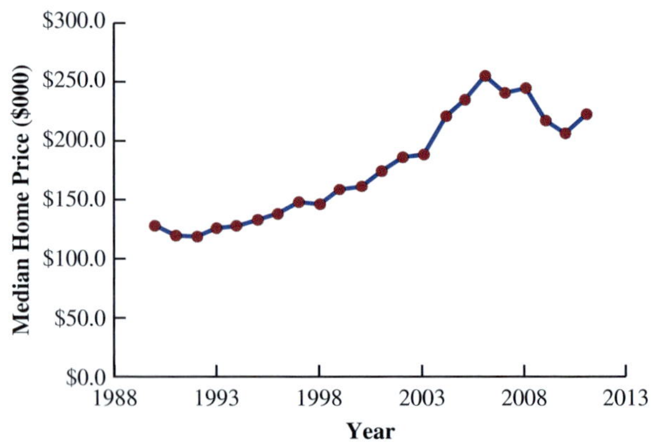

The time series plot exhibits a trend pattern; although the recession of 2008 led to a downturn in prices, the median price rose from 2010 to 2011

b. The methods discussed in this section are only applicable for a time series that has a horizontal pattern; because the time series plot exhibits a trend pattern, the methods discussed in this section are not appropriate

c. In 2003 the median price was $189,500, and in 2004 the median price was $222,300, so, it appears that the time series shifted to a new level in 2004; the time series plot using just the data for 2004 and later follows

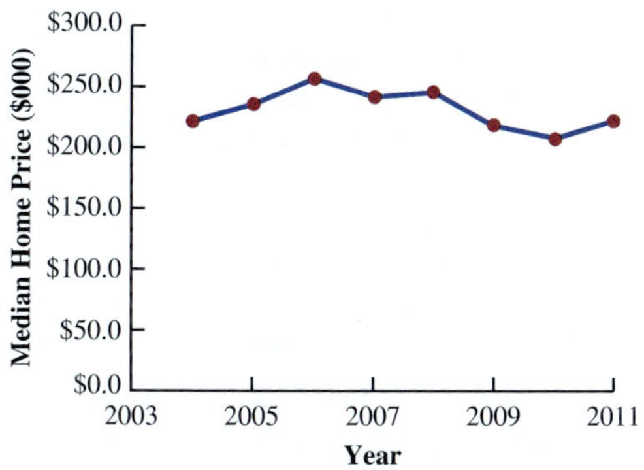

This time series plot exhibits a horizontal pattern; therefore, the methods discussed in this section are appropriate

17. a. The time series plot shows a linear trend

b. $\bar{t} = \frac{\sum_{t=1}^{n} t}{n} = \frac{15}{5} = 3 \quad \bar{Y} = \frac{\sum_{t=1}^{n} Y_t}{n} = \frac{55}{5} = 11$

$\Sigma(t - \bar{t})(Y_t - \bar{Y}) = 21 \quad \Sigma(t - \bar{t})^2 = 10$

$$b_1 = \frac{\sum_{t=1}^{n}(t - \bar{t})(Y_t - \bar{Y})}{\sum_{t=1}^{n}(t - \bar{t})^2} = \frac{21}{10} = 2.1$$

$b_0 = \bar{Y} - b_1\bar{t} = 11 - (2.1)(3) = 4.7$

$T_t = 4.7 + 2.1t$

c. $T_6 = 4.7 + 2.1(6) = 17.3$

18. Forecast for week 6 is 21.16

20. a. The time series plot exhibits a curvilinear trend

b. $T_t = 107.857 - 28.9881t + 2.65476t^2$

c. 45.86

21. a.

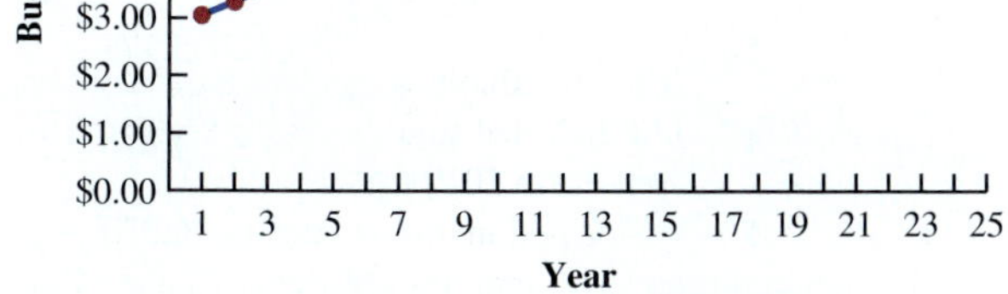

b. $\bar{t} = \frac{\sum_{t=1}^{n} t}{n} = \frac{300}{24} = 12.5 \quad \bar{Y} = \frac{\sum_{t=1}^{n} Y_t}{n} = \frac{148.2}{24} = 6.175$

$\Sigma(t - \bar{t})(Y_t - \bar{Y}) = 290.86 \quad \Sigma(t - \bar{t})^2 = 1150$

$$b_1 = \frac{\sum_{t=1}^{n}(t - \bar{t})(Y_t - \bar{Y})}{\sum_{t=1}^{n}(t - \bar{t})^2} = \frac{290.86}{1150} = .25292$$

$b_0 = \bar{Y} - b_1\bar{x} = 6.175 - (.25292)(12.5) = 3.0135$

c. $\hat{y} = 3.0135 + .25292(25) = 9.34$

Forecast for 2012 is $9.34 billion

22. a.

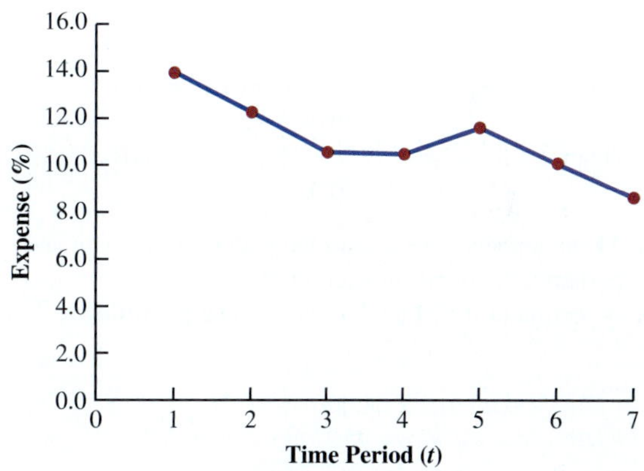

The time series plot shows a downward linear trend

b. $\bar{t} = \frac{\sum_{t=1}^{n} t}{n} = \frac{28}{7} = 4 \quad \bar{Y} = \frac{\sum_{t=1}^{n} Y_t}{n} = \frac{77}{7} = 11$

$\Sigma(t - \bar{t})(Y_t - \bar{Y}) = -19.6 \quad \Sigma(t - \bar{t})^2 = 28$

$$b_1 = \frac{\sum_{t=1}^{n}(t - \bar{t})(Y_t - \bar{Y})}{\sum_{t=1}^{n}(t - \bar{t})^2} = \frac{-19.6}{28} = -.7$$

$b_0 = \bar{Y} - b_1\bar{t} = 11 - (-.7)(4) = 13.8$

$T_t = 13.8 - .7t$

c. 2013 corresponds to time period $t = 8$, $T_8 = 13.8 - .7(8) = 8.2$

d. If SCF can continue to decrease the percentage of funds spent on administrative and fundraising by .7% per year, the forecast of expenses for 2018 is 4.70%

24. a. The time series plot shows a linear trend

b. $T_t = 7.5623 - .07541t$

c. 6.7328

d. Given the uncertainty in global market conditions, making a prediction for December using only time is not recommended

26. a. A linear trend is not appropriate

b. $T_t = 5.702 + 2.889t - 1618t^2$

c. 17.90

28. a. The time series plot shows a horizontal pattern, but there is a seasonal pattern in the data; for instance, in each year the lowest value occurs in quarter 2 and the highest value occurs in quarter 4

b. A portion of the Minitab regression output is shown;

```
The regression equation is
Value = 77.0 - 10.0 Qtr1 - 30.0
        Qtr2 - 20.0 Qtr3
```

c. The quarterly forecasts for next year are as follows:

Quarter 1 forecast = 77.0 − 10.0(1) − 30.0(0) − 20.0(0) = 67
Quarter 2 forecast = 77.0 − 10.0(0) − 30.0(1) − 20.0(0) = 47
Quarter 3 forecast = 77.0 − 10.0(0) − 30.0(0) − 20.0(1) = 57
Quarter 4 forecast = 77.0 − 10.0(0) − 30.0(0) − 20.0(0) = 77

30. a. There appears to be a seasonal pattern in the data and perhaps a moderate upward linear trend

b. A portion of the Minitab regression output follows:

```
The regression equation is
Value = 2492 - 712 Qtr1 - 1512
        Qtr2 + 327 Qtr3
```

c. The quarterly forecasts for next year are as follows:

Quarter 1 forecast is 1780
Quarter 2 forecast is 980
Quarter 3 forecast is 2819
Quarter 4 forecast is 2492

d. A portion of the Minitab regression output follows:

```
The regression equation is
Value = 2307 - 642 Qtr1 - 1465
        Qtr2 + 350 Qtr3 + 23.1 t
```

The quarterly forecasts for next year are as follows:

Quarter 1 forecast is 2058
Quarter 2 forecast is 1258
Quarter 3 forecast is 3096
Quarter 4 forecast is 2769

32. a. The time series plot shows both a linear trend and seasonal effects

b. A portion of the Minitab regression output follows:

```
The regression equation is
Revenue = 70.0 + 10.0 Qtr1 + 105
          Qtr2 + 245 Qtr3
```

Quarter 1 forecast is 80
Quarter 2 forecast is 175
Quarter 3 forecast is 315
Quarter 4 forecast is 70

c. A portion of the Minitab regression output follows

```
The regression equation is
Revenue = -70.1 + 45.0 Qtr1 + 128
          Qtr2 + 257 Qtr3 + 11.7 Period
```

Quarter 1 forecast = is 221
Quarter 2 forecast = is 315
Quarter 3 forecast = is 456
Quarter 4 forecast = is 211

34. a. The time series plot shows seasonal and linear trend effects

b. *Note*: Jan = 1 if January, 0 otherwise; Feb = 1 if February, 0 otherwise; and so on

A portion of the Minitab regression output follows:

```
The regression equation is
Expense = 175 - 18.4 Jan - 3.72 Feb +
          12.7 Mar + 45.7 Apr + 57.1
          May + 135 Jun + 181 Jul + 105
          Aug + 47.6 Sep + 50.6 Oct +
          35.3 Nov + 1.96 Period
```

c. *Note*: The next time period in the time series is Period = 37 (January of Year 4); the forecasts for January–December are 229; 246; 264; 299; 312; 392; 440; 366; 311; 316; 302; 269

35. a. The time series plot indicates a linear trend and a seasonal pattern

b.

Year	Quarter	Time Series Value	Four-Quarter Moving Average	Centered Moving Average
1	1	4		
	2	2		
			3.50	
	3	3		3.750
			4.00	
	4	5		4.125
			4.25	
2	1	6		4.500
			4.75	
	2	3		5.000
			5.25	
	3	5		5.375
			5.50	
	4	7		5.875
			6.25	
3	1	7		6.375
			6.50	
	2	6		6.625
			6.75	
	3	6		
	4	8		

c.

Year	Quarter	Time Series Value	Centered Moving Average	Seasonal-Irregular Component
1	1	4		
	2	2		
	3	3	3.750	0.800
	4	5	4.125	1.212
2	1	6	4.500	1.333
	2	3	5.000	0.600
	3	5	5.375	0.930
	4	7	5.875	1.191
3	1	7	6.375	1.098
	2	6	6.625	0.906
	3	6		
	4	8		

Quarter	Seasonal-Irregular Values		Seasonal Index	Adjusted Seasonal Index
1	1.333	1.098	1.216	1.205
2	0.600	0.906	0.752	0.746
3	0.800	0.930	0.865	0.857
4	1.212	1.191	1.201	1.191
		Total	4.036	

$$\text{Adjustment for seasonal index} = \frac{4.000}{4.036} = 0.991$$

36. a.

Year	Quarter	Deseasonalized Value
1	1	3.320
	2	2.681
	3	3.501
	4	4.198
2	1	4.979
	2	4.021
	3	5.834
	4	5.877
3	1	5.809
	2	8.043
	3	7.001
	4	6.717

b. Let Period = 1 denote the time series value in Year 1—Quarter 1; Period = 2 denote the time series value in Year 1—Quarter 2; and so on; a portion of the Minitab regression output treating Period as the independent variable and the Deseasonlized Values as the values of the dependent variable follows:

```
The regression equation is
Deseasonalized Value = 2.42 + 0.422
                       Period
```

c. The quarterly deseasonalized trend forecasts for Year 4 (Periods 13, 14, 15, and 16) are as follows:

Forecast for quarter 1 is 7.906
Forecast for quarter 2 is 8.328
Forecast for quarter 3 is 8.750
Forecast for quarter 4 is 9.172

d. Adjusting the quarterly deseasonalized trend forecasts provides the following quarterly estimates:

Forecast for quarter 1 is 9.527
Forecast for quarter 2 is 6.213
Forecast for quarter 3 is 7.499
Forecast for quarter 4 is 10.924

38. a. The time series plot shows a linear trend and seasonal effects

b. 0.71 0.78 0.83 0.97 1.02 1.30 1.50 1.23 0.98 0.99 0.93 0.79

c.

Month	Deaseasonalized Expense
1	239.44
2	230.77
3	246.99
4	237.11
5	235.29
6	242.31
7	240.00
8	235.77
9	244.90
10	242.42
11	247.31
12	246.84
13	253.52
14	262.82
15	259.04
16	252.58
17	259.80
18	253.85
19	266.67
20	272.36
21	265.31
22	272.73
23	274.19
24	278.48
25	274.65
26	269.23
27	277.11
28	288.66
29	284.31
30	300.00
31	280.00
32	268.29
33	295.92
34	297.98
35	301.08
36	316.46

d. Let Period = 1 denote the time series value in January—Year 1; Period = 2 denote the time series value in February—Year 2; and so on; a portion of the Minitab regression output treating Period as the independent variable and the Deseasonlized Values as the values of the dependent variable follows:

```
The regression equation is
Deseasonalized Expense = 228 + 1.96
                         Period
```

e.

Month	Monthly Forecast
January	213.37
February	235.93
March	252.69
April	297.21
May	314.53
June	403.42
July	486.42
August	386.52
September	309.88
October	314.98
November	297.71
December	254.44

40. a. The time series plot indicates a seasonal effect; power consumption is lowest in the time period 12–4 A.M., steadily increases to the highest value in the 12–4 P.M. time period, and then decreases again. There may also be some linear trend in the data

b.

Time Period	Adjusted Seasonal Index
12–4 A.M.	0.3256
4–8 A.M.	0.4476
8–12 noon	1.3622
12–4 P.M.	1.6959
4–8 P.M.	1.4578
8–12 midnight	0.7109

c. The following Minitab output shows the results of fitting a linear trend equation to the deseasonalized time series:

```
The regression equation is
Deseasonalized Power = 63108 + 1854 t
```

Deaseasonalized Power (t = 19) = 63,108 + 1854(19) = 98,334

Forecast for 12–4 P.M. = 1.6959(98,334) = 166,764.63 or approximately 166,765 kWh

Deaseasonalized Power (t = 20) = 63,108 + 1854(20) = 100,188

Forecast for 4–8 P.M. = 1.4578(100,188) = 146,054.07 or approximately 146,054 kWh

Thus, the forecast of power consumption from noon to 8 P.M. is 166,765 + 146,054 = 312,819 kWh

42. a. The time series plot indicates a horizontal pattern

b.

$$\text{MSE}(\alpha = .2) = 1.40$$
$$\text{MSE}(\alpha = .3) = 1.27$$
$$\text{MSE}(\alpha = .4) = 1.23$$

A smoothing constant of $\alpha = .4$ provides the best forecast because it has a smaller MSE

c. 31.00

44. a. There appears to be an increasing trend in the data

b. A portion the Minitab regression output follows (*Note*: $t = 1$ corresponds to 2001, $t = 2$ corresponds to 2002, and so on)

```
The regression equation is
Balance($) = 1984 + 146 t
```

The forecast for 2009 ($t = 9$) is Balance($) = 1984 + 146(9) = $3298

c. A portion of the Minitab regression output follows (*Note*: $t = 1$ corresponds to 2001, $t = 2$ corresponds to 2002, and so on)

```
The regression equation is
Balance($) = 2924 - 419 t + 62.7 tsq
```

The forecast for 2009 ($t = 9$) is Balance ($) = 2924 − 419(9) + 62.7(9)^2 = $4232

d. The quadratic trend equation provides the best forecast accuracy for the historical data

e. Linear trend equation

46. a. The forecast for July is 236.97

Forecast for August, using forecast for July as the actual sales in July, is 236.97

Exponential smoothing provides the same forecast for every period in the future; this is why it is not usually recommended for long-term forecasting

b. Using Minitab's regression procedure we obtained the linear trend equation

$$T_t = 149.72 + 18.451t$$

Forecast for July is 278.88

Forecast for August is 297.33

c. The proposed settlement is not fair since it does not account for the upward trend in sales; based upon trend projection, the settlement should be based on forecasted lost sales of $278,880 in July and $297,330 in August

48. a. The time series plot shows a linear trend

b. $T_t = -5 + 15t$

The slope of 15 indicates that the average increase in sales is 15 pianos per year

c. 85, 100

50. a.

Quarter	Adjusted Seasonal Index
1	1.2717
2	0.6120
3	0.4978
4	1.6185

Note: Adjustment for seasonal index $= \dfrac{4}{3.8985} = 1.0260$

b. The largest effect is in quarter 4; this seems reasonable since retail sales are generally higher during October, November, and December

52. a. Yes, a linear trend pattern appears to be present

b. A portion of the Minitab regression output follows:

```
The regression equation is
Number Sold = 22.9 + 15.5 Year
```

c. Forecast in year 8 is or approximately 147 units

54. b. The centered moving average values smooth out the time series by removing seasonal effects and some of the random variability; the centered moving average time series shows the trend in the data

c.

Quarter	Adjusted Seasonal Index
1	0.899
2	1.362
3	1.118
4	0.621

d. Hudson Marine experiences the largest seasonal increase in quarter 2; since this quarter occurs prior to the peak summer boating season, this result seems reasonable, but the largest seasonal effect is the seasonal decrease in quarter 4; this is also reasonable because of decreased boating in the fall and winter

Chapter 18

1. $n = 27$ cases with a value different than 150

Normal approximation $\mu = .5n = .5(27) = 13.5$

$\sigma = \sqrt{.25\,n} = \sqrt{.25(27)} = 2.5981$

With the number of plus signs = 22 in the upper tail, use continuity correction factor as follows

$$P(x \geq 21.5) = P\left(z \geq \frac{21.5 - 13.5}{2.5981}\right) = P(z \geq 3.08)$$

p-value $= (1.0000 - .9990) = .0010$

p-value $\leq .01$; reject H_0; conclude population median > 150

2. Dropping the no preference, the binomial probabilities for $n = 9$ and $p = .50$ are as follows

x	Probability	x	Probability
0	0.0020	5	0.2461
1	0.0176	6	0.1641
2	0.0703	7	0.0703
3	0.1641	8	0.0176
4	0.2461	9	0.0020

Number of plus signs = 7

$P(x \geq 7) = P(7) + P(8) + P(9)$

$= .0703 + .0176 + .0020$

$= .0899$

Two-tailed p-value $= 2(.0899) = .1798$

p-value $> .05$, do not reject H_0; conclude no indication that a difference exists

4. a. H_0: Median ≥ 15

H_a: Median < 15

b. $n = 9$; number of plus signs = 1

p-value $= .0196$

Reject H_0; bond mutual funds have lower median

6. $n = 48$; $z = 1.88$

p-value $= .0301$

Reject H_0; conclude median $> \$56.2$ thousand

8. a. $n = 15$

p-value $= .1186$

Do not reject H_0; no significant difference for the pace

b. 25%, 68.8%; recommend larger sample

10. $n = 600$; $z = 2.41$

p-value $= .0160$

Reject H_0; significant difference, *American Idol* preferred

12. H_0: Median for Additive 1 − Median for Additive 2 = 0

H_a: Median for Additive 1 − Median for Additive 2 ≠ 0

Difference	Absolute Difference	Rank	Signed Ranks Negative	Signed Ranks Positive
2.07	2.07	9		9
1.79	1.79	7		7
−0.54	0.54	3	−3	
2.09	2.09	10		10
0.01	0.01	1		1
0.97	0.97	4		4
−1.04	1.04	5	−5	
3.57	3.57	12		12
1.84	1.84	8		8
3.08	3.08	11		11
0.43	0.43	2		2
1.32	1.32	6		6
	Sum of Positive Signed Ranks			$T^+ = 70$

$$\mu_{T^+} = \frac{n(n+1)}{4} = \frac{12(13)}{4} = 39$$

$$\sigma_{T^+} = \sqrt{\frac{n(n+1)(2n+1)}{24}} = \sqrt{\frac{12(13)(25)}{24}} = 12.7475$$

$$P(T^+ \geq 70) = P\left(z \geq \frac{69.5 - 39}{12.7475}\right) = P(z \geq 2.39)$$

p-value = 2(1.0000 − .9916) = .0168
p-value ≤ .05, reject H_0; conclude significant difference between additives

13. H_0: Median time without Relaxant 1 − Median time with Relaxant ≤ 0
H_a: Median time without Relaxant 1 − Median time with Relaxant > 0

Difference	Absolute Difference	Rank	Signed Ranks Negative	Signed Ranks Positive
5	5	9		9
2	2	3		3
10	10	10		10
−3	3	6.5	−6.5	
1	1	1		1
2	2	3		3
−2	2	3	−3	
3	3	6.5		6.5
3	3	6.5		6.5
3	3	6.5		6.5
	Sum of Positive Signed Ranks		T^+ =	45.5

$$\mu_{T^+} = \frac{n(n+1)}{4} = \frac{10(11)}{4} = 27.5$$

$$\sigma_{T^+} = \sqrt{\frac{n(n+1)(2n+1)}{24}} = \sqrt{\frac{10(11)(12)}{24}} = 9.8107$$

$$P(T^+ \geq 45.5) = P\left(z \geq \frac{45 - 27.5}{12.7475}\right) = P(z \geq 1.78)$$

p-value = (1.0000 − .9925) = .0375
p-value ≤ .05; reject H_0; conclude without the relaxant has a greater median time

14. $n = 11$; $T^+ = 61$; $z = 2.45$
p-value = .0142
Reject H_0; conclude significant difference; on-time % better in 2006

16. $n = 10$; $T^+ = 12.5$; $z = -1.48$
p-value = .1388
Do not reject H_0; conclude no difference between median scores

18. H_0: The two populations of additives are identical
H_a: The two populations of additives are not identical

Additive 1	Rank	Additive 2	Rank
17.3	2	18.7	8.5
18.4	6	17.8	4
19.1	10	21.3	15
16.7	1	21.0	14
18.2	5	22.1	16
18.6	7	18.7	8.5
17.5	3	19.8	11
		20.7	13
		20.2	12
W =	34		

$$\mu_W = \frac{1}{2}n_1(n_1 + n_2 + 1) = \frac{1}{2}7(7 + 9 + 1) = 59.5$$

$$\sigma_W = \sqrt{\frac{1}{12}n_1n_2(n_1 + n_2 + 1)} = \sqrt{\frac{1}{12}7(9)(7 + 9 + 1)}$$

$= 9.4472$

With $W = 34$ in lower tail, use the continuity correction

$$P(W \leq 34) = P\left(z \leq \frac{34.5 - 59.5}{9.4472}\right) = P(z \leq -2.65)$$

p-value = 2(.0040) = .0080
p-value < .05; reject H_0; conclude additives are not identical
Additive 2 tends to provide higher miles per gallon

19. a. H_0: The two populations of salaries are identical
H_a: The two populations of salaries are not identical

Public Accountant	Rank	Financial Planner	Rank
50.2	5	49.0	2
58.8	19	49.2	3
56.3	16	53.1	10
58.2	18	55.9	15
54.2	13	51.9	8.5
55.0	14	53.6	11
50.9	6	49.7	4
59.5	20	53.9	12
57.0	17	51.8	7
51.9	8.5	48.9	1
W =	136.5		

$$\mu_W = \frac{1}{2}n_1(n_1 + n_2 + 1) = \frac{1}{2}10(10 + 10 + 1) = 105$$

$$\sigma_W = \sqrt{\frac{1}{12}n_1n_2(n_1 + n_2 + 1)} = \sqrt{\frac{1}{12}10(10)(10 + 10 + 1)}$$

$= 13.2288$

With $W = 136.5$ in upper tail, use the continuity correction

$$P(W \geq 136.5) = P\left(z \geq \frac{136 - 105}{13.2288}\right) = P(z \geq 2.34)$$

p-value = 2(1.0000 − .9904) = .0192
p-value ≤ .05; reject H_0; conclude populations are not identical
Public accountants tend to have higher salaries

b. Public Accountant $\frac{(55.0 + 56.3)}{2} = \$55.65$ thousand

Financial Planner $\frac{(51.8 + 51.9)}{2} = \$51.85$ thousand

20. a. \$54,900, \$40,400
b. $W = 69$; $z = 2.04$
p-value = .0414
Reject H_0; conclude a difference between salaries; men higher

22. $W = 157$; $z = 2.74$
p-value = .0062

Reject H_0; conclude a difference between ratios; Japan tends to be higher

24. $W = 116$; $z = -.22$
p-value $= .8258$
Do not reject H_0; conclude no evidence prices differ

26. H_0: All populations of product ratings are identical
H_a: Not all populations of product ratings are identical

	A	B	C
	4	11	7
	8	14	2
	10	15	1
	3	12	6
	9	13	5
Sum of Ranks	34	65	21

$$H = \left[\frac{12}{15(16)}\left(\frac{34^2}{5} + \frac{65^2}{5} + \frac{21^2}{5}\right)\right] - 3(16) = 10.22$$

χ^2 table with $df = 2$, $\chi^2 = 10.22$; the p-value is between .005 and .01

p-value $\leq .01$; reject H_0; conclude the populations of ratings are not identical

28. H_0: All populations of calories burned are identical
H_a: Not all populations calories burned are identical

	Swimming	Tennis	Cycling
	8	9	5
	4	14	1
	11	13	3
	6	10	7
	12	15	2
Sum of Ranks	41	61	18

$$H = \left[\frac{12}{15(16)}\left(\frac{41^2}{5} + \frac{61^2}{5} + \frac{18^2}{5}\right)\right] - 3(16) = 9.26$$

χ^2 table with $df = 2$, $\chi^2 = 9.26$; the p-value is between .005 and .01

p-value $\leq .05$ reject H_0; conclude that the populations of calories burned are not identical

30. $H = 8.03$ with $df = 3$
p-value is between .025 and .05
Reject H_0; conclude a difference between quality of courses

32. a. $\Sigma d_i^2 = 52$

$$r_s = 1 - \frac{6\Sigma d_i^2}{n(n^2 - 1)} = 1 - \frac{6(52)}{10(99)} = .685$$

b. $$\sigma_{r_s} = \sqrt{\frac{1}{n - 1}} = \sqrt{\frac{1}{9}} = .3333$$

$$z = \frac{r_s - 0}{\sigma_{r_s}} = \frac{.685}{.3333} = 2.05$$

p-value $= 2(1.0000 - .9798) = .0404$
p-value $\leq .05$, reject H_0; conclude significant positive rank correlation

34. $\Sigma d_i^2 = 250$

$$r_s = 1 - \frac{6\Sigma d_i^2}{n(n^2 - 1)} = 1 - \frac{6(250)}{11(120)} = -.136$$

$$\sigma_{r_s} = \sqrt{\frac{1}{n - 1}} = \sqrt{\frac{1}{10}} = .3162$$

$$z = \frac{r_s - 0}{\sigma_{r_s}} = \frac{-.136}{.3162} = -.43$$

p-value $= 2(.3336) = .6672$
p-value $> .05$, do not reject H_0; we cannot conclude that there is a significant relationship

36. $r_s = -.709$, $z = -2.13$
p-value $= .0332$
Reject H_0; conclude a significant rank correlation

38. Number of plus signs $= 905$, $z = -3.15$
p-value less than .0020
Reject H_0; conclude a significant difference between the preferences

40. $n = 12$; $T^+ = 6$; $z = -2.55$
p-value $= .0108$
Reject H_0; conclude significant difference between prices

42. $W = 70$; $z = -2.93$
p-value $= .0034$
Reject H_0; conclude populations of weights are not identical

44. $H = 12.61$ with $df = 2$
p-value is less than .005
Reject H_0; conclude the populations of ratings are not identical

46. $r_s = .757$, $z = 2.83$
p-value $= .0046$
Reject H_0; conclude a significant positive rank correlation

Chapter 19

2. a. 5.42
b. UCL $= 6.09$, LCL $= 4.75$

4. *R chart:*
UCL $= \bar{R}D_4 = 1.6(1.864) = 2.98$
LCL $= \bar{R}D_3 = 1.6(.136) = .22$
$\bar{x}$ chart:
UCL $= \bar{\bar{x}} + A_2\bar{R} = 28.5 + .373(1.6) = 29.10$
LCL $= \bar{\bar{x}} - A_2\bar{R} = 28.5 - .373(1.6) = 27.90$

6. 20.01, .082

8. a. .0470
b. UCL $= .0989$, LCL $= -0.0049$ (use LCL $= 0$)
c. $\bar{p} = .08$; in control
d. UCL $= 14.826$, LCL $= -0.726$ (use LCL $= 0$)
Process is out of control if more than 14 defective
e. In control with 12 defective
f. *np* chart

10. $f(x) = \frac{n!}{x!(n-x)!} p^x(1-p)^{n-x}$

When $p = .02$, the probability of accepting the lot is

$$f(0) = \frac{25!}{0!(25-0)!}(.02)^0(1-.02)^{25} = .6035$$

When $p = .06$, the probability of accepting the lot is

$$f(0) = \frac{25!}{0!(25-0)!}(.06)^0(1-.06)^{25} = .2129$$

12. $p_0 = .02$; producer's risk = .0599
$p_0 = .06$; producer's risk = .3396
Producer's risk decreases as the acceptance number c is increased

14. $n = 20$, $c = 3$

16. **a.** 95.4
b. UCL = 96.07, LCL = 94.73
c. No

18.

	R Chart	$\bar{x}$ Chart
UCL	4.23	6.57
LCL	0	4.27

Estimate of standard deviation = .86

20.

	R Chart	$\bar{x}$ Chart
UCL	.1121	3.112
LCL	0	3.051

22. **a.** UCL = .0817, LCL = −.0017 (use LCL = 0)

24. **a.** .03
b. $\beta = .0802$

Chapter 20

1. **a.**

Item	Price Relative
A	103 = (7.75/7.50)(100)
B	238 = (1500/630)(100)

b. $I_{2011} = \frac{7.75 + 1500.00}{7.50 + 630.00}(100) = \frac{1507.75}{637.50}(100) = 237$

c. $I_{2011} = \frac{7.75(1500) + 1500.00(2)}{7.50(1500) + 630.00(2)}(100)$
$= \frac{14,625.00}{12,510.00}(100) = 117$

d. $I_{2011} = \frac{7.75(1800) + 1500.00(1)}{7.50(1800) + 630.00(1)}(100)$
$= \frac{15,450.00}{14,130.00}(100) = 109$

2. **a.** 32%
b. \$8.14

3. **a.** Price relatives for A = (6.00/5.45)100 = 110
B = (5.95/5.60)100 = 106
C = (6.20/5.50)100 = 113

b. $I_{2011} = \frac{6.00 + 5.95 + 6.20}{5.45 + 5.60 + 5.50}(100) = 110$

c. $I_{2011} = \frac{6.00(150) + 5.95(200) + 6.20(120)}{5.45(150) + 5.60(200) + 5.50(120)}(100)$
$= 109$
9% increase over the two-year period

4. $I_{2011} = 114$

6.

Item	Price Relative	Base Period Price	Base Period Usage	Weight	Weighted Price Relative
A	150	22.00	20	440	66,000
B	90	5.00	50	250	22,500
C	120	14.00	40	560	67,200
			Totals	1250	155,700

$$I = \frac{155,700}{1250} = 125$$

7. **a.** Price relatives for A = (3.95/2.50)100 = 158
B = (9.90/8.75)100 = 113
C = (.95/.99)100 = 96

b.

Item	Price Relative	Base Price	Quantity	Weight $P_{i0}Q_i$	Weighted Price Relative
A	158	2.50	25	62.5	9,875
B	113	8.75	15	131.3	14,837
C	96	.99	60	59.4	5,702
			Totals	253.2	30,414

$$I = \frac{30,414}{253.2} = 120$$

Cost of raw materials is up 20% for the chemical

8. $I = 105$; portfolio is up 5%

10. **a.** Deflated 2007 wages: $\frac{\$30.04}{207.3}(100) = \$14.49$

Deflated 2011 wages: $\frac{\$33.23}{224.9}(100) = \$14.78$

b. $\frac{33.23}{30.04}(100) = 1.11$; the percentange increase in actual wages is 11%

c. $\frac{14.78}{14.49}(100) = 1.02$; the percentage increase in real wages is 2%

12. a. 2009: $\frac{\$29.1}{216.0}(100) = \$13.47$

2010: $\frac{\$33.3}{218.4}(100) = \$15.25$

2011: $\frac{\$32.9}{226.9}(100) = \$14.50$

b. 2009: $\frac{\$29.1}{173.4}(100) = \$16.78$

2010: $\frac{\$33.3}{180.2}(100) = \$18.48$

2011: $\frac{\$32.9}{192.5}(100) = \$17.09$

c. PPI is more appropriate than CPI because these figures reflect prices paid by retailers (rather than by consumers)

14. $I = \frac{300(18.00) + 400(4.90) + 850(15.00)}{350(18.00) + 220(4.90) + 730(15.00)}(100)$

$= \frac{20{,}110}{18{,}328}(100) = 110$

15. $I = \frac{95(1200) + 75(1800) + 50(2000) + 70(1500)}{120(1200) + 86(1800) + 35(2000) + 60(1500)}(100)$

$= 99$

Quantities are down slightly

16. $I = 83$

18. a. 151, 197, 143, 178

b. $I = 170$

20. $I_{\text{Jan}} = 73.5$, $I_{\text{Mar}} = 70.1$

22.

Item	Price Relatives $(P_{it}/P_{i0})100$	Base Price P_{i0}	Quantity Q_i	Weight $W_i = P_{i0}Q_i$	Weighted Price Relatives $(P_{it}/P_{i0})100\ W_i$
Handle	126.9	7.46	1	7.46	946.67
Blades	153.7	1.9	17	32.30	4964.51
			Totals	39.76	5911.18

$I_{2011} = (5911.18/39.76) = 148.7$

24. 2008 (84810/215.3)100 = \$39,392
2009 (87210/214.5)100 = \$40,657
2010 (87650/218.1)100 = \$40,188
2011 (91060/224.9)100 = \$40,489
(40489/39392) = 1.028

The median salary increased 2.8% over the period

26. $I = 143$; quantity is up 43%

Appendix E: Microsoft Excel 2010 and Tools for Statistical Analysis

Microsoft Excel 2010, part of the Microsoft Office 2010 system, is a spreadsheet program that can be used to organize and analyze data, perform complex calculations, and create a wide variety of graphical displays. We assume that readers are familiar with basic Excel operations such as selecting cells, entering formulas, copying, and so on. But we do not assume readers are familiar with Excel 2010 or the use of Excel for statistical analysis.

The purpose of this appendix is twofold. First, we provide an overview of Excel 2010 and discuss the basic operations needed to work with Excel 2010 workbooks and worksheets. Second, we provide an overview of the tools that are available for conducting statistical analysis with Excel. These include Excel functions and formulas which allow users to conduct their own analyses and add-ins that provide more comprehensive analysis tools.

Excel's Data Analysis add-in, included with the basic Excel system, is a valuable tool for conducting statistical analysis. In the last section of this appendix we provide instruction for installing the Data Analysis add-in. Other add-ins have been developed by outside suppliers to supplement the basic statistical capabilities provided by Excel. In the last section we also discuss StatTools, a commercially available add-in developed by Palisade Corporation.

Overview of Microsoft Excel 2010

A workbook is a file containing one or more worksheets.

When using Excel for statistical analysis, data is displayed in workbooks, each of which contains a series of worksheets that typically include the original data as well as any resulting analysis, including charts. Figure 1 shows the layout of a blank workbook created each time Excel is opened. The workbook is named Book1, and consists of three worksheets named Sheet1, Sheet2, and Sheet3. Excel highlights the worksheet currently displayed (Sheet1) by setting the name on the worksheet tab in bold. To select a different worksheet simply click on the corresponding tab. Note that cell A1 is initially selected.

The wide bar located across the top of the workbook is referred to as the Ribbon. Tabs, located at the top of the Ribbon, provide quick access to groups of related commands. There are nine tabs shown on the workbook in Figure 1: File; Home; Insert; Page Layout; Formulas; Data; Review; View; and Add-Ins. Each tab contains a series of groups of related commands. Note that the Home tab is selected when Excel is opened. Figure 2 displays the groups available when the Home tab is selected. Under the Home tab there are seven groups: Clipboard; Font; Alignment; Number; Styles; Cells; and Editing. Commands are arranged within each group. For example, to change selected text to boldface, click the Home tab and click the Bold button in the Font group.

Figure 3 illustrates the location of the Quick Access Toolbar and the Formula Bar. The Quick Access Toolbar allows you to quickly access workbook options. To add or remove features on the Quick Access Toolbar click the Customize Quick Access Toolbar button on the Quick Access Toolbar.

The Formula Bar (see Figure 3) contains a Name box, the Insert Function button *fx*, and a Formula box. In Figure 3, "A1" appears in the name box because cell A1 is selected. You can select any other cell in the worksheet by using the mouse to move the cursor to another cell and clicking or by typing the new cell location in the Name box. The Formula box is used to display the formula in the currently selected cell. For instance, if you had entered =A1+A2 into cell A3, whenever you select cell A3 the formula =A1+A2 will be

FIGURE 1 BLANK WORKBOOK CREATED WHEN EXCEL IS OPENED

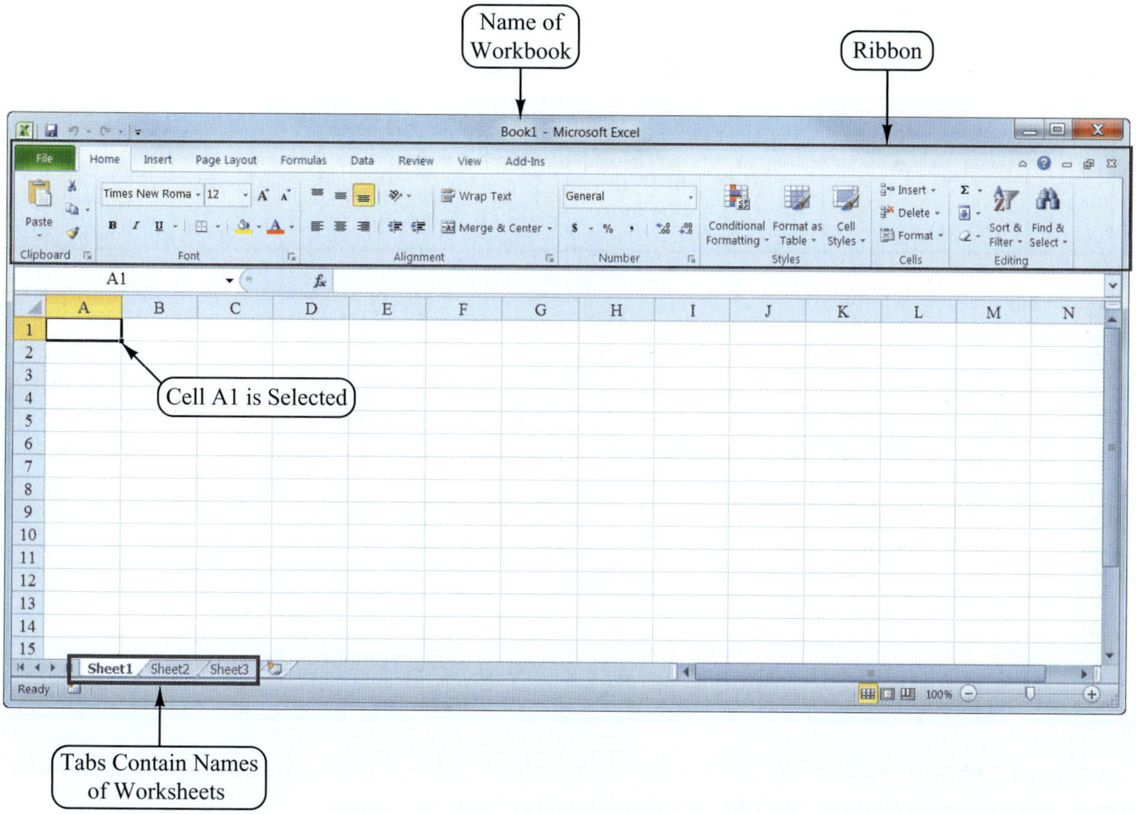

shown in the Formula box. This feature makes it very easy to see and edit a formula in a particular cell. The Insert Function button allows you to quickly access all of the functions available in Excel. Later we show how to find and use a particular function.

Basic Workbook Operations

Figure 4 illustrates the worksheet options that can be performed after right-clicking on a worksheet tab. For instance, to change the name of the current worksheet from "Sheet1" to "Data," right-click the worksheet tab named "Sheet1" and select the Rename option. The current worksheet name (Sheet1) will be highlighted. Then, simply type the new name (Data) and press the Enter key to rename the worksheet.

Suppose that you wanted to create a copy of "Sheet 1." After right-clicking the tab named "Sheet1," select the Move or Copy option. When the Move or Copy dialog box appears, select Create a Copy and click OK. The name of the copied worksheet will appear as "Sheet1 (2)." You can then rename it, if desired.

To add a worksheet to the workbook, right-click any worksheet tab and select the Insert option; when the Insert dialog box appears, select Worksheet and click OK. An additional blank worksheet titled "Sheet 4" will appear in the workbook. You can also insert a new worksheet by clicking the Insert Worksheet tab button that appears to the right of the last worksheet tab displayed. Worksheets can be deleted by right-clicking the worksheet tab and choosing Delete. After clicking Delete a window will appear warning you that any data appearing in the worksheet will be lost. Click Delete to confirm that you do want to

FIGURE 2 PORTION OF THE HOME TAB

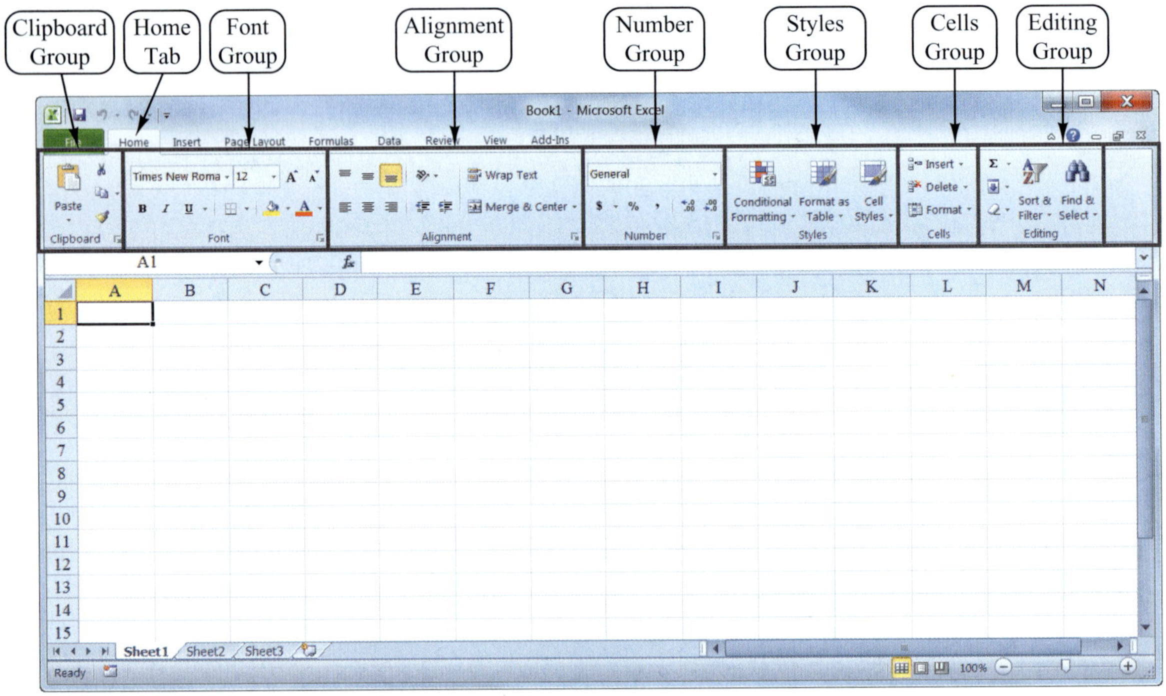

FIGURE 3 EXCEL 2010 QUICK ACCESS TOOLBAR AND FORMULA BAR

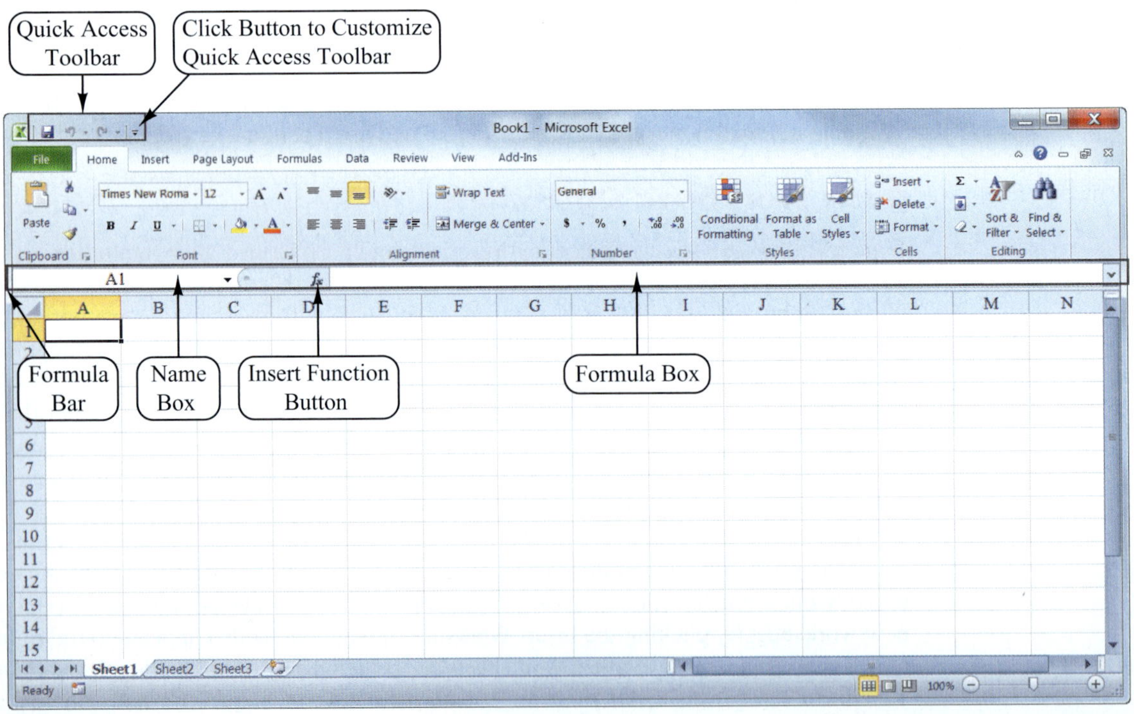

FIGURE 4 WORKSHEET OPTIONS OBTAINED AFTER RIGHT-CLICKING ON A WORKSHEET TAB

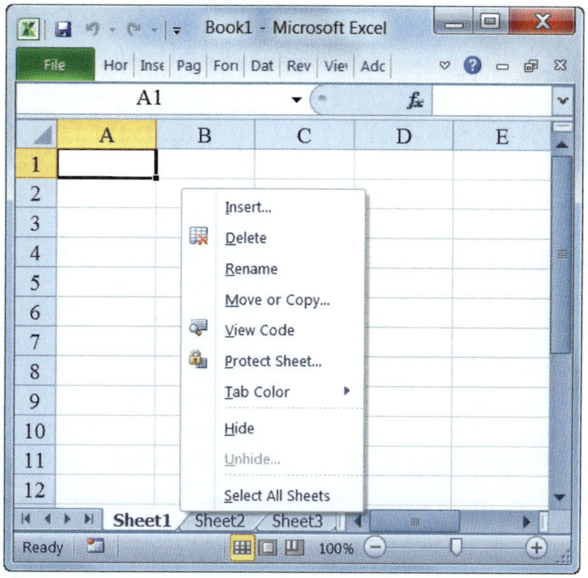

delete the worksheet. Worksheets can also be moved to other workbooks or a different position in the current workbook by using the Move or Copy option.

Creating, Saving, and Opening Files

Data can be entered into an Excel worksheet by manually entering the data into the worksheet or by opening another workbook that already contains the data. As an illustration of manually entering, saving, and opening a file we will use the example from Chapter 2 involving data for a sample of 50 soft drink purchases. The original data are shown in Table 1.

Suppose you just opened Excel and want to work with this data. A blank workbook containing three worksheets will be displayed. The soft drink data can now be entered by simply typing it into one of the worksheets. If Excel is currently running and no blank workbook is displayed, you can create a blank workbook using the following steps:

Step 1: Click the **File** tab
Step 2: Click **New** in the list of options
Step 3: When the Available Templates dialog box appears:
Double-click **Blank Workbook**

A new workbook containing three worksheets labeled Sheet1, Sheet2, and Sheet3 will appear.

Suppose we want to enter the data for the sample of 50 soft drink purchases into Sheet1 of the new workbook. First, we enter the label "Brand Purchased" into cell A1; then, we enter the data for the 50 soft drink purchases into cells A2:A51. As a reminder that this worksheet contains the data, we will change the name of the worksheet from "Sheet1" to "Data" using the procedure described previously. Figure 5 shows the data worksheet that we just developed.

TABLE 1 DATA FROM A SAMPLE OF 50 SOFT DRINK PURCHASES

Coca-Cola	Sprite	Pepsi
Diet Coke	Coca-Cola	Coca-Cola
Pepsi	Diet Coke	Coca-Cola
Diet Coke	Coca-Cola	Coca-Cola
Coca-Cola	Diet Coke	Pepsi
Coca-Cola	Coca-Cola	Dr. Pepper
Dr. Pepper	Sprite	Coca-Cola
Diet Coke	Pepsi	Diet Coke
Pepsi	Coca-Cola	Pepsi
Pepsi	Coca-Cola	Pepsi
Coca-Cola	Coca-Cola	Pepsi
Dr. Pepper	Pepsi	Pepsi
Sprite	Coca-Cola	Coca-Cola
Coca-Cola	Sprite	Dr. Pepper
Diet Coke	Dr. Pepper	Pepsi
Coca-Cola	Pepsi	Sprite
Coca-Cola	Diet Coke	

FIGURE 5 WORKSHEET CONTAINING THE SOFT DRINK DATA

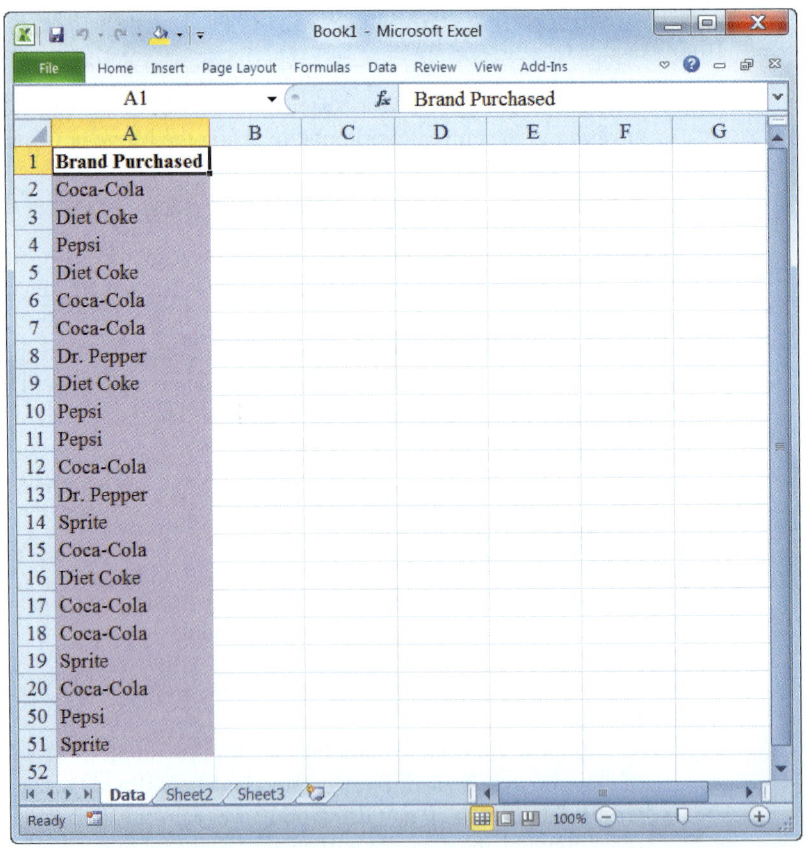

Note: Rows 21–49 are hidden.

Before doing any analysis with these data, we recommend that you first save the file; this will prevent you from having to reenter the data in case something happens that causes Excel to close. To save the file as an Excel 2010 workbook using the filename SoftDrink we perform the following steps:

Step 1: Click the **File** tab
Step 2: Click **Save** in the list of options
Step 3: When the Save As dialog box appears:
Select the location where you want to save the file
Type the filename **SoftDrink** in the **File name** box
Click **Save**

Keyboard shortcut: To save the file, press CTRL+S

Excel's Save command is designed to save the file as an Excel 2010 workbook. As you work with the file to do statistical analysis you should follow the practice of periodically saving the file so you will not lose any statistical analysis you may have performed. Simply click the File tab and select Save in the list of options.

Sometimes you may want to create a copy of an existing file. For instance, suppose you would like to save the soft drink data and any resulting statistical analysis in a new file named "SoftDrink Analysis." The following steps show how to create a copy of the SoftDrink workbook and analysis with the new filename, "SoftDrink Analysis."

Step 1: Click the **File** tab
Step 2: Click **Save As**
Step 3: When the Save As dialog box appears:
Select the location where you want to save the file
Type the filename **SoftDrink Analysis** in the **File name** box
Click **Save**

Once the workbook has been saved, you can continue to work with the data to perform whatever type of statistical analysis is appropriate. When you are finished working with the file simply click the close window button ✕ located at the top right-hand corner of the Ribbon. To access the SoftDrink Analysis file at another point in time you can open the file by performing the following steps:

Step 1: Click the **File** tab
Step 2: Click **Open**
Step 3: When the Open dialog box appears:
Select the location where you previously saved the file
Enter the filename **SoftDrink Analysis** in the **File name** box
Click **Open**

The procedures we showed for saving or opening a workbook begin by clicking File tab to access the Save and Open commands. Once you have used Excel for a while you will probably find it more convenient to add these commands to the Quick Access Toolbar.

Using Excel Functions

Excel 2010 provides a wealth of functions for data management and statistical analysis. If we know what function is needed, and how to use it, we can simply enter the function into the appropriate worksheet cell. However, if we are not sure what functions are available to accomplish a task or are not sure how to use a particular function, Excel can provide assistance. Many new functions for statistical analysis have been added with Excel 2010. To illustrate we will use the SoftDrink Analysis workbook created in the previous subsection.

FIGURE 6 INSERT FUNCTION DIALOG BOX

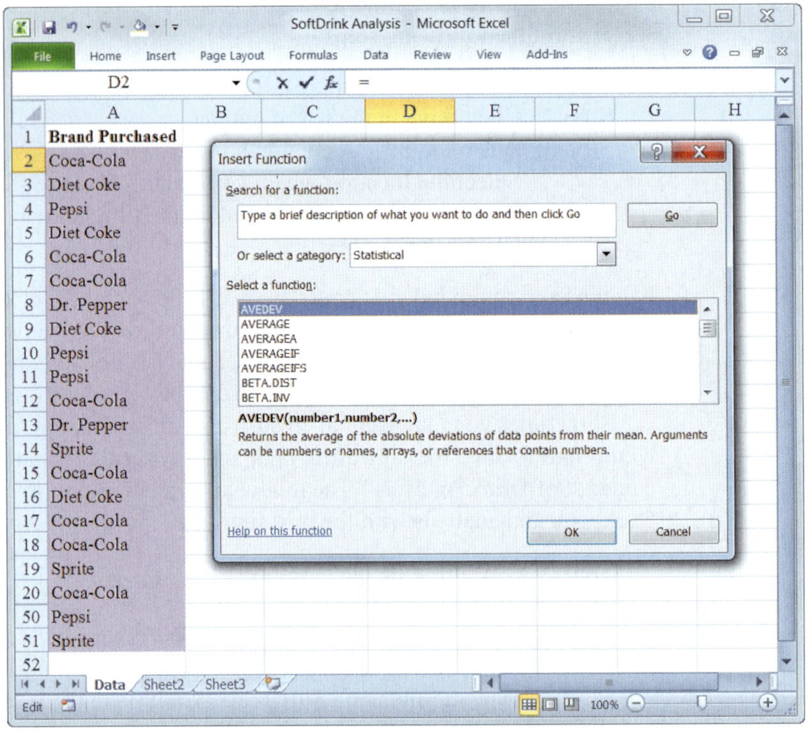

Note: Rows 21–49 are hidden.

Finding the Right Excel Function

To identify the functions available in Excel, select the cell where you want to insert the function; we have selected cell D2. Click the **Formulas** tab on the Ribbon and then click the **Insert Function** button in the **Function Library** group. Alternatively, click the *fx* button on the formula bar. Either approach provides the **Insert Function** dialog box shown in Figure 6.

The **Search for a function** box at the top of the Insert Function dialog box enables us to type a brief description of what we want to do. After doing so and clicking **Go**, Excel will search for and display, in the **Select a function** box, the functions that may accomplish our task. In many situations, however, we may want to browse through an entire category of functions to see what is available. For this task, the **Or select a category** box is helpful. It contains a drop-down list of several categories of functions provided by Excel. Figure 6 shows that we selected the **Statistical** category. As a result, Excel's statistical functions appear in alphabetic order in the Select a function box. We see the AVEDEV function listed first, followed by the AVERAGE function, and so on.

The AVEDEV function is highlighted in Figure 6, indicating it is the function currently selected. The proper syntax for the function and a brief description of the function appear below the Select a function box. We can scroll through the list in the Select a function box to display the syntax and a brief description for each of the statistical functions that are available. For instance, scrolling down farther, we select the COUNTIF function as shown in Figure 7. Note that COUNTIF is now highlighted, and that immediately below the Select a function box we see **COUNTIF(range,criteria)**, which indicates that the COUNTIF function contains two inputs, range and criteria. In addition, we see that the description of the COUNTIF function is "Counts the number of cells within a range that meet the given condition."

FIGURE 7 DESCRIPTION OF THE COUNTIF FUNCTION IN THE INSERT FUNCTION DIALOG BOX

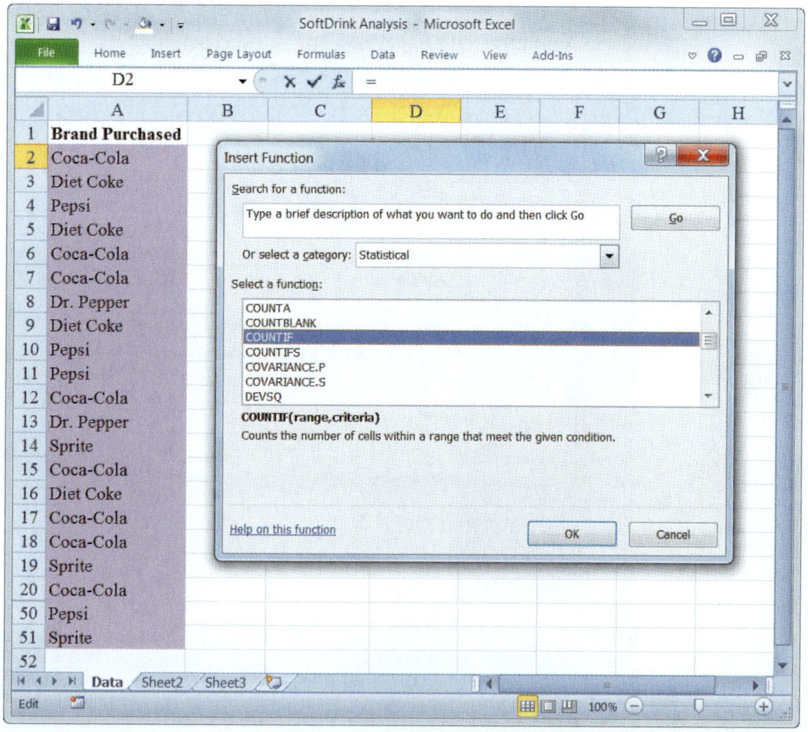

Note: Rows 21–49 are hidden.

If the function selected (highlighted) is the one we want to use, we click **OK**; the **Function Arguments** dialog box then appears. The Function Arguments dialog box for the COUNTIF function is shown in Figure 8. This dialog box assists in creating the appropriate arguments for the function selected. When finished entering the arguments, we click OK; Excel then inserts the function into a worksheet cell.

Inserting a Function into a Worksheet Cell

We will now show how to use the Insert Function and Function Arguments dialog boxes to select a function, develop its arguments, and insert the function into a worksheet cell.

Suppose we want to construct a frequency distribution for the soft drink purchase data in Table 1. Figure 9 displays an Excel worksheet containing the soft drink data and labels for the frequency distribution we would like to construct. We see that the frequency of Coca-Cola purchases will go into cell D2, the frequency of Diet Coke purchases will go into cell D3, and so on. Suppose we want to use the COUNTIF function to compute the frequencies and would like some assistance from Excel.

Step 1. Select cell D2
Step 2. Click *fx* on the formula bar
Step 3. When the Insert Function dialog box appears:
Select **Statistical** in the **Or select a category** box
Select **COUNTIF** in the **Select a function** box
Click **OK**

FIGURE 8 FUNCTION ARGUMENTS DIALOG BOX FOR THE COUNTIF FUNCTION

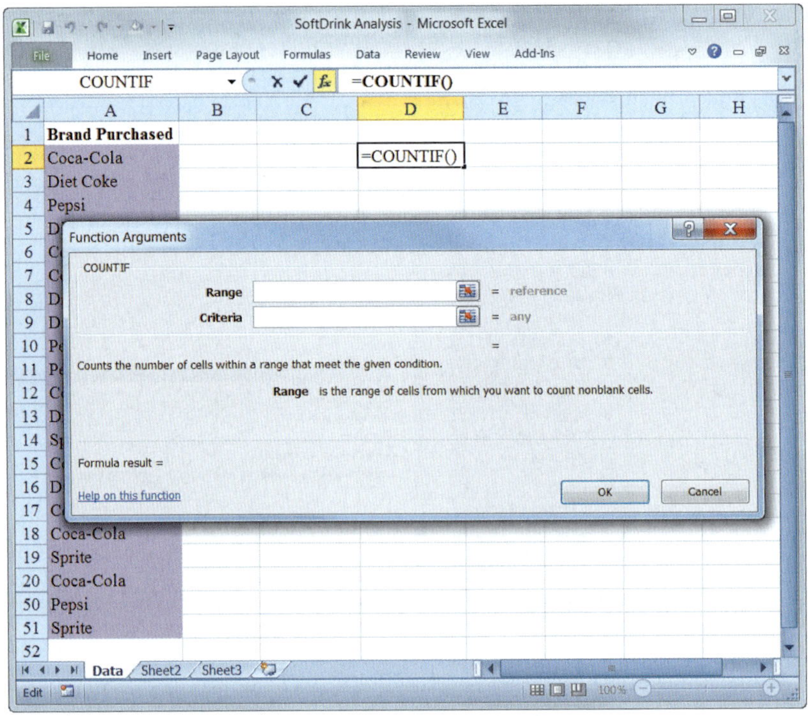

Note: Rows 21–49 are hidden.

FIGURE 9 EXCEL WORKSHEET WITH SOFT DRINK DATA AND LABELS FOR THE FREQUENCY DISTRIBUTION WE WOULD LIKE TO CONSTRUCT

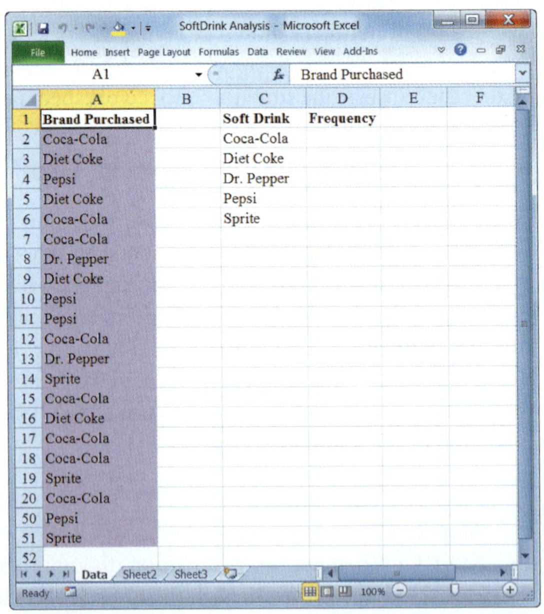

Note: Rows 21–49 are hidden.

FIGURE 10 COMPLETED FUNCTION ARGUMENTS DIALOG BOX FOR THE COUNTIF FUNCTION

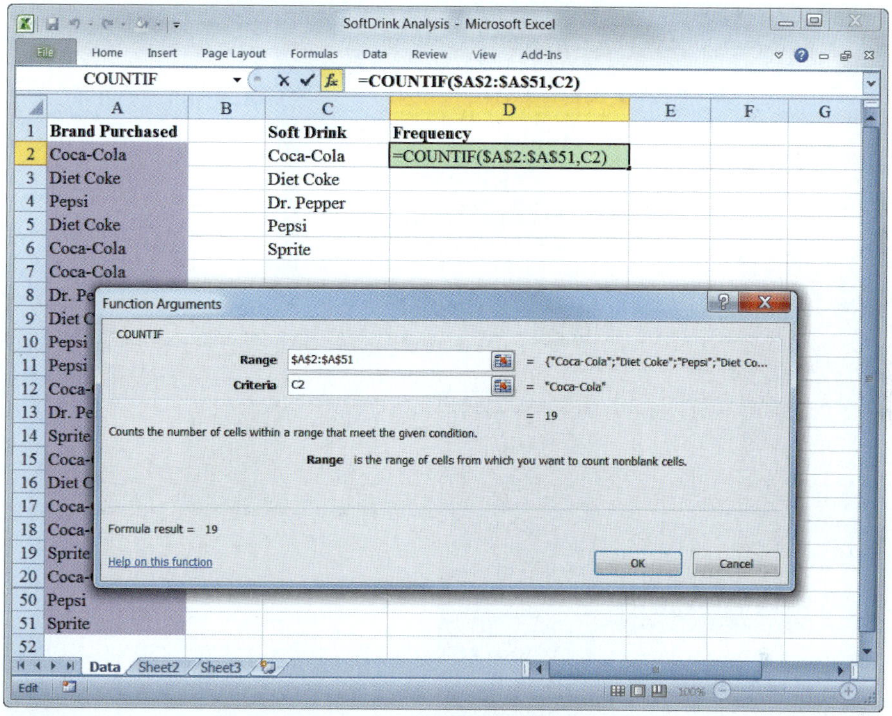

Note: Rows 21–49 are hidden.

Step 4. When the **Function Arguments** dialog box appears (see Figure 10):
Enter $A$2:$A$51 in the **Range** box
Enter C2 in the **Criteria** box (At this point, the value of the function will appear on the next-to-last line of the dialog box. Its value is 19.)
Click **OK**

Step 5. Copy cell D2 to cells D3:D6

The worksheet then appears as in Figure 11. The formula worksheet is in the background; the value worksheet appears in the foreground. The formula worksheet shows that the COUNTIF function was inserted into cells D2:D6. The value worksheet shows the proper class frequencies as computed.

We illustrated the use of Excel's capability to provide assistance in using the COUNTIF function. The procedure is similar for all Excel functions. This capability is especially helpful if you do not know what function to use or forget the proper name and/or inputs required for a function.

Using Excel Add-Ins

Excel's Data Analysis Add-In

Excel's Data Analysis add-in, included with the basic Excel package, is a valuable tool for conducting statistical analysis. Before you can use the Data Analysis add-in it must be installed. To see if the Data Analysis add-in has already been installed, click the Data tab on the Ribbon. In the Analysis group you should see the Data Analysis command. If you do

FIGURE 11 EXCEL WORKSHEET SHOWING THE USE OF EXCEL'S COUNTIF FUNCTION TO CONSTRUCT A FREQUENCY DISTRIBUTION

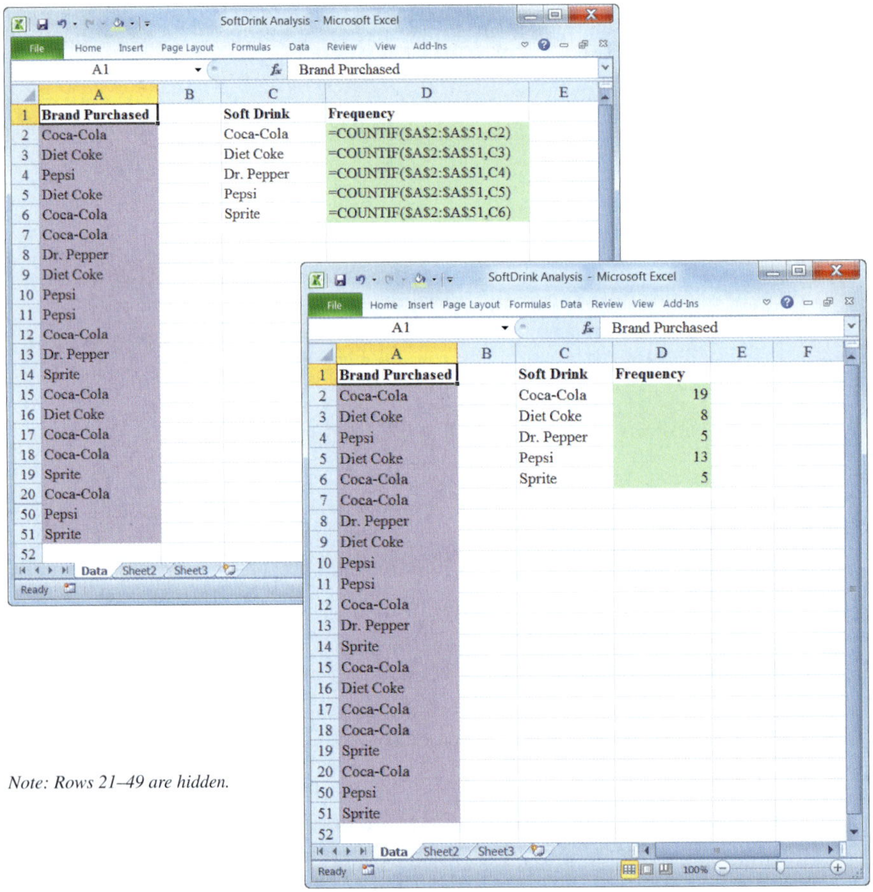

Note: Rows 21–49 are hidden.

not have an Analysis group and/or the Data Analysis command does not appear in the Analysis group, you will need to install the Data Analysis add-in. The steps needed to install the Data Analysis add-in are as follows:

Step 1. Click the **File** tab
Step 2. Click **Options**
Step 3. When the Excel Options dialog box appears:
Select **Add-Ins** from the list of options (on the pane on the left)
In the **Manage** box, select **Excel Add-Ins**
Click **Go**
Step 4. When the Add-Ins dialog box appears:
Select **Analysis ToolPak**
Click **OK**

Outside Vendor Add-Ins

One of the leading companies in the development of Excel add-ins for statistical analysis is Palisade Corporation. In this text we use StatTools, an Excel add-in developed by

Palisade. StatTools provides a powerful statistics toolset that enables users to perform statistical analysis in the familiar Microsoft Office environment.

In the appendix to Chapter 1 we describe how to download and install the StatTools add-in and provide a brief introduction to using the software. In several appendices throughout the text we show how StatTools can be used when no corresponding basic Excel procedure is available or when additional statistical capabilities would be useful.

Typically the add-ins offered with textbooks are designed primarily for classroom use. StatTools, however, was developed for commercial applications. As a result, students who learn how to use StatTools will be able to continue using StatTools throughout their professional career.

Appendix F: Computing p-Values Using Minitab and Excel

Here we describe how Minitab and Excel can be used to compute p-values for the z, t, χ^2, and F statistics that are used in hypothesis tests. As discussed in the text, only approximate p-values for the t, χ^2, and F statistics can be obtained by using tables. This appendix is helpful to a person who has computed the test statistic by hand, or by other means, and wishes to use computer software to compute the exact p-value.

Using Minitab

Minitab can be used to provide the cumulative probability associated with the z, t, χ^2, and F test statistics. So the lower tail p-value is obtained directly. The upper tail p-value is computed by subtracting the lower tail p-value from 1. The two-tailed p-value is obtained by doubling the smaller of the lower and upper tail p-values.

The z test statistic We use the Hilltop Coffee lower tail hypothesis test in Section 9.3 as an illustration; the value of the test statistic is $z = -2.67$. The Minitab steps used to compute the cumulative probability corresponding to $z = -2.67$ follow.

Step 1. Select the **Calc** menu
Step 2. Choose **Probability Distributions**
Step 3. Choose **Normal**
Step 4. When the Normal Distribution dialog box appears:
Select **Cumulative probability**
Enter 0 in the **Mean** box
Enter 1 in the **Standard deviation** box
Select **Input Constant**
Enter -2.67 in the **Input Constant** box
Click **OK**

Minitab provides the cumulative probability of .0038. This cumulative probability is the lower tail p-value used for the Hilltop Coffee hypothesis test.

For an upper tail test, the p-value is computed from the cumulative probability provided by Minitab as follows:

$$p\text{-value} = 1 - \text{cumulative probability}$$

For instance, the upper tail p-value corresponding to a test statistic of $z = -2.67$ is $1 - .0038 = .9962$. The two-tailed p-value corresponding to a test statistic of $z = -2.67$ is 2 times the minimum of the upper and lower tail p-values; that is, the two-tailed p-value corresponding to $z = -2.67$ is $2(.0038) = .0076$.

The t test statistic We use the Heathrow Airport example from Section 9.4 as an illustration; the value of the test statistic is $t = 1.84$ with 59 degrees of freedom. The Minitab steps used to compute the cumulative probability corresponding to $t = 1.84$ follow.

Step 1. Select the **Calc** menu
Step 2. Choose **Probability Distributions**

Step 3. Choose **t**
Step 4. When the t Distribution dialog box appears:
Select **Cumulative probability**
Enter 59 in the **Degrees of freedom** box
Select **Input Constant**
Enter 1.84 in the **Input Constant** box
Click **OK**

Minitab provides a cumulative probability of .9646, and hence the lower tail p-value = .9646. The Heathrow Airport example is an upper tail test; the upper tail p-value is 1 − .9646 = .0354. In the case of a two-tailed test, we would use the minimum of .9646 and .0354 to compute p-value = 2(.0354) = .0708.

The χ^2 test statistic We use the St. Louis Metro Bus example from Section 11.1 as an illustration; the value of the test statistic is $\chi^2 = 28.18$ with 23 degrees of freedom. The Minitab steps used to compute the cumulative probability corresponding to $\chi^2 = 28.18$ follow.

Step 1. Select the **Calc** menu
Step 2. Choose **Probability Distributions**
Step 3. Choose **Chi-Square**
Step 4. When the Chi-Square Distribution dialog box appears:
Select **Cumulative probability**
Enter 23 in the **Degrees of freedom** box
Select **Input Constant**
Enter 28.18 in the **Input Constant** box
Click **OK**

Minitab provides a cumulative probability of .7909, which is the lower tail p-value. The upper tail p-value = 1 − the cumulative probability, or 1 − .7909 = .2091. The two-tailed p-value is 2 times the minimum of the lower and upper tail p-values. Thus, the two-tailed p-value is 2(.2091) = .4182. The St. Louis Metro Bus example involved an upper tail test, so we use p-value = .2091.

The F test statistic We use the Dullus County Schools example from Section 11.2 as an illustration; the test statistic is $F = 2.40$ with 25 numerator degrees of freedom and 15 denominator degrees of freedom. The Minitab steps to compute the cumulative probability corresponding to $F = 2.40$ follow.

Step 1. Select the **Calc** menu
Step 2. Choose **Probability Distributions**
Step 3. Choose **F**
Step 4. When the F Distribution dialog box appears:
Select **Cumulative probability**
Enter 25 in the **Numerator degrees of freedom** box
Enter 15 in the **Denominator degrees of freedom** box
Select **Input Constant**
Enter 2.40 in the **Input Constant** box
Click **OK**

Minitab provides the cumulative probability and hence a lower tail p-value = .9594. The upper tail p-value is 1 − .9594 = .0406. Because the Dullus County Schools example is a two-tailed test, the minimum of .9594 and .0406 is used to compute p-value = 2(.0406) = .0812.

Using Excel

WEB file

p-Value

Excel functions and formulas can be used to compute p-values associated with the z, t, χ^2, and F test statistics. We provide a template in the data file entitled p-Value for use in computing these p-values. Using the template, it is only necessary to enter the value of the test statistic and, if necessary, the appropriate degrees of freedom. Refer to Figure F.1 as we describe how the template is used. For users interested in the Excel functions and formulas being used, just click on the appropriate cell in the template.

The z test statistic We use the Hilltop Coffee lower tail hypothesis test in Section 9.3 as an illustration; the value of the test statistic is $z = -2.67$. To use the p-value template for this hypothesis test, simply enter -2.67 into cell B6 (see Figure F.1). After doing so, p-values for all three types of hypothesis tests will appear. For Hilltop Coffee, we would use the lower tail p-value $= .0038$ in cell B9. For an upper tail test, we would use the p-value in cell B10, and for a two-tailed test we would use the p-value in cell B11.

The t test statistic We use the Heathrow Airport example from Section 9.4 as an illustration; the value of the test statistic is $t = 1.84$ with 59 degrees of freedom. To use the p-value template for this hypothesis test, enter 1.84 into cell E6 and enter 59 into cell E7 (see Figure F.1). After doing so, p-values for all three types of hypothesis tests will appear.

FIGURE F.1 EXCEL WORKSHEET FOR COMPUTING p-VALUES

	A	B	C	D	E	F
1	**Computing *p*-Values**					
2						
3						
4	**Using the Test Statistic z**			**Using the Test Statistic *t***		
5						
6	**Enter *z* -->**	-2.67		**Enter *t* -->**	1.84	
7				***df* -->**	59	
8						
9	***p*-value (Lower Tail)**	0.0038		***p*-value (Lower Tail)**	0.9646	
10	***p*-value (Upper Tail)**	0.9962		***p*-value (Upper Tail)**	0.0354	
11	***p*-value (Two Tail)**	0.0076		***p*-value (Two Tail)**	0.0708	
12						
13						
14						
15						
16	**Using the Test Statistic Chi Square**			**Using the Test Statistic *F***		
17						
18	**Enter Chi Square -->**	28.18		**Enter *F* -->**	2.40	
19	***df* -->**	23		**Numerator *df* -->**	25	
20				**Denominator *df* -->**	15	
21						
22	***p*-value (Lower Tail)**	0.7909		***p*-value (Lower Tail)**	0.9594	
23	***p*-value (Upper Tail)**	0.2091		***p*-value (Upper Tail)**	0.0406	
24	***p*-value (Two Tail)**	0.4181		***p*-value (Two Tail)**	0.0812	
25						

The Heathrow Airport example involves an upper tail test, so we would use the upper tail p-value = .0354 provided in cell E10 for the hypothesis test.

The χ^2 test statistic We use the St. Louis Metro Bus example from Section 11.1 as an illustration; the value of the test statistic is $\chi^2 = 28.18$ with 23 degrees of freedom. To use the p-value template for this hypothesis test, enter 28.18 into cell B18 and enter 23 into cell B19 (see Figure F.1). After doing so, p-values for all three types of hypothesis tests will appear. The St. Louis Metro Bus example involves an upper tail test, so we would use the upper tail p-value = .2091 provided in cell B23 for the hypothesis test.

The F test statistic We use the Dullus County Schools example from Section 11.2 as an illustration; the test statistic is $F = 2.40$ with 25 numerator degrees of freedom and 15 denominator degrees of freedom. To use the p-value template for this hypothesis test, enter 2.40 into cell E18, enter 25 into cell E19, and enter 15 into cell E20 (see Figure F.1). After doing so, p-values for all three types of hypothesis tests will appear. The Dullus County Schools example involves a two-tailed test, so we would use the two-tailed p-value = .0812 provided in cell E24 for the hypothesis test.

Index

Note: Chapters 21 and 22 can be found with the Online Content for this book. Index entries found in these chapters are denoted by the chapter number, hyphen, and page number.

Page numbers followed by a **n** indicate a footnote.

D

E

F

G

H

I

J

K

L

M

Q

R

T

U

V

W

X

Y

Z

Statistics for Business and Economics 12e WEBfiles

Chapter 1

File	Location
Nations	Table 1.1
Norris	Table 1.5
Shadow02	Exercise 25

Chapter 2

File	Location
2011Movies	Case 2
2012Names	Exercise 5
2012Networks	Exercise 6
2012Population	Exercise 46
AirSurvey	Exercise 7
ApTest	Table 2.8
Audit	Table 2.4
BaseballHall	Exercise 8
BBB	Exercise 48
Careers	Exercise 24
CEOTime	Exercise 20
Colleges	Exercises 53, 54, 55, & 56
Computer	Exercise 23
Crosstab	Exercise 27
Crosstab2	Exercise 28
DJIAPrices	Exercise 19
DYield	Exercise 49
FedBank	Exercise 10
Franchise	Exercise 22
Frequency	Exercise 11
FuelData2012	Exercise 35
Hypertension	Exercise 41
LargeCorp	Exercise 21
LivingArea	Exercise 9
ManagerTime	Exercise 43
Marathon	Exercise 26
MPG	Exercise 39
MutualFunds	Exercises 32, 33, & 34
NewSAT	Exercise 44
PelicanStores	Case 1
Restaurant	Table 2.9
Scatter	Exercise 36
SmartPhones	Exercise 42
Snow	Exercise 40
SoftDrink	Table 2.1
StartUps	Exercise 47
Stereo	Table 2.14
SuperBowl	Exercise 45
Syndicated	Exercise 4
Zoo	Exercise 58

Chapter 3

File	Location
2011Movies	Case Problem 2
2012Start Salary	Table 3.1
3Points	Exercise 8
AfricanElephants	Case Problem 5
Ages	Exercise 63
Asian	Case Problem 3
AustralianOpen	Exercise 28
BackToSchool	Exercise 32
BigBangTheory	Exercise 12
BowlGames	Exercise 57
CellService	Exercise 52
Coffee	Exercise 31
CommuteTime	Exercise 7
FairValue	Exercise 71
Flights	Exercise 27
Homes	Exercise 68
Housing	Exercise 59
MajorSalary	Figure 3.8
MLBSalaries	Exercise 53
Mutual	Exercise 54
NCAA	Exercise 44
NFLTickets	Exercise 45
PanamaRailroad	Exercise 75
PelicanStores	Case Problem 1
Penalty	Exercise 66
PovertyLevel	Exercise 69
Runners	Exercise 50
Shoppers	Case Problem 4
SpringTraining	Exercise 72
StateUnemp	Exercise 14
Stereo	Table 3.6
StockMarket	Exercise 60
TaxCost	Exercise 10
Travel	Exercise 70
WaitTracking	Exercise 64
WorldTemp	Exercise 61

Chapter 4

File	Location
Judge	Case Problem

Chapter 6

File	Location
Volume	Exercise 24

Chapter 7

File	Location
EAI	Section 7.1
MetAreas	Appendix 7.2, 7.3, & 7.4
MutualFund	Exercise 14

Chapter 8

File	Location
Alcohol	Exercise 21
Auto	Case Problem 3
CorporateBonds	Exercise 16
Flights	Exercise 48
GulfProp	Case Problem 2
Houston	Exercise 5
Interval p	Appendix 8.2
JobSatisfaction	Exercise 37
JobSearch	Exercise 18
Lloyd's	Section 8.1
Miami	Exercise 17
NewBalance	Table 8.3
Nielsen	Exercise 6
NYSEStocks	Exercise 47
Professional	Case Problem 1
Program	Exercise 20
Scheer	Table 8.4
Standing	Exercise 49
TaxReturn	Exercise 9
TeeTimes	Section 8.4
TicketSales	Exercise 22

Chapter 9

File	Location
Administrator	Exercise 29
AgeGroup	Exercise 39
AirRating	Section 9.4
Bayview	Case Problem 2
ChildCare	Exercise 30
Coffee	Section 9.3
Drowsy	Exercise 44
Eagle	Exercise 43
FirstBirth	Exercise 64
Fowle	Exercise 21
GolfTest	Section 9.3
Hyp Sigma Known	Appendix 9.2
Hyp Sigma Unknown	Appendix 9.2
Hypothesis p	Appendix 9.2
Orders	Section 9.4
Quality	Case Problem 1
UsedCars	Exercise 32
WeeklyPay	Exercise 65
WomenGolf	Section 9.5

Chapter 10

File	Location
AirDelay	Exercise 18
BusinessTravel	Exercise 24
CheckAcct	Section 10.2
CollegeCosts	Exercise 13
ExamScores	Section 10.1
Golf	Case Problem
GolfScores	Exercise 26
HomePrices	Exercise 39
Hotel	Exercise 6
Matched	Table 10.2
Mutual	Exercise 40
Occupancy	Exercise 46
PriceChange	Exercise 42
SATMath	Exercise 16
SoftwareTest	Table 10.1
StockPrices	Exercise 22
TaxPrep	Section 10.4
TestScores	Exercise 25

Chapter 11

File	Location
Bags	Exercise 19
BatteryTime	Exercise 21
BusTimes	Section 11.1
Costco	Exercise 10
Halloween	Exercise 6
PriceChange	Exercise 8
SchoolBus	Section 11.2
Training	Case Problem
Travel	Exercise 25
Yields	Exercise 11

Chapter 12

File	Location
Ambulance	Exercise 32
AutoLoyalty	Table 12.1
AutoQuality	Exercise 14
BeerPreference	Table 12.6
BothWork	Exercise 29
Chemline	Table 12.10
ChiSquare	Appendix 12.2
Demand	Exercise 26
Grades	Exercise 34
M&M	Exercise 22
NYReform	Case Problem
WorkforcePlan	Exercise 12